# AutoCAD® for Interior Design and Space Planning Using AutoCAD® 2002

BEVERLY L. KIRKPATRICK
Adjunct Faculty, Eastfield College

JAMES M. KIRKPATRICK
Eastfield College

Prentice Hall

Upper Saddle River, New Jersey
Columbus, Ohio

**Library of Congress Cataloging-in-Publication Data**

Kirkpatrick, Beverly L.
    AutoCAD for interior design and space planning using AutoCAD 2002 / Beverly L.
Kirkpatrick, James M. Kirkpatrick.--[New ed.].
        p. cm.
    Includes index.
    ISBN 0-13-097107-3
    1. Interior decoration--Computer-aided design. 2. Space
(Architecture)--Planning--Computer-aided design. 3. AutoCAD. I. Kirkpatrick, James
M. II. Title.

NK2113 .K47 2002
729′.0285′5369--dc21                                    2001055494

Editor in Chief: Stephen Helba
Executive Editor: Debbie Yarnell
Media Development Editor: Michelle Churma
Production Editor: Louise N. Sette
Production Supervision: Lisa Garboski, bookworks
Design Coordinator: Diane Ernsberger
Cover Designer: Linda Sorrells-Smith
Cover art: Corbis Stock Market
Production Manager: Brian Fox
Marketing Manager: Jimmy Stephens

This book was set in Times Roman by STELLARViSIONs. It was printed and bound by
Courier Kendallville, Inc. The cover was printed by Phoenix Color Corp.

Pearson Education Ltd., *London*
Pearson Education Australia Pty. Limited, *Sydney*
Pearson Education Singapore Pte. Ltd.
Pearson Education North Asia Ltd., *Hong Kong*
Pearson Education Canada, Ltd., *Toronto*
Pearson Educación de Mexico, S. A. de C.V.
Pearson Education—Japan, *Tokyo*
Pearson Education Malaysia Pte. Ltd.
Pearson Education, *Upper Saddle River, New Jersey*

10 9 8 7 6 5 4 3 2 1
ISBN: 0-13-097107-3

# Preface

AutoCAD has become the industry standard graphics program for interior design and space planning; it is used to complete the many drawings that make up a design project. Many design firms have adopted AutoCAD as their standard because:

☐ it saves time
☐ affiliated professions use it, and these firms need to be able to exchange disks in order to work on the same drawing
☐ their competitors are using it, and
☐ their clients expect it.

To be successful in design today, students must be proficient in the use of AutoCAD as it relates to interior design and space planning. This need for a specific AutoCAD textbook is what led us to write *AutoCAD for Interior Design and Space Planning*.

The newly updated text, for AutoCAD 2002, is divided into four parts:

☐ Part I: Preparing to Draw with AutoCAD (Chapters 1–3)
☐ Part II: Two-Dimensional AutoCAD (Chapters 4–12)
☐ Part III: Special Topics (Chapters 13–16)
☐ Part IV: Three-Dimensional AutoCAD (Chapters 17–18)

This new edition includes many features designed to help the reader master AutoCAD 2002.

☐ A Prompt/Response format leads the reader through each new AutoCAD command to prevent confusion and frustration.
☐ Exercises are geared to architects, interior designers, and space planners, providing students the opportunity to work with real-world situations.
☐ Chapters 2 and 3 are introductory chapters for using AutoCAD 2002. Material in Chapters 4 through 18 progresses from basic to the complex in a step-by-step learning process for users of AutoCAD 2002.
☐ Over 500 figures (many printed to scale) support the text and reinforce the material.
☐ Illustrations located in the margins help the user locate AutoCAD commands within the AutoCAD menus and toolbars. (Margins also contain notes, tips, and warnings that give students additional support and information.)
☐ Chapters 8 through 14 follow the graphic development of a design project called the Tenant Space project; each chapter contains step-by-step instructions for drawing each stage of the project.
☐ Four other projects—obtained from designers presently working in the field—are included in the text as practice exercises.
☐ Practice exercises in every chapter review the commands learned.
☐ Learning objectives and review questions in every chapter reinforce the learning process.
☐ An *Instructor's Manual* is available to support the text.

Most importantly, this text was written to help you, the reader, master the AutoCAD program, which will be a valuable tool in your professional career.

We would like to thank the reviewers of the manuscript: Zane D. Curry, Ph.D., Texas Tech University, and Christine Spangler, George Washington University.

We extend a special thank you to Stephanie Clemons and her students at Colorado State University for testing the manuscript in their classroom.

We would also like to acknowledge the following people, who contributed ideas and drawings: Mary Peyton, IALD, IES, Lighting Consultant; Roy Peyton, John Sample, Katherine Broadwell, Curran C. Redman, S. Vic Jones, W. M. Stevens, John Brooks, Bill Sorrells, and the CAD students at Eastfield College. Finally, we would like to thank Autodesk, Inc.

B.L.K.
J.M.K.

Preface

# Contents

# AutoCAD® for Interior Design and Space Planning Using AutoCAD® 2002

# PART 1

# PREPARING TO DRAW WITH AUTOCAD

## Introduction

## AUTOCAD FOR INTERIOR DESIGN AND SPACE PLANNING

This book is written for interior designers and space planners who want to learn the Auto-CAD program in the most effective and efficient manner—by drawing with it. AutoCAD commands are introduced in tutorial exercises and thoroughly explained. The tutorial exercises specifically cover interior design and space planning drawings.

Nothing in AutoCAD is difficult to learn. AutoCAD is a very powerful program, however, and you can produce any type of graphics with it. As a result, there are many details that must be clearly understood. This book presents these details in a manner that allows them to be easily understood. It can also be used as a reference when you forget a detail.

Chapters 1 through 5 introduce the AutoCAD program and basic two-dimensional AutoCAD commands. Chapter 6 describes how to add text to your drawings, and Chapter 7 explains printing and plotting. Chapter 9 describes dimensioning. Chapter 11 describes adding furniture specifications to and extracting information from the drawing. Chapter 14 describes how to develop client presentations using AutoCAD. Chapter 15 describes the commands used to insert raster images (like photographs) into AutoCAD drawings. Chapter 16 describes how to customize toolbars and menus. Chapters 17 and 18 describe three-dimensional drawing and include the solid modeling capabilities of AutoCAD 2002.

## BENEFITS OF USING AUTOCAD

When you become an experienced AutoCAD user you will be able to:

- ☐ Produce clear, precise, and impressive drawings by printing or plotting your drawings.
- ☐ Draw with precision so that you can measure exact distances.
- ☐ Change your drawings easily and quickly.
- ☐ Use other programs in combination with AutoCAD to produce reliable furniture specifications and total counts of like pieces of furnishings.
- ☐ Store your drawings on disks.
- ☐ Exchange drawings with other professionals.
- ☐ Use the AutoCAD presentation capabilities for client presentations, either printed or on the display screen.
- ☐ Be in the mainstream of today's technology.

# TYPES OF DRAWINGS COMPLETED IN THE CHAPTER EXERCISES

The following are the types of drawings that are completed in the chapter exercises.

### Two-Dimensional Drawings

Figure 1–1 is the first formal drawing that is completed in Chapter 5, a conference room floor plan with furniture. Chapters 8 thorough 12 follow the graphic development of five design projects. Each chapter contains step-by-step descriptions of commands used to draw the progressive stages of the first project, a Tenant Space project. Those commands can then be applied to drawing the same stage of the remaining four projects without a tutorial explanation. The remaining four projects are examples of work from designers presently working in the field.

Figure 1–2 shows the first stage of the tutorial project completed in Chapter 8. The Tenant Space project begins with drawing the floor plan (exterior and interior walls, doors and windows). Figure 1–3 shows the Tenant Space floor plan that is fully dimensioned in Chapter 9. Figure 1–4 shows an elevation, section, and detail that are part of a typical design package (Chapter 10). Figure 1–5 is the Tenant Space furniture plan with furniture specifications (Chapter 11). Figure 1–6 is the Tenant Space reflected ceiling plan (Chapter 12). Figure 1–7 is the Tenant Space power plan (Chapter 12).

### Isometric Drawings

Figure 1–8 shows an isometric drawing of the Tenant Space reception desk, which is completed in Chapter 13.

### Presentation Drawings

Figure 1–9 shows a Tenant Space project presentation drawing, completed in Chapter 14. The presentation drawing uses drawings completed in the previous chapters. Details of developing slide shows and other effective presentations are also included in Chapter 14.

**FIGURE 1–1**
Conference Room Floor Plan

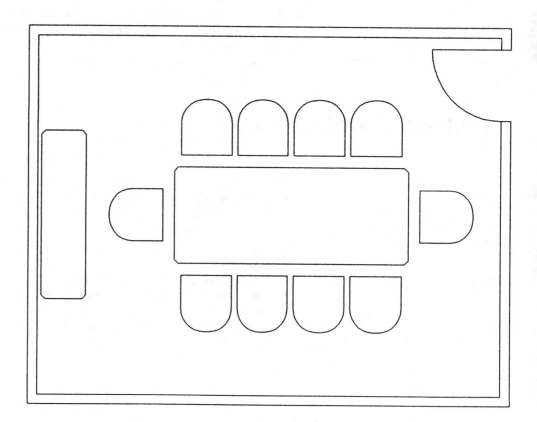

**Part I: Preparing to Draw with AutoCAD**

**FIGURE 1–2**
Tenant Space Floor Plan

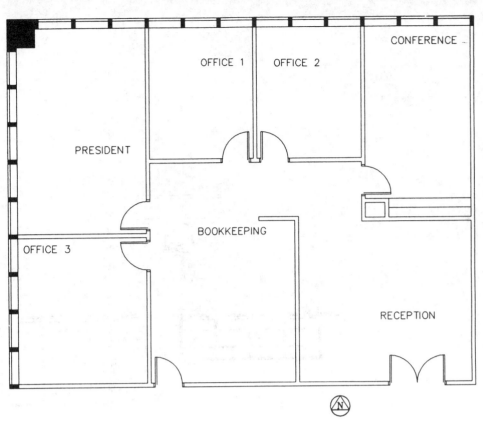

**FIGURE 1–3**
Dimensioned
Tenant Space
Floor Plan

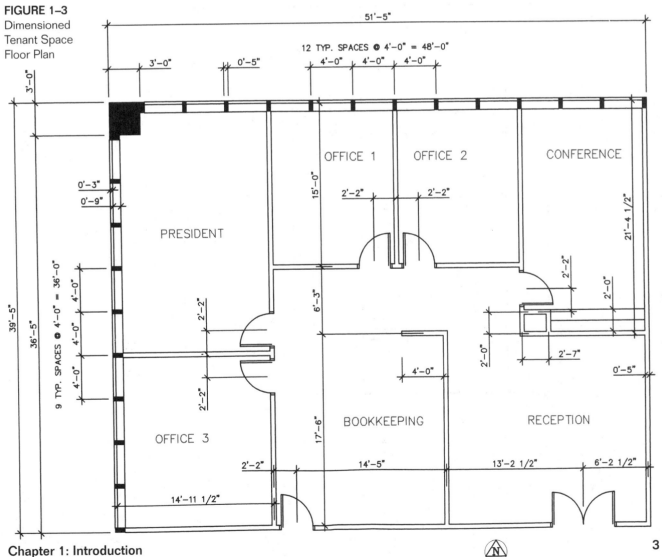

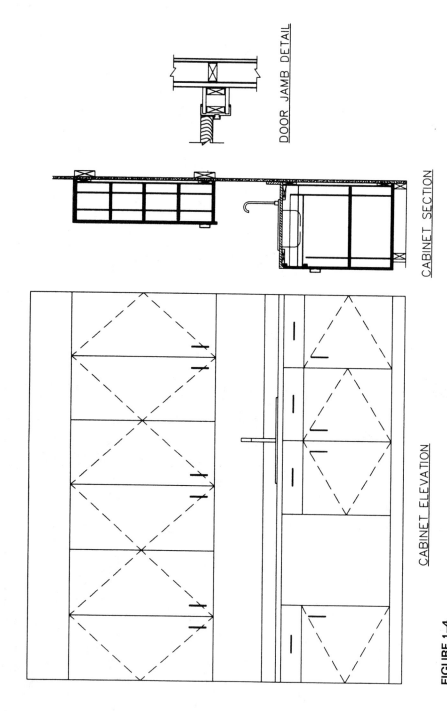

DOOR JAMB DETAIL

CABINET SECTION

CABINET ELEVATION

**FIGURE 1–4**
Tenant Space Elevation, Section, and Detail

4

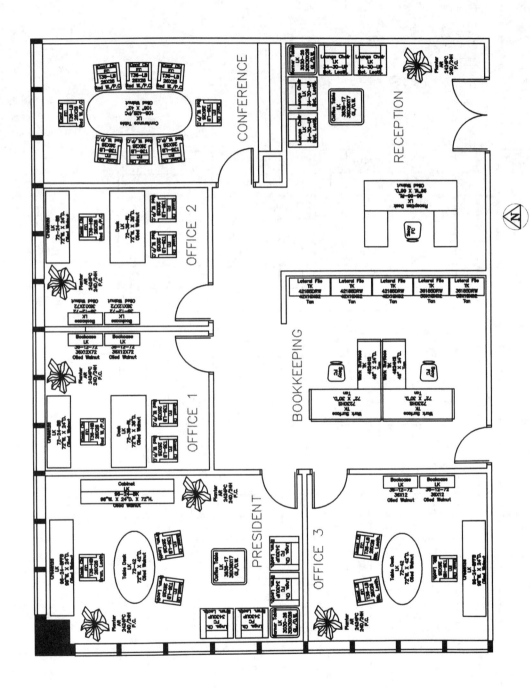

**FIGURE 1-5**
Tenant Space Furniture Plan with Furniture Specifications

5

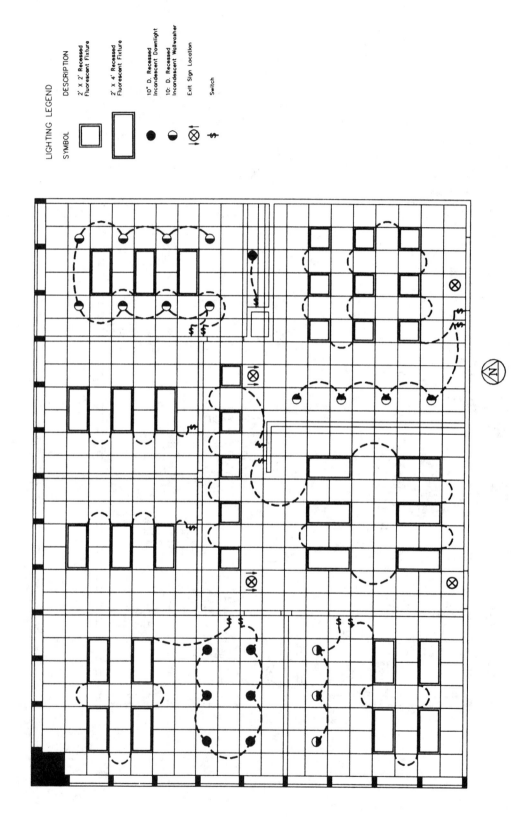

**LIGHTING LEGEND**

| SYMBOL | DESCRIPTION |
|---|---|
| ☐ | 2' X 2' Recessed Fluorescent Fixture |
| ▭ | 2' x 4' Recessed Fluorescent Fixture |
| ● | 10" D. Recessed Incandescent Downlight |
| ◐ | 10: D. Recessed Incandescent Wallwasher |
| ⊗ | Exit Sign Location |
| ⌇ | Switch |

**FIGURE 1-6**
Tenant Space Reflected Ceiling Plan

6

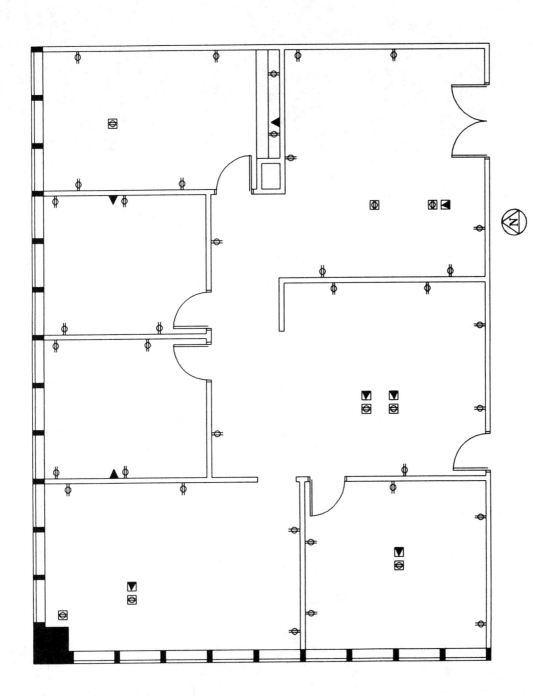

**FIGURE 1-7**
Tenant Space Power Plan

7

**FIGURE 1–8**
Tenant Space Reception Desk in
Isometric

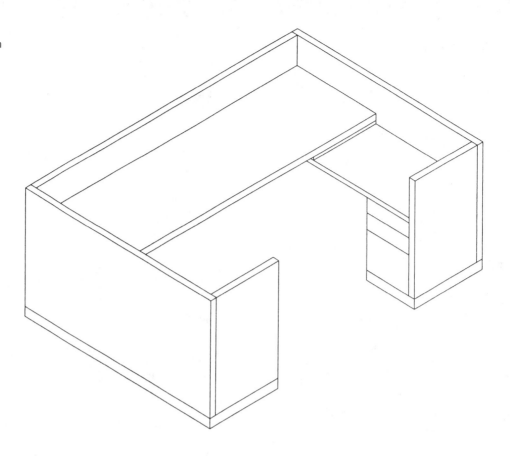

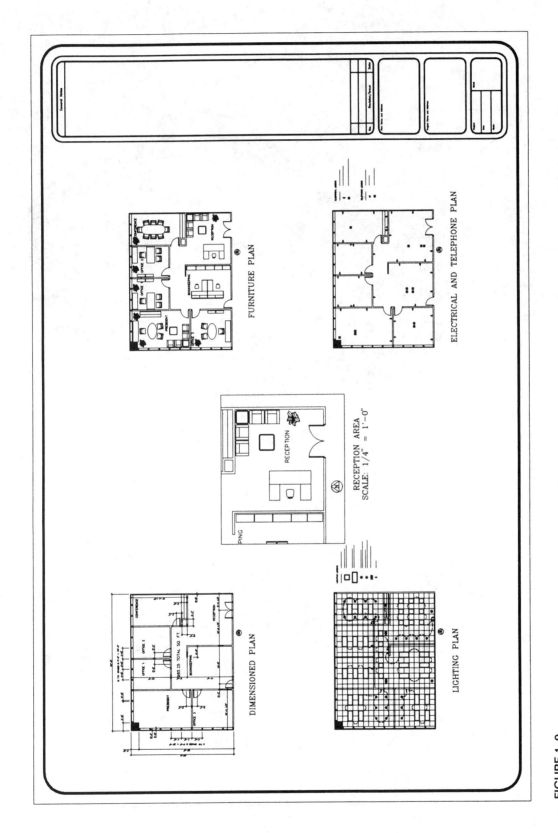

**FIGURE 1-9**
Tenant Space Project Presentation Drawing

9

## Three-Dimensional Models

Figure 1–10 is a typical three-dimensional (3D) model. Basic 3D commands are used to draw the Tenant Space reception desk 3D model completed in Chapter 17. Figure 1–11 shows a complex 3D model of an elaborate patio area developed with solid modeling commands and completed in Chapter 18.

**FIGURE 1–10**
3D Model of the Tenant Space Reception Desk; Shown with Gouraud Shading

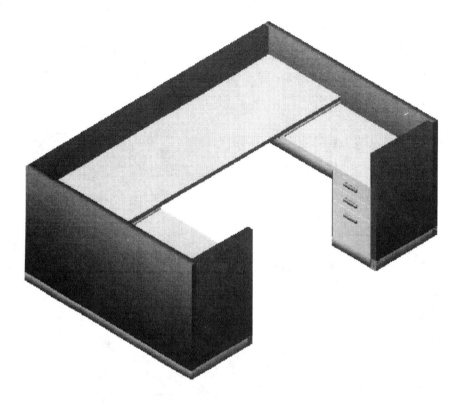

**FIGURE 1–11**
Solid Model of a Patio

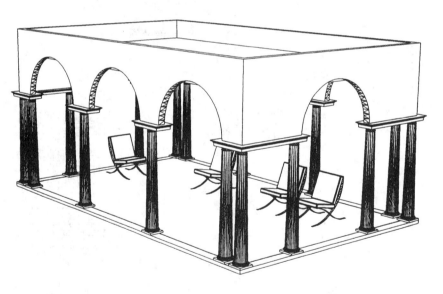

# ADDITIONAL TOPICS DESCRIBED IN THE CHAPTER EXERCISES

Additional topics that are described in this book are:

☐ How to set up your first drawing (Chapter 3).
☐ Adding text to your drawings (Chapter 6).
☐ Printing and plotting drawings (Chapter 7).
☐ Creating a Web page using AutoCAD (Chapter 14).
☐ Using raster images in AutoCAD drawings (Chapter 15).
☐ Customizing AutoCAD menus and toolbars and creating macros (Chapter 16).

AutoCAD is by far the most commonly used CAD program. The time you spend learning to use AutoCAD will give you skills that you can use and develop for the rest of your career. This book has a rich variety of exercises that we hope are fun as well as educational.

# 2

# An Overview of the AutoCAD Program

## OBJECTIVES

After completing this chapter, you will be able to:

☐ Start the Windows operating system.
☐ Start AutoCAD 2002.
☐ Describe the AutoCAD 2002 screen and begin using parts of the screen.
☐ Activate, hide, dock, float, reshape, and resize toolbars.

## EXERCISE 2–1
## Start Microsoft Windows, Start the AutoCAD Program, Examine the AutoCAD Screen, and Exit AutoCAD

Exercise 2–1 provides a step-by-step introduction to Microsoft Windows and AutoCAD 2002. To begin Exercise 2–1, turn on the computer.

### Start Microsoft Windows

**Start Microsoft Windows (Figure 2–1):**
When Windows is started, the Windows opening screen known as the Desktop appears. Figure 2–1 shows a typical display of the Desktop with its icons (an *icon* is a picture). The taskbar appears at the bottom of the screen. It contains the **Start** button, which you can use to start AutoCAD 2002 as follows:

### Start the AutoCAD Program

Start the AutoCAD Program (Figure 2–2):

| Prompt | Response |
|---|---|
| The Desktop is displayed: | CLICK: **the Start button** |
| The Start menu is displayed: | CLICK: **Programs** |
| A submenu of Programs is displayed: | CLICK: **AutoCAD 2002** |
| The AutoCAD 2002 menu is displayed: | CLICK: **AutoCAD 2002** |
| The AutoCAD screen appears with the AutoCAD 2002 Today window (Figure 2–3): | **Close the AutoCAD 2002 Today window by clicking the X in the upper right corner.** |

**Note:** DOUBLE CLICK: means to place your cursor over the selection and press the left mouse button twice rapidly.

You may also double click the AutoCAD 2002 icon shown in the screen in Figure 2–1. This is a shortcut that Windows will create for you, to allow you to activate AutoCAD more quickly.

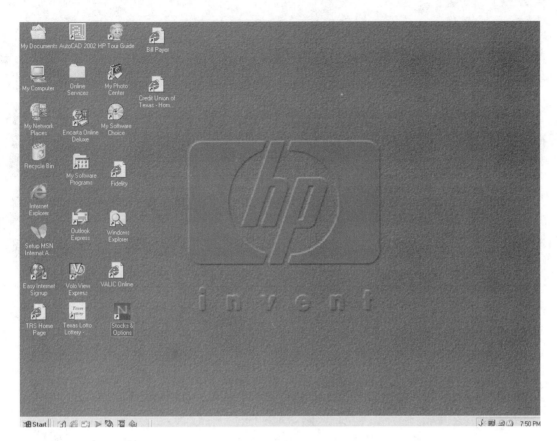

**FIGURE 2–1**
Windows Desktop

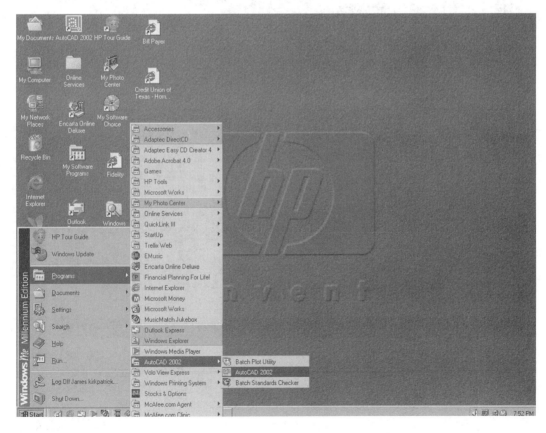

**FIGURE 2–2**
Starting AutoCAD 2002

**FIGURE 2–3**
AutoCAD 2002 Today
Window

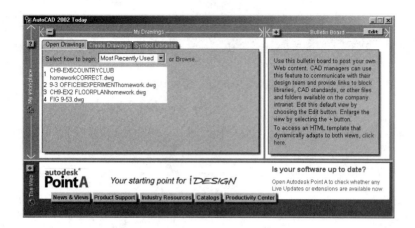

When AutoCAD 2002 is started, the AutoCAD screen appears. It provides the display area for drawing and the commands used to create, modify, view, and plot drawings. For now, you closed the AutoCAD 2002 Today window, which is described in the next chapter. You can begin by naming a new drawing, or you may immediately begin drawing without naming the drawing. When you are ready to end a drawing session, save the drawing using Save or SaveAs..., at which time you must name the drawing. AutoCAD communicates with you on various parts of the screen. You may have a slightly different appearing screen, depending on the preferences selected. A brief introduction to each part of the screen (Figure 2–4) follows.

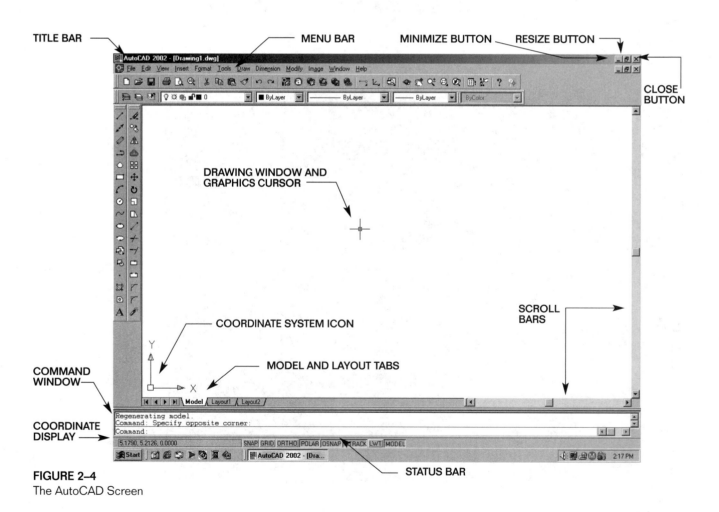

**FIGURE 2–4**
The AutoCAD Screen

Part I: Preparing to Draw with AutoCAD

## The AutoCAD Screen

### Title Bar

The title bar contains the name of the program, AutoCAD 2002, and the name of the current drawing, in this case, [Drawing1], because you have not yet named the drawing.

### AutoCAD Program and Drawing Buttons

This button on the program window minimizes the AutoCAD program. The program remains active, so you can return to it if you choose. To return to it, click the AutoCAD 2002 button on the taskbar at the bottom of the screen. You can also minimize a drawing by clicking this button on the drawing window.

This button resizes the program or drawing window.

This button maximizes the size of the program or drawing window.

This button closes the AutoCAD program or drawing window.

### Drawing Window and Graphics Cursor

The drawing window is where your drawing is displayed. The graphics cursor (or crosshair) follows the movement of a mouse when points of a drawing are entered or a command is selected. To change the graphics cursor to look like the crosshair in Figure 2–4, click Options… under Tools in the menu bar. Click the Display tab of the Options dialog box. Move the slider in the lower left corner to the right to increase the size or left to decrease it.

### Command Window

The command window shown at the bottom of the screen (which may be moved and resized if you want) is where AutoCAD communicates with you once a command is activated. AutoCAD prompts you to enter specific information to further define a command and then responds with action on the screen or additional prompts. Always watch the command window to make sure you and AutoCAD are communicating.

### User Coordinate System Icon

The user coordinate system (UCS) icon in the lower left corner of the drawing window shows the orientation of the X, Y, and Z axes of the current coordinate system. When AutoCAD is started, you are in the world coordinate system (WCS). There are two types of model space UCS icons—2D and 3D. The 3D icon is the default and is shown in Figure 2–4.

### Coordinate Display

Using an X- and Y-axis coordinate system, the coordinate display numbers in the extreme lower left corner tell you where the cursor or crosshair on the screen is located in relation to point 0,0 (the lower left corner). CLICK: on the coordinate display to turn it ON and OFF.

### Status Bar

The status bar at the bottom of the screen keeps you informed about your drawing by displaying the status of modes that affect your drawing: SNAP, GRID, ORTHO, POLAR, OSNAP, OTRACK, LWT, and MODEL. These modes can be turned on and off by clicking on the mode name with the pick button of your mouse. The time is also displayed.

### Scroll Bars

The scroll bars on the bottom and right side of the screen area allow you to move the drawing display at the same magnification up and down, left and right. The scroll bars can be turned on and off using the Display tab of the Options... dialog box under Tools in the menu bar.

### Model and Layout Tabs

The model and layout tabs allow you to select different means of plotting your drawing.

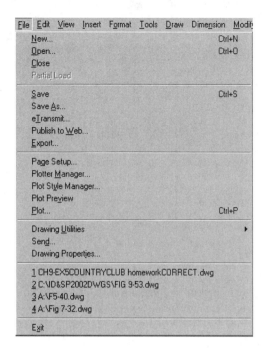

FIGURE 2–5
File Menu

FIGURE 2–6
Edit Menu

FIGURE 2–7
View Menu

**Menu Bar**

**Practice using the menu bar (Figures 2–5 through 2–14):**

You can open a menu item on the menu bar by holding the pointer on the menu name and clicking it; click the menu name again to close the menu, or use the Esc key to cancel any command activated. A pull-down menu will appear for each item on the menu bar when the item is clicked (Figures 2–5 through 2–13). Pull-down menus provide access to many of the same commands that are included on the toolbars. The commands followed by an ellipsis (...) display a dialog box when clicked. Use the Esc key or click the Cancel button in the dialog box to cancel it. Those pull-down menu items with an arrow to the right have a cascading menu.

When you hold your mouse steady over each pull-down menu command or cascading menu command, a text string at the bottom of the display screen (in the coordinate display and status bar area) gives a brief description of the commands. Many of the menu bar commands are used in the following chapters; however, the following brief description of the general content of the menu bar provides an introduction:

**File** (Figure 2–5) This menu bar item contains the commands needed to start a new drawing, open an existing one, save drawings, print or plot a drawing, export data, and exit from AutoCAD. It also shows the most recently active drawings, which may be opened by clicking on them.

**Edit** (Figure 2–6) This item contains the Undo command (allows you to undo or reverse the most recent command) and the Redo command (will redo one undo). It also contains the commands related to the Windows Clipboard such as Cut, Copy, and Paste. Drawings or text from other applications (such as Word or Paintbrush) can be cut or copied onto the Windows Clipboard and then pasted from the Clipboard into an Auto-CAD drawing. The reverse is also possible: AutoCAD drawings can be pasted into other applications. The OLE Links... command is a Windows feature that allows you to link or unlink an AutoCAD drawing and another application's object (document or drawing). When a drawing is copied and placed in a document in another program such as Paintbrush or Word and then linked, editing it updates the information in both the original drawing and the new document.

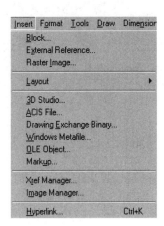

**FIGURE 2–8**
Insert Menu

**FIGURE 2–9**
Format Menu

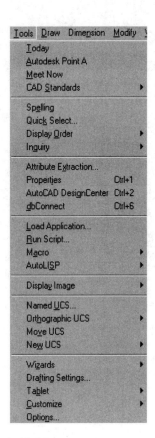

**FIGURE 2–10**
Tools Menu

**View** (Figure 2–7) This menu contains commands that control the display of your drawing. The Redraw command redraws the display screen to remove blips and redraws
any part of the drawing that is missing. Regen is similar to Redraw, but regenerates the
drawing. The Zoom commands control the magnification of the drawing display, and
Pan allows you to move the drawing up and down, left and right. Aerial View allows
you to see a view of your entire drawing and move about the drawing while still in an
enlarged view of a small part of the drawing. The Named Views... command provides
a dialog box that allows you to name drawing views, save them, and restore them as
needed. The Hide, Shade, Render, and 3D Orbit commands are used to render solid
models, and the Toolbars... command allows you to display or hide toolbars.

**Insert** (Figure 2–8) This menu contains the commands that allow you to insert previously drawn objects into an AutoCAD drawing. These objects may be other AutoCAD
drawings or pictures from other drawing programs.

**Format** (Figure 2–9) This menu bar item contains commands that help you set up your
drawing environment and prepare to draw with AutoCAD. The Layer... command creates layers on which different parts of a drawing can be placed. Every drawing entity
(such as an arc, line, or circle) will have a Color, Linetype, and Lineweight. You will
learn in later chapters to create a Text Style and a Dimension Style so you can add text
and dimensions to your drawing. Point Style... allows you to set the style and size for
points that are drawn. Multiline Style... allows you to draw up to 16 lines at a time.
The Units... command establishes the drawing units. For example, an inch is a drawing
unit. Thickness allows you to give an object height in 3D. The Drawing Limits command sets the page size you draw on. The Rename... command allows you to rename
layers, text styles, dimension styles, and more.

**Tools** (Figure 2–10) This menu has a spell checker and a Display Order command that
allows you to place images on top of one another. Inquiry allows you to obtain infor-

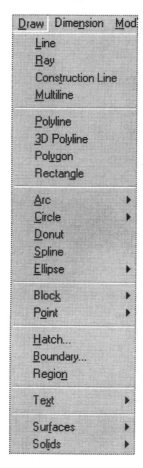

**FIGURE 2–11**
Draw Menu

mation about the size and location of the entities and about the amount of time spent on the drawing when it was done and to place a date and time stamp on your drawing. The AutoCAD DesignCenter is in the Tools menu. It allows you to select pictures and symbols (such as architectural symbols) from other drawings and from a group of symbols supplied by AutoCAD. It also allows you to copy other settings from existing drawings. Tools also has a command for running scripts (described in a later chapter). UCS commands, wizards, and a dialog box for making drawing settings are here. The Tools menu also has a command for customizing menus and toolbars, and activating the Options... dialog box. This dialog box gives you options for customizing Auto-CAD.

**Draw** (Figure 2–11) The Draw menu has all the commands used to draw objects in AutoCAD.

**Dimension** (Figure 2–12) This menu contains the commands used to place dimensions on drawings. All these commands are described in detail in a later chapter.

**Modify** (Figure 2–13) The Modify commands are used to change the position, shape, or number of objects after they have been drawn. Commands to change text are also on this menu.

**Image** (Figure 2–14) This menu provides information about Autodesk CAD overlay software.

**Window** (Figure 2–15) This menu is used to arrange multiple drawings when you are working on more than one drawing at the same time.

**Help** (Figure 2–16) This menu bar item has commands that teach you how to use the Help command. The AutoCAD Help command provides information about how to use AutoCAD commands. It is a very helpful tool for any AutoCAD user. The seven introductory items on this menu, Active Assistance. Developer Help, Support Assistance, Product Support on Point A, What's New, Learning Assistance, and Autodesk User Group International, are very worthwhile. Take the time to run those now to familiarize yourself with the basics of this program.

**FIGURE 2–12**
Dimension Menu

**FIGURE 2–13**
Modify Menu

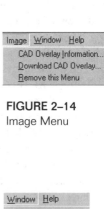

**FIGURE 2–14**
Image Menu

**FIGURE 2–15**
Window Menu

**FIGURE 2–16**
Help Menu

**Part I: Preparing to Draw with AutoCAD**

### Toolbars

The AutoCAD screen shown in Figure 2–4 has four toolbars displayed: a docked Object Properties toolbar (Figure 2–17), a docked Standard Toolbar (Figure 2–18), and the Draw and Modify toolbars docked at the left side of the screen. The Standard Toolbar contains tools that represent frequently used commands. The Object Properties toolbar contains the Layer Properties Manager dialog box, used to create layers and assign properties such as color and linetype to every drawing entity (line, arc, circle, and so on).

**Activate the Standard Toolbar's tooltips (Figure 2–18):**

As you hold the mouse pointer steady (do not click) on each tool of the Standard Toolbar, tooltips will display the name of the command, as shown in Figure 2–18. A text string at the bottom of the display screen (in the coordinate display and status bar area) gives a brief description of the command.

**Activate the Standard Toolbar's flyouts (Figure 2–19):**

Tools with a small black triangle have flyouts. Hold the pointer on the tool, press and hold the pick button, and the flyout will appear, as shown in Figure 2–19. When you posi-

**FIGURE 2–17**
Object Properties Toolbar

**FIGURE 2–18**
Standard Toolbar with Tooltip Displayed

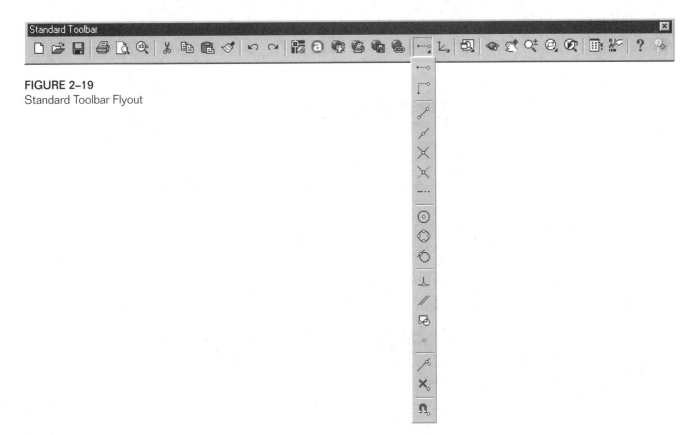

**FIGURE 2–19**
Standard Toolbar Flyout

tion the pointer on a tool in the flyout and release the pick button, the command is activated; a dialog box will appear or a command sequence will begin. The most recently activated tool icon will replace the top icon that was previously visible in the standard toolbar; the location of the icon changes to reflect the most recently used command. Use the Esc key to cancel any command.

**Locate the names of all the toolbars (Figure 2–20):**

| Prompt | Response |
|---|---|
| Command: | CLICK: **Toolbars...** (on the View menu) |
| The Customize dialog box (Figure 2–20) with the Toolbars tab selected appears: | All the toolbar names are displayed in the list. |

**Note:** You can also activate the toolbar list by holding your cursor over any tool icon and clicking the right mouse button. A toolbar may then be opened by clicking on the toolbar name in the list.

**Activate and close the Dimension toolbar:**

To activate a toolbar, pick the check box to the left of the toolbar name, so that a ✔ appears in it. After studying a toolbar, you can close it by clicking the X in the upper right corner of the toolbar. You can also close a toolbar by clicking the ✔ in the Toolbars dialog box next to the toolbar name. Try this by opening and closing the Dimension toolbar, then close the Customize dialog box.

**Close all toolbars at once:**

| Prompt | Response |
|---|---|
| Command: | TYPE: **-TOOLBAR<enter>** (be sure to include the hyphen) |
| Enter toolbar name or [ALL]: | TYPE: **ALL<enter>** |
| Enter an option [Show/Hide]: | TYPE: **H<enter>** |

**FIGURE 2–20**
Customize Dialog Box with the Toolbars Tab Selected, Displaying the Draw Toolbar

### Floating Toolbars

A floating toolbar floats or lies on any part of the AutoCAD screen. A floating toolbar can be moved to another part of the screen and can be reshaped and resized. Any of the top level toolbars can be displayed and will float on the screen as follows:

### Display the Draw toolbar (Figure 2–20):

| Prompt | Response |
|---|---|
| Command: | CLICK: **Toolbars...** (on the View menu) |
| The Customize dialog box with the Toolbars tab selected appears: | CLICK: **the box to the left of Draw** (Figure 2–20) |
| A ✔ appears in the box. | |
| The Draw toolbar appears on the screen: | |

### Display the Modify toolbar:

Use the same steps to display the Modify toolbar as you used to display the Draw toolbar.

To hide any toolbar you do not want visible, click on the X in the upper right corner of the toolbar. Close the Toolbars dialog box by picking the X in the upper right corner, or pick Close.

### Reshape and move the Draw and Modify toolbars (Figure 2–21):

Change the shape of the toolbars to match those shown in Figure 2–21 by changing the width and height. Slowly move the pointer over the borders of each toolbar until you get the double-arrow pointer that allows you to resize it.

Move the Draw and Modify toolbars to the approximate position shown in Figure 2–21 by picking the title bar of each toolbar and dragging it to the new location.

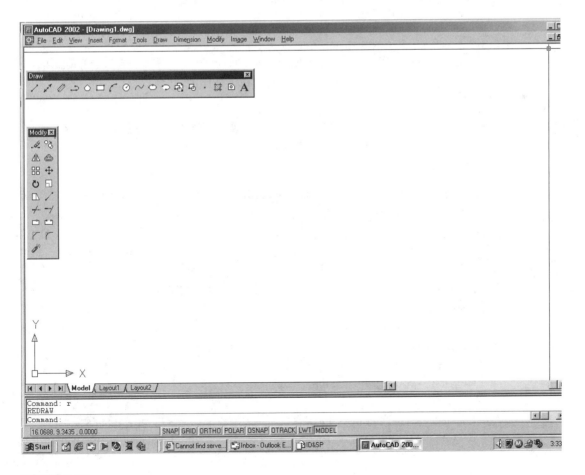

**FIGURE 2–21**
Reshaping and Moving Toolbars

**Chapter 2: An Overview of the AutoCAD Program**

**Change the size of the tool buttons:**

| Prompt | Response |
|---|---|
| Command: | CLICK: **Toolbars...** (from View on the menu bar) |
| The Customize dialog box with the Toolbars tab selected appears: | CLICK: **Large Buttons** (the check box, to put a check in the box, turning it on) |
| A check appears in the Large Buttons check box: | CLICK: **Close** (to exit) |
| All the toolbars are larger: | **Use the same steps to change the tool bars back to the smaller size.** |

### Docked Toolbars

**Display the Standard Toolbar and the Object Properties toolbar:**

| Prompt | Response |
|---|---|
| Command: | CLICK: **Toolbars...** (from View on the menu bar) |
| The Customize dialog box appears: | CLICK: **the box to the left of Standard Toolbar and Object Properties** |
| A ✔ appears in the boxes. Both toolbars appear on the screen: | CLICK: **Close** |

**Dock the Draw, Standard Toolbar, and Object Properties toolbars (Figure 2–22):**
A toolbar can be docked, which means it can be attached to any edge of the drawing window. Once docked, the toolbar does not lie on any part of the drawing area; it also cannot be reshaped. One way to dock a toolbar is to pick on the name of the toolbar and drag it to an edge. When you see an outline of the toolbar along an edge (showing you how the toolbar will look in the docking area), release the pick button on the mouse to dock the toolbar.

To undock the toolbar, pick on the two bars at the top of the toolbar or on the edge of the toolbar, and drag the toolbar away from the edge.

Pick on the name of the Draw toolbar and drag it to the left edge of the drawing area and dock it. Dock the Standard Toolbar and Object Properties toolbar as shown in Figure 2–22.

### Toolbar Command

**Use the Toolbar command to dock the Modify toolbar on the right side of the drawing area (Figure 2–22):**

| Prompt | Response |
|---|---|
| Command: | TYPE: **-TOOLBAR<enter>** (be sure to include the hyphen) |
| Enter toolbar name or [ALL]: | TYPE: **MODIFY<enter>** |
| Enter an option [Show/Hide/Left/Right/ Top/Bottom/Float]<Show>: | TYPE: **R<enter>** |
| Enter new position (horizontal,vertical) <0,0>: | **<enter>** |
| The Modify toolbar is docked on the right side of the drawing area, Figure 2–22. | |

The other options of the Toolbar command, when activated, allow you to dock a toolbar on the left, top, or bottom of the drawing area, float a docked toolbar, show a hidden toolbar, or hide a visible toolbar. You can use the ALL option to make all the toolbars visible or to hide all the toolbars.

**FIGURE 2–22**
Docking the Draw, Standard Toolbar, Object Properties, and Modify Toolbars

### Customizing Toolbars

You can customize toolbars using the Customize dialog box. Using this dialog box, you can add, delete, move, or copy existing tools, or create a new toolbar using existing or new tools.

### Using AutoCAD 2002 with Other Programs

All commands related to the Windows Clipboard such as Cut, Copy, and Paste are available in AutoCAD 2002. Drawings or text from other applications (such as Word or Paintbrush) can be cut or copied onto the Windows Clipboard and then pasted from the Clipboard into an AutoCAD drawing. The reverse is also possible: AutoCAD drawings can be pasted into other applications.

### Exit AutoCAD

The Exit command takes you out of the AutoCAD program. If you have made changes to the drawing and have not saved those changes, AutoCAD will give you the message "Save changes to Drawing1.dwg?" If you have named the drawing, the drawing name will replace the word "Drawing1." This is a safety feature because the Exit command, by itself, does not update or save a drawing. For now, you will not name or save this exercise.

**FIGURE 2–23**
File Menu with Exit Clicked

**Exit AutoCAD (Figure 2–23):**

| Prompt | Response |
| --- | --- |
| Command: | **Exit** (from File on the menu bar) |
| The AutoCAD warning appears: | |
| Save changes to Drawing1.dwg? | CLICK: **No** |
| If you have not drawn anything or made any settings, the message will not appear. | |

## REVIEW QUESTIONS

1. What do you do to display the submenu of programs containing AutoCAD 2002?
   a. TYPE: OPEN<enter>
   b. Double click on the icon
   c. CLICK: the Start icon and then CLICK: Programs
   d. Hold the pointer on the icon and press <enter>
   e. TYPE: Enter<enter>
2. Which tab of the Options dialog box contains the slider bar used to change the size of the crosshair?
   a. File
   b. Display
   c. Drafting
   d. Selection
   e. Profiles
3. Clicking the X in the upper right corner of the AutoCAD program window
   a. Closes the AutoCAD program
   b. Closes the Program Manager and displays the Exit Windows dialog box
   c. Enters the AutoCAD program
   d. Opens the AutoCAD screen
   e. Resizes the AutoCAD screen
4. To maximize the AutoCAD screen
   a. Pick the underscore in the upper right of the screen
   b. Pick the rectangle in the upper right of the screen
   c. Pick the X in the upper right of the screen
   d. Pick the icon to the left of File on the menu bar
   e. The AutoCAD screen cannot be maximized.

5. Which menu on the AutoCAD menu bar contains the command needed to start a new drawing?
   a. File
   b. Edit
   c. Tools
   d. Format
   e. Options

6. Which menu on the AutoCAD menu bar contains the commands related to Windows Clipboard?
   a. File
   b. Edit
   c. Tools
   d. Format
   e. Options

7. Which menu on the AutoCAD menu bar allows you to make and set layers, select drawing units, and set drawing limits?
   a. File
   b. Edit
   c. Tools
   d. Format
   e. Options

8. Which menu on the AutoCAD menu bar takes you to the Toolbars... command?
   a. File
   b. Edit
   c. Tools
   d. Format
   e. View

Complete.

9. List the eight modes displayed on the status bar.

   _____

10. If you have not named a new drawing, what name does AutoCAD assign to it?

   _____

11. Describe the purpose of the command window.

   _____

12. Describe how to open or activate a toolbar.

   _____

13. Describe how to close or hide a toolbar.

   _____

14. Describe how to undock a toolbar.

   _____

15. Describe how to reshape a toolbar.

   _____

16. Describe the function of the scroll bars on the bottom and right side of the AutoCAD for Windows screen.

   _____

17. Describe how to activate a toolbar's tooltips and flyouts.

   Tooltips: _____

   Flyouts: _____

# 3

# Preparing to Draw with AutoCAD

## OBJECTIVES

After completing this chapter, you will be able to:
☐ Begin an AutoCAD drawing using Start from Scratch.
☐ Make settings for an AutoCAD drawing to include Units, Limits, Grid, and Snap.
☐ Create layers and assign color and linetype to each layer.
☐ Use function keys F2 (flip screen), F7 (grid), and F9 (snap) to control the display screen, grid, and snap as required.
☐ Use the commands Save, SaveAs..., and Exit to save work and exit AutoCAD.
☐ Save a drawing as a template.

## INTRODUCTION

When a project is started, decisions are made about the number of drawings required, the appropriate sheet size, scale, and so on. This chapter describes the settings that must be made when preparing to draw with AutoCAD.

The following is a hands-on step-by-step procedure to make the setup for your first drawing exercise in Chapter 4. Each step is followed by an explanation of the command used. To begin, turn on the computer and start AutoCAD.

## FOLLOWING THE EXERCISES IN THIS BOOK

Before you start the exercises in this book, it will help to have a description of how to follow them.

### Drives

This book will assume that the hard drive of the computer is called drive C. It will also assume that there is a floppy disk drive labeled A. You may also save to a network or a zip drive; if so, substitute letters for these drives as needed.

### Prompt and Response Columns

Throughout the exercises in this book, Prompt and Response columns provide step-by-step instructions for starting and completing a command. The Prompt column text repeats the AutoCAD prompt that appears in the command prompt area of the display screen. The text in the Response Column shows your response to the AutoCAD prompt and appears as follows:

1. All responses are shown in bold type.
2. **<enter>** is used to indicate the enter response. Either the right button on the mouse or a key on the keyboard may be used.

3. A response that is to be typed and entered from the keyboard is preceded by the word "TYPE:" and is followed by **<enter>** to indicate the enter response (for example, TYPE: **WALLS<enter>**).

4. If a response is to click a command or command option from a menu or a toolbar, that command is shown in the response column in bold type (for example, **Units**).

5. Most commands can be entered by typing from the keyboard. For example, that option is shown as (or TYPE: **UNITS<enter>**).

6. If the response is to click a button in a dialog box, that button description is shown in the response column in bold type (for example, CLICK: **OK**).

7. Function keys are the keys marked F1 through F12 on the keyboard. If the response is to use a function key, the key name will be preceded by the word "PRESS:" (for example, PRESS: **F7**).

8. Helpful notes, such as (F2 is the flip screen function key), are provided in parentheses.

# EXERCISE 3–1
# Beginning an AutoCAD Drawing Using "Start from Scratch": Setting Units, Limits, Grid, and Snap; Creating Layers; Saving Your Work and Exiting AutoCAD

## Begin a New Drawing Using "Start from Scratch"
## AutoCAD 2002 Today Window

When the AutoCAD program is started, the AutoCAD 2002 Today window appears. It has three tabs: Open Drawings, Create Drawings, and Symbol Libraries (Figure 3–1).

### Open Drawings

This tab allows you to open an existing drawing.

### Create Drawings

This tab allows you to select how you begin a drawing. You may select Template, Start from Scratch, or Wizards.

Template

Any drawing can be saved as a template. You can use one of the templates supplied by AutoCAD, or you can create standard templates to suit your drawing needs or office standards. Templates save time because the drawings environment is already set. Those settings include:

> Unit type and precision
> Drawing limits
> Snap, Grid, and Ortho settings

**FIGURE 3–1**
AutoCAD 2002 Today Window

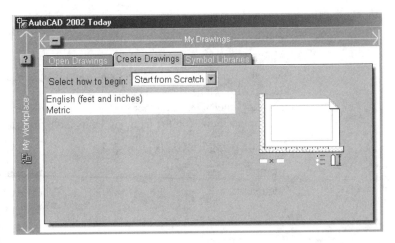

Layer organization
Title blocks, borders, and logos
Dimension and text styles
Linetypes and lineweights

AutoCAD saves the template file in the template folder by default.

Start from Scratch

This button allows you to set up a drawing in English or Metric units.

Wizards

When a new drawing is started by clicking the Wizards tab, AutoCAD leads you through making the drawing setup using a dialog box. The two Wizard options are Quick Setup and Advanced Setup:

**Quick Setup**
The Quick Setup dialog box includes:

Step 1: Units
Step 2: Area (Drawing Limits)

**Advanced Setup**
The Advanced Setup dialog box includes:

Step 1: Units
Step 2: Angle
Step 3: Angle Measure
Step 4: Angle Direction
Step 5: Area (Drawing Limits)

### Symbol Libraries

When this tab is clicked a list of symbol libraries is displayed. The symbols can be used in any drawing. By clicking **DesignCenter Symbol Libraries** or **Edit...** you can add to, delete, or rearrange the available symbol libraries.

**Begin a new drawing (Figure 3–1):**

| Prompt | Response |
|---|---|
| The AutoCAD 2002 Today window appears (Figure 3–1): | CLICK: **the Create Drawings tab** |
| | CLICK: **Start from Scratch** |
| | CLICK: **English** |

Now that you have started a new drawing, select the units that will be used in making this drawing.

## Units

Units refers to drawing units. For example, an inch is a drawing unit. In this book architectural units, which provide feet and fractional inches, are used. The Precision: button in the Drawing Units dialog box allows you to set the smallest fraction to display when showing dimensions and other unit values on the screen. There is no reason to change any of the other settings in the Drawing Units dialog box at this time.

**To set drawing Units... (Figure 3–2):**

| Prompt | Response |
|---|---|
| Command: | (Move the mouse across the top of the display screen on the menu bar. See the menu bar illustration in the book margin to locate the command.) |

**Note:** To cancel a command, PRESS: **Esc** (from the keyboard).

FIGURE 3–2
Drawing Units Dialog Box

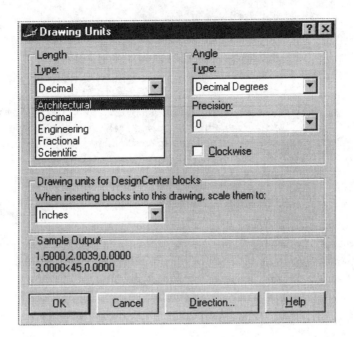

**Note:** The Precision: button has no bearing on how accurately AutoCAD draws. It allows you to set the smallest fraction to display dimensions and other values shown on the screen such as coordinates and defaults. No matter what the Precision: setting, AutoCAD draws with extreme accuracy.

| Prompt | Response |
|---|---|
| | **Units...** |
| | (or TYPE: **UNITS<enter>**) |
| The Drawing Units dialog box appears (Figure 3–2): | CLICK: **Architectural** (for Type: under Length) |
| | CLICK: **0′-0 1/16″** (for Precision: under Length) |
| | CLICK: **OK** |

## Controlling Your Drawing

When you begin drawing with AutoCAD, you may click a tab or drawing aid that you do not need. If you select the Layout1 or Layout2 tabs at the bottom of your drawing window and are not sure where you are in the drawing, simply select the Model tab to return to your drawing. The Layout tabs are used for printing or plotting and will be described later.

The status bar at the bottom of the screen contains various drawing aids. The aids can be turned on and off by clicking on the name with the pick button of your mouse. The drawing aid is on when the button is in, and off when the button is out. Three of these drawing aids that should be on are:

**SNAP** Your crosshair snaps to snap points as you move the cursor across the screen when SNAP is on.

**GRID** A visible pattern of dots you see on the screen when GRID is on.

**MODEL** Model space is where you create your drawing. If you click this button and your drawing changes, or PAPER appears, click the Cancel button on the Page Setup dialog box and also click the Model tab on the drawing to get back into model space.

Drawing aids that you will learn about as you continue through this text but should be off until you learn more about them are:

**ORTHO** Allows you to draw only horizontally and vertically when on.

**POLAR** Shows temporary alignment paths along polar angles when on.

**OSNAP** This is object snap. Osnap contains command modifiers that help you draw very accurately. If you have an osnap mode on that you do not want, it can make your cursor click to points on your drawing that you do not want.

**OTRACK** Shows temporary alignment paths along object snap points when on.

**LWT** Assigns varying lineweights (widths) to different parts of your drawing. When this button is on, the lineweights are displayed on the screen.

## Drawing Scale

A drawing scale factor does not need to be set. While using AutoCAD to make drawings always draw full scale, using real-world feet and inches. Full-scale drawings can be printed or plotted at any scale. Plotting and printing to scale is described in Chapter 7.

## Drawing Limits

**To set drawing limits:**

| Prompt | Response |
|---|---|
| Command: | **Drawing Limits** (or TYPE: **LIMITS** <enter>) |
| Specify lower left corner or [ON/OFF] <0'-0", 0'-0">: | **<enter>** |
| Specify upper right corner <1'-0", 0'-9">: | TYPE: **8-1/2,11 <enter>** |

Think of drawing limits as the sheet size or sheet boundaries. Here 8-1/2,11 was set as the drawing limits. In AutoCAD that value is entered as 8-1/2,11 using a comma with no spaces to separate the X and Y axes. AutoCAD defaults to inches (or any other basic unit of measure), so the inch symbol is not required. The X axis is first (8-1/2) and measures drawing limits from left to right. The Y axis is second (11) and measures drawing limits from bottom to top. You will be drawing in a vertical 8-1/2″ × 11″ area similar to a standard sheet of typing paper.

The lower left corner of the drawing boundaries is 0,0. The upper right corner is 8-1/2,11 (Figure 3–3). These are the limits for Chapter 4 Exercise 1. To turn the 8-1/2″ × 11″ area horizontally, enter the limits as 11,8-1/2.

You can also respond to the Limits: prompt "Specify lower left corner of [ON/OFF] <0'-0", 0'-0">:" by typing ON or OFF. The ON mode, when activated, helps you avoid drawing outside the drawing limits. The OFF mode, when activated, allows you to draw outside the drawing limits.

If you need to change the drawing limits, you may do so at any time by entering new limits to the "Specify upper right corner:" prompt. Changing the drawing limits will automatically show the grid pattern for the new limits.

**FIGURE 3–3**
Drawing Limits

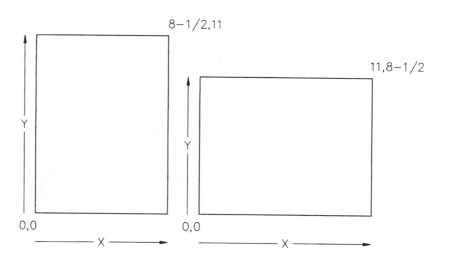

## Grid and Snap

### Set the Grid and Snap Spacing:

| Prompt | Response |
|---|---|
| Command: | TYPE: **GRID<enter>** |
| Specify grid spacing(X) or [ON/OFF/Snap/<br>    Aspect] <0'-0 1/2">: | TYPE: **1/4<enter>** |
| Command: | TYPE: **SN<enter>** |
| Specify snap spacing or [ON/OFF/Aspect/<br>    Rotate/Style/Type] <0'-0 1/2">: | TYPE: **1/8<enter>** |

### Grid

You have just set ¼" as the grid spacing. The grid is the visible pattern of dots on the display screen. With a setting of ¼", each grid dot is spaced ¼" vertically and horizontally. The grid is not part of the drawing, but it helps in getting a sense of the size and relationship of the drawing elements. It is never plotted.

Pressing function key F7 or Ctrl + G turns the grid on or off. The grid can also be turned on or off by selecting either option in response to the prompt "Specify grid spacing(X) or [ON/OFF/Snap/Aspect]" or by clicking GRID at the bottom of the screen.

### Snap

You have set ⅛" as the snap spacing. Snap is an invisible pattern of dots on the display screen. As you move the mouse across the screen, the crosshair will snap, or lock, to an invisible snap grid when SNAP is on. With a setting of ⅛", each snap point is spaced ⅛" horizontally and vertically.

Pressing function key F9 or Ctrl + B turns the snap on or off. The snap can also be turned on or off by selecting either option in response to the prompt "Specify snap spacing or [ON/OFF/Aspect/Rotate/Style]" or by clicking SNAP at the bottom of the screen.

It is helpful to set the snap spacing the same as the grid spacing or as a fraction of the grid spacing so the crosshair snaps to every grid point or to every grid point and in between. The snap can be set to snap several times in between the grid points.

Some drawings or parts of drawings should never be drawn with snap off. Snap is a very important tool for quickly locating or aligning elements of your drawing. You may need to turn snap off and on while drawing, but remember that a drawing entity drawn on snap is easily moved, copied, or otherwise edited.

## Zoom

### To view the entire drawing area:

| Prompt | Response |
|---|---|
| Command: | TYPE: **Z<enter>** |
| Specify corner of window, enter a scale<br>    factor (nX or nXP), or [All/Center/<br>    Dynamic/Extents/Previous/Scale/<br>    Window] <real time>: | TYPE: **A<enter>** |

The Zoom-All command lets you view the entire drawing area. Use it after setting up or entering an existing drawing so that you are familiar with the size and shape of your limits and grid. Otherwise, you may be viewing only a small part of the drawing limits and not realize it.

## Drafting Settings Dialog Box and Components of All Dialog Boxes

You can also set snap and grid by using the Drafting Settings dialog box.

To locate the Drafting Settings dialog box, move the pointer across the top of the display screen and highlight "Tools" on the menu bar. When you CLICK: **TOOLS** a pull-down

menu appears. Move your pointer to highlight Drafting Settings... and CLICK: **Drafting Settings...** . The Drafting Settings dialog box (Figure 3–4) now appears on your screen.

All dialog boxes have some basic components. The following is a description of the components that appear in the Drafting Settings dialog box (Figure 3–4) as well as in other dialog boxes you will use:

1. *Cursor:* Changes to an arrow.

2. *Tabs:* Click the title of the tab to select the part of the dialog box you want to use. The Drafting Settings dialog box has three tabs: Snap and Grid, Polar Tracking, and Object Snap.

3. *OK button:* Click this button to complete the command, leave the dialog box, and return to the drawing. If any changes have been made, they will remain as changes. Pressing **<enter>** has the same effect.

4. *Cancel button:* Click this button to cancel the command, leave the dialog box, and return to the drawing. If any changes have been made, they will be canceled and the original settings will return. Pressing the Esc key has the same effect.

5. *Input buttons:* An input button has two parts, its name and the area where changes can be made by typing new input. Click the second part of the input button Snap X spacing:, located under Snap, and experiment with the text cursor that is attached to the point of the arrow. As you move the mouse and pick a new spot, the text cursor moves also. The following editing keys can be used to edit the text in input buttons:

*Backspace key:* Deletes characters to the left of the text cursor one at a time as it is pressed.
*Delete key:* Deletes characters to the right of the text cursor one at a time as it is pressed.
*Left arrow:* Moves the text cursor to the left without changing the existing text.
*Right arrow:* Moves the text cursor to the right without changing the existing text.

**FIGURE 3–4**
Drafting Settings Dialog Box

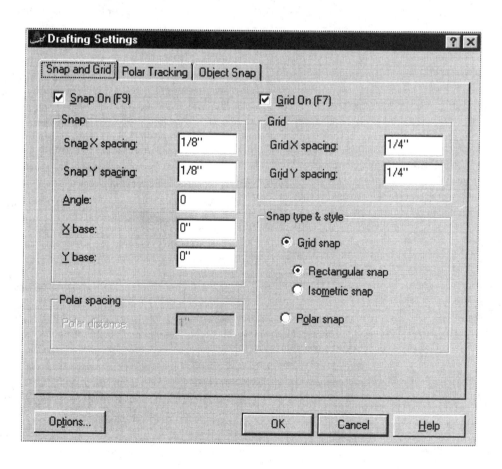

**Part I: Preparing to Draw with AutoCAD**

*Character keys:* After existing settings are deleted, new settings can be typed from the keyboard.

*Snap X spacing input button:* Enter the X spacing in this input button, and the Y spacing is automatically set to the same spacing.

*Grid X spacing input button:* Enter the X spacing in this input button, and the Y spacing is automatically set to the same spacing.

*Snap angle, X base, and Y base input buttons:* These buttons relate to the Rotate option and are discussed in later chapters.

6. *Check buttons:* A check button has two parts, its mode name and the area that can be clicked to toggle the check mark and mode on and off. A check mark in the box indicates the mode is on.

7. *Radio buttons:* A round button within a circle. A dark circle in the selection indicates that selection is picked.

While in the Drafting Settings dialog box, experiment with the different editing keys to become familiar with their functions. The dialog box is a handy tool to use in setting the snap and grid spacing, but if you are a fair typist, typing these commands from the keyboard is faster. After experimenting, be sure to return the grid spacing to ¼ and the snap to ⅛ to have the correct settings for Exercise 4–1.

## Layers

Different parts of a project can be placed on separate layers. The building shell may be on one layer, the interior walls on another, the electrical on a third layer, the furniture on a fourth layer, and so on. There is no limit to the number of layers you may use in a drawing. Each is perfectly aligned with all the others. Each layer may be viewed on the display screen separately, one layer may be viewed in combination with one or more of the other layers, or all layers may be viewed together. Each layer may also be plotted separately or in combination with other layers, or all layers may be plotted at the same time. The layer name may be from 1 to 255 characters in length.

**Create layers using the Layer Properties Manager dialog box (Figures 3–5 and 3–6):**

| Prompt | Response |
|---|---|
| Command: | **Layer...** |
| The Layer Properties Manager dialog box appears (Figure 3–5): | CLICK: **New (three times)** |

**FIGURE 3–5**
Layer Properties Manager
Dialog Box

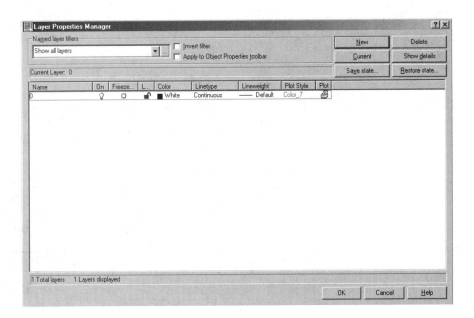

FIGURE 3–6
Layer1, Layer2, Layer3 Appear in
the Layer Name List

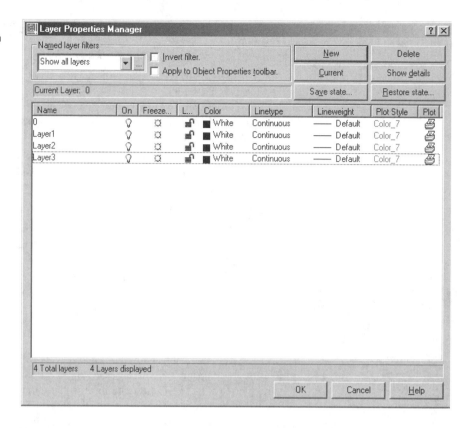

## Prompt

Layer1, Layer2, Layer3 appear in the
Layer Name list (Figure 3–6):

**Assign colors to layers (Figure 3–7):**

## Prompt

The Select Color dialog box appears
(Figure 3–7):

## Response

CLICK: **the black box under Color,
beside Layer1**

## Response

CLICK: **the color Red** (under Standard
Colors)

**FIGURE 3–7**
Select Color Dialog Box

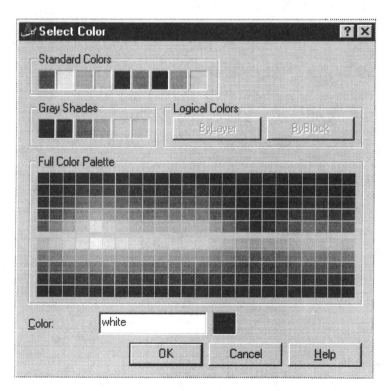

| Prompt | Response |
|---|---|
| | CLICK: **OK** |
| The Layer Properties Manager dialog box appears: | CLICK: **the box under Color, beside Layer2** |
| The Select Color dialog box appears: | CLICK: **the color Magenta** |
| | CLICK: **OK** |
| The Layer Properties Manager dialog box appears: | CLICK: **the box under Color, beside Layer3** |
| The Select Color dialog box appears: | CLICK: **the color Blue** |
| | CLICK: **OK** |

**Assign linetypes to layers (Figures 3–8, 3–9, and 3–10):**

| Prompt | Response |
|---|---|
| The Layer Properties Manager dialog box appears: | CLICK: **the word Continuous under Linetype, beside Layer2** |
| The Select Linetype dialog box appears (Figure 3–8): | CLICK: **Load...** (to load linetypes so they can be selected) |
| The Load or Reload Linetypes dialog box appears (Figure 3–9): | **Move the mouse to the center of the dialog box** and |
| | CLICK: **the right mouse button** |
| | CLICK: **Select All** |
| | CLICK: **OK** |

Linetypes must be loaded before they can be selected. You can load individual linetypes or you can load several by holding down the Shift key as you select. The AutoCAD library of standard linetypes provides you with three different sizes of each standard linetype other than continuous. For example, the DASHED line has the standard size called

**FIGURE 3–8**
Select Linetype Dialog Box

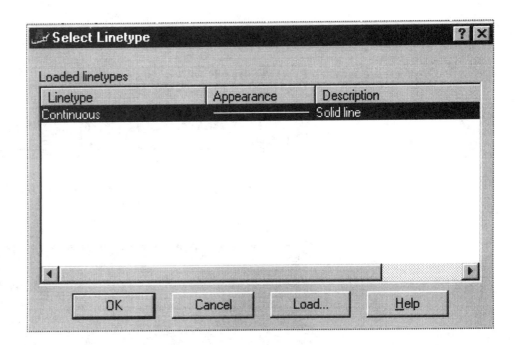

FIGURE 3–9
Load or Reload Linetypes
Dialog Box

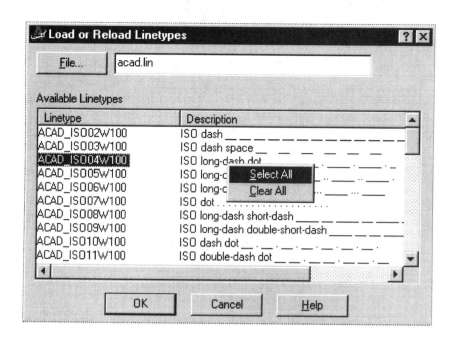

DASHED, a linetype half the standard size called DASHED2(.5x), and a linetype twice the standard size called DASHEDX2(2x).

| Prompt | Response |
|---|---|
| The Select Linetype dialog box appears (Figure 3–10): | CLICK: **Dashed** |
| | CLICK: **OK** |

**Make a layer current (Figure 3–11):**

| Prompt | Response |
|---|---|
| The Layer Properties Manager dialog box appears with layer names, colors, and linetypes assigned as shown in Figure 3–11: | CLICK: **Layer1** (to select it). Be sure to CLICK: on a layer name, not one of the other properties such as lock or color. |

FIGURE 3–10
Select Linetype Dialog Box

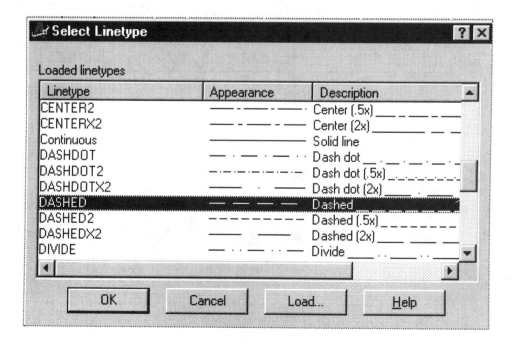

**FIGURE 3–11**
Layers with Colors and Linetypes
Assigned and Layer1 Current

**Note:** In Figure 3–6, the details part of
the Layer Properties Manager dialog box
is not showing. In Figure 3–11, the Show
details button has been clicked to display
the details part of the dialog box.

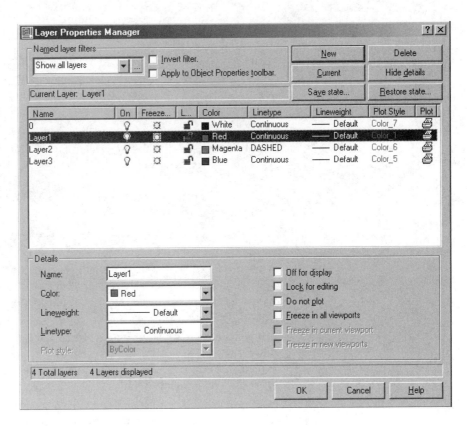

**FIGURE 3–12**
Customize dialog box with the
Toolbars Tab Selected

| Prompt | Response |
|--------|----------|
|  | CLICK: **Current** |
|  | CLICK: **OK** |

Anything drawn from this point until another layer is set current will be on Layer1.

**If the Object Properties toolbar is not visible, make it visible (Figures 3–12 and 3–13):**

| Prompt | Response |
|--------|----------|
| Command: | **Toolbars...** |

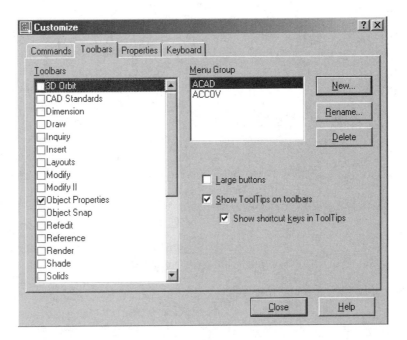

**Chapter 3: Preparing to Draw with AutoCAD**

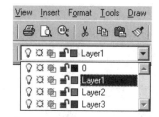

**FIGURE 3–13**
Layer Status on the Object Properties Toolbar

**Note:** With the Object Properties Toolbar displayed, CLICK: the icon showing three sheets of paper to activate the Layer Properties Manager dialog box.

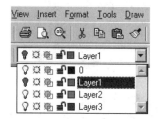

**FIGURE 3–14**
Turn Off Layer1

The Customize dialog box with the
Toolbars tab selected appears
(Figure 3–12):

The Object Properties toolbar appears docked
at the top of the screen with Layer1 current:

CLICK: **the check box beside Object Properties** (so a ✔ appears as shown in Figure 3–12)

CLICK: **Close**

CLICK: **the down arrow** (as shown in Figure 3–13)

The Layer option icons on the Object Properties Toolbar that can be changed, reading from left to right, are:

1. *On or Off:* These pertain to the visibility of layers. When a layer is turned OFF, it is still part of the drawing, but any entity drawn on that layer is not visible on the screen and cannot be plotted. For instance, the building exterior walls layer, interior walls layer, and electrical layer are turned ON and all other layers turned OFF to view, edit, or plot an electrical plan. One or more layers can be turned OFF and ON as required.

2. *Frozen or Thawed in all Viewports:* These also pertain to the visibility of layers. The difference between ON/OFF and FREEZE/THAW is a matter of how quickly the drawing regenerates on the display screen. If a layer is frozen, it is not visible, cannot be plotted, and AutoCAD spends no time regenerating it. A layer that is turned OFF is not visible and cannot be plotted, but AutoCAD does regenerate it.

3. *Frozen or Thawed in Current Viewport:* When you are working with more than one viewport, you may freeze or thaw a layer only in the current viewport. The same layer in other viewports remains unaffected.

4. *Locked or Unlocked:* When a layer is locked, it is visible, and you can draw on it. You cannot use any of the Edit commands to edit any of the drawing entities on the layer. You cannot accidentally change any entity that is already drawn.

To change the state of any layer pick the icon to select the alternate state. For example, Figure 3–14 shows that LAYER1 was turned off by picking the light bulb to turn it off. Experiment with changing the state of layers, then open the Layer Properties Manager dialog box to see the changed state reflected in it. Three additional layer properties that are shown in the Layer Properties Manager dialog box are:

1. *Lineweight:* A lineweight can be assigned to a layer. Lineweights are expressed in millimeters, similar to pen widths. The default lineweight initially set for all layers is .25 mm. The display of the lineweight is controlled by clicking LWT on the status bar. Lineweights are displayed in pixels on the screen; they plot with the exact width of the assigned lineweight. Lineweights can be varied, for example, to show thick lines for a floor plan and thin lines for dimensions, to emphasize something on the drawing, to show existing and new construction, or existing and new furniture.

2. *Plot Style:* Plot styles are created using a plot style table to define various properties such as color, grayscale, and lineweight. A layer's plot style overrides the layer's color, linetype, and lineweight. Plot styles are used when you want to plot the same drawing with different settings or different drawings with the same settings.

3. *Make Layer Plottable or Nonplottable:* This allows you to make visible layers nonplottable. For example, you may not want to plot a layer that shows construction lines. When a layer is nonplottable, it is displayed but not plotted.

Experiment with all parts of the Layer Properties Manager dialog box. If you create some layers that you do not need, delete them by highlighting them and picking the Delete button. To change a layer name, color, or linetype, highlight the layer, and change it in the Details area of the dialog box. Return all layers to their original state before you exit. Pick any open spot on the screen to close the layer list.

**Part I: Preparing to Draw with AutoCAD**

## Options Dialog Box, Open and Save Tab

To locate the Options dialog box, move the pointer across the top of the display screen and highlight **Tools** on the menu bar. CLICK: **Tools,** and a pull-down menu appears. Move your pointer to highlight Options... and CLICK: **Options....** The Options dialog box (Figure 3–15) appears on your screen. CLICK: the **Open and Save tab.**

Controls under the File Save section of the Options dialog box pertain to settings related to saving a file in AutoCAD.

1. *Save as button:* This displays the file formats that can be used when saving an AutoCAD drawing. This option sets the default file format to which drawings will be saved.

2. *Save a thumbnail preview image check button:* When this button is checked, an image of the drawing will be displayed in the Preview area of the Select File dialog box.

3. *Incremental save percentage text box:* Leave this set at 50 to optimize performance. AutoCAD saves only the changes made to a drawing until the percentage of changed space equals the amount set in this box. When the percentage is met, AutoCAD performs a full Save, which eliminates wasted space. When set to 0, AutoCAD will make a full save every time.

Controls under the File Safety Precautions section of the dialog box pertain to preventing data loss and detecting errors.

1. *Automatic Save:* When this box is checked, AutoCAD automatically saves your drawing at the interval you specify in the *Minutes between saves* text box.

2. *Create backup copy with each save:* When this box is checked, AutoCAD will create a backup file each time the drawing is saved. Use the Files tab in this Options dialog box to specify the location of the backup files.

3. *Full-time CRC validation:* CRC means *cyclic redundancy check.* You would check this box if your drawings were being corrupted and you suspected an AutoCAD error or a hardware problem.

**FIGURE 3–15**
Options Dialog Box

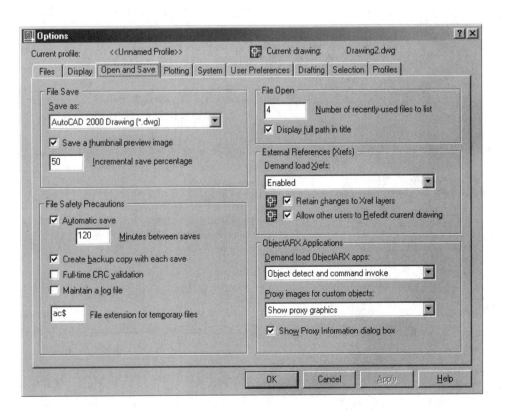

4. *Maintain a log file:* When this box is checked, the contents of the text window are written to a log file. Use the Files tab in this Options dialog box to specify the location of the backup files.

5. *File extension for temporary files:* Used in a network environment to identify temporary files.

## Saving the Drawing and Exiting AutoCAD

You must understand three commands, Save, SaveAs, and Exit (or Quit), and their uses to save your work in the desired drive and directory and to exit AutoCAD after you have saved your work.

### Save

When the command Save is clicked and the drawing has been named, the drawing is saved automatically to the drive and folder in which you are working, and a backup file is created with the same name but with the extension .bak. If the drawing has not been named, Save behaves like SaveAs.

### SaveAs

SaveAs activates the Save Drawing As dialog box whether or not the drawing has been named and allows you to save your drawing to any drive or directory you choose.

Some additional features of the SaveAs command are as follows:

1. A drawing file can be saved and you may continue to work because with the SaveAs command the drawing editor is not exited.

2. If the default drive is used (the drive on which you are working), and the drawing has been opened from that drive, .dwg and .bak files are created when "Create backup copy with each save" is checked on the Open and Save tab on the Options dialog box.

3. If a different drive is specified (a floppy disk in the floppy drive), only a .dwg file is created.

4. To change the name of the drawing, you may save it under a new name by typing a new name in the File Name: button.

5. If the drawing was previously saved, or if a drawing file already exists with the drawing file name you typed, AutoCAD gives you the message "drawing name.dwg already exists. Do you want to replace it?"

   When a drawing file is updated, the old .dwg file is replaced with the new drawing, so the answer to click is Yes. If an error has been made and you do not want to replace the file, click No.

6. A drawing may be saved to as many floppy disks or to as many folders on the hard disk as you wish. You should save your drawing in two different places as insurance against catastrophe.

7. Any drawing can be saved as a template. A drawing template should include settings such as units, limits, grid, snap, layers, title blocks, dimension and text styles, linetypes, and lineweights. When you use the template file to start a new drawing, the settings are already set.

**Save the settings and layers for Exercise 4–1 on the hard drive, or select the drive and folder you want to save in (Figure 3–16):**

| Prompt | Response |
|---|---|
| Command: | **SaveAs...** |

FIGURE 3–16
Save Drawing As Dialog Box;
Save CH4-EX1

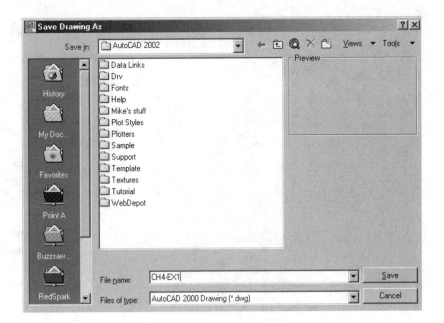

**Prompt**

The Save Drawing As dialog box
appears with the file name highlighted:

**Response**

TYPE: **CH4-EX1** (Because the file
name was highlighted, you were able to
type in that place. If you had used any
other part of the dialog box first, you
would have had to pick to the left of the
file name, hold down the pick button, and
drag the cursor across the name or double
click the text to highlight it and then
begin typing.)

The Save Drawing As dialog box appears
as shown in Figure 3–16:

**Select the drive and/or folder in which
you want to save CH4-EX1.**

CLICK: **Save**

Be sure to make note of the drive and folder where the drawing is being saved so you can
retrieve it easily when you need it.

**OPTIONAL: Save the same drawing to a floppy disk in the A: drive. (Substitute the
drive letter if needed.) (Figure 3–17):**

Insert a formatted diskette into the A drive.

**Prompt**

Command:

The Save Drawing As dialog box appears:

**Response**

Save As…

CLICK: **the down arrow in the
Save in: button, highlight 3½
Floppy [A:]**

FIGURE 3–17
Save CH4-EX1 on the Disk in the
3½ Floppy Drive [A:]

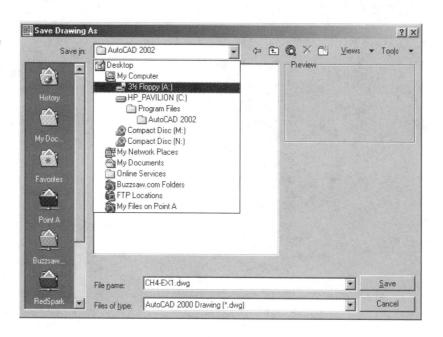

**Prompt**

The Save Drawing As dialog box appears as shown in Figure 3–17:

**Response**

CLICK: **3½ floppy [A:]**

CLICK: **Save**

The light should brighten on the A: drive, indicating that the drawing is being saved. Because the drawing was named when you saved it on the hard drive, you did not have to type the name again to save it with that name on the floppy disk. You could have chosen to give the drawing another name when you saved it on the floppy disk, in which case you would have to type the new name in the File name: input button.

**Save the drawing as a template to a floppy disk in the A: drive, or select the drive and folder you want to save in (Figures 3–18 and 3–19):**

**Prompt**

Command:

The Save Drawing As dialog box appears:

**Response**

**SaveAs...**

CLICK: **the down arrow in the Files of type: button and move the cursor to**

CLICK: **AutoCAD Drawing Template File[*.dwt]**

TYPE: **A-SIZE** (in the File name: input area so the Save Drawing As dialog box appears as shown in Figure 3–18)

CLICK: **the down arrow in the Save in: button, highlight 3½ Floppy [A:]**

CLICK: **3½ Floppy [A:]**

CLICK: **Save**

The Template Description dialog box appears (Figure 3–19):

TYPE: **Setup for 8-1/2,11 sheet** (as shown in Figure 3–19)

CLICK: **OK**

**Note:** If saving on a floppy disk is not convenient, save the drawing as a template in the drive and folder that you use.

**FIGURE 3–18**
Save A-SIZE as a Template on the Disk in the 3½ Floppy Drive [A:]

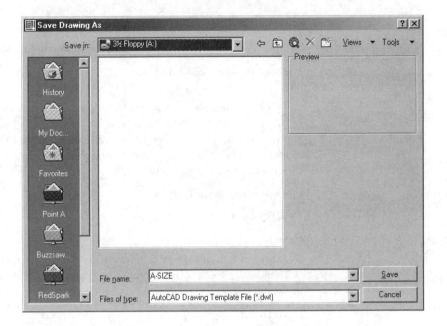

**FIGURE 3–19**
Template Description Dialog Box

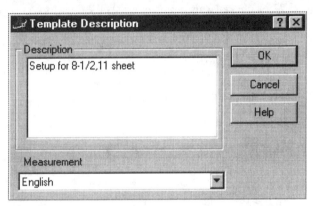

## Drawing Name and File Name Extension

The drawing name can be up to 255 characters long and can have spaces. The drawing name cannot have special characters that the AutoCAD or Microsoft® Windows programs use for other purposes. The special characters that cannot be used include the less-than and greater-than symbols (<>), forward slashes and backslashes (/ \), backquotes (`), equal signs (=), vertical bars (|), asterisks (*), commas (,), question marks (?), semicolons (;), colons (:), and quotation marks ("). As you continue to learn AutoCAD, other objects will be named also, like layers. These naming conventions apply to all named objects.

AutoCAD automatically adds the file extension .dwg to the drawing name and .bak to a backup file. The symbol or icon to the left of the filename describes the type file. If you would also like to see the .dwg and .bak extensions, activate Windows® Explorer and complete the following steps:

1. CLICK: **Folder Options…** on the View menu on the menu bar in Windows 95 and 98, and on the Tools menu in Windows ME. (Earlier versions of Windows will be slightly different, but the labels will be approximately the same.)

2. Remove the check in the check box before the setting "Hide file extensions for known file types."

If you lose a drawing file, the drawing's .bak file can be renamed as a .dwg file and used as the drawing file. Simply keep the name, but change the file extension using Windows® Explorer. If the .dwg file is corrupted, you may give the .bak file a new name and change the extension to .dwg.

## Save Drawing As Dialog Box

The parts and functions of the Save Drawing As dialog box are as follows:

### File name: Input Button

The drawing file name that will be saved appears here.

When you double click any folder, an alphabetized list of all files of the type defined by the Files of type: button in the drive and directory specified in the Save In: button appears. If you want to use one of the names in this list, click it, and that name will replace the one in the File name: button. You will need to use the scroll bar if the list of files is longer than the area shown.

### Files of type: Input Button

Clicking the down arrow reveals a list of file types under which the drawing may be saved.

### Save in:

The drive and folder where the file will be saved is shown here. The list shown in Figure 3–20 indicates that the Template folder under the AutoCAD 2002 folder is open. The list of files in this area shows the files with the .dwt extension that exist in this folder.

### Save Button

When clicked, this button executes the SaveAs... command. If you have already saved the drawing with the same name in the same folder, the warning shown in Figure 3–21 appears. Click Yes if you want to replace the drawing, No if you don't.

### Cancel Button

When clicked, this button cancels the command or closes any open button on the dialog box. The Esc key has the same effect.

FIGURE 3–20
The Template Folder Is Open

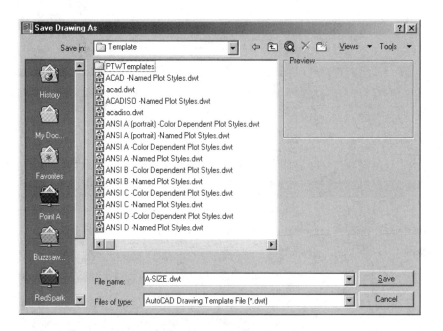

FIGURE 3–21
Save Drawing As Warning

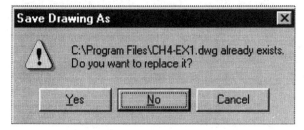

Part I: Preparing to Draw with AutoCAD

File  Edit  View  Insert  Format
New...                    Ctrl+N
Open...                   Ctrl+O
Close
Partial Load
Save                      Ctrl+S
Save As...
eTransmit...
Publish to Web...
Export...
Page Setup...
Plotter Manager...
Plot Style Manager...
Plot Preview
Plot...                   Ctrl+P
Drawing Utilities         ▶
Send...
Drawing Properties...
1 CH4-EX1.dwg
2 A:\A-SIZE.dwt
3 B-SIZE.dwg
4 fIG11-27.dwg
Exit

**Note:** The File menu **Exit** and the Command line: QUIT are the same command.

## Exit (or Quit)

If you have not made any changes to the drawing since you last saved it, the Exit command takes you out of the AutoCAD program. If you have made changes to the drawing and have not saved these changes, AutoCAD will display the message "Save changes to C:\CH4-EX1.dwg?" (or whatever the drawing name is). This is a safety feature because the Exit command, by itself, *does not update or save a drawing*. You have three options: Yes, save the changes; No, do not save changes; or Cancel the Exit command.

If you have just entered a drawing, have made a lot of mistakes, and just want to get rid of everything, respond with No to the Save changes question. If you opened an existing drawing and use the Exit command without making any changes, the stored .dwg file and .bak files are preserved unchanged.

While you are making a new drawing, AutoCAD is creating a .dwg (drawing) file of your drawing. There is no .bak (drawing file backup) file for a new drawing.

Each time an existing drawing file is opened for editing, the original drawing file (.dwg) becomes the drawing file backup (.bak) when "Create backup copy with each save" is checked in the Open and Save tab in the Options dialog box. The new edited version of the drawing becomes the .dwg file. Thus there is a copy of the original drawing file (.bak) and a copy of the new edited version (.dwg).

### Exit AutoCAD:

| Prompt | Response |
|---|---|
| Command: | **Exit** (You may also TYPE: **QUIT<enter>** to exit.) |

## EXERCISE

EXERCISE 3–1. Complete Exercise 3–1 using the procedure described in this chapter.

## REVIEW QUESTIONS

1. Which of the following is *not* on the list of unit length types in the Drawing Units dialog box?
   a. Scientific
   b. Metric
   c. Decimal
   d. Fractional
   e. Architectural
2. The Precision: button on the Drawing Units dialog box does which of the following?
   a. Determines how accurately AutoCAD draws
   b. Has a default value of 1/16″, which may not be changed
   c. Sets decimal places for fractional units
   d. Allows you to set the smallest fraction to display dimensions and other values shown on the screen
   e. Sets decimal places for architectural units
3. While using AutoCAD to make drawings always draw full scale.
   a. True
   b. False
4. The default lower left corner of the drawing limits is 8-1/2,11.
   a. True
   b. False
5. The function key F7 described in this chapter does which of the following?
   a. Provides a check list of the layers created
   b. Turns snap ON or OFF
   c. Flips the screen from the text display to the graphics display
   d. Turns grid ON or OFF
   e. Turns ortho ON or OFF

6. Units, Limits, Grid, and Snap can all be found under the Format menu.
   a. True
   b. False
7. Which of the following function keys is used to turn snap ON or OFF?
   a. F1
   b. F2
   c. F7
   d. F8
   e. F9
8. How many layers may be used in a drawing?
   a. 1
   b. 2
   c. 3
   d. 16
   e. An unlimited number
9. When a layer is OFF, it will regenerate but is not visible.
   a. True
   b. False
10. AutoCAD provides how many sizes of each standard linetype (except continuous)?
   a. 1
   b. 2
   c. 3
   d. 4
   e. As many as you want

Complete.

11. Describe the effect of using the Esc key while in a command.

   _____

12. What is an invisible grid to which the crosshair will lock called?

   _____

13. What Windows® program do you use to change a setting to make all three-letter file name extensions visible?

   _____

14. What special characters cannot be used in a layer and drawing name?

   _____

15. What is the maximum number of characters that may be used in a drawing name?

   _____

16. Explain what .dwg and .dwt files are.
   .dwg: _____
   .dwt: _____

17. Before a linetype other than continuous may be selected or changed in the Layer Properties Manager dialog box, what must be done?

   _____

18. List the toolbar on which the layer status is displayed.

   _____

19. What does the Exit or Quit command do when used by itself?

   _____

20. Describe how Save differs from SaveAs when the drawing has been named.

   _____

# TWO-DIMENSIONAL AUTOCAD

# Drawing with AutoCAD: Basic Commands and Settings

## OBJECTIVES

When you have completed this chapter, you will be able to:

☐ Correctly use the following commands and settings

| | | | | |
|---|---|---|---|---|
| 2D Solid | Ellipse | Ltscale | Pan | Scale |
| Arc | Erase | Move | Redo | Select |
| Blipmode | Highlight | Oops | Redraw | Undo |
| Circle | Line | Ortho | Regen | Zoom |
| Donut | | | | |

☐ Turn ORTHO mode on and off to control drawing as required.
☐ Turn the screen coordinate display off and on.
☐ Correctly use the following selection set options contained in many Modify commands:

| | | | |
|---|---|---|---|
| All | Previous | Add | Window Polygon |
| Window | Crossing Window | Undo | Crossing Polygon |
| Last | Remove | Fence | |

☐ Use the transparent Zoom and Pan commands while another command is in progress.

## INTRODUCTION

Exercises 4–1 and 4–2 provide step-by-step instructions describing how to use many of the AutoCAD commands. Exercises 4–3, 4–4, and 4–5 provide drawings for you to practice the commands learned in Exercises 3–1, 4–1, and 4–2.

Several options are available for each command, and you can access many commands from the Command: line, from the toolbars, or from the menu bar. Experiment with each new command to become familiar with it; you can then decide which options you prefer to use and how you like to access the commands. Upon completion of Chapter 4 and mastery of the commands included in the chapter, you will have a sound foundation upon which to continue learning AutoCAD and the remaining commands.

### Following the Exercises in This Book

Prompt and Response columns continue to provide the steps required to start and complete each new command sequence. A new Response column item used in this and following chapters describes the location of points picked on the screen. Figures are provided throughout the chapters to show the location of the points. Points are indicated in bold type

in the Response column by a **D** followed by a number (for example, **D1,D2**). Look at the figure provided to locate the point on the drawing, and pick a point in the same place on your screen drawing. Another feature added to this and following chapters is that sometimes the response is described generally in the Response column (for example, **Pick the middle of the windowed view**).

## Using the Mouse and Right-Click Customization

You may be using a two-button mouse, a three-button mouse, or a mouse with a small wheel between the buttons. With all three, the left button is the pick button used to select commands and specify points on the screen.

The Right-Click Customization dialog box settings control what happens when the right mouse button (shown as **<enter>** in this book) is clicked. To access the Right-Click Customization dialog box, select Options… under Tools in the menu bar. Select the User Preferences tab of the Options dialog box (Figure 4–1). CLICK: the **Right-Click Customization…** button in the Windows Standard Behavior area, and the Right-Click Customization dialog box (Figure 4–2) appears.

1. Default Mode: In the default mode no objects on the screen are selected, and no command is in progress.
   *Repeat Last Command radio button:* When this button is selected, clicking the right mouse button will repeat the last command.
   *Shortcut Menu radio button:* When this button is selected, a shortcut menu as shown in Figure 4–3 appears when the right mouse button is clicked.

2. Edit Mode: In the edit mode no command is active, and the user selects one or more objects on the screen.
   *Repeat Last Command radio button:* When this button is selected, clicking the right mouse button will repeat the last command.
   *Shortcut Menu radio button:* When this button is selected, and the right mouse button is clicked, a shortcut menu with editing commands will appear (Figure 4–4). The menu may contain edit options specific to the object selected.

**FIGURE 4–1**
Options Dialog Box, User Preferences Tab

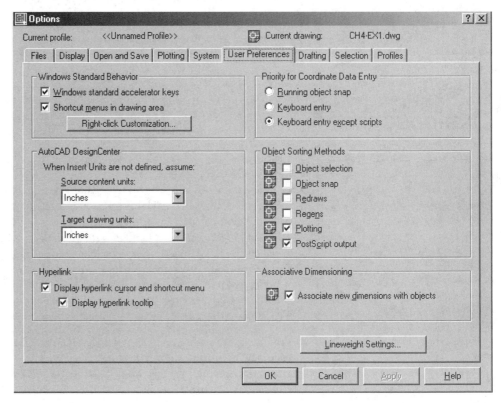

Part II: Two-Dimensional AutoCAD

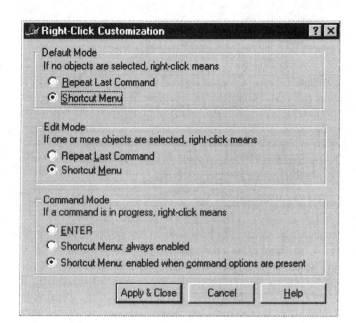

**FIGURE 4–2**
Right-Click Customization Dialog Box

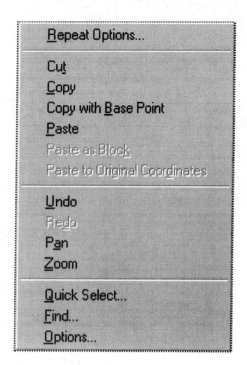

**FIGURE 4–3**
Default Mode Shortcut Menu

3. Command Mode: In the command mode a command is in progress.
   *Enter:* When this button is selected, clicking the right mouse button is the same as pressing the enter key. The shortcut menus are disabled.
   *Shortcut menu; always enabled:* When this button is selected, the shortcut menus are enabled.

**FIGURE 4–4**
Edit Mode Shortcut Menu

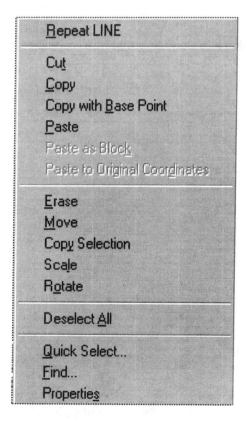

FIGURE 4–5
Command Mode Shortcut Menu

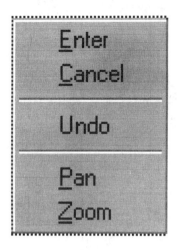

*Shortcut menu; enabled when command options are present:* When this button is selected, a shortcut menu showing command options (Figure 4–5) will appear when the right mouse button is clicked. When no command options are available, right clicking will be the same as pressing the enter key.

In the Response columns of this book **<enter>** indicates that the right mouse button should be clicked. Notes in parentheses are used to clarify how **<enter>** is used. For example, **<enter>** (to return the Line command prompt).

# EXERCISE 4–1
# Drawing Lines and Circles

In Chapter 3, the settings and layers were made for drawing CH4-EX1. In Exercise 4–1, that setup is used to complete your first drawing exercise. When you have completed Exercise 4–1, your drawing will look similar to the drawing in Figure 4–6.

To begin Exercise 4–1, turn on the computer and start AutoCAD. The AutoCAD 2002 Today window is displayed. In the Open Drawings tab of the AutoCAD 2002 Today window, you can use four different methods for locating and opening a file: Most Recently Used, History by Date, History by Filename, and History by Location. Each method shows a file history list of the most recently used drawings. After selecting a method for locating a file hold your mouse over the drawing names in the history list to view the complete drive and folder where the drawing is located and to see a thumbnail preview.

## Open an Existing Drawing on the Hard Drive

If your drawing CH4-EX1 is stored on a floppy disk, proceed with the following. If your drawing CH4-EX1 is stored on the hard disk, skip to the section "To open existing drawing CH4-EX1 on the hard drive when it is stored on the hard disk."

**To open existing drawing CH4-EX1 when it is stored on a floppy disk that has no directories:**

| Prompt | Response |
|---|---|
| The AutoCAD 2002 Today window is displayed: | **Insert the floppy disk in drive A:.** |
| | CLICK: **Open Drawings tab** |
| | DOUBLE CLICK: **A:\CH4-EX1.dwg** |
| | -or- |
| | If A:\CH4-EX1.dwg is not listed in the Select a File: selection: CLICK: **Browse…** |

**Note:** DOUBLE CLICK: means to place your cursor over the selection and press the left mouse button twice rapidly.

**FIGURE 4–6**
Exercise 4–1: Drawing Lines and
Circles

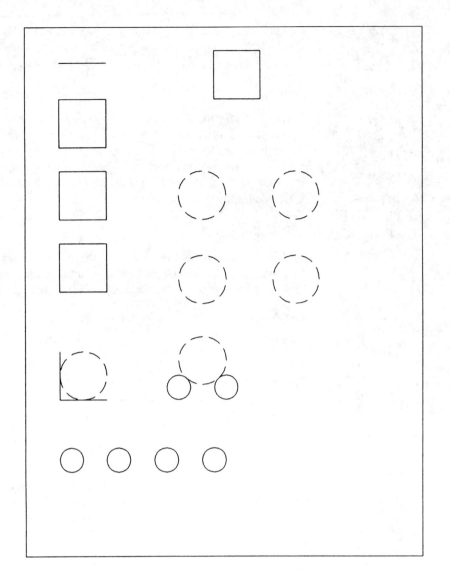

| Prompt | Response |
|---|---|
| The Select File dialog box appears: | CLICK: **3 1/2 Floppy[A:]** |
| | CLICK: **CH4-EX1** |
| | CLICK: **Open** (or DOUBLE CLICK: **CH4-EX1**) |
| CH4-EX1 is opened. | |

**Save the drawing to the hard drive:**

| Prompt | Response |
|---|---|
| Command: | **Save As...** |
| The Save Drawing As dialog box is displayed: | CLICK: **[C:]** (and the correct folder if needed) |
| | CLICK: **Save** |

Now you are working on the hard drive. Do not work on a floppy disk. Always work on the hard drive.

**To open existing drawing CH4-EX1 on the hard drive when it is stored on the hard disk:**

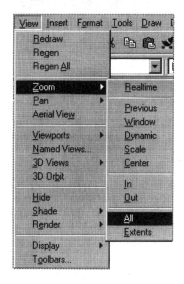

If your drawing is stored on the hard disk, CLICK: **the Open Drawings tab,** and CLICK: C:\CH4-EX1 to open it (include the folder name if you have saved it to a folder).

If your drawing file is not listed, CLICK: **Browse...** to locate it.

## Toolbars

The Object Properties toolbar and the Standard Toolbar are usually visible by default. Illustrations of the AutoCAD menu bar and toolbars of the commands needed to complete the exercises are shown in the book margins. If you plan to use any of the toolbars, be sure to select **Toolbars...** from the **View** menu in the menu bar, and activate the toolbar that contains the tools for the commands that will be used. The name of the toolbar used is included in the margin art.

## ZOOM

The Zoom-All command lets you view the entire drawing area. Use it after setting up or entering a drawing so that you are familiar with the size and shape of your limits and grid. Otherwise, you may be working on a small part of the drawing and not realize it.

**Use Zoom-All to view the entire drawing area:**

| Prompt | Response |
|---|---|
| Command: | **Zoom-All** (or TYPE: **Z\<enter>**) |
| Specify corner of window, enter a scale factor (nX or nXP), or [All/Center/Dynamic/ Extents/Previous/Scale/Window] \<real time>: | TYPE: **A\<enter>** |

## Grid

The grid is visible when it is ON. Press the F7 function key to turn the grid OFF and ON, or CLICK: **GRID** at the bottom of your screen. Turn the grid OFF and ON to clean up any blips that appear on the screen while you are drawing.

## On Your Own

**1. Turn the grid on.**

## Ortho

Press the F8 function key to turn Ortho ON and OFF, or CLICK: **ORTHO** at the bottom of your screen. Ortho mode, when ON, helps you to draw lines perfectly horizontally and vertically. It does not allow you to draw at an angle, so turn Ortho OFF and ON as needed.

## On Your Own

**1. Turn Ortho ON.**

## SNAP

Function key F9 turns Snap ON and OFF, or you may CLICK: **SNAP** at the bottom of your screen. Snap helps you to draw accurately; it is desirable to draw with Snap ON most of the time. If you need to turn Snap OFF to draw or edit a drawing entity, remember to turn it back ON as soon as possible.

## On Your Own

**1. Turn Snap ON.**

**2. Check the Layer Control; Layer1 should be current.**

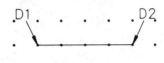

# LINE and ERASE

Use Figure 4–6 as a guide when locating the line and squares drawn using the Line command.

## Drawing Lines Using the Grid Marks

Lines can be drawn by snapping to the grid marks visible on the screen.

**Draw a horizontal line 1″ long, using the grid marks (Figure 4–7):**

**FIGURE 4–7**
Draw a Horizontal Line 1″ Long, Using Grid Marks

| Prompt | Response |
|---|---|
| Command: | **Line** (or TYPE: **L<enter>**) |
| Specify first point: | **D1** (Do not type "D1". Look at Figure 4–7 and click the point D1, approximately three grid spaces down (3/4″) and three grid spaces to the right of the upper left corner of the page.) |
| Specify next point or [Undo]: | **D2** (move four grid marks to the right) |
| Specify next point or [Undo]: | **<enter>** (to complete the command) |

**Erase the line and bring it back again:**

| Prompt | Response |
|---|---|
| Command: | **Erase** (or TYPE: **E<enter>**) |
| Select objects: | **Position the small box that replaces the crosshair any place on the line and click the line.** |
| Select objects: 1 found | |
| Select objects: | **<enter>** (the line disappears) |
| Command: | TYPE: **OOPS<enter>** (the line reappears) |

Do not be afraid to draw with AutoCAD. If you make a mistake, you can easily erase it using the Erase command. When you are using the Erase command, a small box replaces the screen crosshair. The small box is called the *pickbox*. The Oops feature will restore everything erased by the *last* erase command. Oops cannot be used to restore lines erased by a previous command.

**Draw a 1″ square using the grid marks and undo the last two lines (Figure 4–8):**

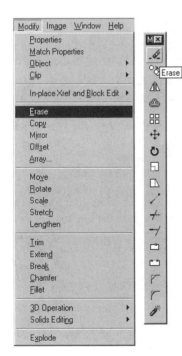

**FIGURE 4–8**
Draw a 1″ Square Using Grid Marks

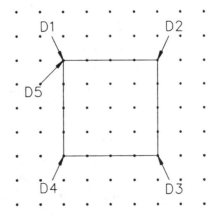

| Prompt | Response |
|---|---|
| Command: | **Line** |
| Specify first point: | **D1** (click a point 3/4″ directly below the left end of the line just drawn) |
| Specify next point or [Undo]: | **D2** (Figure 4–8) |
| Specify next point or [Undo]: | **D3** |
| Specify next point or [Close/Undo]: | **D4** |
| Specify next point or [Close/Undo]: | **D5** |
| Specify next point or [Close/Undo]: | TYPE: **U<enter>** (Move your mouse to see that the line is undone.) |
| Specify next point or [Close/Undo]: | TYPE: **U<enter>** |
| Specify next point or [Close/Undo]: | **<enter>** (to stop and return to the Command: prompt) |

While in the line command if you decide you do not like the last line segment drawn, use the Undo command to erase it and continue on with the "To point:" prompt. Clicking more than one undo will backtrack through the line segments in the reverse of the order in which they were drawn.

**Complete the square (Figure 4–8):**

| Prompt | Response |
|---|---|
| Command: | **<enter>** (to return the Line command prompt) |
| Specify first point: | **<enter>** (the line is attached) |
| Specify next point or [Undo]: | **D4,D5** |
| Specify next point or [Close/Undo]: | **<enter>** (to stop) |

The Line command has a very handy feature: If you respond to the prompt "Specify first point:" by pressing the enter key or the space bar, the line will start at the end of the most recently drawn line.

*The following part of this exercise describes how to draw lines using absolute coordinates, relative coordinates, and polar coordinates. It is important that you are aware of and take the time to understand the various methods, because they apply to drawing other objects also. Of course, you can always refer to this section of the book if you are faced with a situation in which you do not know the best method of drawing.*

### Drawing Lines Using Absolute Coordinates

**Note:** Pressing the Esc key cancels the command selection process and returns AutoCAD to the "Command:" prompt. Use Esc if you get stuck in a command.

Remember, 0,0 is the lower left corner of the page. When you use absolute coordinates to draw, the X-axis coordinate is entered first and identifies a location on the horizontal axis. The Y-axis coordinate is entered second and identifies a location on the vertical axis. The page size is 8-1/2,11. A little adding and subtracting to determine the absolute coordinates will locate the square on the page as follows.

**Draw a 1″ square using absolute coordinates (Figure 4–9):**

| Prompt | Response |
|---|---|
| Command: | **Line** (move the crosshairs to the center of the screen) |
| Specify first point: | TYPE: **4,10-1/2<enter>** (the line begins) |
| Specify next point or [Undo]: | TYPE: **5,10-1/2<enter>** |
| Specify next point or [Undo]: | TYPE: **5,9-1/2<enter>** |
| Specify next point or [Close/Undo]: | TYPE: **4,9-1/2<enter>** |
| Specify next point or [Close/Undo]: | TYPE: **C<enter>** |

**FIGURE 4–9**
Draw a 1″ Square Using Absolute Coordinates

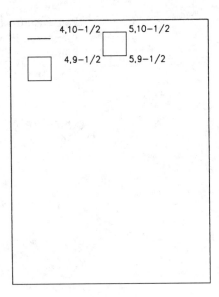

## On Your Own

1. **Function key F6 controls the screen coordinate display located in the lower left corner of the screen. Press the F6 function key to turn the coordinate display off and on. Turn the screen coordinate display on and move your pointer to each corner of the square. Watch how the screen coordinate display shows the X,Y coordinate position of each corner. Compare those coordinates with the coordinates you just typed and entered. They are the same.**

2. **Hold the crosshair of the cursor (with snap on) on the lower left corner of the grid; the coordinate display reads 0′-0″,0′-0″. Move the cursor to the upper right corner of the grid; the coordinate display reads 0′-8 ½″,0′-11″.**

### Drawing Lines Using Relative Coordinates

Relative coordinates are used after a point is entered. (Relative to what? Relative to the point just entered.) After a point has been clicked on the drawing, relative coordinates are entered by typing @, followed by the X,Y coordinates. For example, after a point is entered to start a line, typing and entering @ 1,0 will draw the line 1″ in the X direction, 0″ in the Y direction.

**Draw a 1″ square using relative coordinates:**

| Prompt | Response |
|---|---|
| Command: | **Line** |
| Specify first point: | **Click a point on the grid ½″ below the lower left corner of the first square drawn.** |
| Specify next point or [Undo]: | TYPE: **@1,0<enter>** |
| Specify next point or [Undo]: | TYPE: **@0,−1<enter>** |
| Specify next point or [Close/Undo]: | TYPE: **@−1,0<enter>** |
| Specify next point or [Close/Undo]: | TYPE: **C<enter>** |

A minus sign (−) is used for negative line location with relative coordinates. Negative is to the left for the X axis and down for the Y axis.

### Drawing Lines Using Polar Coordinates

Absolute and relative coordinates are extremely useful in some situations; however, for many design applications (for example, drawing walls) polar coordinates or direct distance entry is used. Be sure you understand how to use all types of coordinates.

Polar coordinates are also relative to the last point entered. They are typed starting with an @, followed by a distance and angle of direction. Figure 4–10 shows the polar coordinate angle directions. The angle of direction is always preceded by a < sign when polar coordinates are entered.

**Draw a 1″ square using polar coordinates:**

FIGURE 4–10
Polar Coordinate Angles

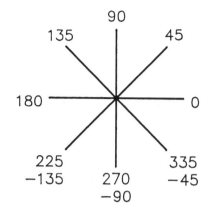

| Prompt | Response |
|---|---|
| Command: | **\<enter\>** (to return the Line command prompt) |
| Specify first point: | **Click a point on the grid 1/2″ below the lower left corner of the last square drawn.** |
| Specify next point or [Undo]: | TYPE: **@1\<0\<enter\>** |
| Specify next point or [Undo]: | TYPE: **@1\<270\<enter\>** |
| Specify next point or [Close/Undo]: | TYPE: **@1\<180\<enter\>** |
| Specify next point or [Close/Undo]: | TYPE: **C\<enter\>** |

## Drawing Lines Using Tracking Along Polar Angles

Function key F10 turns polar tracking on and off, or you may CLICK: **POLAR** at the bottom of your screen. With polar tracking on, as you move the cursor across the screen, alignment paths and tooltips are displayed when you move along polar angles. When polar tracking is on, Ortho mode is automatically off because Ortho restricts the cursor to horizontal and vertical movement.

You can set the polar tracking by using the Drafting Settings dialog box, under Tools in the menu bar. CLICK: the **Polar Tracking** tab (Figure 4–11) of the Drafting Settings dialog box. The following is a description of the components that appear:

1. *Polar Tracking On (F10) check box:* When this box is checked, polar tracking is on.
2. *Polar Angle Settings—Increment angle:* Click the down arrow to select a polar angle increment to track along. You can select 90, 45, 30, 22.5, 18, 15, 10, and 5°.
3. *Polar Angle Settings—Additional angles:* Click the New button to specify in the list box the additional angles you want to track. The Delete button will delete the additional angles.
4. *Polar Angle measurement—Absolute:* Measures polar angles on the X and Y axes of the current UCS.
5. *Polar Angle measurement—Relative to last segment:* Measures polar angles based on the X and Y axes of the last line created.

## On Your Own

1. **Practice drawing lines using polar tracking. Change the settings in the Polar Tracking tab of the Drafting Settings dialog box, and practice different angle**

FIGURE 4–11
Drafting Settings Dialog Box,
Polar Tracking Tab

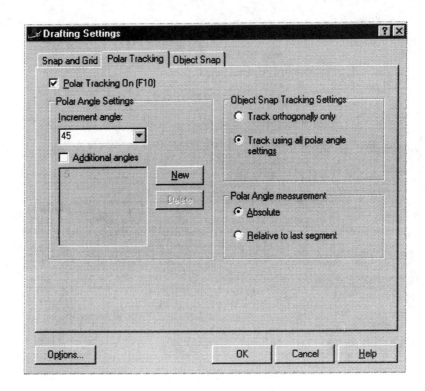

increments. Also, draw lines using absolute and relative to last segment angles so you can understand the difference. Erase your practice session.

2. Use the Erase command to erase the entire last square you just drew using polar coordinates, then replace it using Direct Distance Entry, as described next.

### Drawing Lines Using Direct Distance Entry

Direct Distance Entry is a quick, accurate, and easy way to draw horizontal and vertical lines. (It can also be used to draw at an angle if you know which direction to move your mouse or with any other command that asks you to specify a point.) With ORTHO ON move your mouse in the direction you want to draw, TYPE: **the distance**, and PRESS: **<enter>.**

**Draw a 1″ square using direct distance entry:**

| Prompt | Response |
|---|---|
| Command: | **With ORTHO ON**<br>**Line** (or TYPE: **L<enter>**) |
| Specify first point: | **Click a point on the grid in the same location as the beginning of the square you just erased.** |
| Specify next point or [Undo]: | **Move your mouse to the right.**<br>TYPE: **1<enter>** |
| Specify next point or [Undo]: | **Move your mouse down.**<br>TYPE: **1<enter>** |
| Specify next point or [Close/Undo]: | **Move your mouse to the left.**<br>TYPE: **1<enter>** |
| Specify next point or [Close/Undo]: | TYPE: **C<enter>** |

## CIRCLE

In the following part of this exercise, four circles of the same size are drawn, using four different methods.

## On Your Own

1. **Look at Figure 4–6 to determine the approximate location of the four circles you will draw.**

2. **Set Layer2 current. Layer2 has a dashed linetype.**

### Center, Radius

**Draw a circle with a 1/2″ radius (Figure 4–12):**

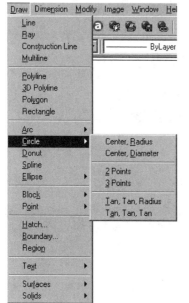

**FIGURE 4–12**
Draw the Same Size Circle Using
Four Different Methods

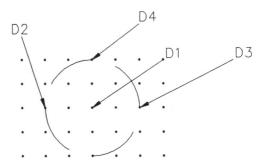

| Prompt | Response |
|---|---|
| Command: | **Circle-Center, Radius** |
| Specify center point for circle or [3P/2P/Ttr (tan tan radius)]: | **D1** |
| Specify radius of circle or [Diameter]: | TYPE: **1/2<enter>** (the circle appears) |

### Center, Diameter

Refer to Figure 4–6 to determine the approximate location of the next circle.

**Draw a circle with a 1″ diameter (Figure 4–12):**

| Prompt | Response |
|---|---|
| Command: | **<enter>** (to return Circle command prompt) |
| Specify center point for circle or [3P/2P/Ttr (tan tan radius)]: | **D1** |
| Specify radius of circle or [Diameter] <0′-0 1/2″>: | TYPE: **D<enter>** (to specify diameter) |
| Specify diameter of circle<0′-1″>: | **<enter>** (the circle appears) |

### 2 points

**Draw a 1″ diameter circle by locating the two endpoints of its diameter (Figure 4–12):**

| Prompt | Response |
|---|---|
| Command: | **Circle-2 Points** |
| Specify center point for circle or [3P/2P/Ttr (tan tan radius)]: _2p | |
| Specify first end point of circle's diameter: | **D2** (on a grid mark) |
| Specify second end point of circle's diameter: | **D3** (move four grid spaces to the right) |

### 3 points

**Draw a 1″ diameter circle by clicking three points on its circumference (Figure 4–12):**

| Prompt | Response |
|---|---|
| Command: | **Circle-3 Points** |

| Prompt | Response |
|---|---|
| Specify center point for circle or [3P/2P/Ttr (tan tan radius)]: _3p | |
| Specify first point on circle: | **D2** |
| Specify second point on circle: | **D3** (move four grid spaces to the right) |
| Specify third point on circle: | **D4** (the center of the top of the circle) |

You have just learned four different methods of drawing the same size circle. You can watch the size of the circle change on the screen by moving the pointer, and you can select the desired size by clicking the point that indicates the size.

## On Your Own

1. **Experiment with different size circles and the different methods until you become comfortable with them.**
2. **Set Layer1 current.**
3. **Draw two 1″ lines that form a corner and two 1/2″ diameter circles, 1″ on center, as shown in Figure 4–13. Figure 4–6 will help you to determine the approximate location of the corner and two circles on your drawing.**
4. **Set Layer2 current again.**

**FIGURE 4–13**
Draw Two 1″ Lines That Form a Corner and Two 1/2″ Diameter Circles, 1″ on Center

## TTR

The next option of the Circle command is Tan, Tan, Radius. This stands for tangent, tangent, and radius. A tangent touches a circle at a single point.

**Draw a circle with a 1/2″ radius tangent to two lines (Figure 4–14):**

**FIGURE 4–14**
Draw a Circle with a 1/2″ Radius Tangent to Two Lines; Draw a Circle with a 1/2″ Radius Tangent to Two Other Circles

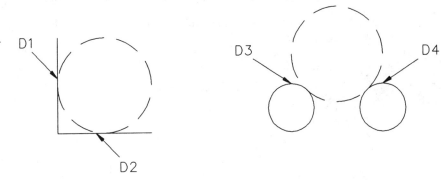

| Prompt | Response |
|---|---|
| Command: | **Circle-Tan, Tan, Radius** |
| Specify center point for circle or [3P/2P/Ttr (tan tan radius): _ttr | |
| Specify point on object for first tangent of circle: | **D1** (pick any place on the line) |

| Prompt | Response |
|---|---|
| Specify point on object for second tangent of circle: | **D2** (pick any place on the line) |
| Specify radius of circle<0′-0 1/4″>: | TYPE: **1/2<enter>** |

**Draw a circle with a 1/2″ radius tangent to two other circles (Figure 4–14):**

| Prompt | Response |
|---|---|
| Command: | **<enter>** (to return Circle command prompt) |
| Specify center point for circle or [3P/2P/Ttr (tan tan radius)]: | TYPE: **TTR<enter>** |
| Specify point on object for first tangent of circle: | **D3** |
| Specify point on object for second tangent of circle: | **D4** |
| Specify radius of circle<0′-0 1/2″>: | **<enter>** |

## On Your Own

1. **Experiment with different size circles. The location of the tangent circle will change with different radius sizes. Also, the location of the tangent circle between the two circles will change, depending on the location of the first and second tangents specified.**

2. **Use the Tangent, Tangent, Tangent option to experiment with drawing circles that are tangent to three objects.**

## LTSCALE

AutoCAD provides a variety of linetypes that you may use. For example, the dashed linetype provided by AutoCAD consists of 1/2″ line segments with 1/4″ spaces in between. The given line segment length (1/2″) and spacing (1/4″) for the dashed linetype are drawn when the global linetype scale factor is set to 1 (the default).

To make the line segment length or spacing smaller, enter a linetype scale factor smaller than 1 but larger than 0 to the Ltscale prompt. To make the line segment length and spacing larger, enter a linetype scale factor larger than 1. Look closely to see the circle's DASHED linetype scale change when the following is entered.

**Use Ltscale to change the size of the DASHED linetype:**

| Prompt | Response |
|---|---|
| Command: | TYPE: **LTSCALE<enter>** |
| Enter new linetype scale factor <1.0000>: | TYPE: **1/2<enter>** |
| Regenerating model. | |

## ZOOM

The different Zoom commands (Realtime, Previous, Window, Dynamic, Scale, Center, In, Out, All, Extents) control how you view the drawing area on the display screen. While drawing the lines and circles for this chapter you have been able to view the entire 8-1/2″ × 11″ drawing limits on the screen. The Zoom-All command was used earlier to assure that view. The Zoom commands are located on the Standard Toolbar and on the menu bar View menu under Zoom.

### Zoom-Window

The Zoom-Window command allows you to pick two opposite corners of a rectangular window on the screen. The cursor changes to form a rubber band that shows the size of

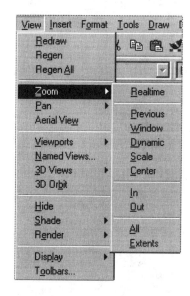

the window on the screen. The size of the window is controlled by the movement of the mouse. The part of the drawing inside the windowed area is magnified to fill the screen when the second corner of the window is clicked.

The following will use the Zoom-Window command to look more closely at the three tangent circles previously drawn.

**Use Zoom-Window to look more closely at the three tangent circles (Figure 4–15):**

| Prompt | Response |
|---|---|
| Command: | TYPE: **Z<enter>** |
| Specify corner of window, enter a scale factor (nX or nXP), or [All/Center/Dynamic/ Extents/Previous/Scale/Window] <real time>: | **D1** (lower left corner of the window) |
| Specify opposite corner: | **D2** (upper right corner of the window) |

The area that was windowed is now displayed to fill the screen.

When the magnification of the circles was enlarged with the Zoom-Window command, to save time AutoCAD did not regenerate the drawing. The part of the drawing that was windowed and magnified was *redrawn* only. That is why the circles are not smooth. Small line segments called vectors make up a circle. When the entire page is displayed, fewer line segments are used to make up the smaller circles. By zooming in and not regenerating, you are able to see the small number of vectors.

**Use REGEN to regenerate the drawing:**

| Prompt | Response |
|---|---|
| Command: | TYPE: **REGEN<enter>** |

By typing and entering REGEN, you issued a regeneration of the drawing. AutoCAD regenerated the circles with the optimal number of line segments (making the circle smoother) for the larger magnification.

**Zoom-All**

Now that you have a windowed area of the drawing, how do you view the entire drawing again? Zoom-All will provide a view of the entire drawing area.

**Use Zoom-All to view the entire drawing:**

| Prompt | Response |
|---|---|
| Command: | **Zoom-All** (or TYPE: **Z<enter>**) |

FIGURE 4–15
Use Zoom-Window

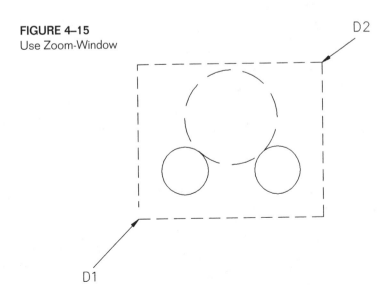

| Prompt | Response |
|---|---|
| Specify corner of window, enter a scale factor (nX or nXP), or [All/Center/Dynamic/Extents/Previous/Scale/Window] <real time>: | TYPE: **A<enter>** |

## Zoom-Previous

Zoom-Previous is a very convenient feature. AutoCAD remembers up to 10 previous views. This is especially helpful and saves time if you are working on a complicated drawing.

**Use Zoom-Previous to see the last view of the tangent circles again:**

| Prompt | Response |
|---|---|
| Command: | **<enter>** |
| Specify corner of window, enter a scale factor (nX or nXP), or [All/Center/Dynamic/Extents/Previous/Scale/Window] <real time>: | TYPE: **P<enter>** |

## Zoom-Dynamic

Another Zoom command that saves time is Zoom-Dynamic.

**Use Zoom-Dynamic to change the display (Figure 4–16):**

| Prompt | Response |
|---|---|
| Command: | **<enter>** |
| Specify corner of window, enter a scale factor (nX or nXP), or [All/Center/Dynamic/Extents/Previous/Scale/Window] <real time>: | TYPE: **D<enter>** |

You now see three areas on the screen (Figure 4–16):

1. The tangent circle area previously windowed.

2. The drawing limits or the drawing extents, whichever is larger.

3. The box with the X in it is the same size as the window that you just made when you windowed the circles. This window can be moved; it follows the movement of your mouse. Experiment by moving it around the screen.

**FIGURE 4–16**
Use Zoom-Dynamic

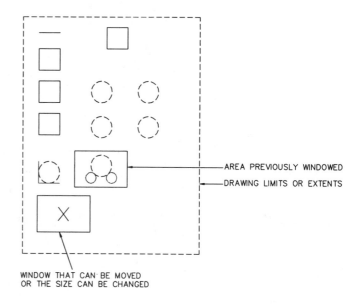

AREA PREVIOUSLY WINDOWED

DRAWING LIMITS OR EXTENTS

WINDOW THAT CAN BE MOVED
OR THE SIZE CAN BE CHANGED

The size of the window can also be changed. Change the size of the window by pressing the pick button on the mouse. The X inside changes to an arrow when you press the left button. When the arrow is in the window, the movement of the pointer changes the size of the window. Experiment with changing the size of the window. Press the left button on the mouse to return the X to the center of the window. With the X in the center of the window, the size remains constant and you may move the window to the area of the drawing that you want to window or zoom in on next.

When you have decided which area of the drawing you want to view next and have the size of window needed, with an X in the center, place the window on the area to be enlarged. When you press the enter button on the mouse, the area inside the window will appear enlarged on the screen.

### Zoom-Extents

Zoom-Extents always performs a regeneration of the drawing. The Zoom-Extents command allows you to view the extents of a drawing. To understand Zoom-Extents, you need to understand the difference between drawing limits and drawing extents. The limits of a drawing are the size of the sheet set with the LIMITS command. The extents of a drawing include whatever graphics are actually drawn on the page. If only half the page is full, the extents will be half the page. Sometimes a drawing entity is drawn outside the limits; this, too, is considered the drawing extents. The Zoom-Extents command provides a view of all drawing entities on the page as large as possible to fill the screen. The Zoom-All command displays the entire drawing limits or extents, whichever is larger. The extents are larger than the limits when a drawing entity is drawn outside of the limits.

**Use Zoom-Extents to view the extents of drawing CH4-EX1:**

| Prompt | Response |
|---|---|
| Command: | **Zoom-Extents** |

The remaining Zoom commands are Scale, Center, Realtime, In, and Out. A brief explanation of each follows.

### Zoom-Scale

Zoom-Scale is stated as "Enter a scale factor (nX or nXP):". The Scale feature allows you to increase or decrease the magnification of the objects on the screen when you are viewing the entire page or a windowed view. If while viewing the entire page or limits of the drawing you type and enter 2 to the Zoom prompt, the new displayed view will have a magnification twice as large as the full view. If you type and enter 1/4, the view will be decreased to one quarter of the full view. To view the entire drawing as displayed within the limits, enter 1 to the Zoom-Scale prompt, "Enter a scale factor (nX or nXP):".

While in a windowed view with an object displayed enter 2 followed by an X (2X) to the Zoom prompt, to increase the magnification of the windowed view by 2. A number followed by an X increases or decreases the object *currently* displayed. If while you are in the windowed area the number 2 is not followed by an X, the full view or entire drawing area (not the windowed area) will be magnified by 2 and displayed.

The "XP" in the Scale part of the Zoom command prompt refers to model space and paper space, which will be discussed in a later chapter.

### Zoom-Center

When Zoom-Center is clicked, AutoCAD asks you for a center point of a window. After you have clicked the center point of the window on the drawing, the prompt asks "Enter magnification or height:". The current height (for example, 11″ on your current drawing) is shown in default brackets. If 2 is typed and entered, a view of 2″ of the current drawing is enlarged to fill the screen. A height larger than the current height (such as 15) decreases the magnification by changing the height of the displayed view to 15″ instead of 11″.

If 2X (an X following the number) is entered to the prompt "Enter magnification or height:", the current drawing display is magnified by 2.

Note: PRESS:<enter> to the Zoom prompt to activate Real-Time Zoom.

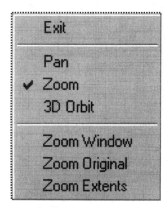

Tip: The Zoom and Pan commands may also be activated by typing **Z** or **P** from the keyboard.

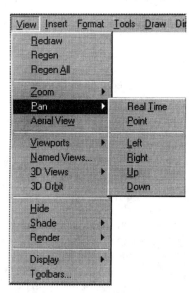

### Real-Time Zoom

The Real-Time Zoom command is located on the Standard Toolbar and on the menu bar View menu under Zoom. You may also TYPE: **RTZOOM <enter>** from the keyboard to activate this command. To zoom in or out, hold down the left mouse button and move the mouse up or down to change the magnification of the drawing. PRESS: **the right mouse button** to get a shortened zoom and pan menu as shown in the margin. CLICK: **Exit** or PRESS: **Esc** to exit the command.

### Zoom-In

Zoom In makes the objects in the drawing appear to be larger.

### Zoom-Out

Zoom Out makes the objects in the drawing appear to be smaller.

## PAN

The Pan command allows you to maintain the current display magnification and see parts of the drawing that may be off the screen and not visible in the display. It allows you to move the entire drawing in any direction. Pan does not change the magnification of the view. It is not necessary to window an area to use the Pan command, but in the following exercise, a windowed view will be used.

## On Your Own

**1. Magnify any portion of the drawing using the Zoom-Window option.**

**Use Pan to move the drawing while in a windowed view:**

| Prompt | Response |
|---|---|
| Command: | **Pan-Point** |
| Specify base point or displacement: | **Click the middle of the windowed view.** |
| Specify second point: | **Click a point two grid marks to the right of the first point.** |

### Real-Time Pan

The Real-Time Pan command is located on the Standard Toolbar and on the menu bar View menu under Pan. You may also TYPE: **P<enter>** to activate this command. To move the view of your drawing at the same magnification, hold down the left button on your mouse and move the mouse in any direction to change the view of your drawing. PRESS: **the right mouse button** while in Real-Time Pan to get a shortened zoom and pan menu. CLICK: **Exit** or PRESS: **Esc** to exit from the command.

### Scroll Bars

The scroll bars on the right side and bottom of the display may also be used to pan from one area of the drawing to another.

## Transparent Commands

A *transparent command* is a command that can be used while another command is in progress. It is very handy to be able to change the display while a command such as Line is in progress. To use the Zoom commands transparently, after you have entered the Line command, TYPE: **'Z<enter>**. An apostrophe (') must precede the command name. The **'Z** prompt is ">>Specify corner of window, enter a scale factor (nX or nXP), or [All/Center/Dynamic/Extents/Previous/Scale/Window] <real time>". The >> preceding the command prompt indicates that the command is being used transparently.

You can also use Pan as a transparent command. While another command is in progress: TYPE: **'P<enter>**, or click it from the View menu in the menu bar.

All the Zoom commands from the View menu in the menu bar may be used transparently; you can simply click them.You can also change grid and snap settings transparently: enter an apostrophe (') before entering the command at any prompt.

## BLIPMODE

**Note:** Sometimes it is very helpful to have Blipmode on, because you can see where your mouse has entered a point on your drawing.

When a point is entered on a drawing, AutoCAD generates small marker blips on the screen. Commands such as Redraw or Regen that redraw or regenerate the drawing erase the marker blips. When you TYPE: **BLIPMODE<enter>**, the Blipmode command has two responses: ON and OFF. When the Blipmode command is OFF, no marker blips are displayed. When the Blipmode command is ON, the marker blips appear.

## REDRAW

When you pick Redraw from the View menu or TYPE: **R<enter>**, AutoCAD redraws and cleans up your drawing. Any marker blips (when a point is entered, AutoCAD generates small marker blips on the screen) on the screen disappear, and drawing entities affected by editing of other objects are redrawn. Pressing function key F7 twice turns the grid off and on and also redraws the screen.

## REGEN

When you click Regen from the View menu, AutoCAD regenerates the entire drawing and redraws the current view. As you have already learned, other View commands do this, and it is seldom necessary to issue a regeneration with the Regen command.

## HIGHLIGHT

When you select any object such as a circle or line to erase, or move, or otherwise modify, the circle or line is highlighted. This highlighting is controlled by the HIGHLIGHT system variable. When you TYPE: **HIGHLIGHT<enter>,** the Highlight command has two responses: enter 1 to turn highlighting ON, or 0 to turn highlighting OFF. You will probably prefer to have this variable on so the items selected are confirmed by the highlighting.

### MOVE and Editing Commands Selection Set

You may want to move some of the items on your page to improve the layout of the page. The Move command lets you do that.

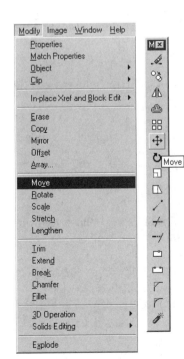

### On Your Own

1. **Set Layer3 current.**
2. **Use Zoom-All to view the entire drawing.**
3. **Set Blipmode to ON.**
4. **Set Highlight to 1 (ON).**
5. **Draw a row of four 1/2″ diameter circles, 1″ on center, as shown in Figure 4–17.**
6. **Pick Move from the Modify menu** (or TYPE: **M<enter>**).

After you pick Move, the prompt in the prompt line asks you to "Select objects:". Also, a pickbox replaces the screen crosshair. The pickbox helps you to select the item or group of items to be moved by positioning the pickbox on the item. The item or group of items selected is called the *selection set*. Many of the AutoCAD Modify commands provide the same prompt, the pickbox, and also the same options used to select the object or objects to be edited. The options are All, Window, Window Polygon, Last, Previous, Crossing, Crossing Polygon, Fence, Remove, Add, and Undo. You can also select an item by clicking any point on it.

The Move command is used in the following part of this exercise to demonstrate the various options many of the Modify commands use to select objects. Notice that when the item is selected AutoCAD confirms your selection by highlighting it.

**FIGURE 4–17**
Draw a Row of Four 1/2″ Diameter Circles, 1″ on Center

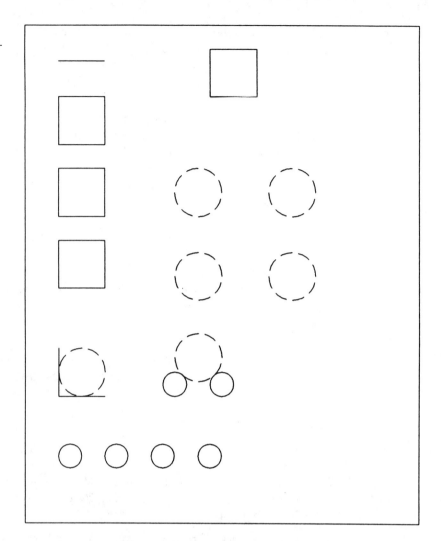

**Tip:** Keep your finger on function key
F9 to turn Snap OFF if it interferes with
clicking on an object; turn it back on as
soon as the object is selected.

**Select a circle by clicking a point on the circle, and move it by clicking a point on the drawing (Figure 4–18):**

| Prompt | Response |
|---|---|
| Select objects: | **D1** (any point on the circumference of the circle) |
| Select objects: 1 found | |
| Select objects: | **<enter>** (you have completed selecting objects) |
| Specify base point or displacement: | **D2** (the center of the circle—be sure SNAP is ON) |
| Specify second point of displacement or <use first point as displacement>: | **Click a point three grid marks (3/4″) to the right.** |

**-or-**

**With ORTHO ON, move your mouse to the right. TYPE: 3/4 <enter>**

**FIGURE 4–18**
Select a Circle by Clicking a Point on the Circle, and Move It by Clicking a Point on the Drawing

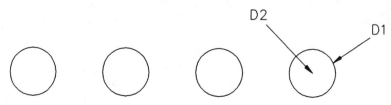

**Select a circle by clicking a point on the circle, and move it by entering relative coordinates (Figure 4–19):**

**FIGURE 4–19**
Select a Circle by Clicking a Point on the Circle, and Move It by Entering Relative Coordinates

**Note:** Keep Snap ON while moving a drawing entity. Snap from one grid point (Base point or displacement) to another (Second point of displacement).

**Tip:** Use transparent Zoom commands to move about your drawing.

| Prompt | Response |
|---|---|
| Command: | **<enter>** (to return Move command prompt) |
| Select objects: | **D1** |
| Select objects: 1 found | |
| Select objects: | **<enter>** |
| Specify base point or displacement: | **D2** (the center of the circle) |
| Specify second point of displacement or <use first point as displacement>: | TYPE: **@ −3/4,0<enter>** |

You can give the second point of displacement by clicking a point on the screen or by using absolute, relative, polar coordinates, or direct distance entry.

**Select items to be edited by using a window, and then remove an item from the selection set (Figure 4–20):**

**FIGURE 4–20**
Select Items to Be Edited by Using a Window, and Then Remove an Item from the Selection Set

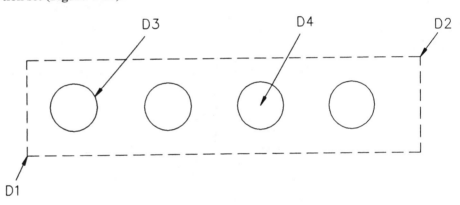

**Tip:** Press F7 twice to clean up the blips (turn grid off and on).

| Prompt | Response |
|---|---|
| Command: | **<enter>** |
| Select objects: | **D1** |
| Specify opposite corner: | **D2** |
| 4 found | |
| Select objects: | TYPE: **R<enter>** |
| Remove objects: | **D3** |
| Remove objects: | **<enter>** |
| Specify base point or displacement: | **D4** (the center of the circle) |
| Specify second point of displacement or <use first point as displacement>: | **Click a point two grid marks down the Y axis.** |

**Window (W), Crossing Window (C), Window Polygon (WP), and Crossing Polygon (CP)**

The Window and Crossing (Window) responses allow you to pick two opposite corners of a rectangular window on the screen. The crosshair of the pointer changes to form a rubber band that shows the size of the window on the screen. The size of the window is controlled by the movement of the pointer. Window Polygon and Crossing Polygon allow you to make a polygon by clicking points that are used to select objects.

**Tip:** Typing W<enter> and C<enter> to activate window and crossing window is helpful when the drawing area is dense and clicking an empty area is difficult or impossible.

With the Window response, only the parts of the drawing that are *entirely contained within the window* are selected to be edited. If the window covers only a part of a drawing entity, that entity is not selected. You may also type and enter **W** to activate the Window response, or **WP** to activate Window Polygon.

When you use the Crossing Window command, any part of the drawing that is contained within or *crossed by the crossing window* is included in the selection set. With a crossing window, a drawing entity such as a line or circle does not have to be entirely contained within the window to be selected.

Picking an empty area on the drawing and moving your mouse to the right creates a window. Picking and moving to the left creates a crossing window.

## On Your Own

1. **Experiment with the difference between Window and Crossing Window. You may also type and enter C to activate the Crossing Window response, or CP to activate Crossing Polygon.**

2. **Return the circles to the approximate location as shown in Figure 4–17.**

### All (All)

Selects all objects on thawed layers.

### Fence (F)

Fence allows you to click points that draw a line that selects any objects it crosses.

### Remove (R) and Add (A)

**Tip:** To remove objects from a selection set, hold the Shift key down and click the object.

The Remove response allows you to remove a drawing part from the selection set. If you are in the remove mode and decide to add another drawing part to the selection set, TYPE: **A<enter>** to return to the add mode.

### Last (L) and Previous (P)

The Last response selects the most recent drawing entity created. The Previous response selects the most recent selection set. Both are handy if you want to use several editing commands on the same drawing entity or the same selection set. You may also type and enter **L** or **P** from the keyboard.

### Undo (U)

While in an editing command, if you decide you do not want something in a selection set, you may use the Undo command to remove it and continue on with the "Select objects:" prompt. Typing **Undo** backtracks through the selection sets in the reverse of the order in which they were selected. You may also type and enter **U** from the keyboard.

## SELECT

The Select command allows you to preselect the items to be edited. Then you can use the "Previous" option in the Modify commands to refer to the selection set. TYPE: **SELECT<enter>** to the Command: prompt.

## Selection Modes Settings

To access the Selection Modes settings, select Options... under Tools in the menu bar. Select the Selection tab of the Options dialog box. The left side of this tab shows Selection Modes and how to change the Pickbox Size. A check mark in the box indicates that the mode is on (Figure 4–21).

*Noun/verb selection:* When this mode is ON, you can select an object *before or after* invoking an edit or inquiry command.

*Use Shift to add to selection:* When this mode is ON, you can add or remove an object from a selection set by holding down the Shift key and selecting the object. To dis-

**FIGURE 4–21**
Options Dialog Box, Selection
Tab

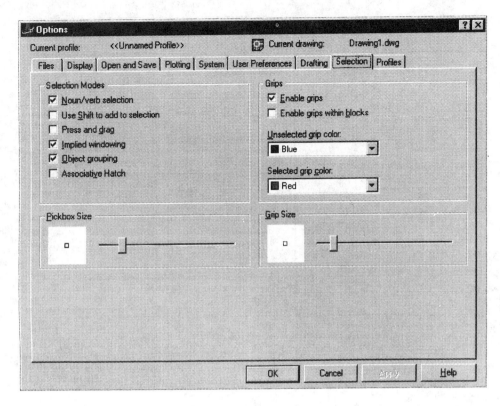

continue this option, click two points to draw a selection window in a blank area of the drawing.

*Press and drag:* When this mode is ON, to draw a selection window, you have to click a point and drag the mouse to the second point. When this mode is not ON, you can click two separate points to draw a selection window.

*Implied windowing:* When this mode is ON, if you click a point outside an object, a selection window will be drawn. Drawing a window from right to left makes a crossing window, and from left to right makes a window.

*Object grouping:* When GROUP is typed and entered at the Command: prompt, the Object Grouping dialog box appears. The dialog box allows you to create and name a group of objects. When Object grouping is on, if you select one item in the object group, the entire object group is selected.

*Associative Hatch:* When using the Hatch command, if this mode is ON, boundary objects are also selected when you use an associative hatch. Hatching is described later in this book.

*Pickbox Size:* Controls the size of the pickbox.

## Save Your Drawing

When you have completed Exercise 4–1, save your drawing in at least two places. You can plot Exercise 4–1 after completing Chapter 7, "Printing and Plotting."

# EXERCISE 4–2
# Drawing Arcs, Ellipses, and Solids

When you have completed Exercise 4–2, your drawing will look similar to the drawing in Figure 4–22. To begin Exercise 4–2, turn on the computer and start AutoCAD. The Auto-CAD 2002 Today window is displayed.

## Begin Drawing CH4-EX2 on the Hard Drive

1. CLICK: **the Create Drawings tab**
2. CLICK: **Wizards**

**FIGURE 4–22**
Exercise 4–2: Drawing Arcs,
Ellipses, and Solids

CLICK: **Quick setup**

3. Set drawing Units: **Architectural**

   CLICK: **Next>**

4. Set drawing Width: **8-1/2″** × Length: **11″**

   CLICK: **Finish**

5. **Use SaveAs... to save the drawing on the hard drive with the name CH4-EX2.**

6. Set Grid: **1/4″**

7. Set Snap: **1/8″**

8. Create the following Layers:

**Note:** To change a layer name after using New to create layers: Make sure the Details part of the Layer Properties Manager dialog box is visible. Click the layer name to highlight it, double click the name in the Name: input area, and type over the existing name. You can also name the layers by clicking New and then typing the layer names separated by commas. When you type the comma you move to the next layer.

| LAYER NAME | COLOR | LINETYPE |
|------------|-------|----------|
| Arcs | Blue | Continuous |
| Ellipses | Green | Continuous |
| Solids | Red | Continuous |

9. Be sure to use **Zoom-All** to view the entire drawing area.

# UNDO

Understanding how to use the Undo command can be very helpful while drawing with AutoCAD.

When **U** is typed from the keyboard to the Command: prompt, and the enter key is pressed (or Undo is selected) the most recent command operation is undone. Most of the time the operation that is undone is obvious, such as when a line that you have just drawn is undone. The most recent mode settings that are not obvious, such as snap, will be undone also. Typing **REDO** and pressing **<enter>** will redo only one undo.

When **U** is typed and entered from the keyboard, no prompt line appears. If **UNDO** is typed and entered, the prompt "Enter the number of operations to undo or [Auto/Control/ BEgin/End/Mark/Back] <1>:" appears.

## <1>

The default is "<1>". You may enter a number for the number of operations to be undone. For instance, if 5 is entered to the prompt, five operations will be undone. If you decide you went too far, you can type and enter **REDO** or select Redo from the standard toolbar, and all five operations will be restored.

Typing **U** from the keyboard and pressing the enter key is the same as entering the number 1 to the Undo prompt. In that instance, **REDO** will redo only one undo, no matter how many times you typed and entered **U**. Right-click menus also have the Undo and Redo commands.

### Mark and Back

The Undo subcommands Mark and Back can be very helpful if you want to practice or experiment while in a drawing. By using Mark and Back you can easily erase a practice session or experiment.

When Mark is selected in response to the Undo prompt, AutoCAD makes a special mark in the undo information; it is not a visible mark. Any drawing or editing that is done after Mark is selected can easily be undone when you click Back in response to the prompt. The Back subcommand will backtrack through the drawing one mark at a time and remove the mark when it's found. An example of the command sequence follows.

### Use UNDO, Mark, and Back for a practice session:

| Prompt | Response |
|---|---|
| Command: | TYPE: **UNDO<enter>** |
| Enter the number of operations to undo or [Auto/Control/BEgin/End/Mark/Back] <1>: | TYPE: **M<enter>** |
| Command: | **Draw several lines and circles.** |
| Command: | TYPE: **UNDO<enter>** |
| Enter the number of operations to undo or [Auto/Control/BEgin/End/Mark/Back] <1>: | TYPE: **B<enter>** |

Everything drawn since Mark was picked is undone.

# ARC

There are many methods from which to choose when you are drawing arcs. Whatever the situation, you can select a method to suit your needs. Experiment with the different methods described next and decide which ones you prefer to use. Use Figure 4–22 as a guide when locating the arcs on your drawing.

## On Your Own

1. **Set Layer Arcs current.**
2. **Set Blipmode ON.**

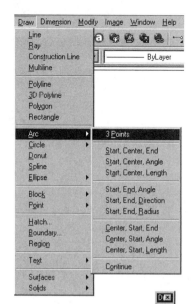

## 3-point

Using the 3-point method, you can draw an arc clockwise or counterclockwise by specifying the start point, second point, and end point of the arc.

**Draw three arcs using the 3-point method (Figure 4–23):**

| Prompt | Response |
|---|---|
| Command: | **Arc-3 Points** (or TYPE: **A<enter>**) |
| Specify start point of arc or [CEnter]: | **D1** (pick a point five grid marks down (1-1/4″) and three grid marks to the right of the upper left corner of the page) |
| Specify second point of arc or [CEnter/ENd]: | **D2** |
| Specify endpoint of arc: | **D3** |
| Command: | **<enter>** (Repeat 3 points) |
| Specify start point of arc or [CEnter]: | **D4** |
| Specify second point of arc or [CEnter/ENd]: | **D5** |
| Specify endpoint of arc: | **D6** |
| Command: | **<enter>** (Repeat 3 points) |
| Specify start point of arc or [CEnter]: | **D7** |
| Specify second point of arc or [CEnter/ENd]: | **D8** |
| Specify endpoint of arc: | **D9** |

## Start, Center, End

The Start, Center, End method allows you to draw an arc only counterclockwise, by specifying the start, center, and end. You can draw the same arc using the Center, Start, End method, which also draws counterclockwise.

**Draw two arcs using the Start, Center, End method (Figure 4–24):**

| Prompt | Response |
|---|---|
| Command: | **Arc-Start, Center, End** |

**FIGURE 4–23**
Draw Arcs Using the
3-Point Method

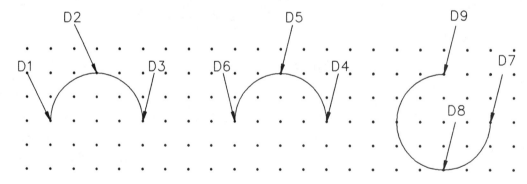

**FIGURE 4–24**
Draw Arcs Using the Start, Center, End Method

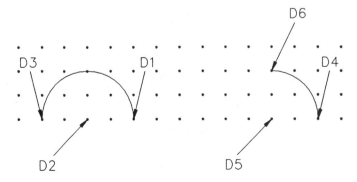

| Prompt | Response |
|---|---|
| Specify start point of arc or [Center]: | **D1** (pick a point 1-3/4″ below the right end of the first arc drawn) |
| Specify second point of arc or [Center/End]:<br>    _c Specify center point of arc: | **D2** |
| Specify endpoint of arc or [Angle/chord Length]: | **D3** |
| Command: | **<enter> (Repeat Start, Center, End)** |
| Specify start point of arc or [Center]: | **D4** |
| Specify second point of arc or [Center/End]:<br>    _c Specify center point of arc: | **D5** |
| Specify endpoint of arc or [Angle/chord Length]: | **D6** |

## Start, Center, Angle

In the Start, Center, Angle method, A is the included angle (the angle the arc will span). A positive angle will draw the arc counterclockwise; a negative angle will draw the arc clockwise.

**Draw an arc using the Start, Center, Angle method (Figure 4–25):**

**FIGURE 4–25**
Draw Arcs Using the Start, Center, Angle and Start, Center, Length Methods

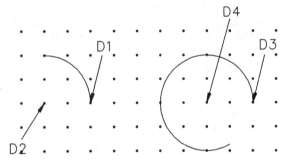

| Prompt | Response |
|---|---|
| Command: | **Arc-Start, Center, Angle** |
| Specify start point of arc or [Center]: | **D1** (2-1/4″ to the right of the last arc drawn) |
| Specify second point of arc or [Center/End]:<br>    _c Specify center point of arc: | **D2** |
| Specify endpoint of arc or [Angle/chord Length]: _a Specify included angle: | **TYPE: 90<enter>** |

## Start, Center, Length

In the Start, Center, Length method, L is the chord length. A *chord* is a straight line that connects an arc's start point and end point. A positive chord length can be entered to draw a minor arc (less than 180°), and a negative chord length can be entered to draw a major arc (more than 180°). Both are drawn counterclockwise. See Figure 4–25.

**Draw an arc using the Start, Center, Length method:**

| Prompt | Response |
|---|---|
| Command: | **Arc-Start, Center, Length** |
| Specify start point of arc or [Center]: | **D3** |
| Specify second point of arc or [Center/End]:<br>    _c Specify center point of arc: | **D4** |
| Specify endpoint of arc or [Angle/chord Length]: _l Specify length of chord: | **TYPE: −1/2<enter>** |

### Start, End, Angle

With the Start, End, Angle method, after the start point and endpoint of the arc have been picked, a positive angle draws the arc counterclockwise; a negative angle keeps the same start and end points but draws the reverse arc or draws clockwise.

### Start, End, Radius

In the Start, End, Radius method, Radius is the arc radius. When you use the method, enter a positive radius to draw a minor arc (less than 180°), and enter a negative radius to draw a major arc (more than 180°). Both are drawn counterclockwise.

### Start, End, Direction

In this method, Direction is the specified direction that the arc takes, from the start point. The direction is specified in degrees. You can also specify the direction by pointing to a single point. Major, minor, counterclockwise, and clockwise arcs can be drawn with the Start, End, Direction method.

### Continue

If Continue is picked at the first prompt of any of the arc methods that start with S, the new arc starts at the end point of the last arc or line drawn. Pressing the enter key has the same effect. The new arc's direction follows the direction of the last arc or line drawn.

## ELLIPSE

Look at Figure 4–22 to determine the approximate location of the ellipses drawn with the Ellipse command.

## On Your Own

**1. Set Layer Ellipses current.**

### Axis, End

The minor axis of an ellipse is its smaller axis, and the major axis is the larger axis.

**Draw an ellipse by entering points for the minor axis of the ellipse (Figure 4–26):**

| Prompt | Response |
|---|---|
| Command: | **Ellipse-Axis, End** |
| | (or TYPE: **EL<enter>**) |
| Specify axis endpoint of ellipse or [Arc/ Center]: | **D1** |
| Specify other endpoint of axis: | **D2** |
| Specify distance to other axis or [Rotation]: | **D3** |

**Draw an ellipse by entering points for the major axis of the ellipse (Figure 4–26):**

| Prompt | Response |
|---|---|
| Command: | **Ellipse-Axis, End** |
| Specify axis endpoint of ellipse or [Arc/ Center]: | **D4** |
| Specify other endpoint of axis: | **D5** |
| Specify distance to other axis or [Rotation]: | **D6** |

**Draw an ellipse at an angle by entering points for the minor axis of the ellipse (Figure 4–26):**

| Prompt | Response |
|---|---|
| Command: | **Ellipse-Axis, End** |
| Specify axis endpoint of ellipse or [Arc/ Center]: | **D7** |

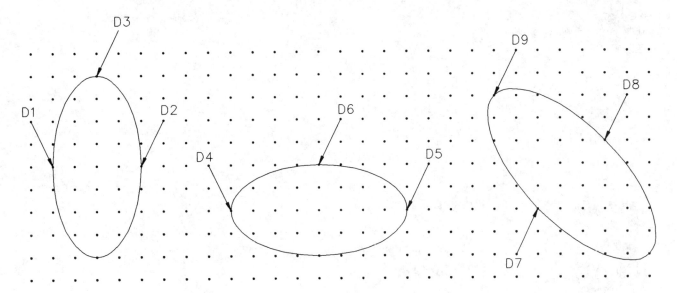

**FIGURE 4–26**
Draw an Ellipse by Entering Points for the Minor and Major Axes of the Ellipse, and Draw an
Ellipse at an Angle

| Prompt | Response |
|---|---|
| Specify other endpoint of axis: | **D8** |
| Specify distance to other axis or [Rotation]: | **D9** |

### Rotation

The Rotation option specifies an actual rotation into the third dimension, around the
major axis. To visualize this, hold a coin between two fingers and rotate it.

**Draw two ellipses by entering points for the major axis and specifying the rotation
angle around the major axis (Figure 4–27):**

| Prompt | Response |
|---|---|
| Command: | **Ellipse-Axis,End** |
| Specify axis endpoint of ellipse or [Arc/ Center]: | **D1** |
| Specify other endpoint of axis: | **D2** |
| Specify distance to other axis or [Rotation]: | TYPE: **R<enter>** (rotation changes the minor axis to the major axis) |
| Specify rotation around major axis: | TYPE: **0<enter>** (a 0° ellipse is a circle) |
| Command: | **<enter>** (Repeat ELLIPSE) |
| Specify axis endpoint of ellipse or [Arc/ Center]: | **D3** |
| Specify other endpoint of axis: | **D4** |
| Specify distance to other axis or [Rotation]: | TYPE: **R<enter>** |
| Specify rotation around major axis: 60 | TYPE: **60<enter>** |

### Center

You may also draw an ellipse by specifying the center point, the endpoint of one axis, and
the length of the other axis. Type **C** and press **<enter>** to the prompt "Specify axis endpoint
of ellipse or [Arc/Center]:" to start with the center of the ellipse. Entering the center point
first is similar to the first two methods described above, and either the minor or major axis
may be constructed first. As with all methods of drawing an ellipse, you can specify the
points either by clicking a point on the drawing or by typing and entering coordinates.

FIGURE 4–27
Draw Ellipses by Specifying the
Rotation Angle

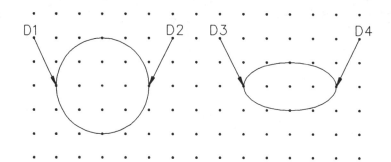

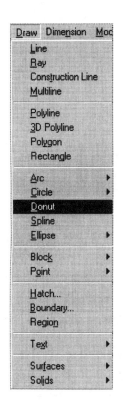

## DONUT

Look at Figure 4–22 to determine the approximate location of the solid ring and solid circle drawn using the Donut command.

### On Your Own

**1. Set Layer Solids current.**

**Use the Donut command to draw a solid ring (Figure 4–28):**

FIGURE 4–28
Use the Donut Command to
Draw a Solid Ring and a Solid
Circle

| Prompt | Response |
|---|---|
| Command: | **Donut** (or TYPE: **DO<enter>**) |
| Specify inside diameter of donut <default>: | TYPE: **1/2<enter>** |
| Specify outside diameter of donut <default>: | TYPE: **1<enter>:** |
| Specify center of donut or <exit>: | **Click a point on the drawing.** |
| Specify center of donut or <exit>: | **<enter>** |

**Use the Donut command to draw a solid circle (Figure 4–28):**

| Prompt | Response |
|---|---|
| Command: | **<enter>** (Repeat DONUT) |
| Specify inside diameter of donut <0′-0 1/2″>: | TYPE: **0<enter>** (so there is no center hole) |
| Specify outside diameter of donut <0′-1″>: | **<enter>** |
| Specify center of donut or <exit>: | **Click a point on the drawing.** |
| Specify center of donut or <exit>: | **<enter>** |

Donut can be used to draw solid dots of any size as well as solid rings with different inside and outside diameters.

## 2D SOLID

With the 2D Solid command you can draw angular solid shapes by entering them as three-sided (triangle) or four-sided (square and rectangle) sections. The trick with the 2D Solid command is entering the third point; to draw a square or a rectangle, you must pick the third point diagonally opposite the second point. If four points are picked in a clockwise or counterclockwise progression, a bow-tie shape is drawn.

In the following part of this exercise, first, the 2D Solid command will be used to draw a solid rectangle and a solid triangle at the bottom of the page. Second, the Scale command will be used to reduce the rectangle and enlarge the triangle.

**Use the 2D Solid command to draw a solid rectangle (Figure 4–29):**

| Prompt | Response |
|---|---|
| Command: | **2D Solid** (or TYPE: **SO<enter>**) |
| Specify first point: | **D1** (Be sure Snap is ON) |
| Specify second point: | **D2** |
| Specify third point: | **D3** (notice that D3 is diagonally opposite D2) |
| Specify fourth point or <exit>: | **D4** |
| Specify third point: | **<enter>** |

**Use the Solid command to draw a solid triangle (Figure 4–29):**

| Prompt | Response |
|---|---|
| Command: | **<enter>** (Repeat SOLID) |
| Specify first point: | **D5** |
| Specify second point: | **D6** |
| Specify third point: | **D7** |
| Specify fourth point or <exit>: | **<enter>** |
| Specify third point: | **<enter>** |

When the "Third point:" prompt appears a second time, you can continue with another section of the shape or press enter to complete a shape.

### FILL ON and FILL OFF

The options FILL ON and FILL OFF affect both the Donut and the 2D Solid commands and any other "filled" areas.

## On Your Own

1. TYPE: **FILL<enter>**, then TYPE: **OFF<enter>**, and then TYPE: **REGEN<enter>** to regenerate the drawing. All the shapes made with the Donut and 2D Solid commands will no longer be solid.

**FIGURE 4–29**
Use the 2D Solid Command to Draw a Solid Rectangle and a Solid Triangle

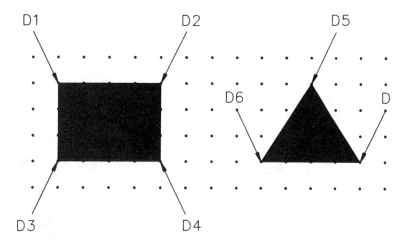

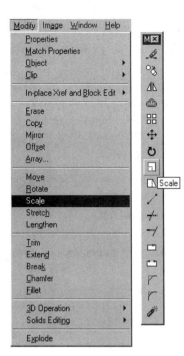

2. TYPE: **FILL<enter>,** then **ON<enter>** to make them solid again.

3. **Regenerate the drawing.**

## SCALE

The Scale command lets you reduce or enlarge either drawing entities or an entire drawing.

### <Scale factor>

**Use the Scale command to reduce the solid rectangle (Figure 4–30):**

| Prompt | Response |
|---|---|
| Command: | **Scale** (or TYPE: **SC<enter>**) |
| Select objects: | **Window the rectangle** (or click the outside edge of the solid). |
| Select objects: | **<enter>** |
| Specify base point: | **D1** |
| Specify scale factor or [Reference]: | TYPE: **.5<enter>** |

The relative scale factor of .5 was used to reduce the rectangle. A relative scale factor of 2 would have enlarged the rectangle.

### Reference

**Use the Scale command to enlarge the solid triangle (Figure 4–30):**

| Prompt | Response |
|---|---|
| Command: | **<enter>** (Repeat SCALE) |
| Select objects: | **Window the triangle** |
| Select objects: | **<enter>** |
| Specify base point: | **D2** |
| Specify scale factor or [Reference]: | TYPE: **R<enter>** |
| Specify reference length <1>: | **<enter>** (to accept 1″ default) |
| Specify new length: | TYPE: **2<enter>** |

The Reference option allows you to type and enter a number for the Reference (current) length of a drawing entity. You can also enter the Reference (current) length by picking two points on the drawing to show AutoCAD the Reference (current) length. You can type and enter the New length by using a number, or you can enter it by picking two points on the drawing to show the New length.

The Reference option is especially useful when you have drawn a project full scale and want to reduce it to scale. To reduce a full-scale drawing to 1/4″ = 1′-0″, the Reference length is 12 and the new length 1/4″. The drawing can then be inserted into a border format. The Insert command is described later in this book.

### Save Your Drawing

When you have completed Exercise 4–2, save your drawing in at least two places. You can plot Exercise 4–2 after completing Chapter 7, "Printing and Plotting."

**FIGURE 4–30**
Use the Scale Command to
Reduce the Solid Rectangle and
Enlarge the Solid Triangle

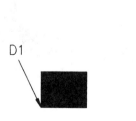
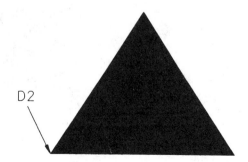

**Part II: Two-Dimensional AutoCAD**

# EXERCISE 4–3
## Drawing Shapes I

Draw, full size, the shapes shown in Figure 4–31. Use the dimensions shown. Locate the shapes approximately as shown. To begin Exercise 4–3, turn on the computer and start AutoCAD. The AutoCAD 2002 Today window is displayed.

### Begin Drawing CH4-EX3 on the Hard Drive

1. CLICK: **the Create Drawings tab**
   CLICK: **Start from Scratch**
   CLICK: **English (feet and inches)**
2. **Use SaveAs... to save the drawing on the hard drive with the name CH4-EX3.**
3. Set drawing Units: **Architectural**
4. Set Drawing Limits: **8-1/2,11**
5. Set Grid: **1/4″**
6. Set Snap: **1/8″**
7. Create the following Layers:

| LAYER NAME | COLOR | LINETYPE |
|------------|-------|----------|
| Single | Blue | Continuous |
| Solid | Red | Continuous |

**FIGURE 4–31**

Exercise 4–3: Drawing Shapes I

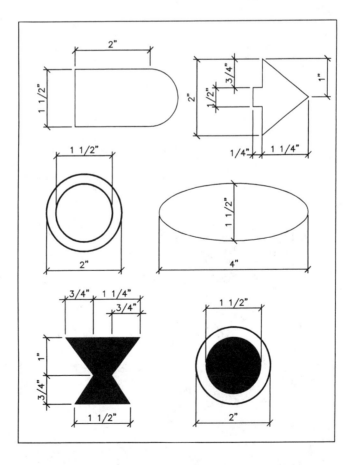

# EXERCISE 4–4
# Drawing a Pattern

Draw the pattern design shown in Figure 4–32. Use a 1/2″ = 1″ architectural scale to measure the pattern design and draw it full scale. Your drawing will be twice the size shown in the figure. To begin Exercise 4–4, turn on the computer and start AutoCAD. The AutoCAD 2002 Today window is displayed.

## Begin Drawing CH4-EX4 on the Hard Drive

1. CLICK: **the Create Drawings tab**

   CLICK: **Start from Scratch**

   CLICK: **English (feet and inches)**

2. **Use SaveAs... to save the drawing on the hard drive with the name CH4-EX4.**

3. Set drawing Units: **Architectural**

4. Set Drawing Limits: **8-1/2,11**

5. Set Grid: **1/4″**

6. Set Snap: **1/8″**

7. Create the Layers on your own.

**FIGURE 4–32**

Exercise 4–4: Drawing a Pattern
(Scale: 1/2″ = 1″)

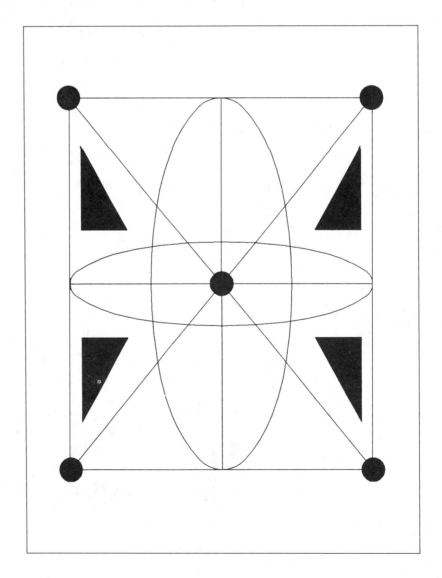

# EXERCISE 4–5
# Drawing Shapes II

Draw the shapes shown in Figure 4–33. Use a 1/2″ = 1″ architectural scale to measure the shapes and draw them full scale. Your drawing will be twice the size shown in the figure. To begin Exercise 4–5, turn on the computer and start AutoCAD. The AutoCAD 2002 Today window is displayed.

## Begin Drawing CH4-EX5 on the Hard Drive

1. CLICK: **the Create Drawings tab**
   CLICK: **Start from Scratch**
   CLICK: **English (feet and inches)**
2. **Use SaveAs... to save the drawing on the hard drive with the name CH4-EX5.**
3. Set drawing Units: **Architectural**
4. Set Drawing Limits: **8-1/2,11**
5. Set Grid: **1/4″**
6. Set Snap: **1/8″**
7. Create the Layers on your own.

**FIGURE 4–33**
Exercise 4–5: Drawing Shapes II
(Scale: 1/2″ = 1″)

# REVIEW QUESTIONS

1. When an existing drawing is stored on a floppy disk, you should open the drawing and immediately save it on the hard disk.
   a. True
   b. False

2. To make the line segment length and spacing larger for a dashed linetype, enter a number higher than 1 to the Ltscale prompt "Enter new scale factor <1.0000>:".
   a. True
   b. False

3. Always use the Zoom-All command after setting up a new drawing.
   a. True
   b. False

4. Snap may be turned OFF and ON while you are drawing.
   a. True
   b. False

5. When polar tracking is ON, Ortho mode is automatically ON also.
   a. True
   b. False

6. To view the entire drawing area, which Zoom command should you use immediately after you have set up a new drawing?
   a. All
   b. Center
   c. Dynamic
   d. Extents
   e. Scale

7. Many of the Modify commands use the same variety of subcommands to select the object or objects to be edited. Which of the following commands is *not* used to select the objects to be edited?
   a. Window
   b. Remove
   c. Circle
   d. Crossing
   e. Add

8. The 3-point method of drawing arcs allows you to draw arcs clockwise or counterclockwise.
   a. True
   b. False

9. The Reference option of the Scale command allows you to pick two points on the drawing to show AutoCAD the current length of the drawing entity to be reduced or enlarged.
   a. True
   b. False

10. Pressing the Esc key cancels a command.
    a. True
    b. False

11. Name the dialog box that has the settings that control what happens when the right mouse button is clicked.

    _____

12. Using relative coordinates to draw a 3″ square, write the information you type and enter in response to the Command: line prompt "Specify next point or [Undo]:" after the first point of the square has been clicked. Draw the square to the right and up.

    1. _____     3. _____

    2. _____     4. _____

13. Using absolute coordinates to draw a 3″ square, write the information that you type and enter in response to the Command: line prompt "Specify next point or [Undo]:" after the first point of the square has been clicked. The first point of the square is at coordinates 4,4. Draw the square to the right and up.

1. _____    3. _____

2. _____    4. _____

14. Using polar coordinates to draw a 3″ square, write the information that you type and enter in response to the Command: line prompt "Specify next point or [Undo]:" after the first point of the square has been clicked. Draw the square to the right and up.

1. _____    3. _____

2. _____    4. _____

15. Write the name of the command that you use to turn on (or off) the generation of marker blips that AutoCAD makes when a point is entered on a drawing.

_____

16. Write the name of the function key that can be pressed twice to redraw the screen.

_____

17. Write the name of the function key that when pressed helps to draw lines perfectly horizontally and vertically.

_____

18. Describe what Direction means in the arc method Start, End, Direction.

_____

_____

_____

_____

19. Describe what Length means in the arc method Start, Center, Length.

_____

_____

_____

_____

20. What command can be typed and entered to the Command: prompt to make the appearance of circles and arcs smoother?

_____

# 5 Drawing with AutoCAD: Conference and Lecture Rooms

## OBJECTIVES

When you have completed this chapter, you will be able to:
□ Correctly use the following pull-down commands and settings:

| | | | |
|---|---|---|---|
| Array | Edit Polyline | Measure | Polyline |
| Break | Explode | Offset | Rectangle |
| Chamfer | Fillet | Osnap | Rotate |
| Copy | From | Pickbox | Tracking |
| Distance | Help | Point | Trim |
| Divide | ID Point | Polygon | |

## EXERCISE 5–1
## Drawing a Rectangular Conference Room Including Furniture

A conference room, including walls and furnishings, is drawn in Exercise 5–1. When you have completed Exercise 5–1, your drawing will look similar to Figure 5–1. To prepare to draw Exercise 5–1, turn on the computer and start AutoCAD. The AutoCAD 2002 Today window is displayed.

1. CLICK: **Create Drawings tab**
2. CLICK: **Wizards**

   CLICK: **Quick Setup**
3. Set drawing Units: **Architectural**

   CLICK: **Next>**
4. Set drawing Width: **25'** × Length: **35'** (Don't forget the foot mark.)

   CLICK: **Finish**
5. **Use SaveAs... to save the drawing on the hard drive with the name CH5-EX1.**
6. Set Grid: **12"**
7. Set Snap: **6"**
8. Create the following Layers:

| LAYER NAME | COLOR | LINETYPE |
|---|---|---|
| Walls | White | Continuous |
| Furniture | Red | Continuous |

9. Set Layer Walls current.
10. Use **Zoom-All** to view the limits of the drawing.

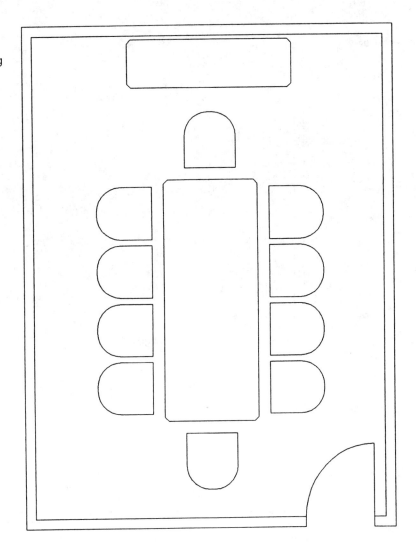

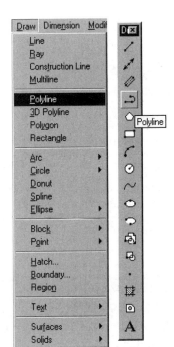

## POLYLINE

We will begin by drawing the conference room walls using the Polyline command. Polylines are different from regular lines in that regardless of the number of segments that make up a polyline, AutoCAD treats a polyline drawn with one operation of the Polyline command as a single entity. This is especially helpful when you are drawing walls, because after you draw the outline of a single room or entire building, the entire polyline can be offset to show the thickness of the walls. Any of the various linetypes may be drawn with Polyline, but the CONTINUOUS linetype will be used to draw the walls of the conference room.

**Use Polyline to draw the inside lines of the conference room walls (Figure 5–2):**

| Prompt | Response |
|---|---|
| Command: | **Polyline** (or TYPE: **PL<enter>**) |
| Specify start point: | TYPE: **5′,5′<enter>** |
| | **Set ORTHO ON** (Press: **F8** or CLICK: **ORTHO**) |
| Current line-width is 0′-0″ | |
| Specify next point or [Arc/Close/Halfwidth/ Length/Undo/Width]: | **Move your mouse to the right and** TYPE: **15′<enter>** |
| Specify next point or [Arc/Close/Halfwidth/ Length/Undo/Width]: | **Move your mouse up and** TYPE: **20′<enter>** |

FIGURE 5–2
Draw the Conference Room
Walls

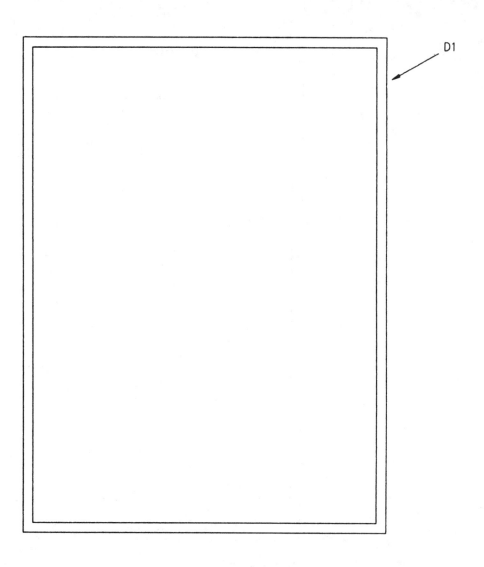

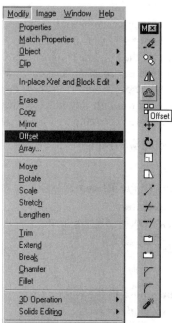

**Prompt**

Specify next point or [Arc/Close/Halfwidth/
    Length/Undo/Width]:

Specify next point or [Arc/Close/Halfwidth/
    Length/Undo/Width]:

**Response**

**Move your mouse to the left and** TYPE:
    **15′<enter>**

TYPE: **C<enter>**

### Undo

The Polyline Undo option is similar to the Line command: If you do not like the last polyline segment drawn, use the Undo option to erase it and continue with the "Specify next point or [Arc/Close/Halfwidth/Length/Undo/Width]:" prompt.

You can enter all the options in the Polyline prompt from the keyboard by typing (upper- or lowercase) the letters that are capitalized in each option. The remaining options in the Polyline prompt will be described later in this chapter.

## OFFSET

Because the polyline is treated as a single entity, when you click one point on the polyline, you are able to offset the entire outline of the conference room at once. If the outline of the room had been drawn with the Line command, using Offset would offset each line segment individually, and the corners would not meet.

**Use Offset to draw the outside line (showing depth) of the conference room walls (Figure 5–2):**

**Part II: Two-Dimensional AutoCAD**

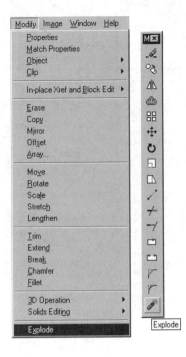

| Prompt | Response |
|---|---|
| Command: | **Offset** (or TYPE: **O<enter>**) |
| Specify offset distance or [Through]<Through>: | TYPE: **5<enter>** |
| Select object to offset or <exit>: | **Click any place on the polyline.** |
| Specify point on side to offset: | **D1** (outside of the rectangle) |
| Select object to offset or <exit>: | **<enter>** |

There are two options in the Offset prompt, Offset distance and Through. To complete the conference room walls, 5″ was set as the offset distance. When the option Through is used, you click the object you want to offset and then click a point on the drawing through which you want the object to be offset.

## EXPLODE

Because the polyline is treated as a single entity, it must be "exploded" before individual line segments can be edited. The Explode command splits the solid polyline into separate line segments. After the polyline is exploded into separate line segments, you will be able to add the conference room door.

**Use Explode to split the two polylines that make the conference room walls:**

| Prompt | Response |
|---|---|
| Command: | **Explode** (or TYPE: **X<enter>**) |
| Select objects: | **Click any place on the outside polyline.** |
| Select objects: | **Click any place on the inside polyline.** |
| Select objects: | **<enter>** |

After you use the Explode command, the walls do not look different, but each line segment is now a separate entity.

## ID POINT

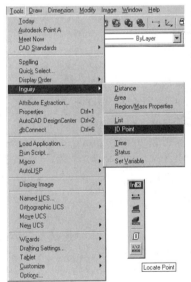

A very useful command, ID Point allows you to locate a point on a drawing and have the position of the point displayed in coordinates. AutoCAD remembers the coordinate location of the point. A command, such as Line, can be initiated immediately after the ID Point command has located a point on the drawing. You can enter the start point of the Line command by using absolute, relative, or polar coordinates, or you may also use direct distance entry, to specify a distance from the established ID Point location.

**On Your Own**

1. **Use Zoom-Window to magnify the corner of the conference room where the door will be located.**

**Use ID Point to locate a point on the drawing. Use Line to draw the right side of the door opening (Figure 5–3):**

| Prompt | Response |
|---|---|
| Command: | **ID Point** (or TYPE: **ID<enter>**) |
| Specify point: | **D1** (with SNAP ON, snap to the inside lower right corner of the conference room) |
| Point: X = 20′-0″ Y = 5′-0″ Z = 0′-0″ | |
| Command: | TYPE: **L<enter>** |
| Specify first point: | TYPE: **@6<180<enter>** (move your mouse so you can see where the line is attached) |
| Specify next point or [Undo]: | TYPE **@5<−90<enter>** |

## FIGURE 5–3

Draw the Door Opening and Door; Draw a Credenza and Conference Table

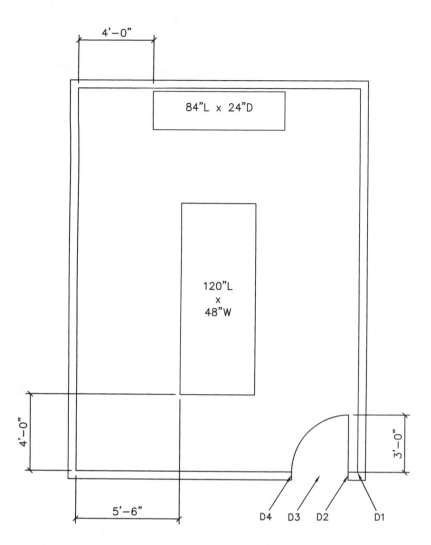

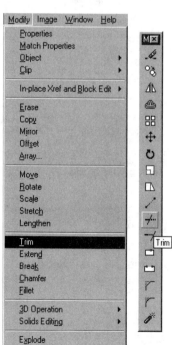

| Specify next point or [Undo]: | **<enter>** |

**Offset the line 3′ to the left to form the door opening:**

| Prompt | Response |
|---|---|
| Command: | **Offset** (or TYPE: **O<enter>**) |
| Specify offset distance or [Through]<0′-5″>: | TYPE: **3′<enter>** |
| Select object to offset or <exit>: | **D2** (the 5″ line you just drew; turn SNAP OFF if necessary) |
| Specify point on side to offset: | **D3** (to the left) |
| Select object to offset or <exit>: | **<enter>** |

## TRIM

**Use Trim to trim the wall lines out of the door opening (Figure 5–3):**

| Prompt | Response |
|---|---|
| Command: | **Trim** (or TYPE: **TR<enter>**) |
| Current settings: Projection=UCS Edge=None Select cutting edges | |
| Select objects: | **D2** |

| Prompt | Response |
|---|---|
| Select objects: 1 found | |
| Select objects: | **D4** |
| Select objects: 1 found, 2 total | |
| Select objects: | **\<enter>** |
| Select object to trim or shift-select to extend or [Project/Edge/Undo]: | **Click the two horizontal wall lines between D2 and D4.** |
| | **\<enter>** (to complete the command; if you turned SNAP OFF to pick the lines, be sure to turn it back ON) |

**Note:** Press enter to the Trim prompt to select all objects as a possible cutting edge.

Watch the Trim prompts carefully. Not until all cutting edges have been selected and the enter key is pressed, so that the prompt "Select object to trim or shift-select to extend or [Project/Edge/Undo]:" appears, can you pick the objects to trim. If you are unable to trim an entity because it does not intersect a cutting edge, hold the Shift key down and click on the entity to extend while still in the Trim command.

## On Your Own

See Figure 5–3.

1. **Use the Line command to draw a 3′ vertical door line. Snap (be sure SNAP is ON) to the upper right corner of the door opening to begin the door line. Draw the line using polar coordinates or direct distance entry.**

2. **Use the Arc-Start, Center, End method to draw the door swing arc, counterclockwise. Note that the start of the arc is the top of the door line, the center is the bottom of the door line, and the end is the upper left corner of the door opening.**

3. **Change the current layer to Furniture.**

4. **Use the Polyline command to draw a credenza (84″ long by 24″ deep) centered on the 15′ rear wall of the conference room, 2″ away from the wall. Locate an ID point by snapping to the inside upper left corner of the conference room. Start the Polyline @48,−2 (relative coordinates) away from the point. Finish drawing the credenza by using direct distance entry or polar coordinates. Use your own personal preference to enter feet or inches. Remember, AutoCAD defaults to inches in Architectural Units, so use the foot (′) symbol if you are using feet. Be sure to draw the credenza using one operation of polyline so it is one continuous polyline.** *Use the Close option for the last segment of the polyline.*

5. **Draw a conference table 120″ long by 48″ wide using the Line command. You can determine the location of the first point by using ID Point or by using grid and snap increments. Use direct distance entry or polar coordinates to complete the table. Refer to Figure 5–3 for the location of the table in the room.**

6. **Use Zoom-Window to zoom in on the table.**

## CHAMFER

A chamfer is an angle (usually 45°) formed at a corner. The following will use the Chamfer command to make the beveled corners of the conference table and credenza.

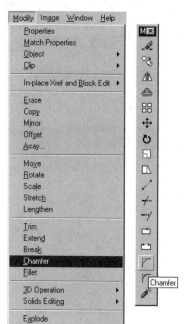

## Use Chamfer to bevel the corners of the table (Figure 5–4):

| Prompt | Response |
|---|---|
| Command: | **Chamfer** (or TYPE: **CHA\<enter>**) |
| (TRIM mode) Current chamfer Dist1 = 0′-0 1/2″, Dist2 = 0′-0 1/2″ | |
| Select first line or [Polyline/Distance/Angle/Trim/Method]: | TYPE: **D\<enter>** |
| Specify first chamfer distance <0′-0 1/2″>: | TYPE: **2\<enter>** |
| Specify second chamfer distance <0′-2″>: | **\<enter>** |
| Select first line or [Polyline/Distance/Angle/Trim/Method]: | **D1** |

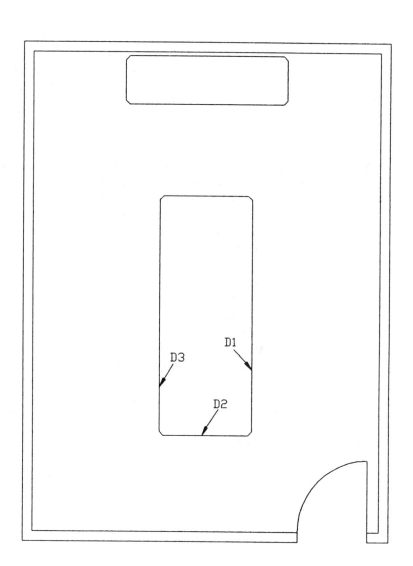

**FIGURE 5–4**
Bevel the Corners of the Table
and Credenza; Draw a Rectangle
Shape

**Part II: Two-Dimensional AutoCAD**

| Prompt | Response |
|---|---|
| Select second line: | **D2** |
| Command: | **<enter>** (Repeat CHAMFER) |
| (TRIM mode) Current chamfer Dist1 = 0'-2", Dist2 = 0'-2" | |
| Select first line or [Polyline/Distance/Angle/ Trim/Method]: | **D2** |
| Select second line: | **D3** |

## On Your Own

1. **Chamfer the other corners of the table (Figure 5–4).**

2. **Use Zoom-Dynamic to zoom in on the credenza.**

### Polyline

Because the credenza was drawn using one operation of the Polyline command, and the Close option was used to complete the credenza rectangle, it is treated as a single entity. The Chamfer command Polyline option chamfers all corners of a continuous polyline with one click.

### Angle

This option of the Chamfer command allows you to specify an angle and a distance to create a chamfer.

### Trim

This option of both the Chamfer and Fillet commands allows you to specify that the part of the original line removed by the chamfer or fillet remains as it was. To do this, TYPE: **T<enter>** at the Chamfer prompt and **N<enter>** at the Trim/No trim <Trim>: prompt. Test this option on a corner of the drawing so you know how it works. Be sure to return it to the Trim option.

### Method

The Method option of the Chamfer command allows you to specify whether you want to use the Distance or the Angle method to specify how the chamfer is to be drawn. The default is the Distance method.

**Use Chamfer distance 2″ to bevel the corners of the credenza (Figure 5–4):**

**Note:** If the last corner of the credenza does not chamfer, this is because the Close option of the Polyline command was not used to complete the polyline rectangle. Explode the credenza symbol and use the Chamfer command to complete the chamfered corner.

| Prompt | Response |
|---|---|
| Command: | **Chamfer** |
| (TRIM mode) Current chamfer Dist1 = 0'-2", Dist2 = 0'-2" | |
| Select first line or [Polyline/Distance/Angle/ Trim/Method]: | TYPE: **P<enter>** (accept 2″ distances as previously set) |
| Select 2D polyline: | **Click any place on the credenza line.** |
| 4 lines were chamfered. | |

When setting the chamfer distance, you can set a different distance for the first and second chamfers. The first distance applies to the first line clicked, and the second distance applies to the second line clicked. You can also set the distance by clicking two points on the drawing.

You can set a chamfer distance of zero and use it to remove the chamfered corners from the table. Using a distance of zero will make 90° corners on the table. Then you can erase the old chamfer lines. This will change the table but not the credenza, because it does not work with a polyline. If you have two lines that do not meet to form an exact corner or that overlap, use the Chamfer command with 0 distance to form an exact corner.

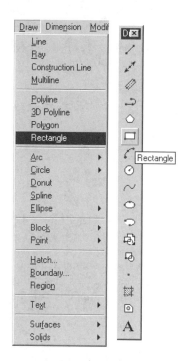

Tip: If you have a two-button mouse, hold down the shift key on your keyboard and press the right mouse button to activate the Osnap menu.

The Chamfer command will chamfer two lines that do not intersect. It automatically extends the two lines until they intersect, trims the two lines according to the distance entered, and connects the two trimmed ends with the chamfer line.

## RECTANGLE

The Rectangle command allows you to draw a rectangle, chamfer or fillet the corners, and give width to the polyline that is created. It also allows you to give elevation and thickness to the polyline. Elevation and thickness are covered in chapters on three-dimensional drawing. To give you an idea of how the Rectangle command works, in the next part of this exercise, you will erase the table and redraw it with the Rectangle command and Osnap-Tracking.

## TRACKING

Tracking, which is similar to the ID Point command, allows you to specify points, except that you can activate Tracking any time AutoCAD asks for a point. You can also specify as many points as you need until you arrive at the desired location, then you press Enter to end the tracking mode. Make sure you turn ORTHO OFF to enter relative coordinates, because after you type and enter TRACK, AutoCAD defaults to ortho mode.

**Erase the table:**

| Prompt | Response |
|---|---|
| Command: | TYPE: **E<enter>** |
| Select objects: | **Window the table<enter>** |

**Draw the table using Rectangle and Osnap-Tracking (Figure 5–3):**

| Prompt | Response |
|---|---|
| Command: | **Rectangle** (or TYPE: **REC<enter>**) |
| Specify first corner point or [Chamfer/ Elevation/Fillet/Thickness/Width]: | TYPE: **C<enter>** |
| Specify first chamfer distance for rectangles <0'-0">: | TYPE: **2<enter>** |
| Specify second chamfer distance for rectangles <0'-2">: | **<enter>** |
| Specify first corner point or [Chamfer/ Elevation/Fillet/Thickness/Width]: | TYPE: **TRACK <enter>** |
|  | **Turn ORTHO OFF (F8);** it automatically turns ON |
| First tracking point: | **With SNAP ON (F9), CLICK: the lower left inside corner of the room.** |
| Next point (Press ENTER to end tracking): | TYPE: **@5'6,4'<enter>** |
| Next point (Press ENTER to end tracking): | **<enter>** (to end tracking) |
| Specify other corner point: | TYPE: **@48,120<enter>** |

## On Your Own

See Figure 5–4.

1. **Zoom in on a portion of the grid outside the conference room walls.**
2. **Draw a rectangle 26" wide by 28" deep using the Line command. Be sure to have SNAP ON when you draw the rectangle. You will now edit this rectangle using the Fillet command to create the shape of a chair.**

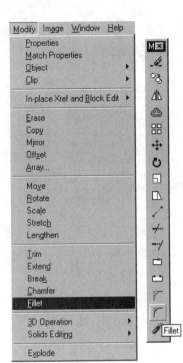

# FILLET

The Fillet command is similar to Chamfer, except the Fillet command creates a round instead of an angle.

**Use Fillet to edit the back of the rectangle to create the symbol of a chair (Figure 5–5):**

**FIGURE 5–5**
Use Fillet to Create the Chair Symbol

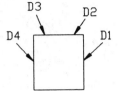

| Prompt | Response |
|---|---|
| Command: | **Fillet** (or TYPE: **F<enter>**) |
| Current settings: Mode = TRIM, Radius = 0'-0 1/2" | |
| Select first object or [Polyline/Radius/Trim]: | TYPE: **R<enter>** |
| Specify fillet radius <0'-0 1/2">: | TYPE: **12<enter>** |
| Select first object or [Polyline/Radius/Trim]: | TYPE: **T<enter>** |
| Enter Trim mode option [Trim/No trim] <Trim>: | TYPE: **T<enter>** (verify Trim option) |
| Select first object or [Polyline/Radius/Trim]: | **D1** |
| Select second object: | **D2** |
| Command: | **<enter>** (Repeat FILLET) |
| Current settings: Mode = TRIM, Radius = 1'-0" | |
| Select first object or [Polyline/Radius/Trim]: | **D3** |
| Select second object: | **D4** |

The Polyline option of Fillet automatically fillets an entire continuous polyline with one click. Remember to set the fillet radius first.

Fillet will also fillet two circles, two arcs, a line and a circle, a line and an arc, or a circle and an arc. When Fillet is used with arcs and circles, AutoCAD uses the select object points to determine the fillet endpoints.

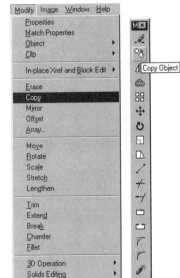

## COPY and OSNAP-Midpoint

The Copy command allows you to copy any part of a drawing either once or multiple times. Object Snap modes when combined with other commands help you to draw very accurately. As you become more familiar with the Object Snap modes you will use them constantly to draw with extreme accuracy. The following introduces the Osnap-Midpoint mode, which helps you to snap to the midpoint of a line or arc.

**Use the Copy command, combined with Osnap-Midpoint, to copy three times the chair you have just drawn (Figure 5–6):**

| Prompt | Response |
|---|---|
| Command: | **Copy** (or TYPE: **CP<enter>**) |
| Select objects: | **Click the first corner of a window that will include the chair.** |
| Specify opposite corner: | **Click the other corner of the window to include the chair.** |

**FIGURE 5–6**
Copy the Chair Three Times; Use
Rotate to Rotate the Chairs

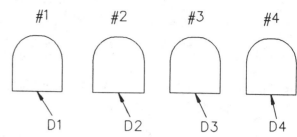

| Prompt | Response |
|---|---|
| Select objects: | <enter> |
| Specify base point or displacement, or [Multiple]: | TYPE: **M<enter>** |
| Specify base point: | TYPE: **MID<enter>** |
| Mid of | **D1** |
| Specify second point of displacement or <use first point as displacement>: | **D2,D3,D4** (be sure SNAP is ON, and leave enough room to rotate the chairs, Figure 5–7) |
| Specify second point of displacement or <use first point as displacement>: | <enter> |

By selecting the option Multiple in response to the Copy prompt, you were able to copy the chairs multiple times. If Multiple is not selected, you can copy the chair only once.

The Osnap-Midpoint mode helped you snap very accurately to the midpoint of the line; you used the midpoint of the line that defines the front of the chair as the base point. When using the Copy command, carefully choose the base point so that it helps you easily locate the copies.

## ROTATE

The Rotate command rotates a selected drawing entity in the counterclockwise direction; 90° is to the left, and 270° (or −90°) is to the right. You select a base point of the entity to be rotated, and the entity rotates about that base point.

**Use the Rotate command to rotate chairs 2 and 3 (Figure 5–6):**

| Prompt | Response |
|---|---|
| Command: | **Rotate** (or TYPE: **RO<enter>**) |
| Current positive angle in UCS: ANGDIR= counterclockwise ANGBASE=0 | |
| Select objects: | **Start the window to include chair 2.** |
| Specify opposite corner: | **Complete the window to include chair 2.** |
| Select objects: | <enter> |
| Specify base point: | TYPE: **MID<enter>** |

**FIGURE 5–7**
Rotated Chairs

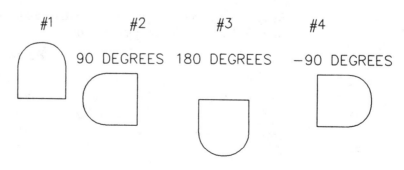

| Prompt | Response |
|---|---|
| Mid of | **D2** |
| Specify rotation angle or [Reference]: | TYPE: **90<enter>** |
| Command: | **<enter>** |
| Current positive angle in UCS: ANGDIR= counterclockwise ANGBASE=0 | |
| Select objects: | **Window chair 3** |
| Select objects: | **<enter>** |
| Specify base point: | TYPE: **MID<enter>** |
| mid of | **D3** |
| Specify rotation angle or [Reference]: | TYPE: **180<enter>** |

**Note:** If part of the entity that is to be rotated lies on the specified base point, that part of the entity remains on the base point while the entity's orientation is changed.

## On Your Own

See Figure 5–7.

**1. Rotate chair 4 using a 270° (or −90°) rotation angle.**

### Reference

The Reference option of the Rotate prompt is sometimes easier to use, especially if you do not know the rotation angle. It allows you to select the object to be rotated and click the base point. Type: **R<enter>** for Reference. Then you can enter the "Reference angle:" (current angle) of the object by typing it and pressing enter. If you don't know the current angle, you can show AutoCAD the "Reference angle:" by picking the two endpoints of the line to be rotated. You can specify the "New angle:" by typing it and pressing enter. If you don't know the new angle, you can show AutoCAD the "New angle:" by picking a point on the drawing.

## POINT

The Point command allows you to draw points on your drawing. Object Snap recognizes these points as nodes. The Osnap mode Node is used to snap to points.

There are many different types of points to choose from. The appearance of these points is determined by the Pdmode (point definition mode) and Pdsize (point definition size) options within the Point command.

**Use the Point Style... command to set the appearance of points:**

| Prompt | Response |
|---|---|
| Command: | **Point Style...** (or TYPE: **DDPTYPE<enter>**) |
| The Point Style dialog box appears (Figure 5–8): | CLICK: **the X box** |
| | CLICK: **Set Size in Absolute Units** |
| | TYPE: **6 in the Point Size: entry box** |

You have just set the points to appear as an X, and they will be 6″ high. The Point Style dialog box shows the different types of points available. The size of the point may be set in a size relative to the screen or in absolute units. Your Point Style dialog box should appear as shown in Figure 5–8.

| | Response |
|---|---|
| | CLICK: **OK** |

## On Your Own

See Figure 5–9.

**1. Use the Explode command on the table** (so you can use the Offset command).

**2. Use the Offset command to offset the two lines that define the long sides of the conference table. The chairs will be placed 6″ from the edge of the able, so set 6″**

**FIGURE 5–8**
Point Style Dialog Box

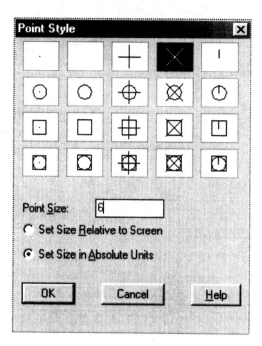

**FIGURE 5–9**
Offset the Two Lines Defining the
Long Sides of the Conference
Table; Divide the Lines Into Eight
Equal Segments; Copy Chair 4

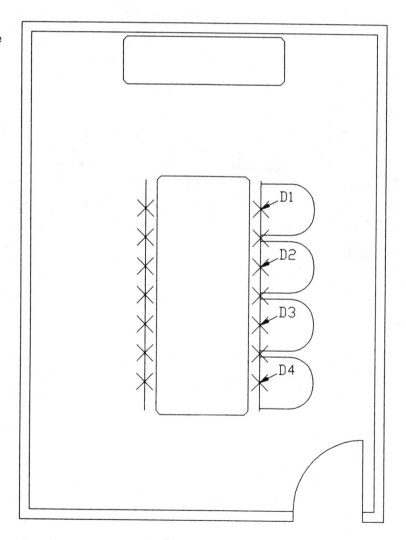

as the offset distance. Offset the lines on each side, outside the table as shown in Figure 5–9. These lines will be used as construction lines to help locate the chairs.

## DIVIDE

The Divide command divides an entity into equal parts and places point markers along the entity at the dividing points. The pdmode has been set to 3 (an X point), so an X will appear as the point marker when you use Divide.

**Use Divide to divide the offset lines into eight equal segments (Figure 5–9):**

| Prompt | Response |
|---|---|
| Command: | **Divide** (or TYPE: **DIV<enter>**) |
| Select object to divide: | **Click any place on one of the offset lines.** |
| Enter the number of segments or [Block]: | TYPE: **8<enter>** |

The X points divide the line into eight equal segments.

You can divide lines, circles, arcs, and polylines by selecting them. The Divide command also draws a specified Block at each mark between the equal segments. You will learn about Blocks in Chapter 8.

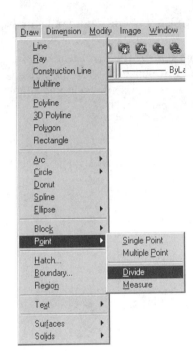

## On Your Own

See Figure 5–9.

1. **Continue with the Divide command and divide the other offset line into eight equal segments.**

## COPY, OSNAP-Midpoint, OSNAP-Node

**Use the Copy command (combined with Osnap-Midpoint and Osnap-Node) to copy chair 4 four times on the right side of the conference table (Figure 5–9):**

| Prompt | Response |
|---|---|
| Command: | **Copy** (or TYPE: **CP<enter>**) |
| Select objects: | **Click below and to the left of chair 4.** |
| Specify opposite corner: | **Window chair 4.** |
| Select objects: | **<enter>** |
| Specify base point or displacement, or [Multiple]: | TYPE: **M<enter>** |
| Specify base point: | TYPE: **MID<enter** |
| _mid of | **Click any place on the straight line that forms the front of the chair symbol.** |
| Specify second point of displacement or <use first point as displacement>: | TYPE: **NOD<enter>** |
| of | **D1** |
| Specify second point of displacement or <use first point as displacement>: | TYPE: **NOD<enter>** |
| of | **D2** |
| Specify second point of displacement or <use first point as displacement>: | TYPE: **NOD<enter>** |
| of | **D3** |
| Specify second point of displacement or <use first point as displacement>: | TYPE: **NOD<enter>** |
| of | **D4** |

| Prompt | Response |
|---|---|
| Specify second point of displacement or <br>    &lt;use first point as displacement&gt;: | &lt;enter&gt; |

By selecting the option Multiple in response to the Copy prompt, you were able to copy the chairs multiple times.

The points act as nodes (snapping exactly on the center of the X) for Object Snap purposes.

## On Your Own

See Figure 5–10.

1. **Continue with the Copy, Osnap-Midpoint, and Osnap-Node commands, and place four chairs on the left side of the table.**
2. **Use the Copy command to place a chair at each end of the conference table. Because you will be copying each chair only once, do not pick Multiple but go immediately to Osnap-Midpoint to specify the base point. Use the grid and snap to determine the "Second point of displacement:" for each chair.**

**FIGURE 5–10**
Complete Exercise 5–1

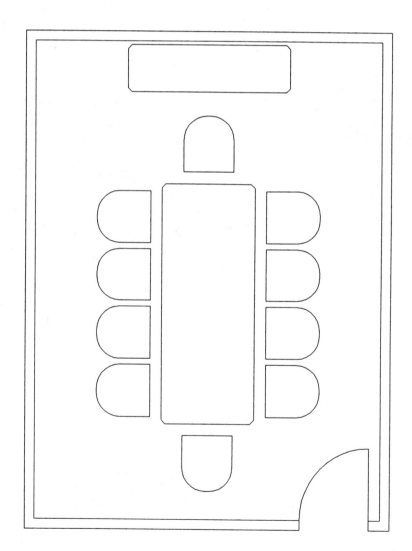

3. TYPE: PDMODE<enter> at the Command: prompt. Set the Pdmode to 1, and the drawing is regenerated. The X's will disappear. You have set the Pdmode to be invisible.

4. Erase the offset lines used to locate the chairs on each long side of the table. Use F7 to redraw when it looks like part of the chairs have been erased.

5. Erase the chairs you have drawn outside the conference room walls.

6. Exercise 5–1 is complete.

## HELP

If you have forgotten the name of a command or the options that are available for a specific command, the Help command is available to refresh your memory. The Help command provides a list of the AutoCAD commands as well as information about specific commands.

**Use HELP to obtain information about a specific command:**

| Prompt | Response |
|---|---|
| Command: | TYPE: **HELP<enter>** |
| The AutoCAD 2002 Help: User Documentation appears on the screen: | CLICK: the Index Tab |
| | TYPE: **DONUT** (or type the name of any other command you have questions about) |
| | DOUBLE CLICK: **DONUT command** |
| The Topics Found dialog box is displayed: | CLICK: **the Display button** |
| Information about the DONUT command is shown: | CLICK: **X** (upper right corner) to close when you are through |

Don't forget that the Help command is available. You can also use the Help command while you are in the middle of another command. If you type 'help (be sure to include the apostrophe) in response to any prompt that is not asking for a text string, information is supplied about the current command. The information is sometimes specific to the current prompt.

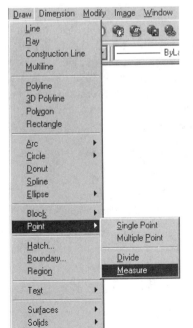

## MEASURE

The Measure command is similar to the Divide command, except that with Measure you specify the distance. Divide calculates the interval to divide an entity into a specified number of equal segments. The Measure command places point markers at a specified distance along an entity.

The measurement and division of a circle start at the angle from the center that follows the current Snap rotation. The measurement and division of a closed polyline start at the first vertex drawn. The Measure command also draws a specified block at each mark between the divided segments.

## PICKBOX SIZE

The Pickbox Size slider bar on the Selection tab under Options... on the Tools menu (Figure 5–11) can be used to change the size of the target box, the small box that rides on the screen crosshair and appears when the Modify commands are used.

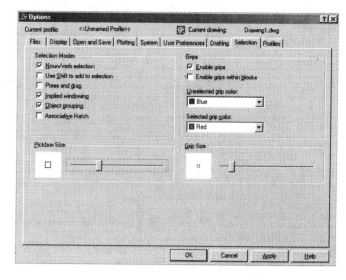

**FIGURE 5–11**
Options Dialog Box, Selection Tab, Pickbox Slider Bar

## On Your Own

1. **Activate a Modify command to confirm visually the current size of the pickbox.**
2. **Cancel the command and complete the following to change the size of the pickbox.**

**Change the size of the pickbox:**

| Prompt | Response |
|--------|----------|
| Command: | TYPE: **PICKBOX<enter>** |
| New value for PICKBOX <default>: | TYPE: **a number larger or smaller than the default<enter>** |

## OSNAP

It is very important that you become familiar with and use Object Snap modes in combination with Draw, Edit, Modify, and other AutoCAD commands while you are drawing. When an existing drawing entity is not located on a snap point, it is impossible to connect a line or other drawing entity exactly to it. You may try, and you may think that the two points are connected, but a close examination (Zoom-Window) will reveal that they are not. Object Snap modes are used in combination with other commands to connect exactly to specific points of existing objects in a drawing. You need to use Object Snap modes constantly for complete accuracy while drawing.

### Activating Osnap

An Osnap mode can be activated in four different ways:

1. Typing the Osnap abbreviation (first three letters of the Object Snap mode) from the keyboard.
2. Pressing Shift and right-clicking in the drawing area, then choosing an Object Snap mode from the Object Snap menu that appears (Figure 5–12).
3. Clicking from the Object Snap flyout on the Standard toolbar (Figure 5–13).
4. Clicking from the Object Snap toolbar (Figure 5–14).

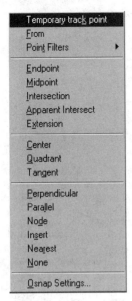

FIGURE 5–12
Activating Osnap by Pressing
Shift and Right-Clicking in the
Drawing Area

FIGURE 5–13
Activating Osnap by Clicking from
the Object Snap Flyout on the
Standard Toolbar

FIGURE 5–14
Activating Osnap by Clicking from
the Object Snap Toolbar

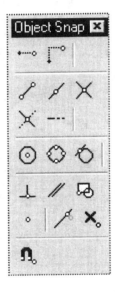

## Osnap Modes That Snap to Specific Drawing Features

You have already used Osnap-Midpoint and Node. They are examples of Osnap modes that snap to specific drawing features. Midpoint snaps to the midpoint of a line or arc, and Node snaps to a point entity.

The following list describes other Osnap modes that snap to specific drawing features. AutoCAD Osnap modes treat each edge of a solid and each polyline segment as a line.

3D faces and viewports (described in later chapters) are treated in the same manner. You will use many of these Osnap modes while completing the exercises in this book.

**Endpoint**  Snaps to the endpoint of a line or arc. The end of the line or arc nearest the point picked is snapped to.

**Midpoint**  Snaps to the midpoint of a line or arc.

**Center**  Snaps to the center of an arc or circle.

**Node**  Snaps to a point (POINT: command) entity.

**Quadrant**  Snaps to the closest quadrant point of an arc or circle. These are the 0°, 90°, 180°, and 270° points on a circle or arc.

**Intersection**  Snaps to the intersection of two lines, a line with an arc or circle, or two circles and/or arcs. You will use this mode often to snap to the intersection of two lines.

**Extension**  Extends a line or arc. With a command and the extension mode active, pause over a line or arc, and after a small plus sign is displayed, slowly move along a temporary path that follows the extension of the line or arc. You can draw objects to and from points on the extension path line.

**Insert**  Snaps to the insertion point of text, attribute, or Block entities. (These entities are described in later chapters.)

**Perpendicular**  Snaps to the point on a line, circle, or arc that forms a 90° angle from that object to the last point. For example, if you are drawing a line, click the first point of the line, then use Perpendicular to connect the line to another line, circle, or arc. The new line will be perpendicular to form a 90° angle with the first pick.

**Tangent**  Snaps to the point on a circle or arc that when connected to the last point entered forms a line tangent to (touching at one point) the circle or arc.

**Nearest**  Snaps to the point on a line, arc, or circle that is closest to the position of the crosshair; also snaps to any point (POINT: command) entity that is visually closest to the crosshair. You will use this mode when you want to be sure to connect to a line, arc, circle, or point, and cannot use another Osnap mode.

**Apparent Intersection**  Snaps to what appears to be an intersection even though one object is above the other in 3D space.

**Parallel**  Draws a line parallel to another line. With the line command active, click the first point of the new line you want to draw. With the parallel mode active, pause over the line you want to draw parallel to, until a small parallel line symbol is displayed. Move the cursor away from but parallel to the original line, and an alignment path is displayed for you to complete the new line.

For the Line command, you can also use the Tangent and Perpendicular modes when picking the first point of the line. This allows you to draw a line tangent to, or perpendicular to, an existing entity.

### Running Osnap Modes

You can use individual Osnap modes while in another command, as you did with Midpoint and Node. You can also set a running Osnap mode. A running Osnap mode is constantly in effect while you are drawing, until it is disabled. For example, if you have many intersections to which you are connecting lines, set the Intersection mode as a running mode. This saves time by eliminating your constant return to the Osnap command for each intersection pick.

You can set a running Osnap mode using Drafting Settings... from the Tools menu. When the Drafting Settings dialog box appears, Figure 5–15, make sure the Object Snap tab is active. Click a check mark beside the desired Osnap mode or modes. Be sure to disable the running Osnap mode when you are through using it, as it will interfere with your drawing. Clicking OSNAP on in the status bar will activate any running Osnap modes you have set in the Object Snap tab, and clicking it off will disable any running Osnap modes you have set. When no running Osnap modes are set and OSNAP is clicked on in the status bar, the Object Snap tab will appear. When running Osnap modes are set, hold your mouse over OSNAP in the status bar and right-click. Click "Settings..." in the menu that appears to access the Drafting Settings dialog box.

Tools Draw Dimension Modify I
- Today
- Autodesk Point A
- Meet Now
- CAD Standards ▶
- Spelling
- Quick Select...
- Display Order ▶
- Inquiry ▶
- Attribute Extraction...
- Properties          Ctrl+1
- AutoCAD DesignCenter Ctrl+2
- dbConnect           Ctrl+6
- Load Application...
- Run Script...
- Macro ▶
- AutoLISP ▶
- Display Image ▶
- Named UCS...
- Orthographic UCS ▶
- Move UCS
- New UCS ▶
- Wizards ▶
- Drafting Settings...
- Tablet ▶
- Customize ▶
- Options...

**FIGURE 5-15**
Drafting Settings Dialog Box,
Object Snap Tab

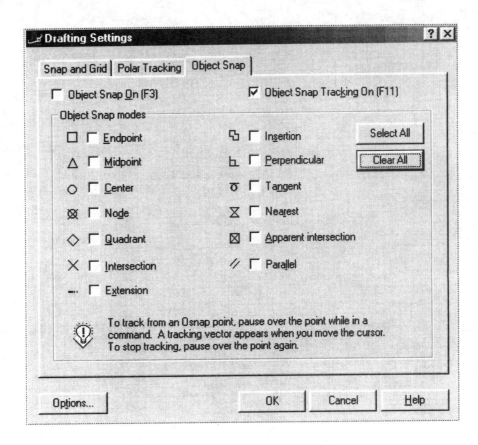

## Osnap Settings: Marker, Aperture, Magnet, Tooltip

Note the markers (small symbols) beside each Object Snap mode in the Drafting Settings dialog box, Object Snap tab (Figure 5–15). The display of the markers is controlled under the Drafting tab of the Options dialog box (Figure 5–16). A check mark beside Marker

**FIGURE 5-16**
Options Dialog Box, Drafting
Tab

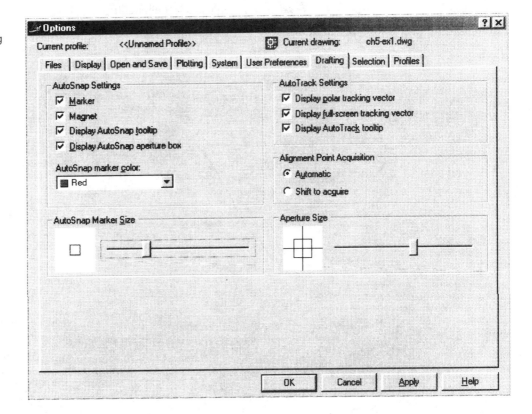

will add the marker symbol to the crosshair. The AutoSnap Marker Size slider bar at the bottom of the dialog box specifies the size of the marker. The color of the marker can be changed also, by clicking the down arrow under AutoSnap marker color:.

When Osnap is activated, a small target box called an *aperture* can also be added to the screen crosshair. This small box shows the area within which AutoCAD will search for Object Snap candidates. The display of the box is controlled under the Drafting tab of the Options dialog box (Figure 5–16). A check mark beside Display AutoSnap aperture box will add the target box to the crosshair. The Aperture Size slider bar on the right side of the dialog box specifies the size of the box.

The Magnet setting (Figure 5–16) locks the aperture box onto the snap point. The AutoSnap tooltip setting (Figure 5–16) will appear on the screen when on.

### Save Your Drawing

When you have completed Exercise 5–1, save your work in at least two places. Exercise 5–1 is printed in Chapter 7.

## EXERCISE 5–2
## Drawing a Rectangular Lecture Room Including Furniture

A lecture room, including walls and furnishings, is drawn in Exercise 5–2. When you have completed Exercise 5–2, your drawing will look similar to Figure 5–17. To prepare to draw Exercise 5–2, turn on the computer and start AutoCAD. The AutoCAD 2002 Today window is displayed.

1. CLICK: **the Create Drawings tab**
2. CLICK: **Wizards**
   CLICK: **Quick Setup**
3. Set drawing Units: **Architectural**
   CLICK: **Next>**
4. Set drawing Width: **25′** × Length: **35′**
   CLICK: **Finish**
5. **Use SaveAs... to save the drawing on the hard drive with the name CH5-EX2.**
6. Set Grid: **12″**
7. Set Snap: **6″**
8. Create the following Layers:

| LAYER NAME | COLOR | LINETYPE |
|---|---|---|
| Walls | White | Continuous |
| Furniture | Red | Continuous |

9. Set Layer Walls current.
10. Use **Zoom-All** to view the limits of the drawing.

### POLYLINE

The Polyline prompt is "Specify next point or [Arc/Close/Halfwidth/Length/Undo/Width]:". In Exercise 5–1, a simple continuous polyline was used to draw the inside lines of the conference room walls, then Offset was used to draw the outside line showing wall depth. The Width option of the Pline prompt allows you to specify a thickness for the polyline. The Width option is used to draw the lecture room walls in Exercise 5–2.

## Width

The Width option allows you to draw wide polylines. In Exercise 5–2, a 5″ wide polyline is used to draw the walls of the lecture room. The *interior dimensions* of the lecture room are 15′ × 20′. The starting and ending points of a wide polyline are the *center* of the polyline's width. Because the starting and ending points of the wide polyline segments are the center of the line segment, 5″ is added to each line length to compensate for the 2-1/2″ wall thickness on each side of the center line.

When a wide polyline is exploded, the width information is lost and the polyline changes to a line segment.

**Use Polyline Width to draw the walls of the lecture room (Figure 5–18):**

| Prompt | Response |
|---|---|
| Command: | **Polyline** (or TYPE: **PL<enter>**) |
| Specify start point: | TYPE: **4′9-1/2,4′9-1/2<enter>** |
| Current line-width is 0′0″ | |
| Specify next point or [Arc/Close/Halfwidth/ Length/Undo/Width]: | TYPE: **W<enter>** |
| Specify starting width <0′0″>: | TYPE: **5<enter>** |
| Specify ending width <0′-5″>: | **<enter>** |

**FIGURE 5–18**
Use a Wide Polyline to Draw the
Lecture Room Walls

| Prompt | Response |
|---|---|
| Specify next point or [Arc/Close/Halfwidth/ Length/Undo/Width]: | **Turn ORTHO ON** <br> **Move your mouse to the right** and TYPE: **15'5<enter>** |
| Specify next point or [Arc/Close/Halfwidth/ Length/Undo/Width]: | **Move your mouse up** and TYPE: **20'5<enter>** |
| Specify next point or [Arc/Close/Halfwidth/ Length/Undo/Width]: | **Move your mouse to the left** and TYPE: **15'5<enter>** |
| Specify next point or [Arc/Close/Halfwidth/ Length/Undo/Width]: | TYPE: **C** |

When you subtract 2-1/2″ (half the polyline width) from coordinates 5',5' to get your starting point of coordinates 4'9-1/2,4'9-1/2, the inside lower left corner of the lecture room is located on the grid mark at coordinates 5',5'. Turn coordinates (F6) on and snap to the lower left inside corner of the lecture room to verify this.

With 5″ added to each measurement, the inside dimensions of the lecture room are 15' × 20'. If we had wanted the *outside* of the lecture room walls to measure 15' × 20', we would have *subtracted* 5″ from each measurement.

Notice that you do not have to insert the inch symbol in the polar coordinates, because architectural units default to inches.

### Close

It is always best to use the Close option when you are completing a wide polyline. The effect of using Close is different from clicking or entering a point to complete the polyline. With the Close option, a beveled corner will appear. A 90° corner will appear if the point is entered or clicked.

### Halfwidth

The Halfwidth option in the polyline prompt is similar to the Width option, except that half the total width is specified.

### Length

The Length option in the Polyline prompt allows you to draw a polyline segment at the same angle as the previously drawn polyline segment, by simply specifying the length of the new segment. It also allows you to return to straight line segments after you have drawn a polyline arc.

### FILL ON, FILL OFF

The settings FILL ON and FILL OFF affect the appearance of the polyline. To have an outline of the polyline, TYPE: **FILL<enter>**, then **OFF<enter>** and regenerate the drawing. To have it appear solid again, TYPE: **FILL<enter>**, then TYPE: **ON<enter>** and regenerate the drawing.

### On Your Own

1. TYPE: **FILL<enter>**, then TYPE: **OFF <enter>** and **regenerate the drawing to create an open polyline.**

2. **Use Zoom-Window to magnify the corner of the lecture room where the door will be drawn.**

## BREAK and FROM

The Break command can be used to erase a part of a drawing entity. From can be used to set a temporary reference point, similar to ID point.

**Use Break to create an opening for the lecture room door (Figure 5–19):**

**FIGURE 5–19**
Use Break to Create an Opening
for the Lecture Room Door

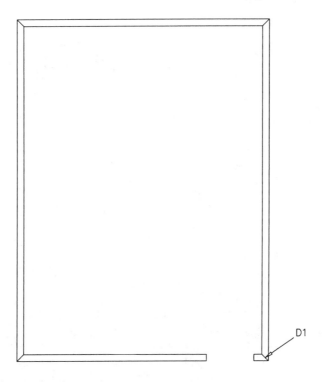

| Prompt | Response |
|---|---|
| Command: | **Break** (or TYPE: **BR<enter>**) |
| Select object: | **Click any place on the polyline** |
| Specify second break point or [First point]: | TYPE: **F<enter>** (for first point) |
| Specify first break point: | TYPE: **FRO<enter>** (abbreviation for FROM) |
| Base point: | TYPE: **INT<enter>** |
| of | **D1** (Figure 5–19) |
| <Offset> | TYPE: **@8-1/2<180<enter>** |
| Specify second break point: | TYPE: **@36<180<enter>** |

### First

When selecting an entity to break, you may use the point entered in the selection process as the first break point, or you may TYPE: **F<enter>** to be able to select the first break point.

### @

Sometimes you need only to break an entity and not erase a section of it. In that case, use @ as the second break point. The line will be broken twice on the same point; no segments will be erased from the line.

### On Your Own

1. **With snap on, use the Line command to draw a 5′ × 5′ square in the approximate location shown in Figure 5–20, and proceed with the following to see how Edit Polyline will join lines to form a single polyline.**

### Edit Polyline

Edit Polyline is a special edit command that is used only to edit polylines. The prompt is "Enter an option [Close/Join/Width/Edit vertex/Fit/Spline/Decurve/Ltypegen/Undo]:".

The following describes how to use the Join and Width options available in the Edit Polyline prompt. All options can be used on either a simple polyline or a wide polyline.

**FIGURE 5–20**
Edit Polyline Join Option

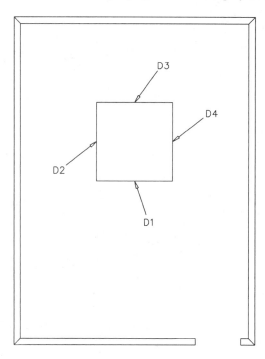

**Part II: Two-Dimensional AutoCAD**

## Join

The Join option joins any line, arc, or other polyline to an existing polyline if it meets that existing polyline's endpoints. The Join option also joins lines or arcs together and changes them into a single polyline. You will do this in the following part of this exercise.

**Use Edit Polyline Join to join four separate lines (drawn with the Line command) to form a single polyline (Figure 5–20):**

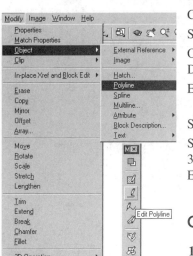

| Prompt | Response |
|---|---|
| Command: | **Edit Polyline** (or TYPE: **PE\<enter>**) |
| Select polyline or [Multiple]: | **D1** |
| Object selected is not a polyline<br>Do you want to turn it into one? \<Y> | **\<enter>** |
| Enter an option [Close/Join/Width/Edit vertex/<br>Fit/Spline/Decurve/Ltype gen/Undo]: | TYPE: **J\<enter>** |
| Select objects: | **D2,D3,D4** |
| Select objects:<br>3 segments added to polyline | **\<enter>** |
| Enter an option [Open/Join/Width/Edit vertex/<br>Fit/Spline/Decurve/Ltype gen/Undo]: | **\<enter>** (to complete the command) |

## On Your Own

1. To verify that all segments of the line have been joined to form a single polyline, use the Erase command and pick a point on the new polyline. If all segments are highlighted, it is a polyline, and you can enter Esc to cancel the Erase command.

### Width

The Width option allows you to change the width of an existing polyline.

**Use Edit Polyline Width to change the width of the polyline that makes the 5′ × 5′ square:**

| Prompt | Response |
|---|---|
| Command: | **Edit Polyline** |
| Select polyline or [Multiple]: | **Click a point on the polyline that forms<br>the 5′ × 5′ square** |
| Enter an option [Open/Join/Width/Edit vertex/<br>Fit/Spline/Decurve/Ltype gen/Undo]: | TYPE: **W\<enter>** |
| Specify new width for all segments: | TYPE: **5\<enter>** |
| Enter an option [Open/Join/Width/Edit vertex/<br>Fit/Spline/Decurve/Ltype gen/Undo]: | **\<enter>** |

## On Your Own

See Figure 5–21.

1. Use the Erase command to erase the 5′ × 5′ square that you have drawn in the middle of the lecture room walls.
2. Use the Line command to draw a 3′ vertical door line:
   a. Use Osnap-From to specify the first point of the line.
   b. Use Osnap-Endpoint to snap to the base point that is the end (center of the polyline's width) of the wide polyline.
   c. The offset is 2 1/2 up to begin the verticle door line at the inside corner of the door opening.
3. Use the Arc-Start, Center, Angle method to draw the counterclockwise door swing arc. Use Osnap-Endpoint for the start and center connections.

4. **Set the current layer to Furniture. To draw the first chair in the group of chairs, zoom in on a portion of the grid inside the lecture room walls in the lower left area.**

5. **Use the Line command to draw a rectangle 26″ wide by 28″ deep. This chair shape will be used to draw the entire group of 16 chairs and will be moved to the correct position later. For now, just be sure it is located in the general area of the lower left corner of the room, shown in Figure 5–21.**

6. **Edit the rectangle, using the Fillet command, 12″ Radius to form the shape of the chair.**

7. **Zoom-Extents after you finish drawing the chair.**

## ARRAY

Array allows you to make multiple copies of an object in a rectangular or polar (circular) array. The rectangular option is used to draw all the chairs in the lecture room; the polar option is described in Exercise 5–3.

**Use the Array command to make a rectangular pattern of 16 chairs (Figure 5–21 and Figure 5–22):**

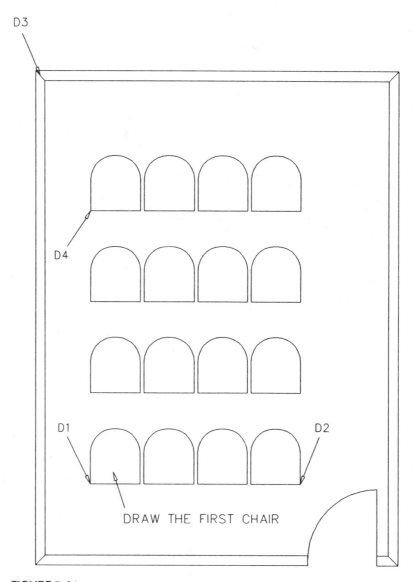

**FIGURE 5–21**
Draw the Chairs for the Lecture Room

Part II: Two-Dimensional AutoCAD

FIGURE 5–22
Array Dialog Box

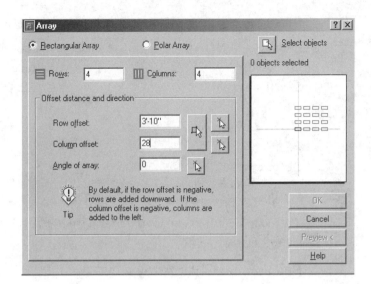

Hint: In the Array command, include the
original cornerstone item in the number
of rows and columns.

Note: To rotate a rectangular array, set
the snap rotation to the desired angle and
then create the array.

| Prompt | Response |
|---|---|
| Command: | **Array** (or TYPE: **AR<enter>**) |
| The Array dialog box appears: | CLICK: **the Select objects button** |
| Select objects: | PICK: **any point to locate the first corner of a window to include the entire chair** |
| Specify opposite corner: | **Window the chair just drawn.** |
| Select objects: | **<enter>** |
| The Array dialog box appears: | CLICK: **the Rectangular Array button** |
| | TYPE: **4 in the Rows: input area** |
| | TYPE: **4 in the Columns: input area** |
| | TYPE: **46 in the Row offset: input area** |
| | TYPE: **28 in the Column offset: input area** |
| | TYPE: **0 in the Angle of array: input area** |
| | CLICK: **OK** |

### Rectangular

The Rectangular option of Array allows you to make multiple copies of an object in a rectangular array. The array is made up of horizontal rows and vertical columns. The direction and spacing of the rows and columns are determined by the distance you specify between each. In the previous example we used the chair as the cornerstone element in the lower left corner of the array. Positive numbers were entered for the distance between the rows and columns, and the array was generated up and to the right. When a positive number is entered for the rows, they proceed up; when a negative number is entered, they proceed down. When a positive number is entered for the columns, they proceed to the right; when a negative number is entered, they proceed to the left.

## DISTANCE

The Distance command can be used to determine measurements. We know the interior width of the room is 15′. To center the array of chairs accurately in the lecture room, we need to measure the width of the array. The depth appears to be fine for the room size.

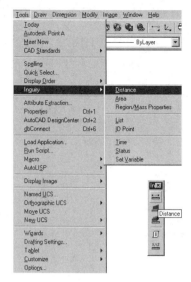

## Use Distance to measure a specified distance (Figure 5–21):

| Prompt | Response |
|---|---|
| Command: | **Distance** (or TYPE: **DIST<enter>**) |
| Specify first point: | TYPE: **INT<enter>** |
| int of | **D1** |
| Specify second point: | TYPE: **INT<enter>** |
| int of | **D2** |

Distance = 9'-2", Angle in XY Plane = 0,
   Angle from XY Plane = 0, Delta X = 9'-2",
   Delta Y = 0'-0", Delta Z = 0'-0"

The room width, 180", minus the array width, 110", is 70". You can leave 35"-wide aisles on each side of the array.

## Position the Chair Array

To locate the chair array precisely, use Move and From as well as some Osnap modes. The array will be located 2" away from the back wall of the lecture room and will have 35"-wide aisles on each side.

The aisle width, 35", plus half the width of the polyline, 2-1/2", is 37-1/2" on the X axis. The chair depth, 28", plus half the width of the polyline, 2-1/2", plus the distance away from the wall, 2", is 32-1/2" on the Y axis. Make sure ORTHO is off.

**To locate the chair array (Figure 5–21):**

| Prompt | Response |
|---|---|
| Command: | **Move** (or TYPE: **M<enter>**) |
| Select objects: | CLICK: **any point to locate the first corner of a window to include the entire array** |
| Specify opposite corner: | **Window the entire array.** |
| Select objects: | **<enter>** |
| Specify base point or displacement: | TYPE: **INT<enter>** |
| int of | **D4** |
| Specify second point of displacement or <use first point as displacement>: | TYPE: **FRO<enter>** |
| Base point: | TYPE: **INT<enter>** |
| Int of: | **D3** |
| <Offset>: | TYPE: **@37-1/2,-32-1/2<enter>** (do not forget the minus (hyphen) in front of the 32-1/2) |

## On Your Own

See Figure 5–23.

1. **Draw the lectern centered on the chair array, as shown.**

2. TYPE: **FILL<enter>**, then TYPE: **ON<enter> and regenerate the drawing to have the walls appear solid again.**

3. **Exercise 5–2 is complete.**

## Save Your Drawing

When you have completed Exercise 5–2, save your work in at least two places. Exercise 5–2 is printed in Chapter 7.

FIGURE 5–23
Complete Exercise 5–2

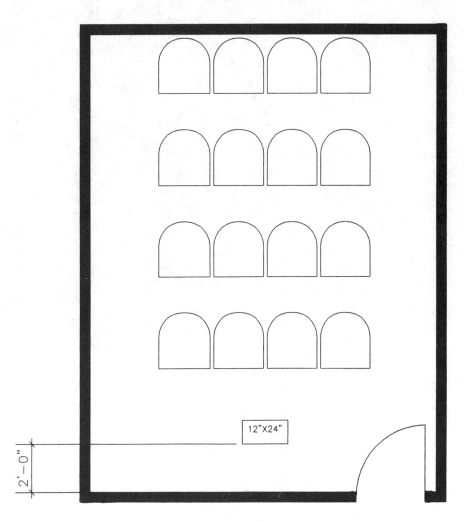

# EXERCISE 5–3
## Drawing a Curved Conference Room Including Furniture

A conference room, including walls and furnishings, is drawn in Exercise 5–3. When you have completed Exercise 5–3, your drawing will look similar to Figure 5–24. To prepare to draw Exercise 5–3, turn on the computer and start AutoCAD. The AutoCAD 2002 Today window is displayed.

1. CLICK: **the Create Drawings tab**
2. CLICK: **Wizards**
   CLICK: **Quick Setup**
3. Set drawing Units: **Architectural**
   CLICK: **Next>**
4. Set drawing Width: **25′** × Length: **35′**
   CLICK: **Finish**
5. **Use SaveAs... to save the drawing on the hard drive with the name CH5-EX3.**
6. Set Grid: **12″**
7. Set Snap: **6″**
8. Create the following Layers:

| LAYER NAME | COLOR | LINETYPE |
|---|---|---|
| Walls | White | Continuous |
| Furniture | Red | Continuous |

FIGURE 5–24

Exercise 5–3: Drawing a Curved
Conference Room Including Furniture (Scale: ¼″ = 1′-0″)

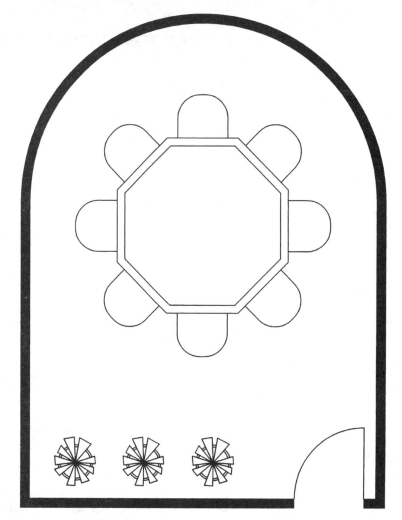

9. Set Layer Walls current.

10. Use **Zoom-All** to view the limits of the drawing.

## POLYLINE

The last option we discuss in the Polyline prompt is Arc. The Polyline Arc command is similar to the Arc command in the Draw menu.

**Hint:** Use the Coordinate Display at the bottom of your screen to determine the absolute coordinates of a point. If the coordinates are grayed out, click on them to turn them on.

**Draw the walls of the conference room, using a wide polyline and wide polyarc (Figure 5–25):**

| Prompt | Response |
|---|---|
| Command: | **Polyline** (or TYPE: **PL<enter>**) |
| Specify start point: | TYPE: **4′9-1/2,4′9-1/2<enter>** |
| Current line-width is 0′-0″ | |
| Specify next point or [Arc/Close/Halfwidth/ Length/Undo/Width]: | TYPE: **W** |
| Specify starting width <0′-0″>: | TYPE: **5<enter>** |
| Specify ending width <0′-5″>: | **<enter>** |
| Specify next point or [Arc/Close/Halfwidth/ Length/Undo/Width]: | TYPE: **@15′5<0<enter>** |
| Specify next point or [Arc/Close/Halfwidth/ Length/Undo/Width]: | TYPE: **@12′9<90<enter>** |
| Specify next point or [Arc/Close/Halfwidth/ Length/Undo/Width]: | TYPE: **A<enter>** |

**FIGURE 5–25**
Draw Exercise 5–3

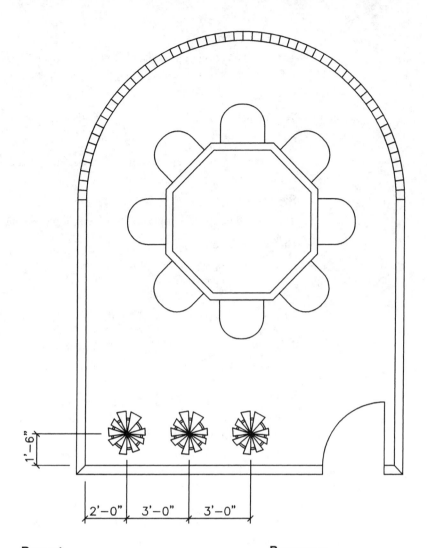

| Prompt | Response |
|---|---|
| Specify endpoint of arc or [Angle/CEnter/ CLose/Direction/Halfwidth/Line/Radius/ Second pt/Undo/Width]: | TYPE: **@15′5<180<enter>** |
| Specify endpoint of arc or [Angle/CEnter/ CLose/Direction/Halfwidth/Line/Radius/ Second pt/Undo/Width]: | TYPE: **L<enter>** |
| Specify next point or [Arc/Close/Halfwidth/ Length/Undo/Width]: | TYPE: **C<enter>** |

### Arc, <Endpoint of arc>

The Arc, <Endpoint of arc> option allows you to pick or specify the end point of the arc, as you did in the preceding exercise.

### Arc, Line

The Arc, Line option returns you to the straight line polyline mode and the Polyline prompts.

### Arc, Angle

If you select Angle from the prompt, you can specify the included angle. A positive angle draws the arc counterclockwise; a negative angle draws the arc clockwise.

### Arc, CEnter

The Arc, CEnter option draws an arc segment tangent to the previous polyline segment unless otherwise specified. This option allows you to specify a center point other than the one AutoCAD automatically calculates.

### Arc, Direction

The Arc, Direction option allows you to specify a direction other than the one AutoCAD automatically sets (the direction equal to the previous segment's ending direction).

### Radius

The Radius option allows you to specify the radius of the arc.

### CLose

The CLose option closes the polyline to be with an arc segment rather than a straight line segment.

### Second pt

The Second pt option allows you to specify a second and third point of the polyarc.

### Halfwidth, Undo, Width

The Halfwidth, Undo, and Width options here are similar to the same options in the straight polyline prompt.

## On Your Own

See Figure 5–25.

1. TYPE: **FILL<enter>**, then TYPE: **OFF<enter>** and regenerate the drawing to create an open polyline.
2. Use the Break command and From (as you did with CH5-EX2) to create a 3′ door opening, 6″ in from the lower inside right corner of the room. Be sure to allow 2-1/2″ for the polyline width on the left side of the center line.
3. Use the Line command to draw a 3′ vertical door line. Use Osnap-From the endpoint of the polyline with a 2-1/2″ offset. Start the door line at the inside corner of the door opening.
4. Use the Arc-Start, Center, Angle method to draw the door swing arc. Use Osnap-Endpoint for the start and center connections.
5. Set the current layer to Furniture.

## POLYGON

The Polygon command draws a polygon with 3 to 1024 sides. After the number of sides is specified, the Polygon prompt is "Specify center of polygon or [Edge]:". When the center of the polygon (default option) is specified, the polygon can then be inscribed in a circle or circumscribed about a circle. When the polygon is inscribed in a circle, all the vertices lie on the circle, and the edges of the polygon are inside the circle. When the polygon is circumscribed about a circle, the midpoint of each edge of the polygon lies on the circle, and the vertices are outside the circle. A polygon, which is actually a closed polyline, must be exploded before it can be edited. Edit Polyline can be used to edit a polygon.

**Use the Polygon command to draw the conference table (Figure 5–25):**

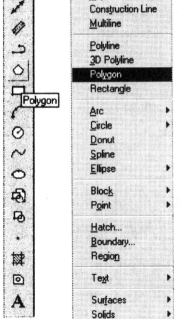

| Prompt | Response |
|---|---|
| Command: | **Polygon** (or TYPE: **POL<enter>**) |
| Enter number of sides <4>: | TYPE: **8<enter>** |
| Specify center of polygon or [Edge]: | TYPE: **12′6,16′6<enter>** |
| Enter an option [Inscribed in circle/ Circumscribed about circle]<I>: | TYPE: **I<enter>** (or just **<enter>** if I is the default |
| Specify radius of circle: | TYPE: **48<enter>** |

The method of specifying the radius controls the orientation of the polygon. When the radius is specified with a number, as above, the bottom edge of the polygon is drawn at the current snap angle—horizontal in the polygon just drawn. When the radius of an inscribed polygon is specified with a point, a vertex of the polygon is placed at the point location. When the radius of a circumscribed polygon is specified with a point, an edge midpoint is placed at the point's location.

### Edge

When the Edge option of the prompt is selected, AutoCAD prompts "Specify first endpoint of edge:" and "Specify second endpoint of edge:". The two points entered to the prompts specify one edge of a polygon that is drawn counterclockwise.

## On Your Own

See Figure 5–25.

1. **To draw the first chair of the eight chairs that are placed around the conference table, zoom in on a portion of the grid inside the conference room walls.**

2. **Use the Line command to draw a rectangle 26″ wide by 28″ deep using polar coordinates or direct distance entry.**

3. **Edit one of the 26″ wide sides of the rectangle, using the Fillet command, 12″ Radius to form the back of the chair.**

4. **The chairs are located 6″ in from the outside edge of the table. Use the Move command, Osnap-Midpoint (to the front of the chair), and From to locate the front of chair 6″ inside the midpoint of an edge of the conference table polygon.**

5. **Use the Trim and Erase commands to erase the part of the chair that is under the conference table.**

6. **Use the Offset command to offset the outside edge of the conference table 4″ to the inside, to form the 4″ band.**

7. **Zoom-Extents after you have finished step 6.**

## ARRAY

**Use the Array command to make a polar (circular) pattern of eight chairs (Figure 5–25):**

| Prompt | Response |
| --- | --- |
| Command: | **Array** (or TYPE: **AR<enter>**) |
| The Array dialog box appears: | CLICK: **the select objects button** |
| Select objects: | CLICK: **the first corner for a window to select the chair just drawn** |
| Specify opposite corner: | **Window the chair just drawn.** |
| Select objects: | **<enter>** |
| | CLICK: **the Polar Array button** |
| | CLICK: **the button that allows you to pick a center point** |
| Specify center point of array: | CLICK: **the center point of the polygon (or TYPE: 12′6,16′6<enter>)** |
| | TYPE: **8 in the Total number of items input area** |
| | TYPE: **360 in the Angle to fill: input area** |
| | **Make sure there is a check in the Rotate items as copied check box.** |
| CLICK: **OK** | |

## Polar

The Polar option of Array allows you to make multiple copies of an object in a circular array. The 360° "Angle to fill" can be specified to form a full circular array. An angle less than 360° can be specified to form a partial circular array. When a positive angle is specified, the array is rotated counterclockwise (+=ccw). When a negative angle is specified, the array is rotated clockwise (−=cw).

AutoCAD constructs the array by determining the distance from the array's center point to a point on the entity selected. If more than one object is selected, the reference point is on the last item in the selection set. When multiple items are arrayed and are not rotated as they are copied, the resulting array depends on the reference point used.

If one of the two array parameters used above—the number of items in the array or the angle to fill—is not specified, AutoCAD will prompt for a third parameter—"Angle between items:". Any two of the three array parameters must be specified to complete an array.

### On Your Own

See Figure 5–25.

1. **Use Zoom-Window to zoom in on the area of the conference room where the plants and planters are located.**
2. **Use the Circle command, 9″ Radius, to draw the outside shape of one planter.**
3. **Use the Offset command, offset distance 1″, offset to the inside of the planter, to give a thickness to the planter.**
4. **Use the Line command to draw multisegmented shapes (to show a plant) in the planter.**
5. **Use Trim to trim any lines you need to remove. Window the entire planter to select the cutting edges, and then select the lines to trim.**
6. **Use the Copy command to draw the next two planters as shown in Figure 5–25.**
7. **Set FILL ON and regenerate the drawing to have the walls appear solid again.**
8. **Exercise 5–3 is complete.**

### Save Your Drawing

When you have completed Exercise 5–3, save your work in at least two places. You can plot Exercise 5–3 after completing Chapter 7.

# EXERCISE 5–4
# Drawing a Rectangular Conference Room Including Furniture

A rectangular conference room including furniture (Figure 5–26) is drawn in Exercise 5–4. To prepare to draw Exercise 5–4, turn on the computer and start AutoCAD. The AutoCAD 2002 Today window is displayed.

1. CLICK: **the Create Drawings tab**
2. CLICK: **Wizards**
   CLICK: **Quick Setup**
3. Set drawing Units: **Architectural**
   CLICK: **Next>**
4. Set drawing Width: **27′** × Length: **22′**
   CLICK: **Finish**
5. **Use SaveAs... to save the drawing on the hard drive with the name CH5-EX4.**
6. Set Grid: **12″**
7. Set Snap: **6″**

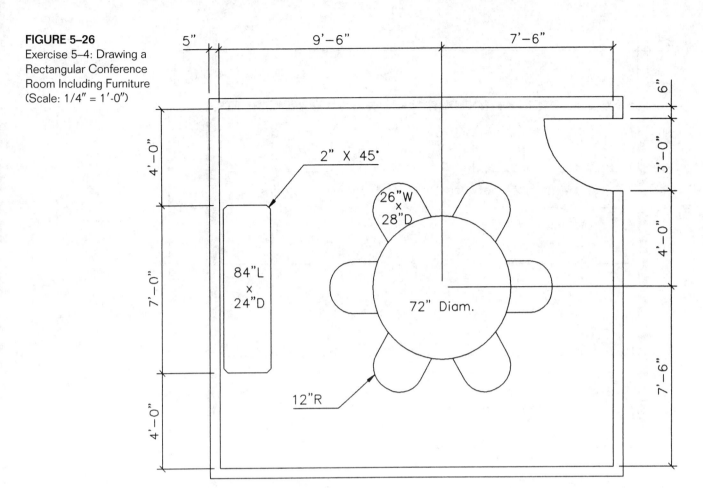

**FIGURE 5–26**
Exercise 5–4: Drawing a Rectangular Conference Room Including Furniture (Scale: 1/4″ = 1′-0″)

8. Create the following Layers:

| LAYER NAME | COLOR | LINETYPE |
|------------|-------|----------|
| Walls | Blue | Continuous |
| Furniture | Red | Continuous |

9. Use the measurements shown in Figure 5–26 to draw the conference room full scale.

10. You can plot Exercise 5–4 after completing Chapter 7.

11. Save the drawing in at least two places.

# EXERCISE 5–5
# Drawing a Rectangular Lecture Room Including Furniture

A lecture room including furniture (Figure 5–27) is drawn in Exercise 5–5. To prepare to draw Exercise 5–5, turn on the computer and start AutoCAD. The AutoCAD 2002 Today window is displayed.

1. CLICK: **the Create Drawings tab**

2. CLICK: **Wizards**

   CLICK: **Quick Setup**

3. Set drawing Units: **Architectural**

   CLICK: **Next>**

4. Set drawing Width: **25′** × Length: **27′**

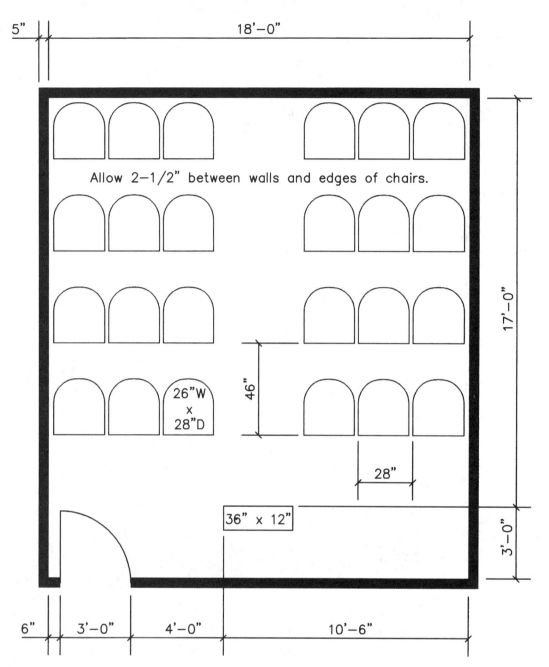

5"

18'-0"

Allow 2-1/2" between walls and edges of chairs.

17'-0"

46"

26"W
x
28"D

28"

36" x 12"

3'-0"

6"  3'-0"  4'-0"  10'-6"

**FIGURE 5–27**
Exercise 5–5: Drawing a Rectangular Lecture Room Including Furniture (Scale: 1/4″ = 1′-0″)

 

CLICK: **Finish**

5. **Use SaveAs... to save the drawing on the hard drive with the name CH5-EX5.**

6. Set Grid: **12″**

7. Set Snap: **6″**

8. Create the following Layers:

| LAYER NAME | COLOR | LINETYPE |
|---|---|---|
| Walls | White | Continuous |
| Furniture | Magenta | Continuous |

Part II: Two-Dimensional AutoCAD

9. Use the measurements shown in Figure 5–27 to draw the lecture room full scale.

10. You can plot Exercise 5–5 after completing Chapter 7.

11. Save the drawing in at least two places.

## REVIEW QUESTIONS

1. When the outline of the walls of a room is drawn with a zero width polyline, which of the following commands can be used to draw most quickly the second line that shows the depth of the walls?
   a. Line
   b. Polyline
   c. Offset
   d. Copy
   e. Array

2. Which of the following commands is used to split a solid polyline into separate line segments?
   a. ID Point
   b. Offset
   c. Array
   d. Trim
   e. Explode

3. Which of the following commands is used to locate, on a drawing, a point that AutoCAD uses as the origin for a command?
   a. ID Point
   b. Inquiry
   c. First point
   d. Aperture
   e. Distance

4. The Chamfer command will chamfer two lines that do not intersect.
   a. True
   b. False

5. Which of the following commands can be used to draw a rounded corner?
   a. Chamfer
   b. Fillet
   c. Offset
   d. Trim
   e. Edit Polyline

6. Which of the following Osnap modifiers is used to snap to a point entity?
   a. Perpendicular
   b. Endpoint
   c. Node
   d. Midpoint
   e. Intersection

7. Which of the following rotation angles is the same as −90°?
   a. 90
   b. 180
   c. 270
   d. 300
   e. 330

8. Which of the following controls the appearance of the markers used in the Divide command?
   a. Aperture Size
   b. Point Style
   c. Osnap
   d. Pickbox Size
   e. ID Point

9. Which of the following settings is used to change the size of the target box that appears when Modify commands are used?
   a. Aperture Size
   b. Point Style
   c. Osnap
   d. Pickbox Size
   e. ID Point

10. Which of the following commands can be used to join lines or arcs together and make them a single polyline?
    a. Explode
    b. Edit Polyline
    c. Polyline
    d. Close
    e. Edit vertex

11. Describe the difference between a square drawn with the Line command and a square drawn with the Polyline command.

    _____

    _____

    _____

12. Describe what the Trim prompt "Select cutting edges... Select objects:" means.

    _____

    _____

13. Describe how to chamfer the corners of a rectangle using only the Rectangle command.

    _____

14. Which Polyline-Arc option allows you to draw an arc in a direction other than the one AutoCAD automatically sets?

    _____

15. Which command is used to determine the exact distance from one point to another?

    _____

16. Describe the difference between a polygon that has been inscribed in a circle and one that has been circumscribed about a circle.

    Inscribed in a circle:    _____

    _____

    Circumscribed about a circle:    _____

    _____

17. When creating a counterclockwise polar array of six chairs arranged in a half circle, which "Angle to fill" would you use to form the partial array?

    _____

18. Describe the use of the option From.

    _____

19. Which Polyline Arc option allows you to draw a straight line polyline after a polyline arc has been drawn?

    _____

20. Describe the use of Tracking.

    _____

# 6 Adding Text to the Drawing

## OBJECTIVES

When you have completed this chapter, you will be able to:

☐ Define the terms *style* and *font* and describe the function of each.
☐ Use different fonts on the same drawing.
☐ Place text on several different parts of the drawing with a single command.
☐ Use the modifiers Center, Align, Fit, Middle, Right, Top, and Style.
☐ Use the Text Style... setting to create condensed, expanded, rotated, backward, inclined, and upside-down text.
☐ Use the Text Style... setting to change any style on the drawing to a different font.
☐ Use standard codes to draw special characters such as the degree symbol, the diameter symbol, the plus and minus symbol, and underscored and overscored text.
☐ Use Mtext (multiline text) to create paragraph text.
☐ Spell check your drawing.

## EXERCISE 6–1
## Placing Text on Drawings

To make complete drawings with AutoCAD, you need to know how text is added to the drawings. The following AutoCAD commands, used to place lettering on drawings, are examined in Exercise 6–1.

**Text Style...**   Used to control the appearance of text.
**Single Line Text (Dtext)**   Used to draw text that is not in paragraph form.
**Multiline Text (Mtext)**   Used to draw text that is in paragraph form.

When you have completed Exercise 6–1, your drawing will look similar to the drawing in Figure 6–1. To begin Exercise 6–1, turn on the computer and start AutoCAD. The AutoCAD 2002 Today window is displayed.

The drawing template A-size, created in Chapter 3, will be used for this exercise.

1. CLICK: **the Create Drawings tab**
2. CLICK: **Template**
3. CLICK: **Browse**
4. LOOK: **in the drive and/or folder where you saved the A-size template**
5. CLICK: **A-size.dwt**
6. CLICK: **Open**
7. **Use SaveAs... to save the drawing on the hard drive with the name CH6–EX1.**
8. Set Layer1 current.
9. Use Zoom-All to view the limits of the drawing.

**FIGURE 6–1**
Exercise 6–1: Placing Text on
Drawings

YOUR NAME                                                    YOUR CLASS NUMBER

**THIS WAS TYPED
WITH THE HEADING STYLE,
AND THE IMPACT FONT,
1/4" HIGH, CENTERED**

THIS WAS TYPED
WITH THE HANDLTR STYLE,
AND THE CITY BLUEPRINT FONT,
3/16" HIGH, CENTERED

STANDARD STYLE, FIT OPTION

<u>OVERSCORE WITH THE OVERSCORE STYLE</u>

<u>OVER</u>SCORE WITH THE STANDARD STYLE

<u>UNDERSCORE WITH THE STANDARD STYLE</u>

STANDARD CODES WITH THE STANDARD STYLE
±1/16"     45°     Ø1/2"

ARIAL FONT
WITH THE UPSIDEDOWN STYLE,
UPSIDE DOWN AND BACKWARD

V
E
R
T
I
C
A
L

S
T
Y
L
E

THIS IS PARAGRAPH OR
MULTILINE TEXT TYPED WITH
THE SANS SERIF FONT, ⅛" HIGH
IN AN AREA THAT MEASURES 3"
X 1".

THIS IS *PARAGRAPH OR
MULTILINE TEXT* CREATED
WITH THE SANS SERIF FONT, ⅛"
HIGH IN AN AREA THAT
MEASURES 3" X 1".

## Making Settings for Text Style...

It is very important to understand the difference between the terms *style name* and *font name* with regard to text:

**Style name:**  This is a general category that can be assigned any name you choose. The style name is used to distinguish fonts. You may use the same name for the style as is used for the font, or you may use a different name, single number, or letter for the style name.

**Font name:**  This is the name of a particular alphabet that you select to assign to a style name. A font has to be in the AutoCAD program before it can be selected and assigned to a style name.

You may have only one font per style, but you can have many styles with the same font. For example,

| Style Name | Font Name |
| --- | --- |
| SIMPLEX | SIMPLEX |
| CLIENT NAME | ITALIC |
| NOTES | SIMPLEX |
| ITALIC | ITALIC |
| BANNER | MONOTEXT |
| COMPANY NAME | ROMAND |
| ROMAND | ROMAND |

In the following procedure, the Text Style... setting is used.

FIGURE 6–2
Select the TechnicLite Font for
the Standard Style

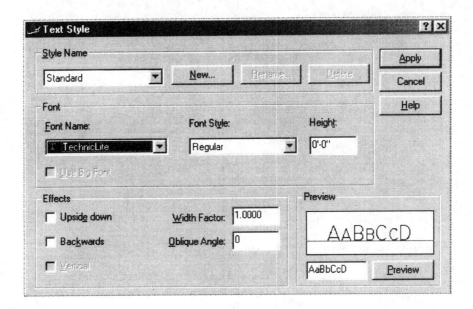

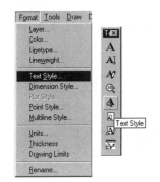

**Make the setting for the STANDARD style (Figure 6–2):**

| Prompt | Response |
|---|---|
| Command: | **Text Style...** (or TYPE: **ST<enter>**) |
| The Text Style dialog box appears: | CLICK: **TechnicLite** (in the Font Name: list) |
| | CLICK: **Apply** |

Any text typed while the STANDARD style is active will now contain the TechnicLite font. Notice the preview area in the lower right corner that shows you what the font looks like. Notice also that the vertical setting is grayed out, indicating that this font cannot be drawn running up and down.

The other settings should be left as they are. If you leave the text height set at 0, you will be able to draw different heights of the same style and you will be able to change the height of text if you need to. Leave the text height set to 0 in all cases. The Width Factor allows you to stretch letters so they are wider by making the width factor greater than 1, narrower by making the width factor less than 1. The Oblique Angle slants the letters to the right if the angle is positive and to the left if the angle is negative.

**Make the settings for a new style that will be used on the drawing (Figures 6–3 and 6–4):**

| Prompt | Response |
|---|---|
| The Text Style dialog box: | CLICK: **New...** |
| The New Text Style dialog box appears with a Style Name that AutoCAD assigns, style1: | TYPE: **HEADING** (to name the style, Figure 6–3) |

FIGURE 6–3
Name the Style, HEADING

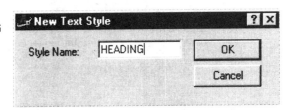

| Prompt | Response |
|---|---|
| | CLICK: **OK** |
| The Text Style dialog box appears: | CLICK: **romand.shx** (in the Font Name: list, Figure 6–4) |
| | CLICK: **Apply** |

You now have two styles that have been defined on your drawing, STANDARD and HEADING.

## On Your Own (Figures 6–5 and 6–6)

1. **Make the settings for the following new styles:**

| Style Name | Font Name: | Other Settings |
|---|---|---|
| HANDLTR | CityBlueprint | None |
| OVERSCORE | Arial | None |

| Style Name | Font Name: | Other Settings |
|---|---|---|
| UPSIDEDOWN | Arial | Place checks in the Effects box labeled Upside down and the box labeled Backwards. |
| VERTICAL | romand.shx | Place a check in the Effects box labeled Vertical, Figure 6–5. |

**Note:** If you make a mistake while making the settings for a new style, go back to the Text Style dialog box, highlight the style name, change or fix the settings, and CLICK: **Apply**.

2. **Click the down arrow in the Style Name list to determine if your list matches the one shown in Figure 6–6.**

3. **Click the HEADING style name to make it current.**

4. **Close the dialog box.**

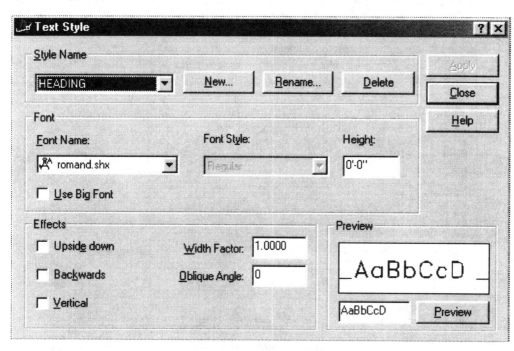

**FIGURE 6–4**
Select the romand.shx Font for the HEADING Style

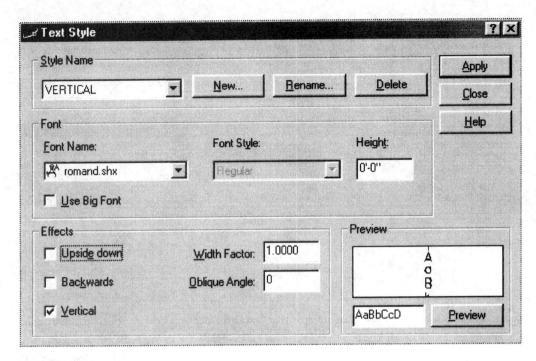

**FIGURE 6–5**
Make Setting for the VERTICAL Style

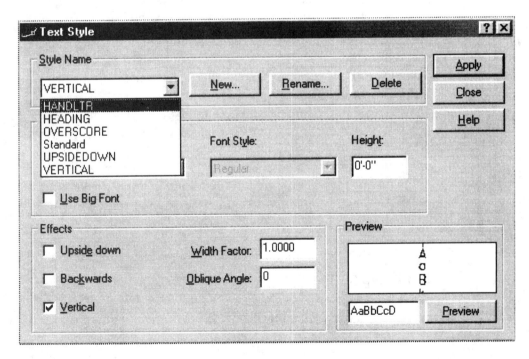

**FIGURE 6–6**
Check the Style Name List

Chapter 7: Adding Text to the Drawing

## Using the Single Line Text Command to Draw Text

The Single Line Text command (also known as Dtext) is used to draw text that is not in paragraph form. Although the name of the command might lead you to believe that only a single line can be drawn, such is not the case. To draw one line under another just PRESS: **<enter>**, and the next line will be ready to be drawn with the same settings as the first line. To demonstrate this, draw several of the lines of text on your current drawing.

If you are not happy with the location of the text, use the Move command to relocate it.

**Draw the first two examples at the top of the page using single line text (Figure 6–7):**

| Prompt | Response |
|---|---|
| Command: | **Single Line Text** (or TYPE: **DT<enter>**) |
| Specify start point of text or [Justify/Style]: | TYPE: **C<enter>** |
| Specify center point of text: | TYPE: **4-1/4,10<enter>** (You are locating the center of the line of text using absolute coordinates, 4-1/4″ to the right and 10″ up.) |
| Specify height <0′-0 3/16″>: | TYPE: **1/4<enter>** |
| Specify rotation angle of text <0>: | **<enter>** |
| Enter text: | TYPE: **THIS WAS TYPED<enter>** |
| Enter text: | TYPE: **WITH THE HEADING STYLE, <enter>** |
| Enter text: | TYPE: **AND THE ROMAND FONT, <enter>** |
| Enter text: | TYPE: **1/4″ HIGH<enter>** |
| Enter text: | **<enter>** |
| Command: | **<enter>** (Repeat DTEXT) |
| Specify start point of text or [Justify/Style]: | TYPE: **S<enter>** (to change styles) |
| Enter style name or [?] <HEADING>: | TYPE: **HANDLTR<enter>** |
| Specify start point of text or [Justify/Style]: | TYPE: **C<enter>** |
| Specify center point of text: | TYPE: **4-1/4,8<enter>** |
| Specify height <0′-0 3/16″>: | TYPE: **3/16<enter>** |
| Specify rotation angle of text <0>: | **<enter>** |
| Enter text: | TYPE: **THIS WAS TYPED<enter>** |
| Enter text: | TYPE: **WITH THE HANDLTR STYLE, <enter>** |
| Enter text: | TYPE: **AND THE CITY BLUEPRINT FONT, <enter>** |
| Enter text: | TYPE: **3/16″ HIGH, CENTERED <enter>** |
| Enter text: | **<enter>** |

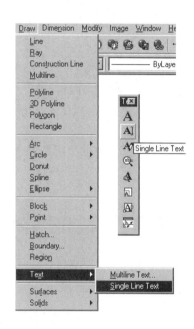

**FIGURE 6–7**
First Two Examples of Single Line Text

THIS WAS TYPED
WITH THE HEADING STYLE,
AND THE ROMAND FONT,
1/4" HIGH

THIS WAS TYPED
WITH THE HANDLTR STYLE,
AND THE CITY BLUEPRINT FONT,
3/16" HIGH, CENTERED

**FIGURE 6–8**
Using the Fit Option of Single
Line Text

THIS WAS TYPED
WITH THE HEADING STYLE,
AND THE ROMAND FONT,
1/4" HIGH

THIS WAS TYPED
WITH THE HANDLTR STYLE,
AND THE CITY BLUEPRINT FONT,
3/16" HIGH, CENTERED

## STANDARD STYLE, FIT OPTION

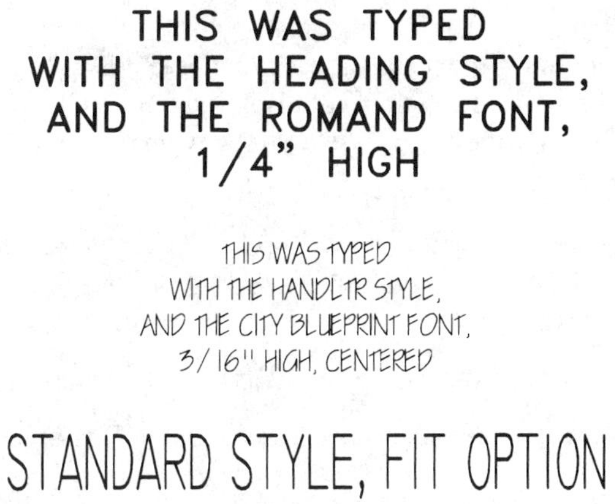

**Draw the next block of text using the Fit option of single line text with the STAN-DARD style (Figure 6–8):**

| Prompt | Response |
|---|---|
| Command: | **Single Line Text** (or TYPE: DT**<enter>**) |
| Specify start point of text or [Justify/Style]: | TYPE: **S<enter>** (to change styles) |
| Enter style name or [?] <HANDLTR>: | TYPE: **STANDARD<enter>** |
| Specify start point of text or [Justify/Style]: | TYPE: **F<enter>** (for Fit) |
| Specify first endpoint of text baseline: | TYPE: **1-1/2,6<enter>** |
| Specify second endpoint of text baseline: | TYPE: **7,6<enter>** |
| Specify height <0'-0 3/16">: | TYPE: **1/2<enter>** |
| Enter text: | TYPE: **STANDARD STYLE,** **FIT OPTION<enter>** |
| Enter text: | **<enter>** |

When you activate the Single Line Text command, the prompt is "Specify start point of text or [Justify/Style]:". The Style option allows you to select a different style (that has already been defined) for the text you are about to draw. If you TYPE: **J<enter>**, the prompt then becomes "Enter an option [Align/Fit/Center/Middle/Right/TL/TC/TR/ML/MC/MR/BL/BC/BR]:".

### Align

Align draws the text between two points that you click. It does not condense or expand the font but instead adjusts the letter height so that the text fits between the two points.

### Fit

Fit draws the text between two clicked points like the Align option, but instead of changing the letter height, Fit condenses or expands the font to fit between the points.

### Center

Center draws the text so that the bottom of the line of lettering is centered on the clicked point. Centering is not displayed until the second return is pressed. You may also choose the top or the middle of the line of lettering by typing TC or MC at the justify prompt.

### Middle

Middle draws the text so that the middle of the line of lettering is centered around a clicked point. This is very useful when a single line of text must be centered in an area such as a box. Middle is not displayed until the second return is pressed. The top or bottom of the line may also be selected by typing MC or MB at the justify prompt.

## Right

Right draws the text so that each line of text is right justified (ends at the same right margin). Right justification is not displayed until the second return is pressed. The top or center of the line may also be selected by typing TR or MR at the justify prompt.

## TL/TC/TR/ML/MC/MR/BL/BC/BR

These are alignment options: Top Left, Top Center, Top Right, Middle Left, Middle Center, Middle Right, Bottom Left, Bottom Center, Bottom Right. They are used with horizontal text.

**Draw a line of text using the VERTICAL style (Figure 6–9)**

(Remember that you checked Vertical in the Text Style dialog box for this text style.)

| Prompt | Response |
|---|---|
| Command: | **<enter>** (Repeat DTEXT) |
| Specify start point of text or [Justify/Style]: | TYPE: **S<enter>** |
| Enter style name or [?] <Standard>: | TYPE: **VERTICAL<enter>** |
| Specify start point of text or [Justify/Style]: | TYPE: **1,6<enter>** |
| Specify height <0'-0 1/2">: | TYPE: **1/4<enter>** |
| Specify rotation angle of text <270>: | **<enter>** |
| Enter text: | TYPE: **VERTICAL STYLE<enter>** |
| Enter text: | **<enter>** |

**FIGURE 6–9**

Using the Vertical Option of Single Line Text

THIS WAS TYPED
WITH THE HEADING STYLE,
AND THE ROMAND FONT,
1/4" HIGH

THIS WAS TYPED
WITH THE HANDLTR STYLE,
AND THE CITY BLUEPRINT FONT,
3/16" HIGH, CENTERED

STANDARD STYLE, FIT OPTION

V
E
R
T
I
C
A
L

S
T
Y
L
E

## Using Standard Codes to Draw Special Characters

Figures 6–10 through 6–14 show the use of codes to obtain several commonly used symbols, such as the degree symbol, the diameter symbol, the plus-minus symbol, and underscored and overscored text. The top line of Figure 6–10 shows the code that must be typed to obtain the degree symbol following the number 45. The top line is displayed until the <enter> is pressed to obtain the degree symbol shown on the bottom line. Two percent symbols followed by the letter D produce the degree symbol.

Figure 6–11 illustrates that two percent symbols followed by the letter C produce the diameter symbol. Any text following the symbol must be typed immediately following the code.

Figure 6–12 shows the code for the plus-minus symbol.

Figure 6–13 shows the code for underscore: two percent symbols followed by the letter U. Notice that the first line contains only one code. The second line contains two codes: one to start the underline and one to stop it.

Figure 6–14 shows the code for overscored text. The same code sequence for starting and stopping the overscore applies.

45%%D

45˚

**FIGURE 6–10**
Degree Symbol Code

%%C.500

Ø.500

**FIGURE 6–11**
Diameter Symbol Code

%%P.005

±.005

**FIGURE 6–12**
Plus–Minus Symbol Code

%%UUNDERSCORE

UNDERSCORE

%%UUNDERSCORE%%U LETTERS

UNDERSCORE LETTERS

**FIGURE 6–13**
Underscore Code

%%OOVERSCORE

OVERSCORE

%%OOVERSCORE%%O LETTERS

OVERSCORE LETTERS

**FIGURE 6–14**
Overscore Code

**Draw five lines containing special codes for the overscore, underscore, plus-minus, degree, and diameter symbols (Figure 6–15):**

| Prompt | Response |
|---|---|
| Command: | <enter> (Repeat DTEXT) |
| Specify start point of text or [Justify/Style]: | TYPE: **S<enter>** |
| Enter style name or [?]<VERTICAL>: | TYPE: **OVERSCORE<enter>** |
| Specify start point of text or [Justify/Style]: | TYPE: **1-1/2,5<enter>** |
| Specify height <0′-0 3/16″>: | TYPE: **3/16<enter>** |
| Specify rotation angle of text <0>: | <enter> |
| Enter text: | TYPE: **%%OOVERSCORE WITH THE OVERSCORE STYLE<enter>** |
| Enter text: | <enter> |
| Command: | <enter> (Repeat DTEXT) |
| Specify start point of text or [Justify/Style]: | TYPE: **S<enter>** |
| Enter style name of [?]<OVERSCORE>: | TYPE: **STANDARD<enter>** |
| Specify start point of text or [Justify/Style]: | TYPE: **1-1/2,4-1/2<enter>** |
| Specify height <0′-0 1/2″>: | TYPE: **3/16 <enter>** |
| Specify rotation angle of text <0>: | <enter> |
| Enter text: | TYPE: **%%OOVERSCORE%%O WITH THE STANDARD STYLE <enter>** |
| Enter text: | <enter> |

**FIGURE 6–15**
Using Single Line Text to Draw Symbols with Standard Codes

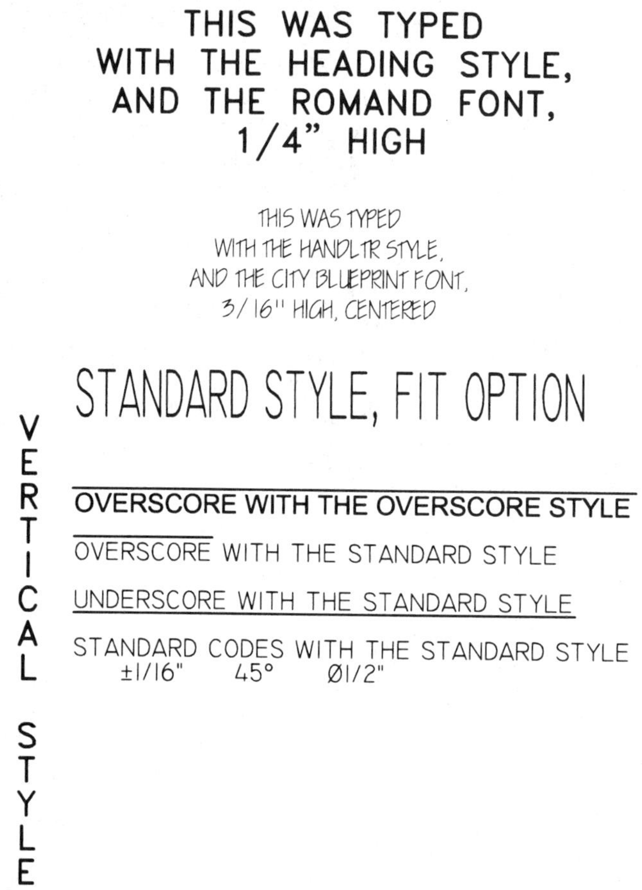
THIS WAS TYPED
WITH THE HEADING STYLE,
AND THE ROMAND FONT,
1/4" HIGH
THIS WAS TYPED
WITH THE HANDLTR STYLE,
AND THE CITY BLUEPRINT FONT,
3/16" HIGH, CENTERED
STANDARD STYLE, FIT OPTION
VERTICAL STYLE
OVERSCORE WITH THE OVERSCORE STYLE
OVERSCORE WITH THE STANDARD STYLE
UNDERSCORE WITH THE STANDARD STYLE
STANDARD CODES WITH THE STANDARD STYLE
±1/16" 45° Ø1/2"

| Prompt | Response |
|---|---|
| Command: | **<enter>** |
| Specify start point of text or [Justify/Style]: | **<enter>** |
| Enter text: | TYPE: **%%UUNDERSCORE WITH THE STANDARD STYLE <enter>** |
| Enter text: | **<enter>** |
| Command: | **<enter>** |
| Specify start point of text or [Justify/Style]: | **<enter>** |
| Enter text: | TYPE: **STANDARD CODES WITH THE STANDARD STYLE <enter>** |
| Enter text: | **<enter>** |
| Command: | **<enter>** |
| Specify start point of text or [Justify/Style]: | CLICK: **a point in the approximate location ± 1/16″ is shown in Figure 6–15** |
| Specify height <0′-0 3/16″>: | **<enter>** |
| Specify rotation angle of text <0>: | **<enter>** |
| Enter text: | TYPE: **%%P1/16″<enter>** |
| Enter text: | CLICK: **a point in the approximate location 45° is shown in Figure 6–15** |
| Enter text: | TYPE: **45%%D<enter>** |

| Prompt | Response |
|---|---|
| Enter text: | CLICK: **a point in the approximate location ⌀1/2″ shown in Figure 6–15** |
| Enter text: | TYPE: **%%C1/2″<enter>** |
| Enter text: | **<enter>** |

## On Your Own

1. **Make the Style Name UPSIDEDOWN current.**
2. **Use Single Line Text to draw the following phrase (3/16 height) upside down and backward with its start point at 7,2-1/2 (Figure 6–16):**

   UPSIDEDOWN AND BACKWARD<enter>
   WITH THE UPSIDEDOWN STYLE, <enter>
   ARIAL FONT <enter> <enter>.

3. **Change the current style to STANDARD.**

## Using the Multiline Text Command to Draw Text Paragraphs

The Multiline Text command (also known as Mtext) is used to draw text in paragraph form. The command activates the Multiline Text Editor, which has many of the same features that other Windows Text Editors have. You can select a defined style, change the text height, boldface and italicize some fonts, select a justification style, specify the width of the line, rotate a paragraph, search for a word and replace it with another, undo, import text, and select symbols for use on your drawing. In this exercise you will create a paragraph using the sans serif font.

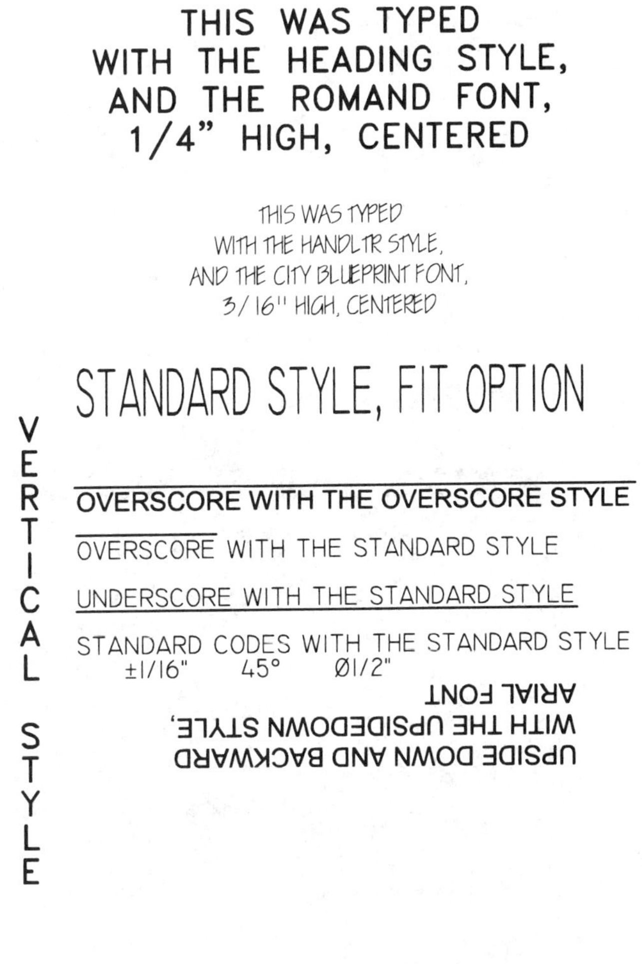

**FIGURE 6–16**
Draw a Phrase Upside Down and Backward with the UPSIDE-DOWN Style

THIS WAS TYPED
WITH THE HEADING STYLE,
AND THE ROMAND FONT,
1/4″ HIGH, CENTERED

THIS WAS TYPED
WITH THE HANDLTR STYLE,
AND THE CITY BLUEPRINT FONT,
3/16″ HIGH, CENTERED

STANDARD STYLE, FIT OPTION

V
E
R
T
I
C
A
L

‾OVERSCORE WITH THE OVERSCORE STYLE‾

‾OVERSCORE‾ WITH THE STANDARD STYLE

UNDERSCORE WITH THE STANDARD STYLE

STANDARD CODES WITH THE STANDARD STYLE
±1/16″    45°    ⌀1/2″

S
T
Y
L
E

UPSIDE DOWN AND BACKWARD
WITH THE UPSIDEDOWN STYLE,
ARIAL FONT

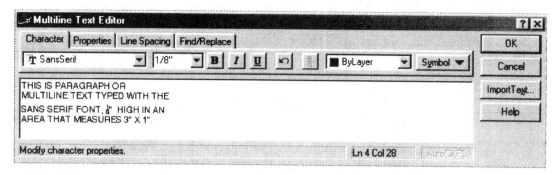

**FIGURE 6–17**
The Multiline Text Editor

**Use Multiline Text to draw a paragraph (Figure 6–17), then copy it 3-1/4″ to the right:**

| Prompt | Response |
|---|---|
| Command: | **Multiline Text** (or TYPE: **MT<enter>**) |
| Specify first corner: | TYPE: **1-1/2,2<enter>** |
| Specify opposite corner or [Height/Justify/ Line spacing/Rotation/Style/Width]: | TYPE: **@3,-1** <enter> (Be sure to include the minus (-) so the vertical side of the text box is down. This makes the paragraph box 3″ × 1″ tall) |
| The Multiline Text Editor appears: | **Change the text height to 1/8 and the font to SansSerif,** then TYPE: **the paragraph shown in Figure 6–17.** When you type 1/8 in the paragraph, the dialog box shown in Figure 6–18 appears. CHECK: **Enable AutoStacking** as shown so the fraction will be stacked with the numerator over the denominator. |
| | After the paragraph is typed correctly, CLICK: **OK** |
| Command: | TYPE: **CP<enter>** |
| Select objects: | CLICK: **any point on the paragraph** |
| Select objects: | **<enter>** |

**FIGURE 6–18**
Enable AutoStacking

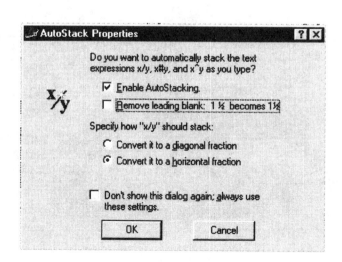

**FIGURE 6–19**

Use Multiline Text to Type a Paragraph, Then Copy It

THIS WAS TYPED
WITH THE HEADING STYLE,
AND THE ROMAND FONT
1/4" HIGH, CENTERED

THIS WAS TYPED
WITH THE HANDLTR STYLE,
AND THE CITY BLUEPRINT FONT,
3/16" HIGH, CENTERED

## STANDARD STYLE, FIT OPTION

**OVERSCORE WITH THE OVERSCORE STYLE**

OVERSCORE WITH THE STANDARD STYLE

UNDERSCORE WITH THE STANDARD STYLE

STANDARD CODES WITH THE STANDARD STYLE
±1/16"     45°     Ø1/2"

ARIAL FONT

UPSIDE DOWN AND BACKWARD
WITH THE UPSIDEDOWN STYLE,

V E R T I C A L   S T Y L E

THIS IS PARAGRAPH OR MULTILINE TEXT TYPED WITH THE SANS SERIF FONT, 1/8" HIGH IN AN AREA THAT MEASURES 3" X 1".

THIS IS PARAGRAPH OR MULTILINE TEXT TYPED WITH THE SANS SERIF FONT, 1/8" HIGH IN AN AREA THAT MEASURES 3" X 1".

| Prompt | Response |
|---|---|
| Specify base point or displacement, or [Multiple]: | CLICK: **any point** |
| Specify second point of displacement or <use first point as displacement>: | TYPE: **@3-1/4,0<enter>** (This copies the paragraph 3-1/4″ directly to the right, Figure 6–19.) |

If you have trouble getting the Multiline Text to change text height, cancel the command and TYPE: **DT** to activate Single Line Text and change the default text height to 1/8. The Multiline Text height will then be set at 1/8, and you can proceed with typing the paragraph. Be sure you do not cancel the Single Line Text command before you have changed the default text height.

## Changing Text Properties

There will be occasions when you will need to change the text font, height, or content. AutoCAD has several commands that can be used to do these tasks:

**Text Style...**   Use this command to change the font of text within a text style that already exists on your drawing.

**CHANGE**   Use this command to change the endpoint of a line or the radius of a circle, and for Single Line Text. When you use it for Single Line Text, you can change the text properties, the insertion point, the text style, the text height, the text rotation angle, or the text content.

**DDEDIT** (Edit Text)   Use this command if you want to change the text contents only for Single Line Text. This command gives you the Multiline Text Editor when you select multiline text and allows you to change all its properties.

**DDMODIFY** (Properties)   Use this command to change any of the text's characteristics: properties, origin, style, height, rotation angle, the text content, or any of several other properties.

**Use the Text Style... command to change the font of text typed with the HEADING name from Romand to Impact (Figure 6–20):**

| Prompt | Response |
|---|---|
| Command: | **Text Style...** (or TYPE: **ST<enter>**) |
| | CLICK: **HEADING** (in the Style Name list) |
| The Text Style dialog box appears: | CLICK: **Impact** (from the Font Name list, Figure 6–20) |
| | CLICK: **Apply** |
| | CLICK: **Close** |

Notice that everything you typed with the HEADING style name is now still the HEADING style but changed to the Impact font.

**Use the CHANGE command to change the height of the phrase "VERTICAL STYLE" to 1/2″ and the contents to "VERTICAL NAME."**

| Prompt | Response |
|---|---|
| Command: | TYPE: **CHANGE<enter>** |
| Select objects: | CLICK: **any point on the words VERTICAL STYLE** |
| Select objects: | **<enter>** |
| Specify change point or [Properties]: | **<enter>** |
| Specify new text insertion point <no change>: | **<enter>** |
| Enter new text style <VERTICAL>: | **<enter>** |
| Specify new height <0′-0 1/4″>: | TYPE:**1/2<enter>** |
| Specify new rotation angle <270>: | **<enter>** |
| Enter new text <VERTICAL STYLE>: | TYPE: **VERTICAL NAME <enter>** |
| Oops! This is too big, and the phrase vertical style is better. | Change this back to the way it was: CLICK: **UNDO** (on the Standard Toolbar), or TYPE: **U, <enter>.** |

**FIGURE 6–20**
Select the Impact Font for the HEADING Style

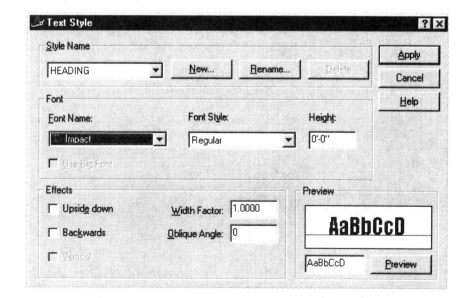

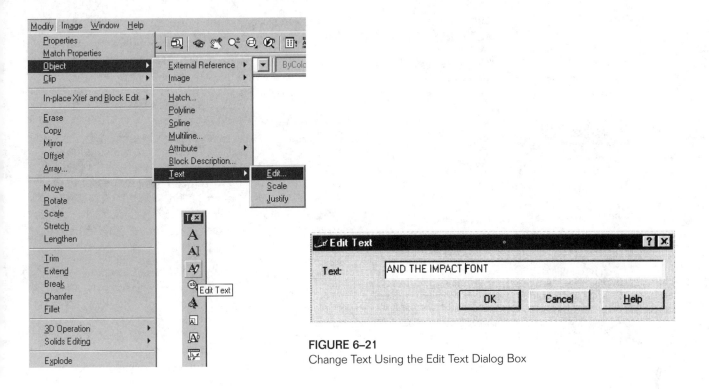

FIGURE 6–21
Change Text Using the Edit Text Dialog Box

Use the DDEDIT (Edit Text) command to change "AND THE ROMAND FONT" at the top of the page to "AND THE IMPACT FONT" and 1/4″ HIGH to 1/4″ HIGH, CENTERED (Figure 6–21):

| Prompt | Response |
|---|---|
| Command: | **Modify-Text...** or TYPE: **DDEDIT<enter>** |
| Select an annotation object or [Undo]: | CLICK: **AND THE ROMAND FONT** |
| The Edit Text dialog box appears: | CLICK: **to the right of ROMAND, backspace over ROMAND** and TYPE: **IMPACT** (Figure 6–21) |
| | CLICK: **OK** |
| Select an annotation object or [Undo}: | **<enter>** |

## On Your Own

1. Use the Edit Text command to change the line of text that reads "1/4″ HIGH" to "1/4″ HIGH, CENTERED."

FIGURE 6–22
Changing Multiline Text to the Italic Font

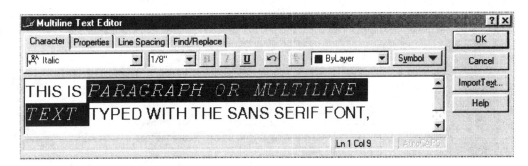

**Continue using the Edit Text command to change the words PARAGRAPH OR MULTILINE TEXT in the copied paragraph to the italic font (Figure 6–22):**

| Prompt | Response |
|---|---|
| Command: | TYPE: **DDEDIT<enter>** |
| Select an annotation object or [Undo]: | CLICK: **any point on the copied paragraph** |
| The Multiline Text Editor (Figure 6–22) appears: | CLICK: **the left mouse button to the left of the word PARAGRAPH, hold it down, and drag to the end to the word TEXT so that PARAGRAPH OR MULTILINE TEXT is highlighted,** then CLICK: **italic** in the font list |
| | CLICK: **OK** |
| Select an annotation object or [UNDO]: | PRESS: **ESC or <enter>** |

**Use the DDMODIFY (Properties) command to change the vertical line of text from Layer1 to Layer2 (Figure 6–23):**

| Prompt | Response |
|---|---|
| Command: | CLICK: **the vertical line of text (VERTICAL STYLE)** |
| Command: | **Properties** (or TYPE: **DDMODIFY <enter>**) |
| The Properties dialog box appears: | CLICK: **Layer** |
| | CLICK: **the down arrow** (Figure 6–23) |
| | CLICK: **Layer2** |
| | CLICK: **the X in the upper right corner to close** |
| | PRESS: **Esc twice** |

VERTICAL STYLE is now changed to Layer2.

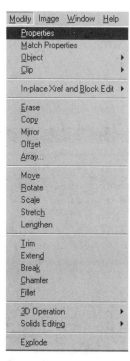

**FIGURE 6–23**
Change Text to Layer2

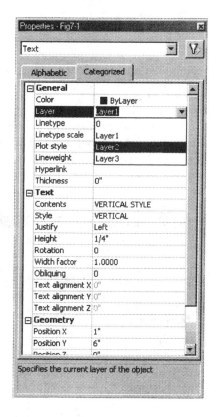

## On Your Own

1. Use Single Line Text, STANDARD style, 1/8″ high to place your name and class number in the upper left and upper right corners, respectively. The start point for your name is 1,10-1/2. Use right-justified text for class number (at the Dtext prompt "Specify start point of text or [Justify/Style]:" TYPE: R<enter>. The right endpoint of text baseline is 7-1/2, 10-1/2.

## Checking the Spelling

AutoCAD has a spell checker that allows you to accurately check the spelling on your drawing. If the word is correctly spelled but is not in the current dictionary, you can select Ignore All to ignore all instances of that word on the drawing. You can also add the word to the current dictionary. You can change the spelling of a single use of a word or all instances of the word on the drawing by picking Change All. AutoCAD also allows you to change dictionaries.

## On Your Own

1. Purposely misspell the word TYPED. Use Edit Text... (or Properties) to change THIS WAS TYPED to THIS WAS TPYED.

Use the Spelling command to check the spelling on your drawing (Figures 6–24 and 6–25):

| Prompt | Response |
|---|---|
| Command: | **Spelling** (or TYPE: **SP<enter>**) |
| Select objects: | TYPE: **ALL<enter>** to select all the text on your drawing |
| Select objects: | **<enter>** |
| The Check Spelling dialog box appears (Figure 6–24): | CLICK: **Ignore All** for all font and command names until you reach the word TPYED |

**FIGURE 6–24**
Change TPYED to TYPED Using Spell Check

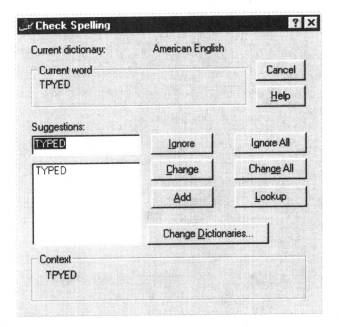

**FIGURE 6–25**
CLICK: **OK** to Complete the Spell Check

**Prompt**

The AutoCAD Message appears:

**Response**

CLICK: the word **TYPED** if it is not already highlighted in the Suggestions: box

CLICK: **Change**

CLICK: **OK** (Figure 6–25)

## Save Your Drawing and Exit AutoCAD

When you have completed Exercise 6–1, save your drawing in at least two places. Exercise 6–1 is printed in Chapter 7.

## REVIEW QUESTIONS

1. The command used in this chapter to place line text (text not in paragraph form) on drawings is
   a. Single Line Text (Dtext)
   b. TXT
   c. Multiline Text (Mtext)
   d. DDedit
   e. MS-DOS Text Editor
2. The command used in this chapter to place paragraph text on drawings is
   a. Single Line Text (Dtext)
   b. TXT
   c. Multiline Text (Mtext)
   d. DDedit
   e. MS-DOS Text Editor
3. Which of the following could be used as a style name?
   a. SIMPLEX
   b. TITLE
   c. NAMES
   d. A
   e. All the above could be used as a style name.
4. Which of the following is a font name?
   a. SIMPLEX
   b. TITLE
   c. NAMES
   d. A
   e. All the above are font names.
5. You can change from one text style to another from within the Single Line Text command.
   a. True
   b. False
6. When you set the text style, which of the following text height settings will allow you to draw different heights of the same text style?
   a. 1/4
   b. 0' - 0"
   c. 1
   d. 1000
   e. -
7. Which of the following Single Line Text options draws text between two clicked points and adjusts the text height so that it fits between the two points?
   a. Fit
   b. Align
   c. Justify
   d. Middle
   e. Style

8. Which of the following Single Line Text options draws text between two clicked points and condenses or expands the text to fit between the two points but does not change the text height?
   a. Fit
   b. Align
   c. Justify
   d. Middle
   e. Style

9. The justification letters MR stand for
   a. Middle, Right-justified
   b. Margin, Right-justified
   c. Midpoint, Left-justified
   d. Bottom, Right-justified
   e. Margin Release

10. Which of the following modifiers should be selected if you want the bottom of the line of text to end 1/2″ above and 1/2″ to the left of the lower right corner of the drawing limits?
    a. TL
    b. BR
    c. BL
    d. TR
    e. MR

11. List three commands that can be used to change or edit text.

    _____    _____    _____

12. List the command that allows you to change only the text contents.

    _____

13. List the command that allows you to change text height, contents, properties, justification, style, and origin.

    _____

14. List the command used to create a paragraph of text.

    _____

15. List the command that will spell check any line or paragraph of text you select.

    _____

16. Describe the difference between text style name and font name.

    _____

    _____

17. List the setting for Style height that must be used for AutoCAD to prompt you for height when Dtext is used.

    _____

18. Write the description for the abbreviations TL, ML, and BR.

    _____

    _____

19. Describe how to quickly change all the text on a drawing done in the STANDARD style, TXT font, to the SIMPLEX font.

    _____

    _____

20. List the standard codes for the following.

    a. Degree symbol: _____

    b. Plus–minus symbol: _____

    c. Diameter symbol: _____

    d. Underscore: _____

    e. Overscore: _____

# 7 Printing and Plotting

## OBJECTIVES

When you have completed this chapter, you will be able to:

☐ Create different layout tabs for your drawing.
☐ Select a title block for a layout tab.
☐ Print or plot from a model or layout tab.
☐ Print drawings on ink-jet or laser printers to scale or to fit on standard sheets.
☐ Plot drawings at various scales using pen, ink-jet, or laser plotters.

## INTRODUCTION

At the bottom of the drawing window are Model, Layout1, and Layout2 tabs. Model space is the 2D (and also 3D) environment in which you have been working to this point. Model space is where your 2D and 3D model (drawing) is created and modified.

When you start a new drawing AutoCAD provides a single Model tab and two Layout tabs. A layout tab (paper space in previous releases) is similar to a piece of illustration board used to paste up a presentation; it helps you lay out your drawings for printing or plotting. You can create as many layouts for a drawing as you need. For example, one layout can be a title sheet, another the floor plan, another the furniture plan, and so on. All the sheets are in the one drawing and are identified with the Layout tab name.

Exercise 7–1 describes print/plot responses for Exercise 7–1 when the Model tab is current, using the Plot dialog box. Exercise 7–2 describes print/plot responses for Exercise 5–1, using a Create Layout Wizard, and adding an ANSI title block supplied by AutoCAD. Exercise 7–3 describes print/plot responses for Exercise 5–2 when a Layout tab is current, and using Page Setup.

## EXERCISE 7–1
## Print/Plot Responses for Exercise 6–1, Using the Model Tab

The following is a hands-on, step-by-step exercise to make a hard copy of Exercise 6–1. To begin, turn on the computer and start AutoCAD. The AutoCAD 2002 Today window is displayed.

### On Your Own

1. **Open drawing CH6-EX1 on the hard drive so it is displayed on the screen. Remember, if your drawing has been saved on a floppy disk, open it from the floppy disk and save it on the hard drive.**
2. **Make sure the Model tab is current.**
3. **Click the Plot command from the Standard Toolbar, or** CLICK: **Plot… from the File menu, or** TYPE: **PLOT<enter> to access the Plot dialog box. Pressing the Ctrl and P keys at the same time will also access the Plot dialog box.**

**FIGURE 7–1**
Plot Dialog Box, Plot Device
Tab

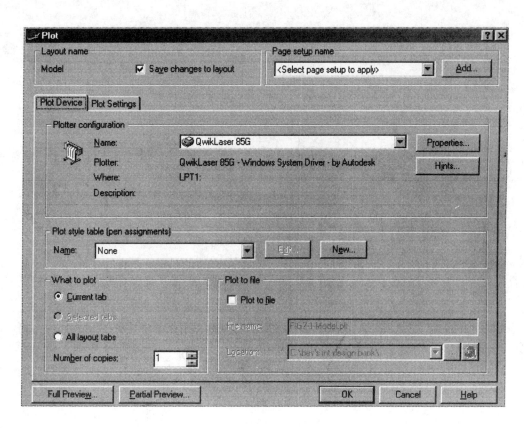

4. **Click the Plot Device tab of the Plot dialog box (Figure 7–1).**

5. **Follow the step-by-step information to make a hard copy of drawing CH6-EX1.**

*The following describes the top part of the Plot dialog box that stays the same, regardless if the Plot Device tab, or the Plot Settings tab, is current.*

## Layout Name

This area at the top of the dialog box displays the current layout tab name or shows if the Model tab is current. It shows "Model" now, because the Model tab is current.

### Save Changes to Layout Check Button

When this button is checked, any settings made in the Plot dialog box are saved with the current layout.

## Page Setup Name

Layout settings (the settings that control the final plot output) are referred to as *page setups*. This list box displays any named or saved page setups that you can select to apply to the current page setup.

### Add...

When this button is clicked, the User Defined Page Setups dialog box is displayed. You can choose to create a new page setup from the settings you are currently making, rename, or delete page setups.

*The following describes the parts of the Plot dialog box with the Plot Device tab current:*

## Plotter Configuration

The Name: line displays the current plot device (plotter or printer). When the down arrow is clicked, a list of the available plotting devices is displayed in the Name list. You can select the plot device that you want to use.

**FIGURE 7–2**
Plotter Configuration Editor

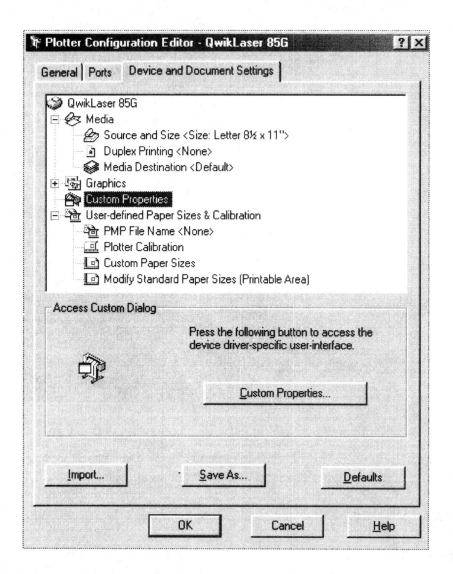

**Properties...**

When this button is clicked, the Plotter Configuration Editor (Figure 7–2) is displayed. The Plotter Configuration Editor allows you to view or modify current plot device information.

> *Custom Properties*  When this button of the Plotter Configuration Editor is clicked, a Custom Properties dialog box for the configured plotter (or printer) appears. Each plotter (or printer) has a unique Custom Properties dialog box; you can customize settings for the vector colors, print quality, and raster corrections for your plotter (or printer) using the Properties dialog box.

**Hints...**

When this button is clicked, information about the current plot device is displayed.

**Step 1.  Select the printer that you will use. If the Name: line does not show the correct plot device, click the down arrow and select the printer that you will use.**

If you need to add a plot device, the Plotter Manager (under File in the menu bar) is used to add or modify plotter and printer configuration files.

## Plot Style Table (Pen Assignments)

Plot styles allow you to plot the same drawing in different ways; a plot style can be assigned to a layer or to an object. AutoCAD provides some plot styles, or you can create your own.

**FIGURE 7–3**
Plot Styles Dialog Box

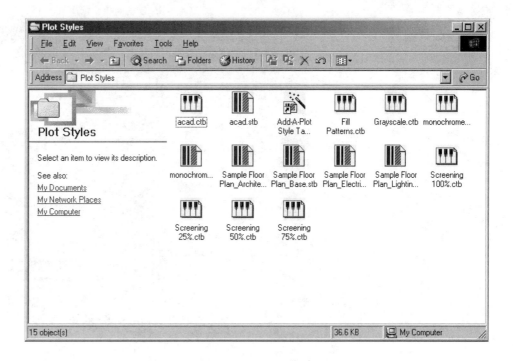

A plot style contains settings that can override an object's color, linetype, and lineweight. Output effects that can be set in the plot style are pen assignments, dithering, gray scale, and screening. End styles, join styles, and fill styles can also be set in plot styles.

The Plot Styles dialog box (Figure 7–3), located under Plot Style Manager... in the File menu, can be used to create, edit, or store plot files. The Add Plot Style Table Wizard (Figure 7–4), located under Wizards in the Tools menu, leads you through creating a plot style. There are two types of plot styles: color dependent (stored with the extension .ctb) and named (stored with the extension .stb). With the color-dependent plot style, all objects of the same color will have the same plot style that is assigned to that color. You can change the plot style of an object by changing the color of the object. With a named plot style, you can assign any plot style to any object regardless of color.

To use a plot style, you must attach it to the model or layout tabs by selecting it in the Name: line, as described next.

**FIGURE 7–4**
Add Plot Style Table Wizard

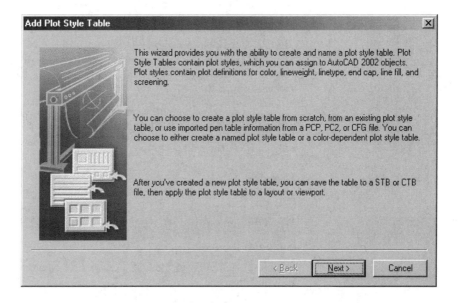

**FIGURE 7-5**
Plot Style Table Editor

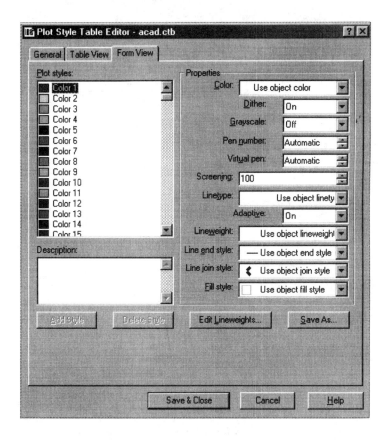

## Name:

Displays the plot style table assigned to the current Model tab or layout tab and a list of the currently available plot style tables. If more than one layout tab is selected and they have different plot style tables assigned, the list displays "Varies."

## Edit...

When this button is clicked (and a plot style other than None is selected in the Name line) the Plot Style Table Editor (Figure 7–5) is displayed. This allows you to edit the selected plot style table that is assigned to the plot style selected in the Name line.

## New...

When this button is clicked, the Add Plot Style Table wizard is displayed, which allows you to create a new plot style table.

**Step 2.** **CLICK: the plot style acad.ctb in the Name: line.**
**CLICK: No when AutoCAD asks "Assign this plot style table to all layouts?"**
**CLICK: the Edit... button to view the Plot Style Table Editor for acad.ctb (Figure 7–5).**
**CLICK: the Cancel button to exit.**
**Do the same to view some of the other plot styles AutoCAD provides.**

**Step 3.** **Set the plot style to None.**

## What to Plot

### Current Tab

When this button is selected, the current Model or Layout tab is plotted.

### Selected Tabs

When this button is selected, all "selected" tabs are plotted. If you want to select multiple tabs, hold down CTRL while clicking the tabs.

### All Layout Tabs

When this button is selected, all the layout tabs are plotted.

### Number of Copies:

Displays the number of copies that are to be plotted.

**Step 4.    Select the button for Current tab, and 1 for the Number of copies.**

## Plot to File

If you do not check the Plot to file button, AutoCAD plots directly from your computer. If there is a cable leading from your computer to the printer or plotter, or if you are plotting from a network, do not check the Plot to file button.

If you do check the Plot to file button, a file is created with the extension .plt.

### File Name:

When Plot to file is selected, the file name is the drawing name plus the tab name (Model or Layout tab name), separated by a hyphen.

### Location:

This line displays where the plot file is stored. The default location for the plot file is the same location as the drawing file.

…

Select this button to browse for a new location to store the plot file.

**Step 5.    Select the correct setting for the Plot to file check button, for your situation.**

**Step 6.    CLICK: the Plot Settings tab of the Plot dialog box (Figure 7–6).**

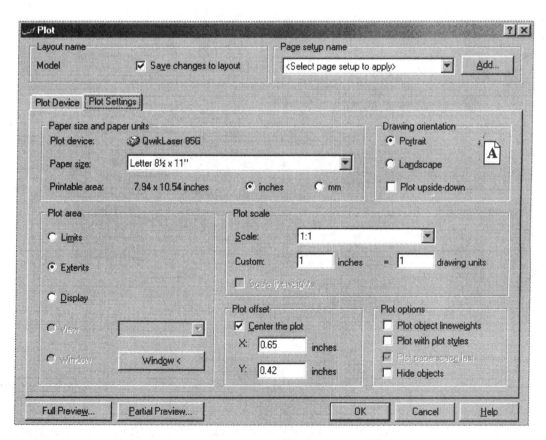

FIGURE 7-6
Plot Dialog Box, Plot Settings Tab

*The following describes the parts of the Plot dialog box when the Plot Settings tab is current:*

## Paper Size and Paper Units

### Paper Size:

The Paper size: line displays the current paper size. When the down arrow is clicked, it lists the paper sizes the printer (Figure 7–7) or plotter (Figure 7–8) can accommodate; the current size is highlighted. An A, B, D, or E displayed beside the size indicates a standard American National Standards Institute (ANSI) paper size. ARCH displayed beside the size indicates a standard architectural paper size.

### Printable Area:

The printable area is the actual part of the paper that the printer or plotter can use.

### Inches and mm

The radio buttons inches and mm allow you to select either inches or millimeters for specifying the paper size.

**Step 7.    Select the inches radio button and the 8½″ × 11″ paper size.**

## Drawing Orientation

The paper icon represents the orientation of the selected paper size. The letter *A* icon represents the orientation of the drawing on the paper.

### Portrait

This button allows you to specify a vertical orientation of the drawing on the page.

### Landscape

This button allows you to specify a horizontal orientation of the drawing on the page. If a plot shows only half of what should have been plotted, the orientation may need to be changed.

**FIGURE 7–7**
Paper Sizes for a Printer

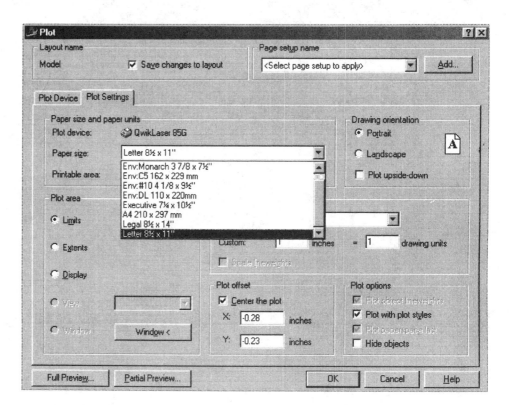

Part II: Two-Dimensional AutoCAD

FIGURE 7–8
Paper Sizes for a Plotter

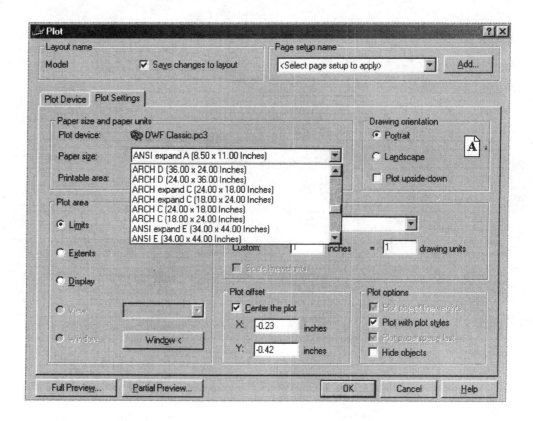

## Plot Upside-Down

This check box allows you to plot the drawing, in a portrait or landscape orientation, upside-down.

**Step 8.   Select the Portrait orientation.**

## Plot Area

A dialog box *radio button* is a button that is part of a group that is mutually exclusive—only one button in the group can be picked. The five radio buttons in the Plot area—Limits, Extents, Display, View, and Window—specify the part of the drawing that is to be printed, and only one can be selected at a time. When the button is selected, a black dot appears inside the button.

### Limits

This option plots the part of the drawing that lies within the drawing limits. The limits for drawing CH6-EX1 are 8-1/2,11.

### Extents

This option plots the drawing extents. The drawing extents are whatever graphics are actually drawn, including any graphics that lie outside the limits of the drawing area.

### Display

This option plots the part of the drawing that is displayed on the screen at the time the plot is made.

### View

This selection plots any view that has been named and saved with the View command. No view was named and saved for drawing CH6-EX1. If you have saved a view, click the View button and select the name of the view you want to print.

### Window

This selection allows you to pick two corners of a window and plot only the part of the drawing that is within the window. When the **Window** < button is clicked, it clears the Plot dialog box so you can view your drawing and use your mouse to click the two corners of a window. AutoCAD then returns to the Plot dialog box.

**Step 9.   CLICK: the Extents radio button to select the drawing extents as the part of the drawing that is to be printed.**

## Plot Scale

### Scale:

The Scale: line displays the scale at which the drawing will be plotted. When the down arrow is clicked, a list of available scales is displayed. You can select the scale that you want to use. To be able to measure a plotted drawing accurately using a scale, you must enter a specific plotting scale.

You may respond by selecting Scaled to Fit instead of entering a specific scale. When you select this option, AutoCAD scales the selected plot area as large as possible to fit the specified paper size.

**Step 10.   Select a scale of 1:1, which is 1 plotted inch = 1 drawing unit.**

## Plot Offsets

### Center the Plot

To center the drawing on the paper, place a check in the Center the plot check box, and the plot will be automatically centered on the paper.

## X and Y Offset

The plot offset specifies the location of the plot, on the paper, from the lowerleft corner of the paper. The X: input line moves the plotted drawing in the X direction on the paper, and the Y: input moves the drawing in the Y direction. You can enter either positive or negative values.

**Step 11.   Place a check in the Center the plot check box.**

Notice that the X and Y inputs are is automatically calculated to center the selected plotting area (extents) in the paper size ($8\frac{1}{2}'' \times 11''$).

## Plot Options

### Plot Object Lineweights

A check mark in this box tells AutoCAD to plot the drawing using the lineweights you have assigned to any object in the drawing.

### Plot with Plot Styles

This option allows you to use a plot style. Since you are not using a plot style, this box will not be checked.

### Plot Paper Space Last

When this option is checked, model space will be plotted first. Usually, paper space drawings are plotted before model space drawings.

### Hide Objects

The Hide objects button refers to 3D objects only. When you use the Hide command, AutoCAD hides any surface on the screen that is behind another surface in 3D space. If you want to do the same on your model space plot, you must click the Hide objects check button so a check appears in the box.

FIGURE 7–9
Partial Plot Preview Dialog Box

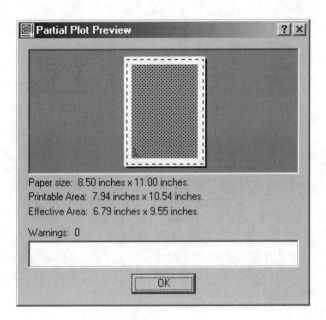

Paper size: 8.50 inches x 11.00 inches.
Printable Area: 7.94 inches x 10.54 inches.
Effective Area: 6.79 inches x 9.55 inches.

Warnings: 0

If you are printing viewports in paper space, this button has no effect. To hide in paper space, select the viewport in which you want to have hidden lines, click Properties under Modify in the menu bar, and turn Hide Plot on.

**Step 12:   Do not put a check in any of these plot option boxes. (Plot paperspace last is grayed out because no layout tabs were used.)**

*The following describes the bottom part of the Plot dialog box that stays the same regardless if the Plot Device tab, or the Plot Settings tab, is current.*

## Partial Preview...

When you click the Partial Preview... button the Partial Plot Preview dialog box (Figure 7–9) appears. This allows you to preview the plot and, if any warnings appear, change the settings. A partial preview shows only an outline of the effective plotting area of the drawing.

The effective plotting area, measured from the plot origin, is the actual size of the graphics to be plotted on the paper. If the maximum size for the printer is exceeded, AutoCAD gives you a warning. If this warning appears and seems to be a problem, or if the effective plotting area appears too small, cancel the plot and recheck the drawing limits, or extents, and any layers that are off or frozen, and see how they relate to the plot settings. Review the plot settings that include the plot offset, paper size, drawing orientation, and plot scale, and change them accordingly to get a successful plot.

## Full Preview...

The Full Preview... button shows you exactly how the final plot will appear on the sheet.

**Step 13.   Click the Full Preview... button.**

Preview your plot for Exercise 6–1. If there is something wrong with the plot, press the spacebar and make the necessary adjustments. If the preview looks OK, press the spacebar to end the preview. You may also click the right mouse button to access the menu shown in Figure 7-10.

**Step 14.   Click OK.**

The plot proceeds from this point. If you have not created a plot file, remove the completed plot from the printer or plotter. If you have created a .plt file, take your floppy disk to the plot station or send your plot via a network.

FIGURE 7–10
Full Preview Right-Click Menu

## Plotting for the Internet

The format of drawings used on the World Wide Web must be different from that of the standard .dwg file. AutoCAD 2002 allows you to create .DWF (drawing web format) or other PublishtoWeb files from the Plot dialog box. To create any of these files do the following:

1. Start the Plot command.
2. Select a DWF or PublishtoWeb plotter for the plot device.
3. When you select a DWF or PublishtoWeb plotter, the Plot to file box is automatically checked as well as the filename and location. If you want to give the file a different name or location, you can do so by editing them in their text boxes.
4. To change the resolution, background color, layer information, or other properties, CLICK: **Properties...**, CLICK: **Custom Properties** in the plotter tree information, then CLICK: **Custom Properties...** when it appears on the tab.
5. CLICK: **OK.**

The file is then created in the location you have specified. DWF or PublishtoWeb files can be viewed on the Internet.

# EXERCISE 7–2
# Print/Plot Responses for Exercise 5–1, Using a Layout Wizard

The following is a hands-on, step-by-step exercise to make a hard copy of Exercise 5–1 using a Create Layout wizard. To begin, turn on the computer and start AutoCAD. The AutoCAD 2002 Today window is displayed.

## On Your Own

**1. Open drawing CH5-EX1 on the hard drive so it is displayed on the screen. Remember, if your drawing has been saved on a floppy disk, open it from the floppy disk and save it on the hard drive.**

## Model, Layout1, and Layout2 Tabs

At the bottom of the drawing window are Model, Layout1, and Layout2 tabs. Model space is the 2D (and also 3D) environment in which you have been working to this point. Model space is where your 2D and 3D model (drawing) is created and modified. A layout tab (paper space) is similar to a piece of illustration board used to paste up a presentation. In Exercise 7–2, the Create Layout wizard creates a layout tab and is used to plot Exercise 5–1.

## On Your Own

**1. Make sure the Model tab is current.**

**2. Create a new layer named Viewport. Make its color green and set it current.**

**3. CLICK: Wizards (in the Tools menu in the menu bar). CLICK: Create Layout... (in the Wizards menu) to access the Create Layout dialog box (Figure 7–10).**

**4. Follow the step-by-step information to make a hard copy of drawing CH5-EX1.**

**Step 1. TYPE: "Furniture Plan" for the new layout name in the input box (Figure 7–11). CLICK: Next>.**

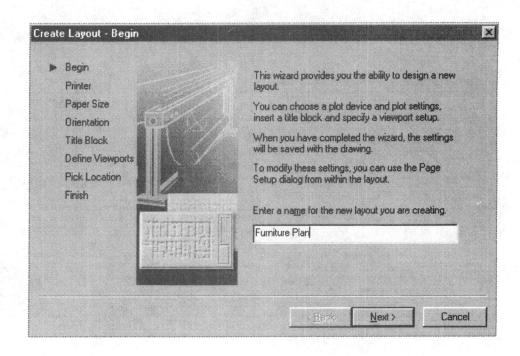

Step 2.   Select a configured printer or plotter for the new layout. CLICK: Next>

Step 3.   Select a paper size of 8½″ × 11″. CLICK: Next>.

Step 4.   Select the Portrait orientation of the drawing on the paper. CLICK: Next>.

Step 5.   Select the ANSI A title block (portrait).dwg for the layout. Select the Block radio button so the title block will be inserted as a block (Figure 7–12). CLICK: Next>.

Step 6.   Select the Single radio button so you will have a single viewport configuration. Select 1/40 = 1900 as the viewport scale (Figure 7–13). CLICK: Next>.

Step 7.   CLICK: Next>. AutoCAD will locate the viewport.

Step 8.   CLICK: Finish. The Layout tab named Furniture Plan is created with CH5-EX1 conference room shown at 1/40 = 1900 scale. The title block is also in the viewport.

FIGURE 7–12
Create Layout Dialog Box; STEP
5. Select an ANSI Title Block
Inserted as a Block

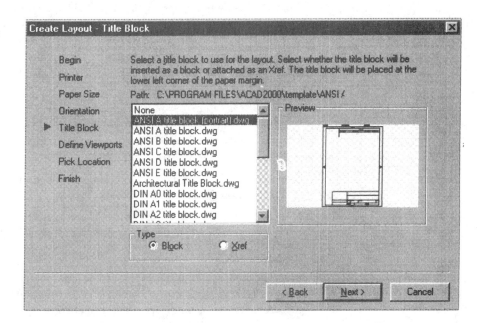

FIGURE 7–13
STEP 6. Select the Single Viewport and ¼″ = 1′0″ as the Viewport Scale

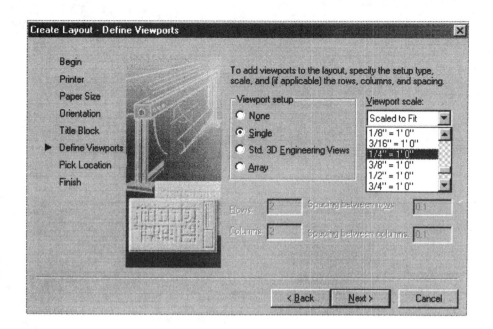

If your conference room is not centered within the ANSI title block, or your title block is outside the dashed lines that show the area that will be plotted, continue with steps 9, 10, and 11.

**Step 9.** **If your conference room is not centered within the ANSI title block,
change to Model space; (TYPE: MS <enter> or CLICK: PAPER on the
status bar to switch to Model space). Use Pan to center the conference
room. CLICK: MODEL on the status bar to return to Paper space.**

> **You may also use the Move command *while in Paper space* to move the
conference room. Click on the *green outline* of the viewport to center the
room within the border. The border of the viewport will also move; see
STEP 10 to change the border's layer and turn the layer off. Be aware
that you must be in Paper space to complete the remaining steps.**

**Step 10.** **The outline of the viewport (shown in green on your screen) needs to be
turned off. Turn the Viewport layer off so it will not print.**

**Note:** If you can't click the green outline
of the viewport without also selecting
the title block, use Zoom-Window to get
closer in.

**Step 11.** **Only the graphics that are within the dashed lines (printable area of your
computer) will be plotted. If the title block is too large for the printable
area of your printer, click the title block and use the Scale command to
reduce it. Specify 0,0 as the base point and TYPE: .98 to reduce the title
block 2%. You may also use the Move command to center the title block
within the dashed lines.**

**Step 12.** **Use Figure 7–14 as a guide. Use the Simplex font, 1/8″ high. to type your
school name and title your drawing. Use the Simplex font, 1/16″ high. to
type the scale and to type the word "NAME" and your name. Complete as
shown in Figure 7–14.**

**Step 13.** **RIGHT CLICK: the Furniture Plan tab. CLICK: Plot. Make sure the
scale is set 1:1.**

**Step 14.** **CLICK: Full Preview… if the preview is OK, right click and CLICK:
<exit>. If not, cancel and correct the problem.**

**Step 15.** **CLICK: OK.**

The plot proceeds from this point. If you have not created a plot file, remove the completed plot from the printer or plotter. If you have created a .plt file, take your floppy disk
to the plot station or send your plot via a network.

**FIGURE 7–14**
Title Your Drawing and Type Your
Name

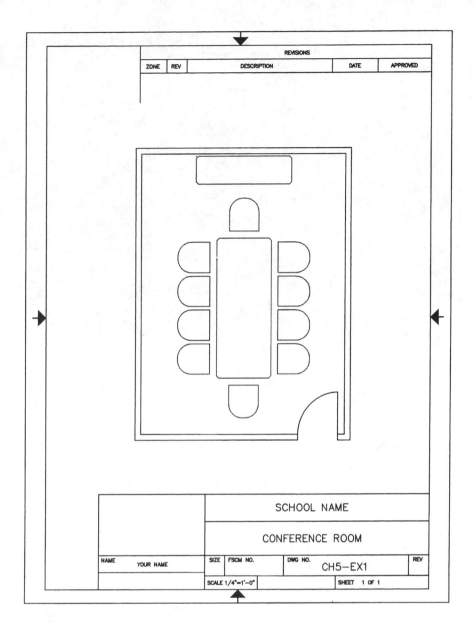

| | | REVISIONS | | |
|---|---|---|---|---|
| ZONE | REV | DESCRIPTION | DATE | APPROVED |

| NAME | | | | | | SCHOOL NAME | | | |
| | YOUR NAME | | | | | CONFERENCE ROOM | | | |
| | | SIZE | FSCM NO. | | DWG NO. | CH5–EX1 | | | REV |
| | | SCALE 1/4"=1'–0" | | | | | SHEET 1 OF 1 | | |

# EXERCISE 7–3
## Print/Plot Responses for Exercise 5–2, Using Page Setup

The following is a hands-on, step-by-step exercise to make a hard copy of Exercise 5–2, using Page Setup. To begin, turn on the computer and start AutoCAD. The AutoCAD 2002 Today window is displayed.

### On Your Own

1. **Open drawing CH5-EX2 on the hard drive so it is displayed on the screen. Remember, if your drawing has been saved on a floppy disk, open it from the floppy disk and save it on the hard drive.**

2. **Create a new layer named Viewport. Make its color green and set it current.**

### Model, Layout1, and Layout2 Tabs

At the bottom of the drawing window are Model, Layout1, and Layout2 tabs. Model space is the 2D (and also 3D) environment in which you have been working to this point. Model space is where your 2D and 3D model (drawing) is created and modified. A Layout tab (paper space) is similar to a piece of illustration board used to paste up a presenta-

**FIGURE 7–15**
Page Setup - Layout Dialog Box;
Plot Device Tab

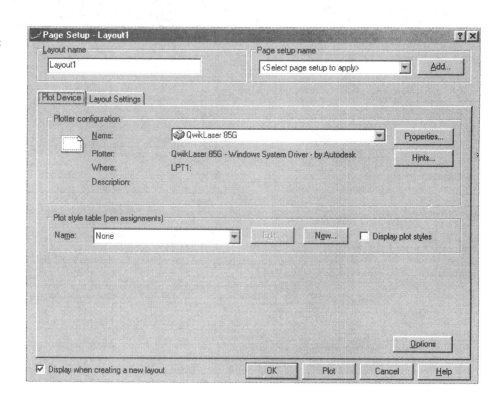

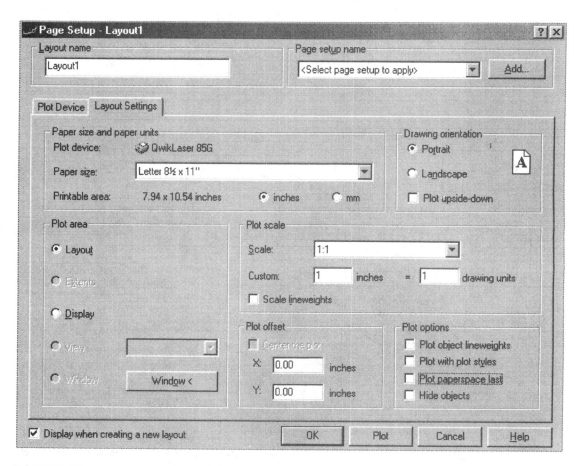

**FIGURE 7–16**
Page Setup—Layout1 Dialog Box; Layout Settings Tab

Part II: Two-Dimensional AutoCAD

tion. Exercise 7–3 describes print/plot responses for Exercise 5–2 when a Layout tab is current and Page Setup is used to plot.

**Step 1.** **CLICK: Layout1 tab at the bottom of drawing CH5-EX2. The Page Setup - Layout1 dialog box appears.** If the dialog box does not appear, right click on the Layout 1 tab and CLICK: **Page Setup....**

**Step 2.** **CLICK: the Plot Device tab of the Page Setup - Layout1 dialog box (Figure 7–15).**

**Step 3.** **Select the printer that you will use.**

**Step 4.** **Set the Plot style table to None.**

**Step 5.** **CLICK: the Layout Settings tab of the Page Setup - Layout1 dialog box.**

**Step 6.** **Make the settings as shown in Figure 7–16 to the Layout Settings tab of the Page Setup - Layout1dialog box.**

**Step 7.** **CLICK: OK.**

AutoCAD returns to the drawing screen with paper space current and the Layout1 tab highlighted. You are now in paper space, a presentation space for AutoCAD. The drawing image you are looking at is not to any scale now—it is "Scaled to fit" within the paper space limits. You need to proceed with the following to make sure your drawing will be printed to a scale of ¼″ = 1′-0″.

**Step 8.** **CLICK: Properties (from Modify in the menu bar). The Properties dialog box for Exercise 5–2 appears (Figure 7–17).**

**FIGURE 7–17**
Set the Model Space Scale to ¼″ = 1′

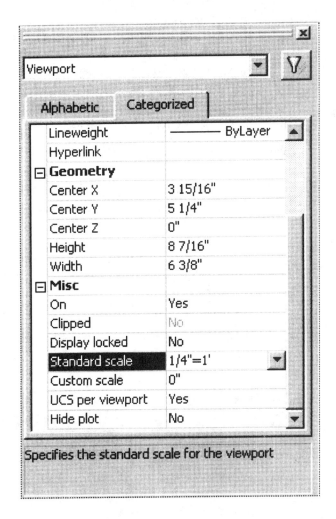

FIGURE 7–18
Select the Paper Space Boundary

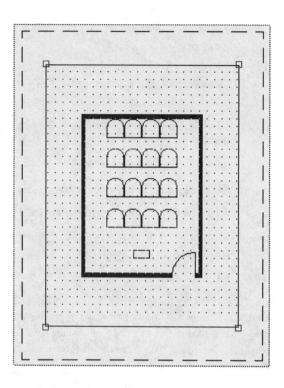

**Step 9.** CLICK: the green line around the drawing showing the paper space boundary (Figure 7–18).

**Step 10.** CLICK: Standard scale in the Properties dialog box. CLICK: the arrow to the right of Standard scale and scroll down to select $1/4'' = 1'0''$. This sets the model space scale to $1/4'' = 1'0''$. This scale is then shown in the paper space viewport. Close the Properties dialog box.

**Step 11.** Create a new layer named Viewport. Change the red line of the paper-space viewport boundary to the new layer called Viewport. Turn the Viewport layer off so it will not print.

**Step 12.** Right-click on the Layout1 tab. CLICK: Plot… from the right-click menu (Figure 7–19).

When you right-click on a layout tab, you get a shortcut menu. This menu allows you to create a new layout tab, create a new layout tab using a template, delete a layout tab, rename a layout tab, move or copy a layout tab, highlight all layouts tabs, use a page setup, or plot the drawing.

FIGURE 7–19
Layout Tab Right-Click Menu

```
New layout
From template...
Delete
Rename
Move or Copy...
Select All Layouts

Page Setup...
Plot...
```

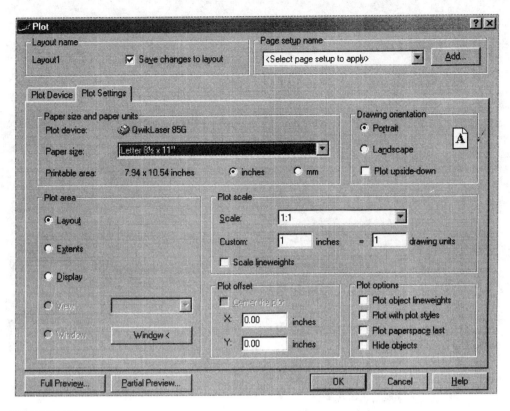

**FIGURE 7–20**
Plotting Layout1 Tab

**Step 13.   Make sure the Plot scale is 1:1 (Figure 7–20).**

Because you are plotting the layout tab that is already scaled 1/4″ = 1′0″ you use the Plot scale of 1:1.

**Step 14.   Click OK.**

The plot proceeds from this point. If you have not created a plot file, remove the completed plot from the printer or plotter. If you have created a .plt file, take your floppy disk to the plot station or send your plot via a network.

## REVIEW QUESTIONS

1. Which of the following pull-down menus contains the Plot... command?
   a.  File
   b.  Edit
   c.  Format
   d.  Tools
   e.  Window
2. Output effects that can be set in a plot style table are
   a.  Pen assignments
   b.  Dithering
   c.  Gray scale
   d.  Screening
   e.  All the above

3. Which of the following will produce a plot of the part of the drawing that is displayed on the screen?
   a. Display
   b. Extents
   c. Limits
   d. View
   e. Window

4. Which of the following will produce a plot of the entire drawing, even if part of it is outside the limits?
   a. All
   b. Extents
   c. Limits
   d. View
   e. Window

5. A plot file has which of the following extensions?
   a. .bak
   b. .dwg
   c. .plt
   d. .cfk
   e. .dwf

6. A plot that shows only half of what should have been plotted could probably be corrected by doing which of the following?
   a. Moving the origin .5
   b. Selecting View instead of Extents
   c. Writing the plot to a file
   d. Selecting Landscape instead of Portrait
   e. Selecting a smaller page

7. The plot option "Hide objects" on the Plot Settings tab of the Plot dialog box refers to which of the following?
   a. 3D objects
   b. Isometric drawings
   c. Hidden linetypes
   d. 2D objects
   e. Slide files

8. A drawing that is to be plotted so that it fits on a particular size sheet without regard to the scale requires which scale response?
   a. 1:1
   b. Full
   c. 1:2
   d. Scaled to Fit
   e. MAX

9. Which of the following pull-down menus used in this chapter contains the command to create a Layout Wizard?
   a. File
   b. Tools
   c. Insert
   d. Format
   e. Window

10. When you are using the Plot command to plot a Layout tab that is already scaled to $1/2'' = 1'0''$, use a Plot scale of:
    a. $1/2'' = 1'0''$
    b. 1:1
    c. 1:2
    d. 1:48
    e. Scaled to Fit

11. Name the three tabs that are at the bottom of the drawing window.

    _____   _____   _____

12. Describe why a Layout tab is used.

   _____

13. Describe why you would use different plot styles for the same drawing.

   _____

14. Describe the two different drawing orientations you can select when plotting.

   _____

15. Describe the difference between model space and a Layout tab (paper space).

   _____

16. List the eight commands that are on the right-click menu of a Layout tab.

   _____  _____  _____  _____
   _____  _____  _____  _____

17. Name the two types of files that can be viewed on the Internet.

   _____

18. When using a Layout Wizard, describe how to center your drawing within an ANSI title block.

   _____

19. When using a Layout Wizard why do you to turn off the outline of the Paper Space viewport.

   _____

20. List the 12 properties listed in the Plot Style Table Editor that can be set.

   _____  _____  _____  _____
   _____  _____  _____  _____
   _____  _____  _____  _____

# 8  Drawing the Floor Plan: Walls, Doors, and Windows

## OBJECTIVES

When you have completed this chapter, you will be able to:
☐ Correctly use the following commands and settings:

| | | | |
|---|---|---|---|
| Base | Extend | List | Named Views |
| Block-Make... | Insert-Block... | MINSERT | Properties... |
| Change | Linetype | Multiline | Status |
| Color | Lineweight | Multiline Style... | Wblock |
| Edit Multiline | | | |

## THE TENANT SPACE PROJECT

The Polyline or Multiline commands can be used to draw walls quickly. Polyline was described and used in Chapter 5. With Polyline, solid walls are drawn. With Multiline, walls with up to 16 lines are drawn. Exercise 8–1 contains step-by-step instructions for using Multiline to draw the exterior and interior walls of a tenant space that is located in the northwest corner of a building. The exercise also contains step-by-step instructions for inserting windows and doors into the plan.

Chapters 9 through 12 provide step-by-step instructions to complete the tenant space project started in Chapter 9. Each chapter will use the building plan drawn in Chapter 8 to complete a part of the project as described next.

*Chapter 9:* The tenant space is dimensioned and the square feet calculated.
*Chapter 10:* Elevations, sections, and details are drawn.
*Chapter 11:* Furniture is drawn, attributes are assigned (furniture specifications), and the furniture is added to the plan.
*Chapter 12:* The reflected ceiling plan and power plan are drawn.

## EXERCISE 8–1
## Tenant Space Floor Plan

When you have completed Exercise 8–1, the tenant space floor plan, your drawing will look similar to Figure 8–1. To prepare to draw Exercise 8–1, turn on the computer and start AutoCAD. The AutoCAD 2002 Today window is displayed.

1. CLICK: **the Create Drawings tab**
2. CLICK: **Wizards**
   CLICK: **Quick Setup**
3. Set drawing Units: **Architectural**
   CLICK: **Next>**
4. Set drawing Width: **75′** × Length: **65′**
   CLICK: **Finish**
5. **Use SaveAs... to save the drawing on the hard drive with the name CH8-EX1.**
6. Set Grid: **12″**
7. Set Snap: **6″**

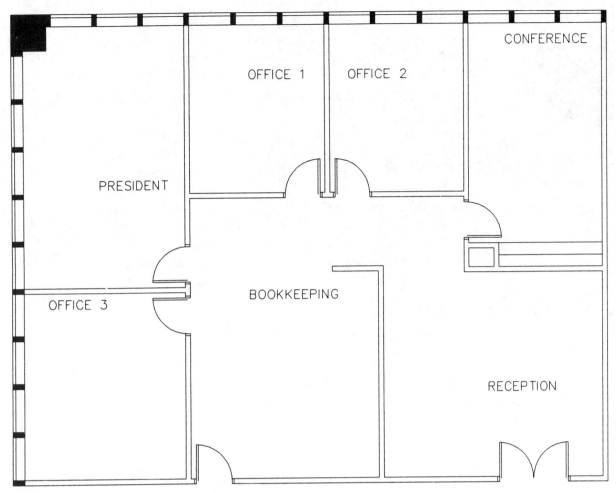

**FIGURE 8–1**
Exercise 8–1: Tenant Space Floor Plan (Scale: 1/8″ = 1′-0″)

8. Create the following Layers. Be sure to type and enter a comma after each layer name. The cursor will move to the next line so you can type the next layer name:

| LAYER NAME | COLOR | LINETYPE |
|---|---|---|
| A-area | White | Continuous |
| A-clng | Green | Continuous |
| A-door | Yellow | Continuous |
| A-flor-iden | White | Continuous |
| A-flor-wdwk | White | Continuous |
| A-furn | Magenta | Continuous |
| A-glaz | White | Continuous |
| A-pflr-dims | Cyan | Continuous |
| A-wall-ext | Blue | Continuous |
| A-wall-int | Red | Continuous |
| E-comm | Green | Continuous |
| E-lite | White | Continuous |
| E-powr | White | Continuous |

The layers listed include those that will be used in Chapters 9, 11, and 12. The layer names are based on the guidelines provided by the document *CAD LAYER GUIDE-LINES Recommended Designations for Architecture, Engineering, and Facility Management Computer-Aided Design*, prepared by the Task Force on CAD Layer Guidelines.

9. Set Layer A-wall-ext current.

10. Use **Zoom-All** to view the limits of the drawing.

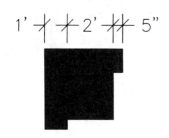

**FIGURE 8-2**
Use the 2D Solid Command to Draw the Corner Column and Two Mullions

## 2D SOLID

The 2D Solid command was described in Chapter 4. The following part of Exercise 8–1 uses the 2D Solid command to draw the window mullions and the 3'-square corner column located in the northwest corner of the tenant space.

**Turn BLIPMODE on and use 2D Solid to draw the 3'-square corner column (Figure 8–2):**

| Prompt | Response |
|---|---|
| Command: | TYPE: **BLIPMODE<enter>** |
| Enter Mode [ON/OFF]<default> | TYPE: **ON<enter>** |
| Command: | **2D Solid** (or TYPE: **SO<enter>**) |
| Specify first point: | TYPE: **17',51'<enter>** |
| Specify second point: | TYPE: **@3'<0<enter>** |
| Specify third point: | TYPE: **@-3',-3'<enter>** |
| Specify fourth point or <exit>: | TYPE: **@3'<0<enter>** |
| Specify third point: | **<enter>** |

### On Your Own

1. Zoom in close around the column, and use the 2D Solid command to draw the two separate mullions (5″ × 12″) that are on the east and south sides of the column just drawn, as shown in Figure 8–2. Use polar and relative coordinates to draw the mullions much like you just drew the corner column.

## ARRAY

The Array command was described in Chapter 5. The following part of Exercise 8–1 uses the Array command to draw the window mullions on the north and west exterior walls.

**Use Array to finish drawing the mullions on the north exterior wall (Figure 8–3):**

| Prompt | Response |
|---|---|
| Command: | **Array** (or TYPE: **AR<enter>**) |
| The Array dialog box appears: | CLICK: **the Select objects button** |
| Select objects: | **Click the mullion located on the east side of the column.** |
| Select objects: 1 found | |
| Select objects: | **<enter>** |
| | CLICK: **the Rectangular Array button** |
| | TYPE: **1 in the Rows: input area** |
| | TYPE: **13 in the Columns: input area** |
| | TYPE: **4' in the Column offset: input area** |
| | TYPE: **0 in the Row offset: input area** |
| | TYPE: **0 in the Angle of array: input area** |
| | CLICK: **OK** |

### On Your Own

1. Use the Array command to draw the remaining mullions on the west exterior wall, as shown in Figure 8–3. Specify 10 rows, 1 column, and −4' distance between rows.

2. Next, you will draw the walls using Multiline after you set Multiline Style.... It is helpful if the column and mullions are not solid. Set **FILL OFF** and regenerate the drawing so that the columns and mullions are not solid.

3. Zoom-Extents to see the entire drawing.

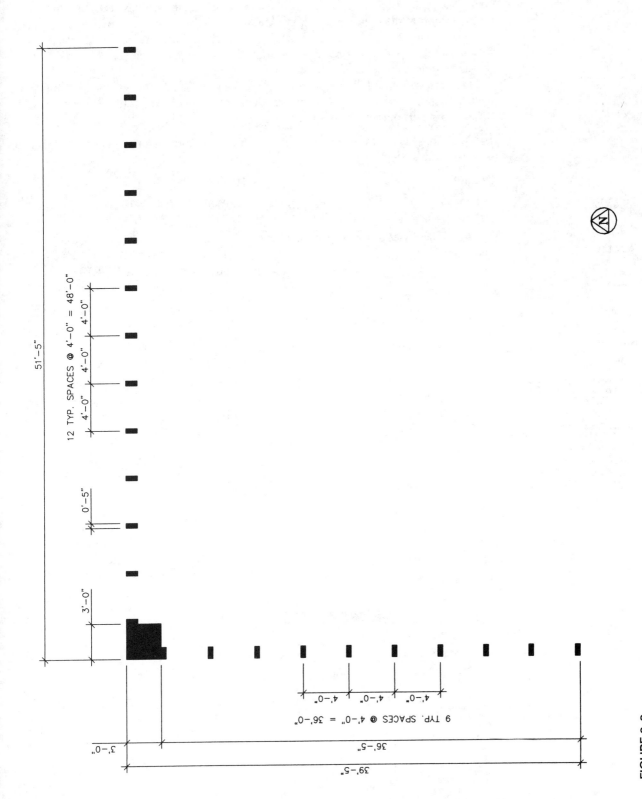

**FIGURE 8-3**
Use the Array Command to Finish Drawing the Mullions (Scale: 1/8" = 1'-0")

## MULTILINE STYLE...

With the column and mullions now completed, you are ready to use Multiline to draw the walls. The Multiline Style... dialog box allows you to make the settings necessary to draw up to 16 lines at the same time with the Multiline command. You can specify color and linetype for any of the 16 lines and endcaps for each multiline. You can specify the walls as solid (background fill) or not. You must add the name of the multiline style to the list of current styles before you can draw with it.

Next, you will use Multiline Style... to make the settings for the north exterior wall of the tenant space. You will have one line at 0, one at 9″, and one at 12″ (the 3″ glass line is offset 3″ from the outside line of the 12″ wall).

**Use Multiline Style... to set a three-line wall that is 12″ thick with a 3″ glass line (Figures 8–4 and 8–5):**

| Prompt | Response |
|---|---|
| Command: | **Multiline Style...** (or TYPE: **MLSTYLE<enter>**) |
| The Multiline Styles dialog box appears (Figure 8–4): | Highlight: **STANDARD** in the Name: input line and TYPE: **THREE** as shown in Figure 8–4 |
| | CLICK: the **Description: input line** and TYPE: **WALLS** |
| | CLICK: **Add** to make the style current |
| | CLICK: **Element Properties...** |
| The Element Properties dialog box appears: | HIGHLIGHT: **0.500** in the Offset input line and TYPE: **9** |
| | CLICK: **Add** |
| | HIGHLIGHT: **0.000** in the Offset input line and TYPE: **12** |
| | CLICK: **Add** |
| | Do you have a scroll bar in the Elements list box that indicates more lines? If so, scroll down to look. If you have a –0.5 offset, CLICK: **−.05** in the list and CLICK: **Delete** to delete an unnecessary offset |

**FIGURE 8–4**
Multiline Style Named THREE

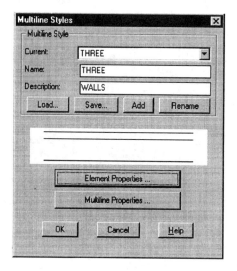

**Part II: Two-Dimensional AutoCAD**

FIGURE 8–5
Element Properties with Offsets
of 0, 9, and 12″

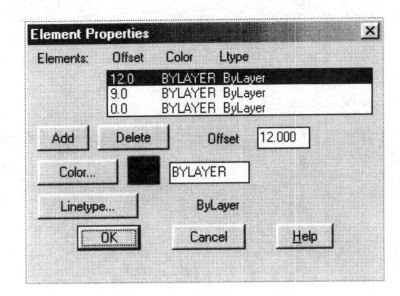

You should now have a 12.0, a 9.0, and 0.0 in the Element Properties list as shown in Figure 8–5 and nothing else—no scroll bar to the right indicating more lines. You could now assign colors and linetypes to the lines. If you do not assign colors or linetypes, the lines will assume the color and linetype of the layer on which the multilines are drawn. Leave colors and linetypes assigned BYLAYER so you can look at the drawing and see which layers they are on.

| Prompt | Response |
|---|---|
| | CLICK: **OK** |
| The Multiline Styles dialog box appears: | CLICK: **OK** |

## MULTILINE

The Multiline prompt is "Specify start point or [Justification/Scale/STyle]:". The Multiline command uses the current Multiline Style to draw up to 16 lines at the same time with or without end caps.

### Style

You can set any style current that has been defined with the Multiline Style... command if it is not already current (TYPE: **ST<enter>** to the Multiline prompt, then TYPE: **the style name<enter>** and begin drawing).

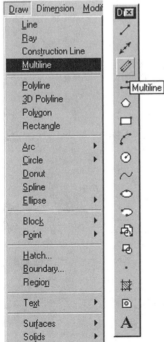

### Justification

This option allows you to select Top, Zero, or Bottom lines to begin drawing multilines. The default is Top. In this case Zero and Bottom are the same because there are no negative offsets. If you have a positive 3 offset, a 0, and a negative 3 offset, your three lines will be drawn from the middle line with justification set to zero.

### Scale

This option allows you to set the scale at which lines will be drawn. If your multiline style has a 10 offset, a 6 offset, and a 0, and you set the scale at .5, the lines will be drawn 5 and 3″ apart. The same style with a scale of 2 draws lines 20 and 12″ apart.

**Use Multiline to draw the north exterior wall of the tenant space (Figure 8–6):**

| Prompt | Response |
|---|---|
| Command: | **Multiline**<br>(or TYPE: **ML<enter>**) |

Current settings: Justification = Top, Scale =
   1.00, Style = THREE

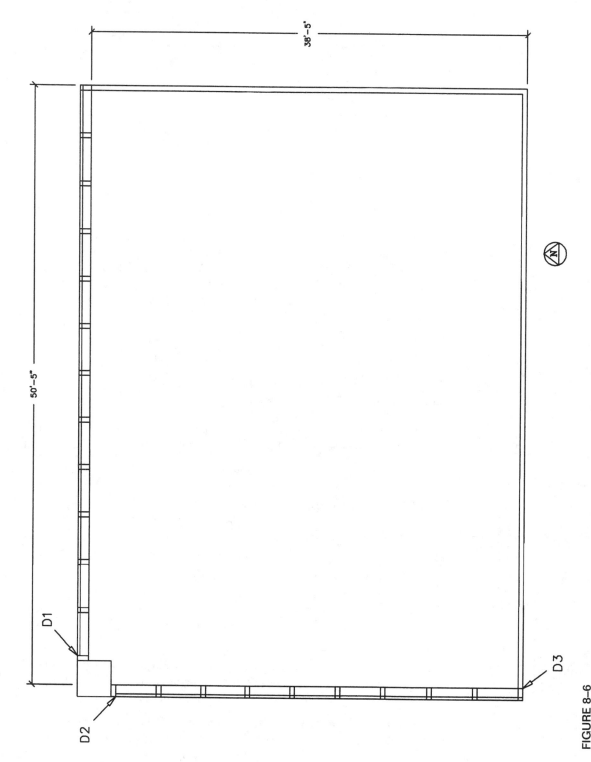

**FIGURE 8-6**
Use Multiline to Draw Exterior Walls with the Multiline Styles THREE, THREE-WEST, and TWO (Scale: 1/8" = 1'-0")

| Prompt | Response |
|---|---|
| Specify start point or [Justification/Scale/ STyle]: | TYPE: **INT\<enter\>** |
| | **D1** (Figure 8–6) |
| of | |
| Specify next point: | **Turn ORTHO ON. Move your mouse to the right** and TYPE: **48'\<enter\>** |
| Specify next point or [Undo]: | **\<enter\>** |

## On Your Own (Figures 8–6, 8–7, and 8–8)

1. Set a new multiline style with the name THREE-WEST; Description, Walls, and offsets of 0, 3, and 12 (Figure 8–7).
2. Use Multiline with a justification of Bottom to draw the west wall of the tenant space with the THREE-WEST multiline style. Use Osnap-Intersection and CLICK: D2 (Figure 8–6) to start the multiline and make the line 36' long (subtract 2'5" from the dimension on the right side of Figure 8–6 to account for the 3'-square corner column and the 5" mullion).
3. Set a new multiline style with the name TWO; Description INTERIOR WALLS, and offsets of 0 and 5 (Figure 8–8).
4. Use Multiline with a justification of bottom to draw the south and east walls of the tenant space. Use Osnap-Intersection and CLICK: D3 (Figure 8–6) and make the line to the right 50'5" and the line up 38'5".
5. Next, the interior walls are drawn. Remember to use transparent Zoom commands to move to different parts of the drawing while in the Multiline command. TYPE: 'Z from the keyboard and press \<enter\>. An apostrophe (') must precede the Z, or use the Zoom commands from the View menu in the menu bar.

**Note:** You cannot edit the Element and Multiline Properties of an mline style that you have used in a drawing. They are grayed out.

Use Multiline with the Multiline Style TWO to draw 5"-wide horizontal and vertical interior walls inside the tenant space. Keep layer A-WALL=EXT current. The layer on which the interior walls are drawn will be changed to A-WALL-INT in this exercise with the Properties... command (Figure 8–9):

| Prompt | Response |
|---|---|
| Command: | **Multiline** (or TYPE: **ML\<enter\>**) |
| Current settings: Justification = Bottom, Scale = 1.00, Style = TWO | |

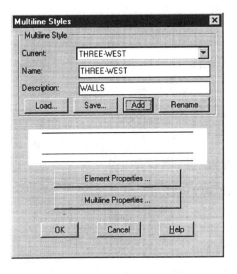

**FIGURE 8–7**
Set a New Multiline Style Named THREE-WEST

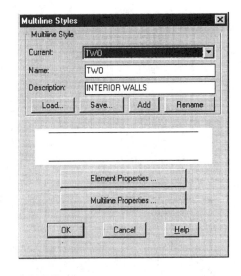

**FIGURE 8–8**
Set a New Multiline Style Named TWO

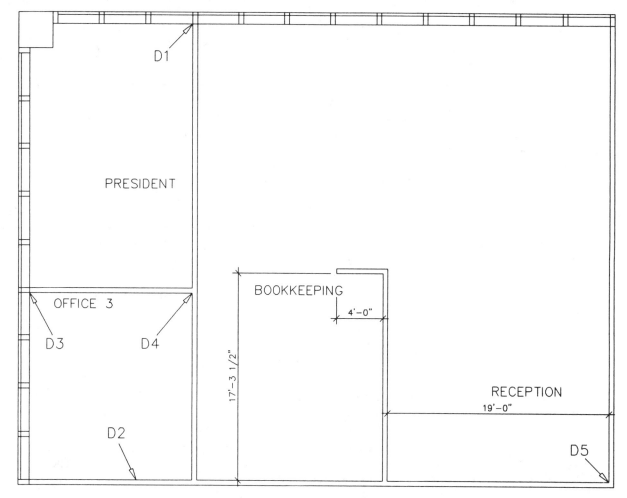

**FIGURE 8–9**
Use Multiline to Draw Interior Walls (Scale: 1/8″ = 1′-0″)

| Prompt | Response |
|---|---|
| Specify start point or [Justification/Scale/STyle]: | **Osnap-Intersection** |
| of | CLICK: **D1** (Figure 8–9) |
| Specify next point: | **Osnap-Perpendicular** |
| to | **D2** |
| Specify next point or [Undo]: | **<enter>** (the intersection will be edited later) |
| Command: | **<enter>** |
| Current settings: Justification = Bottom, Scale = 1.00, Style = TWO: | |
| Specify start point or [Justification/Scale/STyle]: | **Osnap-Intersection** |
| of | **D3** |
| Specify next point: | **Osnap-Perpendicular** |
| to | **D4** |
| Specify next point or [Undo]: | **<enter>** (the intersection will be edited later) |

FIGURE 8–10
Multiline with End Cap

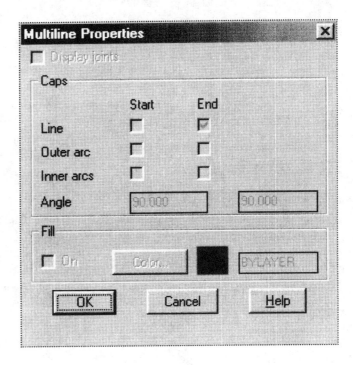

Set a new multiline style that uses the settings of the TWO style but adds an end cap at the end of the line. Then use Multiline and Osnap-From to draw the wall that separates the reception and bookkeeping areas (Figures 8–9 and 8–10):

| Prompt | Response |
| --- | --- |
| Command: | **Multiline Style...** |
| The Multiline Styles dialog box appears: | DOUBLE CLICK: **Name: TWO** and TYPE: **TWO-CAP-END** |
| | CLICK: **Add** |
| | CLICK: **Multiline Properties** |
| The Multiline Properties dialog box appears: | In the caps area CLICK: **End** in the Line row so a check appears in it as shown in Figure 8–10. |
| | CLICK: **OK** |
| The Multiline Styles dialog box appears: | CLICK: **OK** |
| Command: | TYPE: **ML<enter>** |
| Current settings: Justification = Bottom, Scale = 1.00, Style = TWO-CAP-END Specify start point or [Justification/Scale/STyle]: | **Osnap-From** |
| Base point: | **Osnap-Endpoint** |
| of | **D5** (Figure 8–9) |
| <Offset>: | TYPE: **@19'5<180** |
| Specify next point: | **Turn ORTHO ON. Move your mouse up** and TYPE: **17'3-1/2<enter>** |
| Specify next point or [Undo]: | **Move your mouse to the left** and TYPE: **4'<enter>** |
| Specify next point or [Close/Undo]: | **<enter>** (the intersection will be edited next) |

Look at the check box marked On in the Fill area. When this is checked, the walls are drawn with a solid fill.

# EDIT MULTLINE

The Edit Multiline command allows you to change the intersections of multilines in a variety of ways as shown in Figure 8–11. Just CLICK: the change you want, CLICK: **OK**, and then CLICK: the two multilines whose intersection you want to change.

**Use Edit Multiline to trim the intersections of the multilines forming the interior walls to an Open Tee (Figures 8–11 and 8–12).**

| Prompt | Response |
|--------|----------|
| Command: | Under the Modify menu, CLICK: **Object**, then CLICK: **Multiline...** (or TYPE: **MLEDIT<enter>**) |
| The Multiline Edit Tools dialog box appears: | CLICK: **Open Tee** |
| | CLICK: **OK** |
| Select first mline: | CLICK: **the vertical wall separating the reception and bookkeeping areas** |
| Select second mline: | CLICK: **the south horizontal exterior wall** |

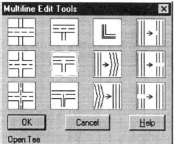

**FIGURE 8–11**
Edit Multiline Open Tee

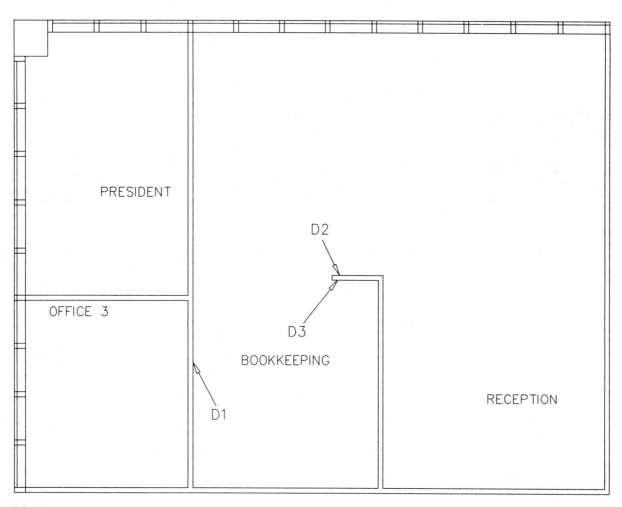

**FIGURE 8–12**
Practice Using the Extend Command (Scale: 1/8″ = 1′-0″)

| Prompt | Response |
|---|---|
| Select first mline (or Undo): | CLICK: **the interior vertical wall of office 3** |
| Select second mline: | CLICK: **the south horizontal exterior wall** |
| Select first mline (or Undo): | CLICK: **the interior horizontal wall of the president's office** |
| Select second mline: | CLICK: **the interior vertical wall of the president's office** |
| Select first mline (or Undo): | **<enter>** |
| | Have part of your walls disappeared? TYPE: **RE<enter>** to get them back. |

If you made a mistake while drawing the walls, the next part of this exercise will show you how to explode the multiline and use a modify command to edit the multiline.

## EXTEND

The Extend command allows you to lengthen an existing line or arc segment to meet a specified boundary edge. You will find it very useful when drawing walls. In the following part of this exercise, a boundary edge will be selected, and the horizontal wall of the bookkeeping area will be extended. The Undo option will then be used to erase it.

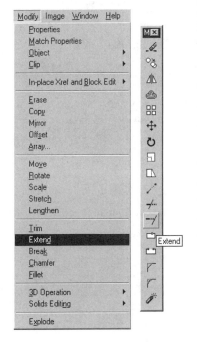

**Practice using the Extend command, and then undo the practice session. You must first Explode the Multilines using the Explode command to make the separate lines. (Figure 8–12):**

| Prompt | Response |
|---|---|
| Command: | **Explode** (or TYPE: **X<enter>**) |
| Select objects: | **D1** |
| Select objects: | **D2** |
| Select objects: | **<enter>** |
| Command: | **Extend** (or TYPE: **EX<enter>**) |
| Select boundary edge(s)... Select objects: | **D1** |
| Select objects: 1 found Select objects: | **<enter>** |
| Select object to extend or shift-select to trim or [Project/Edge/Undo]: | **D2** |
| Select object to extend or shift-select to trim or [Project/Edge/Undo]: | **D3** |
| Select object to extend or shift-select to trim or [Project/Edge/Undo]: | **<enter>** |

The points D2 and D3 were picked close to the left end of the line segment because the selected line (or arc) is extended from the end closest to the point picked. If the boundary edge does not intersect the entity to be extended, the prompt "Entity does not intersect an edge" appears. If you need to trim an entity that intersects the boundary edge, hold the Shift key down and click on the entity to be trimmed while still in the Extend command.

## On Your Own

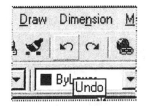

1. **After examining how precisely the lines are extended to meet the selected boundary edge, use the Undo command to erase the practice session.**

# CHANGE

The Change command can be used to change seven properties—Color, Elevation, Layer, Linetype, Linetype scale, Lineweight, and Thickness—of an entity. You are familiar with the Color, Layer, and Linetype properties. The Elevation and Thickness properties, used in drawing basic three-dimensional models, is discussed in Chapter 17.

## On Your Own

**1. Before using the Change command, explode the outside wall line of the exterior north and west walls of the tenant space.**

**Use the Change command to change the layer property of the glass line from the A-wall layer to the A-glaz layer:**

| Prompt | Response |
|--------|----------|
| Command: | TYPE: **CHANGE\<enter>** |
| Select objects: | **Click any points on both glass lines (the middle line on the north and west walls).** |
| Select objects: 1 found | |
| Select objects: 1 found | |
| Select objects: | **\<enter>** |
| Specify change point or [Properties]: | TYPE: **P\<enter>** |
| Enter property to change [Color/Elev/LAyer/ LType/ltScale/LWeight/Thickness]: | TYPE: **LA\<enter>** |
| Enter new layer name \<A-wall-ext>: | TYPE: **A-GLAZ\<enter>** |
| Enter property to change [Color/Elev/LAyer/ LType/ltScale/LWeight/Thickness]: | **\<enter>** |

The prompts for changing the Color and Linetype properties of any entity are the same as for changing the Layer property. To keep your drawing simple, do not mix multiple colors and linetypes within one layer. It is best to create a new layer with the desired linetypes and colors and change the layer property of the entity.

### Change \<Change point>

The \<Change point> option of the Change command will change the location of text. It can also be used to move an endpoint of a line to a new location or to change the radius of a circle.

If a line is picked when the "Select objects:" prompt appears, the endpoint closest to the point picked is moved to the new point picked when the "Specify change point or [Properties]:" prompt appears. If a circle is picked when the "Select objects:" prompt appears, the radius of the circle is changed to pass through the new point picked when the "Specify change point or [Properties]:" prompt appears.

## PROPERTIES...

The Properties Window (Figure 8–13) allows you to change any property that can be changed.

**Use the Properties... command to change the layer of the interior walls from the A-wall-ext layer to the A-wall-int layer.**

| Prompt | Response |
|--------|----------|
| Command: | **Properties...** |
| The Properties window appears: | **Use a crossing window to select all the interior walls.** |
| The Properties window lists all the interior wall properties: | CLICK: **Layer...** |

**FIGURE 8–13**
Properties Window

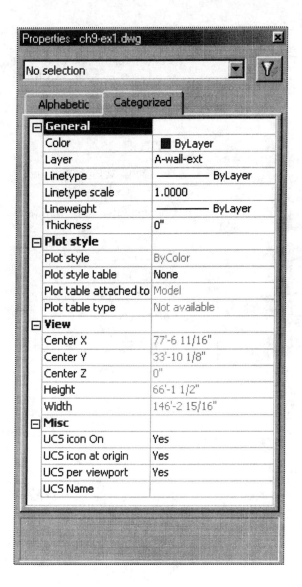

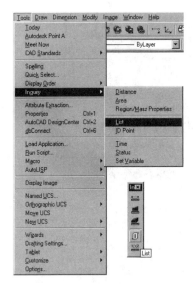

| Prompt | Response |
|---|---|
| | CLICK: **the down arrow** |
| | CLICK: **A-wall-int** |
| | **Close the dialog box and** PRESS: **Esc twice.** |

To change a property using the Properties window, select the object and then either enter a new value or select a new value from a list. You can leave the Properties window open, and you can also right-click in the Properties window to dock it.

## LIST

After you have changed the property of an entity and would like to confirm the change, or if you need additional information about an entity, using the List command is very helpful. The List command provides a screen display of the data stored for an entity.

**Use the List command to examine the data stored for one line of an interior wall:**

| Prompt | Response |
|---|---|
| Command: | **List** (or TYPE: **LIST<enter>**) |
| Select objects: | **Click only one line of an interior wall.** <br> **<enter>** |

Depending on the type of entity selected, the List command displays data information for the entity. For the line selected, this data information includes the Layer on which the line is drawn, the length of the line, and its position relative to the current UCS. If several entities are selected, the list can become very long. Use Esc to cancel the listing and return to the Command: prompt when the listing is longer than needed. PRESS: F2 to return to the graphics screen

## STATUS

The Status command reports the current values of many of the defaults, modes, and extents used by AutoCAD.

**Use the Status command to examine the Status Report for your drawing:**

| Prompt | Response |
| --- | --- |
| Command: | TYPE: **STATUS<enter>** |
| The Status Report appears, | |
| Press ENTER to continue: | **<enter>** |
| Command: | PRESS: **F2** (flip screen) |

## COLOR

To access the Select Color dialog box (Figure 8–14), CLICK: **Color...** under Format in the menu bar.

### Set Color ByLayer

We have discussed and used the entity property of Color as determined by the color assigned to a Layer, thus controlling the entity color "ByLayer." The entity is drawn with a layer current and inherits the color assigned to the layer. The Select Color dialog box sets the color for drawing entities. When ByLayer is selected, the entities subsequently drawn inherit the color of the layer on which they are drawn.

**FIGURE 8–14**
Select Color Dialog Box

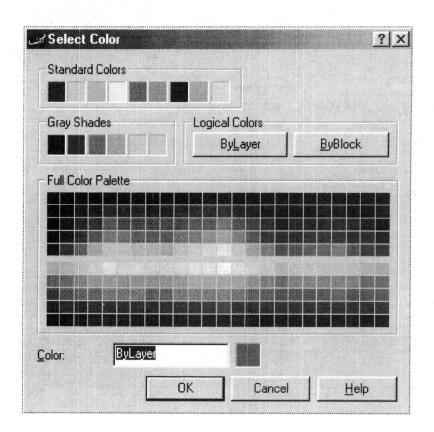

### Set Color Individually

The color property of entities can also be set individually. When a color, such as red, is selected from the Object Properties toolbar, or selected in the Select Color dialog box, the entities subsequently drawn inherit the color property red. The entities will be red regardless of the layer that is current when they are drawn.

To keep your drawing simple, do not mix the two methods of setting color. When a new color is needed, create a layer and assign the new color to that layer.

### Set Color ByBlock

When you have completed drawing the interior walls of the tenant space, you will draw the doors and insert them into the walls. The Wblock (Write Block) command will be used to make blocks of the two different types of doors used in the tenant space. Blocks can be stored on a floppy disk or hard disk and recalled and inserted into a drawing. Thus you can create a library of often-used parts, such as doors, windows, and furniture, using the Wblock command.

Most library parts that are blocks need to be drawn on the 0 Layer, which is the same as setting the color property to ByBlock. The reason for this is explained in the following examples.

### Example 1

A door (library part) is drawn on a Layer named DOOR that is assigned the color property red, and a Wblock is made of the door. The door block is inserted into a new project. Because the block was originally drawn on a layer named DOOR (color red) the layer name is dragged into the new drawing layer listing, and the door will be red, regardless of the layer current in the new drawing.

### Example 2

A door (library part) is drawn on the 0 Layer, Wblock is made of the door, and the door Wblock is inserted into a new project. Because the block was originally drawn on the 0 Layer, the door is generated on the drawing's current layer and inherits all properties of that layer.

Before any drawing entity that will be used as a block is drawn, you need to decide how it will be used in future drawings; that will determine the color property that it is assigned.

## LINETYPE

When the Linetype command is typed and entered or selected from the Format menu the Linetype Manager dialog box appears. Like the Color command, the linetype property can be set to ByLayer, individually, or ByBlock. Most library parts that are blocks should be drawn on the 0 Layer, which is the same as setting the linetype to ByBlock. When inserted as a block, the parts will inherit the linetype of the current layer.

## LINEWEIGHT

When Lineweight… is selected from the Format menu, the Lineweight Settings dialog box (Figure 8–15) is displayed. Like the Color and Linetype commands, the lineweight property

**Tip:** If everything you draw is one color regardless of the layer it is drawn on, check the color setting, and set it to ByLayer.

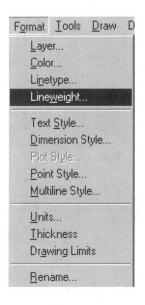

**FIGURE 8–15**
Lineweight Settings Dialog Box

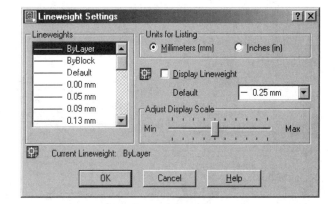

can be set to ByLayer or ByBlock or individually. It can also be set to default. The default value is initially set at .01″ or .25 mm, which you can change. A lineweight value of 0 is displayed in model space as one pixel wide and plots the thinnest lineweight available on the specified plotter. In paper space, lineweight values are displayed in the exact plotting width.

## MAKE OBJECT'S LAYER CURRENT

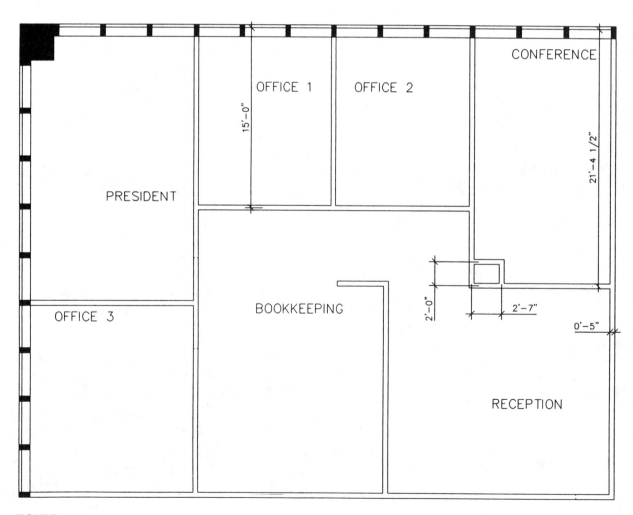

This is another command that is very useful on the Object Properties toolbar. When you activate this command and pick any object, the layer that object is on becomes current.

### On Your Own

1. **Set Layer A-wall-int current. Use Multiline with the correct Multiline Style current to finish drawing the interior walls of the tenant space. Use the dimensions shown in Figure 8–16. Remember that you can use the Modify commands (Extend, Trim, Edit Multiline, and so on) to fix the Multiline. To use Extend and Trim you must first explode the multiline.**

2. **Set FILL ON and regenerate the drawing.**

3. **Set 0 as the current layer. Use the dimensions shown in Figure 8–17 to draw the two door types—single door and double door—that will be defined as blocks and inserted into the tenant space. Pick any open space on your drawing and draw each door full size. In the following part of this exercise the Block and Wblock commands are used to define the doors as blocks.**

**FIGURE 8–16**
Use Multiline to Finish Drawing the Interior Walls (Scale: 1/8″ = 1'-0″)

## FIGURE 8–17
Two Door Types That Will Be Defined As Blocks and Inserted into the Tenant Space

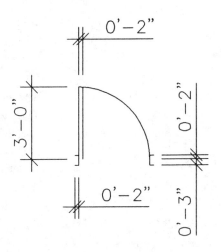

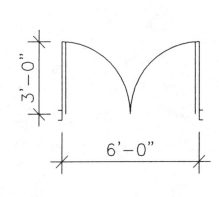

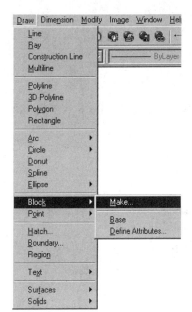

## BLOCK-MAKE...

The Block-Make... command allows you to define any part of a current drawing as a block. Copies of the block can be inserted only into that drawing. Copies of a block defined with the Block-Make... command cannot be used in any other drawing without using the AutoCAD DesignCenter (described in a later chapter).

**Use the Block-Make... command to define the single door drawing as a block named DOOR stored in the current drawing (Figures 8–18 and 8–19):**

| Prompt | Response |
|--------|----------|
| Command: | **Block-Make...** (or TYPE: **B<enter>**) |
| The Block Definition dialog box appears: | TYPE: **DOOR** in the Block name: box |

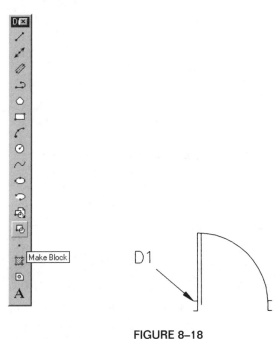

**FIGURE 8–18**
DOOR Block

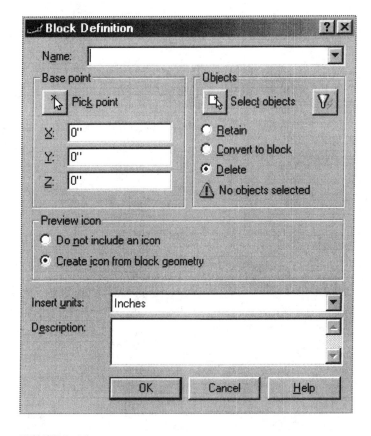

**FIGURE 8–19**
Block Definition Dialog Box

| Prompt | Response |
|---|---|
| | CLICK: **the Delete radio button under Objects** |
| | CLICK: **the Pick point button** |
| Specify block insertion base point: | **Osnap-Endpoint** |
| of: | **D1** (Figure 8–18) |
| The Block Definition dialog box appears: | CLICK: **the Select Objects button** |
| Select objects: | CLICK: **a point to locate the first corner of a selection window** |
| Specify opposite corner: | **Window only the single-door drawing.** |
| Select objects: | **<enter>** |
| The Block Definition dialog box appears: | CLICK: **OK** |
| The single door symbol is gone and is now defined as a block within your drawing. | |

The three radio buttons in the Objects area of the Block Definition dialog box specify what happens to the selected object (in this instance, the door) after you create the block:

**Retain**   After the block is created, the door symbol will remain in the drawing but will not be a block.

**Convert to Block**   After the block is created, the door symbol will remain in the drawing and will be a block.

**Delete**   After the block is created, the door symbol will be deleted.

A Block name can be 1 to 255 characters long. It may include only letters, numbers, and three special characters—$ (dollar sign), - (hyphen), and _ (underscore).

The Insert command is used later in this exercise to insert copies of the DOOR block into your drawing. The "Specify block insertion base point:" is the point on the inserted block to which the crosshair attaches. It allows you to position copies of the block exactly into the drawing. It is also the point around which the block can be rotated when it is inserted.

**Use the Block-Make... command to view a listing of the block just created:**

| Prompt | Response |
|---|---|
| Command: | **Block-Make...** (or TYPE: **B<enter>**) |
| The Block Definition dialog box appears: | CLICK: **the down arrow beside Name:** |
| The block name appears: | CLICK: **<cancel>** |

Blocks defined with the Block command can be inserted only into the drawing in which they are defined. When you want to build a library of parts defined as blocks that can be inserted into any drawing, use the Wblock command, described next.

## WBLOCK

The Wblock command allows you to define any part of a drawing or an entire drawing as a block. Blocks created with the Wblock command can be stored on a floppy disk or on the hard disk. Copies of the blocks can then be inserted into any drawing. These Wblocks become drawing files with a .dwg extension, just like any other AutoCAD drawing.

**Use Wblock to save the double-door drawing as a block on a floppy disk in drive A (Figures 8–20 and 8–21):**

| Prompt | Response |
|---|---|
| Command: | TYPE: **W<enter>** |
| The Write Block dialog box appears: | TYPE: **DOORD** in the File name: box |
| | CLICK: **the ... Button** (to the right of Location:) |

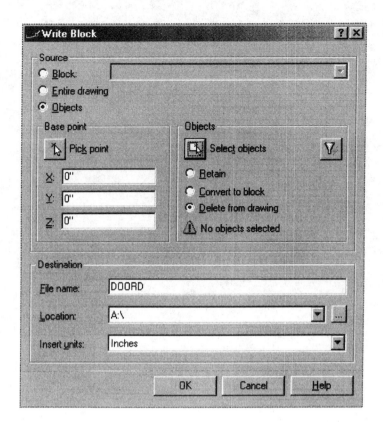

FIGURE 8–20
Write Block Dialog Box

FIGURE 8–21
DOORD Block

Note: You may save the DOORD block
to any drive that is convenient.

| Prompt | Response |
| --- | --- |
| The Browse for Folder dialog box appears: | CLICK: **3-1/2 Floppy A:** |
| | CLICK: **OK** |
| The Write Block dialog box appears: | CLICK: **Delete from drawing** |
| | CLICK: **Pick point button** |
| Specify insertion base point: | **Endpoint** |
| of | **D1** (Figure 8–21) |
| The Write Block dialog box appears: | CLICK: **the Select objects button** |
| Select objects: | **Window the entire double-door drawing.** |
| Select objects: | **<enter>** |
| The Write Block dialog box appears: | CLICK: **OK** |

The double-door drawing disappears and is saved as a block on drive A.

The double-door drawing is now saved as a drawing file with a .DWG file extension on the floppy disk in drive A. Copies of the DOORD drawing can be recalled and inserted into any other drawing. It is obvious that building a library of parts that can be inserted into any drawing saves time.

The three radio buttons in the Source area of the Write Block dialog box specify what you are defining as a Wblock:

**Block**    This helps define a block that is stored in a current drawing as a Wblock.

**Entire drawing**    Not only parts of a drawing but also an entire drawing can be defined as a block. Use 0,0,0 as the base point when defining an entire drawing as a block.

**Objects**    Allows you to select an object to define as a block.

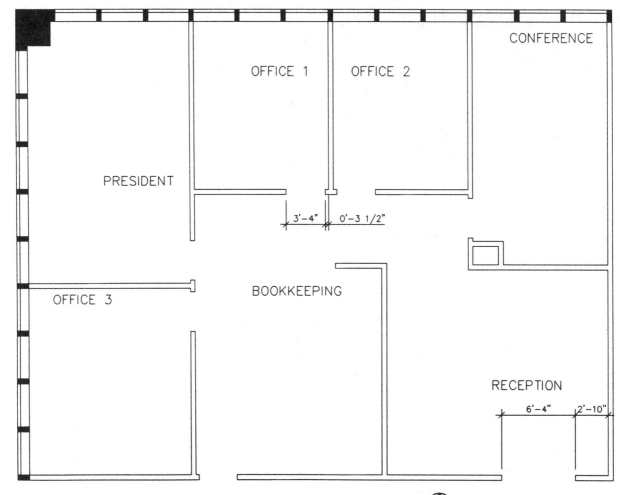

**FIGURE 8–22**
Use the Dimensions Shown to Draw the Openings for All Doors (Scale: 1/8″ = 1′-0″)

## On Your Own

1. **Use the Wblock command to write the DOOR block stored in your current drawing to the disk in drive A.**

2. **In the following part of this exercise, the doors will be inserted into the tenant space. Before the doors are inserted, openings for all doors must be added to the drawing. Each single door is 3′4″ wide, including the 2″ frame, so each opening for a single door is 3′4″ wide. As shown in Figure 8–22, the dimension from the corner of each room to the outside edge of the single door frame is 3-1/2″. The dimensions shown in Figure 8–22 for the door to OFFICE 1 apply to all single-door openings.**

Use the dimensions shown in Figure 8–22 to draw the openings for the five single doors (layer A-wall-int) and for the double-entry door (layer A-wall-ext). A helpful hint: Use Osnap-Tracking or ID with the Line command to draw the first door opening line, and Offset for the second door opening line. Then use Trim to complete the opening. If Trim does not work, explode the multiline first, then trim.

## INSERT-BLOCK...

The Insert-Block... command allows you to insert the defined blocks into your drawing. It may be used to insert a block defined with either the Block-Make command or the Wblock command.

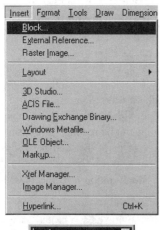

The Insert mode found in the Osnap menu allows you to snap to the insertion point of Text or a Block entity.

The following part of the exercise uses the Insert command to insert the DOOR block into the tenant space. Don't forget to zoom in on the area of the drawing on which you are working. Remember also that the insertion point of the DOOR block is the upper left corner of the door frame.

**Set Layer A-DOOR current. Use the Insert command to insert the block named DOOR into OFFICE 2 (Figures 8–23 and 8–24):**

**FIGURE 8–23**
Insert Dialog Box

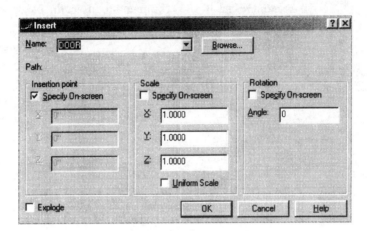

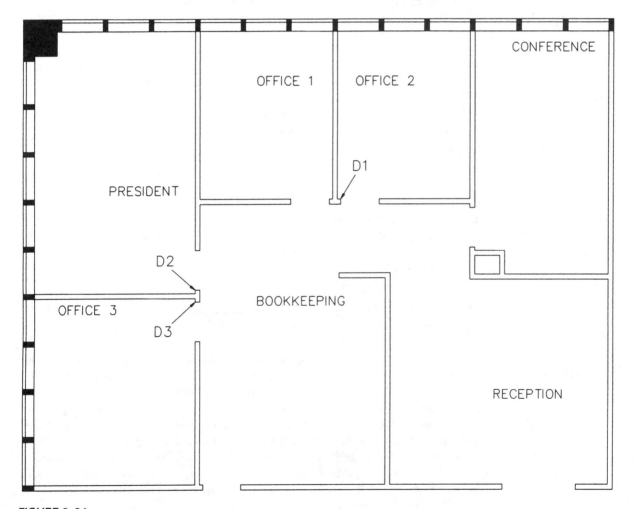

**FIGURE 8–24**
Use the Insert-Block… Command to Insert the Block Named DOOR (Scale: 1/8″ = 1′-0″)

| Prompt | Response |
|---|---|
| Command: | **Insert-Block...** (or TYPE: **I<enter>**) |
| The Insert dialog box appears (Figure 8–23): | CLICK: **DOOR** (in the Name: box) |
| | CLICK: **OK** |
| Specify insertion point or [Scale/X/Y/Z/ Rotate/PScale/PX/PY/PZ/PRotate]: | **Osnap-Intersection** |
| of | **D1** (Figure 8–24) |

**Use the Insert-Block... command to insert the block named DOOR into the president's office (Figure 8–24):**

| Prompt | Response |
|---|---|
| Command: | **Insert-Block...** (or TYPE: **I<enter>**) |
| The Insert dialog box appears with DOOR in the Name: box: | TYPE: **90** (in the Rotation Angle: input box) |
| | CLICK: **OK** |
| Specify insertion point or [Scale/X/Y/Z/ Rotate/PScale/PX/PY/PZ/PRotate]: | **Osnap-Intersection** |
| of | **D2** |

Because the doors were drawn on the 0 Layer, when inserted as blocks on the A-door Layer, they assumed the properties of the A-door Layer and are yellow.

When a copy of a block is inserted into the drawing, it is inserted as a single entity. The openings for the doors were prepared before the blocks were inserted, because the Trim command will not work to trim the walls out using a block as the cutting edge. Before the Trim command can be used, or a copy of a block can be edited, the block must be exploded with the Explode command. When a block is exploded, it returns to separate entities; it also changes color because it returns to the 0 Layer.

If you want a block to be inserted retaining its separate objects, check the Explode box in the lower left corner of the Insert dialog box.

### Insertion Point

The "Insertion point:" of the incoming block is the point where the "insertion base point" specified when the door was defined as a block will be placed. In the preceding exercises, the Osnap mode Intersection was used to position copies of the block exactly into the drawing. You can also use the ID command when inserting a block. Use the ID command to identify a point on the drawing, and then initiate the Insert-Block... command after the point has been located. You can then enter the "Insertion point:" of the block by using relative or polar coordinates to specify a distance from the established point location.

### X Scale Factor, Y Scale Factor

The X and Y scale factors provide a lot of flexibility in how the copy of the block will appear when it is inserted. The default X and Y scale factor is 1. A scale factor of 1 inserts the block as it was originally drawn.

**Note:** The Measure command draws a specified block at each mark between divided segments. The Divide command also draws a specified block at each mark between equal segments.

New scale factors can be typed and entered in response to the prompts. AutoCAD multiplies all X and Y dimensions of the block by the X and Y scale factors entered. By default, the Y scale factor equals the X scale, but a different Y scale factor can be entered separately. This is especially helpful when you are inserting a window block into a wall with windows of varying lengths. The block can be inserted, the X scale factor can be increased or decreased by the desired amount, and the Y scale factor can remain stable by being entered as 1.

Negative X or Y scale factors can be entered to insert mirror images of the block. When the X scale factor is negative, the Y scale factor remains positive. When the Y scale factor is negative, the X scale factor remains positive. Either a negative X or Y scale factor will work in the following example, but negative X will be used.

Use the Insert-Block... command, a negative X scale factor, and rotate the angle of the block to insert the block named DOOR into OFFICE 3 (Figure 8–24):

| Prompt | Response |
|---|---|
| Command: | **Insert-Block...** |

| Prompt | Response |
|---|---|
| The Insert dialog box appears with DOOR in the Name: box: | TYPE: **–1** (in the X scale input box) |
| | TYPE: **90** (in the Rotation Angle: input box) |
| | CLICK: **OK** |
| Specify insertion point or [Scale/X/Y/Z/ Rotate/PScale/PX/PY/PZ/PRotate]: | **Osnap-Intersection** |
| of | **D3** |

## On Your Own

See Figure 8–25.

1. **Use the Insert-Block... command to complete the insertion of all doors in the tenant space.**

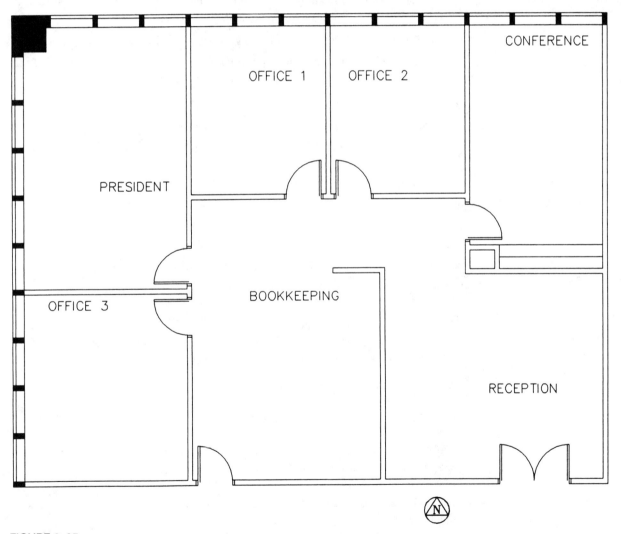

**FIGURE 8–25**
Exercise 8–1: Tenant Space Floor Plan (Scale: 1/8″ = 1′-0″)

2. Set Layer A-flor-wdwk current. Draw two lines to show the cabinets in the conference room. The upper cabinets are 12″ deep.

3. Set Layer A-flor-iden current. Create a new Text Style with the Simplex font. Use Dtext, height 9″, to type the identifying name in each room. Use the approximate locations as shown in Figure 8–25; the names can be moved as needed when furniture is inserted into the drawing.

## Inserting Entire Drawings as Blocks

The Insert-Block... command can be used to insert into the current drawing any drawing that has not been defined as a block and to define it as a block within that drawing. Simply use the Insert-Block... command to insert the drawing. Use the Browse... button in the Insert dialog box to locate the drawing.

## Redefining an Inserted Block Using the Block Command

The appearance of any block, defined as a block within a drawing, and all copies of the block within the drawing may be changed easily. As an example, we use the DOOR block that is defined as a block within the tenant space drawing. The following steps describe how to change the appearance of a block and all copies of the block that have already been inserted within a drawing. If you use this example to change the appearance of the DOOR block, be sure to return it to the original appearance.

1. Insert a copy of the DOOR block in an open space in the tenant space drawing.

2. Explode the DOOR block and edit it so that it is different from the original DOOR block.

3. Use the Block-Make... command as follows to redefine the block.

| Prompt | Response |
|---|---|
| Command: | **Block-Make...** |
| The Block Definition dialog box appears: | TYPE: **DOOR** in the Block name: box |
| | CLICK: **Pick Point** |
| Specify insertion base point: | **Pick the insertion base point**. |
| The Block Definition dialog box appears: | CLICK: **Select Objects** |
| Select objects: | **Window the single door.** |
| Select objects: | <enter> |
| The Block Definition dialog box appears: | CLICK: **OK** |
| The AutoCAD Warning "Door is already defined. Do you want to redefine it?" appears: | CLICK: **Yes** |

The DOOR block is redefined, and all copies of the DOOR block that are in the drawing are redrawn with the new definition of the DOOR block.

## Advantages of Using Blocks

1. A library of drawing parts allows you to draw an often-used part once instead of many times.

2. Blocks can be combined with customized menus to create a complete applications environment around AutoCAD that provides the building and furnishings parts that are used daily. Customized menus are discussed in Chapter 16.

3. Once a block is defined and inserted into the drawing, you can update all references to that block by redefining the block.

4. Because AutoCAD treats a block as a single entity, less disk space is used for each insertion of a block. For example, the door contains an arc and approximately 10 lines. If each door were drawn separately, the arcs and lines would take up a lot of disk space.

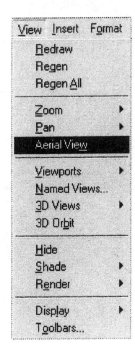

When inserted as a block, the arcs and lines are treated as one definition. The more complicated a block, the greater is the disk space saved. A block that is inserted as exploded is inserted as separate entities and does not save disk space.

## MINSERT

The MINSERT (Multiple Insert) command (TYPE: **MINSERT<enter>**) allows you to insert multiple copies of a block in a rectangular array pattern. Only a single entity reference is created with the MINSERT command, and the standard scaling and rotation option prompts are supplied. There is no way to edit a Minsert because it cannot be exploded.

## Aerial View

Aerial View works in all model space views. It displays a view of the drawing in a separate window that you can move or resize. When you keep Aerial View open, you can zoom or pan without choosing a command.

### On Your Own

**1. Use Aerial View to move around your drawing of the tenant space.**

## NAMED VIEWS

Many of the drawings that architects and space planners work with are large. The Named Views command is useful when you are working with a complex drawing. It allows you to window a portion of the drawing and save it as a named view that can be recalled to the screen with the Named Views-Restore command. For example, you may View Window each room in the tenant space and assign a View Name; then you can recall each room for editing by using the Named Views-Restore command.

**Use Zoom-All to view the entire tenant space drawing. Use the Named Views command to create, name, and restore a view of the president's office:**

| Prompt | Response |
|---|---|
| Command: | **Named Views**<br>(or TYPE: **V<enter>**) |
| The View Control dialog box appears: | CLICK: **New...** |
| The New View dialog box appears: | TYPE: **PRESIDENT** in the View name: box |
| | CLICK: **Define window** (radio button) |
| | CLICK: **Define View Window button**<br>(with the small arrow on it) |
| Specify first corner: | **Window only the president's office.** |
| Specify opposite corner: | |
| The New View dialog box appears: | CLICK: **OK** |
| The View Control dialog box appears: | CLICK: **OK** |
| Command: | **<enter>** |
| The View Control dialog box appears: | CLICK: **PRESIDENT** |
| | CLICK: **Set Current** |
| | CLICK: **OK** |

The View named PRESIDENT appears on the screen.

When you first enter the Drawing Editor, you can recall a named view by using the Named View... command. You can also print or plot a portion of a drawing by supplying the view name.

### Delete

Delete removes one or more views from the list of saved Views. CLICK: **the view name**, then CLICK: **the Delete button** on your keyboard.

### On Your Own

Use the Named Views... command to create and name a view of each room in the tenant space.

## SAVE

When you have completed Exercise 8–1, save your work in at least two places.

## PLOT

Use a Layout Wizard or Page Setup to create a Layout tab named Floor Plan. Plot or print Exercise 8–1 to scale.

# EXERCISE 8–2
# Office I Floor Plan

1. Draw the office I floor plan as shown in Figure 8–26. Use the dimensions shown or use an Architectural scale of 1/8″ = 1′-0″ to measure the office floor plan, and draw it full scale. Use Multiline or Polyline to draw the walls.
2. Plot or print the drawing to scale.

# EXERCISE 8–3
# Office II Floor Plan

1. Draw the office II floor plan as shown in Figure 8–27. Use the dimensions shown or use an Architectural scale of 1/8″ = 1′-0″ to measure the office floor plan, and draw it full scale. Use Multiline or Polyline to draw the walls.
2. Plot or print the drawing to scale.

# EXERCISE 8–4
# House Floor Plan

1. Draw the lower and upper levels of the house floor plan as shown in Figure 8–28. Use the dimensions shown or use an Architectural scale of 1/8″ = 1′-0″ to measure the house floor plan, and draw it full scale. Use Multiline or Polyline to draw the walls.
2. Plot or print the drawing to scale.

# EXERCISE 8–5
# Country Club Floor Plan

1. Draw the country club floor plan as shown in Figure 8–29. Use the dimensions shown or an Architectural scale of 1/16″ = 1′-0″ to measure the country club floor plan, and draw it full scale. Use Multiline or Polyline to draw the walls.
2. Plot or print the drawing to scale.

**FIGURE 8–26** ⟶
Exercise 8–2: Office I Floor Plan
(Scale: 1/8″ = 1′-0″) (Courtesy
of Business Interiors Design
Department, Irving, Texas, and
GTE Directories.)

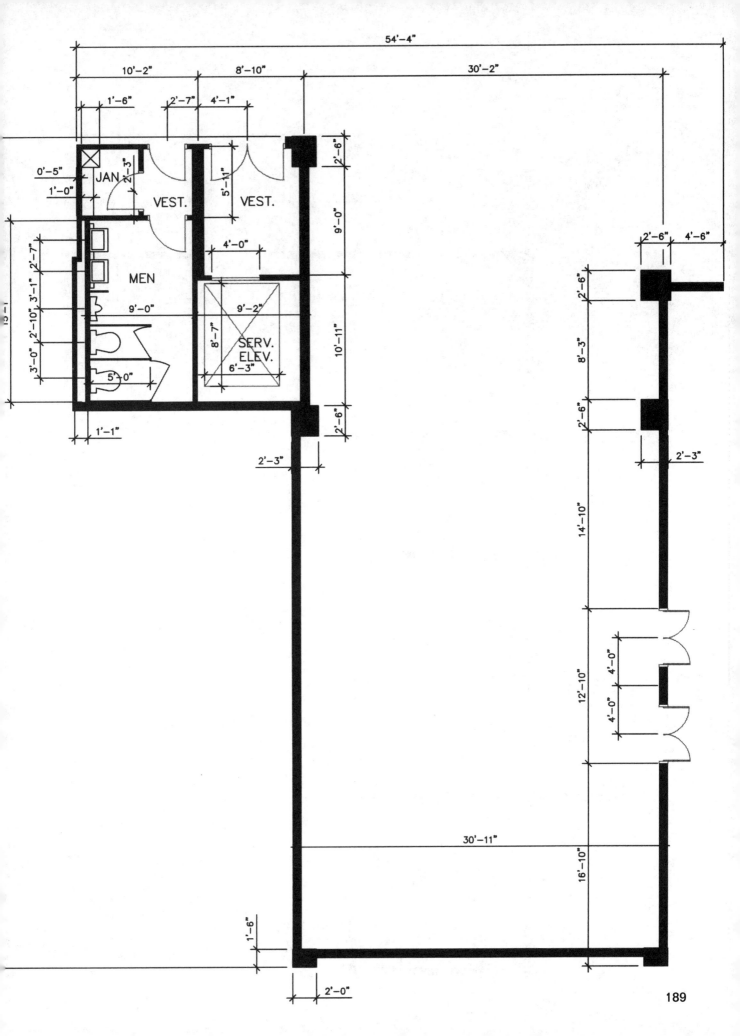

189

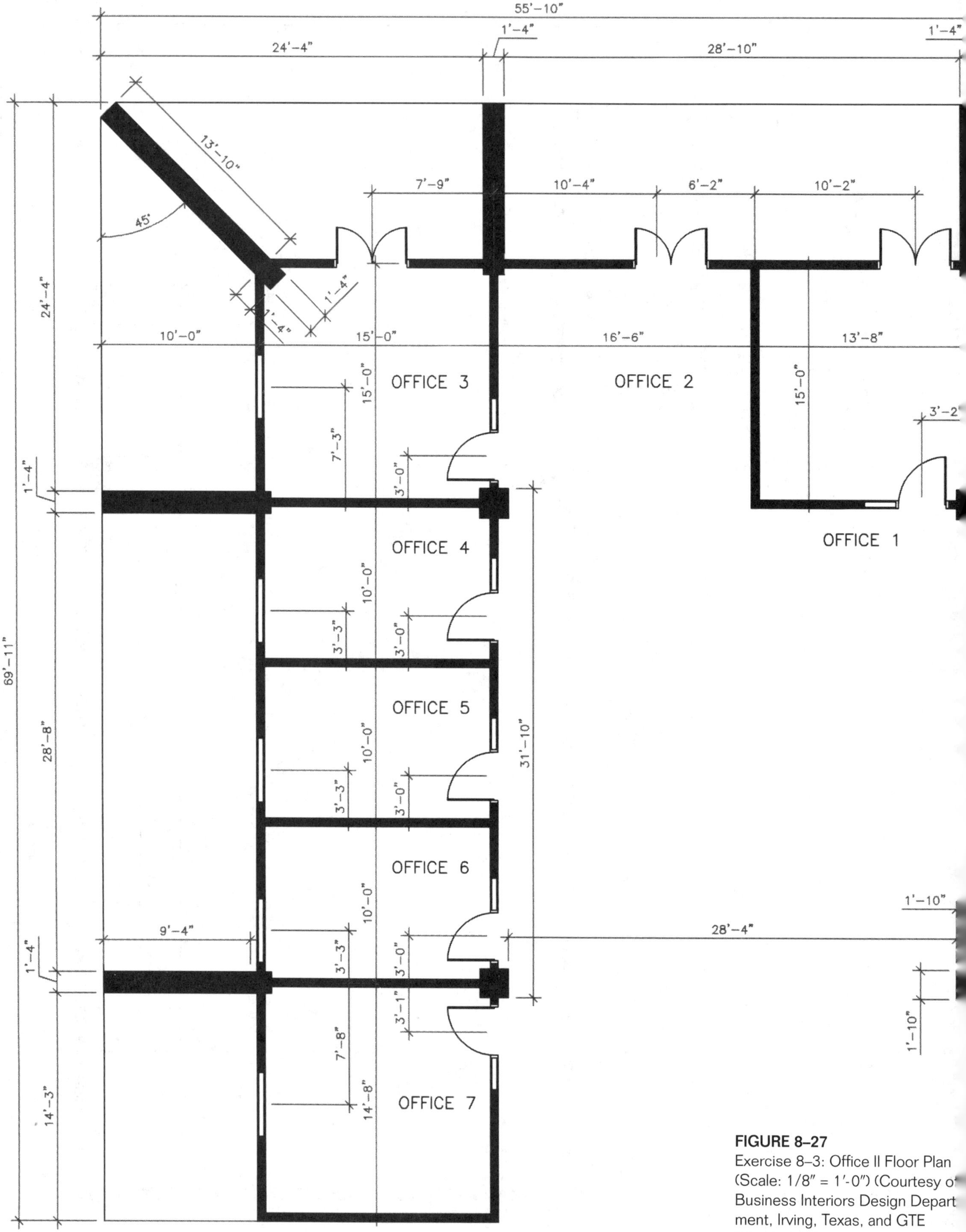

**FIGURE 8–27**

Exercise 8–3: Office II Floor Plan (Scale: 1/8″ = 1′-0″) (Courtesy of Business Interiors Design Department, Irving, Texas, and GTE Directories.)

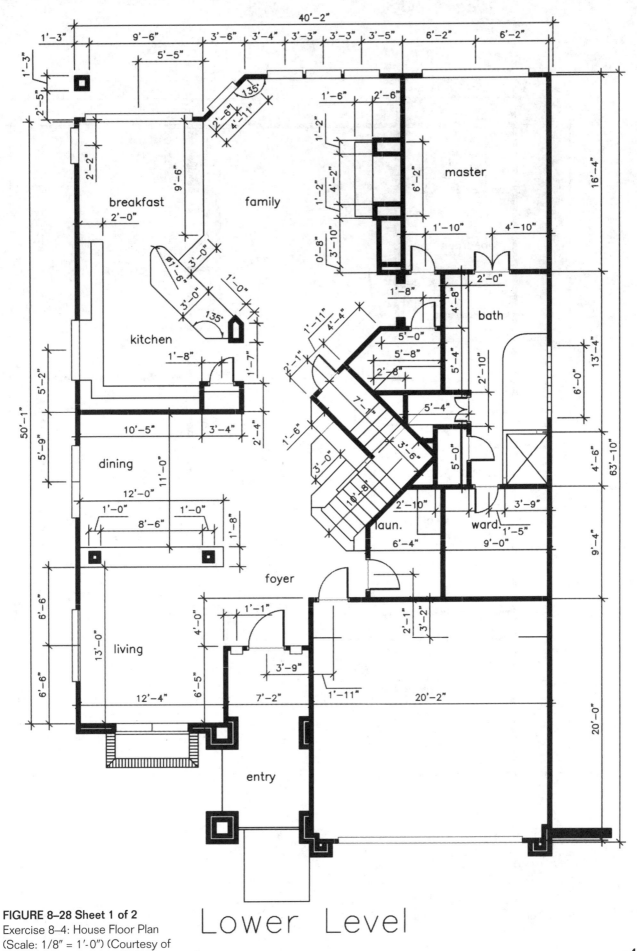

**FIGURE 8–28 Sheet 1 of 2**

Exercise 8–4: House Floor Plan
(Scale: 1/8″ = 1′-0″) (Courtesy of
John Brooks, AIA, Dallas, Texas.)

Lower Level

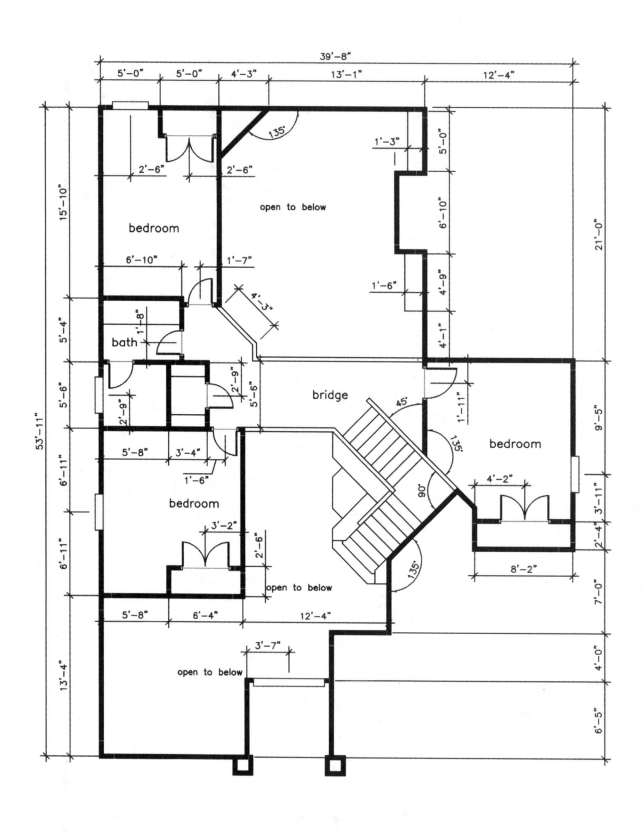

Upper Level

FIGURE 8–28 Sheet 2 of 2

Part II: Two-Dimensional AutoCAD

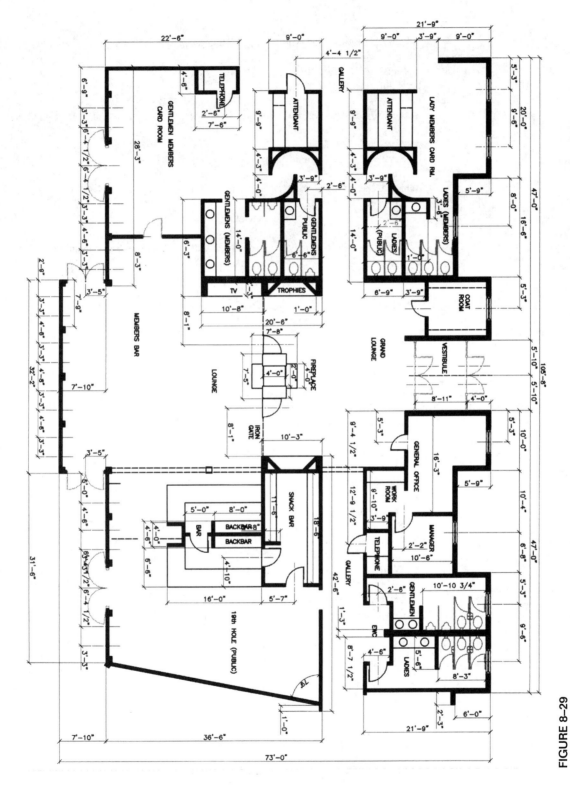

**FIGURE 8–29**

Exercise 8–5: Country Club Floor Plan (Scale: 1/16" = 1'-0") (Courtesy of S. Vic Jones and Associates, AIA, Dallas, Texas.)

# REVIEW QUESTIONS

1. What is the maximum number of lines you can draw at the same time with Multiline?
   - a. 2
   - d. 12
   - b. 4
   - e. 16
   - c. 8

2. Which of the following Multiline justification options can be used to draw a three-line wall using the middle line?
   - a. Top
   - d. Left
   - b. Right
   - e. Zero
   - c. Bottom

3. When you are setting a new Multiline Style what must you pick in the Multiline Style dialog box to set the new style current?
   - a. Add
   - d. Load...
   - b. Save...
   - e. Current
   - c. New

4. Which of the following may *not* be changed with the Change command?
   - a. Color
   - d. Circle radius
   - b. Layer
   - e. Polyline width
   - c. Text position

5. Which of the following may *not* be changed with the Properties... command?
   - a. Color
   - d. Thickness
   - b. Layer
   - e. Drawing name
   - c. Linetype

6. Which of the following commands tells you the layer a line is on and its length?
   - a. Status
   - b. Dist
   - c. Area
   - d. List
   - e. Utility

7. On which layer should most blocks be constructed?
   - a. 0 Layer
   - b. Any layer with a color other than white
   - c. Blocks Layer
   - d. BL Layer
   - e. Any layer other than the 0 Layer

8. If a block is inserted with a check in the Explode block, which of the following is true?
   - a. The block must be exploded before it can be edited.
   - b. Each element of the block is a separate object.
   - c. The block assumes the color of the current layer.
   - d. A Wblock is created with the same name.
   - e. AutoCAD will not accept the block name.

9. The Wblock command does which of the following?
   - a. Creates a block that can be used on the current drawing only
   - b. Creates a drawing file on any disk
   - c. Creates a drawing file on the hard disk only
   - d. Creates blocks of parts of the current drawing only
   - e. Uses only named blocks on the current drawing

10. Which scale factor can be used to create a mirror image of a block with the use of the Insert-Block... command?
    - a. Negative X, Positive Y
    - b. Positive X, Positive Y
    - c. Negative X, Negative Y
    - d. Mirrored images cannot be created with the Insert-Block... command.

11. List the command you must use to set a new multiline style.

12. List five properties that can be changed with the Change command.

    1. _____

    2. _____

    3. _____

    4. _____

    5. _____

13. List the command that allows you to change any property.

    _____

14. Describe how to use the Block-Make.. . command to redefine, on the current drawing, seven insertions of the block DOOR using an updated drawing file named DOOR.

    _____

    _____

15. Describe the basic difference between Block-Make… and Wblock.

    _____

    _____

    _____

16. List the command that allows you to save and restore a view.

    _____

17. Describe what happens when a block is created using the Block-Make… command, and the Retain objects radio button is selected.

    _____

    _____

18. Describe how several entities drawn on a single layer may each be a different color.

    _____

    _____

19. List four advantages of using blocks.

    1. _____

    _____

    2. _____

    _____

    3. _____

    _____

    4. _____

    _____

20. Compare the characteristics of the Minsert command with those of the Insert command.

    _____

    _____

    _____

    _____

# Dimensioning and Area Calculations

## OBJECTIVES

When you have completed this chapter, you will be able to:

☐ Understand the function of each dimensioning variable.
☐ Set dimensioning variables.
☐ Save and restore dimensioning styles.
☐ Correctly use the following commands and settings:

| | | | |
|---|---|---|---|
| Aligned | Cal | Leader | Override |
| Align Text | Center Mark | Linear | Radius |
| Angular | Continue | Newtext | Style. . . |
| Area | Diameter | Oblique | Update |
| Baseline | Dimension Edit | Ordinate | |

## SIX BASIC TYPES OF DIMENSIONS

Dimensioning with AutoCAD can be fun and easy when the many options under the Dimension menu are thoroughly understood. Before dimensioning the tenant space floor plan completed in Chapter 8, we will describe some of those options.

Six basic types of dimensions can be automatically created using AutoCAD. They are linear, aligned, ordinate, radius, diameter, and angular. They are listed in the Dimension menu and are shown on the Dimension toolbar. Each dimension type can be activated by selecting one of the following:

**Linear**   For dimensioning horizontal, vertical, and angled lines.
**Aligned**   For showing the length of features that are drawn at an angle.
**Ordinate**   To display the $x$ or $y$ coordinate of a feature.
**Radius**   To create radius dimensioning for arcs and circles.
**Diameter**   To create diameter dimensioning for arcs and circles.
**Angular**   For dimensioning angles.

Additionally, leaders and center marks can be drawn by selecting Leader or Center Mark.

The appearance of these six basic types of dimensions, leaders, and center marks when they are drawn and plotted is controlled by settings called *dimensioning variables*.

## DIMENSIONING VARIABLES

A list of dimensioning variables and a brief description of each variable appears when STATUS is typed from the Dim: prompt. Figure 9–1 shows the list of dimensioning variables and the default setting for each, as they appear when STATUS is typed from the Dim: prompt and Architectural units have been set.

Some variables do not apply to the standard dimensioning techniques that architects and space planners use for drawings and will be less important to you than others. Once

FIGURE 9–1
Dimensioning Variables

| | | |
|---|---|---|
| DIMASO | Off | Create dimension objects |
| DIMSTYLE | Standard | Current dimension style (read-only) |
| | | |
| DIMADEC | 0 | Angular decimal places |
| DIMALT | Off | Alternate units selected |
| DIMALTD | 2 | Alternate unit decimal places |
| DIMALTF | 25.4000 | Alternate unit scale factor |
| DIMALTRND | 0" | Alternate units rounding value |
| DIMALTTD | 2 | Alternate tolerance decimal places |
| DIMALTTZ | 0 | Alternate tolerance zero suppression |
| DIMALTU | 2 | Alternate units |
| DIMALTZ | 0 | Alternate unit zero suppression |
| DIMAPOST | | Prefix and suffix for alternate text |
| DIMASZ | 3/16" | Arrow size |
| DIMATFIT | 3 | Arrow and text fit |
| DIMAUNIT | 0 | Angular unit format |
| DIMAZIN | 0 | Angular zero supression |
| DIMBLK | ClosedFilled | Arrow block name |
| DIMBLK1 | ClosedFilled | First arrow block name |
| DIMBLK2 | ClosedFilled | Second arrow block name |
| DIMCEN | 1/16" | Center mark size |
| DIMCLRD | BYBLOCK | Dimension line and leader color |
| DIMCLRE | BYBLOCK | Extension line color |
| DIMCLRT | BYBLOCK | Dimension text color |
| DIMDEC | 4 | Decimal places |
| DIMDLE | 0" | Dimension line extension |
| DIMDLI | 3/8" | Dimension line spacing |
| DIMDSEP | | Decimal separator |
| DIMEXE | 3/16" | Extension above dimension line |
| DIMEXO | 1/16" | Extension line origin offset |
| DIMFRAC | 0 | Fraction format |
| DIMGAP | 1/16" | Gap from dimension line to text |
| DIMJUST | 0 | Justification of text on dimension line |
| DIMLDRBLK | ClosedFilled | Leader block name |
| DIMLFAC | 1.0000 | Linear unit scale factor |
| DIMLIM | Off | Generate dimension limits |
| DIMLUNIT | 2 | Linear unit format |
| DIMLWD | -2 | Dimension line and leader lineweight |
| DIMLWE | -2 | Extension line lineweight |
| DIMPOST | | Prefix and suffix for dimension text |
| DIMRND | 0" | Rounding value |
| DIMSAH | Off | Separate arrow blocks |
| DIMSCALE | 1.0000 | Overall scale factor |
| DIMSD1 | Off | Suppress the first dimension line |
| DIMSD2 | Off | Suppress the second dimension line |
| DIMSE1 | Off | Suppress the first extension line |
| DIMSE2 | Off | Suppress the second extension line |
| DIMSOXD | Off | Suppress outside dimension lines |
| DIMTAD | 0 | Place text above the dimension line |
| DIMTDEC | 4 | Tolerance decimal places |
| DIMTFAC | 1.0000 | Tolerance text height scaling factor |
| DIMTIH | On | Text inside extensions is horizontal |
| DIMTIX | Off | Place text inside extensions |
| DIMTM | 0" | Minus tolerance |
| DIMTMOVE | 0 | Text movement |
| DIMTOFL | Off | Force line inside extension lines |
| DIMTOH | On | Text outside horizontal |
| DIMTOL | Off | Tolerance dimensioning |
| DIMTOLJ | 1 | Tolerance vertical justification |
| DIMTP | 0" | Plus tolerance |
| DIMTSZ | 0" | Tick size |
| DIMTVP | 0.0000 | Text vertical position |
| DIMTXSTY | Standard | Text style |
| DIMTXT | 3/16" | Text height |
| DIMTZIN | 0 | Tolerance zero suppression |
| DIMUPT | Off | User positioned text |
| DIMZIN | 0 | Zero suppression |

the variables are set you may make a template (or a prototype drawing) containing all the settings (Layers, Units, Limits, etc.) for a particular type of drawing. Notice that the variable names begin to make sense when you know what they are. For example: DIMSCALE is dimensioning scale, DIMTXT is dimensioning text, and DIMSTYLE is dimensioning style. The following describes the function of each dimensioning variable.

## Dimensioning Variables That Govern Sizes, Distances, and Offsets

Before dimensioning a drawing, you must establish standards for how each element of the dimension will appear. For example, you may decide that the dimension text size will be 1/8″ high and that tick marks (instead of arrows) will be used at the ends of the dimension lines. The following describes the dimensioning variables that govern the sizes, distances, and offsets of the dimensioning elements and provides an example of each element.

### DIMTXT—text height

**Tip:** If the current Text Style height setting is other than 0, the DIMTXT setting has no effect on the height of dimensioning text. Be sure to set Text Style height to 0.

In Chapter 6, how to set a new text style and font was described. The dimension text uses the same font that is current in the Text Style setting. When the current Text Style setting does not have a fixed text height, the value of the DIMTXT variable specifies the height of the dimension text. Figure 9–2 shows dimension text.

**FIGURE 9–2**
Dimension Text and Tick Marks

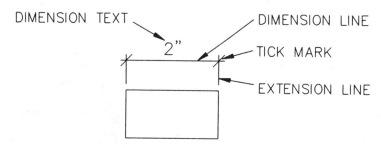

### DIMTSZ—tick size

Tick marks are small, 45° lines drawn at the point where the dimension line meets the extension line. The value of the DIMTSZ variable specifies the size of the tick drawn at the ends of dimension lines for linear, radius, and diameter dimensioning. The value entered specifies half the tick size. For a 1/8″ tick, enter a DIMTSZ value of 1/16″. When the DIMTSZ value is zero and DIMASZ (arrow size) is a positive value, arrows are drawn instead of ticks. Figure 9–2 shows ticks drawn at the ends of linear dimension lines.

### DIMEXO—extension line origin offset

Extension lines extend from the object being measured to the dimension line. The value of the DIMEXO variable specifies how far the extension line is offset from the points picked on the object that is to be dimensioned. For example, you may snap precisely on the corners of a building, but the extension lines will be offset from the corners by the distance specified for the DIMEXO value. Figure 9–3 shows an extension line offset.

### DIMEXE—extension above dimension line

The value of the DIMEXE variable specifies how far the extension line extends above the dimension line. Figure 9–3 shows an extension line extension.

### DIMDLE—dimension line extension

The value of the DIMDLE variable specifies how far the dimension line extends past the extension line when ticks are specified instead of arrows. Figure 9–3 shows a dimension line extension.

**FIGURE 9–3**
Extension Line Offset, Extension Line Extension, and Dimension Line Extension

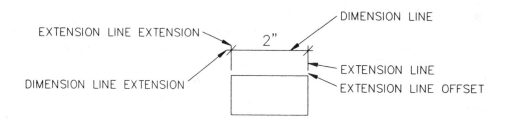

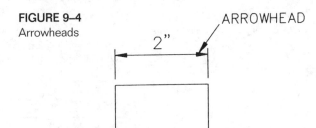

**FIGURE 9-4**
Arrowheads

### DIMASZ—arrow size

Arrowheads instead of ticks may be drawn at the ends of dimension lines. The value of the DIMASZ variable specifies the length of the arrowheads drawn. When DIMTSZ (tick size) is set to a value other than zero, the DIMASZ variable has no effect for linear, aligned, radius, and diameter dimensioning, and ticks are drawn. Figure 9-4 shows arrowheads drawn at the ends of linear dimension lines.

A leader is used to show dimension text or other notes on a drawing. The value of DIMASZ also specifies the length of the arrowhead drawn at the end of a leader when the Leader command is used. When DIMASZ is zero, no arrowhead is attached to the leader. When the value of DIMASZ is other than zero, it specifies the size of the arrowhead at the end of the leader. If the value of DIMASZ is a positive number and an arrowhead is not drawn on the leader, increase the leader length to allow for the arrow. Figure 9-5 shows an arrowhead drawn at the end of a leader.

The value of DIMASZ also specifies the length of arrowheads drawn in angular dimensioning. Figure 9-5 shows arrowheads drawn at the end of an angular dimension line arc.

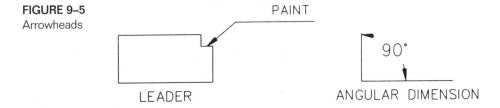

**FIGURE 9-5**
Arrowheads

### DIMDLI—dimension line spacing

After the first segment of a line is dimensioned with a linear dimension, the Continue command automatically continues the next linear dimension. The next linear dimension uses the second extension line of the previous linear dimension as its first extension line. Typically, the dimension lines continue along on the same horizontal line. Sometimes, when the space is small and to avoid drawing over the previous dimension, the continued dimension line is offset. The DIMDLI variable setting determines the size of the offset. Figure 9-6 shows typical linear dimensioning with the Continue command and an offset linear dimension with the Continue command.

After the first segment of a line is dimensioned with a linear dimension, the Baseline command automatically continues the next linear dimension from the baseline (first

**FIGURE 9-6**
Typical Linear Dimensioning with the Continue Command, and an Offset Linear Dimension with the Continue Command

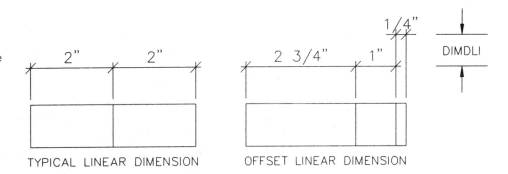

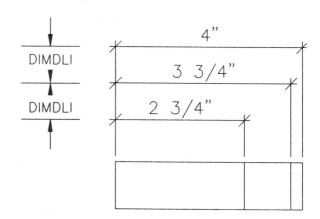

**FIGURE 9–7**
Linear Dimensioning with the Baseline Command

extension line) of the first linear dimension. The new dimension line is offset to avoid drawing on top of the previous dimension. The DIMDLI variable controls the size of the offset. Figure 9–7 shows a linear dimension with the Baseline command.

### DIMCEN—center mark size

A center mark is the "+" that marks the center of a circle or arc. A center line includes the "+" and adds lines that intersect the circumference of the circle or arc. The value of DIM-CEN controls the drawing of circle and arc center marks and center lines by the Diameter, Radius, and Center Mark commands.

The Diameter and Radius commands provide both the center mark (or center line) and dimensions. The Center Mark command is used to draw only a center mark (or center line) and does not provide dimensions.

When the value of DIMCEN is zero, center marks and center lines are not drawn. When the value of DIMCEN is greater than zero, it specifies the size of the center mark. The value of DIMCEN specifies the size of one arm of the "+". For example, if the value of DIMCEN is 1/8″, the center mark is 1/4″ wide and high overall. When the value of DIMCEN is less than zero (negative), center lines are drawn rather than center marks. The negative value specifies the size of one arm of the mark portion of the center line and how far outside the circumference of the circle the center line extends. For Radius and Diameter dimensioning, center marks or center lines are drawn only when the dimension line is placed outside the circle or arc. Figure 9–8 shows a center mark and a center line. The center mark (on the left) is a positive DIMCEN value. The center line (on the right) is a negative DIMCEN value.

**Note:** A center mark or center line is not drawn with the Diameter and Radius commands when the dimension line is inside the circle or arc.

**FIGURE 9–8**
Center Mark and Center line

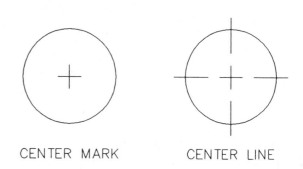

CENTER MARK          CENTER LINE

### DIMGAP—gap from dimension line to text

Dimension text may be placed above a solid dimension line or along the dimension line when the dimension line is broken. The DIMGAP variable specifies the gap or distance AutoCAD maintains on each side of the dimension text when the dimension line is broken. Figure 9–9 shows the gap from the dimension line to the dimension text.

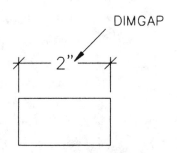

**FIGURE 9–9**
Gap from Dimension Line to Text

DIMGAP

2″

## Dimensioning Variable for Overall Scale Factor

### DIMSCALE—overall scale factor

The preceding section described the dimensioning variables that govern the sizes, distances, and offsets of dimensioning elements. It is important to understand how the value that is entered for a variable that governs a size, distance, or offset of a dimensioning element relates to your drawing as it appears on the screen and when the drawing is plotted.

When a building that is drawn full scale is displayed on the screen, the dimensioning elements will be drawn in a larger scale and will thus measure larger than when plotted at a scale of 1/8″ = 12″. DIMSCALE is the variable that controls the overall scale factor, or how the dimensioning parts appear on the screen display while you are drawing full scale and how they appear when plotted. For example, if you decide that the dimensioning text (DIMTXT) will be 1/8″ high when a drawing is plotted, enter 1/8″ for the DIMTXT value. If you plan to plot the drawing at 1/2″ = 12″, set DIMSCALE to 24. While you are drawing full scale, the text height will be 1/8″ × 24″, or 3″ high, on the screen. When the drawing is plotted at 1/2″ = 12″, the entire drawing including the dimensioning is reduced by a scale factor of 24 (1/2 = 12, 1 = 24).

The DIMSCALE for a drawing that is plotted at 1/4″ = 12″ is 48 (1/4 = 12, 1 = 48), and for a plotting ratio of 1/8″ = 12″ the DIMSCALE is 96 (1/8 = 12, 1 = 96).

## Dimensioning Variable for Length Factor

### DIMLFAC—linear unit scale factor

The DIMLFAC setting is the length factor by which all measured linear distances are multiplied before AutoCAD completes the dimension text on the drawing. The default, 1, is for drawing full scale, where one drawing unit equals one dimensioning unit. When you are drawing at a scale of 1/2″ = 1″ or 6″ = 12″, the DIMLFAC is set to 2 and all measured distances are multiplied by 2. When you are drawing at a scale of 1/4″ = 12″, the DIMLFAC value is 48 and all measured distances are multiplied by 48. Because you will be drawing at full scale only, use the DIMLFAC default setting of 1.

## Dimensioning Variables That Affect Location, Orientation, and Appearance of Dimension Text and Dimension Lines

### DIMDEC—decimal places

This variable sets the number of decimal places to the right of the decimal point for the dimension value.

### DIMDSEP—decimal separator

Specifies a single character to use instead of a period to separate decimal values from whole numbers when decimal values are used.

When prompted, type a single character at the command line. The DIMDSEP character is used instead of the default decimal point.

### DIMTXSTY—text style

Specifies the text style of the dimension. The text style chosen must be defined in the current drawing.

### DIMLUNIT—linear unit format

Sets Units for all dimension types except Angular.

1. Scientific
2. Decimal
3. Engineering
4. Architectural
5. Fractional
6. Windows Desktop (decimal format using Control Panel settings for decimal separator and number grouping symbols)

### DIMFRAC—fraction format

Sets the fraction format when DIMLUNIT is set to 4 (Architectural) or 5 (Fractional).

**0**  Horizontal
**1**  Diagonal
**2**  Not stacked (for example, 1/2)

### DIMLWD—dimension line and leader lineweight

Sets the lineweight for dimension lines and leaders.

### DIMLWE—extension line lineweight

Sets the lineweight for extension lines.

**Note:** When the DIMLWD and DIMLWE setting shows –2, the lineweight is set to ByBlock.

### DIMTAD—place text above the dimension line

The DIMTAD setting controls the vertical placement of dimension text that is drawn inside or outside the extension lines (text is placed outside the extension lines when there is not enough room for it inside the extension lines).

**0**  Centers the dimension text between the extension lines. When DIMTAD is OFF, DIMTVP controls the vertical placement of text. Figure 9–10 shows linear dimension lines and text that is inside the extension lines, with DIMTAD ON (1) and OFF (0).
**1**  When DIMTAD is ON, the dimension text is placed above the dimension line. The dimension line is not broken and is a single, solid line. DIMTIH and DIMTOH (described next) must be OFF for DIMTAD to work for vertical dimensions that are inside or outside the extension lines.
**2**  Places the dimension text on the side of the dimension line farthest away from the defining points.
**3**  Places the dimension text to conform to a Japanese Industrial Standards (JIS) representation.

### DIMTVP—text vertical position

When DIMTAD is OFF, AutoCAD uses the DIMTVP value to determine the vertical placement of text above or below a solid dimension line or along a split dimension line. A value of .6 to −.6 splits the dimension line to accommodate the dimension text. A value of 1 places the text above a single, solid dimension line. A value of −1 places the text below a single, solid dimension line. Figure 9–10 shows dimension lines with different DIMTVP settings.

**FIGURE 9–10**
DIMTAD and DIMTVP Settings

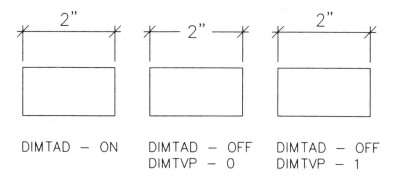

**Part II: Two-Dimensional AutoCAD**

### DIMTIH—text inside extension is horizontal

The DIMTIH setting controls the orientation of dimension text that fits between the extension lines. When DIMTIH is ON, the text is always oriented horizontally. When DIMTAD is ON and DIMTIH is ON, the vertical dimension lines are split to accommodate the horizontal text. When DIMTIH is OFF, the text is aligned with the dimension line. Figure 9–11 shows linear dimension text with DIMTIH ON and OFF.

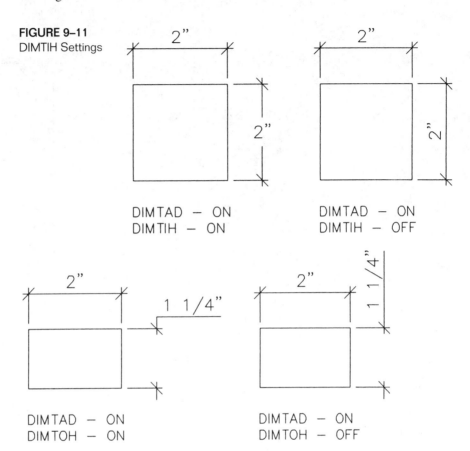

**FIGURE 9–11**
DIMTIH Settings

DIMTAD – ON
DIMTIH – ON

DIMTAD – ON
DIMTIH – OFF

**FIGURE 9–12**
DIMTOH Settings

DIMTAD – ON
DIMTOH – ON

DIMTAD – ON
DIMTOH – OFF

### DIMTOH—text outside horizontal

The DIMTOH setting affects dimension text that is drawn outside the extension lines. When DIMTOH is ON, the text is always oriented horizontally. When DIMTOH is OFF, the text is aligned with the dimension line. Figure 9–12 shows dimension text that is outside the extension lines, with DIMTOH ON and OFF.

### DIMTIX—place text inside extensions

AutoCAD automatically places the dimension text inside the extension lines when there is sufficient room and outside the extension lines when there is not. When DIMTIX is ON, the dimension text is forced between the extension lines. This happens even if Auto-CAD would have automatically placed it outside because of the limited room. When DIMTIX is OFF, the text location for linear, aligned, and angular dimensions varies depending on the type of dimension. If DIMTIX is OFF when you are drawing radius and diameter dimensions, the dimension text is forced outside the circle or arc. Figure 9–13 shows linear and diameter dimensions with DIMTIX ON and OFF.

### DIMSOXD—suppress outside dimension lines

AutoCAD automatically draws dimension lines and text outside the extension lines when there is not sufficient room inside the extension lines for the text. DIMSOXD is effective only when DIMTIX is ON. When DIMTIX and DIMSOXD are both ON, the text is

**FIGURE 9–13**
DIMTIX Settings

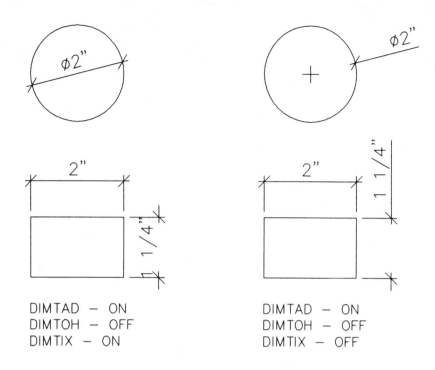

DIMTAD  —  ON
DIMTOH  —  OFF
DIMTIX  —  ON

DIMTAD  —  ON
DIMTOH  —  OFF
DIMTIX  —  OFF

**FIGURE 9–14**
DIMTIX and DIMSOXD Settings

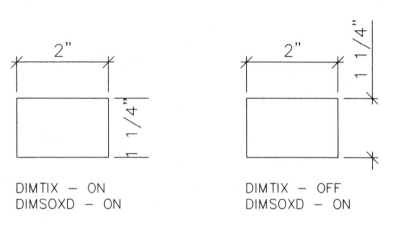

DIMTIX  —  ON
DIMSOXD  —  ON

DIMTIX  —  OFF
DIMSOXD  —  ON

forced inside the extension lines and the dimension line is not drawn. Figure 9–14 shows linear dimensions with DIMTIX and DIMSOXD ON. It also shows the same linear dimensions with DIMTIX OFF and DIMSOXD ON.

### DIMTOFL—force line inside extension lines

When there is not sufficient room for the text and dimension lines between the extension lines, AutoCAD automatically places them outside the extension lines. When DIMTOFL is ON, the dimension line is drawn between the extension lines, even when the text is drawn outside the extension lines. If DIMTOFL is ON and DIMTIX is OFF when radius and diameter dimensions are drawn, the dimension line is drawn inside the circle or arc and the leader and text are drawn outside of the circle or arc. Figure 9–15 shows linear and diameter dimensions with DIMTOFL OFF and ON.

### DIMATFIT—arrow and text fit

This variable controls the placement of text and arrowheads inside or outside extension lines based on the available space between extension lines as follows:

**0**    Places text and arrowheads between the extension lines if space is available. Otherwise places both text and arrowheads outside extension lines.

**FIGURE 9–15**
DIMTOFL Settings

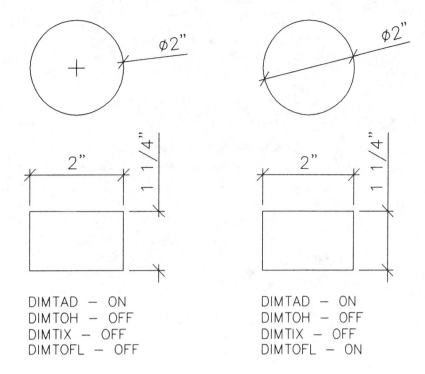

```
DIMTAD — ON          DIMTAD — ON
DIMTOH — OFF         DIMTOH — OFF
DIMTIX — OFF         DIMTIX — OFF
DIMTOFL — OFF        DIMTOFL — ON
```

**1**  If space is available, places text and arrowheads between the extension lines. When enough space is not available for both, AutoCAD moves the arrows first, then the text.

**2**  If space is available, places text and arrowheads between the extension lines. When enough space is not available for both, AutoCAD moves the text first, then the arrows.

**3**  This setting moves either the text or arrows, whichever fits.

### DIMJUST—justification of text on dimension line

This variable controls the horizontal position of the text in the dimension as follows:

**0**  Positions the text centered between the extension lines.
**1**  Positions the text next to the first extension line.
**2**  Positions the text next to the second extension line.
**3**  Rotates the text so that it is aligned above the first extension line
**4**  Rotates the text so that it is aligned above the second extension line.

### DIMUPT—user-positioned text

When this variable is on, it allows you to click the point where you wish the dimension line and the text to appear. If you want the text to appear nearer one end of the dimension line, select a single point that will place the dimension line where you want it and will place the text on the same point. The setting is 0 for OFF and 1 for ON.

### DIMSD1—suppress the first dimension line

When the DIMSD1 value is set to ON, the dimension line nearest the first extension line origin is not drawn.

### DIMSD2—suppress the second dimension line

When the DIMSD2 value is set to ON, the dimension line nearest the second extension line origin is not drawn.

### DIMSE1—suppress the first extension line

Setting the DIMSE1 value to ON suppresses the drawing of the first extension line. Sometimes while you are drawing dimensions, it is convenient to be able to turn off the first extension line. When you are using Continue dimensioning, suppressing the first extension line prevents the overlapping of extension lines with each continuing dimension. When the first extension is suppressed, you have to draw it in (or turn DIMSE1 OFF and UPDATE the first dimension) to complete the first dimension segment drawn.

### DIMSE2—suppress the second extension line

Setting the DIMSE2 value to ON suppresses the drawing of the second extension line.

### DIMZIN—zero suppression

The value of DIMZIN controls how the feet and inches of the dimensions appear. Figure 9–16 shows how DIMZIN affects feet and inches, using Architectural and Decimal units.

**FIGURE 9–16**
DIMZIN Values

| DIMZIN Value | Meaning | Examples | | | |
|---|---|---|---|---|---|
| 0 | Suppress zero feet and inches | ¼″ | 3″ | 2′ | 1′-0½″ |
| 1 | Include zero feet and inches | 0′-0¼″ | 0′-3″ | 2′-0″ | 1′-0½″ |
| 2 | Include zero feet; suppress zero inches | 0′-0¼″ | 0′-3″ | 2′ | 1′-0½″ |
| 3 | Suppress zero feet; include zero inches | ¼″ | 3″ | 2′-0 | 1′-0½″ |
| 4 | Suppress leading zeros in decimal dimensions | .500 | .50 | .0010 | |
| 8 | Suppress trailing zeros in decimal dimensions | 0.5 | 1.5 | .001 | |
| 12 | Suppress leading and trailing zeros in decimal dimensions | .5 | 1.5 | .001 | |

### DIMPOST—prefix and suffix for dimension text

The DIMPOST variable defines a prefix, a suffix, or both for a dimension measurement. It is used when the Decimal unit of measurement is selected. For example, a DIMPOST setting of "<>mm" would produce a measurement of "10.50mm" for a measurement of 10.50 units. Use <> to indicate placement of the text. For example, to display mm 10.50, enter mm <>.

### DIMAUNIT—angular unit format

This variable sets the angle format for angular dimensions as follows:

**0**  Decimal degrees
**1**  Degrees/minutes/seconds
**2**  Gradians
**3**  Radians

### DIMADEC—angular decimal places

Controls the number of decimal places shown in angular dimensions.

### DIMAZIN—angular zero suppression

Suppresses zeros for angular dimensions.

**0**  Displays all leading and trailing zeros.
**1**  Suppresses leading zeros in decimal dimensions (for example, 0.5000 becomes .5000).
**2**  Suppresses trailing zeros in decimal dimensions (for example, 12.5000 becomes 12.5).
**3**  Suppresses leading and trailing zeros (for example, 0.5000 becomes .5).

## Dimensioning Variables for Setting Color

### DIMCLRD—dimension line and leader color

The DIMCLRD setting controls the color of dimension lines, arrowheads, and leaders. When DIMCLRD is set to BYBLOCK the dimension lines and arrowheads take on the color of the current layer. You can also set DIMCLRD by entering a color number or name. For example, setting DIMCLRD to 1 will produce red dimension lines, arrowheads, and leaders. They will be red regardless of the layer that is current when they are drawn. This can be useful when you want different elements of the dimension to have varying line weights. When plotting, you should coordinate the dimension part colors to varying lineweights.

### DIMCLRE—extension line color

Similar to DIMCLRD, the DIMCLRE setting controls the color of the extension line.

### DIMCLRT—dimension text color

Similar to DIMCLRD, the DIMCLRT setting controls the color of the dimension text.

## Dimensioning Variables for Adding Dimension Tolerances, Generating Dimension Limits, and Rounding Dimensions

### DIMTDEC—tolerance decimal places

Sets the number of decimal places in the tolerance value for a dimension.

### DIMTOL—tolerance dimensioning

When DIMTOL is on, dimension tolerances that are specified by the values of DIMTP (Plus Tolerance) and DIMTM (Minus Tolerance) are added to the dimension text. Setting DIMTOL ON forces DIMLIN (Generate Dimension Limits) OFF. When the plus tolerance and minus tolerance values are the same, AutoCAD draws a ± symbol followed by the tolerance value. When the plus and minus tolerances differ, the plus tolerance is drawn above the minus. Examples of dimensioning with dimension tolerances are shown in Figure 9–17.

**FIGURE 9–17**
Dimensioning with DIMTOL On

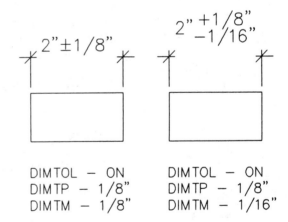

### DIMTOLJ—tolerance vertical justification

Controls the vertical placement of tolerance values relative to the dimension text as follows.

**0**    Bottom
**1**    Middle
**2**    Top

### DIMTZIN—tolerance zero suppression

Suppresses zeros in tolerance values to the right of the value as follows:

**0**    Zeros are not suppressed (are shown; Example: .0500)
**1**    Zeros are suppressed (are not shown; Example: .05)

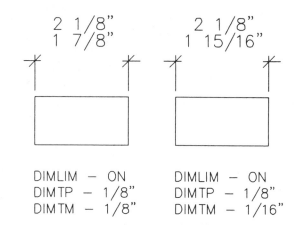

**FIGURE 9–18**
Dimensioning with DIMLIM On

2 1/8"
1 7/8"

2 1/8"
1 15/16"

DIMLIM — ON
DIMTP — 1/8"
DIMTM — 1/8"

DIMLIM — ON
DIMTP — 1/8"
DIMTM — 1/16"

### DIMLIM—generate dimension limits

When DIMLIM is ON, dimension limits that are specified by the values of DIMTP and DIMTM are added to the dimension text. Setting DIMLIM ON forces DIMTOL OFF. Examples of dimensioning with dimension limits are shown in Figure 9–18.

### DIMTP—plus tolerance

The DIMTP setting specifies the plus tolerance used when DIMTOL is ON and the upper dimension limits when DIMLIM is ON.

### DIMTM—minus tolerance

The DIMTM setting specifies the minus tolerance used when DIMTOL is ON and the lower dimension limits when DIMLIM is ON.

### DIMTFAC—tolerance text height scaling factor

Similar to DIMSCALE, DIMTFAC is the scale factor applied to the text height (DIMTXT) of the tolerance values specified in DIMTP and DIMTM. For example, if DIMTFAC is .5 and DIMTXT is 1/8″, the plus and minus tolerances are drawn with text 1/16″ high.

### DIMRND—rounding value

The value of DIMRND is used for rounding dimension distances. It does not apply to angular dimensions. For example, a rounding value of 1/2″ would result in rounding of all distances to the nearest 1/2″ unit; 2-3/4″ would become 3″.

## Dimensioning Variables for Alternate Units of Measurement

### DIMALT—alternate units selected

When DIMALT is ON, dimensions for two different systems of measurement, such as inches and metric, will be drawn. For example, when DIMALT is ON and DIMALTF is set at 25.4, the dimension text appears as 2″ (50.80mm).

### DIMALTD—alternate unit decimal places

The DIMALTD setting determines the number of places to the right of the decimal the alternate text will display. In the preceding alternate unit example, the DIMALTD setting is 2.

### DIMALTF—alternate unit scale factor

The value of DIMALTF is the number by which the basic dimension is multiplied to obtain the value of the alternate unit. The default for DIMALFT is 25.4, the number of millimeters per inch. When DIMALT is on and DIMALTF is 25.4, the inch unit of measurement is multiplied by 25.4 to determine the alternate unit of measurement.

### DIMALTRND—alternate units rounding value

Rounds off the alternate dimension units.

### DIMALTTD—alternate tolerance decimal places

DIMALTTD sets the number of decimal places for the tolerance values of an alternate units dimension.

### DIMALTTZ—alternate tolerance zero suppression

DIMALTTZ suppresses zeros in alternate tolerance values.

### DIMALTU—alternate units

This variable sets units for alternate dimension.

### DIMALTZ—alternate unit zero suppression

DIMALTZ suppresses zeros in alternate dimension values.

### DIMAPOST—prefix and suffix for alternate text

The DIMAPOST value is the prefix or suffix applied to the alternate unit of measurement. For example, when using metric, you enter the value of DIMAPOST as "mm", as shown in the DIMALT alternate unit example.

## Dimensioning Variables for Designing Your Own Arrow Block

### DIMBLK—arrow block name

**Tip:** If you have defined a DIMBLK other than the standard arrowhead or tick and want to return to the standard form, respond with a period (.) to the DIMBLK name. Until you do this, the defined DIMBLK remains in effect.

If you do not want an arrow or tick mark to be used at the ends of dimension lines, you may use other AutoCAD defined arrowhead blocks or design your own mark. AutoCAD provides a variety of predefined blocks such as a dot, that can be used at the end of dimension lines. To see a list of predefined blocks, look under DIMBLK in AutoCAD Help. You may also use the Block command to make a block of your own mark, and AutoCAD will insert it.

At the DIMBLK prompt, enter the name of the block to be drawn at the ends of the dimension line. The DIMASZ variable is used to determine the size of arrow blocks identified by the DIMBLK variable.

### DIMSAH—separate arrow blocks, DIMBLK1—first arrow block name, DIMBLK2—arrow block

You may use different blocks for the marks at the two ends of the dimension line. When DIMSAH is on, the DIMBLK1 and DIMBLK2 variables specify different user-defined arrow blocks to be drawn at the two ends of the dimension line. DIMBLK1 names the block used for the mark drawn at one end of the dimension line, and DIMBLK2 names the block used for the mark drawn at the other end of the dimension line.

### DIMLDRBLK—leader block name

Specifies the arrow type for leaders. If you want to turn off the arrowhead display, enter a single period (.) for the leader block name. To see a list of predefined blocks, look under DIMBLK in AutoCAD Help.

## Dimensioning Variables for Associative Dimensions

The DIMASO variable is obsolete. It was used in AutoCAD releases prior to 2002. The system variable DIMASSOC affects how dimensions are inserted.

### DIMTMOVE—text movement

Sets dimension text movement rules.

**0**  Moves the dimension line with dimension text.
**1**  Adds a leader when dimension text is moved.
**2**  Allows text to be moved freely without a leader.

### Dimension Variable for Naming a Dimension Style

#### DIMSTYLE—current dimension style (read-only)

While dimensioning the same drawing, you may want some of the dimensions to have different variable settings from the rest of the dimensions. For example, you may want a different text height for some dimensions. If you want to use two or more distinct styles of dimensioning in the same drawing, each style (and the variable settings for that style) may be saved separately and recalled when needed. The DIMSTYLE variable tells the name of the current dimension style.

### DIMASSOC System Variable

This new AutoCAD 2002 setting is not one of the dimensioning variables but does affect how dimensions behave in relation to the object being dimensioned. It has three states:

**0**  Creates exploded dimensions. Each part of the dimension (arrowheads, lines, text) is a separate object.
**1**  Creates dimensions that are single objects but are not associated with the object being dimensioned. When the dimension is created, definition points are formed (at the ends of extension lines, for example). If these points are moved, as with the Stretch command, the dimension changes, but it is not directly associated with the object being dimensioned.
**2**  Creates associative dimension objects. The dimensions are single objects, and one or more of the definition points on the dimension are linked to association points on the object. When the association point on the object moves, the dimension location, orientation, and text value of the dimension change. For example: Check DIMASSOC to make sure the setting is 2 (TYPE: **DIMASSOC<enter>**. If the value is not 2, TYPE: **2<enter>**). Draw a 2″ circle and dimension it using the diameter dimensioning command. With no command active, CLICK: any point on the circle so that grips appear at the quadrants of the circle. CLICK: any grip to make it hot and move the grip. The dimension changes as the size of the circle changes.

# EXERCISE 9–1
# Dimensioning the Tenant Space Floor Plan Using Linear Dimensions

Exercise 9–1 provides instructions for setting the dimensioning variables for the tenant space floor plan drawn in Exercise 8–1, saving the dimensioning variables, and dimensioning the exterior and interior of the tenant space floor plan using linear dimensions. When you have completed Exercise 9–1, your drawing will look similar to Figure 9–19. To begin, turn on the computer and start AutoCAD. The AutoCAD 2002 Today window is displayed.

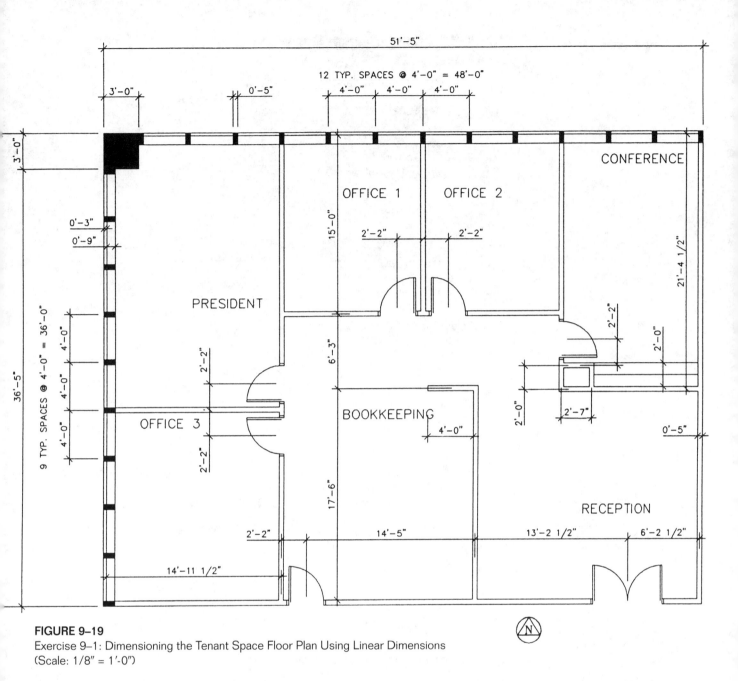

**FIGURE 9–19**

Exercise 9–1: Dimensioning the Tenant Space Floor Plan Using Linear Dimensions
(Scale: 1/8″ = 1′-0″)

**Begin drawing CH9-EX1 on the hard drive by opening existing drawing CH8-EX1 and saving it as CH9-EX1 on the hard drive.**

| Prompt | Response |
|---|---|
| The AutoCAD 2002 Today window is displayed. | CLICK: **Open Drawings tab** |
| | CLICK: **CH8-EX1.dwg** |
| | -or- |
| | If CH8-EX1.dwg is not listed CLICK: **Browse:** |
| | DOUBLE CLICK: **Browse** |
| The Select File dialog box appears: | **Locate: CH8-EX1** |
| | DOUBLE CLICK: **CH8-EX1** |
| CH8-EX1 is opened. | |

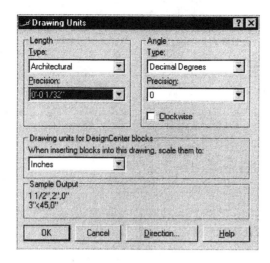

**Save the drawing to the hard drive.**

| Prompt | Response |
|---|---|
| Command: | **SaveAs...** |
| The Save Drawing As... dialog box is displayed: | TYPE: **CH9-EX1** (replace CH8-EX1 in the File Name: input box) |
| | CLICK: the correct drive and folder |
| | CLICK: **Save** |

You are now working on the hard drive with a drawing named CH9-EX1. Do not work on a floppy disk. Always work on the hard drive.

Just to be sure that you have the drawing units correctly set before you begin dimensioning:

**Note:** Be sure to select 32 as the denominator of the smallest fraction to display when setting drawing Units so that the dimensioning variable settings may display the same fraction if they are set in 32nds.

| Prompt | Response |
|---|---|
| Command: | TYPE: **UNITS<enter>** |
| The Drawing Units dialog box appears: | SELECT: **Architectural** in the Type: box |
| | SELECT: **0'-0 1/32″** in the Precision: box |

## Setting the Dimensioning Variables

There are three different ways the dimensioning variables can be set. The following describes how to set dimensioning variables.

**STATUS**

**Use STATUS to view the current status of all the dimensioning variables and change the setting for DIMASZ:**

| Prompt | Response |
|---|---|
| Command: | TYPE: **DIM<enter>** |
| Dim: | TYPE: **STATUS<enter>** |
| (The dimension variables appear on the screen.) | CLICK: **the maximize button** |
| | **Use the scroll bars to move to the top of the list.** |
| Dim: | TYPE: **ASZ<enter>** |
| Dim: asz | |

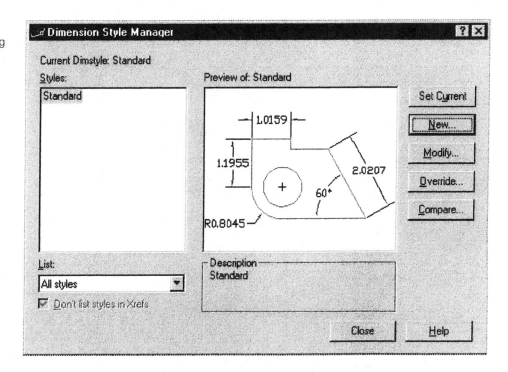
at top of page — Dimension toolbar

Dimension | Standard

Dimension Style

**Prompt**

Enter new value for dimension variable
    <default>:

Dim:

## Dimension Style Manager dialog box

The Dimension Style Manager dialog box (Figure 9–20) allows you to change dimension variables using tabs on the dialog box.

You can modify an existing style (the default style is Standard), or you can name a new style and make that style current when you begin dimensioning. In this exercise you will create a new style that has several dimensioning variables that are different from the Standard style.

### Use the Dimension Style Manager to create a new style (Figures 9–20 through 9–27):

**Prompt**

Command:

The Dimension Style Manager
    (Figure 9–20) appears:
The Create New Dimension Style dialog
    box (Figure 9–21) appears:

**Response**

You can enter a new value for the
    variable. *Do not* enter a new value at
    this time. PRESS: **ESC.**
PRESS: **F2**

**Response**

**Dimension Style...** ( or TYPE:
    **DDIM<enter>**)

CLICK: **New...**

TYPE: **STYLE1** in the New Style Name
    box
CLICK: **Continue** (or PRESS: **<enter>**)

**FIGURE 9–20**
Dimension Style Manager Dialog
Box

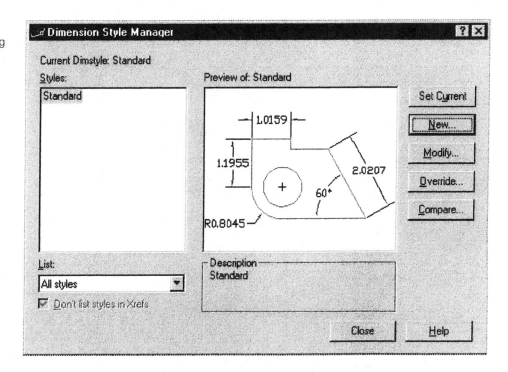

**Dimension Style Manager**

Current Dimstyle: Standard

Styles:
Standard

List:
All styles
☑ Don't list styles in Xrefs

Preview of: Standard

1.0159
1.1955
2.0207
60°
R0.8045

Description
Standard

Set Current
New...
Modify...
Override...
Compare...

Close     Help

**FIGURE 9–21**
Create New Dimension Style Dialog Box

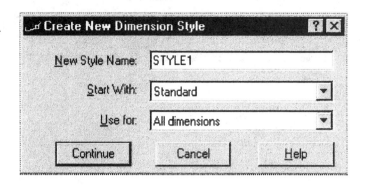

| Prompt | Response |
|---|---|
| The New Dimension Style dialog box appears: | CLICK: **the Primary Units tab** (Figure 9–22) (Setting the Primary Units first will allow you to view how dimensions will appear as you set other variables.) |
| The Primary Units tab is shown: | SELECT: **Architectural** in the Unit format: box |
| | SELECT: **0′-0 1/32″** in the Precision box |
| All other variables for this tab should be set as shown in Figure 9–22. | |
| | CLICK: **the Lines and Arrows tab** (Figure 9–23) |
| The Lines and Arrows tab is shown: | CLICK: **the down arrow so that 1/16″ appears in the Extend beyond dim lines: box** (Figure 9–23) |

**FIGURE 9–22**
Primary Units Tab of the New Dimension Style Dialog Box

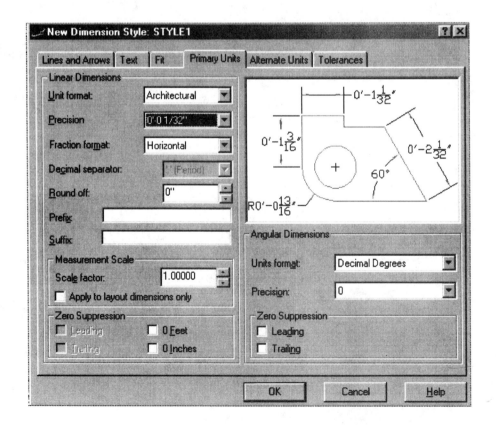

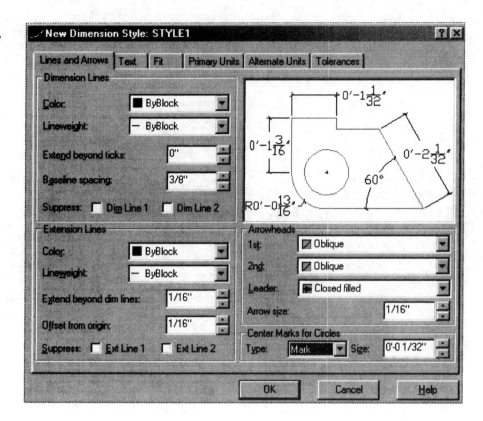

| Prompt | Response |
|---|---|
| | (If 1/16″ is not in the list, highlight the text and TYPE: **1/16.**) |
| | CLICK: **Oblique** in the Arrowheads 1st: list. |
| | CLICK: **1/16″** in the Arrow size: list (If 1/16″ is not in the list, highlight the text and TYPE: **1/16.**) |
| | CLICK: **Mark** in the Center Marks for Circles Type: list |
| | CLICK: **1/32″** in the Center Marks for Circles Size: list |
| All other variables for this tab should be set as shown in Figure 9–23. | |
| | CLICK: **the Text tab** |
| The Text tab is shown: | CLICK: **1/16″** in the Text height: box (Figure 9–24) (If 1/16″ is not in the list, highlight the text and TYPE: **1/16.**) |
| | CLICK: **1/32** in the Offset from dim line: box in the Text Placement area |
| | CLICK: **Above** in the Vertical: box of the Text Placement area (This places dimension text above the dimension line.) |
| | CLICK: the **Aligned with dimension line** radio button in the Text Alignment area |

**FIGURE 9–24**
Text Tab of the New Dimension
Style Dialog Box

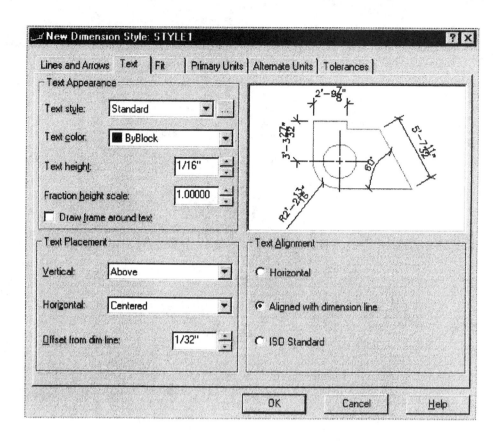

| Prompt | Response |
|---|---|
| All other variables for this tab should be set as shown in Figure 9–24. | |
| | CLICK: **the Fit tab** |
| The Fit tab is shown: | CLICK: the **Always keep text between ext lines** radio button in the Fit Options area (Figure 9–25) |
| | CLICK: the **Use overall scale of:** radio button |
| | HIGHLIGHT: **the text** in the Use overall scale of: text box and TYPE: **96** (This sets a dimscale of 1/8″=1′ (8 × 12) so that all dimensioning variables are multiplied by 96.) For example, as you are dimensioning the drawing, the text height, originally set at 1/16″, will actually measure 1/16 × 96 or 6″. When the layout is created using 1/8″=1′ scale, all variables will be the size set originally. For example, text height will be 1/16″. |
| All other variables for this tab should be set as shown in Figure 9–25. | |
| | CLICK: **OK** |
| The Dimension Style Manager appears (Figure 9–26): | CLICK: **Set Current** |
| | CLICK: **Compare** |

## FIGURE 9–25
Fit Tab of the New Dimension Style Dialog Box

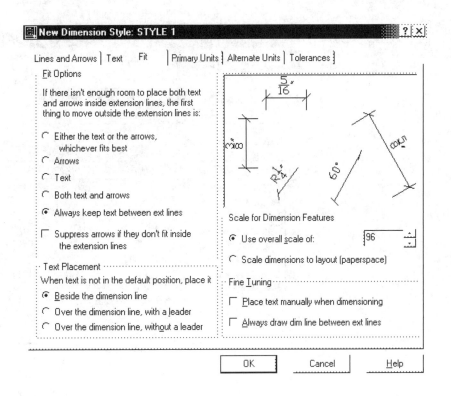

## FIGURE 9–26
Dimension Style Manager Dialog Box with STYLE1 Highlighted

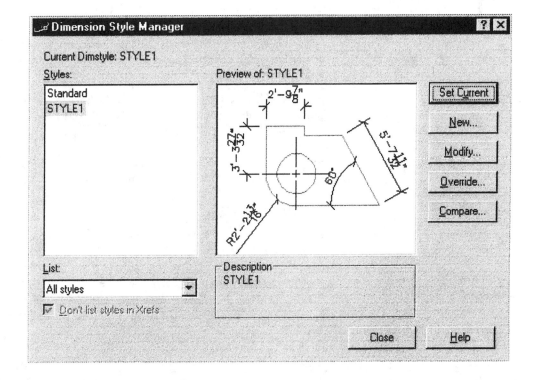

FIGURE 9–27
Compare Dimension Styles Dialog Box

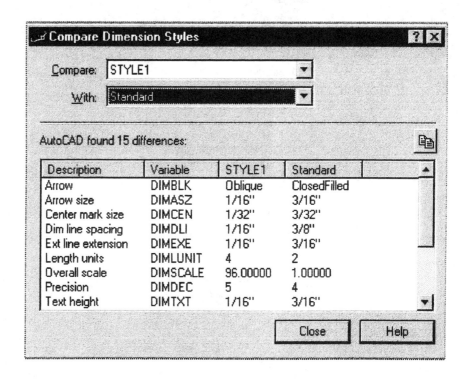

| Description | Variable | STYLE1 | Standard |
|---|---|---|---|
| Arrow | DIMBLK | Oblique | ClosedFilled |
| Arrow size | DIMASZ | 1/16" | 3/16" |
| Center mark size | DIMCEN | 1/32" | 3/32" |
| Dim line spacing | DIMDLI | 1/16" | 3/8" |
| Ext line extension | DIMEXE | 1/16" | 3/16" |
| Length units | DIMLUNIT | 4 | 2 |
| Overall scale | DIMSCALE | 96.00000 | 1.00000 |
| Precision | DIMDEC | 5 | 4 |
| Text height | DIMTXT | 1/16" | 3/16" |

| Prompt | Response |
|---|---|
| The Compare Dimension Styles dialog box appears (Figure 9–27): | CLICK: **Standard** in the With: box |
| | Check to see which variables have changed from the Standard default setting. |
| | CLICK: **Close** |
| The Dimension Style Manager appears: | CLICK: **Close** |

### Alternate and Tolerances tabs

The remaining tabs in the Dimension Style Manager dialog box contain variables for alternate dimensions and tolerances. Alternate dimensions are usually metric dimensions that are displayed with decimal dimensions on mechanical drawings. Tolerances are also associated with mechanical drawings. Because both of these are seldom used on architectural drawings, neither tab will be discussed here.

**From the Command: prompt, type DIMDLE to view the current setting for DIMDLE and change the current setting for DIMDLE**

| Prompt | Response |
|---|---|
| Command: | TYPE: **DIMDLE <enter>** |
| Enter new value for DIMDLE <default>: | TYPE: **1/16<enter>** |

## On Your Own

Use any of the three ways described above to set the dimensioning variables for CH9-EX1. Many of the variables already have the correct setting. If you plan to plot or print CH9-EX1 at a scale of 1/8″ = 12″, using an 8-1/2″ × 11″ plotting size, set the variables as shown in Figure 9–28. Be sure 1/32 is set as the smallest fraction to display when setting drawing Units so the 1/32 dimensioning variable will display that fraction. If you plan to plot CH9-EX1 at a scale of 1/4″ = 12″, using an 18″ × 24″ plotting size, set the variables as shown in Figure 9–29.

**FIGURE 9–28**

Dimensioning Variables (Layout Scale 1/8″ = 1′-0″ on 8½″ × 11″ Sheet).

| | | |
|---|---|---|
| DIMADEC | 0 | Angular decimal places |
| DIMALT | Off | Alternate units selected |
| DIMALTD | 2 | Alternate unit decimal places |
| DIMALTF | 25.40000 | Alternate unit scale factor |
| DIMALTRND | 0″ | Alternate units rounding value |
| DIMALTTD | 2 | Alternate tolerance decimal places |
| DIMALTTZ | 0 | Alternate tolerance zero suppression |
| DIMALTU | 2 | Alternate units |
| DIMALTZ | 0 | Alternate unit zero suppression |
| DIMAPOST | | Prefix and suffix for alternate text |
| DIMASZ | 1/16″ | Arrow size |
| DIMATFIT | 2 | Arrow and text fit |
| DIMAUNIT | 0 | Angular unit format |
| DIMAZIN | 0 | Angular zero supression |
| DIMBLK | Oblique | Arrow block name |
| DIMBLK1 | ClosedFilled | First arrow block name |
| DIMBLK2 | ClosedFilled | Second arrow block name |
| DIMCEN | 1/32″ | Center mark size |
| DIMCLRD | BYBLOCK | Dimension line and leader color |
| DIMCLRE | BYBLOCK | Extension line color |
| DIMCLRT | BYBLOCK | Dimension text color |
| DIMDEC | 5 | Decimal places |
| DIMDLE | 0″ | Dimension line extension |
| DIMDLI | 3/8″ | Dimension line spacing |
| DIMDSEP | | Decimal separator |
| DIMEXE | 1/16″ | Extension above dimension line |
| DIMEXO | 1/16″ | Extension line origin offset |
| DIMFRAC | 0 | Fraction format |
| DIMGAP | 1/32″ | Gap from dimension line to text |
| DIMJUST | 0 | Justification of text on dimension line |
| DIMLDRBLK | ClosedFilled | Leader block name |
| DIMLFAC | 1.00000 | Linear unit scale factor |
| DIMLIM | Off | Generate dimension limits |
| DIMLUNIT | 4 | Linear unit format |
| DIMLWD | -2 | Dimension line and leader lineweight |
| DIMLWE | -2 | Extension line lineweight |
| DIMPOST | | Prefix and suffix for dimension text |
| DIMRND | 0″ | Rounding value |
| DIMSAH | Off | Separate arrow blocks |
| DIMSCALE | 96.00000 | Overall scale factor |
| DIMSD1 | Off | Suppress the first dimension line |
| DIMSD2 | Off | Suppress the second dimension line |
| DIMSE1 | Off | Suppress the first extension line |
| DIMSE2 | Off | Suppress the second extension line |
| DIMSOXD | Off | Suppress outside dimension lines |
| DIMTAD | 1 | Place text above the dimension line |
| DIMTDEC | 5 | Tolerance decimal places |
| DIMTFAC | 1.00000 | Tolerance text height scaling factor |
| DIMTIH | Off | Text inside extensions is horizontal |
| DIMTIX | Off | Place text inside extensions |
| DIMTM | 0″ | Minus tolerance |
| DIMTMOVE | 0 | Text movement |
| DIMTOFL | Off | Force line inside extension lines |
| DIMTOH | Off | Text outside horizontal |
| DIMTOL | Off | Tolerance dimensioning |
| DIMTOLJ | 1 | Tolerance vertical justification |
| DIMTP | 0″ | Plus tolerance |
| DIMTSZ | 0″ | Tick size |
| DIMTVP | 0.00000 | Text vertical position |
| DIMTXSTY | STANDARD | Text style |
| DIMTXT | 1/16″ | Text height |
| DIMTZIN | 1 | Tolerance zero suppression |
| DIMUPT | Off | User positioned text |
| DIMZIN | 1 | Zero suppression |

| | | |
|---|---|---|
| DIMADEC | 0 | Angular decimal places |
| DIMALT | Off | Alternate units selected |
| DIMALTD | 2 | Alternate unit decimal places |
| DIMALTF | 25.40000 | Alternate unit scale factor |
| DIMALTRND | 0″ | Alternate units rounding value |
| DIMALTTD | 2 | Alternate tolerance decimal places |
| DIMALTTZ | 0 | Alternate tolerance zero suppression |
| DIMALTU | 2 | Alternate units |
| DIMALTZ | 0 | Alternate unit zero suppression |
| DIMAPOST | | Prefix and suffix for alternate text |
| DIMASZ | 1/16″ | Arrow size |
| DIMATFIT | 2 | Arrow and text fit |
| DIMAUNIT | 0 | Angular unit format |
| DIMAZIN | 0 | Angular zero supression |
| DIMBLK | Oblique | Arrow block name |
| DIMBLK1 | ClosedFilled | First arrow block name |
| DIMBLK2 | ClosedFilled | Second arrow block name |
| DIMCEN | 1/32″ | Center mark size |
| DIMCLRD | BYBLOCK | Dimension line and leader color |
| DIMCLRE | BYBLOCK | Extension line color |
| DIMCLRT | BYBLOCK | Dimension text color |
| DIMDEC | 5 | Decimal places |
| DIMDLE | 0″ | Dimension line extension |
| DIMDLI | 3/8″ | Dimension line spacing |
| DIMDSEP | . | Decimal separator |
| DIMEXE | 1/16″ | Extension above dimension line |
| DIMEXO | 1/16″ | Extension line origin offset |
| DIMFRAC | 0 | Fraction format |
| DIMGAP | 1/32″ | Gap from dimension line to text |
| DIMJUST | 0 | Justification of text on dimension line |
| DIMLDRBLK | ClosedFilled | Leader block name |
| DIMLFAC | 1.00000 | Linear unit scale factor |
| DIMLIM | Off | Generate dimension limits |
| DIMLUNIT | 4 | Linear unit format |
| DIMLWD | -2 | Dimension line and leader lineweight |
| DIMLWE | -2 | Extension line lineweight |
| DIMPOST | | Prefix and suffix for dimension text |
| DIMRND | 0″ | Rounding value |
| DIMSAH | Off | Separate arrow blocks |
| DIMSCALE | 48.00000 | Overall scale factor |
| DIMSD1 | Off | Suppress the first dimension line |
| DIMSD2 | Off | Suppress the second dimension line |
| DIMSE1 | Off | Suppress the first extension line |
| DIMSE2 | Off | Suppress the second extension line |
| DIMSOXD | Off | Suppress outside dimension lines |
| DIMTAD | 1 | Place text above the dimension line |
| DIMTDEC | 5 | Tolerance decimal places |
| DIMTFAC | 1.00000 | Tolerance text height scaling factor |
| DIMTIH | Off | Text inside extensions is horizontal |
| DIMTIX | Off | Place text inside extensions |
| DIMTM | 0″ | Minus tolerance |
| DIMTMOVE | 0 | Text movement |
| DIMTOFL | Off | Force line inside extension lines |
| DIMTOH | Off | Text outside horizontal |
| DIMTOL | Off | Tolerance dimensioning |
| DIMTOLJ | 1 | Tolerance vertical justification |
| DIMTP | 0″ | Plus tolerance |
| DIMTSZ | 0″ | Tick size |
| DIMTVP | 0.00000 | Text vertical position |
| DIMTXSTY | STANDARD | Text style |
| DIMTXT | 1/16″ | Text height |
| DIMTZIN | 1 | Tolerance zero suppression |
| DIMUPT | Off | User positioned text |
| DIMZIN | 1 | Zero suppression |

## Saving and Then Restoring Saved Dimension Styles

**Note:** Start a drawing, set the dimensioning variables, and save the drawing as a template for future dimensioning projects.

The dimensioning variable settings are saved under a dimension style name. Any dimensions drawn while the style is current will be associated with the style. This is done using the Dimension Style Manager dialog box.

Open the Dimension Style Manager, hold the point over the style name, right click, and CLICK: **Rename**.

### On Your Own

1. **Set Layer A-pflr-dims current.**
2. **Use Zoom-All to view the entire drawing.**

### Linear and Continue Dimensioning

Using Linear, dimension the column and one mullion on the north exterior wall of the tenant space floor plan (Figure 9–30):

| Prompt | Response |
|---|---|
| Command: | **Linear** (or TYPE: **HOR<enter>** from the Dim: prompt) |
| Specify first extension line origin or <select object>: | **D1** (with Snap ON) |
| Specify second extension line origin: | **View, Zoom-Window** (from the menu bar) |
| >>Specify first corner:<br>>>Specify opposite corner: | **Window the northwest corner of the president's office.** |
| Specify second extension line origin: | **D2** |
| Specify dimension line location or [Mtext/<br>Text/Angle/Horizontal/Vertical/Rotated]: | **D3** (on snap, three grid marks up, with 12″ grid) |
| Command: | **<enter> (Repeat Linear)** |
| Specify first extension line origin or <select object>: | TYPE: **INT<enter>** |
| of | **D4** |

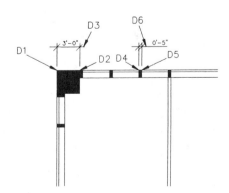

**FIGURE 9–30**
Linear Dimensioning

| Prompt | Response |
|---|---|
| Specify second extension line origin: | TYPE: **INT<enter>** |
| of | **D5** |
| Specify dimension line location or [Mtext/<br>Text/Angle/Horizontal/Vertical/Rotated]: | **D6** (on snap, three grid marks up) |

In the Linear command, after the second extension line origin is selected, the prompt reads:

**Prompt**

Specify dimension line location or
[Mtext/Text/Angle/Horizontal/Vertical/Rotated]:

Before you pick a dimension line location, you may type the first letter of any of the options in the brackets and press <enter> to activate it. These options are as follows:

**Mtext**

To activate the multiline text command for dimensions requiring more than one line of text.

**Text**

To replace the default text with a single line of text. To suppress the text entirely, press the space bar.

**Angle**

To rotate the text of the dimension to a specific angle.

**Horizontal**

To specify that you want a horizontal dimension; this is normally not necessary.

**Vertical**

To specify that you want a vertical dimension; this is normally not necessary.

**Rotated**

To specify that you want to rotate the entire dimension.

**Using Linear and Continue, dimension horizontally (center to center) the distance between four mullions on the north exterior wall of the tenant space (Figure 9–31). (Before continuing, Zoom in or Pan over to the four mullions to be dimensioned.)**

| Prompt | Response |
|---|---|
| Command: | **Linear** |
| Specify first extension line origin or<br>   <select object>: | TYPE: **MID<enter>** |

**FIGURE 9–31**

Linear Dimensioning with the Continue Command to Draw Horizontal Dimensions

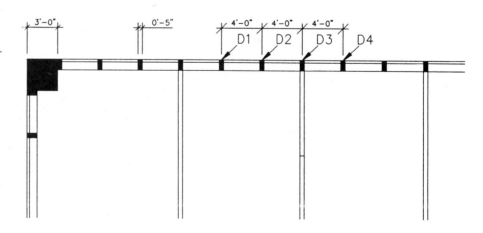

**Part II: Two-Dimensional AutoCAD**

| Prompt | Response |
|---|---|
| of | **D1** |
| Specify second extension line origin: | TYPE: **MID\<enter\>** |
| of | **D2** |
| Specify dimension line location or [Mtext/<br>    Text/Angle/Horizontal/Vertical/Rotated]: | **Click a point on snap, three grid marks<br>    up, to align with previous<br>    dimensions.** |
| Command: | **Continue** (from the Dimension menu or<br>    toolbar) (or TYPE: **CO\<enter\>** from<br>    the Dim: prompt) |
| Specify a second extension line origin or<br>    [Undo/Select\<Select\>]: | TYPE: **MID \<enter\>** |
| of | **D3** |
| Specify a second extension line origin or<br>    [Undo/Select\<Select\>]: | TYPE: **MID\<enter\>** |
| of | **D4** |
| Specify a second extension origin or<br>    [Undo/Select\<Select\>]: | **\<enter\>** |
| Select continued dimension: | **\<enter\>** |

**Using Linear and Continue, dimension vertically (center to center) the distance between four mullions on the west exterior wall of the tenant space (Figure 9–32). (Before continuing, Zoom in on the four mullions to be dimensioned.)**

| Prompt | Response |
|---|---|
| Command: | **Linear** (or TYPE: **VER\<enter\>** from the<br>    Dim: prompt) |
| Specify first extension line origin or<br>    \<select object\>: | TYPE: **MID\<enter\>** |
| of | **Click the first mullion.** (Dimension<br>    south to north.) |
| Specify second extension line origin: | TYPE: **MID\<enter\>** |
| of | **Pick the second mullion.** |
| Specify dimension line location or [Mtext/<br>    Text/Angle]: | **Pick a point on snap, three grid marks<br>    to the left, similar to previous<br>    dimension line locations.** |
| Enter dimension text \<4'-0"\>: | **\<enter\>** |
| Dim: | **Continue** (or TYPE: **CO\<enter\>**) |
| Specify a second extension line origin or<br>    [Select]\<Select\>: | TYPE: **MID\<enter\>** |
| of | **Pick the third mullion.** |
| Enter dimension text \<4'-0"\>: | **\<enter\>\<enter\>** |
| Specify a second extension line origin or<br>    [Select]\<Select\>: | TYPE: **MID\<enter\>** |
| mid of | **Pick the fourth mullion.** |
| Enter dimension text \<4'-0"\>: | **\<enter\>\<enter\>** |
| Specify a second extension line origin or<br>    [Select]\<Select\>: | **\<enter\>** |
| Select continued dimension: | **\<enter\>** |

**Note:** You may change the dimension string at the prompt "Specify dimension line location", by typing **T\<enter\>**, then typing new dimensions from the keyboard and pressing the enter key.

**Tip:** Use Osnap commands often to select extension line origins.

**Note:** You can use the default dimension text, supply your own text, or suppress the text entirely.

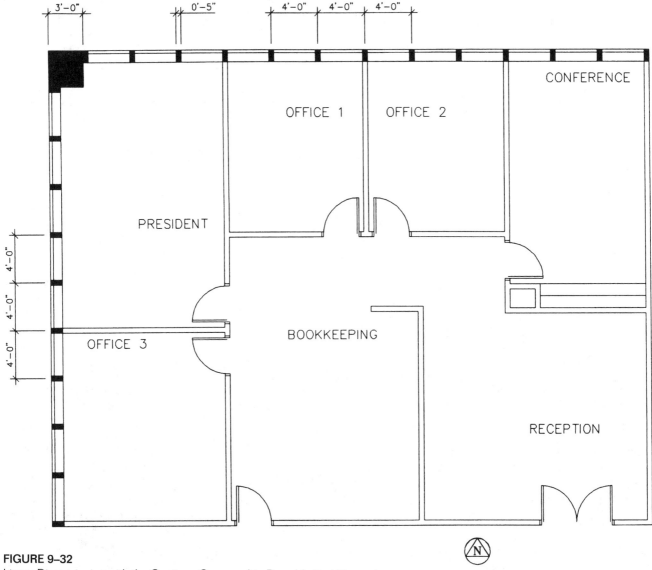

**FIGURE 9–32**
Linear Dimensioning with the Continue Command to Draw Vertical Dimensions
(Scale: 1/8″ = 1′-0″)

ALIGNED

**FIGURE 9–33**
Dimensioning with the Aligned
Command

## Aligned Dimensioning

When Aligned is used, you can select the first and second extension line origin points of a line that is at an angle, and the dimension line will run parallel to the origin points. Figure 9–33 shows an example of aligned dimensioning.

## Baseline Dimensioning

With linear dimensioning, after the first segment of a line is dimensioned, picking the Baseline command in the Dimension menu automatically continues the next linear dimension from the baseline (first extension line) of the first linear dimension. The new dimension line is offset to avoid drawing on top of the previous dimension. The DIMDLI variable controls the size of the offset. Figure 9–34 shows linear dimensioning with the Baseline command.

## On Your Own

See Figure 9–35.

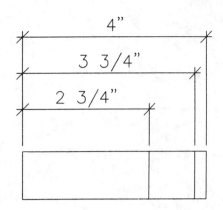

**FIGURE 9–34**
Linear Dimensioning with the
Baseline Command

4"

3 3/4"

2 3/4"

**Tip:** Use the transparent Zoom and Pan commands while in the Dim: mode. You will find them very helpful.

**Caution:** When erasing construction lines, avoid selecting definition points; otherwise the dimension associated with that point will be erased.

**Note:** When stacking dimension lines, locate the first dimension line farther from the object being dimensioned than subsequent dimension lines are from each other. For example, locate the first dimension line three grid marks from the object and the second dimension line two grid marks from the first dimension line.

1. Use Dtext, centered, to add the text "12 TYP. SPACES @4'-0" = 48'-0'" to the plan. Place it two grid marks (on a 12" grid) above the dimension line of the mullions dimension. Set the text height to 6".

2. Use Linear to dimension the overall north exterior wall of the tenant space. You may snap to the tick (intersection) of a previous dimension.

3. Use Dtext, centered, to add the text "9 TYP. SPACES @ 4'-0" = 36'-0'" to the plan. Place it two grid marks (on a 12" grid) above the dimension line of the mullions dimension. Set the text height to 6".

4. Use Linear to dimension from the southwest corner of the tenant space to the southern corner of the column. Use Continue to continue the dimension to the outside northwest corner of the building.

5. Use Linear to dimension the overall west exterior wall of the tenant space.

6. Complete the dimensioning using the Linear dimension commands. Use the Line command and appropriate Osnap modifiers to draw a temporary line across any doorways, or walls that are dimensioned to the center. Using Osnap-Midpoint, pick the lines to locate the extension line origin of the dimensions.

   When you are dimensioning from left to right, any outside dimension line and text will be placed to the right. Dimensioning from right to left draws any outside dimension line and text to the left.

7. **Erase the temporary lines drawn in the doorways and walls.** Be careful not to pick a defpoint (small points on the drawing used to create associative dimensions); otherwise an entire dimension will be erased. Zoom in closely when you are erasing to avoid defpoints.

## SAVE

When you have completed Exercise 9–1, save your work in at least two places.

## PLOT

Use a Layout Wizard or Page Setup to create a Layout tab named Dimensioning Plan1. Select a scale to correspond with the specified DIMSCALE setting. Plot or print Exercise 9–1.

# EXERCISE 9–2
# Associative Dimension Commands and Grips

Exercise 9–2 describes the dimensioning commands that can be used only when DIMASSOC is on. When you have completed Exercise 9–2, your drawing will look similar to Figure 9–36. To begin, turn on the computer and start AutoCAD. The AutoCAD 2002 Today window is displayed.

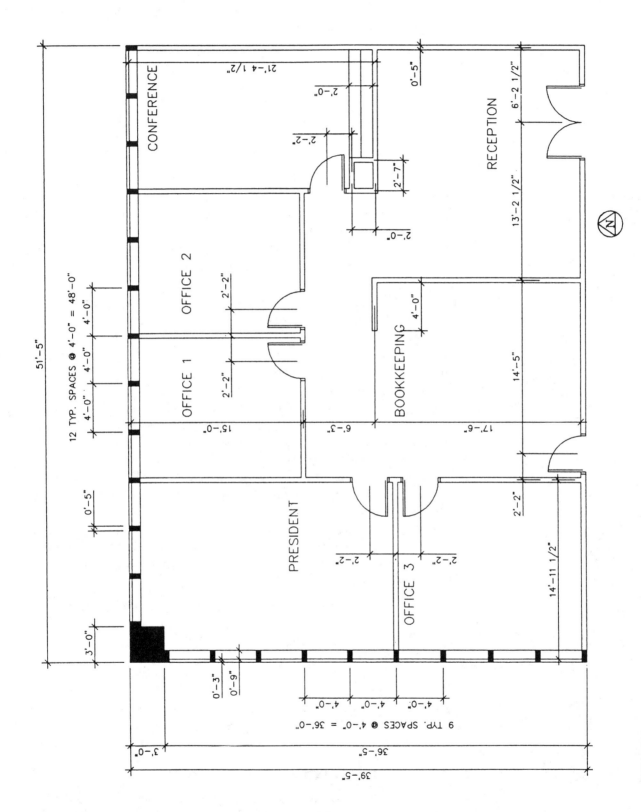

**FIGURE 9-35**
Complete Exercise 9-1 (Scale: 1/8" = 1'-0")

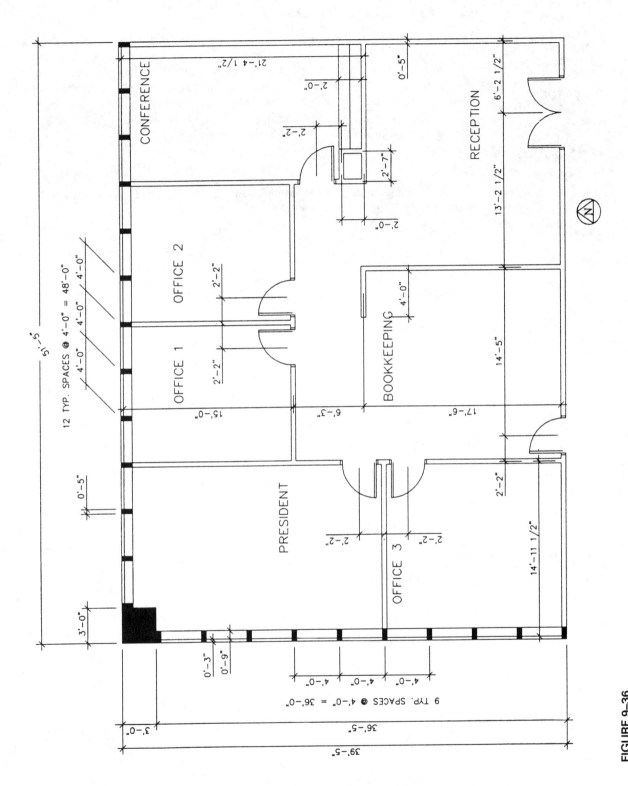

**FIGURE 9–36**

Exercise 9–2: Associative Dimension Commands (Scale: 1/8" = 1'-0")

227

## On Your Own

**1. Open drawing CH9-EX1 and save it as CH9-EX2 to the hard drive.**

## Associative Dimension Commands

When the DIMASSOC variable is on, each dimension that is drawn is created as a block. That means that the extension lines, dimension lines, ticks or arrows, text, and all other parts of the dimensions are entered as a single unit. When DIMASSOC is ON, the dimensions drawn are called *associative dimensions*. When DIMASSOC is OFF, the extension lines, dimension lines and all other parts of the dimension are drawn as separate entities.

Five dimension commands—Oblique, Align Text, Dimension Edit, Override, and Update—can be used only with associative dimensions (if DIMASSOC was ON while you drew the dimensions). The following describes those commands.

### Oblique

**Create an oblique angle for the extension lines of the four mullions on the north exterior wall of the tenant space (Figure 9–37).**

| Prompt | Response |
|---|---|
| Command: | **Oblique** (or TYPE: **OB<enter>** from the DIM: prompt) |

| Prompt | Response |
|---|---|
| Select objects: | **Pick the extension lines of the mullion dimensions on the North exterior wall until they are all highlighted.** |
| Select objects: | **<enter>** |
| Enter obliquing angle (press ENTER for none): | TYPE: **45<enter>** |

The extension lines of the mullion dimensions appear as shown in Figure 9–37.

### Align Text-Angle

**Rotate the text for the overall dimension on the north exterior wall of the tenant space. (Before continuing, Zoom in on the dimension text, "51'-5"".) (Figure 9–38)**

| Prompt | Response |
|---|---|
| Command: | **Align Text-Angle** |
| Select dimension: | **Pick the dimension text, "51'-5"".** |
| Specify angle for dimension text: | TYPE: **30<enter>** |

The text is rotated as shown in Figure 9–38.

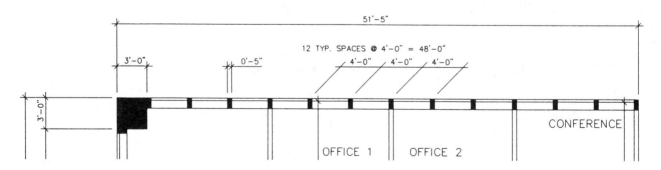

**FIGURE 9–37**
Using the Oblique Command

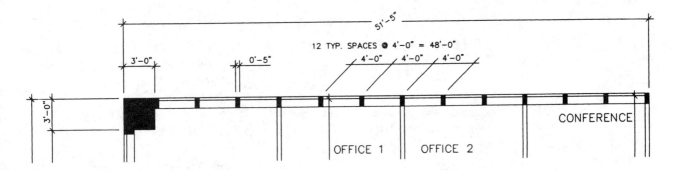

**FIGURE 9–38**
Using the Align Text-Angle Command

**Align Text-Home-Left-Center-Right (Dimension Text Edit from the Dimension toolbar)**

**Change the placement of the text for the overall dimension on the west exterior wall of the tenant space to flush right, and return it to the center position:**

| Prompt | Response |
|---|---|
| Command: | **Align Text-Right** |
| Select dimension: | **Pick the dimension text, 39′-5″.** |
| The text moves to the right side of the dimension line. | |
| Command: | **Align Text-Center** |
| Select objects: | **Pick the same dimension<enter>** |
| The text moves back to the center of the dimension line. | |

The Left option left justifies the text along the dimension line. The Angle option allows you either to type a new text angle (and press enter) or to pick two points to show Auto-CAD new text angle. The Home option returns the dimension text to its home position.

### Dimension Edit

When Dimension Edit is clicked from the Dimension toolbar or **DIMED** is typed at the Command: prompt, the Dimension Edit prompt is "Enter type of dimension editing [Home/New/ Rotate/Oblique]<Home>:" To activate any one of the options type the first letter:

**Home**   Returns the dimension to its default (original) location in the dimension line.
**New**   Allows you to change the existing text. Type the new text, PRESS: **<enter>**, then click the dimension whose text you want to change.
**Rotate**   Allows you to rotate existing text to a specified angle.
**Oblique**   Allows you to make an existing dimension into an oblique one.

### Override

The Override command is helpful when you are in the middle of dimensioning a project or have completed dimensioning a project and decide that one or more of the dimension variables in a named style need to be changed. The Override command can be used to change one or more dimension variables for selected dimensions but does not affect the current dimension style.

**Use Override to change the DIMTXT variable of STYLE1 from 1/16″ to 1/8″:**

| Prompt | Response |
|---|---|
| Command: | **Override** (from the Dimension menu or toolbar) (or TYPE: **OV<enter>** from the DIM: prompt) |
| Enter dimension variable name to override or [Clear overrides]: | TYPE: **DIMTXT<enter>** |
| Enter new value for dimension variable <1/16″>: | TYPE: **1/8<enter>** |
| Enter dimension variable name to override: | **<enter>** |
| Select objects: | **Pick any dimension entity on the drawing.** |
| Select objects: | **<enter>** |
| Command: | TYPE: **DIMTXT <enter>** |
| Enter new value for dimension variable <1/16″>: | **<enter>** |

The DIMTXT of 1/16″ setting has not changed.

### Update

Update differs from Override in that it updates dimensions using the current settings of the dimension style. For example, if you decide a dimension variable needs to be changed in a dimension style, change the variable. You may click the Save button in the Dimension Styles dialog box to save the changed variable to the dimension style. If you do not save the changed variable, AutoCAD prompts you with an ALERT dialog box, "Save changes to current style?" when you change dimension styles. Use Update to include the new variable settings in all or part of the dimensions within the drawing.

**Use Update to change the 1/8″ DIMTXT back to 1/16″:**
Because the Override command did not change DIMTXT within the STYLE1 settings, it is still set at 1/16″.

| Prompt | Response |
|---|---|
| Command: | **Update** (from the Dimension menu or toolbar) (or TYPE: **UP<enter>** from the DIM: prompt) |
| Select objects: | **Click the dimension entity on the drawing changed with Override.** |
| Select objects: | **<enter>** |

## DEFPOINTS Layer

When associative dimensions are created, a special layer named Defpoints is also created. Definition points for associative dimensions are drawn on the Defpoints layer. They are small points on the drawing that are not plotted but are used to create the associative dimension. When an associative dimension is updated or edited, the definition points are redefined.

## Modify Commands

In addition to the preceding commands used to edit associative dimensions, the following Modify commands can be used to edit *the dimensioned object and the accompanying associative dimension*. When editing a dimensioned object, be sure to include the accompanying associative dimension in the selection set.

| | | | |
|---|---|---|---|
| Array | Mirror | Scale | Trim |
| Extend | Rotate | Stretch | |

**Note:** Changing the DIMDLE variable and using Update does not change the dimension line increment for continuation of your drawing, because AutoCAD does not remember which dimensions were drawn using Baseline or Continue.

FIGURE 9–39
Properties Dialog Box

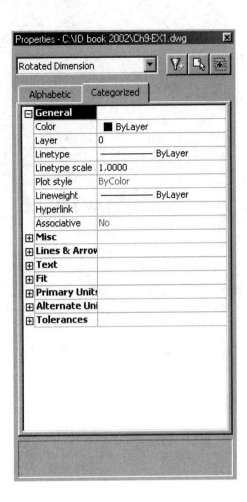

## Modify-Text

Modify-Text from the menu bar works when DIMASSOC is ON or OFF. It activates the Multiline Text Editor and allows you to change the existing text.

## Properties

The Properties command on the Modify menu can be used to change the properties of any dimension, as shown in Figure 9–39. Begin by selecting the dimension to be modified, then CLICK: **Properties** from the Modify menu. The Properties dialog box appears. Clicking the + to the left of the Property group displays a list of those items that can be changed. To change dimension text, CLICK: the + to the left of Text, then CLICK: **Text Override** and TYPE: **the new text** in the box to the right.

## GRIPS

Grips are particularly useful in modifying the placement of dimension text and the location of extension and dimension lines. To use grips to modify a dimension:

| Prompt | Response |
|---|---|
| Command: | CLICK: **the 14'-11 1/2" dimension in OFFICE 3** |
| Five squares appear on the dimension; one at the end of each extension line, one at the center of each tick, and one in the center of the dimension text: | CLICK: **the grip in the center of the dimension text** |

| Prompt | Response |
|---|---|
| The grip changes color (becomes HOT): Specify stretch point or [Base point/ Copy/Undo/eXit]: | **With SNAP ON move your mouse up and** CLICK: **a point two grid marks up.** |
| The dimension is stretched up two grid marks: | CLICK: **the same grip to make it hot, move your mouse to the right, and** CLICK: **a point two grid marks to the right.** |
| The dimension text moves two grid marks to the right: | CLICK: **the grip at the origin of the first extension line to make it hot, and move your mouse up two grid marks** |
| The origin of the first extension line moves up two grid marks: | CLICK: **the grip in the center of the dimension text to make it hot, and press the space bar one time** |
| The prompt changes to Specify move point or [Base point/Copy/Undo/eXit]: | **Move your cursor two grid marks down and** CLICK: **a point.** |
| The entire dimension moves down two grid marks: | PRESS: **Esc twice** |
| The grips disappear: | TYPE: **U<enter>, and continue pressing <enter> until the dimension is returned to its original state.** |

Using grips, you can toggle through STRETCH, MOVE, ROTATE, SCALE, and MIRROR. A more complete description of grips is given in a later chapter.

## SAVE

**When you have completed Exercise 9–2, save your work in at least two places.**

## PLOT

**Use a Layout Wizard or Page Setup to create a Layout tab named Dimensioning Plan2. Select a scale to correspond with the specified DIMSCALE setting. Plot Exercise 9–2.**

# EXERCISE 9–3
# Angular, Diameter, Radius, and Ordinate Dimensioning

Exercise 9–3 describes four types of dimensioning: Angular, Diameter, Radius, and Ordinate dimensioning. It also describes drawing center marks and leaders. When you have completed Exercise 9–3, your drawing will look similar to Figure 9–40. To begin, turn on the computer and start AutoCAD. The AutoCAD 2002 Today window is displayed.

## On Your Own

**1. Open drawing CH9-EX2 and save it as CH9-EX3 to the hard drive.**

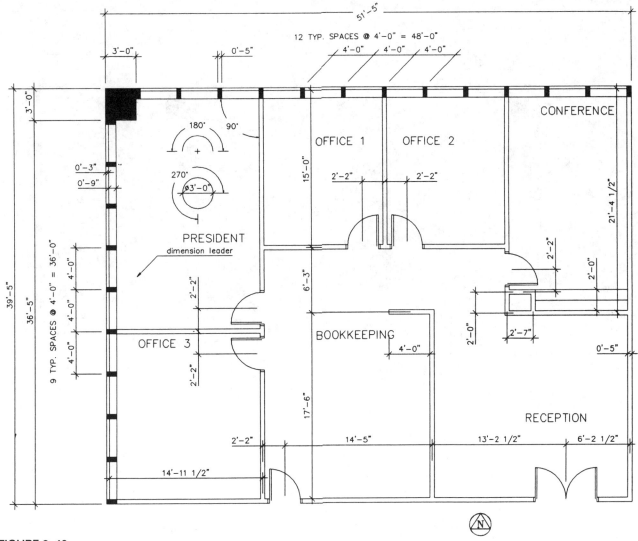

**FIGURE 9–40**
Exercise 9–3: Angular, Diameter, Radius, and Ordinate Dimensioning

2. **The following part of Exercise 9–3 describes angular and radial dimensioning. To practice with both these dimension types, draw an arc (1′-6″ radius) and a circle (1′-6″ radius) in the president's office, as shown in Figure 9–41, on the current A-pflr-dims layer.**

3. **Change the following dimensioning variables:**
   **DIMTAD—to 0**
   **DIMTIH—to on**

## Angular Dimensioning

**With the current layer A-pflr-dims, use the Angular command to dimension the angle of an arc (Figure 9–42):**

| Prompt | Response |
|---|---|
| Command: | **Angular** (from the Dimensioning menu or toolbar) (or TYPE: **AN<enter>** from the Dim: prompt) |

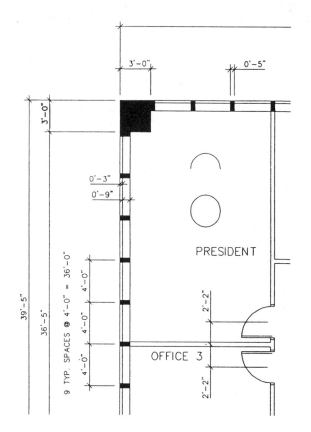

**FIGURE 9-41**
Draw an Arc and a Circle

**FIGURE 9-42**
Using the Angular Command

| Prompt | Response |
|---|---|
| Select arc, circle, line, or <specify vertex>: | **Click any point on the arc just drawn.** |
| Specify dimension arc line location or [Mtext/Text/Angle]: | **Click a point on snap, one grid mark (12″) above the arc.** |
| Dimension text = 180 | |

**Use the Angular command to dimension the angle of two points of a circle (Figure 9–42):**

| Prompt | Response |
|---|---|
| Command: | **Angular** |
| Select arc, circle, line, or <specify vertex>: | **<enter>** |
| Specify angle vertex: | CLICK: **the center of the circle (snap on)** |
| Specify first angle endpoint: | **D1** (snap on) |
| Specify second angle endpoint: | **D2** (snap on) |
| Specify dimension arc line location or [Mtext/Text/Angle]: | CLICK: **a point one grid mark above the circle** |
| Dimension text=270 | |
| Command: | |

**Use the angular command to dimension the angle of two lines (Figure 9–42):**

| Prompt | Response |
|---|---|
| Command: | **Angular** |
| Select arc, circle, line, or <specify vertex>: | **D3** |
| Select second line: | **D4** |
| Specify dimension arc line location or [Mtext/Text/Angle]: | **D5** |
| Dimension text=90 | |
| Command: | |

When dimensioning angles, AutoCAD uses three defining points—the angle vertex and two angle endpoints (the dimension extension lines location). When the arc is dimensioned, the center of the arc is the vertex, and each endpoint of the arc locates the angle endpoints. When a circle is dimensioned, the center of the circle is the vertex, the first point selected is the first angle endpoint, and the second point selected is the second angle endpoint. When two lines are selected, the intersection of the two lines is the angle vertex, and either an arc spans the angle between the two lines or AutoCAD provides extension lines for the arc to span. When <ENTER> is pressed to the Angular prompt, AutoCAD prompts allow you to pick the angle vertex, the first angle endpoint, and the second angle endpoint.

## Center Mark

**Draw a center mark in an arc (Figure 9–43):**

| Prompt | Response |
|---|---|
| Command: | **Center Mark** (from the Dimension menu or toolbar or TYPE: **CEN<enter>** from the Dim: prompt) |
| Select arc or circle: | **Click any place on the arc.** |

A center mark is not associative and cannot be updated.

**FIGURE 9–43**
Using the Center Mark, Diameter, Radius, and Leader Commands

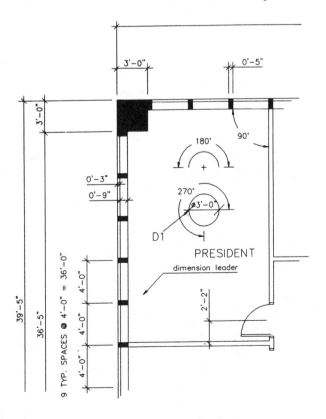

## On Your Own

**1. Change the following dimensioning variables:**

   DIMTAD—to 1
   DIMFIT—to 0

## Diameter

**Dimension the diameter of a circle (Figure 9–43):**

| Prompt | Response |
|---|---|
| Command: | **Diameter** (from the Dimension menu or toolbar or TYPE: **D** from the Dim: prompt) |
| Select arc or circle: | **D1** |
| Enter dimension text <3'-0">: | **<enter>** |
| Specify dimension line location or [Mtext/Text/Angle]: | **D1** (again) |

## Radius

The radius command is similar to the diameter command except that a radius line is drawn.

## Leader

The Leader command draws a leader. It can be used to show dimensions or to place notes on a drawing.

**Practice drawing a Leader (Figure 9–43):**

| Prompt | Response |
|---|---|
| Command: | **Leader** (from the Dimension menu or toolbar or TYPE: L <enter> from the Dim: prompt |
| Specify first leader point, or [Settings] <Settings>: | **Pick a point in the president's office.** |
| Specify next point: | **Pick another point at an angle, two grid marks up.** |
| Specify next point: | **Pick another point, one grid mark to the right.** |
| Specify text width <0'−0"> | **<enter>** |
| Enter first line of annotation text <Mtext>: | TYPE: **dimension leader<enter>** **<enter>** |
| Enter next line of annotated text: | **<enter>** |

**Note:** You can also access the leader command by TYPING: **L <enter>** from the DIM: prompt, but the resulting prompts are shortened.

## Ordinate Dimensioning

Ordinate dimensioning is a method of dimensioning that relates to an identified corner of a part that is the starting point, or point 0,0. The starting point of 0,0 is often called a *datum*. All dimensions are measured from the datum, as shown in Figure 9–44. This type of dimensioning, used for measuring mechanical or sheet-metal parts, is seldom used by architects and space planners. It is similar to baseline dimensioning but does not draw the dimension line.

FIGURE 9–44
Ordinate Dimensioning

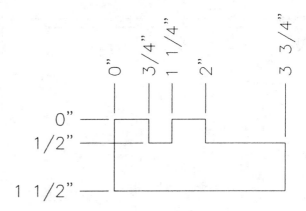

## SAVE

When you have completed Exercise 9–3, save your work in at least two places.

## PLOT

Use a Layout Wizard or Page Setup to create a layout tab named Dimensioning Plan 3. Select a scale to correspond with the specified DIMSCALE setting. Plot or print Exercise 9–3.

# EXERCISE 9–4
# Tenant Space Total Square Feet

Exercise 9–4 provides step-by-step instructions for using the Area command to compute the total square feet of the tenant space floor plan. It also provides instructions for using the Cal (calculator) command. When you have completed Exercise 9–4, your drawing will look similar to Figure 9–45. To begin, turn on the computer and start AutoCAD. The AutoCAD 2002 Today window is displayed.

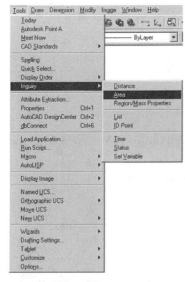

## On Your Own

1. **Open drawing CH9-EX1 from a floppy disk in drive A and save it as CH9-EX4 to the hard drive.**

## AREA

In order for the total square feet of any space to be computed, the exact area that is to be included must be identified. In the tenant space, the face of the exterior building glass on the north and west walls is used as the building's exterior measuring points, and the center of the south and east walls will be used as the interior measuring points.

## On Your Own

Completing the following steps will help you to use the Area command (Figure 9–46):

1. **Freeze layers A-pflr-dims and Defpoints, and set layer A-area current.**
2. **TYPE: FILL<enter> then OFF<enter> so that the column and mullions are not solid. Regenerate the drawing.**
3. **To be able to select the defining points of the exact area, as described above, use the Line command to draw separate lines in each corner of the tenant space to**

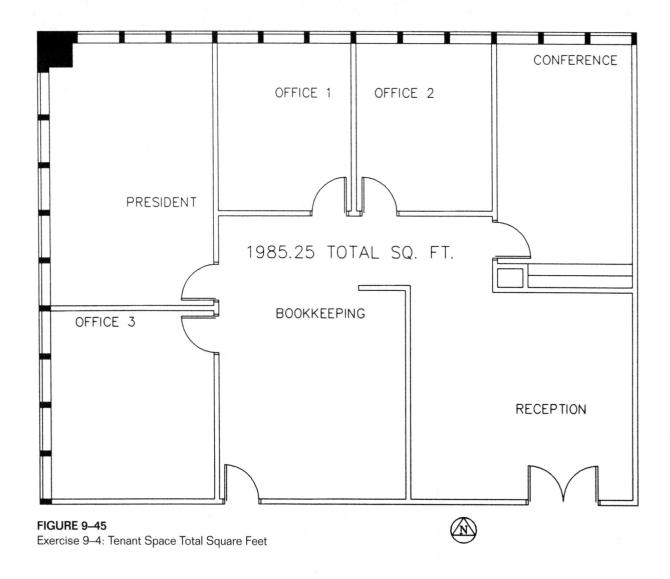

**FIGURE 9–45**
Exercise 9–4: Tenant Space Total Square Feet

which you can snap using Osnap-Intersection-Midpoint. **Each corner with the added lines is shown in Figure 9–46.**

**Compute the total square feet of the tenant space (Figure 9–46):**

| Prompt | Response |
|---|---|
| Command: | **Area (or TYPE: AREA<enter>)** |
| Specify first corner point or [Object/Add/Subtract]: | **TYPE: INT<enter>** |
| | **Use View-Zoom-Window to window around the northwest corner.** |
| of | **D1** (Figure 9–46) |
| | **Use Zoom-Dynamic to window the northeast corner.** |

**FIGURE 9–46**
Defining Points of the Exact Area
Included in the Total Square Feet
of the Tenant Space

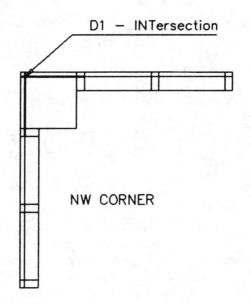

D1 — INTersection

NW CORNER

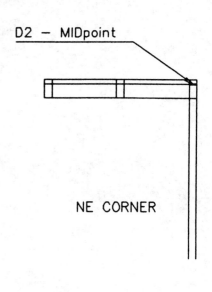

D2 — MIDpoint

NE CORNER

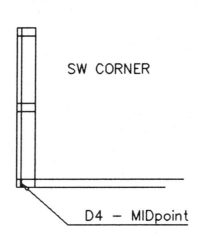

SW CORNER

D4 — MIDpoint

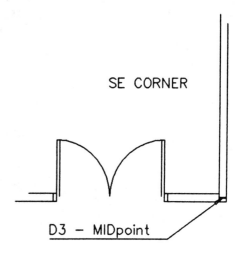

SE CORNER

D3 — MIDpoint

| Prompt | Response |
|---|---|
| Specify next corner point or press ENTER for total: | TYPE: **MID<enter>** |
| of | **D2** |
| | **Use Zoom-Dynamic to window the southeast corner.** |
| Resuming AREA command. | |
| Specify next corner point or press ENTER for total: | TYPE: **MID<enter>** |
| **Prompt** | **Response** |
| of | **D3** |
| | **Use Zoom-Dynamic to window the southwest corner.** |

| Prompt | Response |
|---|---|
| Specify next corner point or press ENTER for total: | TYPE: **MID\<enter>** |
| of | **D4** |
| Specify next corner point or press ENTER for total: | **\<enter>** |
| Area = 285876.25 square in. (1985.2517 square ft), Perimeter = 179′-10″ | |
| Command: | **Use the Dtext command (12″ high) to write the number of total square feet of the drawing.** |

**Add**   When Add is picked, the Area command is placed in an add mode. Add must be picked before the first space (of all the spaces to be added together) is specified. When the first space is specified, the area information is displayed. When the second space is specified, its individual area information is displayed along with the total area information of the two spaces together. Each subsequent space specified is displayed as an individual area total and is added to the running total.

**Subtract**   When Subtract is picked, each subsequent space specified is displayed as an individual area total and is subtracted from the running total.

**Object**   Object allows you to compute the area of a selected circle ellipse, polygon, solid, or polyline. For a circle, the area and circumference are displayed. When a wide, closed polyline is picked, the area defined by the center line of the polyline is displayed (the polyline width is ignored). Object is the fastest way to find the area of a closed polyline.

## On Your Own

**1. When you have completed practicing with the Area command, turn FILL ON.**

## CAL

AutoCAD provides a handy calculator function that functions much like many handheld calculators. The following uses the add and divide features of the calculator. You may want to try other features on your own.

**Use CAL to add three figures:**
+ = add
− = subtract
× = multiply
/ = divide

| Prompt | Response |
|---|---|
| Command: | TYPE: **CAL\<enter>** |
| >>Expression: | TYPE: **2′6″ + 6′2″ + 4′1″\<enter>** |
| 153.0 | **\<enter>** (Because the value is in inches it should be divided by 12 to arrive at feet) |
| >>Expression | TYPE: **153/12\<enter>** |
| 12.75 (or 12′-9″) | |

## SAVE

When you have completed Exercise 9–4, save your work in at least two places.

## PLOT

Use a Layout Wizard or Page Setup to create a layout tab named Dimensioning Plan 4. Select a scale to correspond with the specified DIMSCALE setting. Plot or print Exercise 9–4.

## EXERCISE 9–5
## Use QDIM to Dimension the Conference Room from Exercise 5–1

Exercise 9–5 gives you practice in using the QDIM command from the Dimension menu or toolbar. QDIM allows you to select the objects you want to dimension and to specify which type of dimensioning you want to use and then automatically dimensions the geometry for you. Although you can select any areas to be automatically dimensioned, the more complex the geometry (for example, a complex floor plan), the more careful you have to be in selecting objects because QDIM dimensions everything. To begin, turn on the computer and start AutoCAD. The AutoCAD 2002 Today window is displayed.

### On Your Own

1. **Begin this exercise by opening CH5-EX1 from the floppy disk in drive A and saving it as CH9-EX5 to the hard drive.**

2. **Erase the furniture from the drawing so the drawing appears as shown in Figure 9–47.**

3. **Set dimensioning variables as shown in Figure 9–29.**

4. **TYPE: DIMLUNIT <enter>, TYPE: 4 <enter> to select Architectural Units at the DIMLUNIT prompt.**

**Use Quick Dimension to dimension the drawing (Figures 9–48 and 9–49):**

| Prompt | Response |
|---|---|
| Command: _ | **Quick Dimension** (from the Dimension menu or toolbar) (or TYPE: **QDIM** from the Command: prompt) |
| Select geometry to dimension: | CLICK: **on the outside right side of the floor plan** |

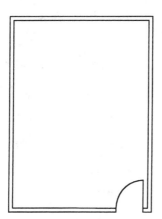

**FIGURE 9–47**
CH5-EX1 with Furniture Erased

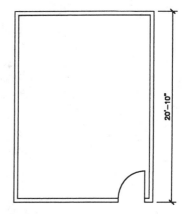

**FIGURE 9–48**
Use Quick Dimension to Dimension the Right Side

| Prompt | Response |
|---|---|
| Select geometry to dimension: | **\<enter\>** |
| Specify dimension line position, or [Continuous/Staggered/Baseline/Ordinate/ Radius/Diameter/datumPoint/Edit] \<Continuous\>: | CLICK: **a point two grid marks to the right of the right side** |

The drawing is dimensioned as shown in Figure 9–48.

| | |
|---|---|
| Command: | **\<enter\>** (Repeat QDIM) |
| Select geometry to dimension: | CLICK: **the bottom line of the floor plan including the door opening** |
| Select geometry to dimension: | **\<enter\>** |
| Specify dimension line position, or [Continuous/Staggered/Baseline/Ordinate/ Radius/Diameter/datumPoint/Edit] \<Continuous\>: | CLICK: **a point two grid marks below the bottom of the floor plan** |

The plan is dimensioned as shown in Figure 9–49.

## On Your Own

1. **If necessary, use grips to move the 11″ dimension to the outside, as shown in Figure 9–50.**

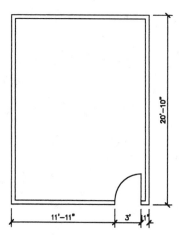

**FIGURE 9–49**
Use Quick Dimension to Dimension the Bottom

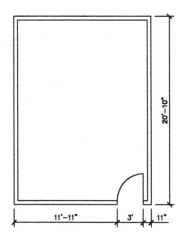

**FIGURE 9-50**
Use Grips to Move the 11″ Dimension to the Outside

## SAVE

When you have completed Exercise 9–5, save your work in at least two places.

## PLOT

Use a Layout Wizard or Page Setup to create a layout tab named Dimensioning Plan. Select a scale to correspond to the specified DIMSCALE setting. Plot or print Exercise 9–5.

# EXERCISE 9–6
# Office I Dimensioned Plan

1. Set dimensioning variables for the office I floor plan completed in Exercise 8–2.
2. Create a new layer for dimensions, and dimension the interior of the office I floor plan (Figure 9–51).
3. Plot the drawing to scale.

# EXERCISE 9–7
# Office II Dimensioned Plan

1. Set dimensioning variables for the office II floor plan completed in Exercise 8–3.
2. Create a new layer for dimensions, and dimension the interior of the office II floor plan (Figure 9–52).
3. Plot the drawing to scale.

# EXERCISE 9–8
# House Dimensioned Plan

1. Set dimensioning variables for the house floor plan completed in Exercise 8–4.
2. Create a new layer for dimensions, and dimension the interior of the house floor plan (Figure 9–53).
3. Plot the drawing to scale.

# EXERCISE 9–9
# Country Club Dimensioned Plan

1. Set dimensioning variables for the country club floor plan completed in Exercise 8–5.
2. Create a new layer for dimensions, and dimension the interior of the country club floor plan (Figure 9–54).
3. Plot the drawing to scale.

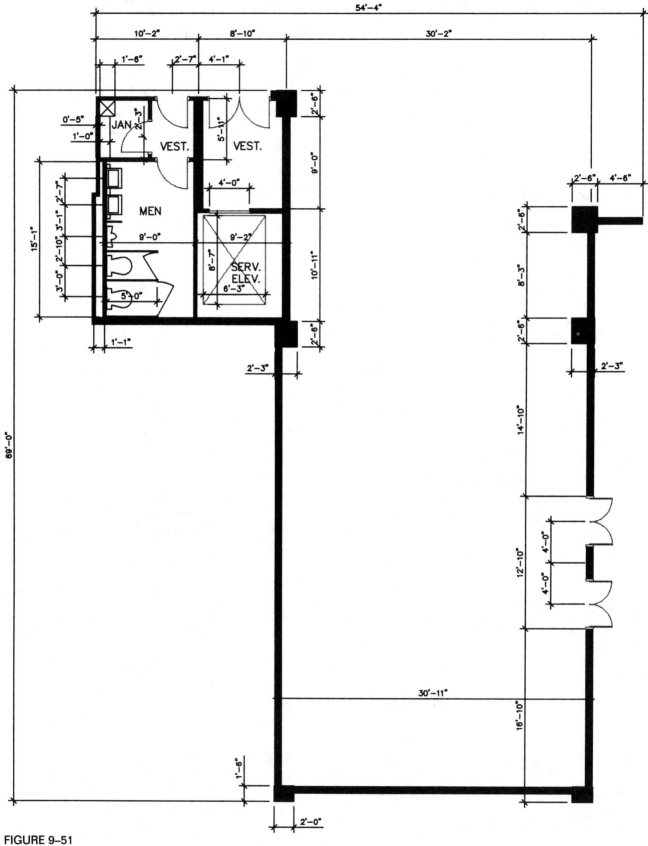

**FIGURE 9–51**
Exercise 9–6; Office I Dimensions

Part II: Two-Dimensional AutoCAD

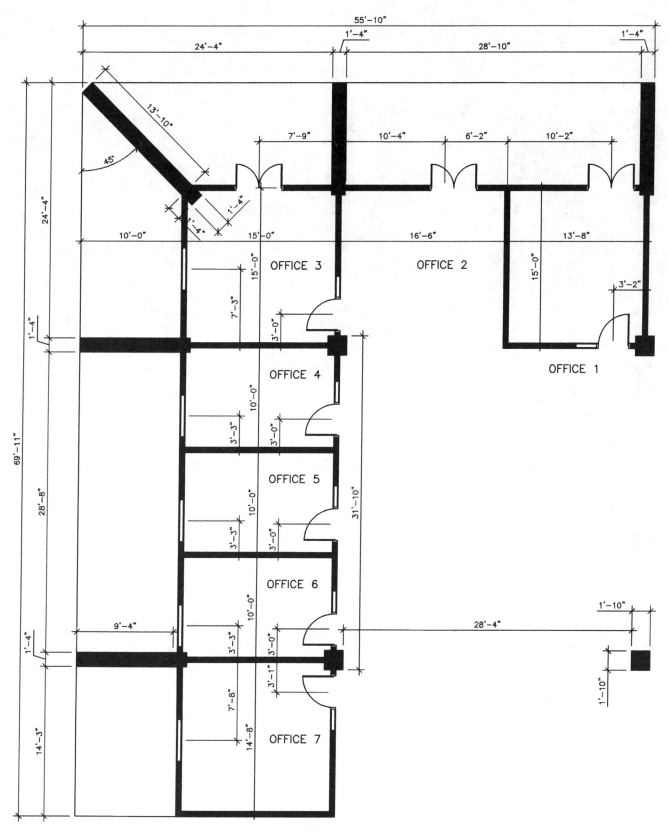

**FIGURE 9–52**
Exercise 9–7; Office II Dimensions

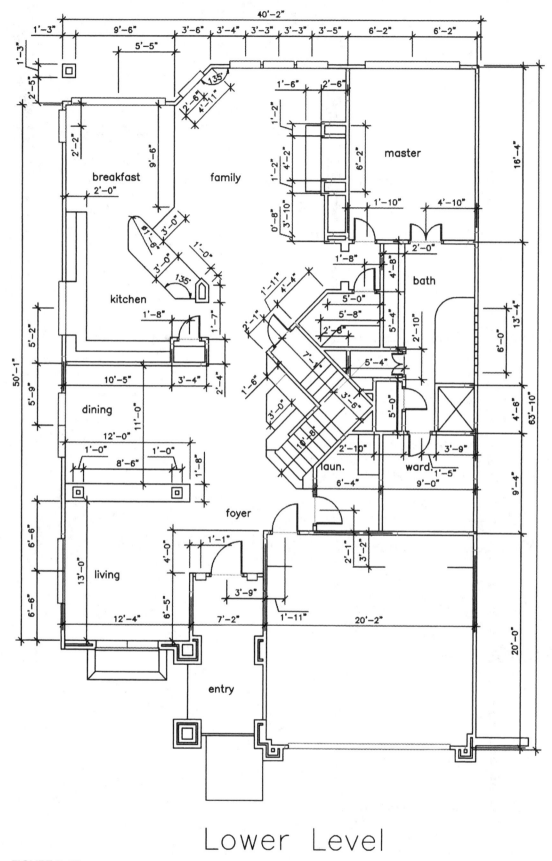

# Lower Level

**FIGURE 9–53**

Exercise 9–8; House Dimensions (Sheet 1 of 2)

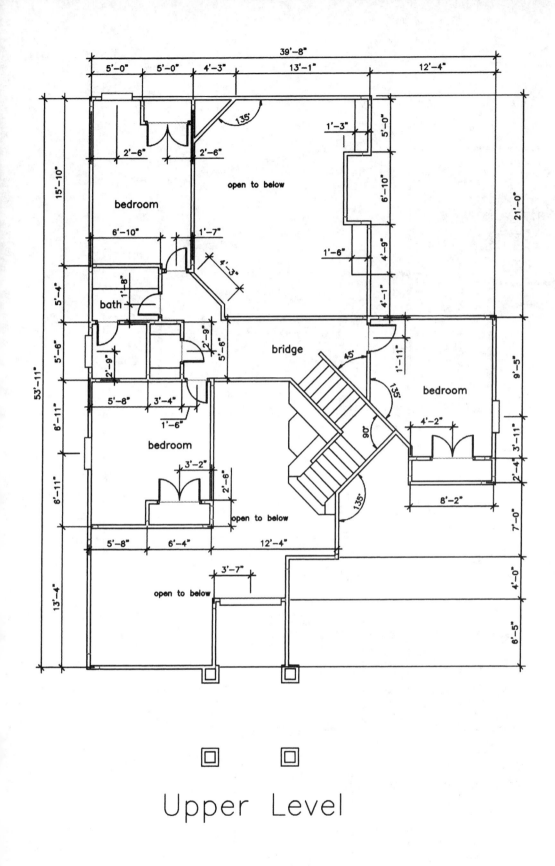

Upper Level

**FIGURE 9–53**
Exercise 9–8; House Dimensions (Sheet 2 of 2)

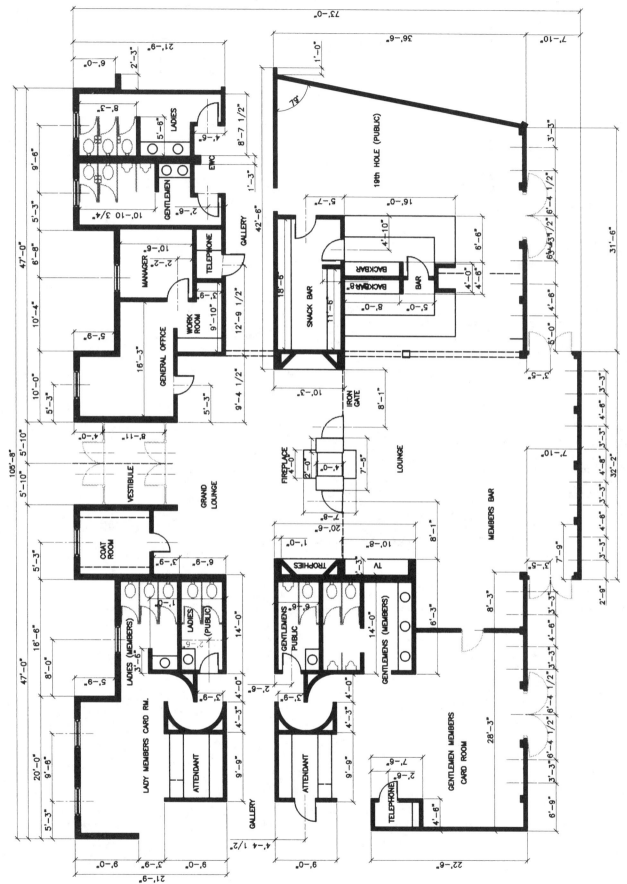

FIGURE 9-54

Exercise 9-9; Country Club Dimensions

248

# REVIEW QUESTIONS

1. A complete list of current dimensioning variables and settings is displayed when which of the following is typed from the Dim: prompt?
   - a. LINEAR
   - b. DIM VARS
   - c. STATUS
   - d. DIMSTYLE
   - e. UPDATE

2. Which of the following dimensioning variables controls the height of text used in the dimension?
   - a. DIMSTYLE
   - b. DIMTSZ
   - c. DIMASZ
   - d. DIMTXT
   - e. DIMTIX

3. Which of the following dimensioning variables controls the length of the arrowhead used in the dimension?
   - a. DIMSTYLE
   - b. DIMTSZ
   - c. DIMASZ
   - d. DIMTXT
   - e. DIMTIX

4. If a full-size drawing is to be plotted at a plotting ratio of 1/8″ = 12″, the DIMSCALE value should be set to
   - a. 1
   - b. 12
   - c. 24
   - d. 48
   - e. 96

5. For DIMTAD to place dimensions above vertical dimension lines, which of the following must be off?
   - a. DIMLIM
   - b. DIMTAD
   - c. DIMTOL
   - d. DIMTP
   - e. DIMTIH

6. Which of the following dimensioning variables forces the dimensioning text between the extension lines?
   - a. DIMTOFL
   - b. DIMTIX
   - c. DIMSOXD
   - d. DIMTIH
   - e. DIMTOH

7. Which of the following commands can be used only on associative dimensions?
   - a. Linear
   - b. Diameter
   - c. Ordinate
   - d. Oblique
   - e. Angular

8. Which of the following commands can be used to change the dimension text string for any dimension?
   - a. Update
   - b. Change
   - c. Trotate
   - d. Modify-Text
   - e. Hometext

9. A DEFPOINTS layer is created when a dimension is drawn with which of the following dimensioning variables set to ON?
   - a. DIMSTYLE
   - b. DIMTOH
   - c. DIMTAD
   - d. DIMASO
   - e. DIMTIH

10. To find the area of a closed polyline most quickly, which of the Area options should be used?
    - a. Object
    - b. Poly
    - c. Add
    - d. Subtract
    - e. First point

11. List the six tabs in the New Dimension Style dialog box:

    1. _____

    2. _____

    3. _____

    4. _____

    5. _____

    6. _____

12. Describe the use of the dimensioning variable DIMDEC.

_____

_____

_____

_____

13. Describe the use of the dimensioning variable DIMLUNIT.

_____

_____

14. Which settings must be made for dimensioning variable values to be displayed in 32nds of an inch?

_____

_____

15. Describe the use of the Continue command for linear dimensioning.

_____

_____

16. Write the name of the dimensioning variable that is used when you design your own arrow block.

_____

17. Describe what happens to the dimension of a 2″-diameter circle when the circle is enlarged to 4″ if DIMASSOC is set to 2.

_____

18. Describe how to save and name a set of dimensioning variables for a drawing.

_____

_____

_____

_____

19. Describe how the Update command differs from the Override command.

_____

_____

_____

_____

20. Describe the use of the QUICK Dimension command.

_____

_____

_____

_____

21. Describe the use of grips to move dimensioning text.

_____

_____

_____

_____

# 10 Drawing Elevations, Wall Sections, and Details

## OBJECTIVES

When you have completed this chapter, you will be able to:

☐ Correctly use the following commands and settings:

| | |
|---|---|
| Edit Hatch | Rename... |
| Filters | Stretch |
| Hatch... | UCS |
| Mirror | UCS Icon |
| Named UCS... (DDUCS) | |

## INTRODUCTION

The AutoCAD program makes it possible to produce clear, accurate, and impressive drawings of elevations, sections, and details. Many of the commands you have already learned are used in this chapter, along with some new commands, to draw an elevation (Exercise 10–1), a section (Exercise 10–2), and a detail (Exercise 10–3) of parts of the tenant space project.

## EXERCISE 10–1
## Tenant Space: Elevation of Conference Room Cabinets

In Exercise 10–1, an elevation of the south wall of the tenant space conference room is drawn. The south wall of the tenant space conference room has built-in cabinets that include a refrigerator and a sink. When you have completed Exercise 10–1, your drawing will look similar to Figure 10–1. To begin, turn on the computer and start AutoCAD. The AutoCAD 2002 Today window is displayed.

1. CLICK: **the Create Drawings tab**
2. CLICK: **Wizards**
   CLICK: **Quick Setup**
3. Set drawing Units: **Architectural**
   CLICK: **Next>**
4. Set drawing Width: **25′** × Length: **24′**
   CLICK: **Finish**
5. **Use SaveAs... to save the drawing on the hard drive with the name CH10-EX1.**
6. Set Grid: **12″**

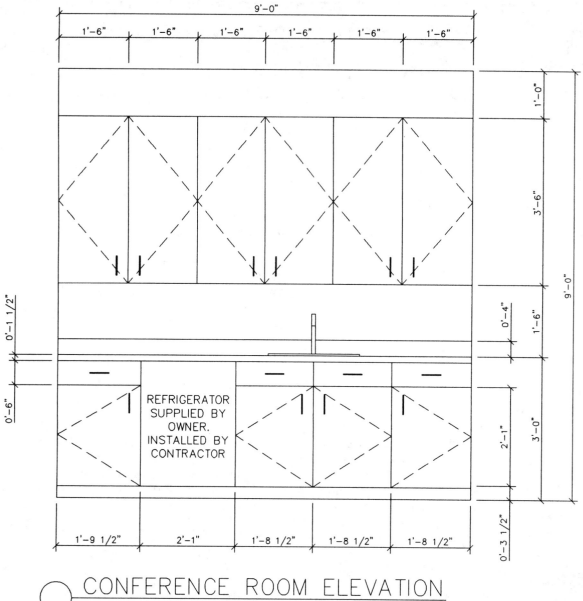

9'-0"

1'-6"  1'-6"  1'-6"  1'-6"  1'-6"  1'-6"

1'-0"

3'-6"

9'-0"

0'-1 1/2"

0'-4"

1'-6"

0'-6"

REFRIGERATOR
SUPPLIED BY
OWNER.
INSTALLED BY
CONTRACTOR

2'-1"

3'-0"

1'-9 1/2"   2'-1"   1'-8 1/2"   1'-8 1/2"   1'-8 1/2"

0'-3 1/2"

CONFERENCE ROOM ELEVATION

SCALE: 1/2"=1'-0"

**FIGURE 10–1**
Exercise 10–1: Tenant Space, Elevation of Conference Room Cabinets (Scale: 1/2″ = 1'-0″)

**FIGURE 10–2**
2D Model Space, 3D Model
Space, and Paper Space
Icons

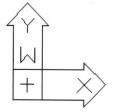

2D MODEL SPACE ICON

3D MODEL SPACE ICON

PAPER SPACE ICON

7. Set Snap: **6″**

8. Create the following Layers:

| LAYER NAME | COLOR | LINETYPE | LINEWIDTH |
|---|---|---|---|
| A-elev | Red | Continuous | Default |
| A-elev-hid | Green | Hidden | Default |
| A-elev-text | White | Continuous | Default |
| A-elev-dim | Blue | Continuous | Default |

9. Set Layer A-elev current.

## UCS

While you were drawing with AutoCAD in previous chapters, the UCS (user coordinate system) icon was located in the lower left corner of your drawings. A coordinate system is simply the X, Y, and Z coordinates used in your drawings. For two-dimensional drawings, only the X and Y coordinates are meaningful. The Z coordinate is used for a three-dimensional model.

Notice that the 2D UCS icon (Figure 10–2) has a W on it. The W stands for world coordinate system. This is the AutoCAD fixed coordinate system, which is common to all AutoCAD drawings.

The UCS command is used to set up a new user coordinate system or to modify the existing one. When UCS is typed from the Command: prompt, the prompt is "Enter an option [New/Move/orthoGraphic/Prev/Restore/Save/Del/Apply/?/World] <World>:"

If you TYPE: **N<enter>,** the following options are available: "Specify origin of new UCS or [ZAxis/3point/OBject/Face/View/X/Y/Z] <0,0,0>:". You can also CLICK: **Move UCS** in the Tools menu to move the origin of the current user coordinate system to another point on the drawing. In two-dimensional drawing the origin of the world UCS is moved, and nothing else is changed.

The Z coordinate is described and used extensively in the chapters that cover three-dimensional modeling. The UCS command options that apply to two dimensions are listed next.

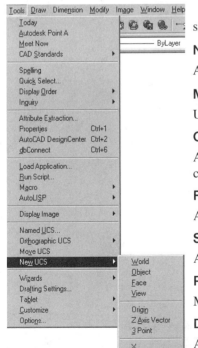

### New

Allows you to specify an origin of a new UCS.

### Move (or Origin)

Used to define a new UCS at a different origin (0,0) point.

### OBject

Allows you to define a new UCS by pointing to a drawing object such as an arc, point, circle, or line.

### Restore

Allows you to recall a UCS, using the name you gave it when you saved it.

### Save

Allows you to name and save a newly created UCS so that you can use it again.

### Previous

Makes the previous UCS current.

### Delete

Allows you to delete one or more saved UCSs.

### ?

Lists the names of the saved user coordinate systems.

### World

This is the AutoCAD fixed coordinate system, which is common to all AutoCAD drawings. In most cases you will want to return to the world coordinate system before plotting any drawing.

**Use the UCS command to change the origin of the current UCS:**

| Prompt | Response |
|---|---|
| Command: | TYPE: **UCS<enter>** |
| Enter an option [New/Move/orthoGraphic/ Prev/Restore/Save/Del/Apply/?/World] <World>: | TYPE: **O<enter>** (to select origin) (or CLICK: **Move UCS**) |
| Specify new origin point <0,0,0>: | TYPE: **8′, 12′<enter>** |

The origin for the current user coordinate system is now 8′ in the X direction and 12′ in the Y direction. The UCS icon may not have moved from where 0,0 was originally located. The UCS Icon command, described next, is used to control the orientation and visibility of the UCS icon.

## UCS Icon

There are two model space icons that you can choose to use: one for 2D drawings and one for 3D drawings. The default is the 3D icon, which you will probably use for both 2D and 3D. The UCS Icon command is used to control the visibility and orientation of the UCS icon (Figure 10–2). The UCS icon appears as arrows (most often located in the lower left corner of an AutoCAD drawing) that show the orientation of the X-, Y-, and Z-axes of the current UCS. It appears as a triangle in paper space (paper space is discussed in Chapter 15). The UCS Icon command options are "ON/OFF/All/Noorigin/ORigin/Properties:". The UCS Icon command options are listed next.

### ON

Allows you to turn on the UCS icon if it is not visible.

### OFF

Allows you to turn off the UCS icon when it gets in the way. This has nothing to do with the UCS location—only the visibility of the UCS icon.

### All

Allows you to apply changes to the UCS icon in all active viewports. (The Viewports command, which allows you to create multiple viewports, is described in Chapter 14.)

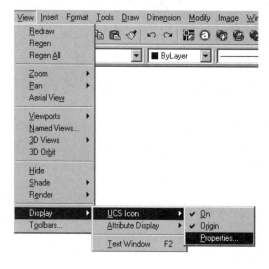

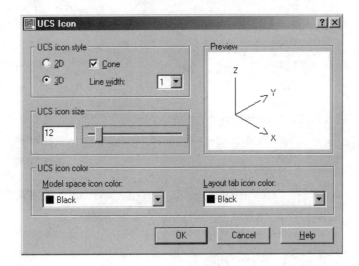

### ORigin

Forces the UCS icon to be displayed at the origin of the current UCS. For example, when USC Icon-Origin is clicked, the new UCS that you just created will appear in its correct position. If the origin of the UCS is off the screen, the icon is still displayed in the lower left corner of the screen.

### Noorigin

When Noorigin is current, the UCS icon is displayed at the lower left corner of the screen.

### Properties

When Properties is selected, the UCS Icon dialog box apppears. This box allows you to select the 2D or 3D model space icon, and to change the size and color of model space and paper space (Layout tab) icons.

**Use the UCS Icon command to force the UCS icon to be displayed at the origin of the new, current UCS:**

| Prompt | Response |
|---|---|
| Command: | TYPE: **UCSICON<enter>** |
| Enter an option [ON/OFF/All/Noorigin/<br>ORigin/Properties] <ON>: | TYPE: **OR<enter>**<br>(or CLICK: **UCS Icon-Origin**) |

The UCS icon now moves to the 8′,12′ coordinate location. You can now begin to draw the cabinets using the new UCS location.

**Using absolute coordinates, draw the lines forming the first upper cabinet door. Start the drawing at the 0,0 location of the new UCS (Figure 10–3):**

| Prompt | Response |
|---|---|
| Command: | **Line** (or TYPE: **L<enter>**) |
| Specify first point: | TYPE: **0,0<enter>** |
| Specify next point or [Undo]: | TYPE: **18,0<enter>** |
| Specify next point or [Undo]: | TYPE: **18,3′6<enter>** |
| Specify next point or [Close/Undo]: | TYPE: **0,3′6<enter>** |
| Specify next point or [Close/Undo]: | TYPE: **C<enter>** |

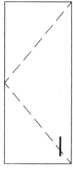

**FIGURE 10–3**
Draw the Lines Forming the First
Upper Cabinet Door

**Use Polyline to draw the door hardware using absolute coordinates (Figure 10–3):**

| Prompt | Response |
|---|---|
| Command: | **Polyline** (or TYPE: **PL<enter>**) |
| Specify start point: | TYPE: **15,2<enter>** |
| Specify next point or [Arc/Close/Halfwidth/ Length/Undo/Width]: | TYPE: **W<enter>** |
| Specify starting width <0'-0">: | TYPE: **1/4<enter>** |
| Specify ending width <0'-0 1/4">: | **<enter>** |
| Specify next point or [Arc/Close/Halfwidth/ Length/Undo/Width]: | TYPE: **15,7<enter>** |
| Specify next point or [Arc/Close/Halfwidth/ Length/Undo/Width]: | **<enter>** |

## On Your Own

**1. Set Layer A-elev-hid current.**

**Draw the dashed lines of the door using absolute coordinates (Figure 10–3):**

| Prompt | Response |
|---|---|
| Command: | **Line** (or TYPE: **L<enter>**) |
| Specify first point: | TYPE: **18,3'6<enter>** |
| Specify next point or [Undo]: | TYPE: **0,21<enter>** |
| Specify next point or [Undo]: | TYPE: **18,0<enter>** |
| Specify next point or [Close/Undo]: | **<enter>** |

## On Your Own

**1. If needed, change the linetype scale of the Hidden linetype to make it appear as dashes, change the linetype to Hidden2, or both. A large linetype scale such as 12 is needed.** (TYPE: **LTSCALE <enter>,** then TYPE: **12 <enter>**.)

## MIRROR

The Mirror command allows you to mirror about an axis any entity or group of entities. The axis can be at any angle.

**Draw the second cabinet door, using the Mirror command to copy part of the cabinet door just drawn. The top and bottom lines of the cabinet door are not mirrored (Figure 10–4):**

| Prompt | Response |
|---|---|
| Command: | **Mirror** (or TYPE: **MI<enter>**) |
| Select objects: | **D1** |
| Specify opposite corner: | **D2** |
| Select objects: | **<enter>** |
| Specify first point of mirror line: | **D3** (with ORTHO and SNAP ON) |
| Specify second point of mirror line: | **D4** |
| Delete source objects? [Yes/No] <N>: | **<enter>** (to complete command) |

## On Your Own

**1. Use the Mirror command to draw the inside and the right vertical cabinet edge of the next two sets of doors.** When this step is completed, your drawing will look like Figure 10–5.

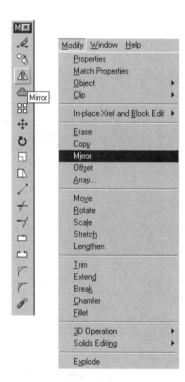

**Note:** If you want to mirror a part of a drawing containing text but do not want the text to be a mirror image, change the MIRRTEXT system variable setting to 0. This allows you to mirror the part and leave the text "right reading." When MIRRTEXT is set to 1 (the default), text is given a mirror image. To change this setting TYPE: **MIRRTEXT<enter>,** then TYPE: **0<enter>.**

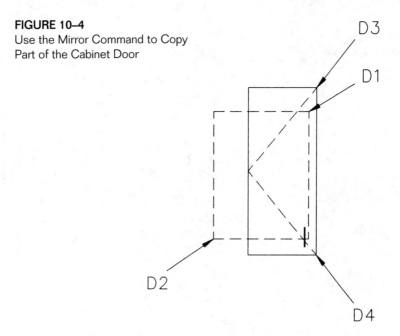

**FIGURE 10–4**
Use the Mirror Command to Copy
Part of the Cabinet Door

**FIGURE 10–5**
Use the Mirror Command to
Draw the Inside of the Cabinet
Doors and the Right Vertical Edge
of the Next Two Sets of Doors

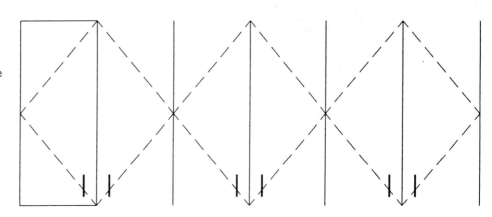

Later you will extend the lines forming the top and bottom of the first cabinet so that you do not have 12 small lines instead of 2 long lines. Having extra line segments increases the size of your drawing file and creates a drawing that is sometimes difficult to change.

**Use the Mirror command to draw the first lower cabinet door (Figure 10–6):**

| Prompt | Response |
|---|---|
| Command: | **Mirror** (or TYPE: **MI<enter>**) |
| Select objects: | **D2** (left to right) |
| Specify opposite corner: | **D1** |
| Select objects: | **<enter>** |
| Specify first point of mirror line: | **D3** (with ORTHO and SNAP on; the lower cabinets will be moved to the accurate location later) |
| Specify second point of mirror line: | **D4** |
| Delete source objects? [Yes/No] <N>: | **<enter>** |

**Note:** A crossing window is clicked right to left.

The lower cabinet door is now too high and too narrow. The Stretch command can be used to shrink the cabinet to the correct height and stretch it to the correct width.

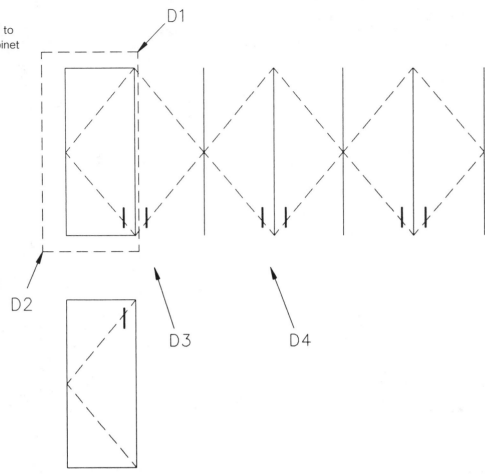

## STRETCH

The Stretch command can be used to stretch entities to make them longer or shorter. It can also be used to move entities that have other lines attached to them without removing the attached lines (described later in this exercise). Stretch requires you to use a crossing window to select objects. As with many other Modify commands, you may select objects initially, then remove or add objects to the selection set before you perform the stretch function.

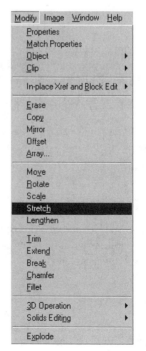

**Use the Stretch command to change the height of the first lower cabinet door just drawn (Figure 10–7):**

| Prompt | Response |
|---|---|
| Command: | **Stretch** (or TYPE: **S<enter>**) |
| Select objects to stretch by crossing-window or crossing-polygon... | |
| Select objects: | **D1** |
| Specify opposite corner: | **D2** |
| Select objects: | **<enter>** |
| Specify base point or displacement: | **D3** (any point) |
| Specify second point of displacement: | TYPE: **@8-1/2<270<enter>** (or move your mouse down and TYPE: **8.5 <enter>**) (the upper door height, 3′6″, minus the lower door height, 2′1″, divided by 2; take half off the top of the door and half off the bottom) |
| Command: | **Stretch** (or PRESS: **<enter>**) |

**FIGURE 10–7**
Use the Stretch Command to
Change the Height of the First
Lower Cabinet Door

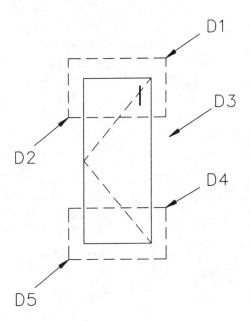

| Prompt | Response |
|---|---|
| Select objects to stretch by crossing-window or crossing-polygon... | |
| Select objects: | **D4** |
| Specify opposite corner: | **D5** |
| Select objects: | **<enter>** |
| Specify base point or displacement: | **D3** (any point) |
| Specify second point of displacement: | TYPE: **@8-1/2<90<enter>** (or move your mouse up and TYPE: **8.5 <enter>**) |

The lower cabinet door should now be 17″ shorter than the upper cabinet door from which it was mirrored (3′6″ minus 17″ equals 2′1″, the cabinet door height). Now let's use Stretch to make the door the correct width.

**Use the Stretch command to change the width of the cabinet door (Figure 10–8):**

| Prompt | Response |
|---|---|
| Command: | **Stretch** |
| Select objects to stretch by crossing-window or crossing-polygon... | |

**FIGURE 10–8**
Use the Stretch Command to
Change the Width of the
Cabinet Door

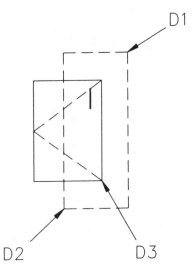

| Prompt | Response |
|---|---|
| Select objects: | **D1** |
| Specify opposite corner: | **D2** |
| Select objects: | **<enter>** |
| Specify base point or displacement: | **D3** (any point) |
| Specify second point of displacement: | TYPE: **@3-1/2<0<enter>** (or move the mouse to the right and TYPE: **3.5 <enter>**) (the upper door width, 1'6", plus 3-1/2", equals the lower door width, 1'9-1/2") |

## Complete the Following Steps to Finish Drawing the Elevation of the South Wall of the Tenant Space Conference Room

**Step 1.  Save the current UCS used to draw the upper cabinets:**

| Prompt | Response |
|---|---|
| Command: | TYPE: **UCS<enter>** |
| Enter an option [New/Move/orthoGraphic/ Prev/Restore/Save/Del/Apply/?/World] <World>: | TYPE: **S<enter>** (or CLICK: **UCS-Save**) |
| Enter name to save current UCS or [?]: | TYPE: **UPPER<enter>** |

**Step 2.  Create a new UCS origin for drawing the lower cabinets by moving the existing UCS origin -4'6" in the Y direction:**

| Prompt | Response |
|---|---|
| Command: | **<enter>** (Repeat UCS) |
| Enter an option [New/Move/orthoGraphic/ Prev/Restore/Save/Del/Apply/?/World] <World>: | TYPE: **O<enter>** |
| Specify new origin point <0,0,0>: | TYPE: **0,-4'6<enter>** (be sure to include the minus sign) |

**Step 3.  Move the lower cabinet door to a point 3-1/2" (the base height) above the origin of the current UCS (Figure 10–9):**

| Prompt | Response |
|---|---|
| Command: | **Move** (or TYPE: **M<enter>**) |
| Select objects: | **D1** |

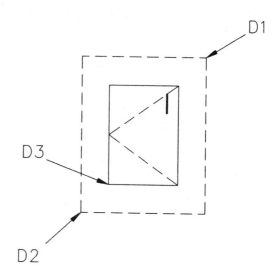

**FIGURE 10–9**
Move the Lower Cabinet Door to a Point 3-1/2" above the Origin of the Current UCS

| Prompt | Response |
|---|---|
| Specify opposite corner: | **D2** |
| Select objects: | **<enter>** |
| Specify base point or displacement: | **Osnap-Intersection** |
| of | **D3** |
| Specify second point of displacement or <use first point as displacement>: | TYPE: **0,3-1/2<enter>** |

## On Your Own

**Step 4.** Copy part of the lower cabinet 3'10-1/2" to the right, as shown in Figure 10–10.

**Step 5.** Stretch the right side of the copied door 1" to the left, making it 1" narrower.

**Step 6.** Use Mirror and Copy to draw the remaining doors, as shown in Figure 10–11.

**Step 7.** Use Extend to extend the top and bottom lines of both the upper and lower cabinets to the right edges of the cabinets, as shown in Figure 10–12.

**Step 8.** Use Offset to draw the bottom line of the base, the top and bottom (top of the drawers line) lines of the countertop, and the backsplash line (Figure 10–13).

**Step 9.** Use Erase and Extend to connect the sides of the upper and lower cabinets and the base with one line on each side (Figure 10–13).

**Step 10.** Set A-elev Layer current, set snap to 1/2", and use Extend, Polyline, and Copy to draw the lower cabinet drawers and their 5" × 1/4" handles. Use Trim to trim the line out of the area where the refrigerator is located (Figure 10–13). (Turn SNAP ON to draw the handles with the 1/4"-wide polyline.

**FIGURE 10–10**
Copy Part of the Lower Cabinet 3'-10-1/2" to the Right

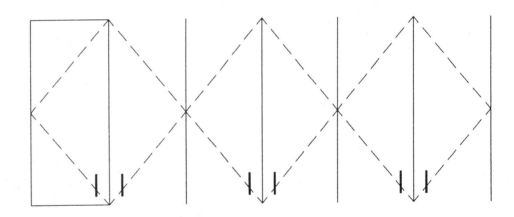

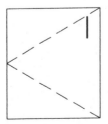

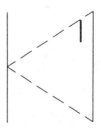

FIGURE 10–11
Use Mirror and Copy to Draw the
Remaining Doors

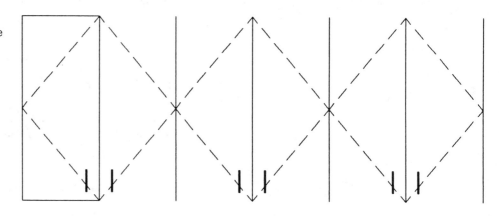

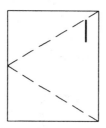
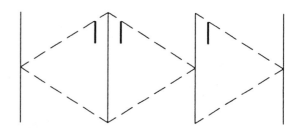

FIGURE 10–12
Use Extend to Extend the Top and
Bottom Lines of Both the Upper
and Lower Cabinets

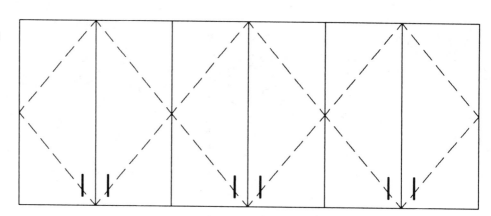

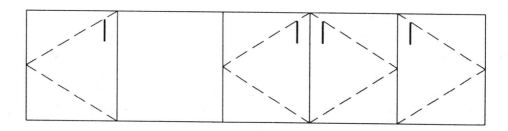

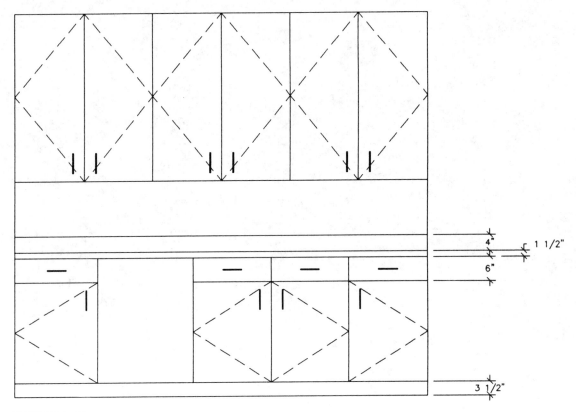

**FIGURE 10–13**
Finish Drawing the Cabinets As Shown

**Step 11.** Draw the sink in the approximate location shown in Figure 10–14 (the Stretch command will be used later to move the sink to the correct location):

| Prompt | Response |
|---|---|
| Command: | **Line** (or TYPE: **L<enter>**) |
| Specify first point: | **D1** (with SNAP on) |
| Specify next point or [Undo]: | TYPE: **@1/2<90<enter>** |
| Specify next point or [Undo]: | TYPE: **@25<0<enter>** |
| Specify next point or [Undo/Close]: | TYPE: **@1/2<270<enter>** |
| Specify next point or [Undo/Close]: | **<enter>** |
| Command: | **<enter>** (Repeat LINE) |
| Specify first point: | **Osnap-Midpoint** |
| of | **D2** |
| Specify next point or [Undo]: | TYPE: **@10<90<enter>** |
| Specify next point or [Undo]: | **<enter>** |
| Command: | **Offset** (or TYPE: **O<enter>**) |
| Specify offset distance or Through <default>: | TYPE: **1/2<enter>** |
| Select object to offset or <exit>: | **D3** (the line just drawn) |
| Specify point on side to offset: | **D4** (to the right) |
| Select object to offset or <exit>: | **D3** |
| Specify point on side to offset: | **D5** (to the left) |
| Select object to offset or <exit>: | **<enter>** |
| Command: | **Line** |

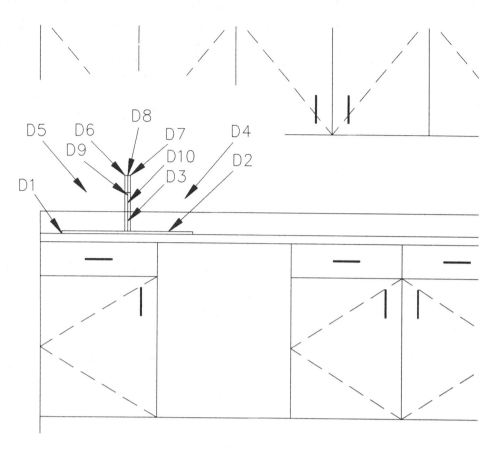

**FIGURE 10–14**
Draw the Sink in the Approximate
Location Shown

| Prompt | Response |
|---|---|
| Specify first point: | **Osnap-Endpoint** |
| of | **D6** |
| Specify next point or [Undo]: | **Osnap-Endpoint** |
| of | **D7** |
| Specify next point or [Undo]: | **<enter>** |
| Command: | **Offset** |
| Specify offset distance or Through <0'-1/2">: | TYPE: **3<enter>** |
| Select object to offset or <exit>: | **D8** |
| Specify point on side to offset: | **D4** |
| Select object to offset or <exit>: | **<enter>** |
| Command: | **Erase** (or TYPE: **E<enter>**) |
| Select objects: | **D9** (the center vertical line) |
| Select objects: | **<enter>** |

## On Your Own

**Step 12.** Trim out the line of the backsplash where it crosses the faucet.

**Step 13.** Set SNAP to 1".

**Step 14.** You can use the Stretch command to move entities that have other lines attached to them without removing the attached lines. Use Stretch to move the sink to its correct location (Figure 10–15):

**FIGURE 10–15**
Use Stretch to Move the Sink to
Its Correct Location

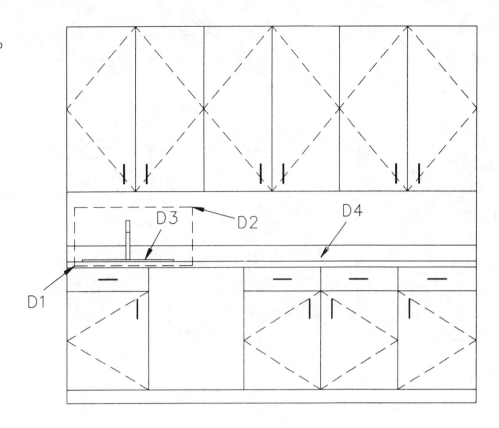

| Prompt | Response |
|---|---|
| Command: | **Stretch** (or TYPE: **S<enter>**) |
| Select objects to stretch by crossing-window or crossing-polygon... | |
| Select objects: | **D2** |
| Specify opposite corner: | **D1** |
| Select objects: | **<enter>** |
| Specify base point or displacement: | **Osnap-Midpoint** |
| of | **D3** |
| Specify second point of displacement or <use first point as displacement> | **D4** (with ORTHO and SNAP ON, pick a point directly above where the two doors meet) |

## On Your Own

**Step 15.** Use Offset and Extend to draw the ceiling line above the cabinets (Figure 10–16).

**Step 16.** Set the A-elev-text Layer current, and use Simplex lettering, 2″ high, to place the note on the refrigerator and to write the name of the elevation, 4″ high.

**Step 17.** Use the UCS command to save the current UCS, and name it LOWER. Set the UCS to World.

**Step 18.** Set the A-elev-dim Layer current, set the dimensioning variables, and add the dimensions as shown in Figure 10–16. You may want to change the GRID and SNAP settings to do the dimensioning.

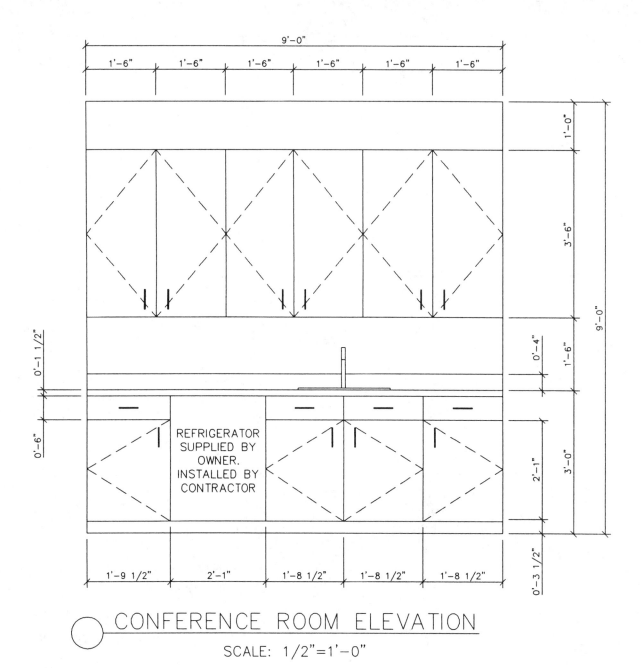

9'-0"

1'-6"  1'-6"  1'-6"  1'-6"  1'-6"  1'-6"

1'-0"

3'-6"

9'-0"

0'-1 1/2"

0'-4"

1'-6"

0'-6"

REFRIGERATOR
SUPPLIED BY
OWNER.
INSTALLED BY
CONTRACTOR

2'-1"

3'-0"

1'-9 1/2"  2'-1"  1'-8 1/2"  1'-8 1/2"  1'-8 1/2"

0'-3 1/2"

CONFERENCE ROOM ELEVATION

SCALE: 1/2"=1'-0"

**FIGURE 10–16**
Complete the Elevation Drawing (Scale: 1/2″ = 1'-0″)

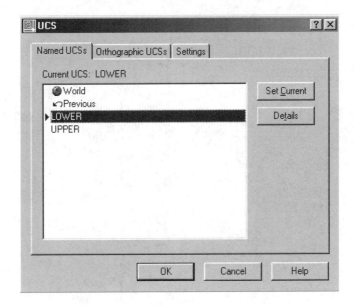

**FIGURE 10–17**
UCS Dialog Box

## NAMED UCS...

The Named UCS... (or TYPE: **DDUCS**) command displays the UCS dialog box (Figure 10–17). This dialog box can be used much like the UCS command.

## RENAME...

The Rename command displays the Rename dialog box, which allows you to rename an existing UCS, as well as many other objects such as Layers, Blocks, Text and Dimension Styles, Views, Linetypes, and Viewport configurations.

## SAVE

When you have completed Exercise 10–1, save your work in at least two places.

## PLOT

Use Layout Wizard or Page Setup to create a layout at a scale of 1/2″ = 1′, and plot or print Exercise 10–1.

# EXERCISE 10–2
# Tenant Space: Section of Conference Room Cabinets with Crosshatching

In Exercise 10–2, a sectional view of the south wall of the tenant space conference room is drawn. The sectional view of the south wall of the conference room (Figure 10–18) shows many construction details that elevation and plan views cannot. Sectional views are imaginary cuts through an area. Crosshatched lines are used to show where the imaginary saw used to make these imaginary cuts, touches the cut objects. This crosshatching is

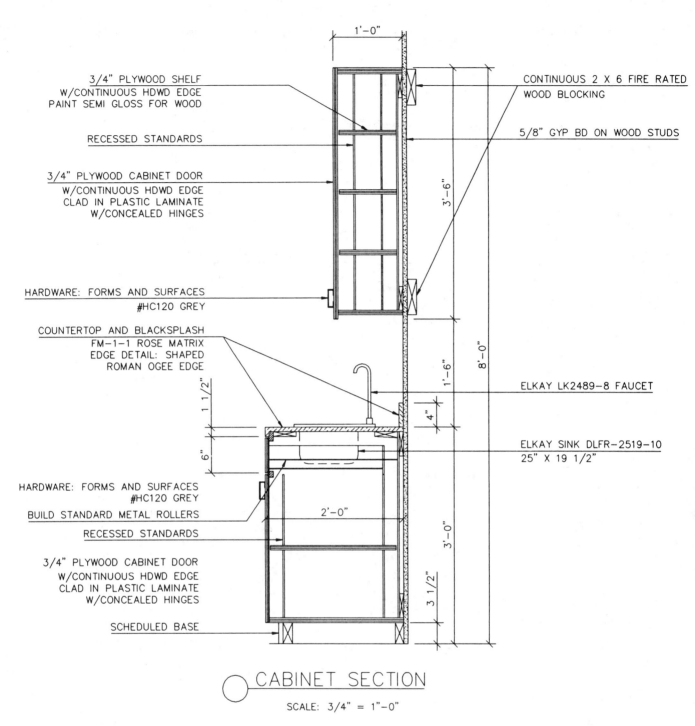

3/4" PLYWOOD SHELF
W/CONTINUOUS HDWD EDGE
PAINT SEMI GLOSS FOR WOOD

RECESSED STANDARDS

3/4" PLYWOOD CABINET DOOR
W/CONTINUOUS HDWD EDGE
CLAD IN PLASTIC LAMINATE
W/CONCEALED HINGES

HARDWARE: FORMS AND SURFACES
#HC120 GREY

COUNTERTOP AND BLACKSPLASH
FM-1-1 ROSE MATRIX
EDGE DETAIL: SHAPED
ROMAN OGEE EDGE

HARDWARE: FORMS AND SURFACES
#HC120 GREY

BUILD STANDARD METAL ROLLERS

RECESSED STANDARDS

3/4" PLYWOOD CABINET DOOR
W/CONTINUOUS HDWD EDGE
CLAD IN PLASTIC LAMINATE
W/CONCEALED HINGES

SCHEDULED BASE

CONTINUOUS 2 X 6 FIRE RATED
WOOD BLOCKING

5/8" GYP BD ON WOOD STUDS

ELKAY LK2489-8 FAUCET

ELKAY SINK DLFR-2519-10
25" X 19 1/2"

1'-0"

3'-6"

8'-0"

1'-6"

4"

1 1/2"

6"

2'-0"

3'-0"

3 1/2"

CABINET SECTION
SCALE: 3/4" = 1"-0"

**FIGURE 10–18**
Exercise 10–2: Tenant Space, Section of Conference Room Cabinets with Crosshatching (Scale: 3/4″ = 1′-0″)

done in AutoCAD by drawing hatch patterns. Exercise 10–2 will describe the Hatch command, used to draw hatch patterns.

When you have completed Exercise 10–2, your drawing will look similar to Figure 10–18. To begin, turn on the computer and start AutoCAD. The AutoCAD 2002 Today window is displayed.

## On Your Own

1. **Begin drawing CH10-EX2 on the hard drive by opening existing drawing CH10-EX1 from a floppy disk in drive A and saving it to the hard drive with the CH10-EX2. You can use all the settings created for Exercise 10–1.**

2. **Reset Drawing Limits, Grid, and Snap as needed.**

3. **Create the following Layers by renaming the existing layers and changing the Hidden linetype to Continuous:**

| LAYER NAME | COLOR | LINETYPE | LINEWEIGHT |
|---|---|---|---|
| A-sect | Red | Continuous | Default |
| A-sect-patt | Green | Continuous | Default |
| A-sect-text | White | Continuous | Default |
| A-sect-dim | Blue | Continuous | Default |

4. **Set Layer A-sect current.**

5. **Use Erase to eliminate the entire drawing or most of the drawing that appears on the screen. After looking closely at Figure 10–18, you may want to keep some of the conference room elevation drawing parts.**

6. **The cabinet section must be drawn before you use the Hatch command to draw the crosshatching. Draw the sectional view of the south wall of the tenant space conference room full size, as show in Figure 10–19. Include the text and the dimensions. Use Layer A-sect to draw the view, Layer A-sect-text for the text and leaders, and Layer A-sect-dim for the dimensions. Hatch patterns as shown in Figure 10–18 will be drawn on Layer A-sect-patt.**

7. **When the cabinet section is complete with text and dimensions, freeze layers A-sect-text and A-sect-dim so that they do not interfere with drawing the hatch patterns.**

## Preparing to Use the Hatch Command with the Select Objects Boundary Option

The most important aspect of using the Hatch command when you use "Select Objects" to create the boundary is to have the boundary of the area to be hatched defined clearly on the drawing. If the boundary of the hatching area is not clearly defined, the hatch pattern will not appear as you want it to. For example, some of the hatch pattern may go outside the boundary area, or the boundary area may not be completely filled with the hatch pattern.

Before you use the Hatch command in this manner, all areas to which hatching will be added must be prepared so that none of their boundary lines extend beyond the area to be hatched. When the views on which you will draw hatching have already been drawn, it is often necessary to use the Break command to break the boundary lines into line segments that clearly define the hatch boundaries. The Break command is used to break any of the lines that define the area to be hatched so that those lines do not extend beyond the boundary of the hatching area.

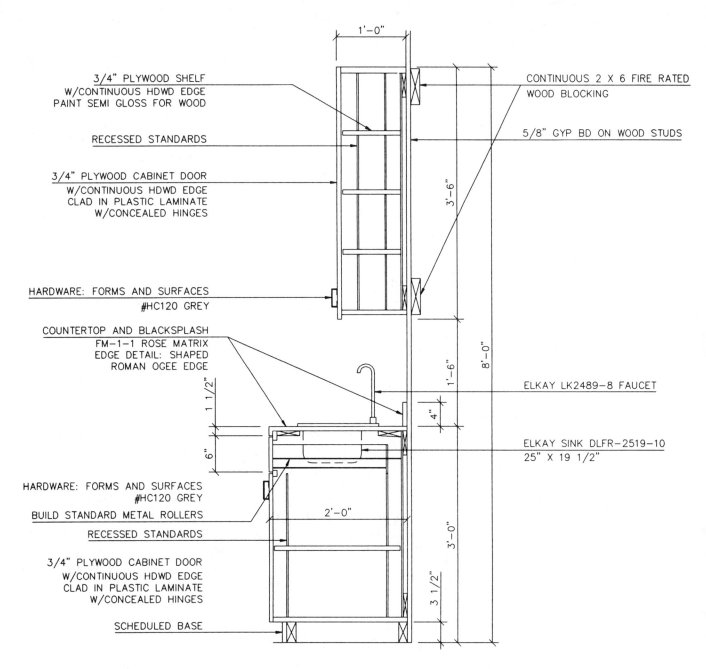

**FIGURE 10–19**

Exercise 10–2: Tenant Space, Section of Conference Room Cabinets Before Crosshatching (Scale: 3/4″ = 1′-0″)

**Use the Break command to help clearly define the right side of the horizontal plywood top of the upper cabinets (Figure 10–20):**

| Prompt | Response |
|---|---|
| Command: | **Break** (or TYPE: **BR\<enter\>**) |
| Select object: | **D1** (to select the vertical line) |
| Specify second break point or [First point]: | TYPE: **F\<enter\>** |
| Specify first break point: | **D2** (use Osnap-Intersection) |
| Specify second break point: | TYPE: **@\<enter\>** (places the second point exactly at the same place as the first point, and no gap is broken out of the line) |

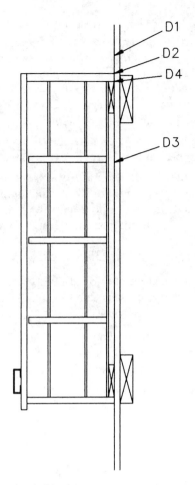

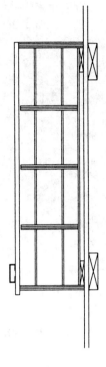

**FIGURE 10–20**
Use the Break Command to Clearly
Define the Right Side of the Horizon-
tal Top Area of the Upper Cabinets

**FIGURE 10–21**
Upper Cabinets with
Hatch Patterns Drawn

| Prompt | Response |
|---|---|
| Command: | **<enter>** (Repeat BREAK) |
| Select object: | **D3** (to select the vertical line) |
| Specify second break point or [First point]: | TYPE: **F<enter>** |
| Specify first break point: | **D4** (use Osnap-Intersection) |
| Specify second break point: | TYPE: **@<enter>** |

You have just used the Break command with the @ option to break the vertical line so that it is a separate line segment that clearly defines the right side of the plywood top area.

The Break command can also be used to erase or break a gap out of an entity. To break a gap out of an entity, simply click the first and second points of the desired gap at the command prompts. As shown in the prompt, "Enter second point (or F for first point):", the point used to "Select object:" can be used as the first point of the break.

## On Your Own

Before using the Hatch command to hatch the plywood top, the three plywood shelves, and the plywood bottom of the upper cabinet as shown in Figure 10–21, you need to define clearly the boundaries of those areas.

1. **Use the Break command to break the vertical line at the intersection of the top and bottom of the left side of the plywood top boundary.**

**Note:** Although the "Pick Points" method of creating hatch boundaries is often much easier, you must know how to use "Select Objects" as well. There are instances when "Pick Points" just does not work.

2. When the boundary of the plywood top is clearly defined, the top, bottom, right, and left lines of the top are separate line segments that do not extend beyond the boundary of the plywood top. To check the boundary, use the Erase command to pick and highlight each line segment. When each line is highlighted, you can see clearly if it needs to be broken. Use the Esc key to cancel the Erase command so that the lines are not actually erased. Use the Break command on the top horizontal line of the plywood top, if needed.

3. Use the Break command to prepare the three plywood shelves and the plywood bottom of the upper cabinet boundaries for hatching.

4. The Hatch command will also not work properly if the two lines of an intersection do not meet, that is, if there is any small gap. If you need to check the intersections of the left side of the plywood shelves to make sure they intersect properly, do this before continuing with the Hatch command as follows.

## HATCH... Boundary Hatch Dialog Box

When the Hatch command is activated (TYPE: **H<enter>**), the Boundary Hatch dialog box with the Quick tab selected appears (Figure 10–22). As listed in the Type: list box, the pattern types can be as follows:

**Predefined**   Makes the Pattern... button available.
**User-defined**   Defines a pattern of lines using the current linetype.
**Custom**   Specifies a pattern from the ACAD.pat file or any other PAT file.

To view the predefined hatch pattern options, CLICK: **the ellipsis (...)** to the right of the Pattern list box. The Hatch Pattern Palette appears (Figure 10–23). Other parts of the Boundary Hatch dialog box are as follows:

### Quick Tab Area

**Pattern**   Specifies a predefined pattern name.
**Custom pattern**   This list box shows a custom pattern name. This option is available when Custom is selected in the Type area.

**Tip:** You may prefer to draw lines on a new layer over the ones existing to form the enclosed boundary area instead of breaking, as described in this procedure. These additional lines may be erased easily with a window after you turn off all layers except the one to be erased. This is sometimes faster and allows the line that was to be broken to remain intact.

**Warning:** Those of you who are still working on your floppy disk are even more likely to lose some of your work with Hatch. Hatching often creates a huge drawing file. Be aware of how large that file is, and be sure it will fit comfortably on your floppy disk when you Save it.

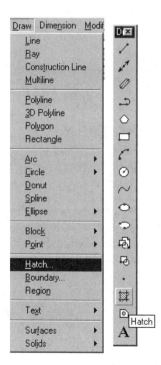

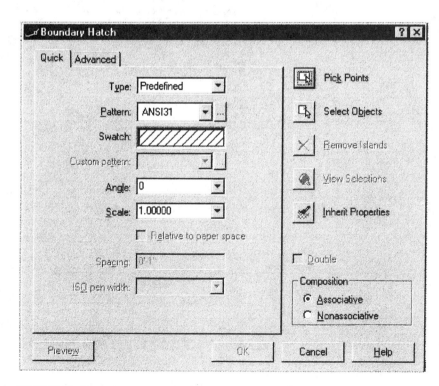

**FIGURE 10–22**
Boundary Hatch Dialog Box

**FIGURE 10–23**
Hatch Pattern Palette

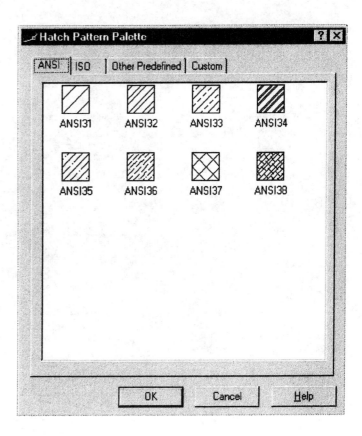

**Angle**   Allows you to specify an angle for the hatch pattern relative to the X axis of the current UCS.

**Scale**   This allows you to enlarge or shrink the hatch pattern to fit the drawing. It is not available if you have selected User-defined in the Type list box.

**Spacing**   Allows you to specify the space between lines on a user-defined hatch pattern.

**ISO pen width**   If you select one of the 14 ISO (International Organization of Standardization) patterns at the bottom of the list of hatch patterns and on the ISO tab of the Hatch Pattern Palette, this option scales the pattern based on the selected pen width. Each of these pattern names begins with ISO.

### General Area

**Pick Points**   Allows you to pick points inside a boundary to specify the area to be hatched.

**Select Objects**   Allows you to select the outside edges of the boundary to specify the area to be hatched.

**Remove Islands**   Allows you to remove from the boundary set objects defined as islands by the Pick Points< option. You cannot remove the outer boundary.

**View Selections**   Displays the currently defined boundary set. This option is not available when no selection or boundary has been made.

**Preview**   Allows you to preview the hatch pattern before you apply it to the drawing.

**Inherit Properties**   Allows you to pick an existing hatch pattern to specify the properties of that pattern. The pattern picked must be associative (attached to and defined by its boundary).

**Double**   When you pick this button so that a ✓ appears in it, the area is hatched with a second set of lines at 90° to the first hatch pattern. This is called a *double hatch*.

### Composition Area

**Associative**   When a ✓ appears in this button, the hatch pattern is a single object and stretches when the area that has been hatched is stretched.

**Nonassociative**   When this button is clicked so that a ✓ appears in it, the hatch pattern is applied as individual line segments instead of a single entity. If you think you may

**FIGURE 10–24**
Boundary Hatch Dialog Box,
Advanced Tab

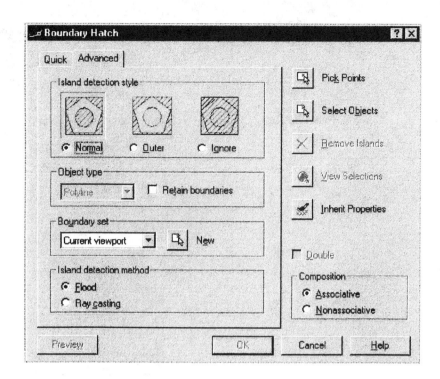

have a hatch pattern that extends outside the hatch boundary, you should bring in the pattern exploded and then use the Trim command to correct the overlap.

## Advanced Tab

When the Advanced tab of the Boundary Hatch dialog box is clicked, the Advanced tab, Figure 10–24, appears.

### Island detection style Area

The following island detection style options are shown in Figure 10–24:

**Normal**   When Normal is clicked (and a selection set is composed of areas inside other areas), alternating areas are hatched, as shown in the Island detection style area.
**Outer**   When Outer is clicked (and a selection set is composed of areas inside other areas), only the outer area is hatched, as shown in the Island detection style area.
**Ignore**   When Ignore is clicked (and a selection set is composed of areas inside other areas), all areas are hatched, as shown in the Island detection style area.

### Object type Area

**List box**   Controls the type of the new boundary object. When the boundary is created, AutoCAD uses a region or polyline. For now, this box should read Polyline. A check must appear in the Retain boundaries box for Object type to be selected.
**Retain boundaries**   Specifies whether the boundary objects will remain in your drawing after hatching is completed.

### Boundary set Area

**List box**   This box allows you to select a boundary set from the current viewport or an existing boundary set.
**New**   When New is clicked, the dialog box temporarily closes and you are prompted to select objects to create the boundary set. AutoCAD includes only objects that can be hatched when it constructs the new boundary set. AutoCAD discards any existing boundary set and replaces it with the new boundary set. If you don't select any objects that can be hatched, AutoCAD retains any current set.

274                                                                    **Part II: Two-Dimensional AutoCAD**

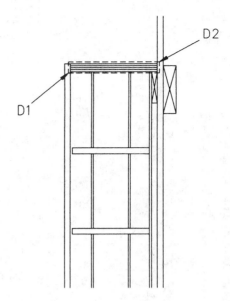

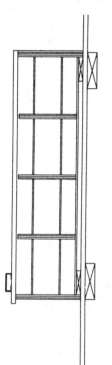

**FIGURE 10–25**
Use the Hatch Command with the
Select Objects< Boundary Option to
Draw a Uniform Horizontal-Line
Hatch Pattern on the Plywood Top of
the Upper Cabinets

### Island detection method

This area allows you to specify whether to include objects within the outermost boundary as boundary objects. These objects are islands.

**Flood**   Includes islands as boundary objects.
**Ray casting**   Excludes islands as boundary objects.

## On Your Own

**1. Set Layer A-sect-patt current.**

**Use the Hatch command with the Select Objects boundary option to draw a uniform horizontal-line hatch pattern on the plywood top of the upper cabinets (Figure 10–25).**

| Prompt | Response |
|---|---|
| Command: | **Hatch** (or TYPE: **H<enter>**) |
| The Boundary Hatch dialog box appears: | CLICK: **User-defined** in the pattern Type: area |
| | Angle: **0** |
| | Spacing: **1/4″** |
| | CLICK: **Select Objects** |
| Select objects: | CLICK: **D1** |
| Specify opposite corner: | CLICK: **D2** |
| Select objects: | **<enter>** |
| The Boundary Hatch dialog box appears: | CLICK: **Preview** |
| A preview of your hatching appears: | **<enter>** |
| The Boundary Hatch dialog box appears: | CLICK: **OK** (if the correct hatch pattern was previewed; if not, CLICK: **Cancel** and fix the problem) |

The plywood top of the upper cabinet is now hatched.

## On Your Own

**1. Use the same hatching procedure to draw a hatch pattern on the three plywood shelves and the plywood bottom of the upper cabinet, as shown in Figure 10–26.**

When you use the Pick Points boundary option to create a boundary for the hatch pattern, AutoCAD allows you to pick any point inside the area, and the boundary is automatically created. You do not have to prepare the boundary of the area as you did with the Select Objects boundary option. The entire area to be hatched must be visible on the screen.

**FIGURE 10–26**
Draw a Hatch Pattern on the
Three Plywood Shelves and the
Plywood Bottom of the Upper
Cabinet

**Tip:** When selecting objects using a
Window, TYPE: **W<enter>** to use the
crosshair.

**Tip:** Turn off or freeze the text and
dimension layers if they interfere with
hatching.

**Note:** Be sure to zoom out so the entire boundary of the area to be hatched is visible or it will not hatch.

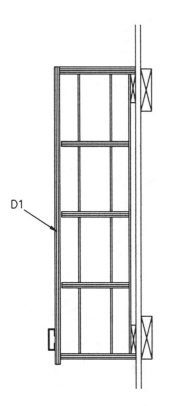

**FIGURE 10–27**
Use the Hatch Command with the Pick Points Boundary Option to Draw a Uniform Vertical-Line Hatch Pattern on the Upper Cabinet Door

**Tip:** You may have to draw a line across the top of the 5/8″ gypsum board to create the hatch pattern.

**Use the Hatch command with the Pick Points boundary option to draw a uniform vertical-line hatch pattern on the upper cabinet door (Figure 10–27):**

| Prompt | Response |
|---|---|
| Command: | **Hatch** (or TYPE: **H<enter>**) |
| The Boundary Hatch dialog box appears: | CLICK: **User-defined** in the Type: area |
| | Angle: **90** |
| | Spacing: **1/4** |
| | CLICK: **Pick Points** |
| Select internal point: | CLICK: **D1** (inside the door symbol) |
| Select internal point: | **<enter>** |
| The Boundary Hatch dialog box appears: | CLICK: **Preview** |
| A preview of your hatching appears: | **<enter>** |
| The Boundary Hatch dialog box appears: | CLICK: **OK** (if the correct hatch pattern was previewed; if not, CLICK: **Cancel** and fix the problem) |

**Use the Hatch command with the Pick Points boundary option to draw the AR-SAND hatch pattern on the 5/8″ gypsum board (Figures 10–28, 10–29, and 10–30):**

| Prompt | Response |
|---|---|
| Command: | **Hatch** |
| The Boundary Hatch dialog box appears: | CLICK: **Predefined** |
| | CLICK: **...** (to the right of the Pattern: list box) |
| The Hatch pattern palette appears: | CLICK: **the Other Predefined tab** |
| | CLICK: **AR-SAND** (Figure 10–28) |
| | CLICK: **OK** |

**FIGURE 10–28**
Select AR-SAND

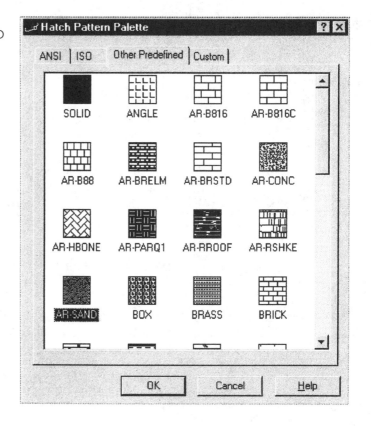

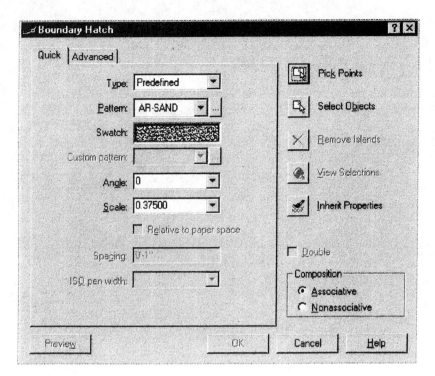

**FIGURE 10–29**
Specify Scale for AR-SAND

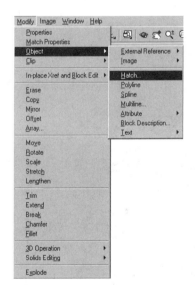

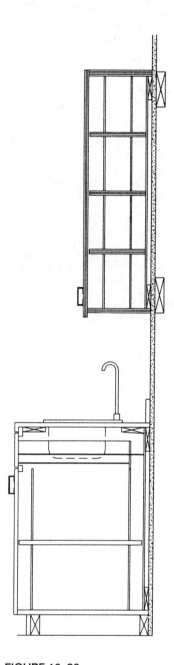

**FIGURE 10–30**
Use the Hatch Command to Draw
the AR-SAND Hatch Pattern on
the 5/8″ Gypsum Board

| Prompt | Response |
|---|---|
| The Boundary Hatch dialog box appears (Figure 10–29): | CLICK: **0** (in the Angle box) |
| | TYPE: **3/8″** (in the Scale: box) |
| | CLICK: **Pick Points** |
| Select internal point: | CLICK: **any point inside the lines defining the 5/8 gypsum board boundary** |
| Select internal point: | **<enter>** |
| The Boundary Hatch dialog box appears: | CLICK: **OK** |
| The 5/8″ gypsum board is now hatched. | |

## Editing Hatch Patterns

If you have prepared a complex drawing to be hatched, and the hatch preview shows one or two lines extending outside the hatch area, click the Nonassociative button in the Boundary Hatch dialog box before you click OK. The hatch pattern will then be inserted as individual lines that can be trimmed or otherwise edited.

If you already have a hatch pattern on the drawing that has one or two lines extending outside the hatch area, select Modify-Hatch..., Edit Hatch (or TYPE: **HE<enter>**), click on the hatch pattern, and click the Nonassociative button in the resulting Hatch edit dialog box (Figure 10–31). If necessary, explode the hatch pattern. The lines may then be trimmed or otherwise edited. The other properties of the hatch pattern may also be edited using the Hatch edit dialog box.

## On Your Own

**Note:** AutoCAD ensures proper alignment of hatch patterns in adjacent areas by generating all lines of every hatch pattern from the same reference point (usually 0,0). Use the Snap, Rotate command, Base point to change the reference point of a hatch pattern to vary the alignment.

1. **Using the patterns described in Figure 10–32, draw hatch patterns by using the Pick Points option on the lower cabinets.**

2. **Thaw layers A-sect-text and A-sect-dim.**

## SAVE

When you have completed Exercise 10–2, save your work in at least two places.

## PLOT

Use Layout Wizard or Page Setup to create a layout at a scale of 3/4″ = 1′ and plot or print Exercise 10–2.

**FIGURE 10–31**
Hatch Edit Using Boundary Hatch Dialog Box

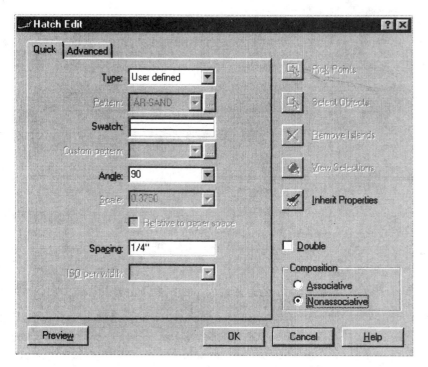

Part II: Two-Dimensional AutoCAD

**FIGURE 10–32**
Draw the Hatch Patterns on the
Lower Cabinets as Shown

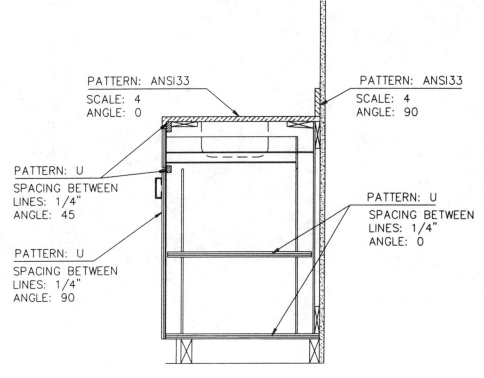

PATTERN: ANSI33
SCALE: 4
ANGLE: 0

PATTERN: ANSI33
SCALE: 4
ANGLE: 90

PATTERN: U
SPACING BETWEEN
LINES: 1/4"
ANGLE: 45

PATTERN: U
SPACING BETWEEN
LINES: 1/4"
ANGLE: 0

PATTERN: U
SPACING BETWEEN
LINES: 1/4"
ANGLE: 90

# EXERCISE 10–3
# Detail of Door Jamb with Crosshatching

In Exercise 10–3, a detail of a door jamb is drawn. When you have completed Exercise 10–3, your drawing will look similar to Figure 10–33. To begin, turn on the computer and start AutoCAD.

## On Your Own

1. **Begin drawing CH11-EX3 on the hard drive by opening existing drawing CH10-EX1 from a floppy disk in drive A and saving it to the hard drive with the name CH10-EX3.** You can use most of the settings you created for Exercise 10–1.

2. **Reset Drawing Limits, Grid, and Snap as needed.**

3. **Create the following Layers by renaming the existing Layers and changing the Hidden linetype to Continuous.**

| LAYER NAME | COLOR | LINETYPE | LINEWEIGHT |
|---|---|---|---|
| A-detl | Red | Continuous | Default |
| A-detl-patt | Green | Continuous | Default |
| A-detl-text | White | Continuous | Default |
| A-detl-dim | Blue | Continuous | Default |

4. **Set Layer A-detl current.**

5. **Use Erase to eliminate the entire drawing that appears on the screen.**

6. **Using the dimensions shown in Figure 10–33, draw all the door jamb components. Drawing some of the components separately and copying or moving them into place will be helpful. Measure any dimensions not shown with a scale of 3″= 1′-0″.**

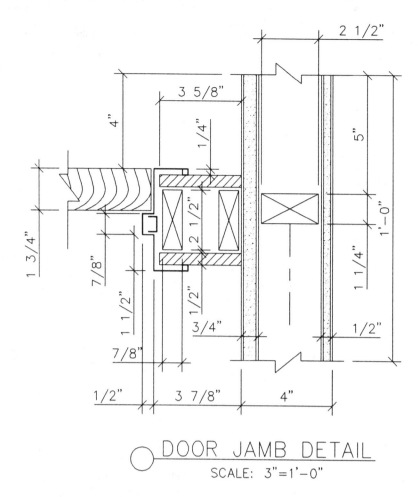

DOOR JAMB DETAIL
SCALE: 3″=1′-0″

7. **Set Layer A-detl-patt current, and draw the hatch patterns as described in Figure 10–34. Use a Spline and array it to draw the curved wood grain pattern.**

8. **Set Layer A-detl-dim current, and draw the dimensions as shown in Figure 10–33.**

9. **Set Layer A-detl-text current, and add the name of the detail as shown in Figure 10–33.**

10. **Save the drawing in two places, create a layout at a scale of 3″ = 1′, and plot or print the drawing.**

**FIGURE 10–34**
Exercise 10–3: Hatch Patterns

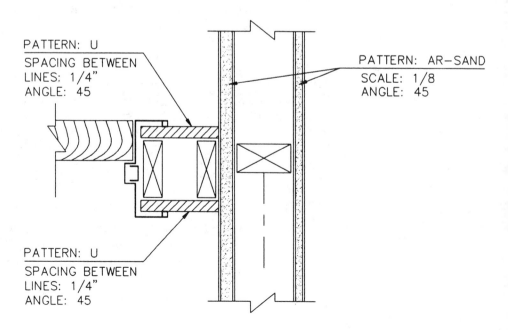

PATTERN: U
SPACING BETWEEN
LINES: 1/4″
ANGLE: 45

PATTERN: AR-SAND
SCALE: 1/8
ANGLE: 45

PATTERN: U
SPACING BETWEEN
LINES: 1/4″
ANGLE: 45

# EXERCISE 10–4
## Using FILTERS to Draw an Orthographic Drawing of a Conference Table

In Exercise 10–4, the AutoCAD feature called FILTERS is used. Using FILTERS is especially helpful when you are making orthographic drawings showing the top, front, and right-side views of an object.

In Exercise 10–4, an orthographic drawing of a conference table, showing the top, front, and right sides, is drawn using FILTERS. When you have completed Exercise 10–4, your drawing will look similar to Figure 10–35. To begin, turn on the computer and start AutoCAD. The AutoCAD 2002 Today window is displayed.

1. CLICK: **the Create Drawings tab**

   CLICK: **Wizards**

2. CLICK: **Quick Setup**

3. Set drawing Units: **Architectural**

   CLICK: **Next>**

4. Set drawing width: **12′** × Length: **9′**

   CLICK: **Finish**

5. **Use SaveAs... to save the drawing on the hard drive with the name CH10-EX4.**

6. Set Grid **2″**

7. Set Snap **1″**

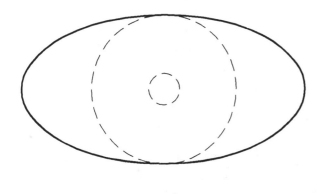

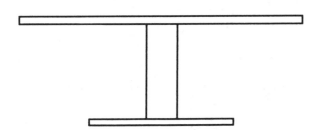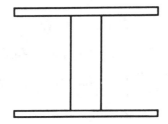

CONFERENCE TABLE

SCALE: 1/2"=1'-0"

**FIGURE 10–35**

Exercise 10–4: Using FILTERS to Draw an Orthographic Drawing of a Conference Table
(Scale: 1/2″ = 1'-0″)

8. Create the following Layers:

| LAYER NAME | COLOR | LINETYPE | LINEWEIGHT |
|------------|-------|----------|------------|
| A-furn-s | Red | Continuous | Default |
| A-furn-h | Green | Hidden | Default |
| A-furn-text | White | Continuous | Default |

9. Set Layer A-furn-h current.

10. Set Ltscale **16**

## POINT FILTERS

In many instances you will find point filters to be a valuable tool for locating points. Point filters relate to the X, Y, and Z coordinates of a point. They allow you to avoid drawing unnecessary construction lines and save considerable time when used effectively. An X filter, for example, says to AutoCAD, "I am pointing to the X location for the point now; then I will point to the Y location." (You will find it helpful to ignore the Z component for now. The Z component is used for drawing 3D models.)

You may filter one or two of the X, Y, and Z components of any point in any command that requires the location of a point. Some of these commands are as follows:

| | |
|------|------|
| Line | Copy |
| Polyline | Move |
| Ellipse | Polygon |
| Circle | |

**Draw the base and column of the table (HIDDEN Line), as shown in the top view (Figure 10–36):**

| Prompt | Response |
|--------|----------|
| Command: | **Circle-Center, Diameter** |
| Specify center point for circle or [3P/2P/Ttr (tan,tan,radius)]: | TYPE: **4′,6′<enter>** |
| Specify diameter of circle: | TYPE: **3′1-1/2<enter>** |
| Command: | **Circle=Center,Diameter** |
| Specify center point for circle or [3P/2P/Ttr (tan,tan,radius)]: | **Osnap-Center** |
| of | **D1** |
| Specify diameter of circle<default>: | TYPE: **8<enter>** (make sure the diameter is specified) |

### On Your Own

**1. Set Layer A-furn-s current.**

**Draw the elliptical top of the table (Continuous Line), as shown in the top view (Figure 10–36):**

| Prompt | Response |
|--------|----------|
| Command: | **Ellipse-Axis, End** |
| Specify axis endpoint of ellipse or [Arc/Center]: | **Osnap-Quadrant** |
| of | **D2** |
| Specify other endpoint of axis: | **Osnap-Quadrant** |
| of | **D3** |
| Specify distance to other axis or [Rotation]: | TYPE: **36-3/4<enter>** |

FIGURE 10–36
Draw the Base, Column, and Top
of the Table

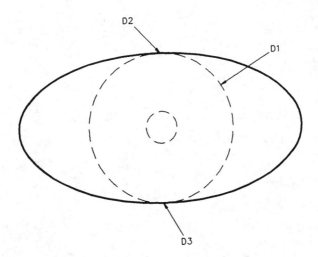

Use **FILTERS** to draw the front view of the top of this odd-size elliptical table (Figure 10–37):

| Prompt | Response |
| --- | --- |
| Command: | **Line** |
| Specify first point: | TYPE: **.X<enter>** |
| of | **Osnap-Quadrant** |
| of | **D1** (Figure 10–37) |
| (need YZ): | **D2** (with SNAP ON, pick a point in the approximate location shown in Figure 10–37) |
| Specify next point or [Undo]: | TYPE: **.X<enter>** |
| of | **Osnap-Quadrant** |
| of | **D3** |
| (need YZ): | **D4** (with ORTHO ON, pick any point to identify the Y component of the point; Ortho says that the Y component of the new point is the same as the Y component of the previous point) |
| Specify next point or [Undo]: | TYPE: **@2<270<enter>** |
| Specify next point or [Undo/Close]: | TYPE: **.X<enter>** |

FIGURE 10–37
Draw the Front View of the Top
of the Table

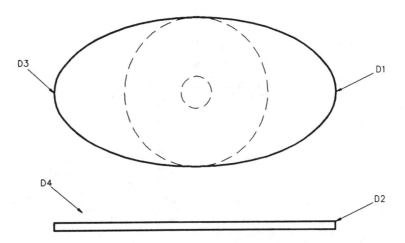

| Prompt | Response |
|---|---|
| of | **Osnap-Endpoint** |
| of | **D2** |
| (need YZ) | With Ortho ON, move your mouse to the right, and pick any point. |
| Specify next point or [Undo/Close]: | TYPE: **C<enter>** |

**Use FILTERS to draw the column of the front view of the table (Figure 10–38):**

| Prompt | Response |
|---|---|
| Command: | **Line** |
| Specify first point: | TYPE: **.X<enter>** |
| of | **Osnap-Quadrant** |
| of | **D1** |
| (need YZ) | **Osnap-Nearest** |
| to | **D2** (any point on this line to identify the Y component of the point) |
| Specify next point or [Undo]: | TYPE: **@24<270<enter>** |
| Specify next point or [Undo]: | **<enter>** |
| Command: | **Offset** (or TYPE: **O<enter>**) |
| Specify offset distance or [Through] <Through>: | TYPE: **8<enter>** |
| Select object to offset or <exit>: | **D3** |
| Specify point on side to offset: | **D4** |
| Select object to offset or <exit>: | **<enter>** |

**Use FILTERS to draw the front view of the base of the table (Figure 10–38):**

| Prompt | Response |
|---|---|
| Command: | **Line** |

**FIGURE 10–38**
Draw the Front View of the Column and Base of the Table

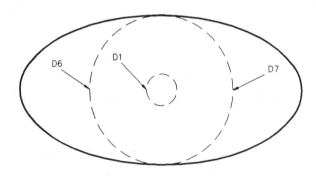

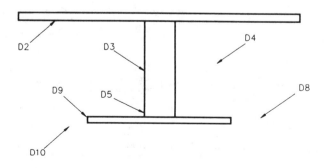

| Prompt | Response |
|---|---|
| Specify first point: | TYPE: **.Y<enter>** |
| of | **Osnap-Endpoint** |
| of | **D5** |
| (need XZ) | **Osnap-Quadrant** |
| of | **D6** |
| Specify next point or [Undo]: | TYPE: **.X<enter>** |
| of | **Osnap-Quadrant** |
| of | **D7** |
| (need YZ) | **D8** (with ORTHO ON, any point will do) |
| Specify next point or [Undo]: | TYPE: **@1-1/2<270<enter>** |
| Specify next point or [Undo/Close]: | TYPE: **.X<enter>** |
| of | **Osnap-Endpoint** |
| of | **D9** |
| (need YZ): | **D10** (with ORTHO ON, any point) |
| Specify next point or [Undo/Close]: | TYPE: **C<enter>** |

## On Your Own

1. **Use FILTERS to draw the right side view of the table with the Line command.** Be sure to get depth dimensions from the top view.

2. **Set Layer A-furn-text current, and add the name of the drawing as shown in Figure 10–39.**

3. **Save the drawing in two places, create a layout at a scale of 1/2″ = 1′, and plot or print the drawing.**

**FIGURE 10–39**
Draw the Right Side View of the Table

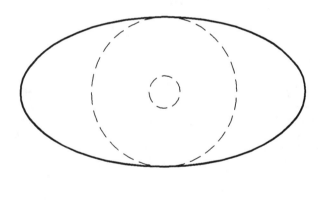

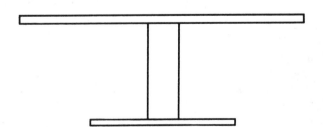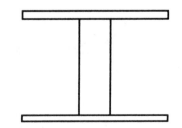

CONFERENCE TABLE

SCALE: 1/2"=1'-0"

# EXERCISE 10–5
## Different Hatch Styles

1. Draw the figure (without hatching) shown in Figure 10–40. Use an Architectural scale of 1/2″ = 1″ to measure the figure, and draw it full scale. Copy it two times, leaving 1″ between figures.

2. Shade each figure with a different Hatch Style as shown: Normal, Outermost, and Ignore. Use the same hatch pattern: User-defined, 1/8 spacing, 45 angle.

3. Save the drawing in two places, and plot or print the drawing to scale.

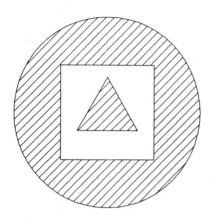 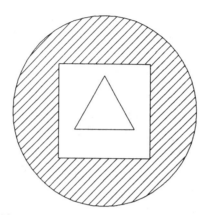 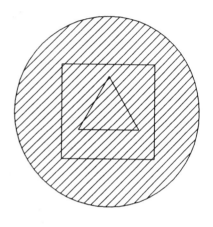

**FIGURE 10–40**

Practice Exercise 10–5: Different Hatch Styles (Scale: 1/2″ = 1″)

# REVIEW QUESTIONS

1. Which of the following patterns produces evenly spaced dots?
   a. U
   b. DOTS
   c. ANSI34
   d. DOLMIT
   e. LINE

**FIGURE 10–41**

2. Which of the following angles produces the User-defined pattern shown in Figure 10–41?
   a. 45
   b. 90
   c. 0
   d. 135
   e. 105

**FIGURE 10–42**

3. Which of the following angles produces the User-defined pattern shown in Figure 10–42?
   a. 45
   b. 90
   c. 0
   d. 135
   e. 105

4. Which of the following commands can be used to correct a hatch pattern that extends outside a hatch boundary, after it has been exploded?
   a. Array
   b. Copy
   c. Move
   d. Trim
   e. Break

**FIGURE 10–43**

5. Which of the following describes the User-defined pattern shown in Figure 10–43?
   a. X pat
   b. 45, 145
   c. Double hatch
   d. Double section
   e. Line-two

6. Which of the following in the Spacing: input area in the Boundary Hatch dialog box produces hatch lines 1/4″ apart (User-defined pattern)?
   a. 1/4″
   b. 1
   c. 1-4
   d. 4
   e. Depends on the size of the drawing.

7. After a Hatch command that spaced lines 1/8″ apart has been performed, what is the default setting in the Spacing: input area for the next hatch pattern?
   a. 0″
   b. 1/4″
   c. 1/8″
   d. 1″
   e. Depends on the size of the drawing.

8. Which setting allows an image to be Mirrored without mirroring the text?
   a. MIRRTEXT = 1
   b. MIRRTEXT = 0
   c. MIRRTXT = 1
   d. MIRRTXT = 0
   e. DTEXT-STYLE = 0

9. The Stretch command is best used for
   a. Stretching an object in one direction
   b. Shrinking an object in one direction
   c. Moving an object along attached lines
   d. All the above
   e. None of the above

10. Which Hatch option allows you to hatch only the outermost boundary of multiple areas within a selection window?
    a. Pattern
    b. Scale
    c. Outer
    d. Normal
    e. Ignore

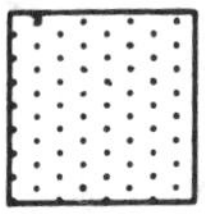

**FIGURE 10–44**

11. What is the correct name of the pattern in Figure 10–44?

   _____

12. How can the predefined Hatch pattern options (Hatch Pattern Palette) be called up on the screen?

   _____

   _____

**FIGURE 10–45**

13. Correctly label the User-defined pattern shown in Figure 10–45. Show angle and spacing at full scale.

   Angle _____     Spacing _____

14. Correctly label the Predefined pattern shown in Figure 10–46. Show pattern and angle.

   Pattern _____     Angle _____

**FIGURE 10–46**

15. How can a hatch pattern line that extends outside a hatch boundary be corrected?

   _____

   _____

   _____

16. What is the name of the UCS Icon command option that forces the UCS icon to be displayed at the 0,0 point of the current UCS?

   _____

17. How can all the lines of an associative 35-line hatch pattern be erased?

   _____

18. List the command that allows you to change a hatch pattern from Associative to Nonassociative.

   _____

19. Describe a practical use for the UCS command for two-dimensional drawing.

   _____

   _____

   _____

   _____

20. List the prompts and responses for getting the UCS icon to move to the UCS origin after the UCS has been moved.

   **Prompt**                           **Response**

   Command:                             _____

   _____              _____

# Drawing and Adding Specifications to Furnishings and the AutoCAD DesignCenter

## OBJECTIVES

When you have completed this chapter, you will be able to:

☐ Correctly use the following commands and settings:

ATTDIA systems variable
ATTEXT (Attribute Extraction)
ATTREDEF (Attribute Redefinition)
Attribute Definition (ATTDEF)
Attribute Display (ATTDISP)
DDATTEXT (Dynamic Dialog Attribute Extraction)
Define Attributes... (DDATTDEF)
Edit Text (DDEDIT)
External Reference (XREF)
Modify Attribute Global (ATTEDIT)
Modify Attribute Single (DDATTE)
XBIND (External Bind)
ADCENTER (AutoCAD DesignCenter)

## INTRODUCTION

This chapter describes the AutoCAD commands that allow specifications to be added to furnishings and how the specifications are extracted from the drawing. These commands are especially important because they reduce the amount of time it takes to add furniture to the plan, and total large amounts of like furniture pieces (with specifications) from the plan. There are many software programs available that can be used with AutoCAD to save even more time. These programs provide furniture symbols already drawn and programs that extract specification information in a form that suits your individual needs. Although you may ultimately combine one of these programs with the AutoCAD program, learning the commands included in this chapter will help you to understand how they interact with AutoCAD.

## EXERCISE 11–1: PART 1
## Tenant Space Furniture Plan with Furniture Specifications

When you have completed Exercise 11–1, your drawing will look similar to Figure 11–1. To draw Exercise 11–1 turn on the computer and start AutoCAD. The AutoCAD 2002 Today window is displayed.

1. Begin drawing CH11-EX1 on the hard drive by opening existing drawing CH10-EX1 from a floppy disk in drive A and saving it as CH11-EX1 on the hard drive.

2. Set Layer 0 current.

3. Freeze Layers A-pflr-dims, Defpoints, and A-area.

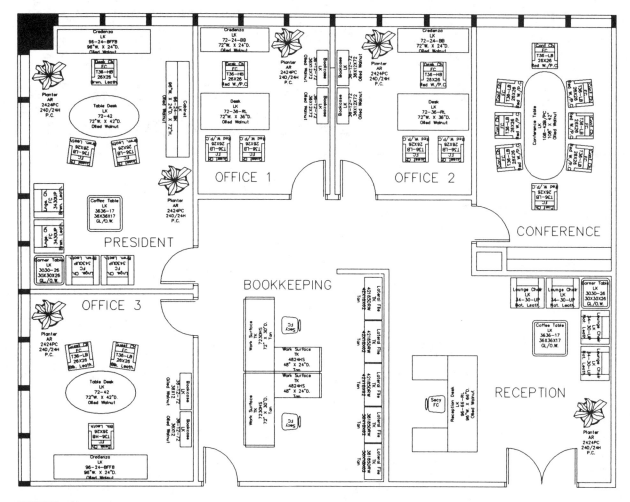

**FIGURE 11-1**

Exercise 11-1: Tenant Space Furniture Plan with Furniture Specifications (Scale: 1/8″ = 1-′0″)

4. Use Zoom-All to view the limits of the drawing.

## On Your Own

1. The furniture symbols must be drawn in plan view before you use the -ATTDEF (Attribute Definition) command to add specifications. Draw the tenant space reception furniture symbols as shown in Figure 11–2. Use a 1/4″ = 1′-0″ architectural scale to measure the symbols, and draw each piece full scale on your drawing. Pick any open space on your drawing to draw the furniture. Draw each symbol on the 0 Layer. Blocks will be made of each symbol after you use the Define Attributes... command, so it does not matter where the furniture is drawn on the plan. Use short, straight sections of a polyline to draw the plant inside the planter.

## -ATTDEF and Define Attributes... (DDATTDEF-Dynamic Dialog Attribute Definition)

The -ATTDEF (Attribute Definition) command allows you to add attributes (furniture specifications) to the furniture symbols drawn in plan view using prompts from the command line. Define Attributes... (DDATTDEF-Dynamic Dialog Attribute Definition) allows you to do the same thing using a dialog box. In this exercise you will use both commands. After the attributes are added, a block is made of the symbol. When the block is inserted into a drawing, the specifications appear on the drawing if they have been

# TENANT SPACE — RECEPTION

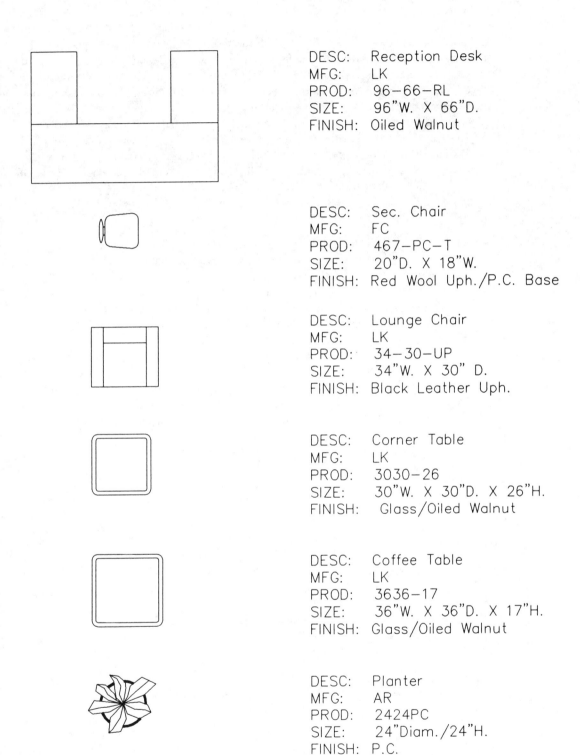

DESC:   Reception Desk
MFG:    LK
PROD:   96—66—RL
SIZE:   96"W. X 66"D.
FINISH: Oiled Walnut

DESC:   Sec. Chair
MFG:    FC
PROD:   467—PC—T
SIZE:   20"D. X 18"W.
FINISH: Red Wool Uph./P.C. Base

DESC:   Lounge Chair
MFG:    LK
PROD:   34—30—UP
SIZE:   34"W. X 30" D.
FINISH: Black Leather Uph.

DESC:   Corner Table
MFG:    LK
PROD:   3030—26
SIZE:   30"W. X 30"D. X 26"H.
FINISH: Glass/Oiled Walnut

DESC:   Coffee Table
MFG:    LK
PROD:   3636—17
SIZE:   36"W. X 36"D. X 17"H.
FINISH: Glass/Oiled Walnut

DESC:   Planter
MFG:    AR
PROD:   2424PC
SIZE:   24"Diam./24"H.
FINISH: P.C.

**FIGURE 11–2**
Reception Furniture Symbols and Specifications (Scale: 1/4" = 1-'0")

defined as visible (attributes can be visible or invisible). You can then extract the attribute information from the drawing using the -ATTEXT command or DDATTEXT using the Attribute Extraction dialog box.

As shown in Figure 11–2, each piece of furniture in the reception area has five attributes. An attribute is made up of two parts, the *tag* and the *value*. The tag is used to help define the attribute but does not appear on the inserted drawing. It does appear on the drawing while attributes are being defined and before it is made into a block. The tags on the reception area furnishings are DESC., MFG., PROD., SIZE, and FINISH. The tag is used when the attribute information is extracted from the drawing. The ATTEXT command lists each occurrence of an attribute in the drawing. The attribute tag may contain any characters, but no spaces, and it is automatically converted to uppercase.

The value is the actual specification, such as Reception Desk, LK, 96-66-RL, 96″W. × 66″D., and Oiled Walnut. The attribute value may contain any characters, and it may also have spaces. The value appears on the drawing after it is inserted as a block. It appears exactly as it was entered.

There are five optional modes for the value of -ATTDEF; these are set at the beginning of the attribute definition:

**Invisible** This value is not displayed on the screen when the block is inserted. You may want to use the Invisible mode for pricing, or you may want to make some attributes invisible so that the drawing does not become cluttered.

**Constant** This value is fixed and cannot be changed. For example, if the same chair is used throughout a project but the fabric varies, then the furniture manufacturer value of the chair will be constant, but the finish value will vary. A Constant value cannot be edited.

**Verify** This mode allows the value to be variable and allows you to check (verify) the value you have entered. Changes in the value may be entered as needed when the block is inserted. A second set of prompts appears while you are inserting the block. These prompts allow you to verify that the value you entered is correct.

**Preset** This mode allows the value to be variable, but the changes are not requested as the block is inserted. It is similar to Constant in that fewer prompts appear. But unlike a Constant value, the Preset value can be changed with ATTEDIT, DDATTE, DDEDIT, and Properties... commands.

**Variable** If none of the above modes is selected, the value is Variable. The Variable mode allows the value to be changed and prompts you once when the block is inserted to type any value other than the default value.

## On Your Own

**1. Keep the 0 Layer current.**

**2. Zoom in on the reception desk.**

**Use -ATTDEF to define the attributes of the reception desk. Make all the attributes of the reception desk Constant (Figure 11–3):**

| Prompt | Response |
|---|---|
| Command: | TYPE: **-ATT<enter>** (be sure to include the hyphen) |

**FIGURE 11–3**
Use -ATTDEF to Define the
Attributes of the Reception
Desk

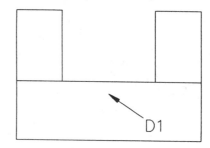

| Prompt | Response |
|---|---|
| Current attribute modes: Invisible=N<br>    Constant=N Verify=N Preset=N<br>Enter an option to change [Invisible/Constant/<br>    Verify/Preset] <done>: | TYPE: **C<enter>** (to set the mode to<br>    Constant) |
| Current attribute modes: Invisible=N<br>    Constant=Y Verify=N Preset=N<br>Enter an option to change [Invisible/Constant/<br>    Verify/Preset] <done>:<br>(NOTE: The "N" after Constant has<br>    changed to "Y.") | <enter> |
| Enter attribute tag name: | TYPE: **DESC<enter>** |
| Enter attribute value: | TYPE: **Reception Desk<enter>** |
| Specify start point of text or [Justify/Style]: | TYPE: **C<enter>** |
| Specify center point of text: | **D1** |
| Specify height <default>: | TYPE: **3<enter>** |
| Specify rotation angle of text <0>: | <enter> |
| (The first attribute is complete; the<br>    Attribute tag appears on the drawing.) | |
| Command: | <enter> (Repeat -ATTDEF) |
| Current attribute modes: Invisible=N<br>    Constant=Y Verify=N Preset=N<br>Enter an option to change [Invisible/Constant/<br>    Verify/Preset] <done>: | <enter> (to keep the Constant mode) |
| Enter attribute tag name: | TYPE: **MFG<enter>** |
| Enter attribute value: | TYPE: **LK<enter>** |
| Specify start point of text or [Justify/Style]: | <enter> (AutoCAD automatically aligns<br>    each new definition below the previous<br>    attribute definition) |
| (The second attribute is complete.) | |
| Command: | <enter> (to return the ATTDEF prompt) |
| Current attribute modes: Invisible=N<br>    Constant=Y Verify=N Preset=N<br>Enter an option to change [Invisible/Constant/<br>    Verify/Preset] <done>: | <enter> |
| Enter attribute tag name: | TYPE: **PROD<enter>** |
| Enter attribute value: | TYPE: **96-66-RL<enter>** |
| Specify start point of text or [Justify/Style]: | <enter> |
| Command: | <enter> (Repeat -ATTDEF) |
| (The third attribute is complete.) | |
| Current attribute modes: Invisible=N<br>    Constant=Y Verify=N Preset=N<br>Enter an option to change [Invisible/Constant/<br>    Verify/Preset] <done>: | <enter> |
| Enter attribute tag name: | TYPE: **SIZE<enter>** |
| Enter attribute value: | TYPE: **96"W X 66"D<enter>** |
| Specify start point of text or [Justify/Style]: | <enter> |
| (The fourth attribute is complete.) | |
| Command: | <enter> |

## FIGURE 11–4
Reception Desk with Attribute Tags

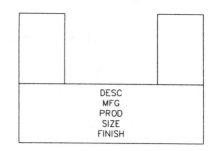

DESC
MFG
PROD
SIZE
FINISH

| Prompt | Response |
|--------|----------|
| Current attribute modes: Invisible=N Constant=Y Verify=N Preset=N | |
| Enter an option to change [Invisible/Constant/ Verify/Preset] <done>: | <enter> |
| Enter attribute tag name: | TYPE: **FINISH<enter>** |
| Enter attribute value: | TYPE: **Oiled Walnut<enter>** |
| Specify start point of text or [Justify/Style]: | <enter> |
| (The fifth attribute is complete.) | |
| Command: | |

When you have completed defining the five attributes, your drawing of the reception desk will look similar to the desk in Figure 11–4.

In the next part of this exercise, you will see how the ATTDEF prompts for a Constant attribute differ from an attribute defined with the Verify mode.

## On Your Own

**1. Keep the 0 Layer current.**

**2. Zoom in on the corner table.**

**Use ATTDEF to define the attributes of the corner table. Make the DESC. and MFG. attributes of the corner table Constant, and use the Verify mode for the PROD., SIZE, and FINISH attributes (Figure 11–5):**

| Prompt | Response |
|--------|----------|
| Command: | TYPE: **-ATT<enter>** |
| Current attribute modes: Invisible=N Constant=Y Verify=N Preset=N | |
| Enter an option to change [Invisible/Constant/ Verify/Preset] <done>: | |
| (*Note:* The "Y" indicates Constant is still the current mode.) | <enter> |
| Enter attribute tag name: | TYPE: **DESC<enter>** |
| Enter attribute value: | TYPE: **Corner Table<enter>** |
| Specify start point of text or [Justify/Style]: | TYPE: **C<enter>** |
| Specify center point of text: | **D1** |
| Specify height <0'-3">: | <enter> |
| Specify rotation angle of text <0>: | <enter> |
| (The first attribute is complete; the Attribute tag appears on the drawing.) | |
| Command: | <enter> (Repeat -ATTDEF) |
| Current attribute modes: Invisible=N Constant=Y Verify=N Preset=N | |

**Note:** If you are not happy with the location of the Attribute Tags, use the Move command to relocate them before using the Block command.

D1

## FIGURE 11–5
Use ATTDEF to Define the Attributes of the Corner Table

| Prompt | Response |
|---|---|
| Enter an option to change [Invisible/Constant/<br>    Verify/Preset] <done>: | <enter> (to keep the Constant mode) |
| Enter attribute tag name: | TYPE: **MFG<enter>** |
| Enter attribute value: | TYPE: **LK<enter>** |
| Specify start point or text or [Justify/Style]: | <enter> |
| (The second attribute is complete.) | |
| Command: | <enter> |
| Current attribute modes: Invisible=N<br>    Constant=Y  Verify=N  Preset=N | |
| Enter an option to change [Invisible/Constant/<br>    Verify/Preset] <done>: | TYPE: **C<enter>** (to cancel the Constant<br>    mode) |
| Current attribute modes: Invisible=N<br>    Constant=N  Verify=N  Preset=N | |
| Enter an option to change [Invisible/Constant/<br>    Verify/Preset] <done>: | TYPE: **V<enter>** (to set the Verify mode) |
| Current attribute modes: Invisible=N<br>    Constant=N  Verify=Y  Preset=N | |
| Enter an option to change [Invisible/Constant/<br>    Verify/Preset] <done>: | <enter> |
| Enter attribute tag name: | TYPE: **PROD<enter>** |
| Enter attribute prompt: | TYPE: **Enter product number<enter>** |
| Enter default attribute value: | TYPE: **30-30-26<enter>** |
| Specify start point of text or [Justify/Style]: | <enter> |
| (The third attribute is complete.) | |
| Command: | <enter> |
| Current attribute modes: Invisible=N<br>    Constant=N  Verify=Y  Preset=N | |
| Enter an option to change [Invisible/Constant/<br>    Verify/Preset] <done>: | <enter> |
| Enter attribute tag name: | TYPE: **SIZE<enter>** |
| Enter attribute prompt: | TYPE: **Enter product size<enter>** |
| Enter default attribute value: | TYPE: **30″W X 30″D X 26″H<enter>** |
| Specify start point of text or [Justify/Style]: | <enter> |
| (The fourth attribute is complete.) | |
| Command: | <enter> |
| Current attribute modes: Invisible=N<br>    Constant=N  Verify=Y  Preset=N | |
| Enter an option to change [Invisible/Constant/<br>    Verify/Preset] <done>: | <enter> |
| Enter attribute tag name: | TYPE: **FINISH<enter>** |
| Enter attribute prompt: | TYPE: **Enter product finish<enter>** |
| Enter default attribute value: | TYPE: **Glass/Oiled Walnut<enter>** |
| Specify start point of text or [Justify/Style]: | <enter> |
| (The fifth attribute is complete.) | |
| Command: | |

**Note:** The Constant mode must be canceled for the Verify and Preset modes to function. The Constant mode overrides the other two.

**Note:** The "Attribute prompt:" line may say whatever you want it to say.

When the attribute mode is set to Verify, two additional ATTDEF prompts appear—"Attribute prompt:" and "Default attribute value:". The attribute prompt information that is typed and entered will appear when the block of the corner table is inserted into the drawing; it will appear and prompt you to enter the product finish, size, and number. The default

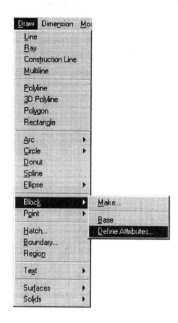

attribute value appears if a different value is not typed and entered. These ATTDEF prompts do not appear while you are defining Constant attributes, because a Constant attribute value cannot vary.

In the following part of this exercise, you will use DDATTDEF and notice that the prompts for the Variable and Preset modes are the same as for the Verify mode. If none of the modes—Constant, Verify, or Preset—is set, the mode is Variable. You will also use the Invisible mode to define attributes.

## On Your Own

**1. Keep the 0 Layer current.**

**2. Zoom in on the secretarial chair.**

**3. If you need to, rotate your secretarial chair to appear oriented like the chair in Figure 11–6.**

**Use Define Attributes... (DDATTDEF-Dynamic Dialog Attribute Definition) to define the attributes of the secretarial chair. Make the DESC. and MFG. attributes of the secretarial chair variable. Use the Preset and Invisible modes for the PROD., SIZE, and FINISH attributes (Figures 11–6, 11–7, 11–8, 11–9, 11–10, and 11–11):**

| Prompt | Response |
|---|---|
| Command: | **Define Attributes...** <br> or TYPE: **ATT\<enter\>** |
| The Attribute Definition dialog box appears: | **Clear all the checks in the Mode area.** <br> (The attribute will now be variable.) |
| | TYPE: **DESC** in the Tag: box |
| | TYPE: **Enter product description** in the Prompt: box |
| | TYPE: **Secy** in the Value: box |
| | CLICK: **the down arrow** in the Justification: box and CLICK: **Center** |

**FIGURE 11–6**
Use DDATTDEF to Define the Attributes of the Secretarial Chair

**FIGURE 11–7**
Defining the First Attribute for the Secretarial Chair

All other parts of the dialog box should be as shown in Figure 11–7.

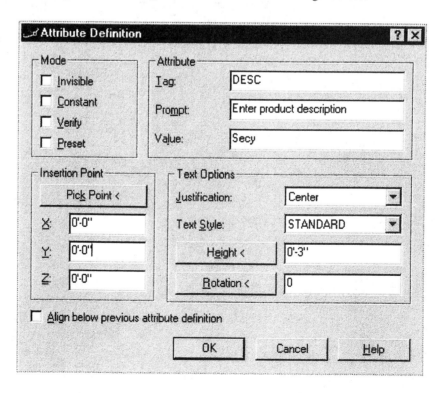

**FIGURE 11–8**
Defining the Second Attribute for
the Secretarial Chair

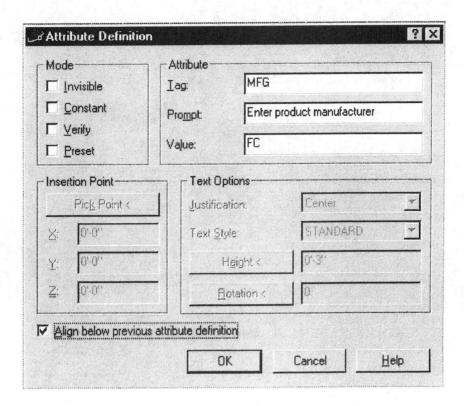

| Prompt | Response |
|---|---|
| | CLICK: **Pick Point<** |
| Start point: | **D1** (Figure 11–6) |
| The Attribute Definition dialog box reappears: | CLICK: **OK** |
| The first attribute is complete; the Attribute Tag appears on the drawing. | |
| Command: | **<enter>** (Repeat ATTDEF) |
| The Attribute Definition dialog box appears: | **Complete the dialog box as shown in Figure 11–8. Notice that the Align below previous attribute definition button is checked, so the Insertion Point and Text Options areas are grayed out.** |
| | CLICK: **OK** |
| The second attribute is complete; the Attribute Tag appears on the drawing aligned below the first attribute. | |
| Command: | **<enter>** (Repeat ATTDEF) |
| The Attribute Definition dialog box appears: | **Complete the dialog box as shown in Figure 11–9. Notice that the Align below previous attribute definition button is checked again and that the Preset and Invisible modes are checked.** |
| | CLICK: **OK** |
| The third attribute is complete; the Attribute Tag appears on the drawing aligned below the second attribute. | |

FIGURE 11–9
Defining the Third Attribute for the
Secretarial Chair

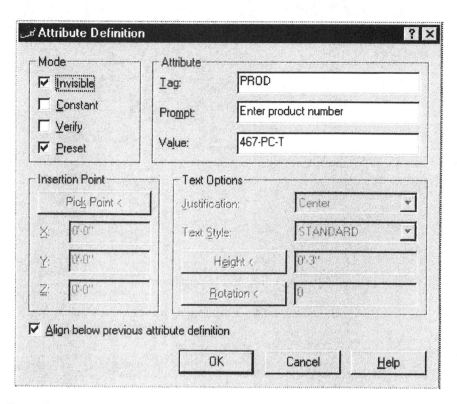

| Prompt | Response |
|---|---|
| Command: | **<enter>** (Repeat ATTDEF) |
| The Attribute Definition dialog box appears: | **Complete the dialog box as shown in Figure 11–10. Notice that the Align below previous attribute definition button is checked again and that the Preset and Invisible modes are checked.** |

FIGURE 11–10

Defining the Fourth Attribute for
the Secretarial Chair

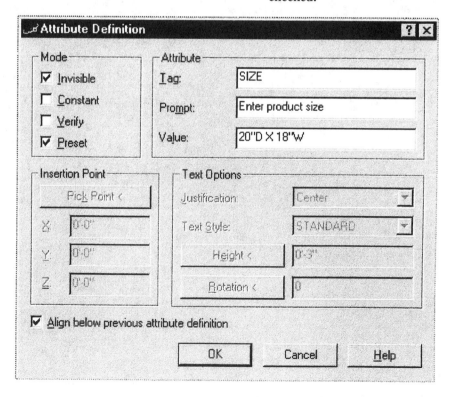

| Prompt | Response |
|---|---|
| | CLICK: **OK** |
| The fourth attribute is complete; the Attribute Tag appears on the drawing aligned below the third attribute. | |
| Command: | **<enter>** (Repeat ATTDEF) |
| The Attribute Definition dialog box appears: | **Complete the dialog box as shown in Figure 11–11. Notice that the Align below previous attribute definition button is checked again and that the Preset and Invisible modes are checked.** |
| | CLICK: **OK** |

The fifth attribute is complete; the Attribute Tag appears on the drawing aligned below the fourth attribute.

## Edit Text (DDEDIT)

Did you make a mistake while responding to the "Attribute tag," "Attribute prompt," or "Default attribute value" prompts? The Edit Text command allows you to use the Edit Attribute Definition dialog box (Figure 11–12) to correct any typing mistakes you may have made while defining the attributes. The Edit Text prompt is "Select an annotation object or [Undo]:". When you pick a tag, the Edit Attribute Definition dialog box appears and allows you to change the attribute tag, prompt, or default value for a Variable, Verify, or Preset attribute. The tag and the default (actually the Value) can be changed for a Con-

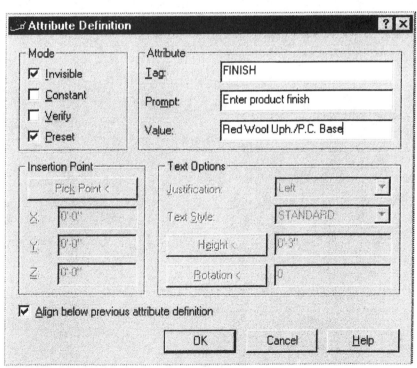

FIGURE 11–11
Defining the Fifth Attribute for the Secretarial Chair

**FIGURE 11–12**
Edit Attribute Definition Dialog
Box

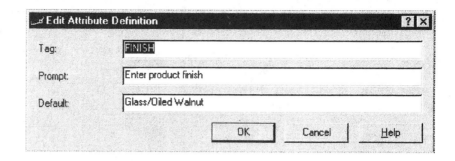

stant attribute; adding a prompt for an attribute defined as Constant does not change the attribute mode, and the prompt does not appear.

The Edit Text command can be used only before the symbol is made into a block.

## On Your Own

1. **Use Wblock to save the reception desk as a Wblock (a drawing) on a floppy disk in drive A. Name the Wblock RDSK. Use the insertion base point as shown in Figure 11–13. Have the desk oriented as shown in Figure 11–13.**

2. **Use Wblock to save the corner table as a Wblock (a drawing) on a floppy disk in drive A. Name the Wblock CRTBL. Use the insertion base point as shown in Figure 11–13. If the table was drawn on snap, you can use the snap point of the two sides of the table as if they met at a 90° angle.**

3. **Use Wblock to save the secretarial chair as a Wblock on a floppy disk in drive A. Name the block SECY. Pick the center of the chair as the insertion base point.**

## Inserting a Block with Attributes—Using the Command: Prompt Line

The Insert command is used to insert the blocks with attributes into the tenant space floor plan. Let's insert the reception desk into the drawing. Remember, all five attribute values were defined as Constant. They will appear on the drawing as you entered them.

**FIGURE 11–13**
Save the Reception Desk and
the Corner Table as a Wblock
(a Drawing) on a Floppy Disk

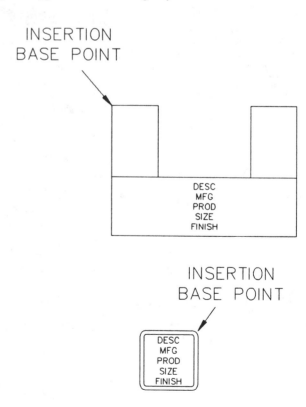

## On Your Own

1.   Set the A-furn Layer current.

**Use the Insert command to insert the RDSK block stored on a floppy disk in drive A into the tenant space floor plan. Use the ID command to help position the block (Figure 11–14):**

| Prompt | Response |
|---|---|
| Command: | TYPE: **ID<enter>** |
| Specify point: | **Osnap-Intersection** |
| of | **D1** |
| ID Point: Int of | |
| X = 49'-0″  Y = 12'-0″  Z = 0'-0″ | |
| Command: | TYPE: **-I<enter>** |
| Enter block name (or ?): | TYPE: **A:RDSK<enter>** |
| Specify insertion point or [Scale/X/Y/Z/ Rotate/PScale/PX/PY/PZ/PRotate]: | TYPE: **@24,30<enter>** |
| Enter X scale factor, specify opposite corner, or [Corner/XYZ]<1>: | **<enter>** |
| Enter Y scale factor <use X scale factor>: | **<enter>** |
| Specify rotation angle <0>: | TYPE: **90<enter>** (the RDSK block is inserted; the Values appear on the block) |

**FIGURE 11–14**
Use the Insert Command to Insert the RDSK Block into the Tenant Space Floor Plan

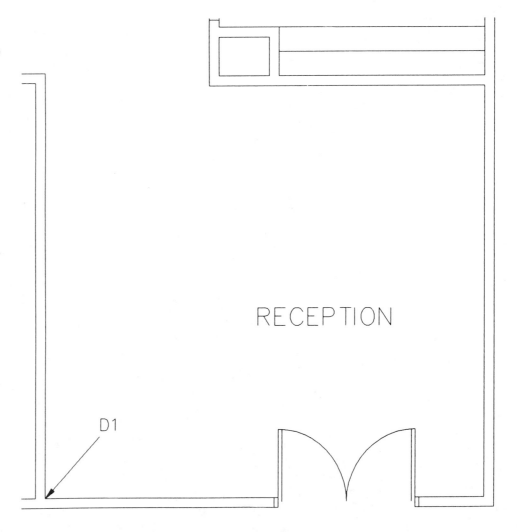

RECEPTION

D1

Let's insert the corner table into the drawing. Remember, the Description and Manufacturer attribute values of the corner table were defined with the Constant mode. The Product, Size, and Finish attribute values were defined with the Verify mode. The prompts entered during the ATTDEF command for the values defined with Verify will appear while you insert the CRTBL block. Those prompts allow you to change the attribute value or accept the Default attribute value that was also entered during the ATTDEF command.

**Keep the A-furn Layer current. Use the Insert command to insert the CRTBL block stored on a floppy disk in drive A into the tenant space floor plan. Use the From option to help position the block (Figure 11–15):**

| Prompt | Response |
|---|---|
| Command: | TYPE: **-I<enter>** |
| Enter block name or [?] <RDSK>: | TYPE: **A:CRTBL<enter>** |
| Specify insertion point or [Scale/X/Y/Z/ Rotate/PScale/PX/PY/PZ/PRotate]: | TYPE: **FRO<enter>** |
| Base point: | **Osnap-Intersection** |
| of | **D1** |
| <Offset> | TYPE: **@-2,-2<enter>** |

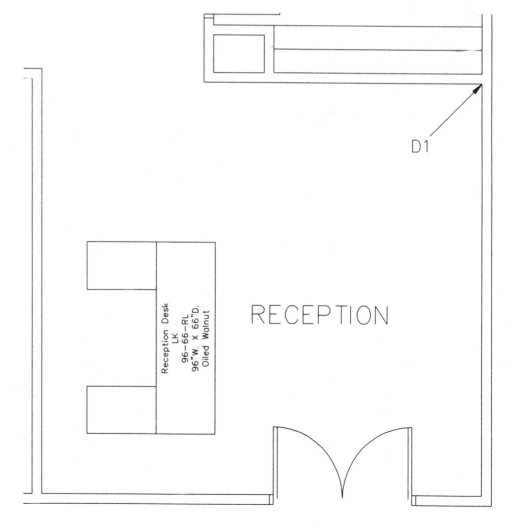

FIGURE 11–15
Use the Insert Command to Insert the CRTBL Block into the Tenant Space Floor Plan

Reception Desk
LK
96–66–RL
96"W. X 66"D.
Oiled Walnut

RECEPTION

**Part II: Two-Dimensional AutoCAD**

| Prompt | Response |
|---|---|
| Enter X scale factor, specify opposite corner, or [Corner/XYZ]<1>: | <enter> |
| Enter Y scale factor <use X scale factor>: | <enter> |
| Specify rotation angle <0>: | <enter> |
| Enter attribute values | |
| Enter product finish <Glass/Oiled Walnut>: | <enter> (to accept the default) |
| Enter product size <30"W × 30"D × 26"H>: | <enter> |
| Enter product number <30-30-26>: | <enter> |
| Verify attribute values | |
| Enter product finish <Glass/Oiled Walnut>: | <enter> |
| Enter product size <30"W × 30"D × 26"H>: | <enter> |
| Enter product number <30-30-26>: | <enter> |

**Note:** If the Enter Attributes dialog box appears, escape from the command, and turn the dialog box off. TYPE: **ATTDIA** **<enter>** and **0<enter>** for the new value.

Some of the values that appeared on the corner table are too long; they go outside the table symbol. We will fix this later in the exercise with the ATTEDIT command.

**Tip:** If you are not happy with a Block location after insertion, use the Move command to relocate it.

When you insert a block with attributes defined using the Verify mode, you may type and enter a new value or accept the default value at the first prompt. A second prompt appears, allowing you to verify that the attribute values you entered by accepting the default or typing from the keyboard are correct.

### Inserting a Block with Attributes—Using an Enter Attributes Dialog Box

The Enter Attributes dialog box (Figure 11–16) can be used to insert blocks with attributes. The dialog box allows you to change or accept the default values of the attributes you defined using the Variable, Verify, or Preset modes. Its appearance is controlled by the ATTDIA system variable.

**FIGURE 11–16**
Enter Attributes Dialog Box

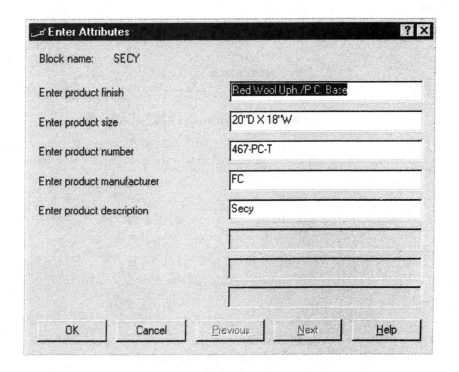

**Set the ATTDIA system variable to 1 to make the dialog box appear while you insert blocks with attributes:**

| Prompt | Response |
|---|---|
| Command: | TYPE: **ATTDIA<enter>** |
| Enter new value for ATTDIA <0>: | TYPE: **1<enter>** |

Let's insert the secretarial chair into the drawing. Remember, the DESC and MFG attributes were defined as Variable, and PROD, SIZE, and FINISH attributes were defined as Preset and Invisible.

**Keep the A-furn Layer current. Use the Insert command to insert the SECY block stored on a floppy disk in drive A into the tenant space reception area:**

Tip: Change your SNAP setting if it helps your accuracy when inserting a Block.

| Prompt | Response |
|---|---|
| Command: | **Insert** (or TYPE: **I<enter>**) |
| The Insert dialog box appears: | CLICK: **Browse...** |
| The Select Drawing File dialog box appears: | In the File name: box TYPE: **A: SECY** (or CLICK: **the down arrow in the Look in: box**, CLICK: **3-1/2 Floppy [A:]** and CLICK: on the **SECY** drawing file) |
| | CLICK: **Open** |
| The Insert dialog box appears with SECY in the Name: box. | CLICK: **OK** |
| Specify insertion point or [Scale/X/Y/Z/ Rotate/PScale/PX/PY/PZ/PRotate]: | **The block is dragged in with the crosshair on the insertion point of the chair. Click a point behind the reception desk close to the location of the center of the chair.** |
| (The Enter Attributes dialog box appears.) | CLICK: **OK** |

Note: The Preset ATTDEF mode is used to eliminate prompts and save time but still allows you to edit the attributes after insertion.

The last three attributes, because they were defined using the Invisible mode, are not visible on the inserted chair.

Using the dialog box, you may change the values for attributes defined using the Verify, Preset, or Variable modes. Prompts do not appear in the Command: prompt area for the values defined with the Preset mode, but with a dialog box, the Preset mode values can be changed as they are inserted.

## Attribute Display (ATTDISP)

The Attribute Display (ATTDISP) command allows you to turn on the Invisible attributes of the secretarial chair. The prompt is "Enter attribute visibility setting [Normal/ON/OFF] <OFF>:".

### ON

Pick ON to make the Invisible attributes appear. Try this, and you will be able to see the Invisible attributes of the secretarial chair.

### OFF

Pick OFF to make all the attributes on the drawing Invisible. Try this, and you will see that all the attributes are not visible.

### Normal

Pick Normal to make visible attributes defined as Visible and to make invisible attributes defined as Invisible. Set Normal as the default.

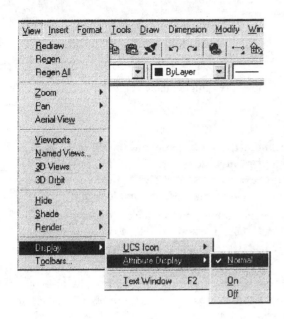

## Modify-Attribute-Single (DDATTE-Dynamic Dialog Attribute Edit)

The Modify-Attribute-Single (Dynamic Dialog Attribute Edit) command uses the Enhanced Attribute Editor dialog box (Figure 11–17) to edit Variable, Verify, and Preset Attributes values of an inserted block. Attributes defined with the Constant mode cannot be edited.

Some of the values on the corner table are too long. Let's use the Modify-Attribute-Single command to make them shorter.

**Use the Modify-Attribute-Single command to edit the values (created with the Verify mode) on the inserted corner table:**

| Prompt | Response |
|---|---|
| Command: | **Modify-Attribute-Single** (or TYPE: **EATTEDIT<enter>**) |
| Select block reference: | **Pick any place on the corner table.** |
| (The Enhanced Attribute Editor dialog box appears.) | **Use the dialog box to insert the following two new values: (Highlight the attribute, then change the value in the Value: text box, then CLICK: Apply.)** |
| | **Enter product finish: GL/O.W.** |

**FIGURE 11–17**
Enhanced Attribute Editor Dialog
Box

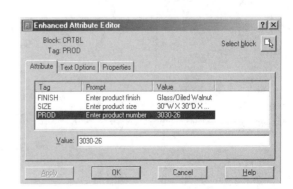

| Prompt | Response |
|---|---|
| | Enter product size..: **30X30X26.** |
| | CLICK: **OK** |

The values that appear on the corner table now fit within the table symbol.

## On Your Own

1. **Set the 0 Layer current. Use the Define Attributes... command to add to the lounge chair, coffee table, and planter the attributes shown in Figure 11–2. Make each attribute Variable and Visible. Set the text height at 3″. Refer to the inserted blocks in Figure 11–18 for the value text (may be abbreviated to fit) and location.**

2. **Use Wblock to save the lounge chair, coffee table, and planter as blocks on a floppy disk in drive A. Name the blocks LGCH, CFTBL, and PLANT. Look at the location of each inserted block in Figure 11–18, and select a point for the insertion base point of each block.**

3. **Set the A-furn Layer current. Use the Insert command to complete the insertion of all furniture in the tenant space reception area. Changing the SNAP setting to 2″ may help with insertion of the blocks. Remember, once a block is inserted, it can be moved to a new location.**

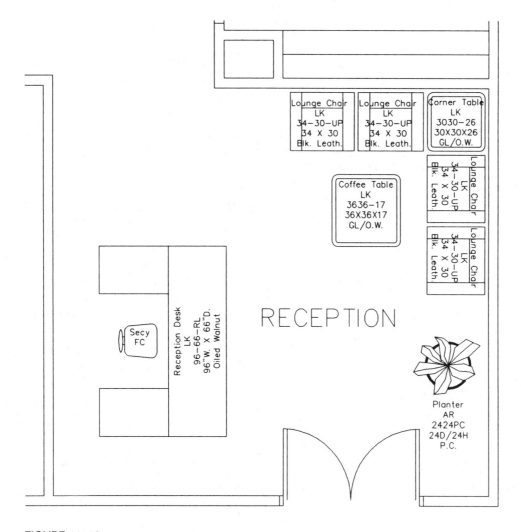

**FIGURE 11–18**
Tenant Space Reception Area (Scale: 1/4″ = 1′-0″)

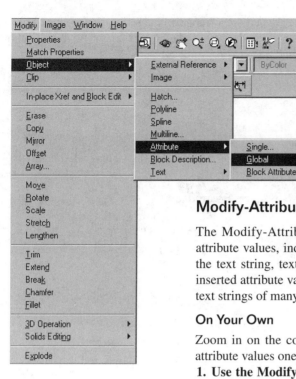

## Modify-Attribute-Global (ATTEDIT-Attribute Edit)

The Modify-Attribute-Global (Attribute Edit) command allows you to edit inserted attribute values, independent of their block reference. It allows you to edit one at a time the text string, text string position, text height, text angle, text style, layer, or color of inserted attribute values. It also provides prompts that allow you globally to edit the value text strings of many attributes all at once. Constant values cannot be edited.

### On Your Own

Zoom in on the coffee table. We will begin by using Modify-Attribute-Global to edit attribute values one at a time.

1. **Use the Modify-Attribute-Global command to edit the text height of the description value, "Coffee Table," and the manufacturer value, "LK":**

**Tip:** To save time while using the ATTDEF command, press the enter key at the "Attribute prompt:" prompt line. The Attribute prompt will then automatically be the same as the tag.

| Prompt | Response |
|---|---|
| Command: | **Modify-Attribute-Global** (or TYPE: **-ATTEDIT\<enter>**) |
| Edit attributes one at a time? [Yes/No] \<Y>: | **\<enter>** |
| Enter block name specification \<*>: | **\<enter>** |
| Enter attribute tag specification \<*>: | **\<enter>** |
| Enter attribute value specification \<*>: | **\<enter>** |
| Select Attributes: | **Pick the text strings "Coffee Table" and "LK"** |
| Select Attributes: | **\<enter>** |
| 2 attributes selected. | |
| Enter an option [Value/Position/Height/Angle/ Style/Layer/Color/Next] \<N>: | |
| ("Coffee Table" is highlighted and an X appears at the beginning of the text string.) | TYPE: **H\<enter>** |
| Specify new height \<0'-3">: | TYPE: **4\<enter>** |
| Enter an option [Value/Position/Height/Angle/ Style/Layer/Color/Next] \<N>: | **Next** (or PRESS:**\<enter>**) |
| Enter an option [Value/Position/Height/Angle/ Style/Layer/Color/Next] \<N>: | |
| ("LK" is highlighted) | TYPE: **H\<enter>** |
| Specify new height \<0'-3">: | TYPE: **4\<enter>** |
| Enter an option [Value/Position/Height/Angle/ Style/Layer/Color/Next] \<N>: | **\<enter>** |

The Modify-Attribute-Global prompts allow you to narrow the value selection by entering a specific block name, tag specification, and value specification. In the preceding exercise, we accepted the default "*" to include all of the blocks.

Only visible attributes can be edited when you respond with "Yes" to the prompt "Edit attributes one at a time?". If you respond with "No" to the prompt, visible and invisible attribute value text strings can be edited.

Let's use the Modify-Attribute-Global command to edit all at once a value on the four lounge chairs.

## On Your Own

Zoom in on the four lounge chairs.

1. **Use the Modify-Attribute-Global command to edit the text string of the finish value on all the chairs at once:**

| Prompt | Response |
|---|---|
| Command: | **Modify-Attribute-Global** (or TYPE: **-ATTEDIT<enter>**) |
| Edit attributes one at a time? [Yes/No] <Y> | TYPE: **N<enter>** |
| Edit only attributes visible on screen? [Yes/No] <Y> | **<enter>** |
| Enter block name specification <*>: | TYPE: **LGCH<enter>** |
| Enter attribute tag specification <*>: | TYPE: **FINISH<enter>** |
| Enter attribute value specification <*>: | TYPE: **Blk. Leath.<enter>** |
| Select Attributes: | **Window all four chairs and the coffee table<enter>** |
| 4 attributes selected. | |
| Enter string to change: | TYPE: **Blk. Leath.<enter>** |
| Enter new string: | TYPE: **Brwn. Leath.<enter>** |

When you use this option of the Modify-Attribute-Global command, the wild-card character "*" is interpreted literally by AutoCAD, so it cannot be used. Type and enter the block name, tag, and value exactly. You may also enter "No" in response to the prompt "Edit only attributes visible on screen?" and invisible attribute values may also be changed.

## On Your Own

1. **Use the Modify-Attribute-Global command to change the text height of the coffee table description value, "Coffee Table," and the manufacturer value, "LK," back to 30.**

## ATTREDEF

Any drawing defined as a block with the Wblock command and inserted into a drawing then becomes available for use as a block in the current drawing. Once inserted, these blocks are similar to blocks defined with the Block command.

The ATTREDEF command allows you to redefine a block within the drawing and updates all previous insertions of the block in your drawing. In the following part of this exercise, the LGCH block will be redefined. Before redefining the block, you must complete a new definition of the block attributes.

## On Your Own

1. **Select "?" from the Command: line Block prompt, and view the list of blocks available within the drawing.**

2. **Set 0 Layer current.**

3. **Insert a copy of the LGCH block in an open space in the tenant space drawing.**

4. **Explode the LGCH block and erase the tags.**

5. **Use the ATTDEF command to create the following new attributes. Make all the attributes variable.**

| Tag | Value |
|-----|-------|
| DESC | Lnge. Ch. |
| MFG | FC |
| PROD | 34-30-UP |
| UPH | Nat. Leath. |

**Use ATTREDEF to redefine the LGCH block:**

| Prompt | Response |
|--------|----------|
| Command: | TYPE: **ATTREDEF<enter>** |
| Enter name of block you wish to redefine: | TYPE: **LGCH<enter>** |
| Select objects for new Block… | |
| Select objects: | **Window the newly drawn lounge chair.** |
| Other corner: 11 found | |
| Select objects: | **<enter>** |
| Specify insertion base point of new Block: | **Select the same insertion base point you previously selected.** |

The drawing is regenerated and all previous insertions of the LGCH block are redefined (Figure 11–19). The values on the block may not have changed exactly as you thought they would. When ATTREDEF is used to redefine a block:

1. New attributes to existing block references are given their default values.
2. Old attributes to existing block references retain their old values.
3. Old attributes not included in the new block definition are deleted from the existing block references.

The shape of the block can also be changed with ATTREDEF. If the lounge chair needed to be smaller, it could have been redrawn before you redefined the block.

## On Your Own

Future insertions of the block will use the redefined variable attribute tags and values. To see how future insertions of the block appear:

1. **Use the Insert command to insert a copy of the redefined LGCH block in an open space in the tenant space drawing.**
2. **Erase the block after comparing the differences between the existing redefined blocks and the newly inserted redefined block.**

**Tip:** Be consistent with the position of the "Insertion base point" location of the furniture symbol blocks. For example, always pick up the upper right or upper left corner. This helps you to remember the "Insertion base point" location when inserting the furniture symbols. It is especially necessary to be consistent when using ATTREDEF so the newly redefined block is oriented correctly.

**FIGURE 11–19**
Redefined LGCH Block

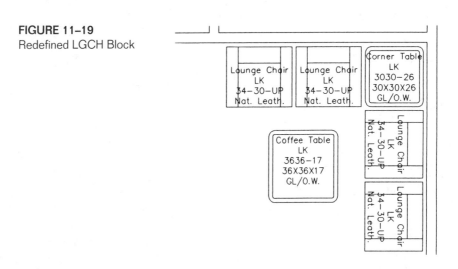

### Redefining an Inserted Block with Attributes Using the BLOCK Command

As described in Chapter 8, you can redefine a block using the Block command. When a block that has attributes assigned is redefined using the Block command, previous insertions of the block are affected as follows:

1. Old constant attributes are lost, replaced by new constant attributes, if any.

**Tip:** If the furniture symbols are inserted on the wrong layer, use the Properties... command to change the symbols to the correct layer.

2. Variable attributes remain unchanged, even if the new block definition does not include those attributes.

3. New variable attributes are not added.

Future insertions of the block will use the new attributes. The previous insertions of the block must be erased and inserted again to use the new attributes.

### On Your Own

1. **Set the 0 Layer current. Draw the remaining furniture symbols as shown in Figures 11–20 through 11–24 for the tenant space. Be sure to note furniture pieces that are repeated, and draw them only once. For example, the planter and secretarial chair symbols have already been drawn, attributes have been added, and a block has been made.**

2. **Use the ATTDEF command to add the attributes shown in Figures 11–20 through 11–24 to the furniture symbols. Make all attributes Variable. Make all the attributes Visible, except the attributes of the bookkeeping systems panels, which need to be Invisible. Set the Text height at 3″. Refer to the inserted blocks in Figure 11–25 for the value text (may be abbreviated to fit) and location.**

3. **Use Wblock to save the new furniture symbols as blocks on a floppy disk in drive A. Create a name for each new block. Look at the location of each inserted block in Figure 11–25, and select a point for the insertion base point of each block.**

4. **Set the A-furn Layer current, and use the Insert command to complete the insertion of all furniture symbols in the tenant space reception plan.**

```
DESC:    Conference Table
MFG:     LK
PROD:    108-42B/PC
SIZE:    108" X 42"
FINISH:  Oiled Walnut
```

```
DESC:    Conference Chair
MFG:     FC
PROD:    T36-LB
SIZE:    26"W. X 26"D.
FINISH:  Red Wool Uph./P.C. Base
```

**FIGURE 11–20**
Conference Room Furniture Symbols and Specifications (Scale: 1/4″ = 1′-0″)

# TENANT SPACE — OFFICE 1 and OFFICE 2

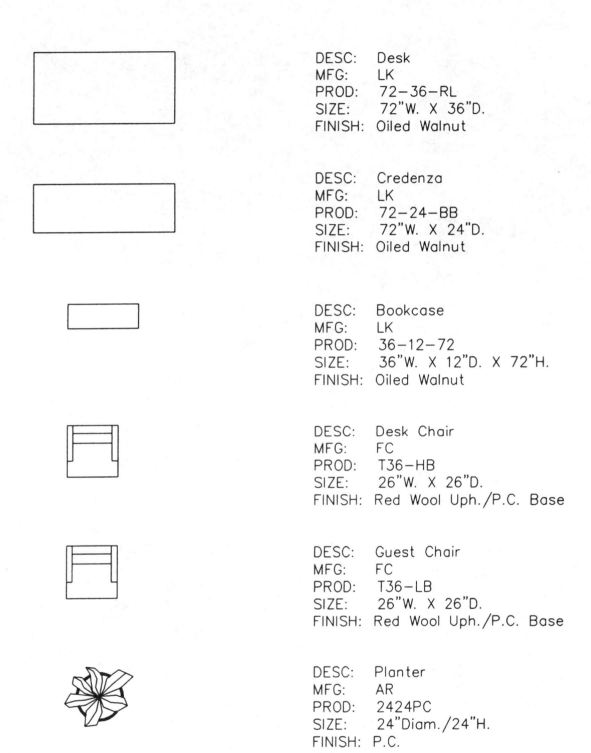

DESC:    Desk
MFG:     LK
PROD:    72-36-RL
SIZE:    72"W. X 36"D.
FINISH:  Oiled Walnut

DESC:    Credenza
MFG:     LK
PROD:    72-24-BB
SIZE:    72"W. X 24"D.
FINISH:  Oiled Walnut

DESC:    Bookcase
MFG:     LK
PROD:    36-12-72
SIZE:    36"W. X 12"D. X 72"H.
FINISH:  Oiled Walnut

DESC:    Desk Chair
MFG:     FC
PROD:    T36-HB
SIZE:    26"W. X 26"D.
FINISH:  Red Wool Uph./P.C. Base

DESC:    Guest Chair
MFG:     FC
PROD:    T36-LB
SIZE:    26"W. X 26"D.
FINISH:  Red Wool Uph./P.C. Base

DESC:    Planter
MFG:     AR
PROD:    2424PC
SIZE:    24"Diam./24"H.
FINISH:  P.C.

**FIGURE 11-21**
Office 1 and Office 2 Furniture Symbols and Specifications (Scale: 1/4" = 1'-0")

# TENANT SPACE — OFFICE 3

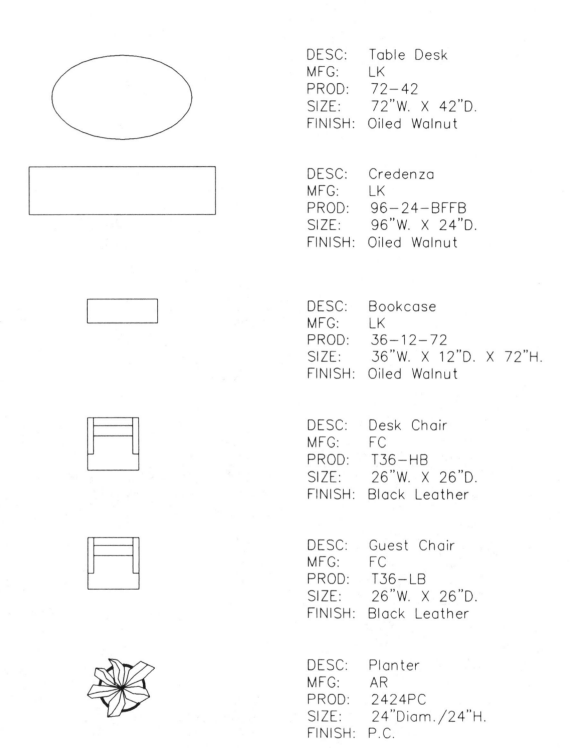

DESC:    Table Desk
MFG:     LK
PROD:    72—42
SIZE:    72"W. X 42"D.
FINISH:  Oiled Walnut

DESC:    Credenza
MFG:     LK
PROD:    96—24—BFFB
SIZE:    96"W. X 24"D.
FINISH:  Oiled Walnut

DESC:    Bookcase
MFG:     LK
PROD:    36—12—72
SIZE:    36"W. X 12"D. X 72"H.
FINISH:  Oiled Walnut

DESC:    Desk Chair
MFG:     FC
PROD:    T36—HB
SIZE:    26"W. X 26"D.
FINISH:  Black Leather

DESC:    Guest Chair
MFG:     FC
PROD:    T36—LB
SIZE:    26"W. X 26"D.
FINISH:  Black Leather

DESC:    Planter
MFG:     AR
PROD:    2424PC
SIZE:    24"Diam./24"H.
FINISH:  P.C.

**FIGURE 11–22**
Office 3 Furniture Symbols and Specifications (Scale: 1/4" = 1'-0")

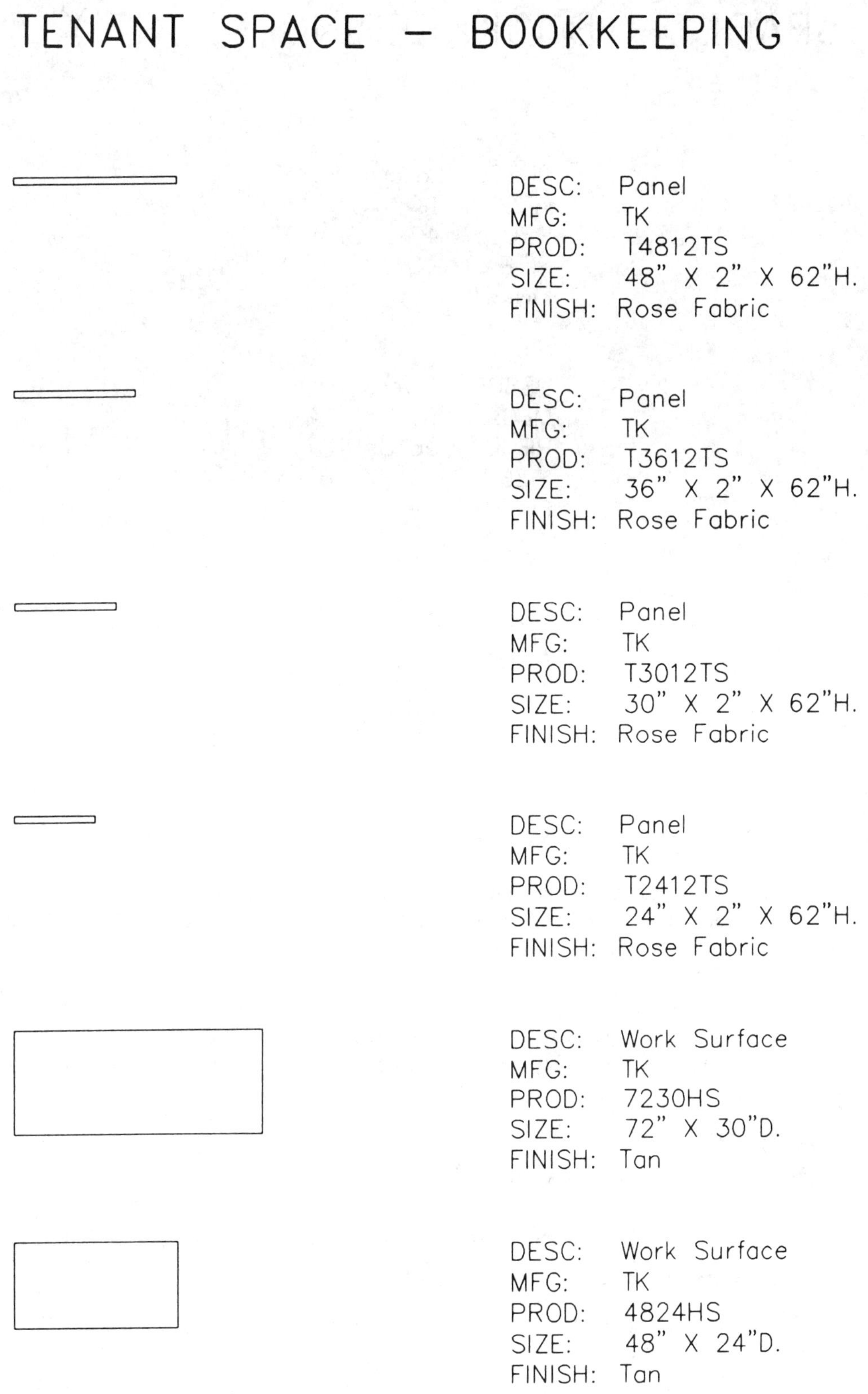

# TENANT SPACE — BOOKKEEPING

DESC:   Panel
MFG:    TK
PROD:   T4812TS
SIZE:   48" X 2" X 62"H.
FINISH: Rose Fabric

DESC:   Panel
MFG:    TK
PROD:   T3612TS
SIZE:   36" X 2" X 62"H.
FINISH: Rose Fabric

DESC:   Panel
MFG:    TK
PROD:   T3012TS
SIZE:   30" X 2" X 62"H.
FINISH: Rose Fabric

DESC:   Panel
MFG:    TK
PROD:   T2412TS
SIZE:   24" X 2" X 62"H.
FINISH: Rose Fabric

DESC:   Work Surface
MFG:    TK
PROD:   7230HS
SIZE:   72" X 30"D.
FINISH: Tan

DESC:   Work Surface
MFG:    TK
PROD:   4824HS
SIZE:   48" X 24"D.
FINISH: Tan

**FIGURE 11–23**
Bookkeeping Furniture Symbols and Specifications (Scale: 1/4″ = 1′-0″)

# TENANT SPACE — BOOKKEEPING (CONT.)

DESC:    Lateral File
MFG:     TK
PROD:    42185DRW
SIZE:    42" X 18" X 62"H.
FINISH:  Tan

DESC:    Lateral File
MFG:     TK
PROD:    36185DRW
SIZE:    36" X 18" X 62"H.
FINISH:  Tan

DESC:    Sec. Chair
MFG:     FC
PROD:    467−PC−T
SIZE:    20"D. X 18"W.
FINISH:  Red Wool Uph./P.C. Base

**FIGURE 11–23** *continued*

## EXTRACTING ATTRIBUTES

The Attribute Extraction wizard in AutoCAD 2002 can be used to produce a parts list or bill of materials directly from a drawing that contains blocks with attributes. The drawing you made in this chapter is an excellent example of this type of drawing. With the Attribute Extract Wizard you can extract existing attributes and save them to an external file in one of two formats. You can then use this file in another software program to produce the exact form you want. Exercise 11–1, Part 2, is used to extract the attributes from the drawing done for Exercise 11–1, Part 1, save it to a txt format, and print it as an external file.

## EXERCISE 11–1 PART 2
## Extracting Attributes from Drawing CH11-EX1

Step 1.   To begin Exercise 11–1 Part 2, turn on the computer and start AutoCAD.

Step 2.   Open drawing CH11-EX1.

Step 3.   Extract attributes from this drawing using the Enhanced Attribute Extraction command.

| Prompt | Response |
|---|---|
| Command: | **Attribute Extraction...** (or TYPE: **EATTEXT**) |
| The Attribute Extraction wizard with Select Drawing tab selected appears: | **With the Current Drawing radio button selected CLICK: Next>** |

# TENANT SPACE — PRESIDENT

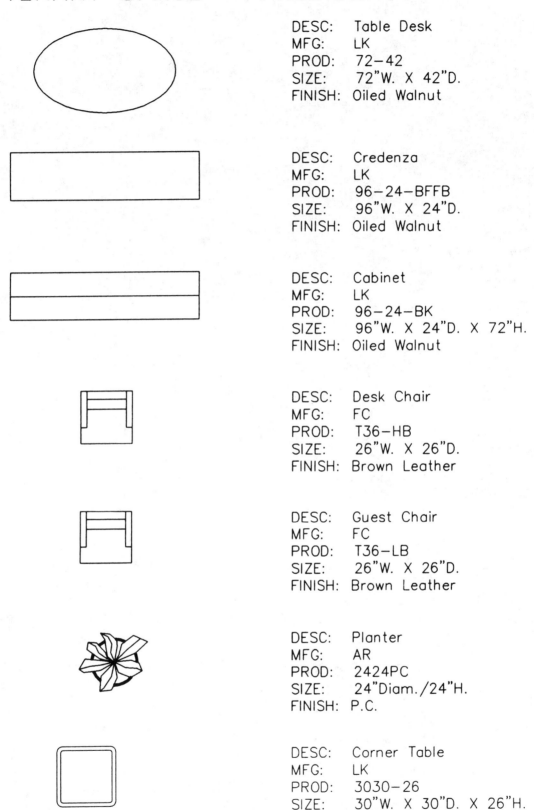

DESC:    Table Desk
MFG:     LK
PROD:    72—42
SIZE:    72"W. X 42"D.
FINISH:  Oiled Walnut

DESC:    Credenza
MFG:     LK
PROD:    96—24—BFFB
SIZE:    96"W. X 24"D.
FINISH:  Oiled Walnut

DESC:    Cabinet
MFG:     LK
PROD:    96—24—BK
SIZE:    96"W. X 24"D. X 72"H.
FINISH:  Oiled Walnut

DESC:    Desk Chair
MFG:     FC
PROD:    T36—HB
SIZE:    26"W. X 26"D.
FINISH:  Brown Leather

DESC:    Guest Chair
MFG:     FC
PROD:    T36—LB
SIZE:    26"W. X 26"D.
FINISH:  Brown Leather

DESC:    Planter
MFG:     AR
PROD:    2424PC
SIZE:    24"Diam./24"H.
FINISH:  P.C.

DESC:    Corner Table
MFG:     LK
PROD:    3030—26
SIZE:    30"W. X 30"D. X 26"H.
FINISH:  Glass/Oiled Walnut

**FIGURE 11–24**
President's Furniture Symbols and Specifications (Scale: 1/4" = 1'-0")

# TENANT SPACE — PRESIDENT (CONT.)

DESC:  Coffee Table
MFG:   LK
PROD:  3636-17
SIZE:  36"W. X 36"D. X 17"H.
FINISH: Glass/Oiled Walnut

DESC:  Lounge Chair
MFG:   FC
PROD:  3430UP
FINISH: Brown Leather

**FIGURE 11–24** *continued*

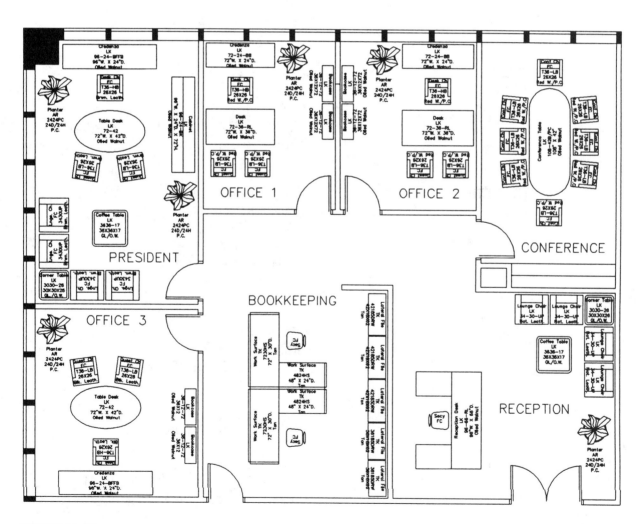

**FIGURE 11–25**
Exercise 11–1: Tenant Space Furniture Plan with Furniture Specifications (Scale: 1/8" = 1'-0")

FIGURE 11–26
Attribute Extraction—Select
Blocks and Attributes

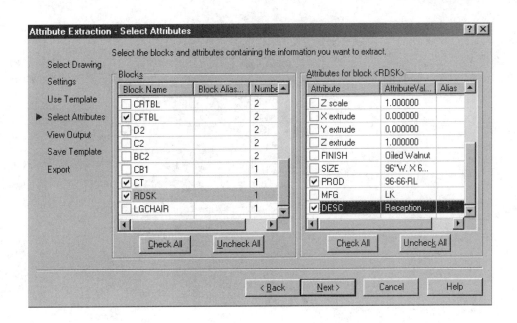

**Attribute Extraction - Select Attributes**

Select the blocks and attributes containing the information you want to extract.

Select Drawing
Settings
Use Template
► Select Attributes
View Output
Save Template
Export

Blocks

| Block Name | Block Alias... | Numbe |
|---|---|---|
| ☐ CRTBL | | 2 |
| ☑ CFTBL | | 2 |
| ☐ D2 | | 2 |
| ☐ C2 | | 2 |
| ☐ BC2 | | 2 |
| ☐ CB1 | | 1 |
| ☑ CT | | 1 |
| ☑ RDSK | | 1 |
| ☐ LGCHAIR | | 1 |

Check All    Uncheck All

Attributes for block <RDSK>

| Attribute | AttributeVal... | Alias |
|---|---|---|
| ☐ Z scale | 1.000000 | |
| ☐ X extrude | 0.000000 | |
| ☐ Y extrude | 0.000000 | |
| ☐ Z extrude | 1.000000 | |
| ☐ FINISH | Oiled Walnut | |
| ☐ SIZE | 96"W. X 6... | |
| ☑ PROD | 96-66-RL | |
| ☐ MFG | LK | |
| ☑ DESC | Reception ... | |

Check All    Uncheck All

< Back    Next >    Cancel    Help

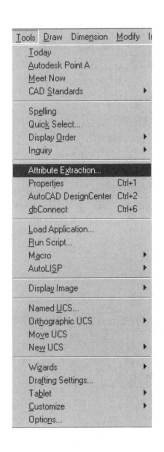

Tools  Draw  Dimension  Modify  I

Today
Autodesk Point A
Meet Now
CAD Standards ▶

Spelling
Quick Select...
Display Order ▶
Inquiry ▶

Attribute Extraction...
Properties        Ctrl+1
AutoCAD DesignCenter Ctrl+2
dbConnect          Ctrl+6

Load Application...
Run Script...
Macro ▶
AutoLISP ▶

Display Image ▶

Named UCS...
Orthographic UCS ▶
Move UCS
New UCS ▶

Wizards ▶
Drafting Settings...
Tablet ▶
Customize ▶
Options...

**Prompt**

Settings tab is selected:

Use Template tab is selected:

Select Attributes tab is selected:

**Response**

CLICK: **Next>**

**With the No Template radio button
selected** CLICK: **Next>**

There should be checks to the left of
all the blocks in the Block Name: list.

CLICK: **Uncheck All** under the
Blocks area.

CHECK: **SECY** in the Block Name list.

CLICK: **Uncheck All** in the Attributes
for block <SECY> list, then CHECK:
the **DESC** and **PROD** attributes
(Figure 11–26).

CHECK: **CFTBL**, CLICK: **Uncheck All**
in the Attributes for block list, then
CHECK: the **DESC** and **PROD**
attributes for that block.

CHECK: **CT**, CLICK: **Uncheck All** in
the Attributes for block list, then
CHECK: the **DESC** and **PROD**
attributes for that block.

CHECK: **RDSK, Uncheck All** in the
Attributes for block list then CHECK:
the **DESC** and **PROD** attributes for
that block.

CLICK: **Next>**

View Output tab is selected:

CLICK: **Alternate View** once or twice so
the screen appears as shown in
Figure 11–27.

CLICK: **Next>**

Save Template tab is selected:

CLICK: **Next>**

**FIGURE 11–27**
Select the Alternate View of the
Output

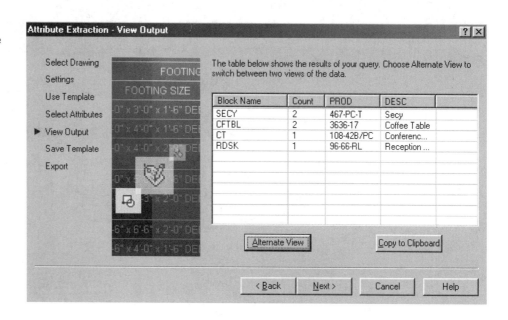

| Block Name | Count | PROD | DESC | |
|---|---|---|---|---|
| SECY | 2 | 467-PC-T | Secy | |
| CFTBL | 2 | 3636-17 | Coffee Table | |
| CT | 1 | 108-42B/PC | Conferenc... | |
| RDSK | 1 | 96-66-RL | Reception ... | |

| Prompt | Response |
|---|---|
| Export tab is selected: | In the File Name text box, TYPE: **A:CH11-1 PART 2** (Figure 11–28). |
| | In the File Type text box, SELECT: **CSV (Comma delimited) (\*.csv))**. |
| | CLICK: **Finish** |

**Step 4. Open Notepad in Windows.**

| CLICK: | **Start** |
|---|---|
| CLICK: | **Accessories** |
| CLICK: | **Notepad** |

**Step 5. Open CH11-EX1-PART 2 from the floppy disk in the A: drive (Figure 11–29).**

| CLICK: | **File** |
|---|---|
| CLICK: | **Open** |

**FIGURE 11–28**
TYPE: The Export File Name,
**A:CH11-1 PART 2**

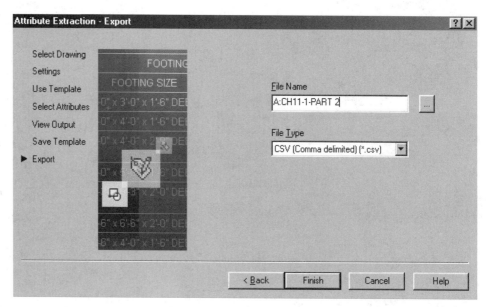

File Name

A:CH11-1-PART 2

File Type

CSV (Comma delimited) (\*.csv)

FIGURE 11–29
Open the CH11-1 PART 2 File in
Notepad

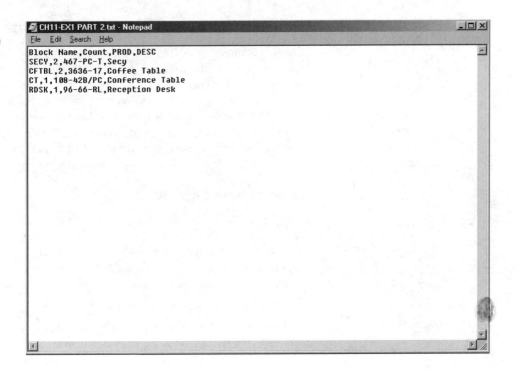

```
CH11-EX1 PART 2.txt - Notepad
File  Edit  Search  Help
Block Name,Count,PROD,DESC
SECY,2,467-PC-T,Secy
CFTBL,2,3636-17,Coffee Table
CT,1,108-42B/PC,Conference Table
RDSK,1,96-66-RL,Reception Desk
```

CLICK: **3 1/2 Floppy [A:]**     (Be sure to CLICK: **All Files (*.*)** in the
Files of Type: box.)

**Step 6. Fix the text file and add your name, class, and section (Figure 11–30).**

CLICK: To the right of the Block Name (between Name and the comma) and press the
Delete key, then press the Tab key. Use Tab, Delete, Backspace, and Return keys to
complete the exercise as shown.

**Step 7. Save this file and plot or print it to complete the exercise.**

FIGURE 11–30
Exercise 11–1 Part 2 Complete

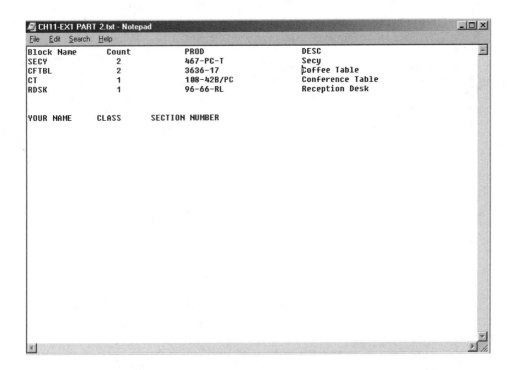

```
CH11-EX1 PART 2.txt - Notepad
File  Edit  Search  Help
Block Name     Count          PROD           DESC
SECY           2              467-PC-T       Secy
CFTBL          2              3636-17        Coffee Table
CT             1              108-42B/PC     Conference Table
RDSK           1              96-66-RL       Reception Desk

YOUR NAME       CLASS      SECTION NUMBER
```

## Furniture Symbol and Specification Software Programs

Creating a library of all the furniture symbols you may need while completing a furniture plan can be very time consuming. Many programs are available on the market today that have the furniture symbols already drawn. Most of the major furniture manufacturers' furniture symbols and catalog specifications are available in programs that work easily with AutoCAD. Some already have the specifications or attributes assigned and allow you to enter variables. Programs are also available that extract attribute information from a drawing and provide a list of information that can be tailored to include such data as item totals, specifications, total costs, and total selling price.

## External Reference (XREF)

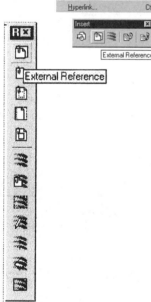

The External Reference command allows you to attach an external reference (xref) (drawing) to a primary drawing. For each drawing, the data is stored in its own separate file. Any changes made to the external reference drawing are reflected in the primary drawing each time the primary drawing is loaded into the Drawing Editor.

There are three distinct advantages to using external references:

1. The primary drawing always contains the most recent version of the external reference.
2. There are no conflicts in layer names and other similar features (called named objects), such as linetypes, text styles, and block definitions. AutoCAD automatically precedes the external reference layer name or other object name with the drawing name of the xref and a slash (/). For example, if the primary drawing and the external reference (named CHAIR) have a layer named Symbol, then the current drawing layer retains the name Symbol, and the external reference layer in the current drawing becomes Chair/symbol.
3. Drawing files are often much smaller.

External references are used, for example, when drawing a large furniture plan containing several different levels of office types, such as assistant, associate, manager, vice president, and president. Each office typical (furniture configuration used in the office) is attached to the current drawing as an external reference. When changes are made to the external reference drawing of the manager's office (as a result of furniture substitution, for example), the change is reflected in each instance of a manager's office in the primary large furniture plan when it is loaded into the Drawing Editor.

When the External Reference command is activated, the Select Reference File dialog box appears. After you attach a drawing to your current drawing, the following options are available in the Xref Manager dialog box:

### Attach

The Attach option allows you to attach as an external reference any drawing to the current drawing. There is no limit to the number of external references that you can attach to your drawing.

### Detach

The Detach option lets you remove unneeded external references from your drawing.

### Reload

The Reload option allows you to update the current drawing with an external reference that has been changed since you began the current drawing. You do not have to exit from the current drawing to update it with an external reference that you or someone else changed while in the current drawing.

### Unload

Temporarily clears the external reference from the current drawing until the drawing is reloaded.

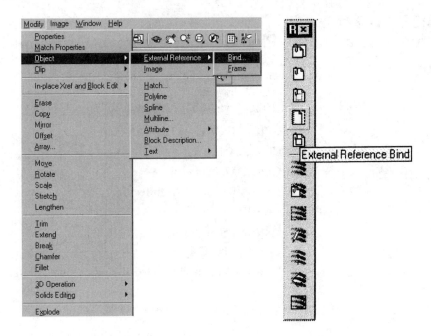

### Bind...

The Insert option in the Bind dialog box creates a block of the external reference in the current drawing and erases any reference to it as an external reference. The Bind option binds the selected xref to the drawing and renames layers in a manner similar to that of the attached xref.

### Features of External References

1. An external reference cannot be exploded.
2. An external reference can be changed into a block with the Bind-Insert option and then exploded. The advantage of using the external reference is then lost. The Bind option would be used if you wanted to send a client a disk containing only the current drawing without including external references on the same disk.
3. External references can be nested. That means that a current drawing containing external references can itself be used as an external reference on another current drawing. There is no limit to the number of drawings you can nest like this.

## XBIND

The XBIND (External Bind) command allows you to bind a selected subset of an external reference's dependent symbols to the current drawing. For example, if you did not want to create a block of the entire external reference but wanted permanently to add only a dimension style of the external reference to the drawing, you could use XBIND.

## SAVE

When you have completed Exercise 11–1, save your work in at least two places.

## PLOT

Plot Exercise 11–1 to scale.

# EXERCISE 11-2
## Reception Area Furniture Plan Using the AutoCAD DesignCenter

When you have completed Exercise 11–2, your drawing will look similar to Figure 11–31. To draw Exercise 11–2 turn on the computer and start AutoCAD. The AutoCAD 2002 Today window is displayed.

1. CLICK: **the Create Drawings tab**

   CLICK: **Wizards**

2. CLICK: **Quick Setup**

3. Set drawing Units: **Architectural**

   CLICK: **Next>**

4. Set drawing Width: **44′** × Length: **34′**

   CLICK: **Finish**

5. **Use SaveAs... to save the drawing to the hard drive with the name CH11–EX2.**

6. Set Grid: **12″**

7. Set Snap: **6″**

You will now use several of the features of the AutoCAD DesignCenter to set up and draw Exercise 11–2.

## THE AUTOCAD DESIGNCENTER

The AutoCAD DesignCenter allows you to do several things that can save you a great deal of time:

Use several existing blocks arranged in categories that AutoCAD has provided.

Use blocks, layers, linetypes, text and dimension styles, and external references from any existing drawing using drag and drop.

Examine drawings and blocks as either drawing names or pictures.

Search for drawings and other files.

**FIGURE 11–31**
Exercise 11–2 Complete

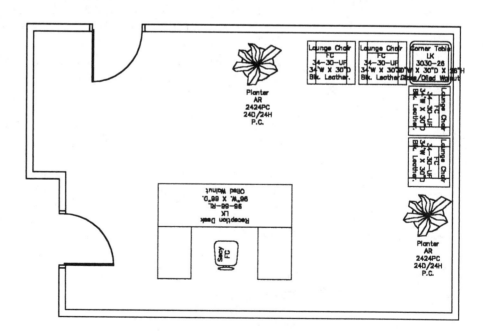

**Now open the AutoCAD DesignCenter and examine it:**

| Prompt | Response |
|---|---|
| Command: | **AutoCAD DesignCenter** (or TYPE: **ADC<enter>**) |
| The DesignCenter appears: | DOUBLE CLICK: **the Desktop icon** (on the extreme left), then DOUBLE CLICK: **the DesignCenter folder** |
| The folders of predefined blocks and other items, Figure 11–32, appear: | DOUBLE CLICK: **Home-Space Planner.dwg** |
| The defined folders under Home-Space Planner appear: | DOUBLE CLICK: **Blocks** |
| All the predefined blocks for this folder appear: | |

You can now click on any of these drawings, hold down the left mouse button, drag the drawing into the current drawing, and drop it. Do not do that for this exercise. Now, examine the other buttons in the DesignCenter, then use layers and blocks from CH11–EX1 to do CH11–EX2.

## DesignCenter Buttons

The icons at the top of the DesignCenter allow you to access all the following options of the DesignCenter:

### Desktop

Clicking this button shows you the Windows Desktop.

### Open Drawings

Shows you the drawings that are currently open.

**FIGURE 11–32**
The AutoCAD DesignCenter

### History

Shows you a list of the most recently opened drawings.

### Tree View Toggle

Displays and hides the tree view. The tree view shows the structure of the files and folders in the form of a chart.

### Favorites

Shows what you have in the Favorites folder. You can save your most often used items here.

### Load

Allows you to load drawings and other items that you want to use in your current drawing.

### Find

Allows you to search for and locate data you need.

### Up

Moves you to the drawing or folder one level above the active one.

### Preview

Allows you to look at a preview of any selected item. If there is no preview image saved with the selected item, the Preview area will be empty.

### Description

Shows a text description of any selected item.

### Views

Provides you with different display formats for the selected items. You can select a view from the View list or choose the View button again to cycle through display formats.

The down arrow at the far right gives you the following:

### Large Icon

Shows the names of loaded items with large icons.

### Small Icon

Shows the names of loaded items with small icons.

### List View

Shows a list of loaded items.

### Detail View

Gives you additional information about the loaded items.

Now, proceed to use the DesignCenter to complete your drawing.

**Use the A-FURN, A-DOOR, and A-WALL-INT layers from CH11–EX1 in the new drawing:**

| Prompt | Response |
|---|---|
| Command: | **Place the floppy disk containing CH11–EX1 in the A: drive** |
| | CLICK: **Load** |
| | CLICK: **3½ Floppy (A:)** and DOUBLE CLICK: **CH11–EX1** |
| | DOUBLE CLICK: **Layers** |

**FIGURE 11-33**
Layers in CH12-EX1

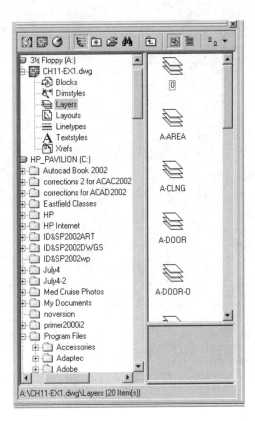

| Prompt | Response |
|---|---|
| The display (Figure 11–33) appears: | CLICK: **Layer A-DOOR, hold down the pick button, drag it into the current drawing (to the right of the DesignCenter), and release the pick button.** |
| | Repeat the previous for Layers **A-FURN and A-WALL-INT** |

**Draw the outside walls of the reception area using the dimensions from Figure 11–34:**

## On Your Own

1. **Set Layer A-WALL-INT current.**
2. **Use Multiline to draw the outside walls of the reception area using the dimensions from Figure 11–34. Set an offset of 5″ for the wall thickness.**

**Use the block DOOR from CH11–EX1 to draw doors in the current drawing:**

## On Your Own

1. **CLICK: Blocks under CH11–EX1, find the block named DOOR, and drag and drop it into the currrent drawing.**
2. **Use the Mirror and Rotate commands if necessary to correctly position the door.**
3. **Place doors in the correct location using the dimensions from Figure 11–34.**
4. **Explode the doors and use the Trim command to trim the walls from the door openings.**

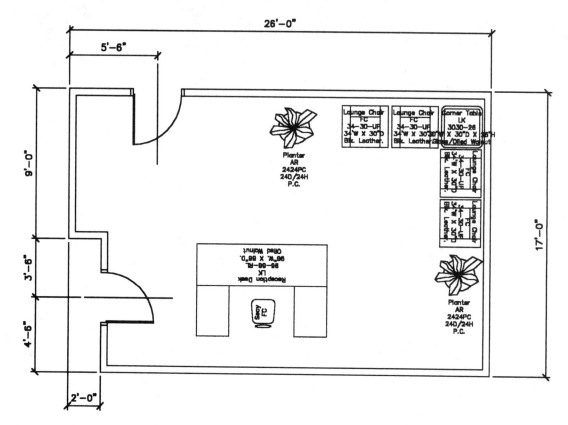

**FIGURE 11–34**
Dimensions for Exercise 11–2

Use the blocks PLANT, CRTBL, RDSK, SECY, and LGCHAIR to draw furniture in the current drawing.

1. CLICK: Blocks under CH11–EX1, find the blocks named PLANT, CRTBL, RDSK, SECY, and LGCHAIR, and drag and drop them into the currrent drawing.

2. Use the Mirror and Rotate commands if necessary to correctly position each item.

3. Place furniture in the approximate locations shown in Figure 11–34.

## SAVE

When you have completed Exercise 11–2 save your work in at least two places.

## PLOT

Plot Exercise 11–2 to scale.

# EXERCISE 11–3
# Office I Furniture Plan

1. Start a new drawing named CH11-EX3 by copying the Office I floor plan drawn in Exercise 8–2 or by copying the Office I floor plan dimensioned in Exercise 9–6.

2. Create a new layer for furniture, and draw the furniture as shown in Figure 11–35 for the Office I furniture plan. Use a 1/8″ = 1′-0″ architectural scale to measure the furniture, and draw it full scale.

3. Save the drawing in two places, and plot or print the drawing to scale.

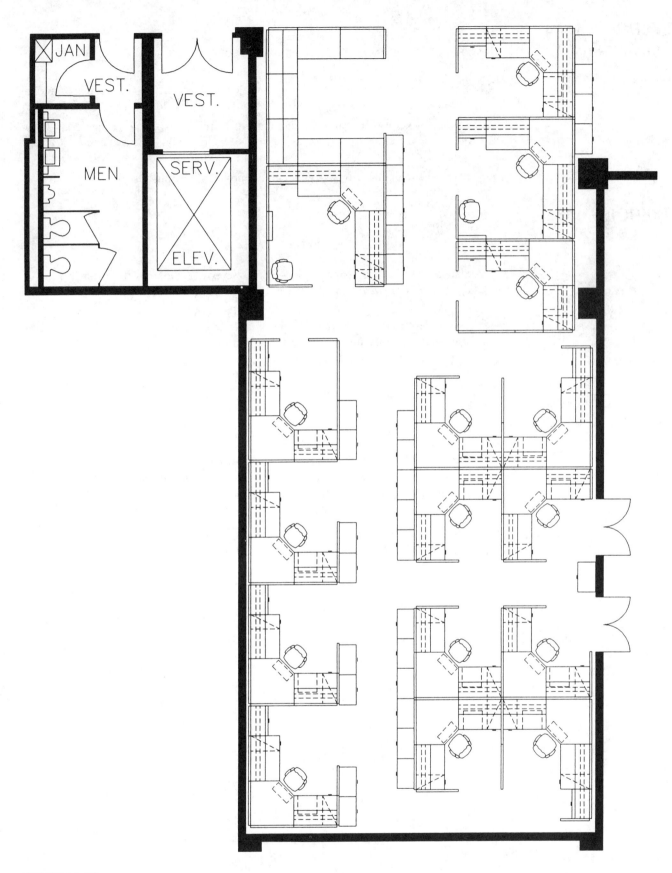

**FIGURE 11-35**
Exercise 11-3: Office I Furniture Plan (Scale: 1/8" = 1'-0")
(Courtesy of Business Interiors Design Department, Irving, Texas, and GTE Directories.)

**Chapter 11: Drawing and Adding Specifications to Furnishings**

# EXERCISE 11–4
## Office II Furniture Plan

1. Start a new drawing named CH11-EX4 by copying the Office II floor plan drawn in Exercise 8–3 or by copying the Office II floor plan dimensioned in Exercise 9–6.
2. Create a new layer for furniture, and draw the furniture as shown in Figure 11–36 for the Office II furniture plan. Use a 1/8″ = 1′-0″ architectural scale to measure the furniture, and draw it full scale.
3. Save the drawing in two places, and plot or print the drawing to scale.

# EXERCISE 11–5
## House Furniture Plan

1. Start a new drawing named CH11-EX5 by copying the house floor plan drawn in Exercise 8–4 or by copying the house floor plan dimensioned in Exercise 9–8.
2. Create a new layer for furniture, and draw the furniture as shown in Figure 11–37, Lower and Upper Levels, for the house furniture plan. Use a 1/8″ = 1′-0″ architectural scale to measure the furniture, and draw it full scale.
3. Save the drawing in two places, and plot or print the drawing to scale.

# EXERCISE 11–6
## Country Club Furniture Plan

1. Start a new drawing named CH11-EX6 by copying the country club floor plan drawn in Exercise 8–5 or by copying the country club floor plan dimensioned in Exercise 9–9.
2. Create a new layer for furniture, and draw the furniture as shown in Figure 11–38 for the country club furniture plan. Use a 1/8″ = 1′-0″ architectural scale to measure the furniture, and draw it full scale.
3. Save the drawing in two places, and plot or print the drawing to scale.

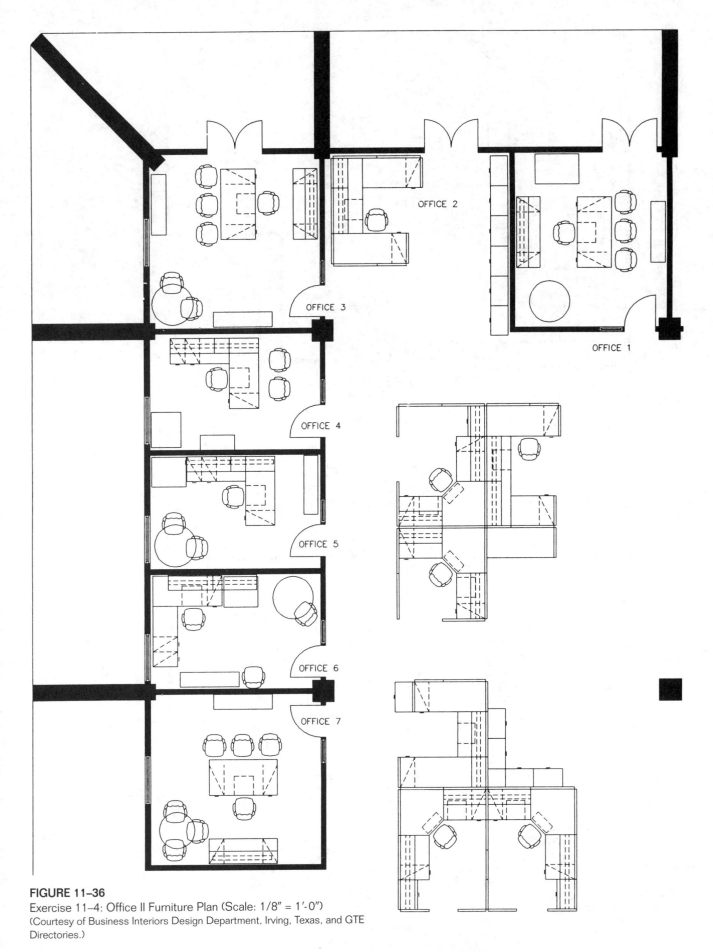

OFFICE 2

OFFICE 1

OFFICE 3

OFFICE 4

OFFICE 5

OFFICE 6

OFFICE 7

**FIGURE 11–36**
Exercise 11–4: Office II Furniture Plan (Scale: 1/8″ = 1′-0″)
(Courtesy of Business Interiors Design Department, Irving, Texas, and GTE
Directories.)

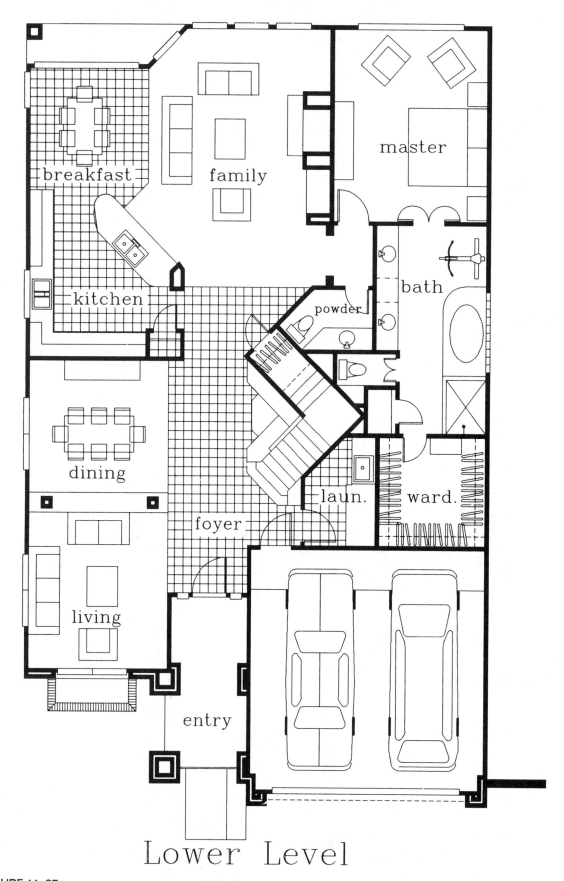

master

breakfast

family

kitchen

bath

powder

dining

laun.

ward.

foyer

living

entry

Lower Level

**FIGURE 11–37**

Exercise 11–5: House Furniture Plan (Scale: 1/8″ = 1′-0″)
(Courtesy of John Brooks, AIA, Dallas, Texas.)

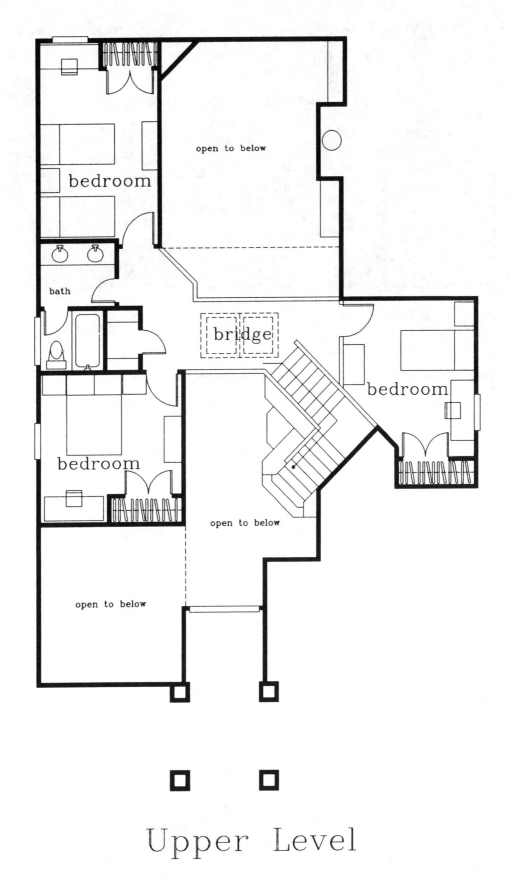

open to below

bedroom

bath

bridge

bedroom

bedroom

open to below

open to below

Upper Level

FIGURE 11–37 *continued*

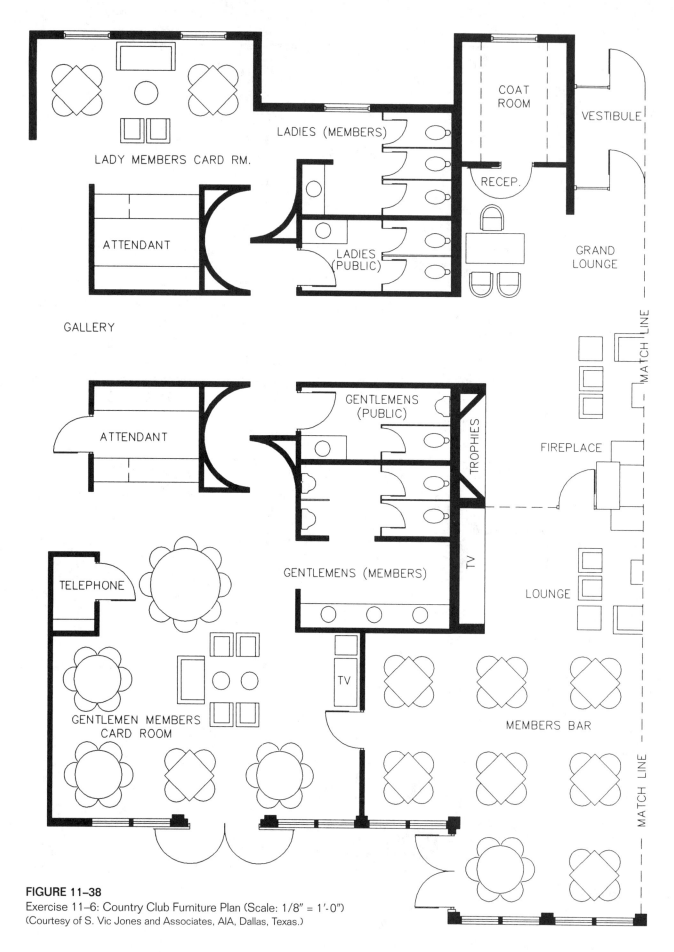

COAT ROOM

VESTIBULE

RECEP.

GRAND LOUNGE

LADIES (MEMBERS)

LADY MEMBERS CARD RM.

ATTENDANT

LADIES (PUBLIC)

GALLERY

MATCH LINE

ATTENDANT

GENTLEMENS (PUBLIC)

TROPHIES

FIREPLACE

TV

GENTLEMENS (MEMBERS)

LOUNGE

TELEPHONE

TV

GENTLEMEN MEMBERS CARD ROOM

MEMBERS BAR

MATCH LINE

**FIGURE 11–38**
Exercise 11–6: Country Club Furniture Plan (Scale: 1/8″ = 1′-0″)
(Courtesy of S. Vic Jones and Associates, AIA, Dallas, Texas.)

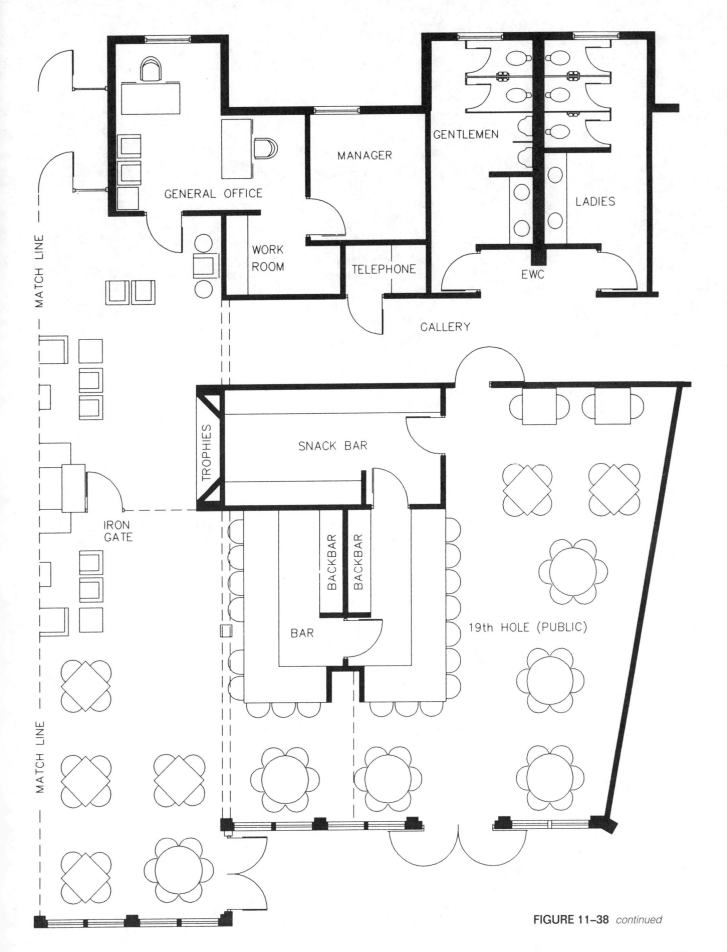

FIGURE 11–38 continued

333

# REVIEW QUESTIONS

1. Which of the following modes must be selected to create a variable attribute that gives you two chances to type the correct value?
   a. Invisible
   b. Constant
   c. Verify
   d. Preset
   e. Do not select any of these.

2. The prompt "Attribute modes–Invisible:Y  Constant:Y  Verify:N  Preset:N" indicates which of the following?
   a. Verify mode is active.
   b. Preset mode is active.
   c. Invisible and Constant modes are active.
   d. Verify and Preset modes are active.
   e. Invisible mode only is active.

3. To change the prompt in Question 2 to "Attribute modes—Invisible:N  Constant:N  Verify:N  Preset:N," you must:
   a. TYPE: IC, then N
   b. TYPE: I, then CI, then N
   c. TYPE: I, then C
   d. TYPE: IC, then OFF
   e. TYPE: IC, then Y

4. In which of the following may spaces *not* be used?
   a. Value
   b. Default Value
   c. Prompt
   d. Tag
   e. Spaces may be used in all the above.

5. AutoCAD automatically places an attribute definition below one that was defined with the previous ATTDEF command.
   a. True
   b. False

6. Which of the following part of an attribute appears on the inserted furniture symbol when the attribute mode is *not* Invisible?
   a. Tag
   b. Prompt
   c. Value
   d. Mode
   e. Block name

7. If you insert a block with attributes into a drawing and no attribute prompts occur, which of the following is true?
   a. All attributes are Constant.
   b. All attributes are Variable.
   c. All attributes are Verify.
   d. All attributes are Invisible.
   e. The block has not been inserted on the correct layer.

8. To use the Enter Attributes dialog box to change or accept default values of attributes, which of the following system variables must be set to 1?
   a. ATTREQ
   b. ATTDIA
   c. ATTMODE
   d. ANGDIR
   e. AUPREC

9. Which of the following commands can be used to make invisible all the visible attributes on the drawing?
   a. DDATTE
   b. ATTEXT
   c. ATTDEF
   d. ATTEDIT
   e. ATTDISP

10. Which of the following commands can be used to edit Variable, Verify, Preset, and Constant attribute values of an inserted block using a dialog box?
    a. ATTEXT
    b. ATTDEF
    c. ATTEDIT
    d. ATTDISP
    e. Constant attributes cannot be edited.

11. The command used to edit attribute values without a dialog box is:

    _____

12. After you have selected several attribute values for editing using ATTEDIT, how do you know which attribute you are currently editing?

    _____

13. Which command will change all the attribute values "Black" to "Brown" on all occurrences of the Tag "COLOR" at the same time, independent of the block reference?

    _____

14. The command that allows you to redefine a block within a drawing and update all previous insertions of the block in your drawing is:

    _____

15. When a block that has attributes assigned is redefined with the Block command, what happens to existing Variable attributes on the drawing?

    _____

16. The command that uses a dialog box to extract attributes from a drawing is:

    _____

17. Describe how an external reference drawing differs from a block drawing.

    _____

    _____

18. Which External Reference option allows you to make an external reference a block on the present drawing?

    _____

19. Describe the main purpose of using blocks with attributes.

    _____

    _____

20. List three advantages of using external references.

    _____

    _____

    _____

# 12 Drawing the Reflected Ceiling Plan and Power Plan

## OBJECTIVES

When you have completed this chapter, you will be able to:

☐ Draw a lighting legend.
☐ Draw a reflected ceiling plan.
☐ Draw electrical and telephone legends.
☐ Draw a power plan.

## INTRODUCTION

Previously learned commands are used to draw the tenant space reflected ceiling plan in Exercise 12–1, Part 1, and power plan in Exercise 12–1, Part 2. Helpful guidelines for drawing Exercise 12–1, Parts 1 and 2, are provided.

## EXERCISE 12–1, PART 1
## Tenant Space Lighting Legend and Reflected Ceiling Plan

In Exercise 12–1, Part 1, two separate drawings are drawn—a lighting legend and a reflected ceiling plan for the tenant space. The lighting legend is drawn first and then inserted into the tenant space reflected ceiling plan. When you have completed Exercise 12–1, Part 1, your reflected ceiling plan drawing will look similar to Figure 12–1.

### Tenant Space Lighting Legend Drawing

#### On Your Own

1. **Begin the lighting legend drawing on the hard drive.**

2. **Create a Layer named E-lite-txt, color Green.**

3. **Draw the lighting legend as shown in Figure 12–2, full scale. Draw the lighting symbols on the 0 Layer, and the text and the two arrows on the E-lite-txt Layer. Typically, the lighting symbols and related circuitry have heavier lineweights than the floor plan. You may accomplish this using one of three methods:**

☐ **Plot the lighting symbols and circuitry with a thicker pen.**
☐ **Draw the lighting symbols and circuitry with a thicker line (polyline or donut).**
☐ **Draw the lighting symbols and circuitry on a layer to which you have assigned a thicker lineweight.**

4. **Wblock the lighting legend drawing to a floppy disk in drive A with the name LIGHTING.**

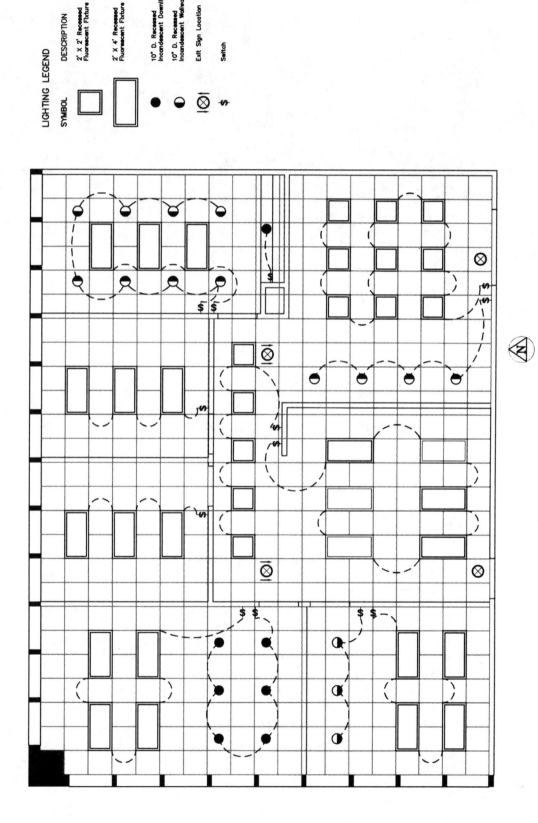

**LIGHTING LEGEND**

| SYMBOL | DESCRIPTION |
|---|---|
| ☐ | 2' x 2' Recessed Fluorescent Fixture |
| ▭ | 2' x 4' Recessed Fluorescent Fixture |
| ● | 10" D. Recessed Incandescent Downlight |
| ◑ | 10" D. Recessed Incandescent Wallwasher |
| ⊗| | Exit Sign Location |
| $ | Switch |

**FIGURE 12–1**

Exercise 12–1, Part 1: Tenant Space Reflected Ceiling Plan (Scale: 1/8" = 1'-0")

FIGURE 12–2
Tenant Space Lighting Legend
(Scale: 1/4" = 1'-0")

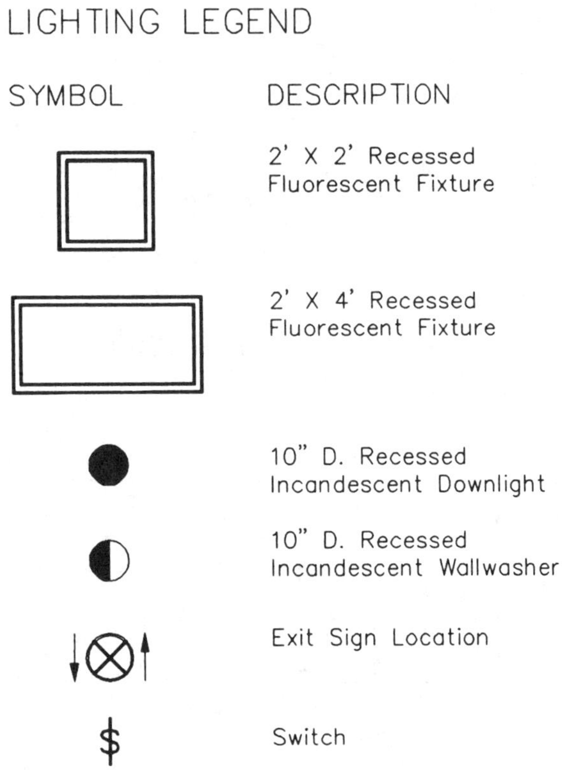

## LIGHTING LEGEND

| SYMBOL | DESCRIPTION |
|---|---|
| ▢ | 2' X 2' Recessed Fluorescent Fixture |
| ▭ | 2' X 4' Recessed Fluorescent Fixture |
| ● | 10" D. Recessed Incandescent Downlight |
| ◑ | 10" D. Recessed Incandescent Wallwasher |
| ↓⊗↑ | Exit Sign Location |
| $ | Switch |

## Tenant Space Reflected Ceiling Plan

### On Your Own

1. **Begin drawing CH12-EX1 on the hard drive by opening existing drawing CH11-EX1 from a floppy disk in drive A and saving it as CH12-EX1 on the hard drive.**

2. **Freeze the following Layers that have objects drawn that are not needed to draw the reflected ceiling plan:**

   **A-area**
   **A-door**
   **A-flor-iden**
   **A-furn**
   **A-pflr-dims**

3. **Create a layer named E-lite-d, color red, lineweight default, and make it current. Draw lines across the door openings as shown in Figure 12–1 (A-door Layer is frozen) on Layer E-lite-d.**

   If you plan to plot the exterior and interior walls with different thicknesses, you may create two separate layers to draw these lines: one for the interior walls (red) and one for the exterior walls (blue). A running Osnap-Intersection mode will help you draw the lines quickly. Be sure to cancel the Osnap mode when you are finished.

4. **Set Layer A-clng current and draw the 2' × 2' ceiling grid: Draw half of a 2' × 2' ceiling tile symbol, as shown in Figure 12–3, in the lower left corner of the tenant space floor plan. Use the Array command to complete the ceiling grid, making it rectangular with 19 rows and 25 columns and having 2' distance between rows and columns.**

FIGURE 12–3
Draw Half of the 2' × 2' Ceiling Grid in the Lower Left Corner of the Tenant Space Floor Plan

Erase the extra ceiling line out of the larger corner column. You may erase or leave the ceiling grid lines that are drawn on top of the south and west interior wall lines of the tenant space floor plan.

5. Set Layer E-lite current and Insert-Block... the lighting legend drawing (LIGHTING), full scale, into the location shown on the tenant space reflected ceiling plan in Figure 12–1. Check the Explode box in the Insert dialog box so that each symbol is inserted as a separate entity.

6. Prepare the ceiling grid for insertion of the $2' \times 4'$ recessed fixture symbols by using the Erase command to erase the ceiling grid lines that will cross the centers of the symbols.

Use the Copy (Multiple) command and an Osnap modifier to copy the lighting symbols from the legend and place them on the plan, as shown in Figure 12–1. You may also snap to a grid point when possible.

The wallwasher, $2' \times 4'$ fixture, and switch symbols appear on the reflected ceiling plan in several different orientations. Copy each symbol and Rotate the individual symbols into the various positions, then use Copy (Multiple) to draw the additional like symbols in the correct locations on the plan.

7. Create an E-lite-w Layer, color white, with a DASHEDX2 linetype, lineweight 0.3 mm, and set it current. Use the Arc command to draw the symbol for the circuitry. Adjust LTSCALE as needed so lines appear as dashed.

8. When you have completed Exercise 12–1, Part 1, save your work in at least two places.

9. Use a Layout Wizard or Page Setup to create a Layout tab named Reflected Ceiling Plan to the appropriate scale for your printer or plotter. Plot or print Exercise 12–1, Part 1.

# EXERCISE 12–1, PART 2
## Tenant Space Power Plan

In Exercise 12–1, Part 2, three separate drawings are drawn—an electrical legend, a telephone legend, and a power plan for the tenant space project. The electrical and telephone legends are drawn first and then inserted into the tenant space power plan. When you have completed Exercise 12–1, Part 2, your tenant space power plan drawing will look similar to Figure 12–4.

### Tenant Space Electrical Legend Drawing

On Your Own

1. Begin the drawing of the electrical legend on the hard drive.

2. Create a Layer named E-power-txt, color Green.

3. Draw the electrical legend as shown in Figure 12–5, full scale. Draw the electrical symbols on the 0 Layer, and the text on the E-power-txt Layer. Draw the symbols with a heavier lineweight than shown.

4. Wblock the electrical legend drawing to a floppy disk in drive A with the name ELECTRIC.

### Tenant Space Telephone Legend Drawing

On Your Own

1. Begin the drawing of the telephone legend on the hard drive.

2. Draw the telephone legend as shown in Figure 12–6, full scale, on the 0 Layer (both text and symbols).

3. Wblock the telephone legend drawing to a floppy disk in drive A with the name TELEPHON.

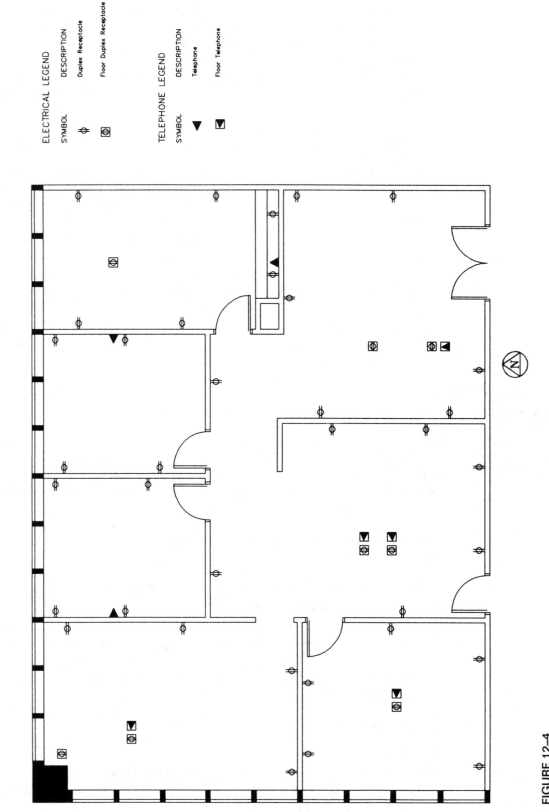

ELECTRICAL LEGEND

| SYMBOL | DESCRIPTION |
|--------|-------------|
| ⊕ | Duplex Receptacle |
| ⊟ | Floor Duplex Receptacle |

TELEPHONE LEGEND

| SYMBOL | DESCRIPTION |
|--------|-------------|
| ▼ | Telephone |
| ▼ | Floor Telephone |

**FIGURE 12–4**
Exercise 12–1, Part 2: Tenant Space Power Plan (Scale: 1/8" = 1'-0")

**FIGURE 12–5**
Tenant Space Electrical Legend
(Scale: 1/4″ = 1′-0″)

## ELECTRICAL LEGEND

SYMBOL                DESCRIPTION

                Duplex Receptacle

                Floor Duplex Receptacle

**FIGURE 12–6**
Tenant Space Telephone Legend
(Scale: 1/4″ = 1′-0″)

## TELEPHONE LEGEND

SYMBOL                DESCRIPTION

                Telephone

                Floor Telephone

## Tenant Space Power Plan

### On Your Own

1. Open drawing CH12-EX1 and save it on the hard drive.

2. Freeze all layers that are not required to draw the power plan.

3. Set Layer E-powr current, change its lineweight to 0.30 mm, and Insert-Block... the electrical legend drawing (ELECTRIC) full scale in the location shown on the tenant space power plan in Figure 12–4. Check the Explode box in the Insert dialog box to separate the symbols into individual entities.

4. Use the Copy (Multiple) command and an Osnap modifier to copy the electrical symbols from the legend and place them on the plan as shown in Figure 12–4. You may also snap to a grid point when possible.

   The duplex receptacle symbol appears on the plan in several different orientations. Copy the symbol, and use Rotate to obtain the rotated positions as shown on the plan. Use the Copy command to draw like rotated symbols in the correct locations on the plan.

   It is helpful to draw a line connecting the two endpoints of the two lines in the duplex receptacle. Use the midpoint of this line to locate the duplex receptacle along the walls. Do not include this line in the selection set of the Copy command. Use Osnap-Center to help locate the floor receptacle symbol.

5. Set Layer E-comm current, change its lineweight to 0.30 mm, and Insert the telephone legend drawing (TELEPHON) full scale in the location shown on the tenant space power plan in Figure 12–4. Check the Explode box in the Insert dialog box.

6. Copy the telephone symbols from the legend, and place them on the plan as shown in Figure 12–4.

7. When you have completed Exercise 12–1, Part 2, save your work in at least two places.

8. Use a Layout Wizard or Page Setup to create a Layout tab named Power Plan to the appropriate scale for your printer or plotter. Plot or print Exercise 12–1, Part 2, to scale.

# EXERCISE 12–2
## Office I Reflected Ceiling Plan and Power Plan

In Exercise 12–2, a reflected ceiling plan and power plan are drawn for Office I.

### On Your Own

1. Begin drawing CH12-EX2 on the hard drive by opening existing drawing CH11-EX3 and saving it as CH12-EX2 on the hard drive.

2. Freeze the layers that are not needed to draw the reflected ceiling plan.

3. Insert-Block... on the correct layer of the lighting legend (LIGHTING) drawn in Exercise 12–1, Part 1, into drawing CH12-EX2. Check the Explode box in the Insert dialog box so that each symbol is inserted as a separate entity. Modify the inserted legend for Office I as shown in Figure 12–7.

4. Complete the Office I reflected ceiling plan as shown in Figure 12–8. Use a Layout Wizard or Page Setup to create a Layout tab named Reflected Ceiling Plan to the appropriate scale for your printer or plotter.

5. Freeze the layers that are not needed to draw the power plan.

6. Insert-Block... on the correct layers of the electrical and telephone legends (ELECTRIC, TELEPHON) drawn in Exercise 12–1, Part 2. Check the Explode box in the Insert dialog box. Modify the inserted legends for Office I as shown in Figure 12–7.

7. Complete the Office I power plan as shown in Figure 12–9. Use a Layout Wizard or Page Setup to create a Layout tab named Power Plan to the appropriate scale for your printer or plotter.

8. When you have completed Exercise 12–2, save your work in at least two places.

9. Plot or print the drawings to scale.

**FIGURE 12–7**
Office I Lighting, Electrical, and Telephone Legends
(Scale: 1/4″ = 1′-0″)

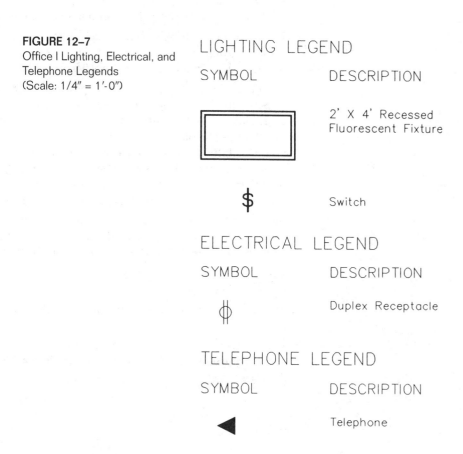

LIGHTING LEGEND

SYMBOL                    DESCRIPTION

                         2′ X 4′ Recessed
                         Fluorescent Fixture

$                        Switch

ELECTRICAL LEGEND

SYMBOL                    DESCRIPTION

                         Duplex Receptacle

TELEPHONE LEGEND

SYMBOL                    DESCRIPTION

                         Telephone

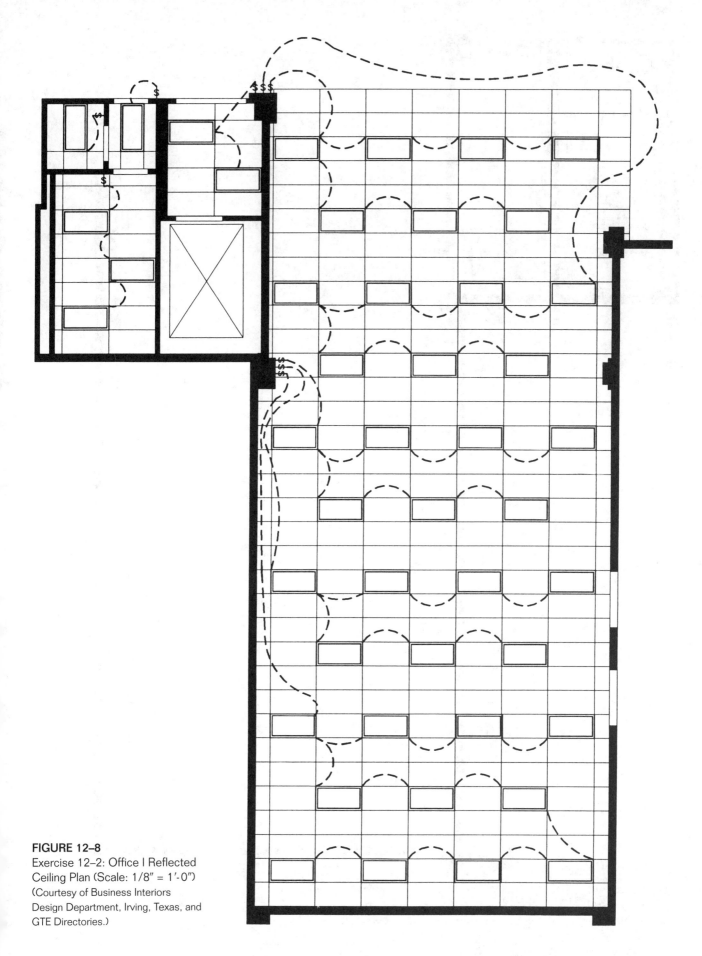

**FIGURE 12–8**
Exercise 12–2: Office I Reflected
Ceiling Plan (Scale: 1/8″ = 1′-0″)
(Courtesy of Business Interiors
Design Department, Irving, Texas, and
GTE Directories.)

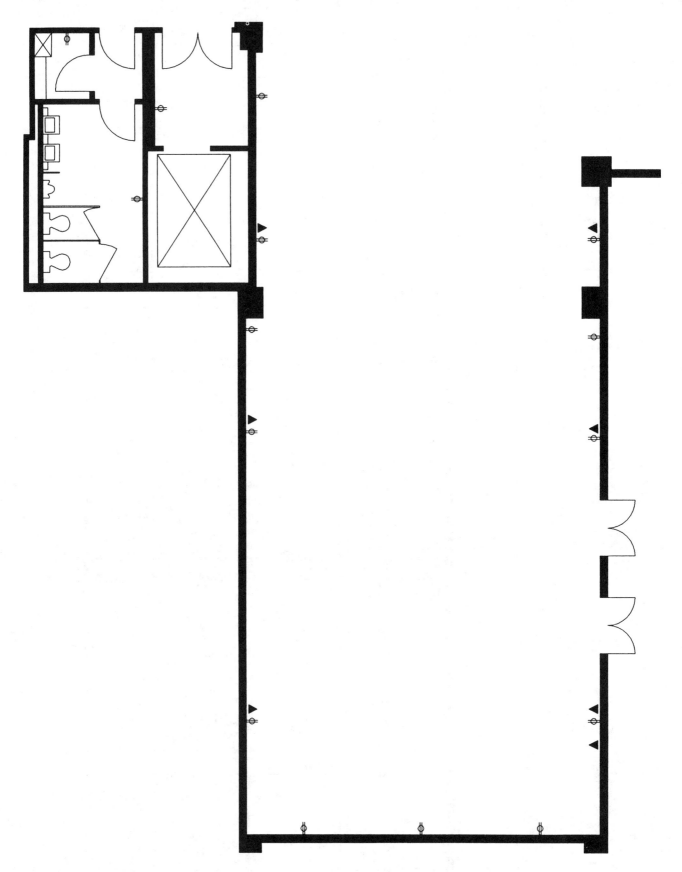

**FIGURE 12–9**
Exercise 12–2: Office I Power Plan (Scale: 1/8″ = 1′-0″)
(Courtesy of Business Interiors Design Department, Irving, Texas, and GTE Directories.)

# EXERCISE 12–3
## Office II Reflected Ceiling Plan and Power Plan

In Exercise 12–3, a reflected ceiling plan and power plan are drawn for Office II.

### On Your Own

1. **Begin drawing CH12-EX3 on the hard drive by opening existing drawing CH11-EX4 and saving it as CH12-EX3 on the hard drive.**

2. **Freeze the layers that are not needed to draw the reflected ceiling plan.**

3. **Insert-Block... on the correct layer of the lighting legend drawn in Exercise 12–1, Part 1 (LIGHTING), into drawing CH12-EX3. Check the Explode box in the Insert dialog box so that each symbol is inserted as a separate entity. Modify the inserted legend for Office II as shown in Figure 12–10.**

4. **Complete the Office II reflected ceiling plan as shown in Figure 12–11. Use a Layout Wizard or Page Setup to create a layout tab named Reflected Ceiling Plan to the appropriate scale for your printer or plotter.**

5. **Freeze the layers that are not needed to draw the power plan.**

6. **Insert-Block... on the correct layers of the electrical and telephone legends (ELECTRIC, TELEPHON) drawn in Exercise 12–1, Part 2. Check the Explode box in the Insert dialog box.**

7. **Complete the Office II power plan as shown in Figure 12–12. Use a Layout Wizard or Page Setup to create a Layout tab named Power Plan to the appropriate scale for your printer or plotter.**

8. **When you have completed Exercise 12–3, save your work in at least two places.**

9. **Plot or print the drawing to scale.**

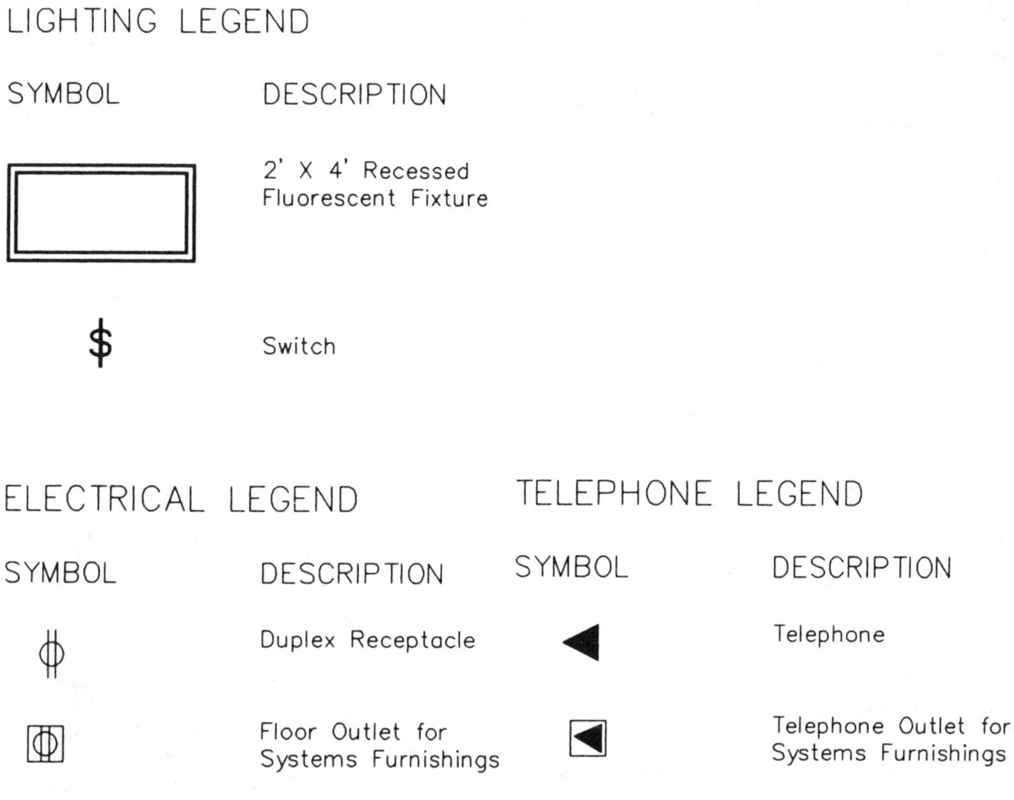

## LIGHTING LEGEND

SYMBOL          DESCRIPTION

2' X 4' Recessed
Fluorescent Fixture

$          Switch

## ELECTRICAL LEGEND          ## TELEPHONE LEGEND

SYMBOL      DESCRIPTION          SYMBOL      DESCRIPTION

Duplex Receptacle          Telephone

Floor Outlet for          Telephone Outlet for
Systems Furnishings          Systems Furnishings

**FIGURE 12–10**
Office II Lighting, Electrical, and Telephone Legends
(Scale: 1/4" = 1'-0")

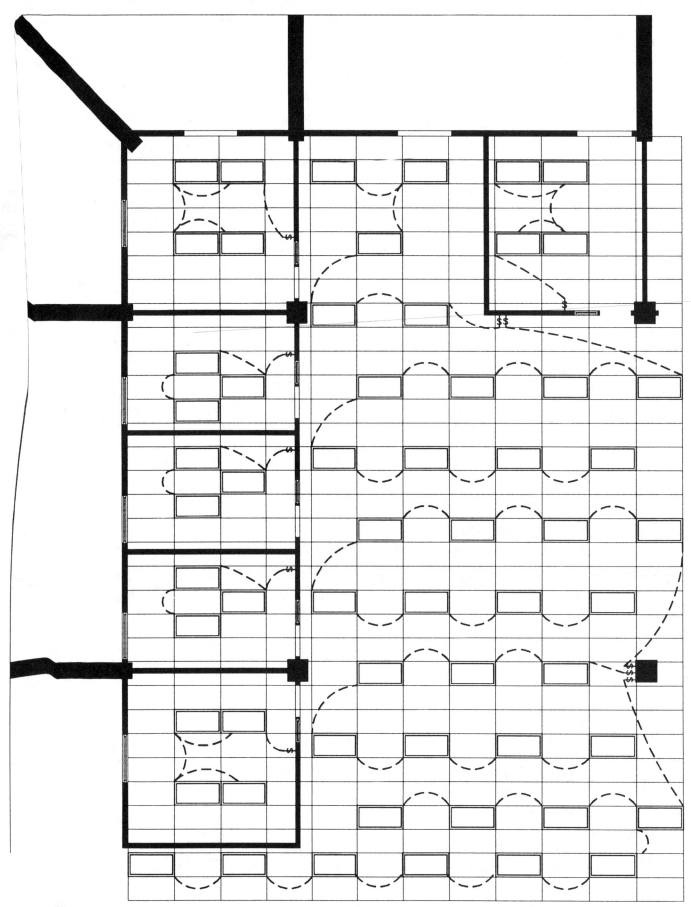

**FIGURE 12–11**

Exercise 12–3: Office II Reflected Ceiling Plan (Scale: 1/8″ = 1′-0″)
(Courtesy of Business Interiors Design Department, Irving, Texas, and GTE Directories.)

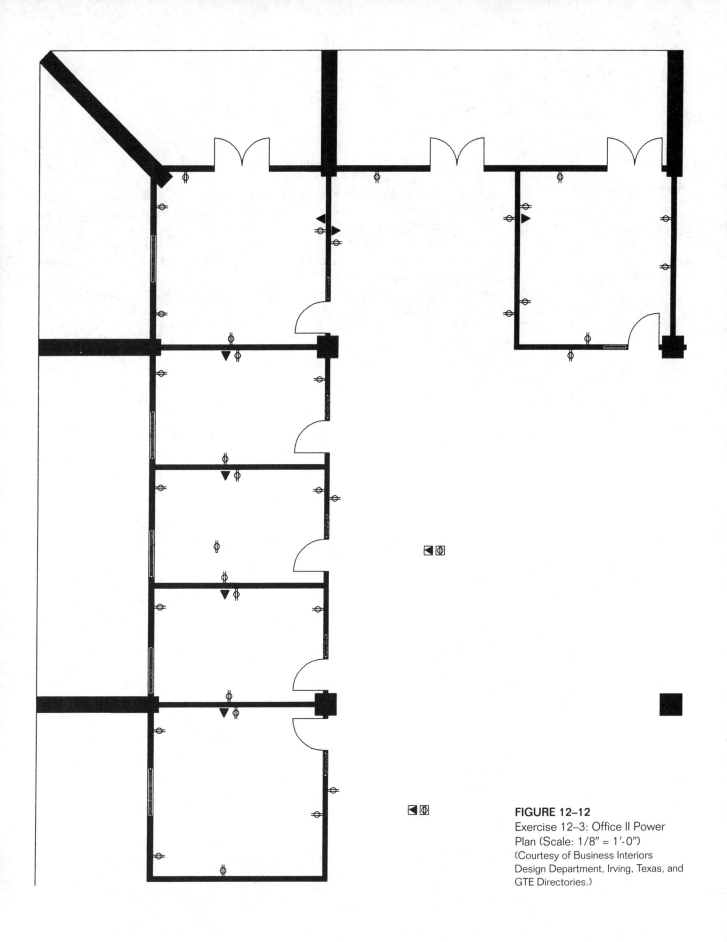

**FIGURE 12–12**
Exercise 12–3: Office II Power
Plan (Scale: 1/8″ = 1′-0″)
(Courtesy of Business Interiors
Design Department, Irving, Texas, and
GTE Directories.)

# EXERCISE 12–4
## House Lighting and Outlet Plan

In Exercise 12–4, a lighting and outlet plan is drawn for the house.

### On Your Own

1. Begin drawing CH12-EX4 on the hard drive by opening existing drawing CH11-EX5 and saving it as CH12-EX4 on the hard drive.

2. Freeze the layers that are not needed to draw the lighting and outlet plan.

3. Insert-Block... on the correct layers of the lighting, electrical, and telephone legends (LIGHTING, ELECTRIC, TELEPHON) drawn in Exercise 12–1, Parts 1 and 2, into drawing CH12-EX4. Check the Explode box in the Insert dialog box so that each symbol is inserted as a separate entity. Modify the inserted legends as shown in Figure 12–13.

4. Complete the lighting and outlet plan for the house as shown in Figure 12–14. Use a Layout Wizard or Page Setup to create a Layout tab named Lighting and Outlet Plan to the appropriate scale for your printer or plotter.

5. When you have completed Exercise 12–4, save your work in at least two places.

6. Plot or print the drawing to scale.

## LIGHTING LEGEND

| SYMBOL | DESCRIPTION |
|---|---|
| | Surface Mounted Incandescent Track Lighting |
| | Chandelier |
| R | Recessed Incandescent Fixture |
| S | Surface Mounted Incandescent Fixture |
| R wp | Recessed Fixture Weatherproof |
| | Wall Fixture |
| wp | Wall Fixture Weatherproof |
| P | Pendant Fixture |
| [ - - - - - - - ] | Fluorescent Fixture |
| $ | Switch |
| $₃ | 3–Way Switch |

## ELECTRICAL LEGEND

| SYMBOL | DESCRIPTION |
|---|---|
| | Duplex Receptacle |
| WP | Duplex Receptacle Weatherproof |
| | Heavy Duty Duplex Receptacle |
| | Floor Duplex Receptacle |

## TELEPHONE LEGEND

| SYMBOL | DESCRIPTION |
|---|---|
| ◀ | Telephone |

**FIGURE 12–13**
House Lighting, Electrical, and Telephone Legends
(Scale: 1/4″ = 1′-0″)

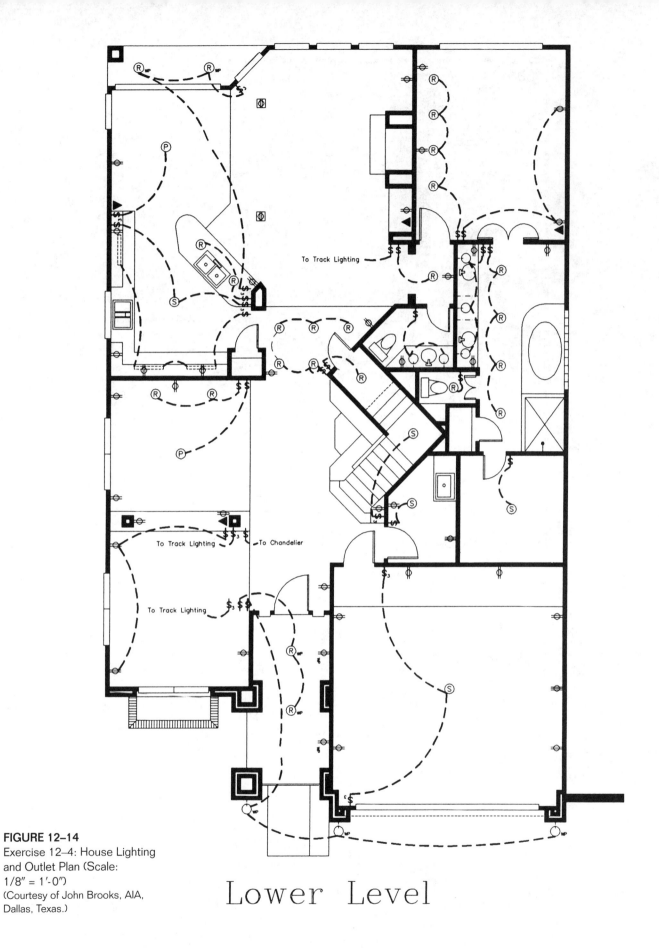

**FIGURE 12–14**

Exercise 12–4: House Lighting
and Outlet Plan (Scale:
1/8″ = 1′-0″)
(Courtesy of John Brooks, AIA,
Dallas, Texas.)

To Track Lighting

To Track Lighting — To Chandelier

To Track Lighting

Lower Level

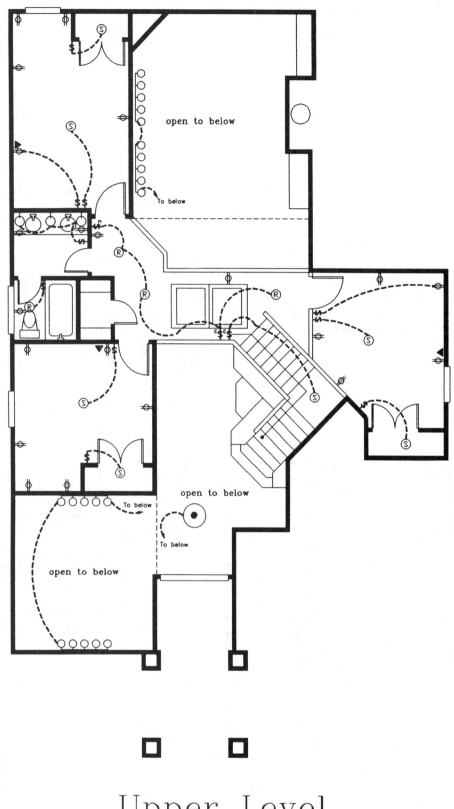

# Upper Level

FIGURE 12–14 continued

# EXERCISE 12–5
## Country Club Reflected Ceiling Plan and Power Plan

In Exercise 12–5, a reflected ceiling plan and power plan are drawn for the country club.

### On Your Own

1. **Begin drawing CH12-EX5 on the hard drive by opening existing drawing CH11-EX6 and saving it as CH12-EX5 on the hard drive.**
2. **Freeze the layers that are not needed to draw the ceiling plan.**
3. **Insert-Block... on the correct layer of the lighting legend (LIGHTING) drawn in Exercise 12–1, Part 1, into drawing CH12-EX5. Check the Explode box in the Insert dialog box so that each symbol is inserted as a separate entity. Modify the inserted legend for the country club as shown in Figure 12–15.**
4. **Complete the country club reflected ceiling plan as shown in Figure 12–16. Use a Layout Wizard or Page Setup to create a Layout tab named Reflected Ceiling Plan to the appropriate scale for your printer or plotter.**
5. **Freeze the layers that are not needed to draw the power plan.**
6. **Insert-Block... on the correct layers of the electrical and telephone legends (ELECTRIC, TELEPHON) drawn in Exercise 12–1, Part 2. Check the Explode box in the Insert dialog box. Modify the inserted legends for the country club as shown in Figure 12–15.**
7. **Complete the country club power plan as shown in Figure 12–17. Use a Layout**

## LIGHTING LEGEND

| SYMBOL | DESCRIPTION |
|---|---|
| ▢ | 2' X 2' Recessed |
| Ⓡ | Recessed Ceiling Fixture |
| Ⓢ | Surface Mounted Ceiling Fixture |
| ⊥◯ | Wall Fixture |
| Ⓟ | Pendant Fixture |
| ↓⊗↑ | Exit Sign Location |
| $ | Switch |
| $₃ | 3–Way Switch |
| $_D | Switch with Dimmer |
| $₃₋D | 3–Way Switch with Dimmer |

## ELECTRICAL LEGEND

| SYMBOL | DESCRIPTION |
|---|---|
| ⌽ | Duplex Receptacle |
| ⌽ | Heavy Duty Duplex Receptacle |
| ⊡ | Floor Duplex Receptacle |

## TELEPHONE LEGEND

| SYMBOL | DESCRIPTION |
|---|---|
| ◀ | Telephone |
| ◀ | Floor Telephone |

**FIGURE 12–15**
Country Club Lighting, Electrical, and Telephone Legends (Scale: 1/4" = 1'-0")

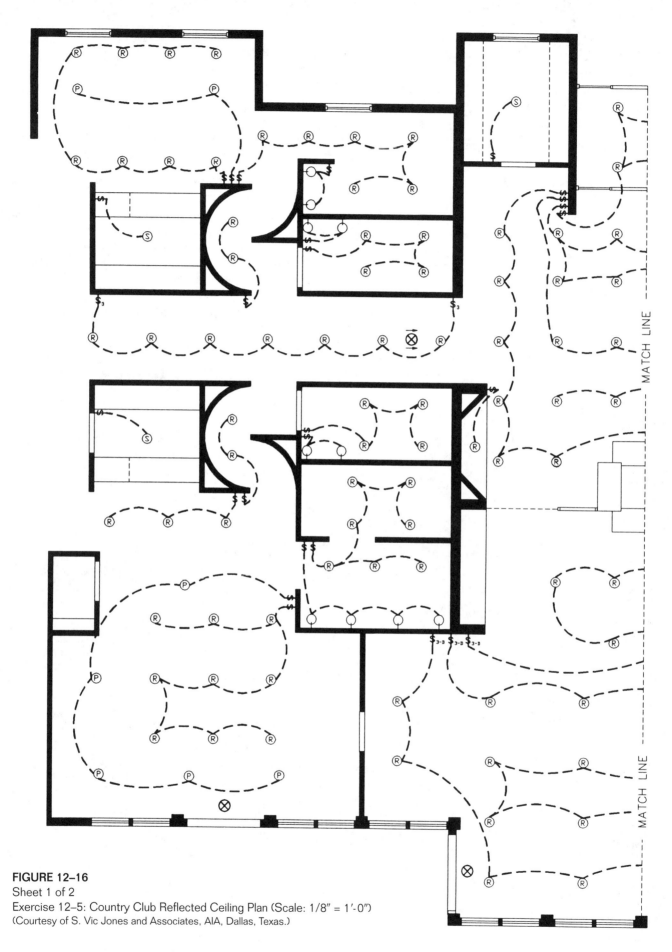

MATCH LINE

MATCH LINE

**FIGURE 12–16**
Sheet 1 of 2
Exercise 12–5: Country Club Reflected Ceiling Plan (Scale: 1/8″ = 1′-0″)
(Courtesy of S. Vic Jones and Associates, AIA, Dallas, Texas.)

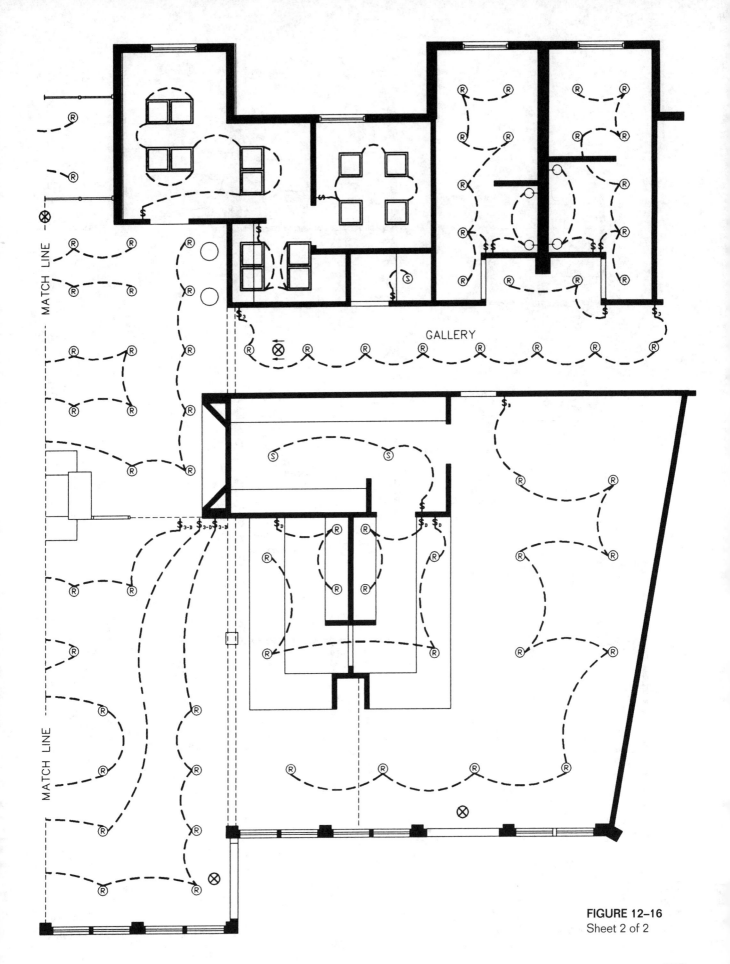

GALLERY

FIGURE 12–16
Sheet 2 of 2

353

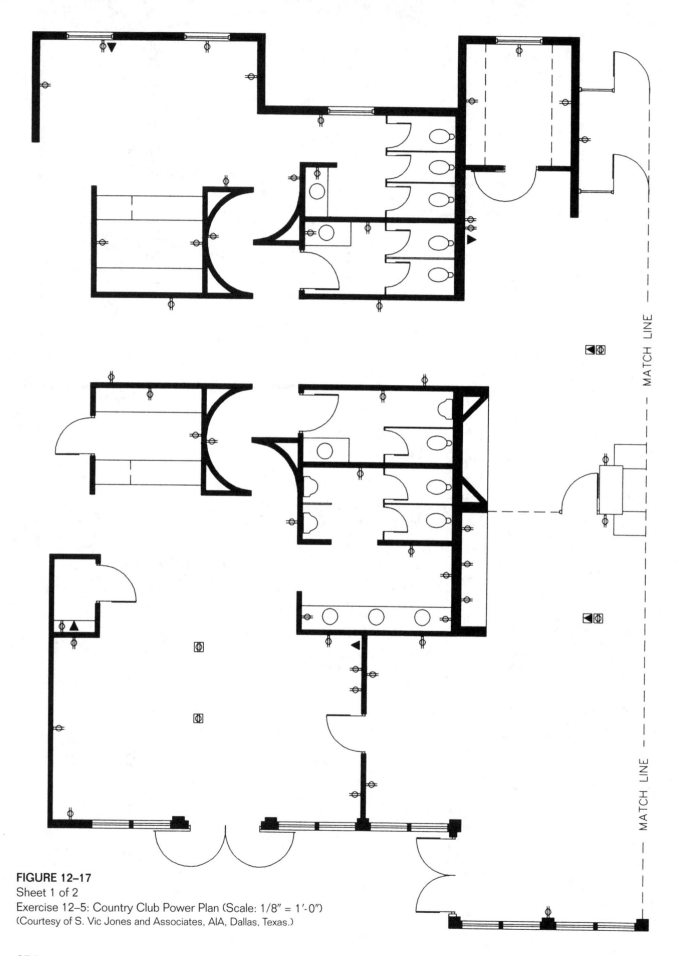

**FIGURE 12–17**
Sheet 1 of 2
Exercise 12–5: Country Club Power Plan (Scale: 1/8″ = 1′-0″)
(Courtesy of S. Vic Jones and Associates, AIA, Dallas, Texas.)

MATCH LINE

MATCH LINE

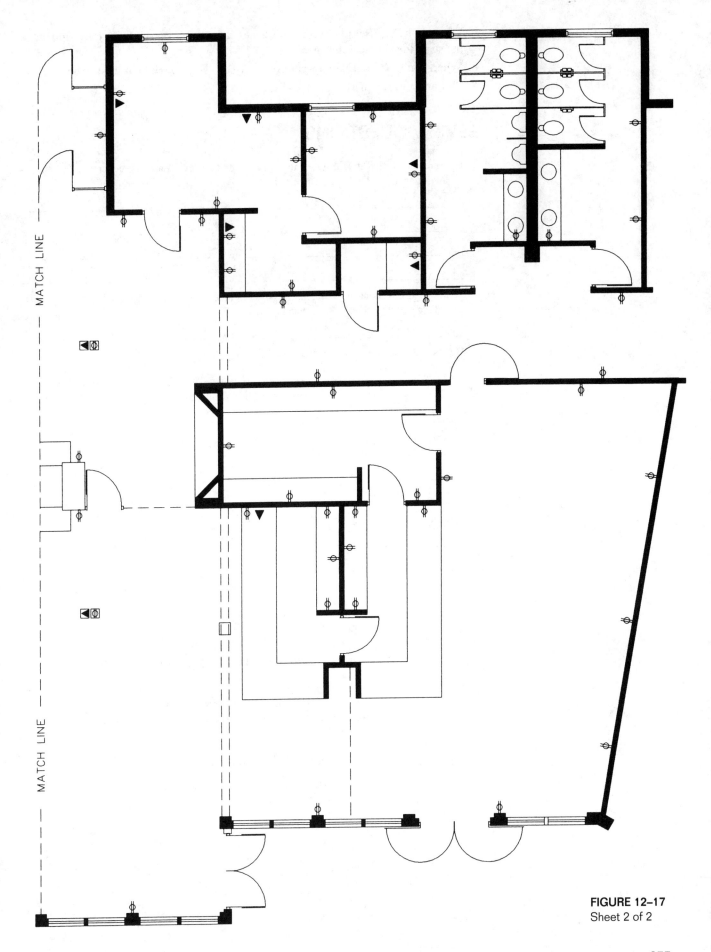

**FIGURE 12–17**
Sheet 2 of 2

Wizard or Page Setup to create a Layout tab named **Power Plan** to the appropriate scale for your printer or plotter.

8. **When you have completed Exercise 12–5, save your work in at least two places.**

9. **Plot or print the drawings to scale.**

## REVIEW QUESTIONS

1. List three methods that you can use to have the lighting symbols and related circuitry have heavier lineweights than the floor plan when plotted.

_____

_____

_____

_____

2. Write the drawing name you used when you Wblocked the lighting legend to a floppy disk. Include the floppy drive destination in the name.

_____

3. How do you use an existing drawing to create a new drawing?

_____

4. List the steps needed to set a running Osnap-Intersection mode.

_____

5. Describe what checking the Explode box in the Insert dialog box does when a drawing is inserted into another drawing, using the Insert-Block... command.

_____

_____

6. Why do you freeze layers instead of turning them off?

_____

_____

7. List the numbers of rows and columns and the spacing used to create an array of the ceiling grid.

Rows _____     Columns _____

Row spacing _____     Column spacing _____

8. List the setting that controls the sizes of linetypes as they appear on the screen.

_____

9. If a Wblock is created on a layer that has the color property green, what color does it assume when it is inserted on a layer with the color property red?

_____

10. How do you insert a block so that all its lines are separate objects?

_____

# III

# SPECIAL TOPICS

# 13 Isometric Drawing

## OBJECTIVES

When you have completed this chapter, you will be able to:

☐ Make isometric drawings to scale from two-dimensional drawings.
☐ Correctly use the following commands and settings:

    ELLIPSE-Isocircle      SNAP-Style Iso

☐ Use the Ctrl-E or F5 keys to change from one isoplane to another.

## INTRODUCTION

Isometric drawing is commonly used to show how objects appear in three dimensions. This drawing method is a two-dimensional one (you are drawing on a flat sheet of paper) that is used to give the appearance of three dimensions. It is not a 3D modeling form such as those that are covered in later chapters. In 3D modeling you actually create three-dimensional objects that can be viewed from any angle and can be placed into a perspective mode.

    You can make isometric drawings quickly and easily using AutoCAD software. Once the proper Grid and Snap settings are made, the drawing itself proceeds with little difficulty. The three isometric axes are 30° right, 30° left, and vertical.

## EXERCISE 13–1
## Fundamentals of Isometric Drawing

Seven isometric shapes are drawn in this exercise to acquaint you with the fundamentals of making isometric drawings using AutoCAD. We will begin with a simple isometric box (Figure 13–1, shape 1) so that you can become familiar with drawing lines on an isometric axis. All seven of these shapes are drawn on the same sheet and plotted on one 8 1/2″ × 11″ sheet. When you have completed Exercise 13–1, your drawing will look similar to Figure 13–1. To begin Exercise 13–1, turn on the computer and start AutoCAD. The AutoCAD 2002 Today window is displayed.

1. CLICK: **the Create Drawings tab**
2. CLICK: **Wizards**
   CLICK: **Quick Setup**
3. Set drawing Units: **Architectural**
   CLICK: **Next>**
4. Set drawing Width: **11′** × Length: **8′6″**
   CLICK: **Finish**

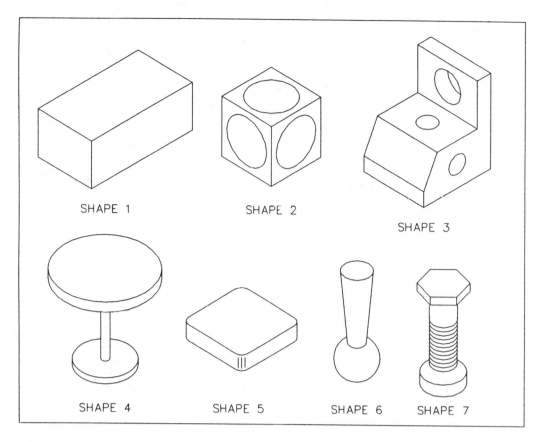

**FIGURE 13–1**
Exercise 13–1: Fundamentals of Isometric Drawing (Scale: 1/2″ = 1′-0″)

5. **Use SaveAs... to save the drawing on the hard drive with the name CH13-EX1.**

6. Set Snap as follows.

**Set Snap for an isometric grid:**

| Prompt | Response |
|---|---|
| Command: | TYPE: **SN<enter>** |
| Specify snap spacing or [ON/OFF/Aspect/ Rotate/Style/Type] <0′-0 ½″>: | TYPE: **S<enter>** |
| Enter snap style [Standard/Isometric]<S>: | TYPE: **I<enter>** |
| Specify vertical spacing <0′-6″>: | TYPE: **1<enter>** (if 1″ is not the default) |

When you want to exit the isometric grid, TYPE: **SN<enter>** and then TYPE: **S<enter>**, then TYPE: **S<enter>** again to select the standard grid. Keep the isometric grid for this exercise.

7. Set Grid: **3″**

8. **Create the following Layers:**

| LAYER NAME | COLOR | LINETYPE | LINEWEIGHT |
|---|---|---|---|
| A-furn-iso-r | Red | Continuous | Default |
| A-furn-iso-g | Green | Continuous | Default |

9. **Set Layer A-furn-iso-g current.**

10. **Zoom-All.**

FIGURE 13–2
Drafting Settings Dialog Box

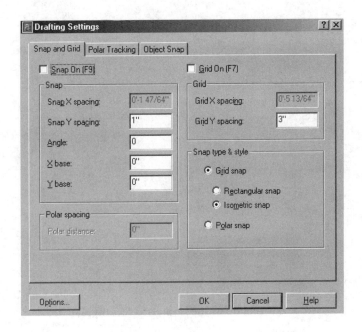

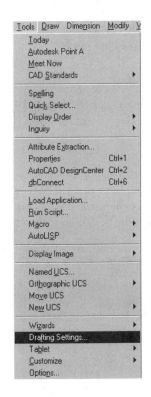

## Drafting Settings Dialog Box

You may also use the Drafting Settings dialog box from the Tools menu on the pull-down menu bar (Figure 13–2) to make the settings. Click the Snap and Grid tab.

When the isometric snap (and the grid) is set, and the Snap and Grid tab of the Drafting Settings dialog box is entered, the 1″ Snap and 3″ Grid settings will appear as shown in Figure 13–2.

### Shape 1: Drawing the Isometric Rectangle

Drawing shape 1 (Figure 13–3) helps you become familiar with drawing lines using isometric polar coordinates.

**Draw the right face of an isometric rectangular box measuring 12″ × 16″ × 30″ using isometric polar coordinates:**

| Prompt | Response |
|---|---|
| Command: | **Line** (or TYPE: **L<enter>**) |
| Specify first point: | **D1** (Figure 13–3) (absolute coordinates 1′7-1/16, 4′11″) |
| Specify next point or [Undo]: | TYPE: **@30<30<enter>** |
| Specify next point or [Undo]: | TYPE: **@12<90<enter>** |
| Specify next point or [Close/Undo]: | TYPE: **@30<210<enter>** |
| Specify next point or [Close/Undo]: | TYPE: **C<enter>** |

**Draw the left face of the isometric rectangular box:**

| Prompt | Response |
|---|---|
| Command: | **<enter>** (Repeat LINE) |
| Specify first point: | **D1 (Osnap-Endpoint)** |
| Specify next point or [Undo]: | TYPE: **@16<150<enter>** |
| Specify next point or [Undo]: | TYPE: **@12<90<enter>** |
| Specify next point or [Close/Undo]: | TYPE: **@16<330<enter>** |
| Specify next point or [Close/Undo]: | **<enter>** |

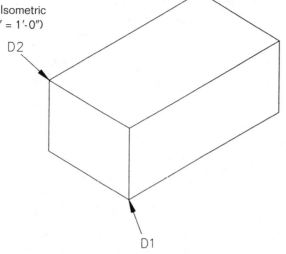

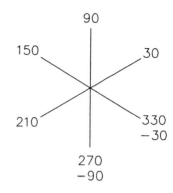

POLAR COORDINATES
FOR ISOMETRIC DRAWING

**Draw the top of the isometric rectangular box:**

| Prompt | Response |
|---|---|
| Command: | **<enter>** (Repeat LINE) |
| Specify first point: | **D2** |
| Specify next point or [Undo]: | TYPE: **@30<30<enter>** |
| Specify next point or [Undo]: | TYPE: **@16<-30<enter>** |
| Specify next point or [Close/Undo]: | **<enter>** |

When using polar coordinates to draw lines in isometric, you can ignore Isoplanes. Isoplanes are isometric faces—Top, Right, and Left. Pressing two keys, Ctrl and E, at the same time toggles your drawing to the correct Isoplane—Top, Right, or Left. The function key F5 can also be used to toggle to the correct Isoplane.

## Shape 2: Drawing Isometric Ellipses

Shape 2 (Figure 13–4) has a circle in each of the isometric planes of a cube. When drawn in isometric, circles appear as ellipses. You must use the isoplanes when drawing isometric circles using the Ellipse command. The following part of the exercise starts by drawing a 15″ isometric cube.

**Draw the right face of a 15″ isometric cube using direct distance entry:**

**FIGURE 13–4**

Shape 2: Drawing Isometric
Ellipses (Scale: 3/4″ = 1′-0″)

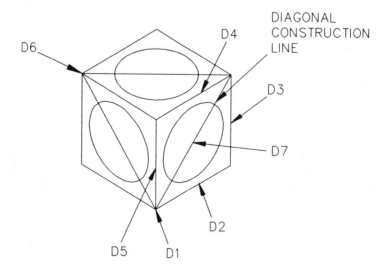

| Prompt | Response |
|---|---|
| Command: | **Toggle to the right isoplane and CLICK: Line** (or TYPE: **L<enter>**) |
| Specify first point: | **D1** (absolute coordinates 5'5-13/16,5') |
| Specify next point or [Undo]: | **With ORTHO ON, move your mouse upward 30° to the right and** TYPE: **15<enter>** |
| Specify next point or [Undo]: | **Move the mouse straight up and** TYPE: **15<enter>** |
| Specify next point or [Close/Undo]: | **Move the mouse downward 30° to the left and** TYPE: **15<enter>** |
| Specify next point or [Close/Undo]: | TYPE: **C<enter>** |

**Use the Mirror command to draw the left face of the isometric cube:**

| Prompt | Response |
|---|---|
| Command: | **Mirror** (or TYPE: **MI<enter>**) |
| Select objects: | **D2,D3,D4<enter>** |
| Specify first point of mirror line: | **D1** (be sure Ortho is on) (**Osnap-Endpoint**) |
| Specify second point of mirror line: | **D5** (PRESS: **F5** to be sure you are in either the right or left isoplane.) |
| Delete source objects? [Yes/No]<N>: | **<enter>** |

**Complete the top face of the isometric cube:**

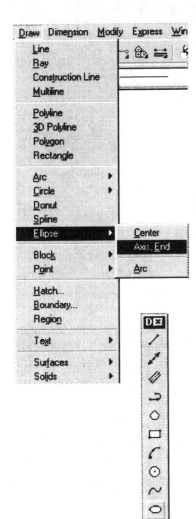

| Prompt | Response |
|---|---|
| Command: | **Toggle to the top isoplane and CLICK: Line** (or TYPE: **L<enter>**) |
| Specify first point: | **D6** (Osnap-Endpoint) |
| Specify next point or [Undo]: | **Move the mouse upward 30° to the right and** TYPE: **15<enter>** |
| Specify next point or [Undo]: | **Move the mouse downward 30° to the right and** TYPE: **15<enter>** |
| Specify next point or [Close/Undo]: | **<enter>** |

## On Your Own

1. Draw construction lines, as shown in Figure 13–4, across diagonally opposite corners in each of the visible surfaces. Be sure a running Osnap of Endpoint is ON. The construction lines will be used to locate accurately the centers of the ellipses.

**Draw an isometric ellipse (6″ radius) that represents a circle in the RIGHT ISO-PLANE:**

| Prompt | Response |
|---|---|
| Command: | **Ellipse** (or TYPE: **EL<enter>**) |
| Specify axis endpoint of ellipse or [Arc/Center/Isocircle]: | TYPE: **I<enter>** |
| Specify center of isocircle: | **Osnap-Midpoint** |
| mid of | **D7** |
| Specify radius of isocircle or [Diameter]: | PRESS: **the F5 function key until the command line reads <Isoplane Right>, then** TYPE: **6<enter>** |

When you type and enter **D** in response to the prompt "Specify radius of Isocircle or Diameter:", you can enter the diameter of the circle. The default is radius.

**Note:** If you do not have the isometric snap style active, the Ellipse command will not prompt you with ISO as one of the options for the command.

**Note:** Select Ellipse-Axis, End if you select from the menu bar. Ellipse-Center or Ellipse-Arc does not allow you to draw an isometric ellipse.

## On Your Own

1. **Follow a similar procedure to draw ellipses in the left and top isoplanes. Be sure to specify Isocircle after you have selected the Ellipse command, and be sure you are in the correct isoplane before you draw the ellipse. Use F5 to toggle to the correct isoplane.**

2. **Erase the construction lines.**

When you have completed this part of the exercise, you have the essentials of isometric drawing. Now you are going to apply these essentials to a more complex shape.

## Shape 3: Drawing Angles in Isometric and Drawing Ellipses to Show the Thickness of a Material

Shape 3 (Figure 13–5) has an angle and also a hole that shows the thickness of the material that makes up the shape. This part of the isometric exercise describes how to draw an angle and how to draw two ellipses to show the thickness of the material. Begin by drawing the front face of the shape.

**Begin to draw the front face of shape 3:**

| Prompt | Response |
| --- | --- |
| Command: | **Toggle to the right isoplane and** CLICK: **Line** (or TYPE: **L<enter>**) (Be sure ORTHO is ON.) |
| Specify first point: | **D1** (Figure 13–5) (Pick a point in the approximate location (8′9-13/16, 4′7) shown in Figure 13–1.) |
| Specify next point or [Undo]: | **Move your mouse upward 30° to the right and** TYPE: **1′8<enter>** |
| Specify next point or [Undo]: | **Move your mouse straight up and** TYPE: **2′<enter>** |
| Specify next point or [Close/Undo]: | **Move your mouse downward 30° to the left and** TYPE: **4<enter>** |
| Specify next point or [Close/Undo]: | **Move your mouse straight down and** TYPE: **1′<enter>** |
| Specify next point or [Close/Undo]: | **Move your mouse downward 30° to the left and** TYPE: **1′<enter>** |
| Specify next point or [Close/Undo]: | **<enter>** |

**Tip:** After you become familiar with isometric angles and toggling to isoplanes, use direct distance entry with Ortho on to draw lines. Just move your mouse in the isometric direction and TYPE: the number that tells AutoCAD how far you want to go. This is the fastest way to draw lines that are on isometric axes.

Because you do not know the angle for the next line, you must locate the other end of it and connect the two endpoints. This is a common practice in isometric drawing. Any time you encounter an angle in isometric, locate the two endpoints of the angle and connect those points to draw a line that is not one of the isometric axes.

**Locate the two endpoints of the angle, and draw the line that is at an angle to complete the front face of shape 3:**

| Prompt | Response |
| --- | --- |
| Command: | **Line** (or TYPE: **L<enter>**) |
| Specify first point: | **D1 (Osnap-Endpoint)** |
| Specify next point or [Undo]: | TYPE: **@4<90<enter>** |
| Specify next point or [Undo]: | **Osnap-Endpoint** |
| of | **D2** |
| Specify next point or [Close/Undo]: | **<enter>** |

**FIGURE 13–5**
Shape 3: Drawing Angles in Isometric and Drawing Ellipses to
Show the Thickness of the Material (Scale: 3/4″ = 1′-0″)

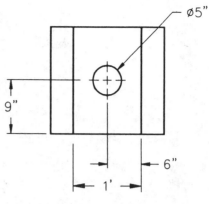

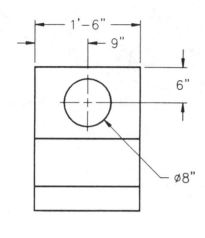

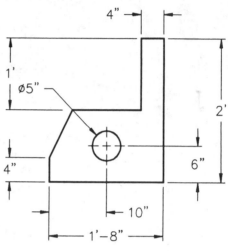

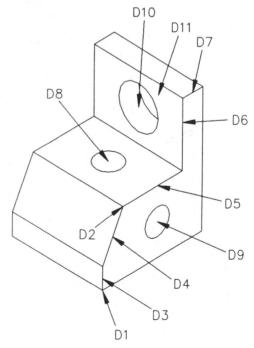

Use the Copy command to draw the identical back plane:

| Prompt | Response |
|---|---|
| Command: | **Copy** (or TYPE: **CP\<enter\>**) |
| Select Objects: | **D3,D4,D5,D6,D7\<enter\>** |

| Prompt | Response |
| --- | --- |
| Specify base point or displacement, or [Multiple]: | **D1** |
| Specify second point of displacement or <use first point as displacement>: | TYPE: **@1'6<150<enter>** |

## On Your Own

1. **Draw lines connecting the front and back surfaces.**

**Draw an isometric ellipse (5″ diameter) that represents a circle in the top isoplane:**

| Prompt | Response |
| --- | --- |
| Command: | **Ellipse** (or TYPE: **EL<enter>**) **(Toggle to the top isoplane using F5.)** |
| Specify axis endpoint of ellipse or [Arc/Center/Isocircle]: | TYPE: **I<enter>** |
| Specify center of isocircle: | **D8** (Count the 3″ grid marks (1″ snap) to locate the center of the plane, or draw construction lines from the midpoints of two parallel sides.) |
| Specify radius of isocircle or [Diameter]: | TYPE: **D<enter>** |
| Specify diameter of isocircle: | TYPE: **5<enter>** |

## On Your Own

1. **Toggle to the right isoplane, and draw a 5″-diameter ellipse in the right isometric plane using D9 as its center.**
2. **Two ellipses are required in the left isoplane, on the part of the shape that sits on top. One is needed on the front surface and part of one is needed on the back surface to describe the thickness of the material. To do this:**

   ☐ **Toggle to the left isoplane, and draw an 8″-diameter ellipse in the left isometric plane using D10 as its center.**
   ☐ **Copy the 8″-diameter ellipse 4″ upward 30° to the right (@4<30<enter>).**
   ☐ **Use the Trim command to trim the back part of the second ellipse.**

## Shape 4: Drawing a Shape That Has a Series of Ellipses Located on the Same Centerline

Shape 4 (Figure 13–6), similar to a round table, will help you become familiar with drawing a shape that has a series of ellipses located on the same center line. Five ellipses must be drawn. The centers of two of them, the extreme top and bottom ellipses, can be located by using endpoints of the centerline. Centers for the other three can be located by using construction lines or the ID command. Construction lines are used for this exercise so that you can see where the centers are.

The following part of the exercise begins by drawing a centerline through the entire height of the object.

**Begin to draw a shape containing several ellipses of different sizes located on the same centerline by drawing the centerline:**

| Prompt | Response |
| --- | --- |
| Command: | **Line** (or TYPE: **L<enter>**) |
| Specify first point: | **D1** (1'11-7/16, 1'4-1/2) |
| Specify next point or [Undo]: | TYPE: **@24<90<enter>** |
| Specify next point or [Undo]: | **<enter>** |

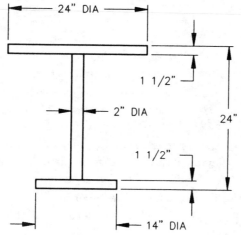

FIGURE 13–6
Shape 4: Drawing a Shape
That Has a Series of Ellipses
Located on the Same Center-
line (Scale: 3/4″ = 1′-0″)

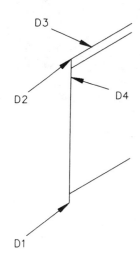

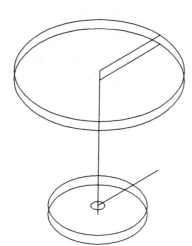

**Draw construction lines used to locate the centers of three ellipses:**

| Prompt | Response |
|---|---|
| Command: | **<enter>** (to repeat line) |
| Specify first point: | **<enter>** (starts from the endpoint of the last point entered) |
| Specify next point or [Undo]: | TYPE: **@12<30<enter>** |
| Specify next point or [Undo]: | **<enter>** |
| Command: | **Copy** (or TYPE: **CP<enter>**) |
| Select objects: | **D3** |
| Select objects: | **<enter>** |
| Specify base point or displacement, or [Multiple]: | TYPE: **M<enter>** |
| Specify base point: | **Osnap-Endpoint** |
| of | **D4** |
| Specify second point of displacement or <use first point as displacement>: | TYPE: **@1-1/2<270<enter>** |
| Specify second point of displacement or <use first point as displacement>: | TYPE: **@22-1/2<270<enter>** |
| Specify second point of displacement or <use first point as displacement>: | **<enter>** |

## On Your Own

Draw the five ellipses:

1. **Toggle to the top isoplane and use Endpoint to locate the center of the uppermost isometric ellipse on the endpoint of the vertical line. Draw it with a diameter of 24″.**

2. **Draw a second 24″-diameter isometric ellipse using as its center the Intersection of the construction line that is located 1-1/2″ from the top end of the vertical line, or copy the 24″ ellipse 1-1/2″ down.**

3. **Draw two isometric ellipses with their centers located at the Intersection of the construction line located 1-1/2″ from the bottom of the vertical line. One ellipse is 2″ in diameter; the other is 14″ in diameter.**

4. **Draw the 14″-diameter ellipse again using the bottom Endpoint of the vertical line as its center, or copy the 14″ ellipse 1-1/2″ down.**

## On Your Own

See Figure 13–7.

See Figure 13–7.

1. **To draw the 2″ column, toggle to the right or left isoplane (the top isoplane does not allow you to draw vertical lines using a pointing device if Ortho is ON). Turn Ortho (F8) ON. Draw a vertical line from the Quadrant of one side of the 2″-diameter ellipse to just above the first 24″-diameter ellipse. Draw a similar line to form the other side of the column.**

2. **With Ortho (F8) ON and toggled to the right or left isoplane, draw vertical lines from the quadrants of the ellipse segments to connect ellipses as shown in Figure 13–7.**

3. **Use Trim and Erase to remove unneeded lines. The drawing is complete as shown in the lower right corner of Figure 16–6.**

**Note:** Although Osnap-Nearest can be used to end an isometric line on another line, the position is not exact. A more exact method is to draw the line beyond where it should end and trim it to the correct length.

**FIGURE 13–7**
Shape 4: Drawing Tangents to the Ellipses (Scale: 3/4″ = 1′-0″)

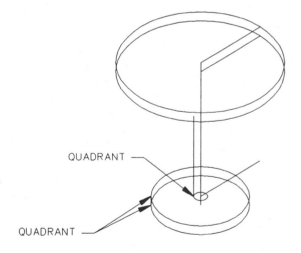

QUADRANT

QUADRANT

## Shape 5: Isometric Detail with Rounded Corners

The fifth drawing (Figure 13–8) in this exercise is a shape that has rounded corners. Rounded corners are common in many items. In two-dimensional drawing, the Fillet command allows you to obtain the rounded corners quickly and easily. This is not so in isometric. Drawing shape 5 will help you become familiar with how rounded corners must be constructed with isometric ellipses.

**Turn Ortho and Snap ON, and toggle to the top isoplane. Draw an 18″ × 18″ square shape in the top isoplane:**

| Prompt | Response |
|--------|----------|
| Command: | **Line** (or TYPE: **L<enter>**) |

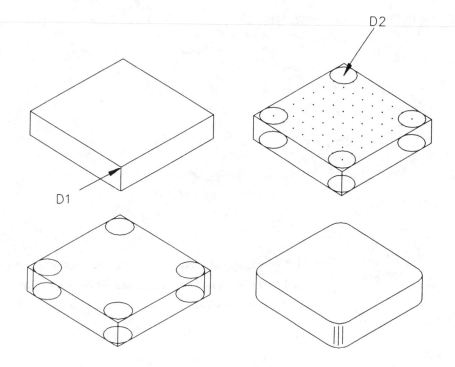

| Prompt | Response |
|---|---|
| Specify first point: | **D1** (on a grid mark) (4′10-7/8, 1′10) |
| Specify next point or [Undo]: | TYPE: **@18<30<enter>** |
| Specify next point or [Undo]: | TYPE: **@18<150<enter>** |
| Specify next point or [Close/Undo]: | TYPE: **@18<210<enter>** |
| Specify next point or [Close/Undo]: | TYPE: **C<enter>** |

## On Your Own

1. Copy the front two edges of the square to form the bottom of the shape. Copy using @4<270 (4″ is the depth) as the polar coordinates for the second point of displacement.

2. Draw lines connecting the top and bottom edges. (These lines are for reference only. You may skip this step if you choose.)

**Draw a 2″ radius ellipse in the top isoplane:**

| Prompt | Response |
|---|---|
| Command: | **Ellipse** (or TYPE: **EL<enter>**) (Toggle to the top isoplane.) |
| Specify axis endpoint of ellipse or [Arc/Center/Isocircle]: | TYPE: **I<enter>** |
| Specify center of isocircle: | **D2** (Count 2″ from the corner to locate the center of the ellipse.) |
| Specify radius of isocircle or [Diameter]: | TYPE: **2<enter>** |

## On Your Own

Complete shape 5:

1. Copy the ellipse just drawn to the other four top corners, locating them in a similar manner.

2. Copy the front three ellipses 4″ in the 270 direction to form corners in the bottom plane.

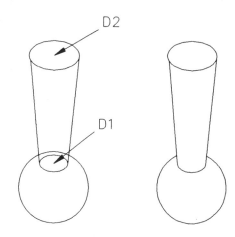

FIGURE 13–9
Shape 6: Isometric Detail—A
Rounded Shape Intersecting a
Sphere (Scale: 3/4″ = 1′-0″)

3. **Draw lines connecting the two outside ellipses using Osnap-Quadrant.**

4. **Use the Trim and Erase commands to remove the extra lines.**

5. **Add highlights on the front corner to complete the drawing.**

## Shape 6: Isometric Detail—A Rounded Shape Intersecting a Sphere

While drawing in isometric, you may encounter a cylinder intersecting a sphere (Figure 13–9). The cylinder in Figure 13–9 is also tapered.

**Draw the sphere:**

| Prompt | Response |
|---|---|
| Command: | **Circle-Center, Radius** (or TYPE: **C<enter>**) |
| Specify center point for circle or [3P/2P/Ttr (tan tan radius)]: | **Click the center of the circle on a grid mark, in the approximate location shown in Figure 13–1.** (7′7-13/16, 1′7) |
| Specify radius of circle or [Diameter]: | TYPE: **6<enter>** |

**Draw the bottom ellipse of the tapered cylinder:**

| Prompt | Response |
|---|---|
| Command: | **Ellipse** (or TYPE: **EL<enter>**) (Toggle to the top isoplane.) |
| Specify axis endpoint of ellipse or [Arc/Center/Isocircle]: | TYPE: **I<enter>** |
| Specify center of isocircle: | **D1** (2″ down from the top quadrant of the circle) |
| Specify radius of isocircle or [Diameter]: | TYPE: **2<enter>** |

**Draw the top ellipse of the tapered cylinder:** (Before you start, **draw a construction 18″ straight up from the center of the first ellipse.**)

| Prompt | Response |
|---|---|
| Command: | **<enter>** |
| Specify axis endpoint of ellipse or [Arc/Center/Isocircle]: | TYPE: **I<enter>** |
| Specify center of isocircle: | **D2** (Click a point 18″ above the center of the first ellipse.) |
| Specify radius of isocircle or [Diameter]: | TYPE: **3.5<enter>** |

## On Your Own

1. **Complete the shape by drawing lines connecting the top and bottom ellipses using Osnap-Quadrant.**

2. **Trim the circle and the bottom ellipse to complete the shape. Erase any construction lines.** Although the true shape of the intersection between the cylindrical shape and the sphere is a compound curve, it is often simplified in isometric, as you have done here. The compound curve is difficult to construct and looks no better than the simplified version.

### Shape 7: Isometric Detail—A Polygon and a Threaded Shape

The final shape in this exercise combines several features (Figure 13–10).

**Draw the hexagonal head of a threaded spacer (Figure 13–10A):**

| Prompt | Response |
|---|---|
| Command: | **Polygon (or TYPE: POL\<enter\>)** |
| Enter number of sides \<4\>: | **TYPE: 6\<enter\>** |
| Specify center of polygon or [Edge]: | **Click a point on a grid mark, in the approximate location shown in Figure 13–1 (with SNAP ON).** |
| Enter an option [Inscribed in circle/ Circumscribed about circle] \<I\>: | **TYPE: C\<enter\>** |
| Specify radius of circle: | **TYPE: 6\<enter\>** |

Now you have a hexagon that cannot be used in isometric drawing. To use it, you must block the hexagon and then insert it with different X and Y values. **Be sure to toggle to the top isoplane when you insert the hexagonal block.**

**Block and insert the hexagon (Figure 13–10B):**

| Prompt | Response |
|---|---|
| Command: | **Block (or TYPE: B\<enter\>)** |
| The Block Definition dialog box appears: | TYPE: **HEX** in the Block name: box. |
| | **Make sure Delete is selected.** |
| | CLICK: **Pick point** |
| Specify insertion base point: | CLICK: **the center of the hexagon** |
| The Block Definition dialog box appears: | CLICK: **Select objects** |
| Select objects: | CLICK: **any point on the hexagon** |
| Select objects: | **\<enter\>** |
| The Block Definition dialog box appears: | CLICK: **OK** |

**FIGURE 13–10**
Shape 7: Isometric Detail—A Polygon and a Threaded Shape
(Scale: 3/4″ = 1′-0″)

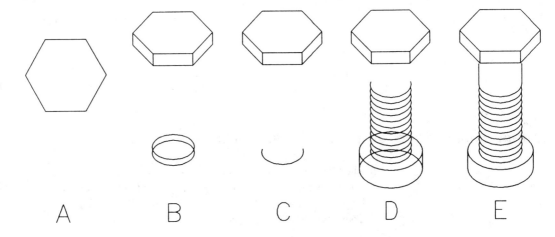

A    B    C    D    E

| Prompt | Response |
|---|---|
| The hexagon disappears: | |
| Command: | **Insert-Block...** (or TYPE: **I\<enter>**) |
| The Insert dialog box appears: | CLICK: **the down arrow in the Name: box** |
| | CLICK: **HEX** (if it is not already in the Name: box) |
| | CHANGE: **Y: in the Scale area to .58** (This is a very close approximation to the isometric scale factor.) |
| | CLICK: **OK** |
| Specify insertion point or [Scale/X/Y/Z/ Rotate/PScale/PX/PY/PZ/PRotate]: | **Pick the location of the isometric hexagon as shown in Figure 13–1 (ON SNAP)** (9'6-1/2, 3'3). |

## On Your Own

Complete drawing shape 7, and add text to your drawing as follows:

1. **Draw 2″ vertical lines from each of the visible corners of the hexagon in the 270 direction (Figure 13–10B).**

2. **Using Osnap-Endpoint, draw lines to form the bottom of the hexagon (Figure 13–10B).**

3. **At a center point 20″ below the center of the isometric hexagon, draw an isometric ellipse with a 3″ radius in the top isoplane. Copy the ellipse 1″ in the 90 direction (Figure 13–10B).**

4. **Trim the back of the bottom ellipse using the top ellipse as the cutting edge. Erase the top ellipse (Figure 13–10C).**

5. **Array the trimmed ellipse using 12 rows, 1 column, and a space between rows of +1″ (Figure 13–10D).**

6. **Draw a 10″-diameter isometric ellipse using the center of the bottom thread ellipse. Copy the ellipse 3″ in the 270 direction (Figure 13–10D).**

7. **Draw lines connecting the quadrants of the two 10″ ellipses (Figure 13–10D).**

8. **Draw lines from the top thread to just below the lower surface of the hexagon (Figure 13–10E).**

9. **Trim and Erase as needed to complete the drawing (Figure 13–10E).**

10. **Set Layer A-furn-iso-r current, and use Single Line Text, 2″H, Simplex font to identify shapes 1 through 7 as shown in Figure 13–1.**

## SAVE

When you have completed Exercise 13–1, save your work in at least two places.

## PLOT

CLICK: **Layout1** and plot or print the drawing on an 8-1/2″ × 11″ sheet of paper.

## EXERCISE 13–2
## Tenant Space Reception Desk in Isometric

The tenant space solid wood reception desk is drawn in isometric in Exercise 13–2. When you have completed Exercise 13–2, your drawing will look similar to Figure 13–11. To begin Exercise 13–2, turn on the computer and start AutoCAD. The AutoCAD 2002 Today window is displayed.

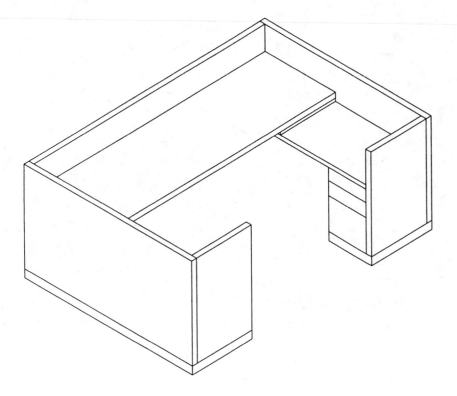

1. CLICK: **the Create Drawings tab**
2. CLICK: **Wizards**
   CLICK: **Quick Setup**
3. Set drawing Units: **Architectural**
   CLICK: **Next>**
4. Set drawing Width: **15′** × Length: **15′**
   CLICK: **Finish**
5. **Use SaveAs... to save the drawing on the hard drive with the name CH13-EX2.**
6. Set Snap: **Style-Isometric-1″**
7. Set Grid: **4″**
8. Create the following Layer:

| LAYER NAME | COLOR | LINETYPE |
|---|---|---|
| A-furn-iso-g | Green | Continuous |

9. Set Layer A-furn-iso-g current.
10. **Zoom-All**

This exercise is a series of straight lines, all of which are on the isometric axes. It is suggested that you follow the step-by-step procedure described next so that you get some ideas about what you can and cannot do when using the isometric drawing method. To draw an isometric view of the reception desk (Figure 13–11) use the dimensions shown in Figure 13–13.

**Set Snap and Ortho on. Toggle to the top isometric plane. Draw the top edge of the panels (Figure 13–12):**

| Prompt | Response |
|---|---|
| Command: | **Line** (or TYPE: **L<enter>**) |

**Tip:** This is a good opportunity to use POLAR tracking. Click Settings… from the shortcut menu. Click the Polar Tracking tab and set the Increment angle: to 15. Select Track using all polar angle settings. CLICK: OK. Now use direct distance entry on all polar angles. Be sure to toggle to the correct isometric plane when using POLAR tracking.

FIGURE 13–12
Drawing the Top Edge of the
Panels

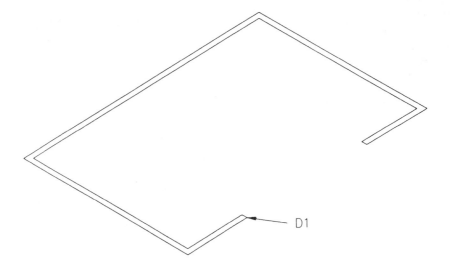

| Prompt | Response |
|---|---|
| Specify first point: | **D1** (Figure 13–12) (absolute coordinates 8'1,7'4) |
| Specify next point or [Undo]: | TYPE: **@24<210<enter>** (or **move the mouse downward 30° to the left and** TYPE: **24<enter>**) |
| Specify next point or [Undo]: | TYPE: **@66<150<enter>** |
| Specify next point or [Close/Undo]: | TYPE: **@96<30<enter>** |
| Specify next point or [Close/Undo]: | TYPE: **@66<-30<enter>** |
| Specify next point or [Close/Undo]: | TYPE: **@24<210<enter>** |
| Specify next point or [Close/Undo]: | TYPE: **@2<150<enter>** |
| Specify next point or [Close/Undo]: | TYPE: **@22<30<enter>** |
| Specify next point or [Close/Undo]: | TYPE: **@62<150<enter>** |
| Specify next point or [Close/Undo]: | TYPE: **@92<210<enter>** |
| Specify next point or [Close/Undo]: | TYPE: **@62<330<enter>** |
| Specify next point or [Close/Undo]: | TYPE: **@22<30<enter>** |
| Specify next point or [Close/Undo]: | TYPE: **C<enter>** |

**Use the Extend command to extend the inside lines of the panels to form the separate panels (Figure 13–14):**

| Prompt | Response |
|---|---|
| Command: | **Extend** (or TYPE: **EX<enter>**) |
| Select objects: | **D1** |
| Other corner: | **D2** |
| Select objects: | **<enter>** |
| Select object to extend or shift-select to trim or [Project/Edge/Undo]: | **D3,D4,D5,D6<enter>** |

**Copy the top edges of the panels to form the lower kickplate surfaces (Figure 13–15):**

| Prompt | Response |
|---|---|
| Command: | **Copy** (or TYPE: **CP<enter>**) |
| Select objects: | **D1,D2,D3,D4** |
| Select objects: | **<enter>** |
| Specify base point or displacement, or [Multiple]: | TYPE: **M<enter>** |

**Tip:** You can also use Polar Tracking and direct distance to specify distances when you copy.

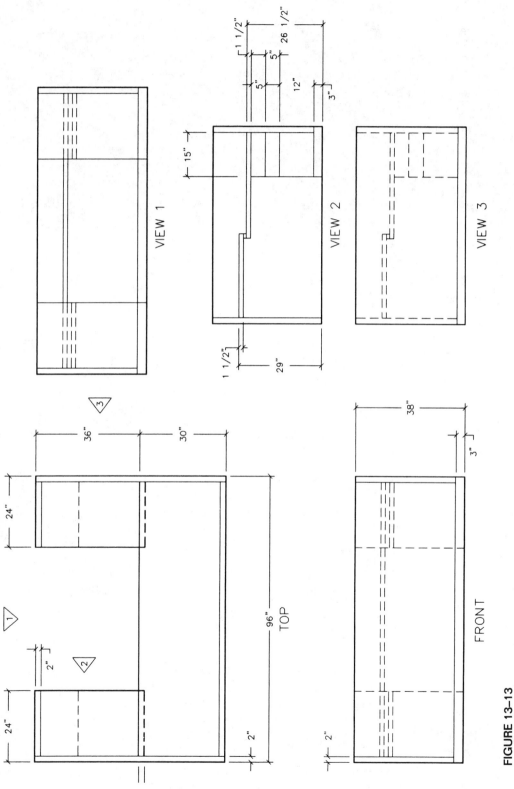

VIEW 1

VIEW 2

VIEW 3

1 1/2"

26 1/2"

5"

5"

12"

3"

15"

1 1/2"

29"

36"

30"

24"

24"

2"

96"

TOP

38"

3"

2"

FRONT

**FIGURE 13–13**
Dimensions of the Tenant Space Reception Desk (Scale: 3/8" = 1'-0")

**FIGURE 13–14**
Extending Lines to Form the
Separate Panels

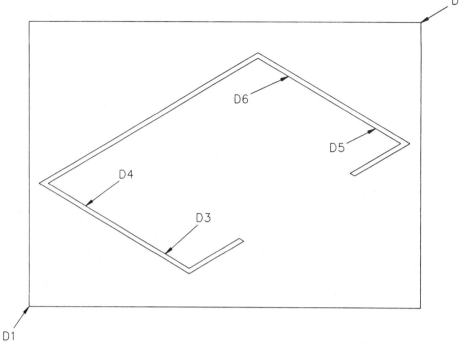

| Prompt | Response |
|---|---|
| Specify base point: | **D1** (any point is OK) |
| Specify second point of displacement or <use first point as displacement>: | TYPE: **@35<270<enter>** |
| Specify second point of displacement or <use first point as displacement>: | TYPE: **@38<270<enter>** |
| Specify second point of displacement or <use first point as displacement>: | **<enter>** |

**Repeat the Copy command to draw the edge of the main work surface against the inside of the panel (Figure 13–15):**

| Prompt | Response |
|---|---|
| Command: | **<enter>** |
| Select objects: | **D5** |
| Select objects: | **<enter>** |
| Specify base point or displacement, or [Multiple]: | **D5** (any point is OK) |
| Specify second point of displacement or <use first point as displacement>: | TYPE: **@9<270<enter>** |

## On Your Own

See Figure 13–16.

1. **Set a running Osnap mode of Endpoint and draw vertical lines connecting top and bottom outside lines and the inside corner above the work surface. Turn the running Osnap mode OFF when you have completed this part of the exercise. Next, you will draw the work surface.**

**Draw the work surfaces (Figure 13–16):**

| Prompt | Response |
|---|---|
| Command: | **Line** (or TYPE: **L<enter>**) |
| Specify first point: | **Osnap-Endpoint, D1** |

## FIGURE 13–15
Copy the Top Edges to Form the
Lower Kickplate Surfaces and the
Edge of the Main Work Surface

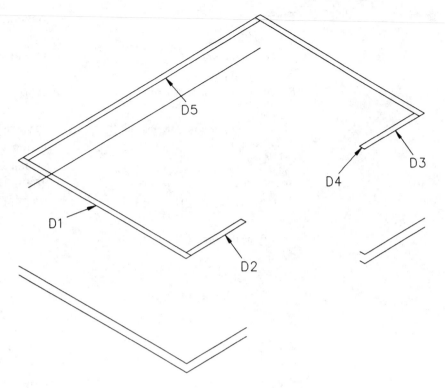

| Prompt | Response |
|---|---|
| Specify next point or [Undo]: | TYPE: **@28<330<enter>** |
| Specify next point or [Undo]: | **D2** (With Ortho ON and the top isoplane active, move your mouse downward 30° to the left and pick any point beyond the inside of the left partition; you can Trim these later.) |
| Specify next point or [Close/Undo]: | **<enter>** |

## FIGURE 13–16
Drawing the Vertical Lines Con-
necting Top and Bottom Edges;
Drawing the Work Surfaces

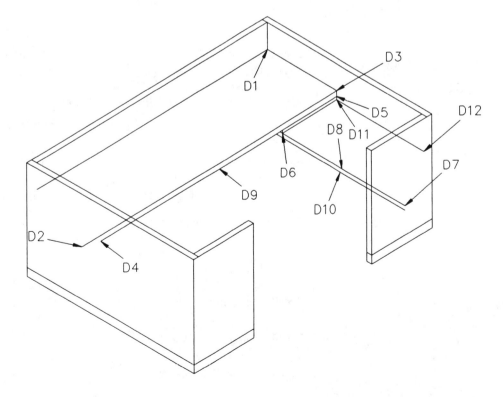

| Prompt | Response |
|---|---|
| Command: | **<enter>** (Repeat LINE) |
| Specify first point: | **Osnap-Endpoint, D3** |
| Specify next point or [Undo]: | TYPE: **@1-1/2<270<enter>** |
| Specify next point or [Undo]: | **D4** (Pick another point outside the left partition.) |
| Specify next point or [Close/Undo]: | **<enter>** |
| Command: | **<enter>** (Repeat LINE) |
| Specify first point: | **Osnap-Endpoint, D5** |
| Specify next point or [Undo]: | TYPE: **@1<270<enter>** |
| Specify next point or [Undo]: | TYPE: **@22<210<enter>** |
| Specify next point or [Close/Undo]: | TYPE: **@1<90<enter>** |
| Specify next point or [Close/Undo]: | **<enter>** |
| Command: | **<enter>** (Repeat LINE) |
| Specify first point: | **Osnap-Endpoint, D6 (Figure 13–16)** |
| Specify next point or [Undo]: | **D7** (Move the mouse downward 30° to the right and pick a point outside the right rear panel.) |
| Specify next point or [Undo]: | **<enter>** |
| Command: | **<enter>** (Repeat LINE) |
| Specify first point: | **Osnap-Endpoint, D11** |
| Specify next point or [Undo]: | **D12** (Pick a point outside the right rear panel.) **<enter>** |
| Command: | **Copy** (or TYPE: **CP<enter>**) |
| Select objects: | **D8** |
| Select objects: | **<enter>** |
| Specify base point or displacement, or [Multiple]: | **D8 (any point)** |
| Specify second point of displacement or <use first point as displacement>: | TYPE: **@1-1/2<270<enter>** |
| Command: | **Extend** (or TYPE: **EX<enter>**) |
| Select objects: | **D9<enter>** |
| Select object to extend or [Project/Edge/Undo]: | **D8, D10<enter>** |

**Trim lines that extend outside the panels (Figure 13–17):**

| Prompt | Response |
|---|---|
| Command: | **Trim** (or TYPE: **TR<enter>**) |
| Select objects: | **D1,D2,D3<enter>** |
| Select object to trim or shift-select to extend or [Project/Edge/Undo]: | **D4,D5,D6,D7,D8,D9<enter>** |

**Draw the drawer pedestal (Figure 13–17):**

| Prompt | Response |
|---|---|
| Command: | **Line** (or TYPE: **L<enter>**) |
| Specify first point: | **Osnap-Endpoint, D10** |
| Specify next point or [Undo]: | **Toggle to the left isoplane and** TYPE: **@15<150<enter>** |
| Specify next point or [Undo]: | **D11** (With Ortho ON, pick a point above the bottom edge of the desktop.) |
| Specify next point or [Close/Undo]: | **<enter>** |

FIGURE 13–17
Trimming Lines and Drawing the
Drawer Pedestal

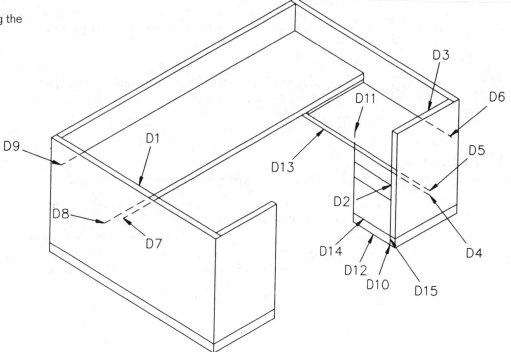

| Prompt | Response |
|---|---|
| Command: | **Copy** (or TYPE: **CP<enter>**) |
| Select objects: | **D12** (Figure 13–17) |
| Select objects: | **<enter>** |
| Specify base point or displacement, or [Multiple]: | TYPE: **M<enter>** |
| Specify base point: | **D12 (any point)** |
| Specify second point of displacement, or <use first point as displacement>: | TYPE: **@3<90<enter>** |
| Specify second point of displacement, or <use first point as displacement>: | TYPE: **@15<90<enter>** |
| Specify second point of displacement, or <use first point as displacement>: | TYPE: **@20<90<enter>** |
| Specify second point of displacement, or <use first point as displacement>: | **<enter>** |

**Trim the extra lines:**

| Prompt | Response |
|---|---|
| Command: | **Trim** (or TYPE: **TR<enter>**) |
| Select objects: | **D13,D14<enter>** |
| Select object to trim or shift-select to extend or [Project/Edge/Undo]: | **D15,D11<enter>** |

## Dimensioning in Isometric

You can resolve the problem of placing dimensions on an isometric drawing by buying a third-party software dimensioning package designed specifically for isometric. Other methods, such as using the aligned option in dimensioning and using an inclined font with the style setting, solve only part of the problem. Arrowheads must be constructed and individually inserted for each isoplane. If you spend a little time blocking the arrowheads and customizing your menu, you can speed up the process significantly.

## SAVE

When you have completed Exercise 13–2, save your work in at least two places.

## PLOT

CLICK: **Layout1**, CLICK: the viewport boundary, and use Properties from the Modify menu to set a standard scale of 1/2″=1′. Plot or print the drawing on an 8-1/2″ × 11″ sheet of paper.

# EXERCISE 13–3
# Tenant Space Reception Seating Area in Isometric

1. Make an isometric drawing, full size, of the chairs, coffee table, and corner table to show the entire reception room seating area. Use the dimensions shown in Figure 13–18.
2. CLICK: **Layout1**, CLICK: the viewport boundary, and use Properties from the Modify menu to set a standard scale of 1/2″=1′. Plot or print the drawing on an 8-1/2″ × 11″ sheet of paper.

**FIGURE 13–18**
Exercise 13–3: Tenant Space
Reception Seating Dimensions
(Scale: 3/8″ = 1′-0″)

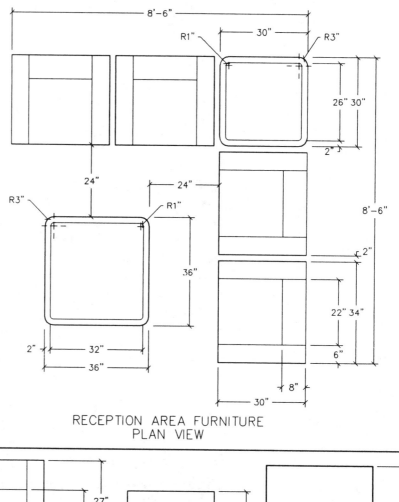

RECEPTION AREA FURNITURE
PLAN VIEW

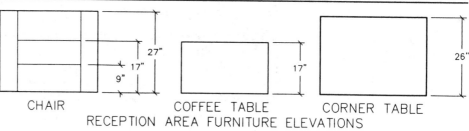

CHAIR  COFFEE TABLE  CORNER TABLE
RECEPTION AREA FURNITURE ELEVATIONS

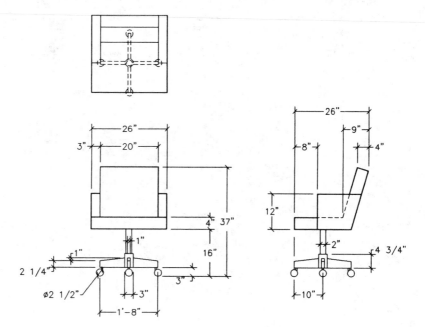

# EXERCISE 13–4
## Tenant Space Conference Chair in Isometric

1. Make an isometric drawing, full size, of the conference room chair. Use the dimensions shown in Figure 13–19.

2. CLICK: **Layout1**, CLICK: the viewport boundary, and use Properties from the Modify menu to set a standard scale of 1/2"=1'. Plot or print the drawing on an 8-1/2" × 11" sheet of paper.

# EXERCISE 13–5
## Conference Room Walls and Furniture in Isometric

1. Make an isometric drawing, full size, of the conference room shown in Figure 13–20. Draw a view from the direction shown by the arrow in Figure 13–20(A).

   The following figures provide the information needed to complete Exercise 13–5:

   □ Figure 13–19: Tenant space conference chair dimensions.
   □ Figure 13–20(A): Plan view of the conference room.
   □ Figure 13–20(B): Elevation of the north wall of the conference room.
   □ Figure 13–20(C): Elevation of the east wall of the conference room.
   □ Figure 13–20(D): Plan and elevation views of the conference table.

   Show the chairs 6″ under the conference table. Two chairs on each side of the table are rotated at a 10° angle. You will have to draw a rectangular box (parallel to the walls) touching the outside points of the plan view of the rotated chairs. Project lines from points on the plan view to the rectangular box, and measure points of intersection with the box to get accurate measurements on the left and right isometric axes.

2. CLICK: **Layout1**, CLICK: the viewport boundary, and use Properties from the Modify menu to set a standard scale of 1/2"=1'. Plot or print the drawing on an 8-1/2" × 11" sheet of paper.

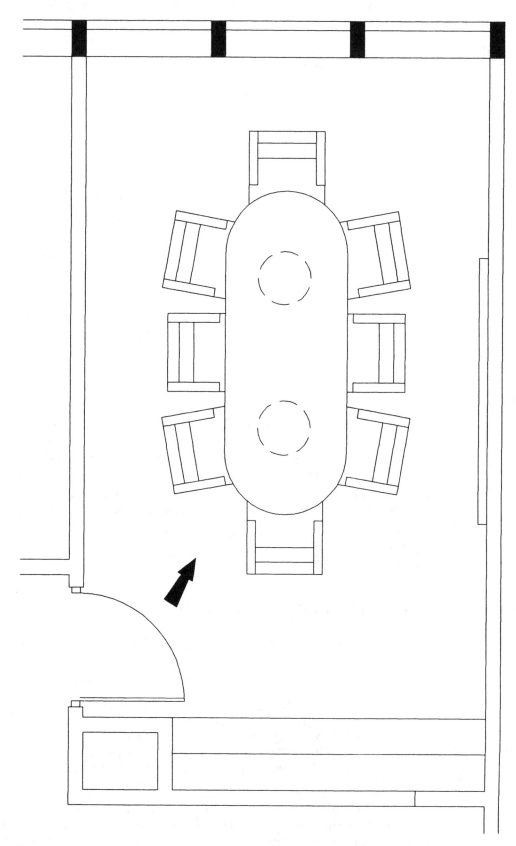

**FIGURE 13–20 (A)**
Exercise 13–5: Plan View of the Conference Room (Scale: 3/8″ = 1′-0″)

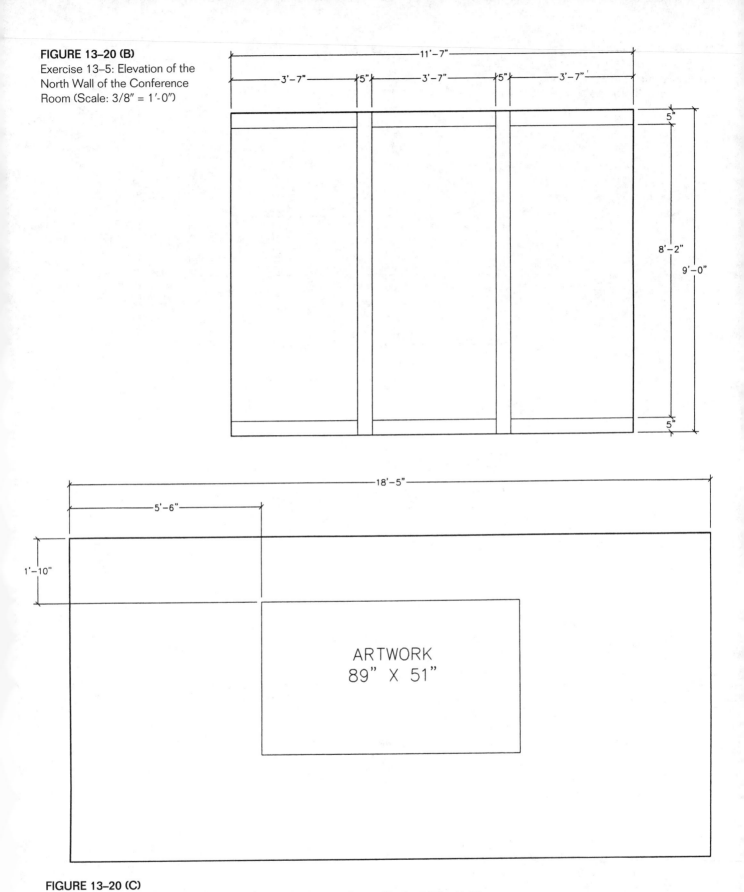

**FIGURE 13–20 (B)**
Exercise 13–5: Elevation of the North Wall of the Conference Room (Scale: 3/8″ = 1′-0″)

**FIGURE 13–20 (C)**
Exercise 13–5: Elevation of the East Wall of the Conference Room (Scale: 3/8″ = 1′-0″)

**FIGURE 13–20 (D)**

Exercise 13–5: Plan and Elevation
Views of the Conference Table
(Scale: 3/8″ = 1′-0″)

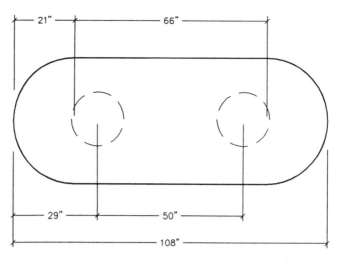

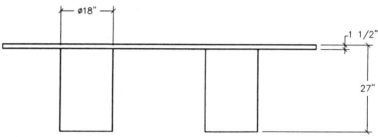

# REVIEW QUESTIONS

1. From which of the following selections on the Tools menu on the menu bar are the isometric snap and grid obtained?
   a. Layer Control...
   b. Drafting Settings…
   c. Set SysVars
   d. Grid On/Off
   e. UCS Control...

2. From which of the Snap options is the isometric snap obtained?
   a. ON
   b. OFF
   c. Aspect
   d. Rotate
   e. Style

3. Which of the following is *not* one of the normal isometric axes?
   a. 30      e. 330
   b. 60      d. 210
   c. 90

4. From which of the Ellipse prompts is the isometric ellipse obtained?
   a. <Axis endpoint 1>
   b. Center
   c. Isocircle
   d. Axis endpoint 2
   e. Rotation

5. Which isoplane is used to draw the ellipse shown in Figure 13–21?
   a. Top
   b. Left
   c. Right

6. Which isoplane is used to draw the ellipse shown in Figure 13–22?
   a. Top
   b. Left
   c. Right

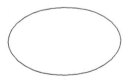

**FIGURE 13–21**

**FIGURE 13–22**

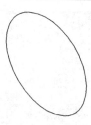

**FIGURE 13–23**

7. Which isoplane is used to draw the ellipse shown in Figure 13–23?
   a. Top
   b. Left
   c. Right

8. Which key(s) toggle from one isoplane to another?
   a. Ctrl-C    d. F5
   b. F9        e. Alt-F1
   c. F7

9. Which of the following is the same as −30°?
   a. 60°    d. 210°
   b. 150°   e. 330°
   c. 180°

10. Which of the following isoplanes will *not* allow vertical lines to be drawn with a mouse when ORTHO is ON?
    a. Top
    b. Left
    c. Right

11. Which function key is used to turn the isometric grid ON and OFF?

    _____

12. Write the correct syntax (letters and numbers) to draw a line 5.25″ at a 30° angle upward to the right.

    _____

13. Write the correct sequence of keystrokes, using polar coordinates, to draw the right side of the isometric rectangle shown in Figure 13–24, after the first point (lower left corner) has been picked. Draw to the right and up.

    1. _____    3. _____
    2. _____    4. _____

2″

4″

**FIGURE 13–24**

14. In Exercise 13–2, why were lines drawn beyond where they should stop and then trimmed to the correct length?

    _____

    _____

15. Which command used in this chapter has a feature labeled "Multiple"?

    _____

16. List the six angles used for polar coordinates in drawing on isometric axes.

    _____

17. Describe how to draw an angled line that is not on one of the isometric axes.

    _____

    _____

18. Describe how to draw a cylindrical object in isometric that has several ellipses of different sizes located on the same centerline.

    _____

    _____

19. Describe two problems that must be solved to place dimensions on an isometric drawing.

    _____

    _____

20. Describe the difference between isometric drawing and 3D modeling.

    _____

    _____

# 14

## Creating Presentations and Creating a Web Page Using AutoCAD

## OBJECTIVES

When you have completed this chapter, you will be able to:

☐ Correctly use the following commands and settings:

| | |
|---|---|
| EDIT | RegenAll |
| Model Space | RESUME |
| MSLIDE | SCRIPT |
| MVIEW | SLDSHOW |
| MVSETUP | Tilemode |
| Paper Space | VPLAYER |
| Redraw | Viewports (VPORTS) |
| RedrawAll | VSLIDE |
| Regen | |

## MODEL SPACE AND PAPER SPACE

This chapter presents the details of how to use model space and paper space and how to plot multiple viewports. It also describes how to write a script file and prepare a slide presentation of your work. Let's begin with the concepts of model space and paper space.

### Model Space

Model space is the 2D environment (and also 3D, as you will discover in Chapters 16 and 17) in which you have been working to this point. While in model space you can use the Viewports (VPORTS) command to divide the display screen into multiple viewports, as shown in Figure 14–1. Model space is limited in that although several viewports may be visible on the display screen, only one viewport can be active on the display screen at a time and only one viewport can be plotted. Model space is where your 2D or 3D model (drawing) is created and modified. When you start a new drawing, you are in model space. When the Model tab is clicked, you are in model space.

### Paper Space

Paper space is similar to a piece of illustration board used to paste up a presentation. The MVIEW command, which operates only when Tilemode is OFF (0), is used to create and

**FIGURE 14–1**
Viewports Created in Model
Space

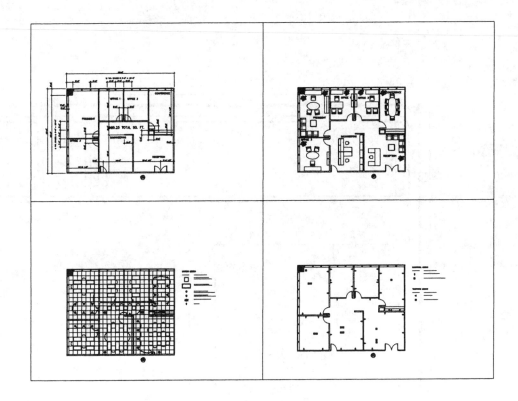

control viewport display; the display screen can be divided into multiple viewports. Each viewport can be treated as a single sheet of paper (on the illustration board) and can be copied, stretched, erased, moved, or scaled, as shown in Figure 14–2. You cannot edit the drawing within the viewport while it is in paper space; however, you can draw something over the viewport—for example, you can add dimensions or labels to a drawing. You can even overlap a viewport over one or more of the other viewports. You can also place the viewports into a single architectural format sheet, and you can plot all the viewports at the same time. When you click any of the Layout tabs, your drawing is placed into paper space.

# EXERCISE 14–1
## Creating a Printed Presentation of the Tenant Space Project by Combining Multiple Plans on One Sheet of Paper

When you have completed Exercise 14–1, your drawing will look similar to Figure 14–3. To begin Exercise 14–1, turn on the computer and start AutoCAD. The AutoCAD 2002 Today window is displayed.

1. **Open existing drawing CH12-EX1 from a floppy disk in drive A and save it as CH14-EX1 to the hard drive.**

2. **Use Zoom-All to view the limits of the drawing.**

### VIEWPORTS (VPORTS)

Begin by dividing the screen into four viewports. Remember that while it is in model space the model (drawing) is the same in each viewport. If you edit the model in any one viewport,

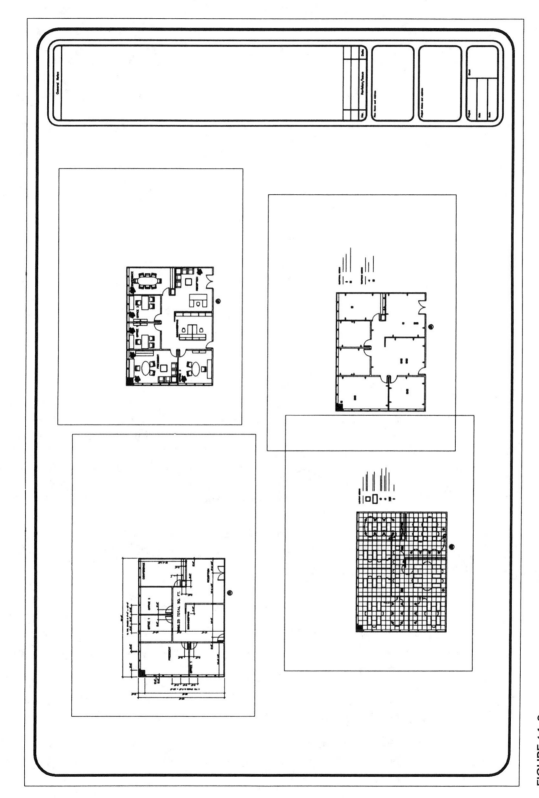

**FIGURE 14-2**
Viewports Modified in Paper Space

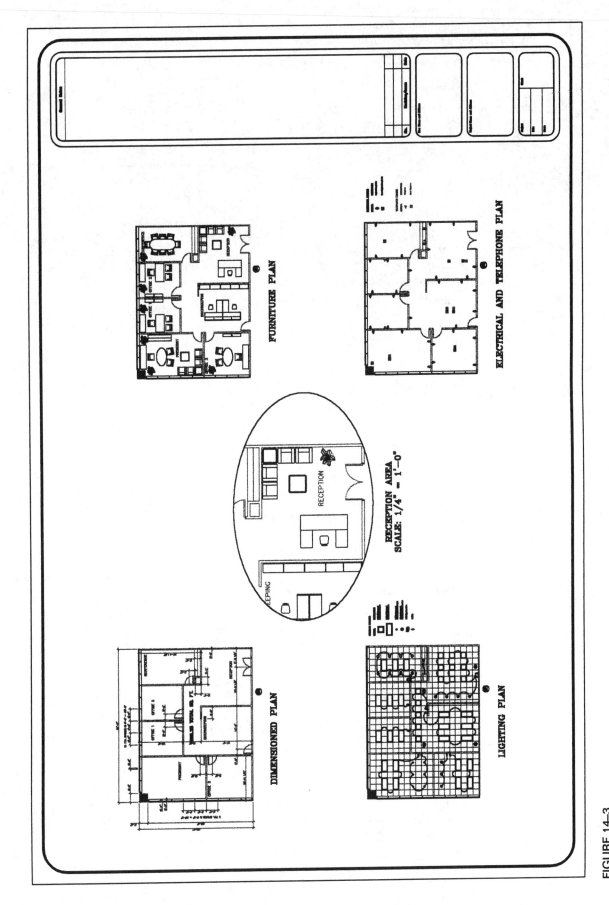

**FIGURE 14–3**

Exercise 14–1: Creating a Printed Presentation of the Tenant Space by Combining Multiple Plans on One Sheet of Paper

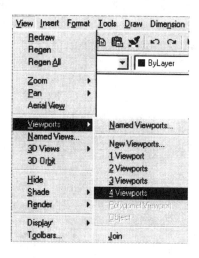

you are doing it in all viewports. You may, however, freeze different layers in each viewport, which you will do later in this exercise; display a different UCS in each viewport, and you may zoom in or out in a viewport without affecting other viewport magnification.

**Divide the screen into four viewports:**

| Prompt | Response |
|---|---|
| Command: | TYPE: **-VPORTS<enter>** |
| Enter an option [Save/Restore/Delete/Join/ SIngle/?/2/<3>/4]<3>: | TYPE: **4<enter>** (or CLICK: **Viewports: 4 viewports**) (or CLICK: **Viewports- New Viewports…** then CLICK: **Four Equal**) |

The screen is now divided into four viewports. The active viewport, outlined with a solid line, displays the lines of the cursor when the cursor is moved into it. Inactive viewports display an arrow when the cursor is moved into those areas. To make a different viewport active, position the arrow in the desired viewport and press the CLICK button on your mouse. The options of the viewports command are:

### Save

Allows you to name a set of viewports and save it for future use. Restore recalls the saved viewports. Any number of sets of viewports may be named, saved, and recalled.

### Restore

Restores a saved set of viewports. AutoCAD prompts you for the name of the saved viewport.

### Delete

Deletes a named viewport set. AutoCAD prompts you for the name of the saved viewport set to be deleted.

### Join

Joins two viewports into a larger one. The resulting view is the dominant viewport. AutoCAD prompts for the following when Join is picked:

| Prompt | Response |
|---|---|
| Select dominant viewport <current viewport>: | **<enter>** (to accept the current active viewport, or CLICK the one you want) |
| Select viewport to join: | Click: **the other viewport.** |

### Single

Returns the display to a single viewport. The resulting view is the current active viewport before single was selected.

### ?

Lists the identification numbers and the screen positions of the current arrangement of viewports and all previously saved viewports by name if you accept the default <*> when AutoCAD prompts you for the viewport configuration to list.

### 2,3,4

Divides the current viewport into two, three, or four viewports with the same view, snap, grid, and layer settings. Selections 2 and 3 also allow you to select a vertical or horizontal arrangement. Selection 3 allows for two smaller viewports to the left or right of one larger one. You can divide the screen into as many as 64 viewports depending on your display.

**FIGURE 14–4**
Start a Command in One Viewport and End It in Another

Part III: Special Topics

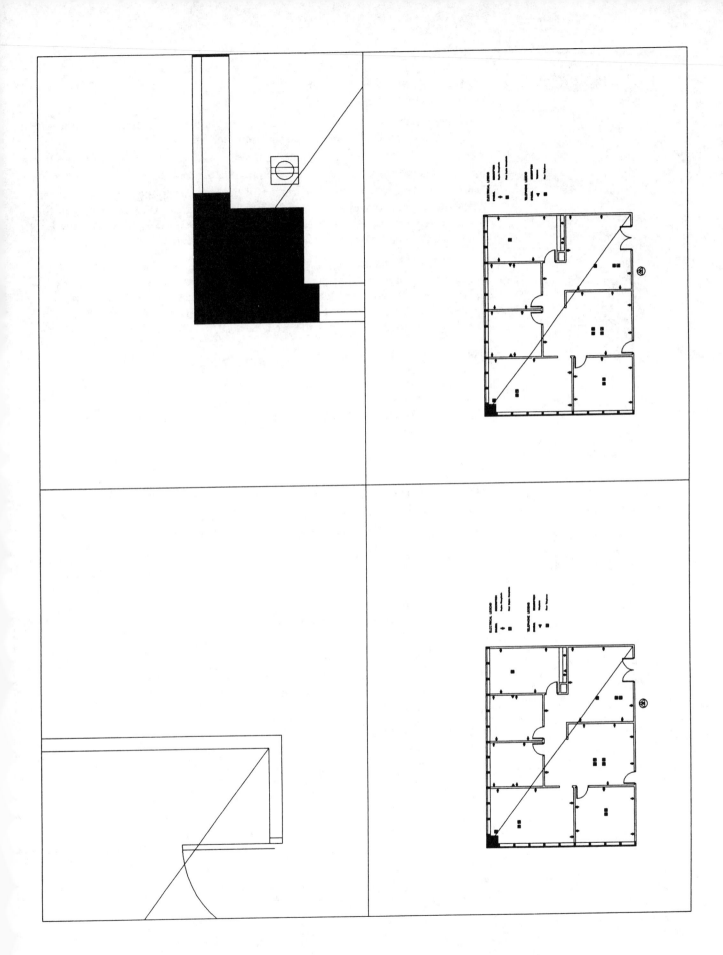

389

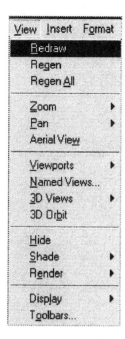

## On Your Own

See Figure 14–4. Experiment with the viewports so that you can get an idea of how viewports can be useful in drawing as well as in presentation:

1. **Click the upper left viewport to make it active, and zoom a window around the lower right corner of the building in the upper left viewport.**
2. **Click the upper right viewport to make it active, and zoom a window around the upper left corner of the building in the upper right viewport.**
3. **Draw a line from the lower right corner of the building to the upper left corner. Click the upper left viewport to make it active, start the Line command in the upper left viewport, and then click the upper right viewport to make it active, ending the line in the upper right viewport. (Be sure Ortho is OFF.)**

When you begin a command in any viewport you must first click the viewport to make it active, so ending the line in the upper right viewport requires two picks: one to make the viewport active and one to complete the Line command. Experiment with this a little, and then use Undo or Zoom-All in each viewport to return all displays to their original magnification. Use Redraw in the View menu to refresh the display in all viewports at the same time.

## REDRAW, REDRAWALL, REGEN, and REGENALL

The Redraw and Regen commands redraw or regenerate the drawing in the current viewport only. The RedrawAll and RegenAll commands redraw or regenerate the drawing in all viewports at the same time. When you TYPE: **R<enter>** you activate Redraw. When you CLICK: **Redraw** on the View menu you activate RedrawAll.

## TILEMODE

Two types of viewports, tiled and nontiled, are available to you in AutoCAD.

**Tiled Viewport Characteristics**  (When you CLICK: the **Model tab,** Tilemode is ON.) Tiled viewports are those that exist in model space with Tidemode ON. They have the following characteristics:

☐ They fill the graphics screen, lie side-by-side like ceramic tiles, and cannot be moved.
☐ They are fixed and cannot overlap.
☐ They can be deleted only by changing the viewport configuration.
☐ Only one tiled viewport can be active at a time.
☐ Only the active viewport can be plotted.
☐ Nothing drawn in a tiled viewport can be edited in a nontiled viewport.

**Nontiled Viewport Characteristics**  (When you CLICK: the **Layout tab,** Tilemode is OFF.) Nontiled viewports are those that exist in paper space or model space. They have the following characteristics:

☐ They may or may not fill the graphics screen.
☐ They can overlap.
☐ They can be moved, copied, scaled, stretched, or erased while they are in paper space.
☐ They can have different layers frozen in any viewport.
☐ All nontiled viewports can be plotted at the same time when they are in paper space.
☐ Nothing drawn in paper space can be edited in model space.

**Tilemode Settings**  Settings for Tilemode are 1 (ON) and 0 (OFF). The Tilemode setting determines whether the viewports displayed are tiled (1— ON) or nontiled (0— OFF).

- You can work in model space with Tilemode set either to 1 (ON) or 0 (OFF). You can move from paper space to model space with Tilemode OFF by clicking PAPER on the status bar at the bottom of your display or typing **MS<enter>**.
- Tilemode must be 0 (OFF) for you to work in paper space.
- The default for Tilemode is 1 (ON).

## MVIEW

The MVIEW command operates only when Tilemode is set to 0 (OFF) and is used to create and control viewport display in model space and paper space. When you TYPE: **MV<enter>**, the Tilemode setting must first be set to 0 (OFF). The MVIEW options are:

### OFF

Think of each viewport as a single sheet of paper (on the illustration board). The viewport can be copied, stretched, erased, moved, or scaled. The drawing within the viewport cannot be edited while it is in paper space. The OFF option turns off the views inside the viewport and saves regeneration time while you are editing the viewports. When the viewports are located so that you are pleased with the format, you can turn the views back on.

### ON

Turns ON the model space view (drawing inside the viewport).

### Hideplot

Used to hide surfaces covered by other surfaces in a 3D model. This option is used in Chapter 16.

### Lock

Allows you to lock a viewport so no one else can edit it.

### Object

Allows you to create a new viewport by selecting an existing object such as a circle.

### Polygonal

Allows you to draw an irregular-shaped viewport using polyline lines and arcs.

### Fit

Creates a single viewport to fill current paper space limits. Other viewports can be erased before or after the Fit option is used.

### 2,3,4

Creates two, three, or four viewports in a specified area or to fit the current paper space limits.

### Restore

Restores saved model space viewports (saved with the Viewports (VPORTS) command) into paper space.

### <First point>

Creates a new viewport defined by picking two corners or by typing the X and Y coordinates of lower left and upper right corners.

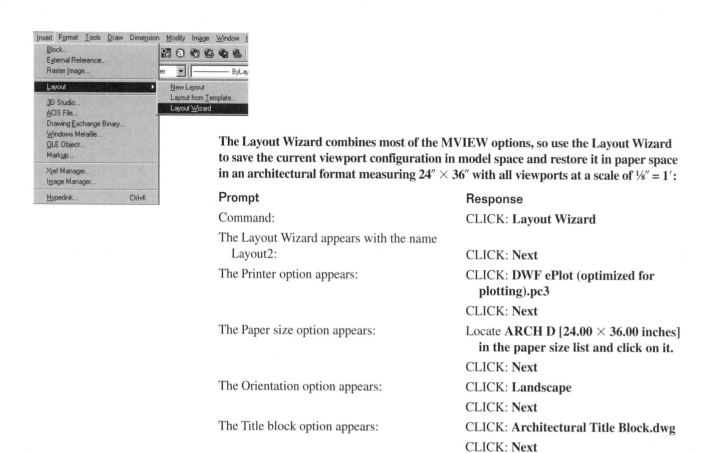

The Layout Wizard combines most of the MVIEW options, so use the Layout Wizard to save the current viewport configuration in model space and restore it in paper space in an architectural format measuring 24″ × 36″ with all viewports at a scale of ⅛″ = 1′:

| Prompt | Response |
|---|---|
| Command: | CLICK: **Layout Wizard** |
| The Layout Wizard appears with the name Layout2: | CLICK: **Next** |
| The Printer option appears: | CLICK: **DWF ePlot (optimized for plotting).pc3** |
| | CLICK: **Next** |
| The Paper size option appears: | Locate **ARCH D [24.00 × 36.00 inches]** in the paper size list and click on it. |
| | CLICK: **Next** |
| The Orientation option appears: | CLICK: **Landscape** |
| | CLICK: **Next** |
| The Title block option appears: | CLICK: **Architectural Title Block.dwg** |
| | CLICK: **Next** |
| The Define viewports option appears: | CLICK: **Array in the Viewport Setup: box** (Figure 14–5) |
| | CLICK: **1/8″=1′ in the Viewport scale: box** |

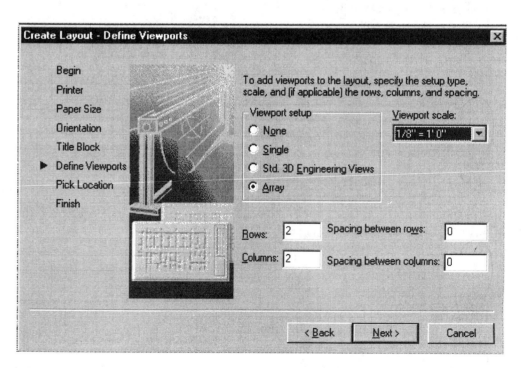

**FIGURE 14–5**
Defining Viewports in the Layout Wizard

| Prompt | Response |
|---|---|
| | TYPE: **2 in the Rows: box** |
| | TYPE: **2 in the Columns: box** |
| | TYPE: **0 in the Spacing between rows box:** |
| | TYPE: **0 in the Spacing between columns box:** |
| | CLICK: **Next** |
| The Pick Location option appears: | CLICK: **Select location:** |
| Specify first corner: | CLICK: **2,2<enter>** |
| Specify opposite corner: | CLICK: **28,22<enter>** |
| The Finish option appears: | CLICK: **Finish** |
| Command: | **Paper Space** (or TYPE: **PS<enter>** or DOUBLE CLICK: **MODEL** on the status bar if you are not already in paper space) |

**Note:** The UCS icon appears as a triangle in paper space.

The Model Space command (with Tilemode OFF) switches you from paper space to model space with paper space viewports active. You may work in model space with Tilemode either ON or OFF.

Since you are presently in paper space, you know that Tilemode is 0 because paper space cannot be active unless Tilemode is 0. To return to model space, TYPE: **MS<enter>** or CLICK: **PAPER** on the status bar (not the Model tab).

**Return to model space with Tilemode set to 0:**

| Prompt | Response |
|---|---|
| Command: | TYPE: **MS<enter>** (or CLICK: **PAPER** on the status bar) |

## On Your Own

In the next part of this exercise, the VPLAYER command is used to freeze different layers in each viewport, to create a unique drawing in each viewport.

1. **Before continuing with the VPLAYER command, thaw all frozen layers. When all layers are thawed, they will all be visible in each viewport.**

2. **Set Attribute Display (TYPE: ATTDISP<enter>, then TYPE: OFF<enter>) to OFF so that the attributes will not appear on the furniture symbols.**

3. CLICK: **each model space viewport and Zoom-All so that all viewports show the entire drawing.**

## VPLAYER

The VPLAYER command allows you to freeze different layers in any viewport. It works in either paper space or model space. To use the VPLAYER command, you must set TILEMODE to 0 (OFF) (CLICK: **any Layout tab**).

In model space, you can use the Layer Properties Manager dialog box to freeze layers in individual viewports by clicking the Freeze/Thaw button under the Active heading beside the layer name. When you click the Freeze/Thaw button under the New heading, that layer is frozen for all new viewports created. Both of these buttons should be picked to freeze layers for newly created viewports.

The VPLAYER command options are:

**?**

Lists layers frozen in selected paper space viewports.

### Freeze

Prompts you to list the names of layers you want to freeze, then prompts you for the viewports in which you want to freeze the layers. The viewport options are:

*All*—All viewports, while in model space or paper space.
*Select*—Switches to paper space (when you are in model space) and allows you to pick viewports for layer freeze.
*Current*—Selects the current viewport while in model space for layer freeze.

### Thaw

Prompts you as before to name the layers you want to thaw, then prompts you for the viewports in which you want to thaw the layers.

### Reset

After you use the Freeze or Thaw option to change a layer's visibility, you can use the Reset option to restore the default visibility setting for a layer in a selected viewport.

### Newfrz

Creates new layers that are frozen in all viewports. If you then want to thaw a layer in a single viewport, use the Thaw option.

### Vpvisdfl

If a layer is frozen in some viewports and thawed in others, you can use the Vpvisdfl option to set the default visibility per viewport for any layer. This default setting then determines the layer's visibility in any new viewport created with the MVIEW command.

**Use the VPLAYER command to freeze layers in the upper left viewport:**

| Prompt | Response |
|---|---|
| Command: | **Click the upper left viewport to make it active.** |
| Command: | **TYPE: VPLAYER<enter>** |
| Enter an option [?/Freeze/Thaw/Reset/ Newfrz/Vpvisdfl]: | **TYPE: F<enter>** |
| Enter layer name(s) to freeze: | **TYPE: A-AREA,A-FURN,A-CLNG, E-LITE,E-LITE-D,E-LITE-W, E-POWR,E-COMM, E-POWER-TXT<enter>** |
| Enter an option [All/Select/Current] <Current>: | **<enter>** (the current viewport) |
| Enter an option [?/Freeze/Thaw/Reset/ Newfrz/Vpvisdfl]: | **<enter>** |

## On Your Own

**Tip:** If you cannot see the Current column, hold the cursor over the right border of the dialog box and when the double arrow appears hold down the left mouse button and drag the border to the right so the current column is visible.

1. **Click the upper right viewport to make it active. Use the Layer Properties Manager dialog box to freeze layers in the current viewport. CLICK: the Freeze/Thaw icons in the Current... column so snowflakes appear as shown in Figure 14–6. CLICK: OK.**

   The layers to be frozen in the upper right viewport (just in case you cannot identify them in the illustration) are:

   A-AREA
   A-CLNG
   A-FLOR-WDWK
   A-PFLR-DIMS
   E-COMM
   E-LITE
   E-LITE-D
   E-LITE-W

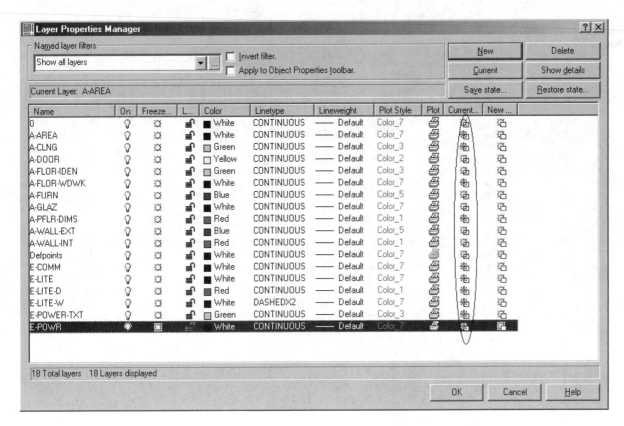

FIGURE 14–6
Frozen Layers in the Upper Right Viewport

E-POWR
E-POWER-TXT

2. CLICK: **the lower left viewport to make it active. Use the Layer Properties Manager dialog box to freeze layers in the current viewport.** CLICK: **"the Freeze/Thaw icons" in the Current… column as shown in Figure 14–7.** CLICK: **OK.**

   The layers to be frozen in the lower left viewport (just in case you cannot identify them in the illustration) are:

   A-AREA
   A-DOOR
   A-FLOR-WDWK
   A-FLOR-IDEN
   A-FURN
   A-PFLR-DIMS
   E-COMM
   E-POWR
   E-POWER-TXT

3. CLICK: **the lower right viewport to make it active. Use the Layer Properties Manager dialog box to freeze layers in the current viewport.** CLICK: **"the Freeze/Thaw icons" in the Current… column as shown in Figure 14–8.** CLICK: **OK.**

   The layers to be frozen in the lower right viewport (just in case you cannot identify them in the illustration) are:

   A-AREA
   A-CLNG
   A-FLOR-IDEN
   A-FLOR-WDWK

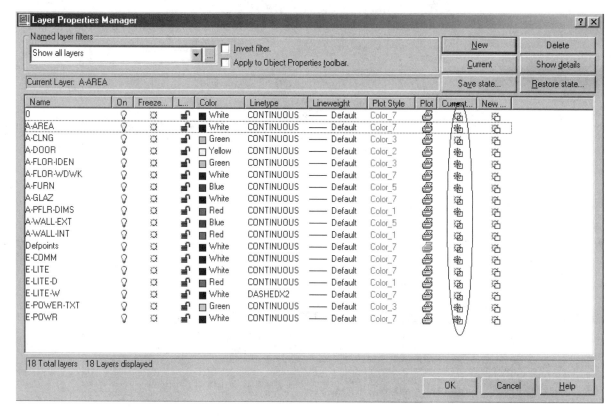

**FIGURE 14–7**
Frozen Layers in the Lower Left Viewport

A-FURN
A-PFLR-DIMS
E-LITE
E-LITE-D
E-LITE-W

There will be occasions when you will want to select or deselect all Layers at the same time. To do that, position the cursor in an open area in the dialog box and press the right mouse button, then CLICK: **Select All** or **Clear All.**

## PAPER SPACE

The Paper Space command switches you from model space to paper space. Tilemode must be 0 (OFF) for Paper Space to work. Tilemode is still set to 0. You have been working in model space with Tilemode set to 0.

**Use the Paper Space command to return to paper space:**

| Prompt | Response |
|---|---|
| Command: | **Paper Space** (or TYPE: **PS<enter>**) |
| | (or DOUBLE CLICK: **MODEL** on the status bar—not the Model tab) |

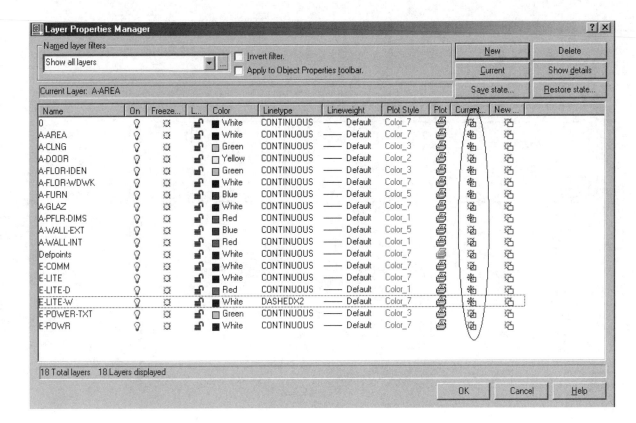

**FIGURE 14–8**
Frozen Layers in the Lower Right Viewport

### On Your Own

1. You now have a 36″ × 24″ architectural format with the four viewports in it. Use the Move command to move the viewports so that they are centered in the space approximately as shown in Figure 14–9. You will have to pick the outside edge of any viewport to move it, or select all four viewports by using a crossing window.

2. Make sure you are still in PAPER SPACE. In the next part of this exercise the Modify Properties command is used to make sure each viewport is still a standard size of 1/8″ = 1′-0″.

3. CLICK: the boundary of all paper space viewports, then CLICK: Properties from the Modify menu and set a standard scale of 1/8″ = 1′ in all four viewports, as shown in Figure 14–10. Use Pan to center images in each viewport.

4. Use the MVIEW command (TYPE: MV<enter>) to turn OFF the model space views (drawings inside the viewports), as shown in Figure 14–10. Turning the viewports off decreases regeneration time and allows you to work faster on complex drawings. Pick the boundary of the viewport to turn the views off.

5. Use the Move command to move all viewports to the approximate locations as shown in Figure 14–11.

6. Use the Mview command (TYPE: MV<enter>) to turn ON the model space views.

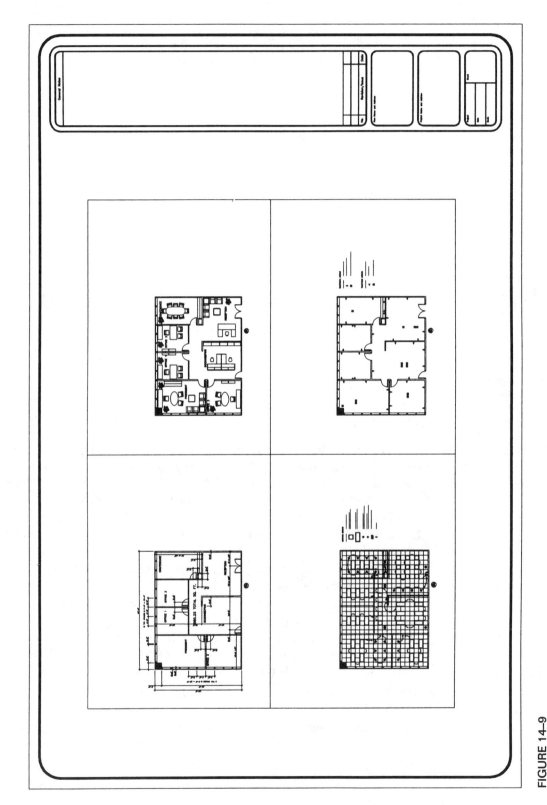

**FIGURE 14-9**
Position the Paper Space Viewports in the Architectural Format

398

**FIGURE 14-10**
Use Modify Properties to Set
a Scale of 1/8″ = 1′ for All
Four Viewports

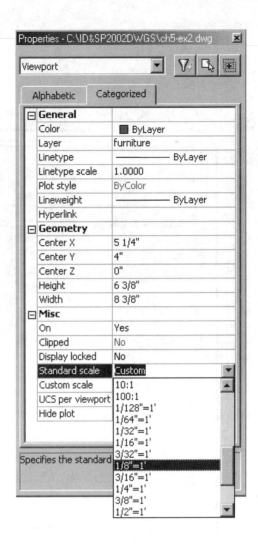

## MVSETUP

Because the viewports have been moved, it is likely that your model space views are not lined up vertically and horizontally. The Mvsetup command can be used to align the views (drawings) within each viewport.

**Use the Mvsetup command to align viewports in model space (Figure 14–12):**

| Prompt | Response |
|---|---|
| Command: | TYPE: **MVSETUP<enter>** |
| Enter an option [Align/Create/Scale viewports/ Options/Title block/Undo]: | TYPE: **A<enter>** |
| Enter an option [Angled/Horizontal/Vertical alignment/Rotate view/Undo]: | TYPE: **H<enter>** (AutoCAD changes to model space) |
| Specify basepoint: | CLICK: **the lower right viewport to make it active.** |
| | **Osnap-Intersection** |
| of | **D1** |
| Specify point in viewport to be panned: | CLICK: **the lower left viewport to make it active.** |
| | **Osnap-Intersection** |
| of | **D2** |

**FIGURE 14–11**
Turn Off the Model Space Views and Move the Viewports

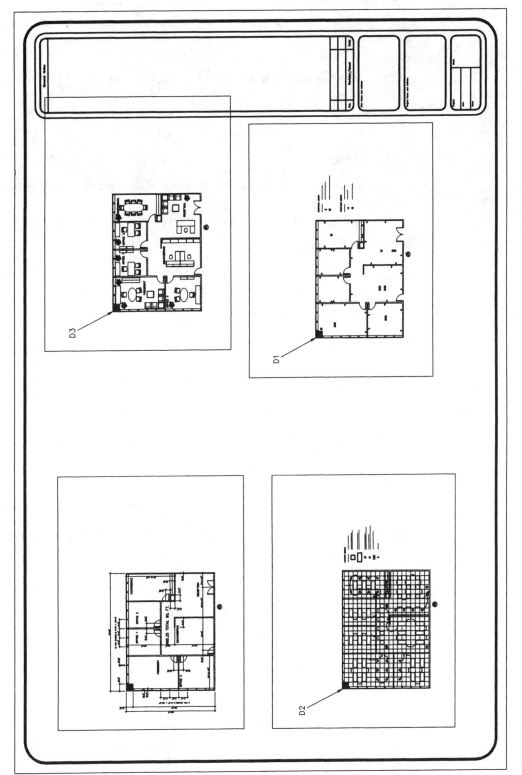

**FIGURE 14–12**
Use MVSETUP to Align the Views within Each Viewport

| Prompt | Response |
|---|---|
| Enter an option [Angled/Horizontal/Vertical alignment/Rotate view/Undo]: | TYPE: **V\<enter\>** |
| Specify basepoint: | **Osnap-Intersection** |
| of | CLICK: **the upper right viewport to make it active.** |
| | **D3** |
| Specify point in viewport to be panned: | CLICK: **the lower right viewport to make it active.** |
| | **Osnap-Intersection** |
| of | **D1** |

## On Your Own

1. **Align, horizontally and vertically, any remaining model space views that need to be aligned.**

   A brief description of the MVSETUP options follows:

### Tilemode Set to 1 (ON)

When Tilemode is ON, MVSETUP acts just like SETUP in earlier versions of AutoCAD. You set Units, Scale, and Paper Size using prompts for each setting.

### Tilemode Set to 0 (OFF)

When Tilemode is OFF, MVSETUP has the following options:

**Align**  This option lets you pan the view so that it aligns with a basepoint in another viewport. You may align viewports horizontally and vertically; you may align them at a specified distance and angle from a basepoint in another viewport; and you may rotate the view in a viewport about a basepoint. This option also has an undo feature.

**Create**  This option allows you to delete existing viewports. It also allows you to create one or more standard-size viewports. If more than one is created, this option allows you to specify the distance between viewports. It also allows you to create an array of viewports. This option also has an undo feature.

**Scale viewports**  This option allows you to set the scale of the drawing displayed in the viewports; it is similar to the Zoom XP feature.

**Options**  This option allows you to specify a layer for the title block, reset paper space limits, change different units, or attach an Xref as the title block.

**Title block**  This option allows you to delete objects from paper space and to select the origin point for this sheet. It then prompts you to select one of 13 standard formats. This option also has an undo feature.

**Undo**  This is an undo option for the major routine.

## Adding Details and Annotating Paper Space Viewports

**Add another viewport (Figure 14–13):**

## On Your Own

1. **Draw an ellipse in paper space the approximate size and location of the one in Figure 14–13.**

   **Now use the MVIEW command to make a new viewport of the ellipse.**

| Prompt | Response |
|---|---|
| Command: | TYPE: **MV\<enter\>** |
| Specify corner of viewport or [ON/OFF/Fit/Hideplot/Lock/Object/ Polygonal/Restore/2/3/4] \<Fit\>: | TYPE: **O\<enter\>** |
| Select object to clip viewport: | CLICK: **the ellipse** |

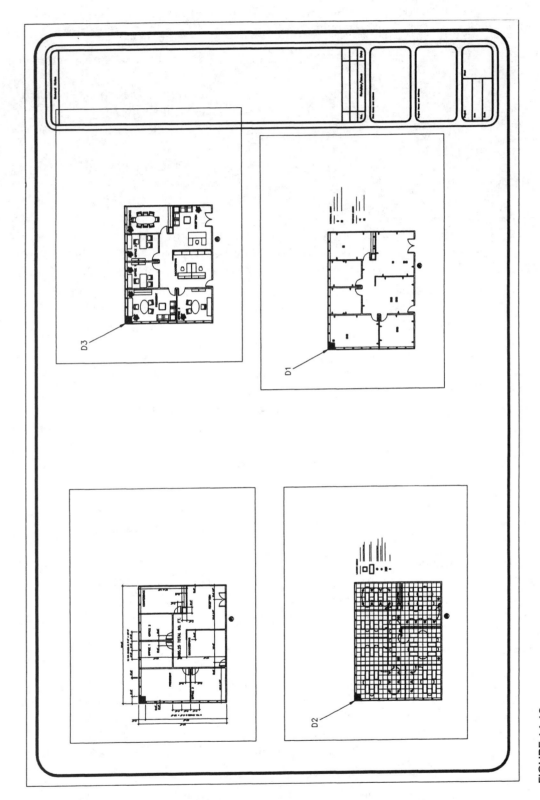

**FIGURE 14-13**
Use MVIEW to Create Another Viewport

403

You are now in model space and have a viewport containing a view of the active model space viewport. All the layers are turned ON. Later in the exercise, the borders of the large viewports will be frozen.

**Use the Modify Properties command to scale the view:**

| Prompt | Response |
| --- | --- |
| Command: | TYPE: **PS <enter> to return to paper space.** |
| Command: | CLICK: **the elliptical viewport boundary** |
| | CLICK: **Properties from the Modify menu** |
| | CLICK: **1/4″ = 1′-0″ from the Standard scale list** |

## On Your Own

1. **Use the Layer Properties Manager dialog box to freeze layers in the newly added, current viewport. Freeze the same layers as you did for the upper right viewport.**

2. **Use Zoom-Dynamic to obtain a view of the reception area of the tenant space.**

3. **If needed, use the Move command to locate the views so that they are located approximately as shown in Figure 14–14. Align them as needed.**

4. **Create a new layer named VPORT. While in paper space change the outside edges of the four large viewports to the VPORT layer. Do not select the outside edge of the viewport that has the detail of the reception area in it. Use the Layer list on the Object Properties toolbar to turn the VPORT Layer OFF. The outside edges of the viewports will no longer be visible.**

5. **Label the views using Dtext (single line text) with the STYLE name Label, FONT—Complex. HEIGHT—1/4, as shown in Figure 14–14. Use the Zoom-Window command to zoom in on the viewports so that the text is visible.**

6. **Fill in the title block information as appropriate using the Dtext (single line text) command.**

## SAVE

**When you have completed Exercise 14–1, save your work in at least two places.**

## PLOT

**Plot or print Exercise 14–1 at a plotting ratio of 1 = 1. You will be plotting a 36″ × 24″ sheet.**

# EXERCISE 14–2
# Creating a Slide Show of the Tenant Space Project Drawings

Another means of creating a presentation is with the use of slides. A slide is made of a drawing while it is active on the display screen; it is a file containing a "snapshot" (a raster image) of the display on the screen. A script file is used to display the slides in the correct order and with an appropriate amount of delay between slides.

Use the following steps to create a slide show:

**Step 1. Select and organize the drawings to be included in the slide show:**

Decide which drawings you wish to include in your slide show. Make a storyboard consisting of quick sketches of the drawings in the order in which you want them to appear. Identify each drawing by the name under which you have it stored. You may include as many drawings as you want (for this exercise use a minimum of 10).

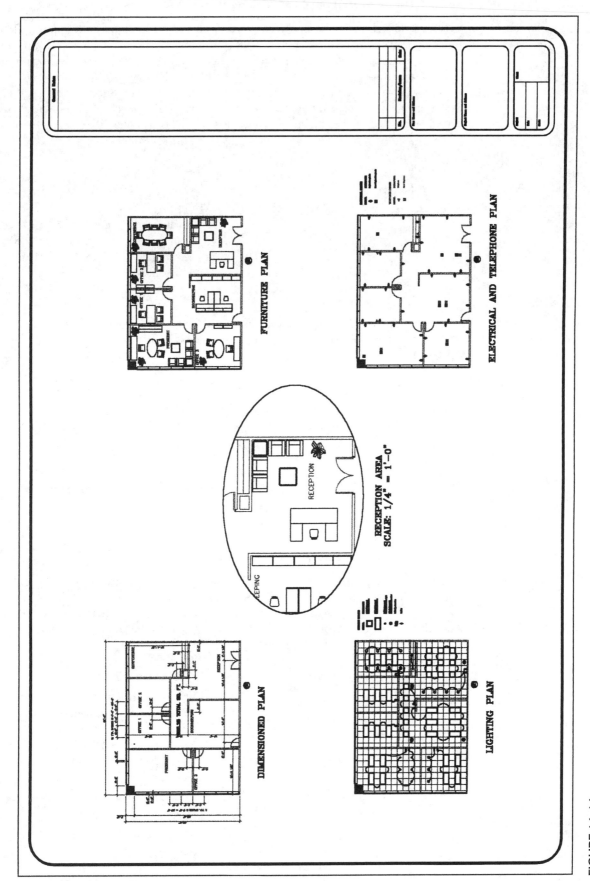

FURNITURE PLAN

ELECTRICAL AND TELEPHONE PLAN

RECEPTION AREA
SCALE: 1/4" = 1'-0"

RECEPTION

SLEEPING

DIMENSIONED PLAN

LIGHTING PLAN

**FIGURE 14–14**
Exercise 14–1 Complete

405

## Step 2. Use MSLIDE to make slides of each drawing:

Using AutoCAD, bring each drawing to be included in the slide show from the floppy disk to the hard drive, one at a time. Zoom a window around a drawing so that it fills the screen. Inserting drawings into a blank area may be the fastest means of accomplishing this. Insert, make the slide, then Undo to get rid of the drawing.

You may also use the Layer Properties Manager dialog box to control the display of different layers to create different drawings and make slides of each drawing. The view of the drawing as displayed on the screen is what your slide will look like.

Make slides of each displayed drawing by using the following procedure:

| Prompt | Response |
|---|---|
| Command: | TYPE: **MSLIDE\<enter\>** |
| The Create Slide File dialog box appears: | TYPE: **A:SLIDE1** in the File name: input area (use an empty floppy disk so that all your slides and the script file will fit on it; label each slide with a different consecutive number) |
| | CLICK: **Save** |

Continue this procedure for each drawing until all slides are made. Number each slide with a different consecutive number. Be sure to save the slides on the floppy disk in drive A by including A: as the destination.

## Step 3. Use VSLIDE to view any slide that you have created:

When the VSLIDE command is used, the slide recalled replaces the current drawing on the display screen. View any slide that you have created by using the following procedure:

| Prompt | Response |
|---|---|
| Command: | TYPE: **VSLIDE\<enter\>** |
| The Select Slide File dialog box appears: | CLICK: **SLIDE1** (on the 3-1/2 Floppy [A:] drive) |
| | CLICK: **Open** (to view Slide1) |

## Step 4. Make a script file for your slide show:

AutoCAD provides the Script command, which allows other commands to be read and executed from a script file. The following procedure describes how to use the Edit command to make a script file for 10 slides while you are in the drawing editor. Read through the description first, and if you have more than 10 slides, you will be able to add to the script file.

| Prompt | Response |
|---|---|
| Command: | TYPE: **EDIT\<enter\>** |
| File to edit: | TYPE: **A:SLDSHOW.SCR\<enter\>** (SLDSHOW is the name of your script file—it can be any standard eight characters, the SCR extension identifies this as a script file to AutoCAD) |
| The MS-DOS Editor appears: | Type the following exactly as described: |
| | TYPE: **VSLIDE A:SLIDE1\<enter\>** (VSLIDE is the VSLIDE command that tells AutoCAD to display a slide; A:SLIDE1 tells AutoCAD where the slide is located and its name) |

**Note:** Leave one space only between the following:
**VSLIDE** and **A:**
**VSLIDE** and **\*A:**
**DELAY** and **2500**

**Note:** Press \<enter\> only once at the end of each line, otherwise your script file will not work.

| Prompt | Response |
|---|---|
| | TYPE: **VSLIDE \*A:SLIDE2\<enter\>** (tells AutoCAD to load the next file— \* means load; A:SLIDE2 is the name of the slide located on a floppy disk in drive A) |
| | TYPE: **DELAY 2500\<enter\>** (tells AutoCAD to delay 2500 milliseconds before proceeding to the next line) |
| | TYPE: **VSLIDE\<enter\>** (tells AutoCAD to display the slide that was loaded with line 2—Slide 2) |
| | TYPE: **VSLIDE \*A:SLIDE3\<enter\>** |
| | TYPE: **DELAY 2500\<enter\>** |
| | TYPE: **VSLIDE** |
| | TYPE: **VSLIDE \*A:SLIDE4\<enter\>** |
| | TYPE: **DELAY 2500\<enter\>** |
| | TYPE: **VSLIDE\<enter\>** |
| | TYPE: **VSLIDE \*A:SLIDE5\<enter\>** |
| | TYPE: **DELAY 2500\<enter\>** |
| | TYPE: **VSLIDE\<enter\>** |
| | TYPE: **VSLIDE \*A:SLIDE6\<enter\>** |
| | TYPE: **DELAY 2500\<enter\>** |
| | TYPE: **VSLIDE\<enter\>** |
| | TYPE: **VSLIDE \*A:SLIDE7\<enter\>** |
| | TYPE: **DELAY 2500\<enter\>** |
| | TYPE: **VSLIDE\<enter\>** |
| | TYPE: **VSLIDE \*A:SLIDE8\<enter\>** |
| | TYPE: **DELAY 2500\<enter\>** |
| | TYPE: **VSLIDE\<enter\>** |
| | TYPE: **VSLIDE \*A:SLIDE9\<enter\>** |
| | TYPE: **DELAY 2500\<enter\>** |
| | TYPE: **VSLIDE\<enter\>** |
| | TYPE: **VSLIDE \*A:SLIDE10\<enter\>** |
| | TYPE: **DELAY 2500\<enter\>** |
| | TYPE: **VSLIDE\<enter\>** |
| | TYPE: **RSCRIPT\<enter\>** (tells AutoCAD to rerun the script file) |

**You must now check each line of your file to be sure it contains no errors:**

Check each line of your script file to be sure there are no extra spaces or returns.

**Save your script file:**

| Prompt | Response |
|---|---|
| | CLICK: **File-Save** |
| | CLICK: **File-Exit** |

You now have a floppy disk containing your script file named Sldshow.Scr and 10 (or more) slides named SLIDE1.sld through SLIDE10.sld.

**Step 5. Test your slide show and script file:**

| Prompt | Response |
|---|---|
| Command: | TYPE: **SCRIPT\<enter\>** |
| (The Select Script File dialog box appears.) | CLICK: **Sldshow.scr** (on the 3-1/2 Floppy [A:]) |
| | CLICK: **Open** |

If all is well, your slide show will run uninterrupted until you decide to stop it. To stop the slide show at any point, press Esc. To start it again, TYPE: **RESUME\<enter\>**.

If the file does not run, make sure the script file and your slide files are on the floppy disk and your script file is correct. Also make sure you have typed the script file name correctly. If the delay period is not what you want, you may edit your script file and make the delay longer or shorter as you wish.

**To edit your script file:**

| Prompt | Response |
|---|---|
| Command: | TYPE: **EDIT\<enter\>** |
| File to edit: | TYPE: **A:SLDSHOW.SCR\<enter\>** |
| The MS-DOS Editor appears with the script file displayed: | **Edit the file as needed.** |

# EXERCISE 14–3
# Creating a Web Page

The Publish to Web Wizard allows you to create a Web page for the Internet using the following options.

**Image Types**   You can choose from three image types (file formats).
**Templates**   You can select one of four templates for the layout of your Web page, or you can design your own template.
**Themes**   You can choose a theme for the template. Themes allow you to change the colors and fonts in your Web page.
**i-drop**   You can select the i-drop property for your Web page so that visitors to your page can drag drawing files into AutoCAD. The i-drop feature is ideally suited for publishing block libraries (a group of drawings) to the Internet.
**Select Drawings**   This option allows you to select any of your drawings and choose any or all of the layouts in that drawing to display on your Web page.
**Generate Images**   Here you can regenerate images for drawings that have changed, or regenerate all images.
**Preview and Post**   This option allows you to see what your Web page will look like before you post it onto the Internet.

**Use the Publish to Web Wizard to create a Web page (Figure 14–15):**

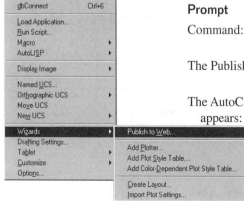

| Prompt | Response |
|---|---|
| Command: | CLICK: **Wizards-Publish to Web** (from the Tools menu) |
| The Publish to Web Begin Wizard appears: | CLICK: **the Create New Web Page button** if it is not already active |
| The AutoCAD drawing information box appears: | CLICK: OK |

FIGURE 14–15
Publish to Web Wizard

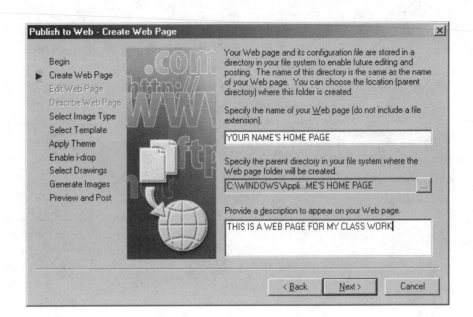

| Prompt | Response |
|---|---|
| The Publish to Web dialog box appears | **Locate a drawing you like and open it.** |
| | CLICK: **Next>** |
| The Create Web Page screen appears: | TYPE: **(YOUR NAME)'s HOME PAGE** in the upper open box (Figure 14–15) |
| | TYPE: **THIS IS A WEB PAGE FOR MY CLASS WORK** in the Provide a description to appear on your Web page box |
| | CLICK: **Next>** |
| The Select Image Type screen appears: | CLICK: **Next>** (or select another of the three types from the list) |
| The Select Template screen appears: | CLICK: **List plus summary** (or another template if you choose) |
| | CLICK: **Next>** |
| The Apply Theme screen appears: | CLICK: **Any of the seven themes from the list** (I chose Supper Club) |
| | CLICK: **Next>** |
| The Enable I-drop screen appears: | CLICK: **Enable-idrop** |
| | CLICK: **Next>** |
| The Select Drawings screen appears: | CLICK: **the ellipsis (the three dots to the right of the Drawing: list) and go find your drawing of CH14-EX1 on a disk or in a folder on the hard drive. When you find it** CLICK: **Open.** |
| | CLICK: **the Layout list:** |
| | CLICK: **Each one of the Layouts** and CLICK: **Add>** |
| | When all the Layouts are in the Image list, CLICK: **Next>** |
| The Generate Images screen appears: | CLICK: **Next>** |

| Prompt | Response |
|---|---|
| The Preview and Post screen appears: | CLICK: **Preview** |
| A preview of your Web page appears: | CLOSE the PREVIEW page |
| The Preview and Post screen appears: | CLICK: **Post Now (or** CLICK: **<Back if you want to change something. (You can also edit this page with this wizard.)** |
| The Posting Web dialog box appears: | CLICK: **Save** |
| The Posting successfully completed message appears: | CLICK: **OK** |
| The Preview and Post screen appears: | CLICK: **Send Email and send yourself an e-mail if you have an e-mail address so you have a link to your Web page.** |
| The Preview and Post screen appears: | CLICK: **Finish** |

# EXERCISE 14–4
## Creating a Presentation

Use the procedures described in Exercise 14–1 to prepare a 36″ × 24″ sheet containing the architectural format and similar plans of one of the other projects you have completed. All viewports should be at a standard scale (1/8″ = 1′-0″ or 1/4″ = 1′-0″). Your final sheet should contain five paper space viewports and should appear similar to Figure 14–14.

# EXERCISE 14–5
## Creating a Presentation

Use the procedures described in Exercise 14–1 to prepare a 36″ × 24″ sheet containing the architectural format and similar plans of still another of the projects you have completed. All viewports should be at a standard scale (1/8″ = 1′-0″ or 1/4″ = 1′-0″). Show two details of different spaces at a scale of 1/4″ = 1′-0″. Your final sheet should contain six paper space viewports and should appear similar to Figure 14–14.

# EXERCISE 14–6
## Creating a Slide Show

Prepare a slide show containing 20 slides of your work plus a title slide. The title slide should contain the following:

Your Name
Title of the Class
Course and Section Number
Instructor's Name
Date

Make your title slide as fancy or as simple as you like. Make a drawing of the title slide, and then use MSLIDE to create the slide.

1. Which of the following is a characteristic of paper space?
   a. Viewports are tiled.
   b. Tilemode is set to 1.
   c. Viewports can overlap.
   d. Models are created.
   e. The VPORTS command will work.
2. How many model space viewports can be created on any one drawing?
   a. 2
   b. 4
   c. 16
   d. 64
   e. Unlimited
3. The Layout Wizard does *not* do which of the following?
   a. Turn viewport ON and OFF
   b. Scale viewports
   c. Allow you to specify the corners of a viewport's location
   d. Allow you to name the Layout
   e. Allow you to create an array of viewports
4. Which command shows you all the viewport options on the New Viewports tab of the Viewports dialog box?
   a. Named Views
   b. Named Viewports
   c. New Viewports
   d. MView
   e. Aerial View
5. A command can be started in one viewport and completed in a different viewport.
   a. True
   b. False
6. Which of the following is a characteristic of a nontiled viewport?
   a. Fills the graphics screen and touches all other viewports
   b. Is fixed and cannot overlap
   c. Can be erased or moved
   d. Only one of these viewports may be plotted at one time.
   e. Only one viewport may be active at one time.
7. Model space may be active with Tilemode set at either 0 or 1.
   a. True
   b. False
8. Which of the following MVIEW options creates several viewports at the same time?
   a. ON
   b. OFF
   c. Fit
   d. 2,3,4
   e. <First point>
9. Which command can be used to set a standard scale of 1/4″ = 1′ in paper space viewports?
   a. Paper Space
   b. Tilemode
   c. Modify Properties
   d. Scale
   e. Model Space
10. Which of the following can be used to align viewports accurately in model space?
    a. MVIEW
    b. VPORTS
    c. Move
    d. MVSETUP
    e. Align

11. Which option of the MVSETUP command is used to obtain a 24″ × 36″ architectural format?

_____

12. List the command and its option that will insert a set of saved model space viewports into paper space.

_____

13. List the prompts and responses needed to freeze layers A-AREA and A-FURN in one of four model space viewports (Tilemode is OFF). The viewport is active.

| Prompt | Response |
|---|---|
| Command: | TYPE: VPLAYER<enter> |
| _____ | TYPE: _____ |
| _____ | TYPE: _____ |
| _____ | _____ |

14. List the command used to switch from model space to paper space when Tilemode is OFF.

_____

15. List four characteristics of tiled viewports that are different from those of nontiled viewports.

_____

_____

_____

_____

16. List the prompts and responses needed to create a slide named SLD1 on a floppy disk in drive A.

| Prompt | Response |
|---|---|
| Command: | TYPE: _____ |
| _____ | TYPE: _____ |
| _____ | CLICK: _____ |

17. Write the command used to view a slide.

_____

18. Write the command used in this chapter to create a script file.

_____

19. Describe what each line of the following script file does.

VSLIDE A:DRAW1 _____

VSLIDE *A:DRAW2 _____

DELAY 1500 _____

VSLIDE _____

20. To run the script file described in this chapter, what files must be contained on the floppy disk in drive A?

_____

_____

# 15 Using Raster Images in AutoCAD Drawings

## OBJECTIVES

When you have completed this chapter, you will be able to:

- □ Define the terms *vector* and *raster images.*
- □ List file types for raster images.
- □ Insert raster images into AutoCAD drawings.
- □ Select raster images for editing.
- □ Use grips to stretch, move, scale, copy, rotate, and mirror raster images.
- □ Clip raster images.
- □ Change the order of images lying on top of each other.
- □ Adjust the brightness and contrast of raster images.
- □ Turn image boundaries ON and OFF.
- □ Delete and detach raster images.

## INTRODUCTION

AutoCAD 2002 allows raster images to be easily imported into and exported from Auto-CAD drawings. A raster image is one made up of dots similar to the photographs you find printed in newspapers and magazines. A vector image is one made up of lines and solids. Most AutoCAD drawings are made up entirely of vector images.

Being able to use raster images easily in AutoCAD drawings means that you can now bring many different types of images into your drawings. For example, you can use files from CorelDraw, Paintbrush, Powerpoint and many other popular graphics programs and place people, trees, cars, and other pictures in your drawing. You can also take photographs with a digital camera and import them into your drawing. AutoCAD uses 14 image file types that you will find listed in the Select Image File dialog box.

Many of the same commands you use with vector images can be used with raster images. How these commands are used, however, varies a little. The following exercise will give you some experience in using raster images.

## EXERCISE 15–1
## Inserting and Modifying Raster Images

The drawing template A-size, created in Chapter 3, will be used for this exercise. You will use that template to create a new drawing and then insert some raster images that are in the AutoCAD 2002 program. After the images are inserted some standard commands will be used to modify the images. Your final drawing will look similar to Figure 15–1.

To prepare to draw Exercise 15–1, turn on the computer and start AutoCAD. The AutoCAD 2002 Today window is displayed.

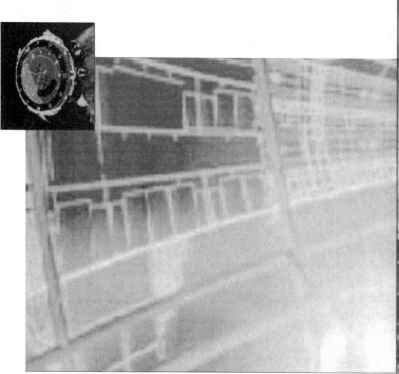

**FIGURE 15–1**
Exercise 15–1: Inserting and Modifying Raster Images (This material has been reprinted with permission from and under the copyright of Autodesk, Inc.)

## On Your Own

1. **CLICK: Create Drawing-select how to begin-Template-CLICK: the A-SIZE template created in Chapter 3 (Figure 15–2).**

2. **Use SaveAs... to save the drawing on the hard drive with the name CH15-EX1.**

3. **Use Zoom-All to view the limits of the drawing.**

4. **Turn GRID and SNAP ON.**

5. **Set Layer1 current.**

## Inserting Raster Images into AutoCAD Drawings

**Find the sample raster files that are in AutoCAD 2002 and insert the one named acadsig (Figure 15–3):**

| Prompt | Response |
|---|---|
| Command: | CLICK: **Raster Image...** (from the Insert menu) |
| The Select Image File dialog box appears: | DOUBLE CLICK: **acadsig** (in the AutoCAD 2002 folder) |
| The Image dialog box appears: | CLICK: **OK** |

**FIGURE 15–2**
Select the Template File

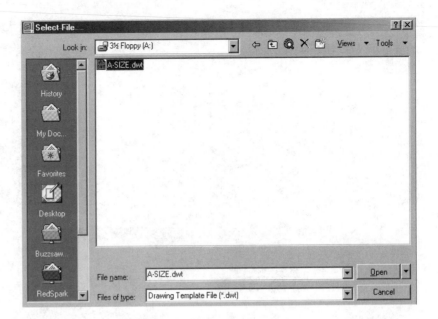

**FIGURE 15–3**
DOUBLE CLICK: the acadsig File
in the AutoCAD 2002 Folder

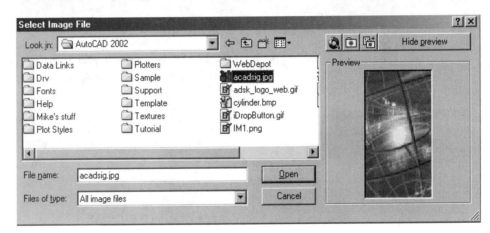

| Prompt | Response |
|---|---|
| Specify insertion point <0,0>: | <enter> (This locates the lower left corner of the picture at 0,0.) |
| Base image size: Width: 1.000000, Height: 1.837500, Inches Specify scale factor <1>: | TYPE: **5<enter>** (This enlarges the picture to five times its original size.) |

The acadsig image is inserted into the drawing.

## Modifying Raster Images

Before you can do anything to an image you have to select it. Raster images have to be selected by using a window or by clicking any point on the image frame. After selecting the object, you may then move, stretch, scale, copy, mirror, or rotate it using grips or one of the standard commands.

You may also use any of the commands on the Reference toolbar to clip, adjust, and otherwise edit the image. Start by clipping this image to a more manageable size.

**FIGURE 15–4**
Show the Reference Toolbar

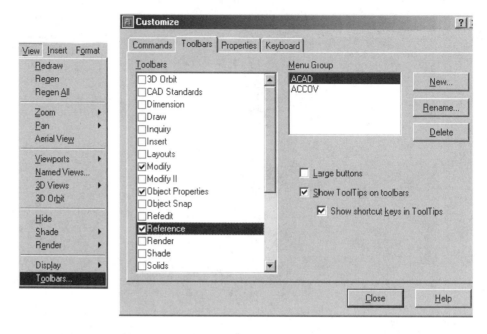

## On Your Own (Figure 15–4)

1. **Activate the Reference toolbar by CLICKING: Toolbars....**
2. **Check the box to the left of Reference on the Toolbars tab and Close the Customize dialog box (Figure 15–4).**

**Clip an area from the enlarged acadsig image (Figure 15–5):**

| Prompt | Response |
|---|---|
| Command: | **Image Clip** |
| Select image to clip: | CLICK: **any point on the frame (the outside edge) of the acadsig image** |
| Enter image clipping option [ON/OFF/Delete/ New boundary] <New>: | **<enter>** |
| Enter clipping type [Polygonal/Rectangular] <Rectangular>: | **<enter>** |
| Specify first corner point: <Osnap off> | TYPE: **0,6-3/4<enter>** |

**FIGURE 15–5**
The Clipped acadsig Image

| Prompt | Response |
|---|---|
| Specify opposite corner point: | TYPE: **5-1/4,3-1/4<enter>** |

**Move the acadsig image toward the center of the drawing limits:**

| Prompt | Response |
|---|---|
| Command: | CLICK: **any point on the image frame** |
| Small blue squares (called Grips) appear on each corner of the image: | CLICK: **the square (Grip) on the lower left corner of the image (to make it Hot—it becomes a solid color)** |
| ** STRETCH ** | |
| Specify stretch point or [Base point/Copy/ Undo/eXit]: | PRESS: **the space bar** |
| ** MOVE ** | |
| Specify move point or [Base point/Copy/ Undo/eXit]: | TYPE:**1-1/4,3-1/2<enter>** |

**Insert the acadsig image again on the right side of the page (Figure 15–6):**

| Prompt | Response |
|---|---|
| Command: | **Raster Image…** |
| The Select Image File dialog box appears with acadsig already selected: | CLICK: **Open** |
| The Image dialog box appears: | CLICK: **OK** |
| Specify insertion point <0,0>: | TYPE: **5-1/4,3<enter>** |
| Base image size: Width: 1.000000, Height: 1.837500, Inches Specify scale factor <1>: | TYPE: **2.5<enter>** |

**Insert another image (a picture of a watch) on the left side of the page:**

| Prompt | Response |
|---|---|
| Command: | **Raster Image…** |

FIGURE 15–6
Insert acadsig Again

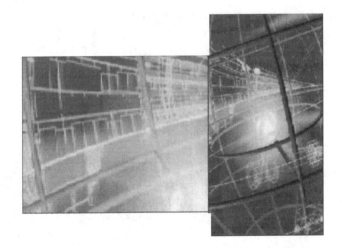

| Prompt | Response |
|---|---|
| The Select Image File dialog box appears with acadsig already selected: | DOUBLE CLICK: **the Sample folder (Figure 15–7)** |
| | CLICK: **Watch** |
| | CLICK: **Open** |
| The Image dialog box appears: | CLICK: **OK** |
| Specify insertion point <0,0>: <Osnap off> | TYPE: **1,6<enter>** |
| Base image size: Width: 1.000000, Height: 1.124464, Inches Specify scale factor <1>: | TYPE: **4<enter>** |

The watch picture is too big, so you will have to scale it down.

**Select the watch raster image.**

| Prompt | Response |
|---|---|
| Command: | CLICK: **any point on the frame of the watch image** |
| Small blue boxes (grips) appear at each corner of the image: | **Center the pickbox on the lower left grip.** |
| | CLICK: **the lower left grip** |

The lower left grip changes to a solid color.

**Scale the watch image to 1/4 its size:**

| Prompt | Response |
|---|---|
| **STRETCH** | |
| Specify stretch point or [Base point/Copy/ Undo/eXit]: | PRESS: **<enter> until the prompt reads as shown in the following Prompt column.** |
| **SCALE** | |
| Specify scale factor or [Base point/Copy/ Undo/Reference/eXit]: | TYPE:**1/4<enter>** |

The watch image is reduced to a smaller size (Figure 15–8).

**FIGURE 15–7**
Select the Watch Image

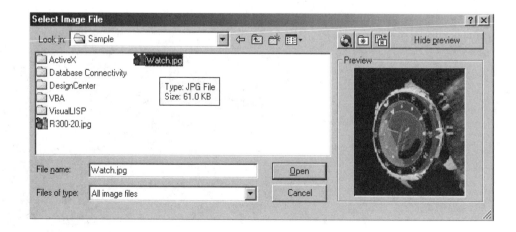

**FIGURE 15–8**
Insert the Watch Image and Scale
It to 1/4 Size

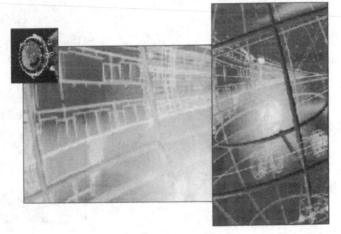

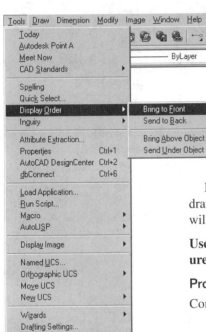

Notice that Figure 15–9 shows the clipped image behind the original image. Your drawing may show the clipped image in front. In any case, complete the next step so you will know how to arrange images in overlapping order.

**Use Display Order to move the clipped image in front of the full acadsig image (Figure 15–9):**

| Prompt | Response |
|---|---|
| Command: | CLICK: **Display Order** |
|  | CLICK: **Bring to Front** |
| Select objects: | CLICK: **any point on the boundary of the clipped image** |
| Select objects: | **<enter>** |

**FIGURE 15–9**
Move the Clipped Image to the Front

FIGURE 15–10
Exercise 15–1 Final Image

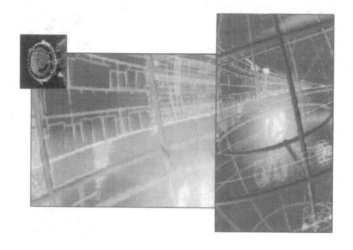

Practice a little with these commands on the Display Order menu. After you are through, your final images should look similar to Figure 15–10.

## Adjusting the Brightness and Contrast of a Raster Image

**Adjust the brightness and contrast of the full acadsig image (Figure 15–11):**

| Prompt | Response |
|---|---|
| Command: | CLICK: **Image Adjust** |
| Select image(s): | CLICK: **any point on the boundary of the full acadsig image and** CLICK: **<enter>** |
| The Image Adjust dialog box appears: | **Move the slider for brightness to 40 and the contrast to 78 as shown in Figure 15–11.** |
| | CLICK: **OK** |

FIGURE 15–11
Image Adjust Dialog Box

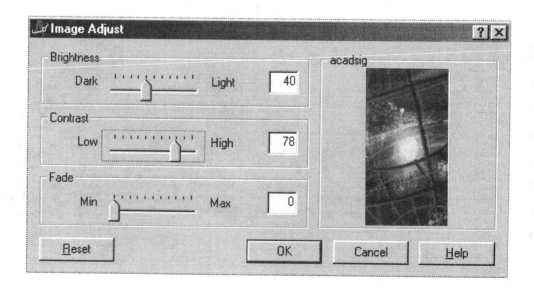

Image Frame

## Turning Raster Image Frames On and Off

**Turn image frames off:**

| Prompt | Response |
|---|---|
| Command: | CLICK: **Image Frame** |
| Enter image frame setting [ON/OFF]<ON>: | TYPE: **OFF<enter>** |

You cannot select an image with the frame turned OFF. If you need to select an image later, you will have to turn the image frame ON again using the Image Frame command.

## Deleting and Detaching Images

When you want to delete one or more images, select them and press the Delete key on your keyboard. You should not delete any of the images you presently have unless you have made a mistake and have more images than are shown in Figure 15–10.

Deleting the images does not detach the image from your drawing. To detach the image, activate the Image Manager (Figure 15–12), select the image file name and CLICK: **Detach**. When the image is detached, it is removed from the drawing database, and all those images are erased from the drawing.

## Save Your Drawing and Exit AutoCAD

When you have completed Exercise 15–1, save your drawing in at least two places, and you can plot or print it.

**FIGURE 15–12**
Image Manager Dialog Box

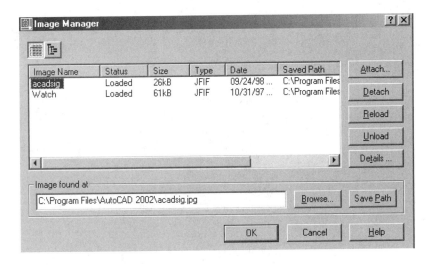

## REVIEW QUESTIONS

1. A raster image is made up of dots.
   a. True     b. False
2. How many raster file types does AutoCAD use?
   a. 1
   b. 4
   c. 14
   d. 25
   e. an unlimited number

3. Which of the following folders contains the Watch raster image used in this chapter?
   a. Sample
   b. AutoCAD 2002
   c. Support
   d. Template
   e. Fonts
4. To select a raster image
   a. Click any point inside the frame.
   b. Click any point outside the frame.
   c. Use a dialog box to select it.
   d. Click any point on the frame.
   e. Type the name of the image.
5. When a raster image is selected
   a. It changes color.
   b. Small blue squares called grips appear on each corner.
   c. Vertical white lines appear on the image.
   d. Horizontal white lines appear on the image.
   e. A round dot appears in the center of the image.
6. When a Scale factor of 1/4 is used with the grips Scale mode
   a. The selected image is reduced to 1/4 its original size.
   b. The selected image is reduced to 1/2 its original size.
   c. The selected image is reduced to 1/25 its original size.
   d. The selected image is enlarged to 4 times its original size.
   e. The selected image is enlarged to 25 times its original size.
7. To activate the Move Grip mode, select the image, pick a grip, and press **<enter>**
   a. Once
   b. Twice
   c. Three times
   d. Four times
   e. Do not press <enter> at all.
8. An image can be made larger or smaller with grips.
   a. True
   b. False
9. When you select Image Clip you have a choice of two types of boundaries to specify. They are
   a. Circular/<Rectangular>
   b. Rectangular/<Elliptical>
   c. Polygonal/<Rectangular>
   d. Circular/<Polygonal>
   e. Elliptical/<Circular>
10. The Display Order command is used to
    a. Show which image was inserted first
    b. Move an image from the bottom of a stack of images to the top
    c. Arrange images in alphabetical order
    d. Arrange images in rows
    e. Arrange images in columns
11. List the command that is used to insert a raster image.

    _____

12. List the command that is used to clip a raster image.

    _____

13. List the command that is used to turn off the frame around raster images.

    _____

14. Write the name of the small blue squares that appear at the corners of a raster image when it is selected.

    _____

15. Describe how to detach a raster image from your drawing.

    _____

# 16 Customizing Toolbars and Menus

## OBJECTIVES

After completing this chapter, you will be able to

- Make new toolbars.
- Add tools to a toolbar.
- Delete tools from a toolbar.
- Move tools from one toolbar to another toolbar.
- Copy tools from one toolbar to another toolbar.
- Delete toolbars.
- Position toolbars.
- Display toolbars.
- Hide toolbars.
- Create and edit tools.
- Make a new menu bar.
- Make a new .mnu (menu) file.
- Copy the acad.mnu file under another name.
- Add macros to a menu.
- Delete commands from a menu.
- Move commands from one position to another.
- Copy commands from one menu to another.
- Delete menus.
- Position menus on the menu bar.
- Load menus.
- Unload menus.

## EXERCISE 16–1
## Customizing Toolbars

AutoCAD allows you to create custom toolbars that allow you to be more productive by arranging tools so they can be found easily and quickly. When you make a new toolbar it has no tools. You have to drag tools onto the new toolbar from the Customize dialog box. In Exercise 16–1 you will start a new toolbar and load it with tools you use frequently. Your final toolbar will look similar to the one shown in Figure 16–1. Turn on the computer and start AutoCAD. The AutoCAD 2002 Today window is displayed.

1. CLICK: **the Create Drawings tab**
2. CLICK: **Wizards**
   CLICK: **Quick Setup**
3. Set drawing Units: **Architectural**
   CLICK: **Next**
4. Set Width: **=11″**
   Set Length: **=8-1/2″**

CLICK: **Finish**

5. **Use SaveAs... to save the drawing on the hard drive with the name CH16-EX1.**

## Making a New Toolbar

**Make a new toolbar (Figures 16–2 and 16–3):**

| Prompt | Response |
|---|---|
| Command: | **Toolbars...** (or CLICK: **any tool with the RETURN button of your pointing device,** then CLICK: **Customize...** at the bottom of the list) |
| The Customize dialog box appears: | CLICK: **the Toolbars tab,** then CLICK: **New...** |
| The New Toolbar dialog box (Figure 16–2) appears: | TYPE: **(your initials)TOOLS** in the Toolbar Name: text box |
| | CLICK: **OK** |

Your new toolbar (Figure 16–3) is displayed. (If the toolbar is not visible, it is hidden behind other toolbars. Either move the other toolbars or turn them off.)

**FIGURE 16–1**
Your New Toolbar

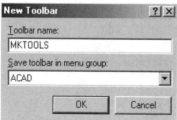

**FIGURE 16–2**
New Toolbar Dialog Box with Your New Name

**FIGURE 16–3**
Your New Toolbar

**FIGURE 16–4**
Move the New Toolbar to the Left
Side of the Screen

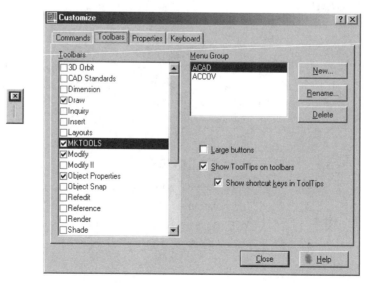

**Part III: Special Topics**

## On Your Own (Figure 16–4)

1. Move your new toolbar to the left side of the screen (Figure 16–4) so it will be to the left of the Customize dialog box. Position your cursor over the toolbar title area, hold down the click button on your mouse, and release the click button when the toolbar is where you want it to be.

### Adding Tools to Toolbars

Add tools to your new toolbar from the Customize dialog box (Figures 16–5, 16–6, 16–7, and 16–8):

Note: If the shape of your toolbar is different from that in the illustration, wait until you have finished adding tools to change its shape. This is explained later in the chapter.

| Prompt | Response |
|--------|----------|
| With the Customize dialog box displayed: | CLICK: **the Commands tab** |
| | CLICK: **Draw** from the list of categories |

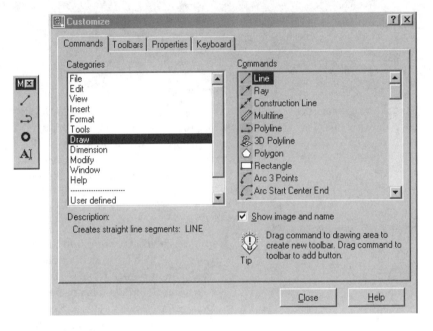

**FIGURE 16–5**
Customize Dialog Box with Draw Category

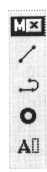

**FIGURE 16–6**
New Toolbar with Line, Polyline, Donut, and Dtext Tools

**FIGURE 16–7**
Select Tools from the Modify Category

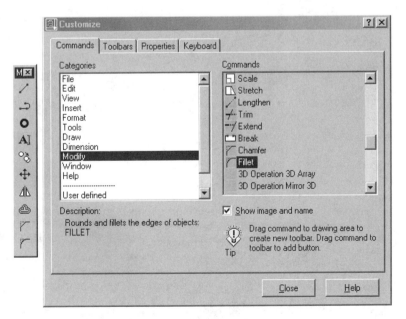

FIGURE 16–8
Select Tools from the Dimension
Category

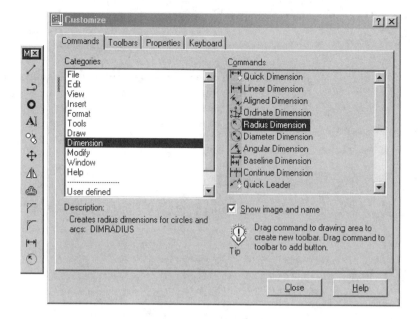

**Prompt**

The tools on the Draw toolbar appear on the right side of the dialog box:

**Response**

Copy the Line tool from the Draw category to your toolbar by moving the cursor so it is over the Line tool, then press the click button and hold it down while you drag the Line tool and release it inside your new toolbar.

Your new toolbar now contains the Line tool:

Copy the Polyline, Donut, and Single Line Text: icons to your toolbar as shown in Figure 16–6. (You will have to click the scroll bar to find the Dtext icon.)

CLICK: the Modify category (Figure 16–7).

Copy the Move, Copy Object, Mirror, Offset, Chamfer, and Fillet tools to your toolbar as shown in Figure 16–7.

CLICK: the Dimension category (Figure 16–8).

Copy the Linear Dimension and Radius Dimension tools to your toolbar as shown in Figure 16–8.

CLICK: Close.

## Deleting Tools from Toolbars

Delete the dimensioning tools from your new toolbar (Figure 16–9):

**Prompt**

Command:

**Response**

Toolbars... (or CLICK: any tool with the RETURN button of your mouse, then CLICK: Customize... at the bottom of the list)

FIGURE 16–9
Customize Toolbars Dialog Box

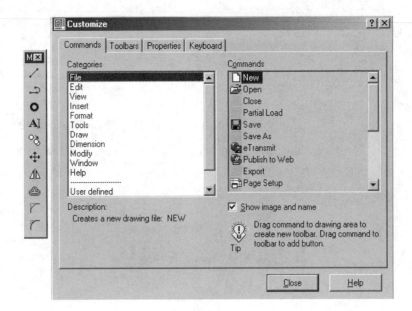

| Prompt | Response |
|---|---|
| The Customize dialog box (Figure 16–9) appears: | CLICK: **the Linear Dimension tool on your toolbar by moving the cursor over the Linear Dimension tool and holding down the click button. Continue holding down the click button and drop the tool into the Customize dialog box.** |
| | **Delete the Radius Dimension tool in a similar manner.** |
| | CLICK: **Close** |

If you accidentally delete a standard tool from a toolbar, you can replace it from the Customize dialog box. If you delete a tool you have customized, you cannot retrieve it.

## Displaying Toolbars

You can display all toolbars (and eliminate your drawing area) or only the ones you use often.

**Display all toolbars:**

| Prompt | Response |
|---|---|
| Command: | TYPE: **-TOOLBAR<enter>** (Be sure to include the hyphen.) |
| Toolbar name (or ALL): | TYPE: **ALL<enter>** |
| Show/Hide: | TYPE: **S<enter>** |

## On Your Own

1. **Hide all toolbars. Follow the same procedure but substitute H<enter> for S<enter>.**

**Display your new toolbar and the Inquiry toolbar (Figure 16–10):**

| Prompt | Response |
|---|---|
| Command: | **Toolbars...** (from the View menu) |

FIGURE 16–10
Display the Inquiry and (your initials)TOOLS Toolbars

| Prompt | Response |
|---|---|
| The Customize dialog box appears: | CHECK: the Inquiry and (your initials)-TOOLS toolbars to display them as shown in Figure 16–10. |
| | CLICK: Close |

## Moving Tools from One Toolbar to Another

**Move the Distance icon from the Inquiry toolbar to your new toolbar (Figure 16–11):**

| Prompt | Response |
|---|---|
| Command: | **Toolbars... (or CLICK: any tool with the RETURN button of your mouse, then CLICK: Customize… at the bottom of the list).** |
| The Customize dialog box appears: | **Hold down the click button over the Distance icon on the Inquiry toolbar and drop it onto your new toolbar (Figure 16–11).** |

When the Customize dialog box is displayed, you can move or copy a tool from one toolbar to another.

## Copying Tools from One Toolbar to Another

**Copy the Distance icon from your new toolbar back to the Inquiry toolbar (Figure 16–11):**

| Prompt | Response |
|---|---|
| With the Customize dialog box still displayed: | **PRESS and HOLD: the Ctrl key while you hold down the click button over the Distance icon on your new menu and drop it onto the Inquiry toolbar (Figure 16–11).** |

FIGURE 16–11
Copying and Moving Tools

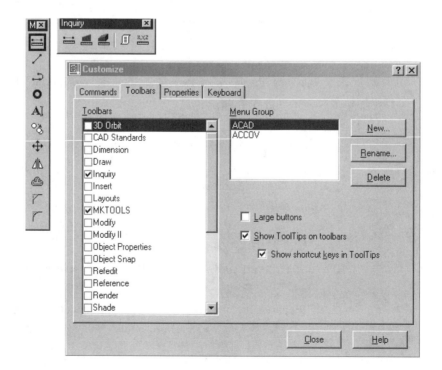

## On Your Own

1. **Copy (not move) the Area icon from the Inquiry toolbar to your new toolbar.**
2. **Close the Customize dialog box.**

## Making New Toolbars and Letting AutoCAD Name Them

You can also make new toolbars by choosing the Commands tab in the Customize dialog box and dragging an icon off the dialog box and dropping it anywhere but onto another toolbar.

**Make two new toolbars and let AutoCAD name them for you (Figure 16–12):**

| Prompt | Response |
|---|---|
| Command: | **Toolbars...** (or CLICK: **any tool with the RETURN button of your mouse, then** CLICK: **Customize… at the bottom of the list**). |
| The Customize dialog box appears | CLICK: **the Command tab** |
| | **Hold down the click button over any of the icons in the Commands list (any category will do) and drop it onto an open area off the Customize dialog box (Figure 16–12).** |
| | **Repeat the preceding procedure so you have two toolbars as shown in Figure 16–12.** |
| | CLICK: **Close** |

You could now proceed to load tools onto these toolbars as described previously.

## Deleting Toolbars

You may delete toolbars from the Customize dialog box. AutoCAD will ask you if you really want to delete the toolbar because you cannot undo this action. If you delete one of the major toolbars such as the Draw toolbar, you can recreate it by making a new toolbar, naming it the Draw toolbar and dragging tools onto it from the Draw Category after clicking the Com-

**FIGURE 16–12**
Creating Two New Toolbars, Toolbar1 and Toolbar2

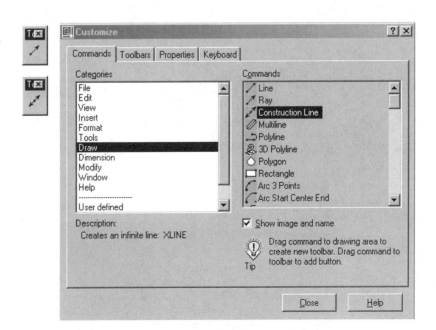

mands tab in the Customize dialog box. You can also reload the acad.mnu file from Options on the Tools menu on the menu bar. To reload the acad.mnu DOUBLE CLICK: **Menu, Help,** and **Miscellaneous File Names,** then DOUBLE CLICK: **Menu File,** then DOUBLE CLICK: **C:\program files\AutoCAD 2002\support\acad.mnu file,** then CLICK: the **acad.mnu** file, then CLICK: **Open,** then CLICK: **OK.** When the warning appears, CLICK: **Yes.** You will replace any customizing you have done with the standard ACAD menu.

**Delete the two new toolbars that AutoCAD named for you:**

| Prompt | Response |
|---|---|
| With the Customize dialog box displayed: | **Use the scroll bars in the Toolbars list box to locate Toolbar1, and use the click button to highlight it.** |
| | CLICK: **Delete** |
| The AutoCAD warning appears —Delete toolbar ACAD.Toolbar1? | CLICK: **Yes** |
| | **Delete Toolbar2 in a similar manner.** |
| | CLICK: **Close** |

## Changing the Shape of a Floating Toolbar

You can change the shape, name, and appearance of a floating toolbar, move it, dock it, float a docked toolbar, reposition tools on a toolbar, and add space between tools.

Let's start with a relatively uncluttered screen.

**Hide all toolbars:**

| Prompt | Response |
|---|---|
| Command: | TYPE: **-TOOLBAR<enter>** |
| Enter toolbar name or [ALL]: | TYPE: **ALL<enter>** |
| Enter an option [Show/Hide]: | TYPE: **H<enter>** |

**Display the (your initials)TOOLS Toolbar:**

| Prompt | Response |
|---|---|
| Command: | **Toolbars . . .** |
| The Customize dialog box appears: | CHECK: **the (your initials)TOOLS check box** |
| | CLICK: **Close** |
| The floating (your initials)TOOLS toolbar appears: | |

A floating toolbar can be reshaped from vertical to horizontal or somewhere in between. The horizontal toolbar can also be reshaped to vertical. Docked toolbars cannot be reshaped.

**Change the shape of the floating (your initials)TOOLS toolbar:**

If your toolbar is vertical:

| Prompt | Response |
|---|---|
| Command: | CLICK: **the bottom border so that the cursor changes to a double arrow and hold down the click button while you move your mouse up.** (You will have to move it over halfway before a change occurs.) |

**Note:** You can also CLICK: the top border, hold down the click button, and move your mouse down.

If your toolbar is horizontal:

| Prompt | Response |
|--------|----------|
| | CLICK: a side border so that the cursor changes to a double arrow and hold down the click button while you move your mouse to the left or right. |

## Renaming a Toolbar

There will be a time when you will need to change the name of a toolbar. This is how to do it.

**Rename the (your initials)TOOLS toolbar (Figure 16–13):**

| Prompt | Response |
|--------|----------|
| Command: | **Toolbars...** |
| The Customize dialog box appears: | **Locate (your initials)TOOLS in the Toolbars list box and highlight it as shown in Figure 16–13.** |
| | CLICK: **Rename...** |
| The Rename Toolbar dialog box appears with the word (your initials)TOOLS highlighted: | TYPE: **MY TOOLBAR** |
| | CLICK: **OK** |
| The Cutomize dialog box appears: | CLICK: **Close** |

The (your initials)TOOLS toolbar is now renamed MYTOOLBAR.

## On Your Own

1. **Rename the MYTOOLBAR to the (your initials)TOOLS toolbar.**

**FIGURE 16–13**

Selecting the (your initials)TOOLS Toolbar and Renaming It

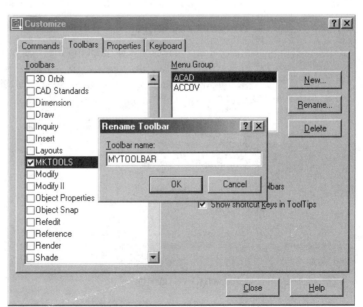

FIGURE 16–14
Check Large Buttons

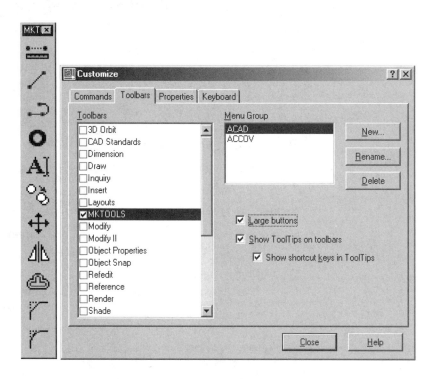

## Changing the Appearance of the Toolbar

The Customize dialog box allows you to change the size of the tools on the toolbar, whether toolbars are displayed in color or black and white, or whether tooltips (the text that appears when you hold the cursor over the tool) are displayed.

**Change the appearance to large buttons (Figure 16–14):**

| Prompt | Response |
|---|---|
| Command: | **Toolbars...** |
| The Customize dialog box appears: | CHECK: **Large buttons as shown in Figure 16–14.** |
| | CLICK: **Close** |

The (your initials)TOOLS toolbar now has large tools.

## Moving Toolbars

You can move toolbars by clicking the toolbar name area and holding down the click button while dragging the toolbar. You can also move toolbars by clicking the area between the outside border of the toolbar and the area surrounding the tools, holding down the click button, and moving the toolbar where you want it.

**Move the (your initials)TOOLS toolbar:**

| Prompt | Response |
|---|---|
| Command: | CLICK: **the area between the outside border of the (your initials)TOOLS toolbar and the area surrounding the tools (or the area at the top of the toolbar), hold down the click button, and move the toolbar to another area.** |

## Docking a Toolbar

FIGURE 16–15
A Docked Toolbar

It is sometimes helpful to get the toolbars out of the drawing area. They can be placed on the outside edges of the screen in what is known as a *docked position*, as shown in Figure 16–15.

## On Your Own (Figure 16–15)

1. Change the icons back to small buttons.
2. Dock the (your initials)TOOLS toolbar on the left side of the screen by moving it as you did previously, except move it to the extreme left side so it appears as shown in Figure 16–15.

## Floating a Docked Toolbar

Toolbars can be removed from their docked position by clicking the area between the tool squares and the toolbar border or the title area, holding down the click button, and moving the toolbar.

## On Your Own

1. Float the (your initials)TOOLS toolbar.

## Repositioning the Tools on a Toolbar

You can change the position of tools on a toolbar from the Customize dialog box. When you click the tool and move it, you must drag the tool more than halfway across the tool that already exists in the new location.

**Reposition a tool on the (your initials)TOOLS toolbar (Figure 16–16):**

FIGURE 16–16
(your initials)TOOLS Toolbar with
Area Tool Position Changed

| Prompt | Response |
|---|---|
| Command: | **Toolbars...** |
| The Customize dialog box appears: | **Position your cursor over the Area tool, hold down the click button, and move the Area tool so it is a little more than halfway past the Distance tool.** |

The (your initials)TOOLS toolbar appears as shown in Figure 16–16.

## Adding Space between Tools on a Toolbar

If you prefer to have a little space between tools on the toolbar, you can change the spacing from the Customize dialog box.

**Add space between tools on the (your initials)TOOLS toolbar (Figure 16–17):**

| Prompt | Response |
|---|---|
| The Customize dialog box appears: | **Position your cursor over the Area tool, hold down the click button, and move the Area tool to the right or left or down but not more than half the distance of the next tool.** |
| | **Repeat the preceding steps for all tools on the (your initials)TOOLS toolbar so it appears as shown in Figure 16–17, then return them to their original position.** |
| | **Close the Customize dialog box.** |

FIGURE 16–17
Adding Space between Tool Icons

## Creating and Modifying Tools

You can create your own tools by modifying or combining the tools that are supplied with AutoCAD.

### Basic Keystrokes Used to Modify Tool Macros

AutoCAD recognizes commands in a macro (a command line) as if they were typed from the keyboard. The following keystrokes represent pressing the Enter key, an operator response, canceling a command, a transparent command, and international versions:

| | |
|---|---|
| ; | The semicolon is the same as pressing Enter. |
| \ | The backslash tells AutoCAD to wait for the operator to do something. |
| ^C^C | Two Ctrl-Cs cancel a previous command and any option of that command. |
| ' | An apostrophe preceding the command allows it to be used transparently. |
| __ | An underscore enables commands to work on international versions of AutoCAD. |

The best way to understand how these work is to create a tool using some of these keystrokes.

### Creating Tools

**Create a tool (Figures 16–18 and 16–19):**

| Prompt | Response |
|---|---|
| Command: | **Place your cursor over the Donut tool on the (your initials)TOOLS toolbar and press the RETURN button on your mouse, then** CLICK: **Customize… at the bottom of the list.** |
| The Customize dialog box appears: | **Place your cursor over the Donut tool on the (your initials)TOOLS toolbar and press the RETURN button on your mouse again.** |
| The right click menu appears: | CLICK: **Properties** |
| The Button Properties tab (Figure 16–18) appears: | **Change the information in the Name: box, the Description: box, and the Macro associated with this button: box as shown in Figure 16–19.** |

**FIGURE 16–18**
Button Properties Tab

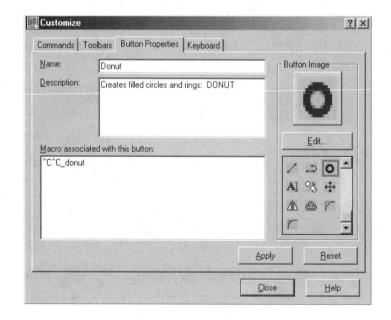

**FIGURE 16–19**
Button Properties Tab for Solid
1/8″ Donut

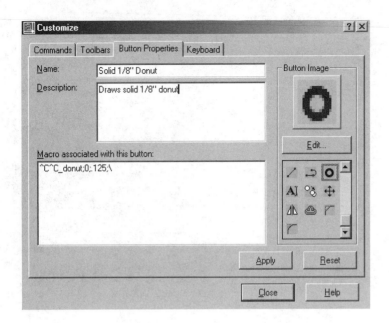

**Prompt**

**Response**

(The line in the Macro associated with
this button: box should read:
^C^C_donut;0;.125;\)

Let's look at the elements of this line:

**^C^C_donut**    This is already here and it means that you are canceling previous commands (^C^C), making the command available to international ver-
sions (_), and activating the Donut command (donut).

**;**    This acts as <enter>, as if you had typed DONUT and then pressed <enter>.

The donut command then asks you for an inside diameter.

**0;**    This tells AutoCAD you want an inside diameter of 0, as if you had typed 0 and
pressed <enter>.

The donut command then asks you for an outside diameter.

**.125;**    This tells AutoCAD you want an outside diameter of .125, as if you had typed
.125 and pressed <enter>.

The donut command then asks you to pick (or type coordinates for) the Center of the
donut.

**\**    The backslash tells AutoCAD you will pick the center or type coordinates—an opera-
tor response.

### Changing or Making Tool Icons

When you create a new command, AutoCAD allows you to change an existing icon or
create an entirely new one with the Button Editor. When you open the Button Editor (Figure 16–20), you have an abbreviated paint program available to you. The four tools at the
top of the editor from left to right are:

**Pencil tool**    Changes one pixel at a time.
**Line tool**    Draws lines in a selected color.
**Circle tool**    Draws circles in a selected color. Hold down the click button on your
mouse to select the center of the circle; continue to hold the click button as you drag the circle to the desired radius.
**Erase tool**    Erases pixels as you move the cursor with the click button depressed
over the area you want to erase.

FIGURE 16–20
Button Editor Dia-
log Box

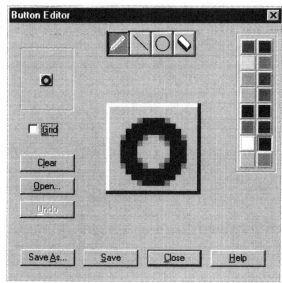

The color bar to the right allows you to select from 16 colors by selecting one with the click button.

The **Grid** button gives you a grid.
The **Clear** button clears the image.
The **Open** button opens images you have saved previously.
The **Undo** button undoes the previous single action.

SaveAs... , Save, Close, and Help perform the standard functions for the tool icons.

**Change the new tool icon to a solid circle (Figures 16–21 and 16–22):**

| Prompt | Response |
|---|---|
| With the Button Properties tab displayed: | CLICK: **Edit...  in the Button Image area.** |
| The Button Editor dialog box appears: | **Click the same color in the color bar as the donut image if it is not already selected.** |
| | **Use the Pencil tool to color all pixels of the inside of the donut as shown in Figure 16–21.** (Hold down the click |

FIGURE 16–21
Color the Inside of the Donut Icon

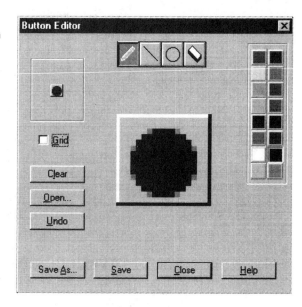

**FIGURE 16-22**
(your initials TOOLS Toolbar with the Solid Donut Tool

**FIGURE 16-23**
(your initials)TOOLS Toolbar with the Donut Tool Added

| Prompt | Response |
|---|---|
| | button with the Pencil tool selected and move it across the area.) |

You could now save this icon to a file but you do not need to at this time.

| Prompt | Response |
|---|---|
| Button Editor dialog box appears: | CLICK: **Close** |
| Would you like to save the changes made to your button? | CLICK: **Yes** |
| The Button Properties tab appears: | CLICK: **Apply** |
| | CLICK: **Close** |

Your (your initials)TOOLS toolbar should now look like Figure 16–22. When you hold the cursor over the new tool, its tooltip now reads Solid 1/8″ Donut.

### On Your Own (Figure 16–23)

1. **Add the original donut command to the (your initials)TOOLS toolbar (from the Draw category) so it appears as shown in Figure 16–23.**

2. **Close the Customize dialog box.**

3. **Save your drawing in two places.**

4. **Exit AutoCAD.**

## EXERCISE 16–2
## Customizing Menus

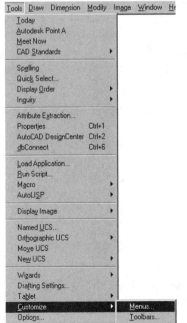

The structure of the AutoCAD menu makes it easy to customize by rearranging commands on the menus, adding new commands, rearranging the menus, and creating keyboard aliases. Sometimes having fewer menus on the menu bar is better than having the full menu. If you occasionally need a command that is no longer on the menu bar, you can type it from the keyboard or access it from a toolbar. Exercise 16–2 will assume that you need a menu bar that has only the File, Edit, View, Insert, Format, Tools, Draw, and Modify menus. Your final menu will look similar to the one shown in Figure 16–24. Turn on the computer and start AutoCAD. The AutoCAD 2002 Today window is displayed.

### Removing and Replacing Menus from the Menu Bar

1. CLICK: **the Create Drawings tab**

2. CLICK: **Wizards**

3. CLICK: **Quick Setup**

4. Set drawing Units: **Architectural**
   CLICK: **Done**

5. **Use SaveAs... to save the drawing on the hard drive with the name CH16-2.**

**FIGURE 16–24**
Shortened Menu Bar

FIGURE 16–25
CLICK: File in the Menu Bar: List
to Remove

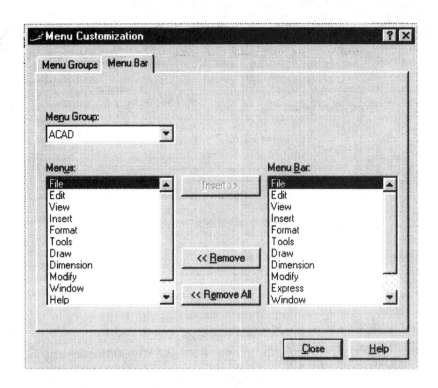

**Remove the File and Edit menus from the menu bar (Figure 16–25):**

| Prompt | Response |
|---|---|
| Command: | CLICK: **Customize, then Menus...** |
| The Menu Customization dialog box appears: | CLICK: **the Menu Bar tab** |
| | CLICK: **ACAD** in the Menu Group list |
| The Menu Bar page appears: | CLICK: **File** in the Menu Bar: list as shown in Figure 16–25 |
| | CLICK: << **Remove** |
| File is removed from the Menu Bar list: | CLICK: **Edit** in the Menu Bar: list |
| | CLICK: << **Remove** |
| Edit is removed from the Menu bar list. | |

**Replace the File and Edit Menus on the menu bar (Figure 16–26):**

| Prompt | Response |
|---|---|
| Menu Customization dialog box: | With **View** highlighted on the Menu Bar: list, CLICK: **File** in the Menus: list as shown in Figure 16–26. |
| | CLICK: **Insert>>** |
| File appears in the menu bar list: | With **View** highlighted on the Menu Bar: list, CLICK: **Edit** in the Menus: list |
| | CLICK: **Insert>>** |
| Edit appears in the menu bar list. | |

## On Your Own

**1. Remove the Dimension, Image, Window, and Help menus from the menu bar.**

**2. Your menu bar appears as shown in Figure 16–27.**

Exercise 16–2 is now complete. Continue with Exercise 16–3.

FIGURE 16–26
CLICK: File in the Menus: List to
Insert

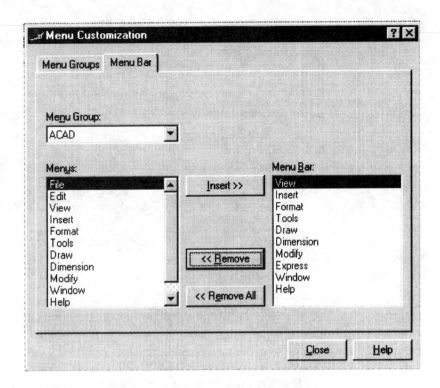

FIGURE 16–27
Your New Menu Bar

# EXERCISE 16–3
## Making a New Menu File

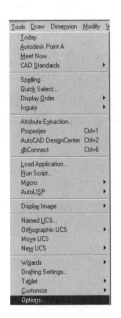

### Returning the Complete Menu Bar

### On Your Own (Figure 16–28)

1. **Exercise 16–3 requires that the complete menu bar be present, so begin by return-ing all menus to their original location as shown in Figure 16–28 using Customize, then Menus.... You will have to remove and insert some menus twice to get the cor-rect location.**

2. **Close the Menu Customization dialog box.**

In Exercise 16–3 you will make a new menu file that contains new macros that you add to menus on the menu bar. Commands in the new menu file are also rearranged, deleted, and copied. To do that you must begin by copying the standard AutoCAD menu file under another name.

### Locating the File Containing the Standard AutoCAD Menu (acad.mnu)

**Find out where the acad.mnu file is located so you can copy it to a floppy disk under the name menu1.mnu (Figure 16–29):**

| Prompt | Response |
|---|---|
| Command: | **Options...** |
| The Options dialog box appears: | CLICK: **the Files tab** |
| The Files tab appears as shown in Figure 16–29: | DOUBLE CLICK: **Menu, Help, and Miscellaneous File Names** |

**FIGURE 16–28**
Original Menu Bar Arrangement

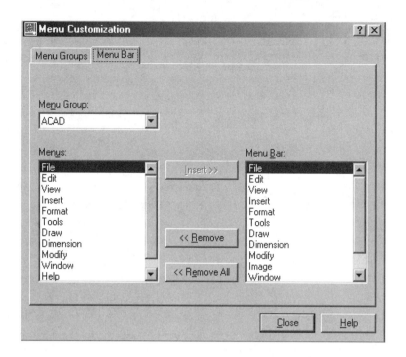

**FIGURE 16–29**
Locating the Menu File

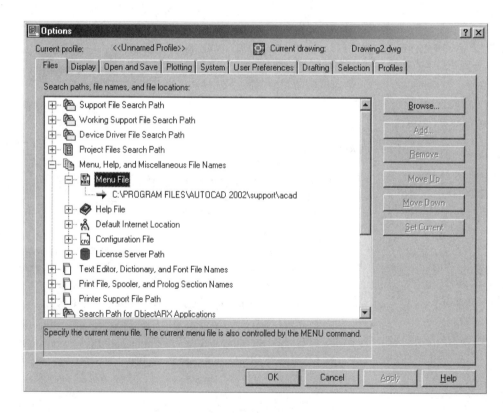

| Prompt | Response |
|--------|----------|
| | DOUBLE CLICK: **Menu File** |
| | **Make a note of the drive, directory, and subdirectory where the Menu File is located. In this case: C:\PROGRAM FILES\AUTOCAD 2002\support\acad** |
| | CLICK: **OK** |

## Copying the acad.mnu File to an Empty Floppy Disk in the A or B Drive

Copy the acad.mnu file to a floppy disk (Figures 16–30, 16–31, and 16–32):

| Prompt | Response |
|---|---|
| | Place an empty floppy disk in the A drive. |
| Command: | CLICK: **Start** |
| | CLICK: **Program Files** |
| | CLICK: **Windows Explorer** (Figure 16–30) |
| The Exploring dialog box appears: | CLICK: **the Program Files folder** |
| The contents of the Program Files folder are displayed: | DOUBLE CLICK: **AutoCAD 2002 folder** |
| The contents of the folder are displayed: | DOUBLE CLICK: **the Support folder** |
| The Support files are displayed: | **Hold down the ctrl key and** CLICK: **the acad.mnu and acad.mnl files** (Figure 16–31). |
| | CLICK: **File- Send To- 3-1/2 Floppy [A:]** or to whichever drive contains your floppy disk (Figure 16–32). (You may also drag and drop the file onto the floppy diskette.) |
| The copying From "SUPPORT to A:" message appears. | |

**FIGURE 16–30**
Start Windows Explorer

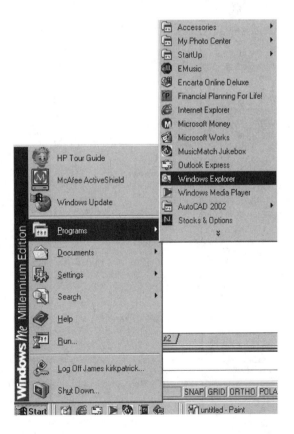

FIGURE 16–31
CLICK: the acad.mnl and
acad.mnu Files While Holding
Down the Ctrl Key

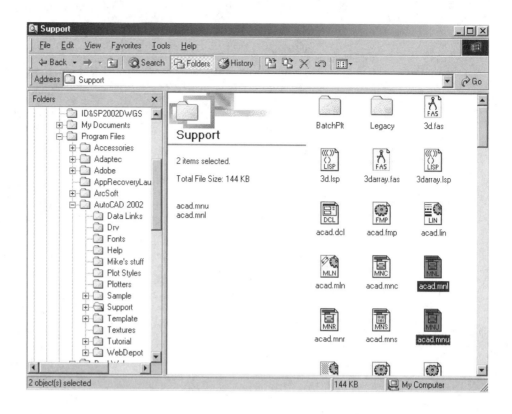

FIGURE 16–32
Send the File to a Floppy Disk

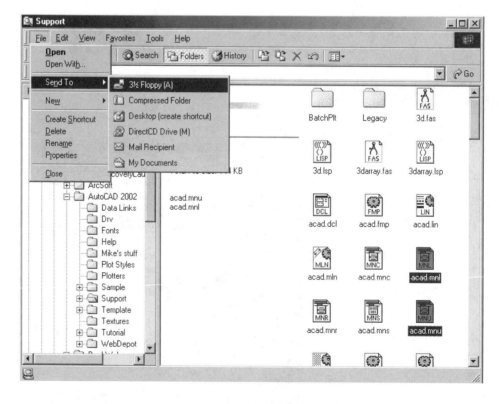

## Renaming the acad.mnu File

**Rename the acad.mnu file on the floppy disk Menu1.mnu (Figures 16–33 and 16–34):**

| Prompt | Response |
|---|---|
| | CLICK: **the vertical scroll bar in the Folders box and scroll up to the floppy drive containing the copied acad.mnu file.** |

**FIGURE 16–33**
Rename the acad.mnu File
Menu1.mnu

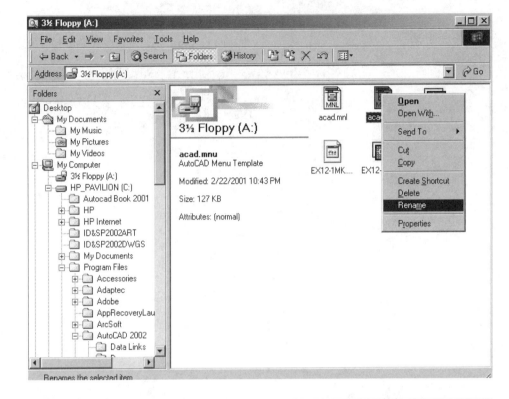

**FIGURE 16–34**
TYPE: **Menu1.mnu** to Rename
the acad.mnu File

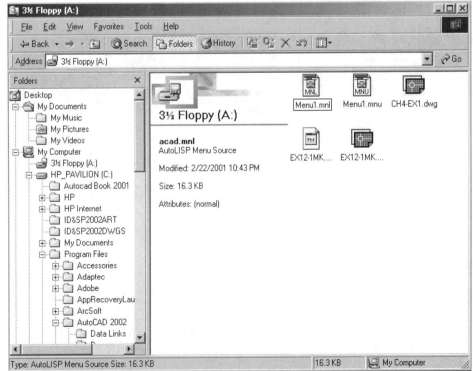

| Prompt | Response |
|---|---|
| | CLICK: **the floppy drive** |
| The contents of the floppy drive are displayed in the right panel: | RIGHT CLICK: **the acad.mnu file** |
| | CLICK: **Rename** (Figure 16–33) |
| The acad.mnu file is highlighted: | TYPE: **Menu1.mnu <enter>** (Figure 16–34) |

## On Your Own

1. **Rename the acad.mnl file to Menu1.mnl in a similar manner.**

## Opening the Menu1.mnu File So You Can Modify the Menu

**Open the Menu1.mnu file on the floppy disk using a text editor such as WordPad (Figure 16–35):**

| Prompt | Response |
|---|---|
| | CLICK: **File-Open** (Figure 16–35) |
| | CLICK: **All documents in the files of type: list** |
| The Menu1.mnu file is displayed: | **Maximize the display.** |

## Relabeling the MENUGROUP

**Relabel the MENUGROUP so AutoCAD will recognize this as a menu different from the original (Figure 16–36):**

| Prompt | Response |
|---|---|
| The Menu1.mnu file is displayed: | **Scroll down to the label ***MENUGROUP = ACAD and change ACAD to MENU1** (Figure 16–36). |

**FIGURE 16–35**
Open the Menu1.mnu File with WordPad in Accessories

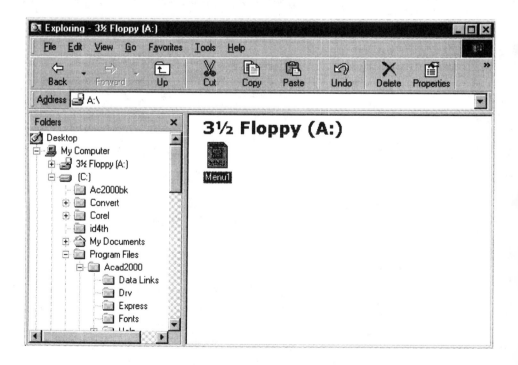

```
//          (Rights in Technical Data and Computer Software), as applicable.
//
//
//       NOTE:  AutoCAD looks for an ".mnl" (Menu Lisp) file whose name is
//              the same as that of the menu file, and loads it if
//              found.  If you modify this menu and change its name, you
//              should copy acad.mnl to <yourname>.mnl, since the menu
//              relies on AutoLISP routines found there.
//
//
//
//       Default AutoCAD NAMESPACE declaration:
//
***MENUGROUP=MENU1|

//
//    Begin AutoCAD Digitizer Button Menus
//
***BUTTONS1
```

**FIGURE 16–36**
Change ***MENUGROUP=ACAD to ***MENUGROUP=MENU1

## On Your Own

1. **Scroll down through the menu through the AutoCAD Button Menus (PRESS: the down arrow) so you become familiar with what the menu looks like.**

2. **Locate the line "Begin AutoCAD Pull-down Menus."**

## Deleting Commands from a Menu on the Menu Bar

You will now find the menus on the menu bar labeled ***POP0 through ***POP11. Begin modifying this menu by deleting some commands on ***POP7 that are not used a great deal.

**Locate the ***POP7 pull-down menu:**

| Prompt | Response |
|---|---|
| | CLICK: **Find...** (from Search or Edit on the menu bar) |
| The Find dialog box (Figure 16–37) appears: | TYPE: ***POP7 in the Find what: text box |
| | CLICK: **Find Next** |
| | **Close the Find dialog box by clicking the X in the upper right corner.** |

**Delete the following commands from the ***POP7 menu:**

| | | |
|---|---|---|
| Line | CircleTTR | Boundary |
| Ray | Splinex | Mtext |
| Xline | Spline | Solid |
| Circle3pt | | |

To delete a line of text, move your cursor to one end of the line, hold down the click button on your mouse, drag the cursor across the line to highlight the text, or CLICK: at the start of the line and press the Delete key. PRESS: **Backspace** to delete the space between lines.

If you make a mistake, CLICK: **Undo** from the Edit menu.

## Adding Macros to a Menu on the Menu Bar

Adding macros to a menu requires that you know what the command is going to ask, and what response is required. For example, the Insert command when typed from the keyboard asks:

FIGURE 16–37
Find Dialog Box

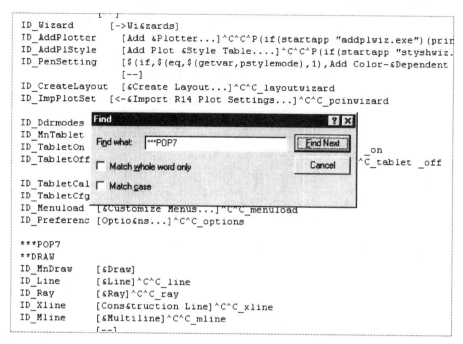

```
ID_Wizard        [->Wi&zards]
ID_AddPlotter    [Add &Plotter...]^C^C^P(if(startapp "addplwiz.exe")(prin
ID_AddPlStyle    [Add Plot &Style Table....]^C^C^P(if(startapp "styshwiz.
ID_PenSetting    [$(if,$(eq,$(getvar,pstylemode),1),Add Color-&Dependent
                 [--]
ID_CreateLayout  [&Create Layout...]^C^C_layoutwizard
ID_ImpPlotSet    [<-&Import R14 Plot Settings...]^C^C_pcinwizard

ID_Ddrmodes
ID_MnTablet
ID_TabletOn                                                      _on
ID_TabletOff                                               ^C_tablet _off

ID_TabletCal
ID_TabletCfg
ID_Menuload      [&Customize Menus...]^C^C_menuload
ID_Preferenc     [Optio&ns...]^C^C_options

***POP7
**DRAW
ID_MnDraw        [&Draw]
ID_Line          [&Line]^C^C_line
ID_Ray           [&Ray]^C^C_ray
ID_Xline         [Cons&truction Line]^C^C_xline
ID_Mline         [&Multiline]^C^C_mline
                 [--]
```

Find dialog box:

Find what: ***POP7   [Find Next]   [Cancel]

☐ Match whole word only
☐ Match case

| Prompt | Response |
|---|---|
| Enter block name or [?]: | **Your response is to TYPE: the block name and PRESS: <enter>.** |
| Insertion point: | **Your response is to CLICK: a point with your mouse, or TYPE: X and Y coordinates and PRESS: <enter>. The symbol in a macro that requires an operator response is the backslash (\).** |
| X scale factor <1>/Corner/XYZ: | **If you want the X scale factor to be 1, the correct response is to PRESS: <enter>. The symbol in a macro that represents <enter> is the semicolon (;).** |
| Y scale factor (default = X): | **If you want the Y scale factor to be the same as the X scale factor, the correct response is to PRESS: <enter>. The symbol in a macro that represents <enter> is the semicolon (;).** |
| Rotation angle <0>: | **If you want the rotation angle to be the same as the original block orientation, the correct response is to PRESS: <enter>. If you want to change the rotation angle often, leave this semicolon off the end of the macro.** |

In this exercise you will add four macros to the Draw pull-down menu. The first macro when clicked will execute the Insert command, insert a drawing named BLOCK1 (which you will have to make and save on a floppy disk in the A drive), insert it at an X scale factor of 1, Y scale factor of X, and it will ask you for a rotation angle. The other three macros will do the same thing for BLOCK2, BLOCK3, and BLOCK4.

Now add the macros to ***POP7 on the menu bar.

**Type the four lines at the top of the ***POP7 menu as shown in Figure 16–38:**

Give careful attention to the arrangement of the text and the exact position of each character. If you make even the slightest change, it will most likely be reflected in your menu.

FIGURE 16–38
Four Macros at the Top of
***POP7

```
***POP7
**DRAW
ID_MnDraw      [&Draw]
ID_BLOCK1      [BLOCK1]^C^C-INSERT;A:BLOCK1;\;;
ID_BLOCK2      [BLOCK2]^C^C-INSERT;A:BLOCK2;\;;
ID_BLOCK3      [BLOCK3]^C^C-INSERT;A:BLOCK3;\;;
ID_BLOCK4      [BLOCK4]^C^C-INSERT;A:BLOCK4;\;;
ID_Mline       [&Multiline]^C^C_mline
               [--]
ID_Pline       [&Polyline]^C^C_pline
ID_3dpoly      [&3D Polyline]^C^C_3dpoly
ID_Polygon     [Pol&ygon]^C^C_polygon
ID_Rectang     [Rectan&gle]^C^C_rectang
               [--]
ID_MnCircle    [->&Circle]
ID_CircleRad   [Center, &Radius]^C^C_circle
ID_CircleDia   [Center, &Diameter]^C^C_circle \_d
               [--]
ID_Circle2pt   [&2 Points]^C^C_circle _2p

ID_CircleTTT   [<-T&an, Tan, Tan]^C^C_circle _3p _tan \_tan \_tan \
ID_Donut       [&Donut]^C^C_donut
ID_MnEllipse   [->&Ellipse]
ID_EllipseCe   [&Center]^C^C_ellipse _c
ID_EllipseAx   [Axis, &End]^C^C_ellipse
```

## Moving Commands from One Position to Another

Commands are easily moved from one position to another. Now that you have deleted several commands, the arrangement of the commands on the Draw menu does not follow any particular pattern. Move the commands so that they are in alphabetical order. Begin by moving the Arc commands to the top of the menu.

**Move the Arc commands to the top of the menu (Figures 16–39 and 16–40):**

FIGURE 16–39
Highlight the Arc Commands and
Cut Them to the Windows Clipboard

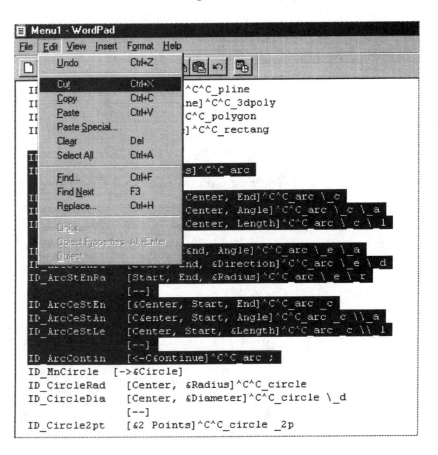

FIGURE 16–40
Arc Commands Are Moved

```
***POP7
**DRAW
ID_MnDraw      [&Draw]
ID_MnArc       [->&Arc]
ID_Arc3point   [3 &Points]^C^C_arc
               [--]
ID_ArcStCeEn   [&Start, Center, End]^C^C_arc \_c
ID_ArcStCeAn   [S&tart, Center, Angle]^C^C_arc \_c \_a
ID_ArcStCeLe   [St&art, Center, Length]^C^C_arc \_c \_l
               [--]
ID_ArcStEnAg   [Start, E&nd, Angle]^C^C_arc \_e \_a
ID_ArcStEnDi   [Start, End, &Direction]^C^C_arc \_e \_d
ID_ArcStEnRa   [Start, End, &Radius]^C^C_arc \_e \_r
               [--]
ID_ArcCeStEn   [&Center, Start, End]^C^C_arc _c
ID_ArcCeStAn   [C&enter, Start, Angle]^C^C_arc _c \\_a
ID_ArcCeStLe   [Center, Start, &Length]^C^C_arc _c \\_l
               [--]
ID_ArcContin   [<-C&ontinue]^C^C_arc ;
ID_BLOCK1      [BLOCK1]^C^C-INSERT;A:BLOCK1;\;;
ID_BLOCK2      [BLOCK2]^C^C-INSERT;A:BLOCK2;\;;
ID_BLOCK3      [BLOCK3]^C^C-INSERT;A:BLOCK3;\;;
ID_BLOCK4      [BLOCK4]^C^C-INSERT;A:BLOCK4;\;;
```

| Prompt | Response |
|---|---|
| Command: | **Position your cursor at the beginning of the Arc commands, hold down the click button, and drag the cursor so that the lines are highlighted as shown in Figure 16–39.** |
| | CLICK: **Cut** |
| | **Position your cursor to the left of ID_BLOCK1.** |
| | CLICK: **Paste** |

The menu appears as shown in Figure 16–40.

## Copying Commands from One Menu to Another

You may decide that you would like to have other commands from other menus on the Draw menu. You can copy them from other menus using the Copy command found on the Edit menu of WordPad, then use Paste to place the copy in the correct locations.

## Saving Menu1.mnu and Returning to AutoCAD

## On Your Own

1. Save your Menu1.mnu file to your floppy disk using the Save command from the WordPad File menu. Be sure to include the .mnu extension.

2. Exit WordPad and Explorer.

3. Activate AutoCAD.

4. Make four drawings of items you often use and WBLOCK or save them on the floppy disk in the A drive with the names BLOCK1, BLOCK2, BLOCK3, and BLOCK4.

## Loading a Menu

Menus are loaded with the MENULOAD command. You can TYPE: **MENULOAD <enter>** from the keyboard, or CLICK: **Customize,** then **Menus...** from Tools on the AutoCAD menu bar. Then CLICK: the Menu Groups tab, then Browse... and locate your menu. When the menu is loaded, it then displays the commands in the new menu arrangement. You must also CLICK: the menu file from Options on the Tools menu on the menu bar. To provide a shortcut for loading the menu go directly to Options.

**Load Menu1.mnu from the floppy disk in the A drive (Figures 16–41, 16–42, and 16–43):**

| Prompt | Response |
|---|---|
| Command: | **Options...** |
| The Options dialog box with the Files tab is displayed: | DOUBLE CLICK: **Menu, etc.** |
| | DOUBLE CLICK: **Menu File** |
| | HIGHLIGHT: **the location of the Menu File** |
| | CLICK: **Browse** |
| | CLICK: **3-1/2 Floppy [A:] or whichever drive contains your floppy disk with the Menu1.mnu file on it.** |
| | CLICK: **Template Menu (*.mnu) in the Files of type: box** |
| | CLICK: **Menu1.mnu so the name appears in the File name: box as shown in Figure 16–41.** |
| | CLICK: **Open** |
| The Options dialog box (Figure 16-42) appears with A:\ menu1 highlighted: | CLICK: **OK** |
| The AutoCAD customization warning appears: | CLICK: **Yes** |
| The Menu1.mnu file loads: | CLICK: **OK** |
| | CLICK: **Draw on the menu bar** |

**FIGURE 16–41**
Select the Menu1.mnu File on the Floppy Disk

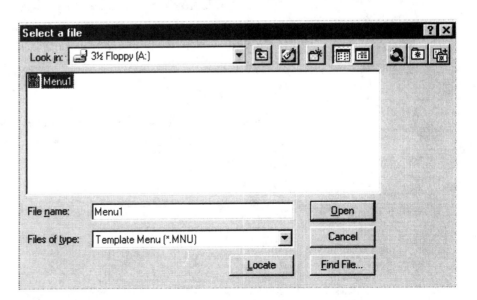

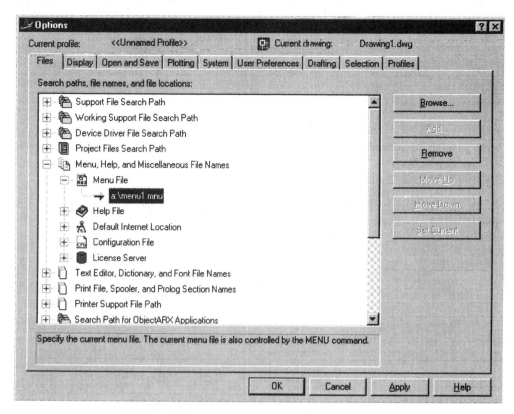

FIGURE 16–42
Options Dialog Box with a:\menu1.mnu as the Menu File

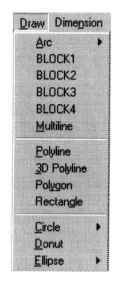

FIGURE 16–43
***POP7 on the Menu1 Menu

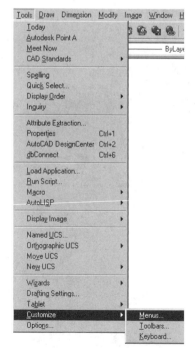

Your menu should appear as shown in Figure 16–43. Test the commands.

If you have any errors, CLICK: **Menu1.mnu** at the bottom of the screen to return to WordPad and the Menu1.mnu file. Make any necessary changes and return to AutoCAD.

Because you loaded the Menu1.mnu file previously, you will get the "Error loading menu file" message when you try to load the file again. You will have to unload the Menu1.mnu file before you can load your new version of it again.

## Unloading, Reloading, and Saving a Menu

To unload a menu, CLICK: **Customize,** then **Menus...,** CLICK: **the Menu Groups tab,** then CLICK: **Unload** to unload the Menu1.mnu file, since it will be the one highlighted. Then CLICK: **Browse** and locate the Menu1.mnu file on your floppy disk again to reload it.

## On Your Own

1. **When your menu is correct, use WordPad SaveAs... to save it on two floppy disks.**

2. **Return to AutoCAD and load the acad.mnu file.**

3. **Exit AutoCAD.**

**Note:** If you lose the Menu Bar, TYPE: **MENU<enter>** and open the acad.mnu file or the acad.mnc to reload it.

# EXERCISE 16–4
## Making a New Toolbar

Make a toolbar named My Blocks containing four of your most commonly used blocks.

1. Make four drawings of items you use often or call them up from an old drawing.

2. Wblock each drawing onto a floppy disk in the A drive using the names A:BLOCK1, A:BLOCK2, A:BLOCK3, and A:BLOCK4 or any other names you want.

3. Make a new toolbar named My Blocks.

4. Create four tools using icons that you will recognize as tools that insert your blocks. Name and describe them as you choose. Use the following as the Macro: for BLOCK1:

   ^C^C_insert;A:BLOCK1;
   Repeat the Macro: for BLOCK2, BLOCK3, and BLOCK4.

   Place the four tools on the new toolbar My Blocks.

# EXERCISE 16–5
## Modifying a Menu File

Modify Menu1 in the following manner:

1. Move the Find... command from the Edit menu on the menu bar to the Modify menu on the menu bar.

2. Rearrange the Modify menu on the menu bar so that all commands are in alphabetical order.

# REVIEW QUESTIONS

1. To make a new toolbar, CLICK: Toolbars..., then CLICK: the Toolbars tab in the Customize dialog box and SELECT:
   a. New
   b. Delete
   c. Customize
   d. Custom
   e. File

2. When you delete a standard tool from a toolbar you cannot retrieve it.
   a. True      b. False

3. To display all toolbars, TYPE: **-TOOLBAR <enter>**, then TYPE: **ALL <enter>**, then TYPE:
   a. **S <enter>**
   b. **D <enter>**
   c. **H <enter>**
   d. **A <enter>**
   e. **T <enter>**

4. To copy a tool from one toolbar to another, CLICK: the tool and drag it to the other toolbar while holding down which key?
   a. Shift
   b. Alt
   c. Ctrl
   d. Esc
   e. F1

5. AutoCAD will make a new toolbar and name it for you when you CLICK: the Commands tab from the Customize dialog box, CLICK: any tool from any category, and
   a. PRESS: New
   b. Drop it on an existing toolbar
   c. Drop it in an open area
   d. PRESS: Ctrl
   e. PRESS: Esc

6. The standard AutoCAD menu file is named
   a. aclt
   b. Menu1
   c. acad
   d. AutoCAD
   e. lt

7. The Windows program used to copy and rename the AutoCAD menu file in this chapter was
   a. WordPad
   b. Files
   c. Windows Explorer
   d. Notepad
   e. StartUp

8. The item that was changed to allow AutoCAD to recognize the Menu1 menu file as different from the standard AutoCAD menu file was
   a. MENU1
   b. The File menu on the menu bar
   c. ***POP0
   d. ***MENUGROUP=
   e. The Button menu

9. The first response AutoCAD asks from you when the Insert command is activated is
   a. Insertion point:
   b. X scale factor
   c. Y scale factor
   d. Block name
   e. Rotation angle:

10. Which of the following displays the macro command name on the menu?
    a. [BLOCK1]
    b. _BLOCK1
    c. BLOCK1<enter>
    d. BLOCK1
    e. (BLOCK1)

Complete.

11. To change tools to large buttons, which dialog box is used?

_____

12. List the areas where toolbars can be docked.

_____

13. Describe how to move a tool from one position on a toolbar to another position.

_____

_____

14. Describe what the ; character is used for in making macros.

_____

15. Describe what ^C^C is used for in making macros.

_____

16. Write a macro to draw a donut with a .125 inside diameter and a .250 outside diameter.

_____

17. What do you pick from the Button Properties dialog box to change a tool's icon?

_____

18. Which command do you use to load a menu?

_____

19. List the name of the menu that is numbered ***POP2.

_____

20. List the name and the extension of the standard AutoCAD menu file.

_____

## OBJECTIVES

After completing this chapter, you will be able to

☐ Describe the differences between working in 2D and 3D.
☐ Use Elevation, Thickness, UCS, and Viewports to create 3D objects in space.
☐ Use 3D Views to display different views of the same object.
☐ Change the location and orientation of the UCS while creating 3D models.
☐ Correctly use the following commands and settings:

| | |
|---|---|
| Properties... | Mview |
| 2D Solid | UCS |
| Elevation | Plan |
| Thickness | 3D Views |
| Hide | Pspace |
| Mspace | Viewports |

## INTRODUCTION

While creating the drawings in previous chapters you were working in two-dimensional AutoCAD and making two-dimensional drawings of objects. This chapter introduces you to drawing in three dimensions; now you will be creating models. Although all the Auto-CAD Draw and Modify commands work in 3D, your concept of what you are drawing must now change. You are creating models, not drawing pictures.

## EXERCISE 17–1, PART 1
### Creating 3D Models Using Elevation and Thickness

When you have completed Exercise 17–1, Part 1, your drawing will look similar to Figure 17–1. In Figure 17–1, four viewports display different viewpoints of a 3D model containing several shapes of varying heights. These heights are called *thicknesses*. Until now you have worked in only the X and Y directions. The Z dimension will now be added to give thickness (vertical shape) to your models. Creating the model in Exercise 17–1, Part

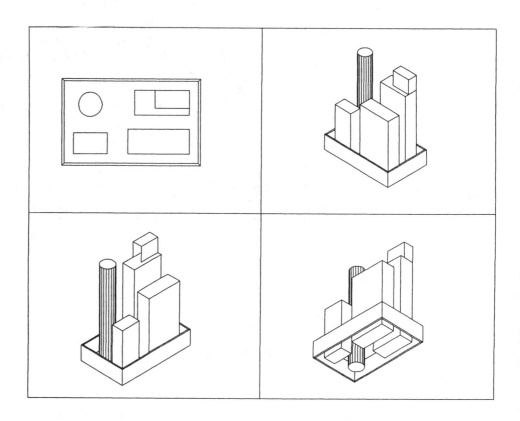

1, demonstrates drawing in 3D using the command ELEV (Elevation) and thickness. When you have finished drawing the model, you will use the VPORTS and VPOINT commands to create the four-viewport display.

To begin Exercise 17–1, Part 1, turn on the computer and start AutoCAD. The Auto-CAD 2002 Today window is displayed.

1. CLICK: **the Create Drawings tab**

2. CLICK: **Wizards**

   CLICK: **Quick Setup**

3. Set drawing Units: **Architectural**

   CLICK: **Next>**

4. Set drawing Width: **60′** × Length: **60′**

   CLICK: **Finish**

5. **Use SaveAs... to save the drawing on the hard drive with the name CH17-EX1.**

6. Set Grid: **12″**

7. Set Snap: **6″**

8. Create the following Layers:

| LAYER NAME | COLOR | LINETYPE | LINEWEIGHT |
|------------|-------|----------|------------|
| 3d-r | Red | Continuous | Default |
| 3d-b | Blue | Continuous | Default |
| 3d-g | Green | Continuous | Default |

The dimensions of the model are shown in Figures 17–2 and 17–3.

**FIGURE 17–2**
Front Elevation Dimensions

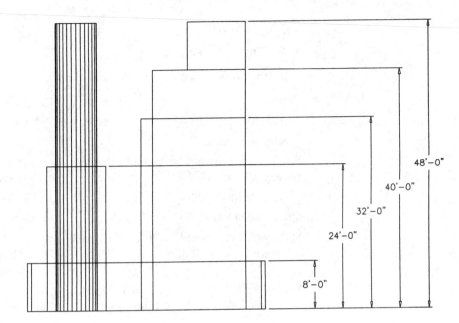

48'-0"
40'-0"
32'-0"
24'-0"
8'-0"

**FIGURE 17–3**
Plan View Dimensions

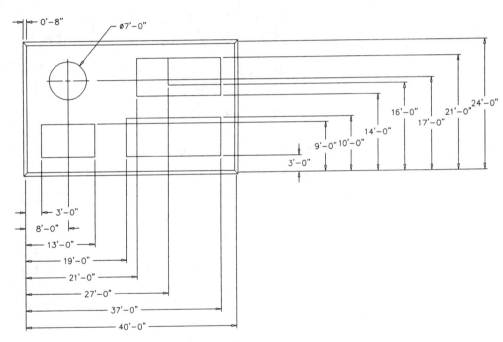

0'-8"
ø7'-0"
24'-0"
21'-0"
17'-0"
16'-0"
14'-0"
10'-0"
9'-0"
3'-0"
3'-0"
8'-0"
13'-0"
19'-0"
21'-0"
27'-0"
37'-0"
40'-0"

# ELEV

**Set the elevation and thickness for the outside wall (Figure 17–2):**

| Prompt | Response |
|---|---|
| Command: | TYPE: **ELEV<enter>** |
| Specify new default elevation <0'-0">: | **<enter>** |
| Specify new default thickness <0'-0">: | TYPE: **8'<enter>** |

**Note:** The plan view of an object has a viewpoint of 0,0,1, meaning that you are above the object looking straight down on it.

Now everything you draw will be at elevation 0'-0" (the ground level for this model) with a thickness of 8'. Don't be concerned when you don't see any thickness for your shapes when you draw them in the following part of this exercise. Remember, you are looking directly down on the plan view of the model (0,0,1 coordinates). You will see the thickness of the model shapes when you change the viewpoint of the model later in the exercise.

## On Your Own

**1. Set Layer 3d-r current.**

**Draw the outside wall (Figure 17–3):**

| Prompt | Response |
|---|---|
| Command: | **Polyline** (or TYPE: **PL<enter>**) |
| Specify start point: | TYPE: **10',32'<enter>** |
| Specify next point or [Arc/Close/Halfwidth/ Length/Undo/Width]: | TYPE: **W<enter>** |
| Specify starting width <0'-0">: | TYPE: **8<enter>** |
| Specify ending width <0'-8">: | **<enter>** |
| Specify next point or [Arc/Close/Halfwidth/ Length/Undo/Width]: | **With Ortho ON, move the mouse to the right and** TYPE: **40'<enter>** |
| Specify next point or [Arc/Close/Halfwidth/ Length/Undo/Width]: <Ortho on> | **Move the mouse down and** TYPE: **24'<enter>** |
| Specify next point or [Arc/Close/Halfwidth/ Length/Undo/Width]: | **Move the mouse to the left and** TYPE: **40'<enter>** |
| Specify next point or [Arc/Close/Halfwidth/ Length/Undo/Width]: | TYPE: **C<enter>** |

The outside wall is complete. Setting the UCS origin to the lower left corner of the polyline (outside wall) will simplify drawing.

**Set the UCS origin to the lower left corner of the polyline:**

| Prompt | Response |
|---|---|
| Command: | TYPE: **UCS<enter>** |
| Enter an option [New/Move/orthoGraphic/ Prev/Restore/Save/Del/Apply/?/World] <World>: | TYPE: **O<enter>** |
| Specify new origin point <0,0,0>: | TYPE: **INT<enter>**(or CLICK: **Osnap-Intersection**) |
| of | CLICK: **the lower left corner of the polyline** |

**Set the elevation and thickness for the cylinder (Figure 17–2):**

| Prompt | Response |
|---|---|
| Command: | TYPE: **ELEV<enter>** |
| Specify new default elevation <0'-0">: | **<enter>** |
| Specify new default thickness <8'-0">: | TYPE: **48'<enter>** |

Now everything you draw will be at elevation 0 with a thickness of 48'.

## On Your Own

**1. Set Layer 3d-b current.**

**Draw the cylinder (Figure 17–3):**

| Prompt | Response |
|---|---|
| Command: | **Circle-Center,Diameter** |

| Prompt | Response |
|---|---|
| Specify center point for circle or [3P/2P/Ttr (tan tan radius)]: | TYPE: **8',17'<enter>** |
| Specify diameter of circle: | TYPE: **7' <enter>** |

The circle is complete. Next, the rectangle shape in front of the circle is drawn. Don't change the elevation or thickness. Draw the rectangle with a thickness of 48', instead of 24', as Figure 17–2 shows. Later in this exercise, the Properties... command will be used to change the thickness to the correct 24'.

**Using the 2D Solid command, draw the rectangle shape in front of the circle (Figure 17–3):**

| Prompt | Response |
|---|---|
| Command: | **2D Solid** (or TYPE: **SO <enter>**) |
| Specify first point: | TYPE: **3',3'<enter>** |
| Specify second point: | TYPE: **13',3'<enter>** |
| Specify third point: | TYPE: **3',9'<enter>** |
| Specify fourth point or <exit>: | TYPE: **13',9'<enter>** |
| Specify third point: | **<enter>** |

**Set the elevation and thickness for the front right rectangle shape (Figure 17–2):**

| Prompt | Response |
|---|---|
| Command: | TYPE: **ELEV<enter>** |
| Specify new default elevation <0'-0">: | TYPE: **<enter>** |
| Specify new default thickness <48'-0">: | TYPE: **32'<enter>** |

**Using the 2D Solid command, draw the front right rectangle shape (Figure 17–3):**

| Prompt | Response |
|---|---|
| Command: | **2D Solid** (or TYPE: **SO <enter>**) |
| Specify first point: | TYPE: **19',3'<enter>** |
| Specify second point: | TYPE: **37',3'<enter>** |
| Specify third point: | TYPE: **19',10'<enter>** |
| Specify fourth point or <exit>: | TYPE: **37',10'<enter>** |
| Specify third point: | **<enter>** |

**Set the elevation and thickness for the bottom rear right rectangle shape (Figure 17–2):**

| Prompt | Response |
|---|---|
| Command: | TYPE: **ELEV<enter>** |
| Specify new default elevation <0'-0">: | **<enter>** |
| Specify new default thickness <32'-0">: | TYPE: **40'<enter>** |

**Using the 2D Solid command, draw the bottom rear right rectangle shape (Figure 17–3):**

| Prompt | Response |
|---|---|
| Command: | **2D Solid** (or TYPE: **SO <enter>**) |
| SOLID Specify first point: | TYPE: **21',14'<enter>** |
| Specify second point: | TYPE: **37',14'<enter>** |
| Specify third point: | TYPE: **21',21'<enter>** |
| Specify fourth point or <exit>: | TYPE: **37',21'<enter>** |

| Prompt | Response |
|---|---|
| Specify third point: | <enter> |

The smallest rectangle shape is sitting on top of the shape you just created, so its *elevation* will be the *thickness* of the previous solid. You can set that now.

**Set the elevation and thickness for the smallest rectangle shape (Figure 17–2):**

| Prompt | Response |
|---|---|
| Command: | TYPE: **ELEV<enter>** |
| Specify new default elevation <0'-0">: | TYPE: **40'<enter>** |
| Specify new default thickness <40'-0">: | TYPE: **8'<enter>** |

**Note:** The values of both the Elevation and Thickness settings can be positive or negative.

Now everything you draw will be at elevation 40' (the top of the 40' tall solid) with a thickness of 8'.

## On Your Own

**1. Set Layer 3d-g current.**

**Draw the smallest rectangle shape (Figure 17–3):**

| Prompt | Response |
|---|---|
| Command: | **2D Solid** (or TYPE: **SO <enter>**) |
| Specify first point: | TYPE: **27',16'<enter>** |
| Specify second point: | TYPE: **37',16'<enter>** |
| Specify third point: | TYPE: **27',21'<enter>** |
| Specify fourth point or <exit>: | TYPE: **37',21'<enter>** |
| Specify third point: | <enter> |

The AutoCAD System Variables ELEVATION and THICKNESS can also be used to set elevation and thickness. They are described in Exercise 17–2.

## Viewports (VPORTS)

**Note:** For the VPORTS command to work, the system variable TILEMODE must be set to 1 (ON). This is the default, so if VPORTS does not work, set TILEMODE to 1.

**Use the Viewports command to divide the screen into four viewports:**

| Prompt | Response |
|---|---|
| Command: | TYPE: **VPORTS<enter>** or CLICK: **Viewports-4 Viewports** |

The Viewports dialog box appears with the
New Viewports tab:

CLICK: **Four: Equal**

CLICK: **OK**

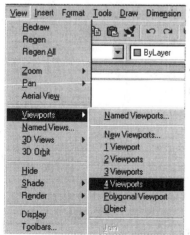

The display area is now divided into four viewports. The active viewport, outlined with a solid line, displays the lines of the cursor when the cursor is moved into the active viewport.

# 3D VIEWPOINT (VPOINT) Command Line Options

Now let's take a look at the model you have drawn. 3D Viewpoint is the command used in this chapter for viewing 3D models. There are three means of selecting a viewing point (the location of the eye that is looking at your model) when you TYPE: **VPOINT** **<enter>**. (3D Orbit can also be used. This command is discussed in detail in Chapter 18.)

**<View point>**  Using this option, you may TYPE: the X, Y, and Z coordinates of the viewpoint from the keyboard, and PRESS: <enter>.

**axes**  PRESS: <enter> at the VPOINT prompt. The AutoCAD compass and axis tripod appear. You can select a viewpoint by picking a point on the AutoCAD compass.

**Viewpoint Presets**  This option allows you to specify the viewpoint by entering two angles—one determines the angle in the X-Y plane from the X axis and the other determines the Z angle from the X-Y plane.

## On Your Own

1. TYPE: **FILL<enter>, then** TYPE: **OFF<enter> to save regeneration time.**

2. **Use Regen All to regenerate all viewports.**

3. **Select the upper right viewport as the current viewport by moving the cursor to any point in that viewport and picking it.**

4. **Set ELEVATION and THICKNESS to 0.**

Next, the 3D Viewpoint command is used to select different viewpoints for the model in each viewport.

**Select the viewpoint for the upper right viewport by typing the X, Y, and Z coordinates of the viewpoint (Figure 17–4):**

| Prompt | Response |
|---|---|
| Command: | TYPE: **VPOINT<enter>** |
| Specify a viewpoint or [Rotate] <display compass and tripod>: | TYPE: **1,-1,1<enter>** |

Figure 17–4 shows the view that appears. Figure 17–5 shows the results of typing other coordinates:

- □ The upper left viewport is the plan view (0,0,1).
- □ The upper right viewport shows the viewpoint 1,-1,1. This means that the viewing eye has been moved one unit to the right, one unit in front, and one unit above the object.
- □ The lower left viewport (-1,-1,1) shows that the viewing eye has been moved one unit to the left, one unit in front, and one unit above the object.
- □ The lower right viewport (1,-1,-1) shows the view resulting from moving the viewing eye one unit to the right, one unit in front, and one unit below the object.

## On Your Own

1. **Experiment with typing different viewpoints if you like.**

2. **Return to the arrangement shown in Figure 17–4.** TYPE: **PLAN<enter>, then <enter> again, or** TYPE: **0,0,1 for the X, Y, and Z coordinates to return to the plan view.**

3. **Click the lower right viewport to make it active.**

**Note:** Using the VPOINT command always causes a regeneration of the model drawing and displays the drawing as Zoom Extents.

**Note:** If a display in any viewport is off center, use Pan to center the display. If it is too large, use Zoom-Dynamic to reduce the size and to center the display in the viewport.

**FIGURE 17–4**
Four Viewports with One 3D
Viewpoint

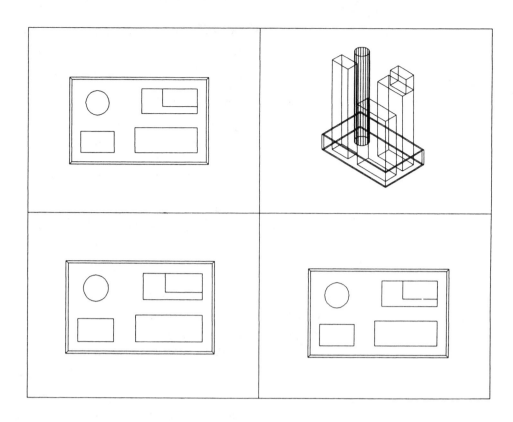

**FIGURE 17–5**
Standard Viewpoints

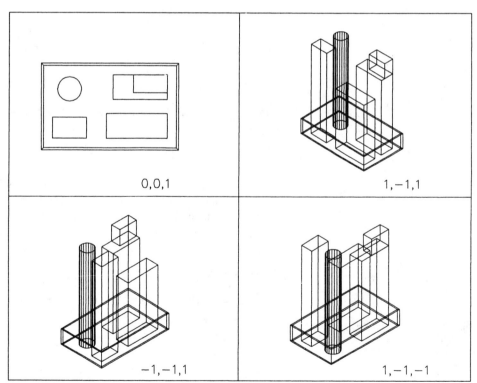

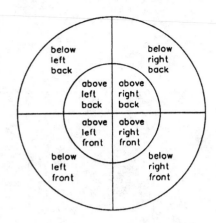

**FIGURE 17–6**
The AutoCAD Compass

**Use the VPOINT command to view the AutoCAD compass (Figure 17–6):**

| Prompt | Response |
|---|---|
| Command: | TYPE: **VPOINT<enter>** |
| | (The AutoCAD tripod may also be selected from the 3D Views on the View menu on the menu bar.) |
| Specify a viewpoint or [Rotate] <display compass and tripod>: | **<enter>** |

The AutoCAD compass (Figure 17–6) and axis tripod appear. As you move the cursor inside the circles, the tripod with its X, Y, and Z axes moves to give you an idea of what the resulting display will be. When the tripod appears to have the desired orientation, pick that spot inside the compass to produce the desired viewpoint.

Study Figure 17–6 for a few moments to obtain an understanding of what each area on the compass signifies. Any point selected within the four parts of the smaller, inner circle is a viewpoint above the object. Any point selected within the four parts of the larger outer circle is a viewpoint below the object. Any point above the horizontal line is a viewpoint behind the object. Any point below the horizontal line is a viewpoint in front of the object. Any point to the right of the vertical line is looking at the right side of the object; any point to the left of the vertical line is the left side. Figure 17–7 shows examples of eight different clicks on the compass.

**Select the viewpoint for the lower right viewport by clicking a point on the AutoCAD compass (Figure 17–5):**

| Prompt | Response |
|---|---|
| The AutoCAD compass is visible. | **Click a point below the horizontal line and to the right of the vertical line, in between the inner circle line and the outer circle line, to create a view similar to the view shown in Figure 17–7B.** |

**Warning:** 3D Viewpoint is only a point from which the view is taken. Nothing is moved; nor are multiple objects displayed. This is all the same model, so if you do anything to move or alter the model itself in one view, you are doing it to all views. Keep in mind the distinction between viewing and creating a model.

## 3D Views Menu Options

**Viewpoint Presets**   The Viewpoint Presets dialog box, Figure 17–8, appears when 3D Views-Viewpoint Presets is clicked from the View menu in the menu bar.

*Absolute to WCS*—When this button is selected, the resulting viewpoint is relative to the World UCS.

*Relative to UCS*—When this button is selected, the resulting viewpoint is relative to the UCS that is current in the drawing at the time.

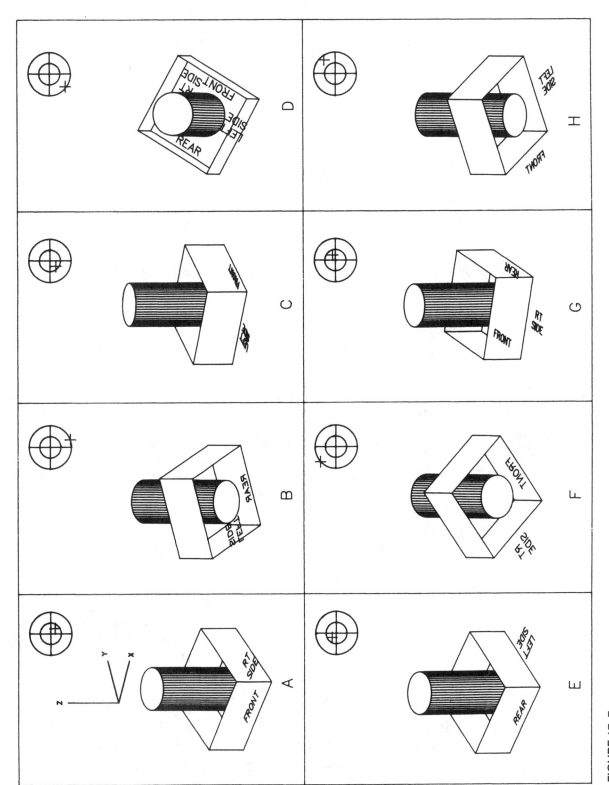

**FIGURE 17-7**
Compass Viewpoints

462

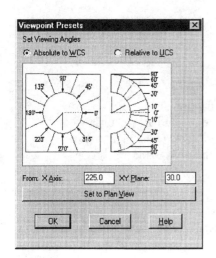

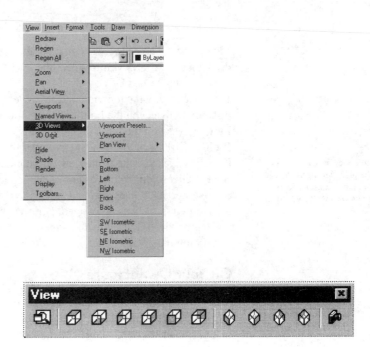

**FIGURE 17–8**
Viewpoint Presets Dialog Box

*From X Axis: Button and Chart*—Specifies the viewing angle from the X axis. The button allows you to type the angle; the chart above it allows you to specify a new angle by clicking the inner region on the circle. The red arm indicates the current angle; the black arm, the new angle. The chart, consisting of a square with a circle in it, may be thought of as a viewpoint looking down on the top of an object:

| | |
|---|---|
| **270** | Places your view directly in front of the object. |
| **315** | Places your view to the right and in front of the object. |
| **0** | Places your view on the right side of the object. |
| **45** | Places your view to the right and behind the object. |
| **90** | Places your view behind the object. |
| **135** | Places your view to the left and behind the object. |
| **180** | Places your view on the left side of the object. |
| **225** | Places your view to the left and in front of the object. |

*From XY Plane: Button and Chart*—Specifies the viewing angle from the X-Y plane. The button allows you to type the angle, and the chart above it allows you to specify a new angle by clicking the inner region on the half circle. Consisting of two semicircles, the chart allows you to specify whether the viewpoint is to be above or below the object:

| | |
|---|---|
| **0** | Places your view directly perpendicular to the chosen angle. For example, a view of 270 on the left chart and 0 on the right chart places the viewpoint directly in front of the object. |
| **10 to 60** | Places your view above the object. |
| **90** | Places your view perpendicular to the top view of the chosen angle. |
| **−10 to −60** | Places your view below the object. |
| **−90** | Places your view perpendicular to the bottom view of the chosen angle. |

*Set to Plan View*—Sets the viewing angles to plan view (270,90) relative to the selected UCS.

Now, let's look at other 3D Views options:

**Viewpoint**  The AutoCAD compass and Axis tripod appear.
**Plan View**  Allows you to select the plan view of the current UCS, the World UCS, or a saved and named UCS.
**Top**  Gives you the top view of the model.
**Bottom**  Gives you the bottom view of the model.
**Left**  Gives you the left side view of the model.
**Right**  Gives you the right side view of the model.
**Front**  Gives you the front view of the model.
**Back**  Gives you the back view of the model.
**SW Isometric**  Gives you an isometric view from the front, to the left, above.
**SE Isometric**  Gives you an isometric view from the front, to the right, above.
**NE Isometric**  Gives you an isometric view from the back, to the right, above.
**NW Isometric**  Gives you an isometric view from the back, to the left, above.

## On Your Own (Figure 17–8)

1. **Click the lower left viewport to make it current.**

2. **Use the Viewport Presets dialog box to set the viewpoint of the lower left viewport; click the 225° angle in the left chart, and the 30° angle in the right chart as shown in Figure 17–8.**

Your view should now look similar to the view in Figure 17–5.

Study the different methods for selecting viewpoints in 3D until you find the one or two methods you feel most comfortable with.

Next, let's correct the height of the rectangle shape that is in front of the cylinder.

## To Change the Thickness of Part of a Model

The Properties or CHPROP command can be used to change to 24′ the thickness of the solid (the rectangle shape in front of the circle) that is presently 48′. Any viewport may be current; it may be easiest to use the plan view.

**Use the Properties command to change the thickness of the solid in front of the circle:**

| Prompt | Response |
|---|---|
| Command: | **Click the rectangle shape in front of the circle.** |
| Command: | **Properties...** (or TYPE: **MO<enter>**) |
| The Properties-Solid dialog box appears: | DOUBLE CLICK: **the 48′ in the Thickness box and** TYPE: **24′** |
| | CLICK: **the X in the upper right corner to close** |
| | PRESS: **the Esc key twice** |

## To Change the Elevation of Part of a Model

Elevation can be changed in the same manner. You can also use the Move command and use relative coordinates to move any object in the Z direction. (For example, @0,0,48′ moves the object 48′ upward; @0,0,-48′ moves the object 48′ downward.) You may also change the elevation by typing **CHANGE<enter>** then selecting Properties by typing **P<enter>** and the Elevation option by typing **E<enter>**.

## HIDE

When you use the Hide command, the drawing is regenerated and all lines of the model that are covered by surfaces in front of them are suppressed. The next time the drawing is regenerated, all lines of the model become visible again.

**Note:** The front view is a 90° clockwise rotation of the plan view of the object looking straight into it. Left side, right side, and rear views are also 90° rotations.

**Note:** Single Line Text (DTEXT) does not accept a THICKNESS setting. You can, however, change the thickness of some text fonts from 0 to any positive value. Use the Properties... command to change text thickness.

## On Your Own

**1. Select the upper right viewport to make it current.**

**Use the Hide command to hide surfaces that are behind other surfaces (Figure 17–9):**

| Prompt | Response |
|---|---|
| Command: | **Hide** (or TYPE: **HI\<enter\>**) |

The resulting display in the upper right viewport is shown in Figure 17–9. Sometimes when surfaces touch, the Hide command produces incorrect results. If your display does not show the bottom line of the top block as a solid line, as in Figure 17–10, the following section will help you correct it.

**FIGURE 17–9**
Correct Result of the Hide
Command

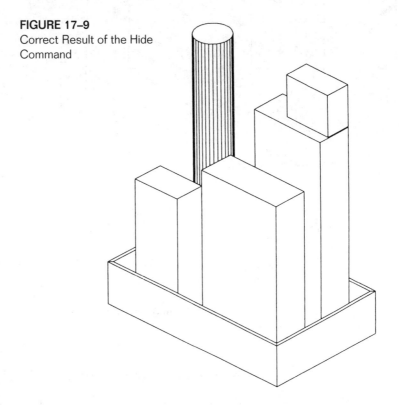

## Incorrect Results of the Hide Command

The bottom line of the top solid does not show (Figure 17–10). When surfaces touch, the Hide command displays unpredictable results. To correct the display, either move the top box up a little or make the supporting box a little shorter (less thick).

**Correct the display (Figure 17–11):**

Note: Properties… can also be used to correct this hide problem.

| Prompt | Response |
|---|---|
| Command: | TYPE: **CHPROP\<enter\>** |
| Select objects: | **D1** (click the lower box) |
| Select objects: | **\<enter\>** |
| Enter property to change [Color/LAyer/ LType/ltScale/LWeight/Thickness]: | TYPE: **T\<enter\>** |
| Specify new thickness <40'-0">: | TYPE: **39'11\<enter\>** |
| Enter property to change [Color/LAyer/ LType/ltScale/LWeight/Thickness]: | **\<enter\>** |
| Command: | TYPE: **HI\<enter\>** |

The display now looks like Figure 17–9.

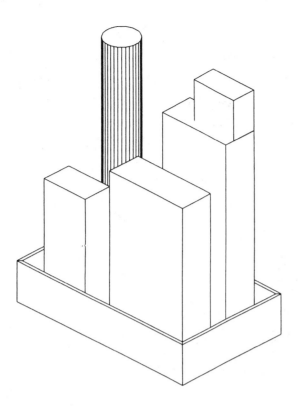

**FIGURE 17–10**
Incorrect Results of the Hide Command

**FIGURE 17–11**
Correcting Incorrect Results of the Hide Command

You may solve in a similar manner other problems that you encounter. Cylinders inside other cylinders, such as a vertical support inside of a circular base, may produce lines that do not hide correctly. To correct the problem, increase the distance between the cylinder and the base by making the hole slightly bigger or the cylinder slightly smaller. A little experimentation will be required.

When you have corrected your hiding problem (if you had one) the drawing is complete.

## Saving the Viewport Configuration and Restoring It in Paper Space

You have been working in model space. Next, the current viewport configuration (four viewports) is saved and restored in paper space. In paper space all four viewports can be plotted.

**Save the current viewport configuration:**

| Prompt | Response |
|---|---|
| Command: | **Viewports-New Viewports** |
| The Viewports dialog box appears: | TYPE: **VP1 in the New name: box** |
| | CLICK: **OK** |

**Restore the viewport configuration in paper space:**

| Prompt | Response |
|---|---|
| Command: | CLICK: **Layout1** |
| The Page Setup-Layout1 dialog box appears: | CLICK: **Cancel** |
| The Active model space viewport is displayed: | **Erase the viewport by clicking its outside edge and pressing Delete.** |
| Command: | TYPE: **MV<enter>** |
| Specify corner of viewport or [ON/OFF/Fit/ Hideplot/Lock/Object/Polygonal/Restore/ 2/3/4] <Fit>: | TYPE: **R<enter>** |

**Note:** As discussed in Chapter 15, all construction for 2D and 3D is done in model space, as you have done in all previous chapters. Paper space (Layouts) allows you to plot all your viewports at once and permits annotation within and across viewports. Paper space also allows viewports to overlap, creating a varied and flexible drawing space. These viewports may be erased, moved, or otherwise edited. Model space does not allow viewports to overlap, and only one model space viewport may be plotted at a time.

| Prompt | Response |
|---|---|
| Enter viewport configuration name or [?] <*Active> | TYPE: **VP1 <enter>** |
| Specify first corner or [Fit] <Fit>: | **<enter>** |

## MVSETUP

The MVSETUP command allows you to do the following:

**Align**  This option allows you to align a view so that it lines up with a view in another viewport.

**Create**  Create allows you to create viewports similar to the Layout Wizard, so that you can create a single viewport, four views (top, front, right side, and isometric), and an array of viewports.

**Scale viewports**  This option allows you to scale viewports so that they are all the same scale or different scales using the ratio of model space to paper space viewports.

**Title block**  This option allows you to select one of a number of title blocks to place around viewports similar to the Layout Wizard.

**Undo**  Undo allows you to undo any part of the MVSETUP command.

**Use the Scale option of the MVSETUP command to scale all viewports uniformly:**

Note: You can also use the Properties... command to set a uniform scale for all viewports. Use a crossing window to select all four viewports, then CLICK: **Properties...** from the Modify menu and select a scale of 1/16″ = 1′ from the standard scale list.

| Prompt | Response |
|---|---|
| Command: | TYPE: **MVSETUP<enter>** |
| Enter an option [Align/Create/Scale viewports/Options/Title block/Undo]: | TYPE: **S<enter>** |
| Select the viewports to scale... | |
| Select objects: | **Use a crossing window to select all four viewports.** (or TYPE: **ALL<enter>**) |
| Select objects: | |
| Set zoom scale factors for viewports Interactively/<Uniform>: | **<enter>** |
| Set the ratio of paper space units to model space units... | |
| Enter the number of paper space units <1.0>: | **<enter>** |
| Enter the number of model space units <1.0>: | TYPE: **200<enter>** |
| Enter an option [Align/Create/Scale viewports/Options/Title block/Undo]: | **<enter>** |

(This sets a ratio of 1 paper space units to 200 model space units—a little less than 1/16″=1′. These ratios will vary depending on the size of the model you create in model space.)

**Use the Hideplot option of MVIEW (Floating Viewports) to remove hidden lines in a selected viewport when the drawing is plotted:**

| Prompt | Response |
|---|---|
| Command: | TYPE: **MV<enter>** |
| Specify corner of viewport or [ON/OFF/Fit/ Hideplot/Lock/Object/Polygonal/Restore/ 2/3/4] <Fit>: | TYPE: **H<enter>** |
| Hidden line removal for plotting [ON/OFF]: | TYPE: **ON<enter>** |
| Select objects: | CLICK: **the boundary of the upper right viewport** |
| Select objects: | **<enter>** |

You may now plot all viewports at the same time; on the plot Full Preview the upper right viewport displays a view with hidden lines removed, as shown in Figure 17–12.

## SAVE

When you have completed Exercise 17–1, save your work in at least two places.

## PLOT

1. **Use the Hideplot option of the MVIEW command to select all three-dimensional viewports and produce a plot similar to Figure 17–13.**
2. **Plot or print Exercise 17–1 on an 11″ × 8-1/2″ sheet. Make sure you are in paper space and plot at 1:1 scale.**

# EXERCISE 17–1, PART 2
## 3D Shapes

**Note:** Although many of the Draw commands can be extruded to create 3D objects, the Hide command treats differently the objects drawn with the various commands. For example, a cube drawn with the Line command (extruded using THICKNESS) is treated as a square cube with no top or bottom; a cube drawn with the 2D Solid command (extruded using THICKNESS) is treated as a solid object with four sides, a top, and a bottom; a polyline with width has a top and bottom; a polyline with 0 width is treated as a line, with no top or bottom.

In Exercise 17–1, Part 2, you can practice drawing 3D objects and using 3D Viewpoint to look at them. You may erase or plot this practice session. Some of the 3D objects are shown in Figure 17–14.

### On Your Own

1. **Return to model space.**
2. **Return to a single viewport.**

### Experiment with Extruded Objects

You can draw 3D objects by setting the THICKNESS and using the Arc, Circle, Donut, Ellipse, Line, Pline, Polygon, and 2D Solid commands. The objects are extruded because

**FIGURE 17–12**
Hideplot in Paper Space

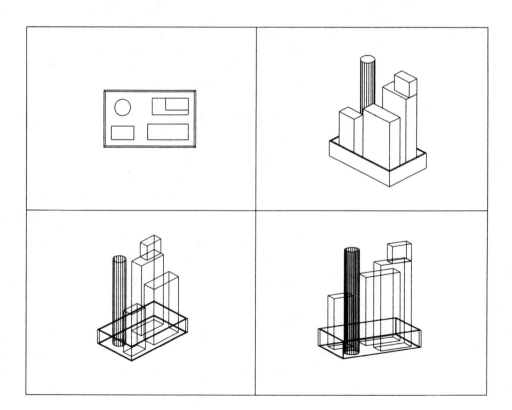

**FIGURE 17–13**
Print or Plot Exercise 17–1, Part 1

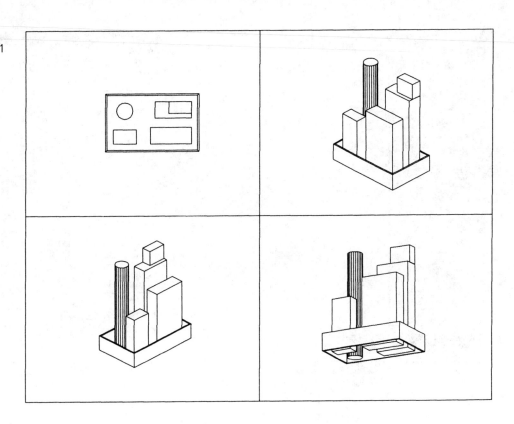

**Note:** Practice using Osnap modifiers to snap to 3D objects created with different commands. Each edge of a 3D object drawn with the 2D Solid command is treated as a separate line entity. Osnap snaps to the center of a wide 3D polyline.

they have thickness. Return the viewport to plan view, and practice using these Draw commands with different ELEVATION and THICKNESS settings to create 3D objects. Then practice using 3D Viewpoint to select different viewpoints. Try drawing some 3D objects while you are in a viewpoint different from the plan view.

## 3D Objects

AutoCAD provides some 3D object shapes—box, cone, dish, dome, mesh, pyramid, sphere, torus, and wedge—that can be selected from the menu bar with a single click. AutoCAD then provides you with prompts to draw the object. Objects such as box and

**FIGURE 17–14**
3D Objects

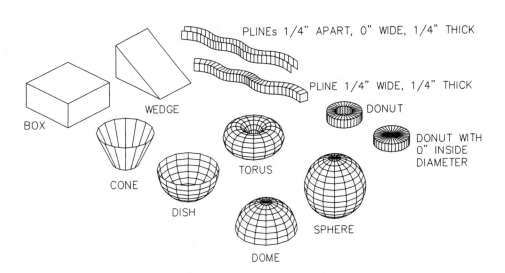

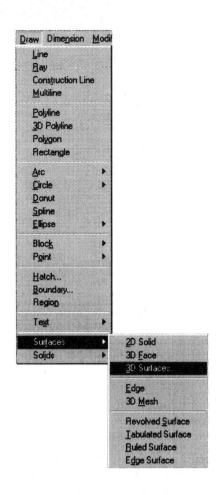

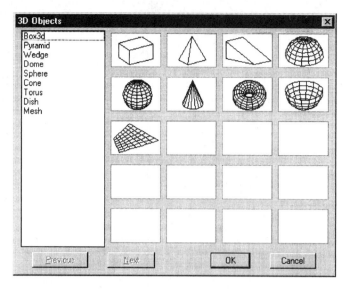

FIGURE 17–15
3D Objects Dialog Box

wedge ask for a rotation angle about the Z axis, allowing you to rotate the object in the plan view. Be aware that these are surface models, not solids. Solid modeling is covered in Chapter 18. You cannot use surface models with solids commands.

**Draw the 3D object torus (Figure 17–15):**

| Prompt | Response |
|---|---|
| Command: | **3D Surfaces...** |
| The 3D Objects dialog box (Figure 17–15) appears: | **CLICK: Torus** |
| | **CLICK: OK** |
| Specify center point of torus: | **Click a point on the screen.** |
| Specify radius of torus or [Diameter]: | **Click a point to indicate the radius** (or TYPE: **the radius size**). |
| Specify radius of tube or [Diameter]: | **Click a point** (or TYPE: **the radius size**). (The DIAMETER of the tube—the inside circle—must be less than the RADIUS of the torus—the outside circle). **If you wish to use diameter, TYPE: D<enter> and then the diameter.** |
| Enter number of segments around tube circumference <16>: | **<enter>** (You may specify more or fewer segments than the default: more makes the object look more round but Hide |

**Part IV: Three-Dimensional AutoCAD**

| Prompt | Response |
|---|---|
| | takes longer; fewer looks less round and Hide is shorter.) |
| Enter number of segments around torus circumference <16>: | <enter> |

## On Your Own

1. **Experiment with 3D objects for a while. Use 3D Views to select different viewpoints. Then erase or plot this practice session.**

# EXERCISE 17–2
# Creating a 3D Model of the Tenant Space Reception Desk

To begin Exercise 17–2, turn on the computer and start AutoCAD. The AutoCAD 2002 Today window is displayed.

1. CLICK: **the Create Drawings tab**

2. CLICK: **Wizards**

   CLICK: **Quick Setup**

3. Set drawing Units: **Architectural**

   CLICK: **Next>**

4. Set drawing Width: **24′** × Length: **15′**

   CLICK: **Finish**

5. **Use SaveAs... to save the drawing on the hard drive with the name CH17-EX2.**

6. Set Grid: **2″**

7. Set Snap: **1″**

8. Create the following Layers:

| LAYER NAME | COLOR | LINETYPE | LINEWEIGHT |
|---|---|---|---|
| 3d-dr1-3 | Blue | Continuous | Default |
| 3d-dr2 | White | Continuous | Default |
| 3d-kick | White | Continuous | Default |
| 3d-panel | Red | Continuous | Default |
| 3d-sp | Blue | Continuous | Default |
| 3d-ws1 | White | Continuous | Default |
| 3d-ws2 | Green | Continuous | Default |

9. Zoom-All

## On Your Own

1. **Create a 3D model of the tenant space reception desk using the dimensions shown in Figure 17–16.**

2. **Set the different layers as needed.**

3. **Use the correct elevation and thickness and the following commands:**

□ *Kickplates*—Layer 3d-kick, Polyline, 2″ width, 0 elevation, 3″ thickness. Use a continuous polyline. Don't forget to draw the kickplate in front and on the inside of the smaller pedestals. Take dimensions from the top view (with ortho on the polyline should go: start point: 15′, 10′, 21 left, 15 up, 22 right, 64 down, 94 left, 64 up, 22 right, 15 down, and 21 left).

□ *Panels*—Layer 3d-panel, Polyline, 2″ width, 3″ elevation, 35″ thickness. Draw a separate polyline section for each panel. (A continuous polyline draws a diagonal line in the

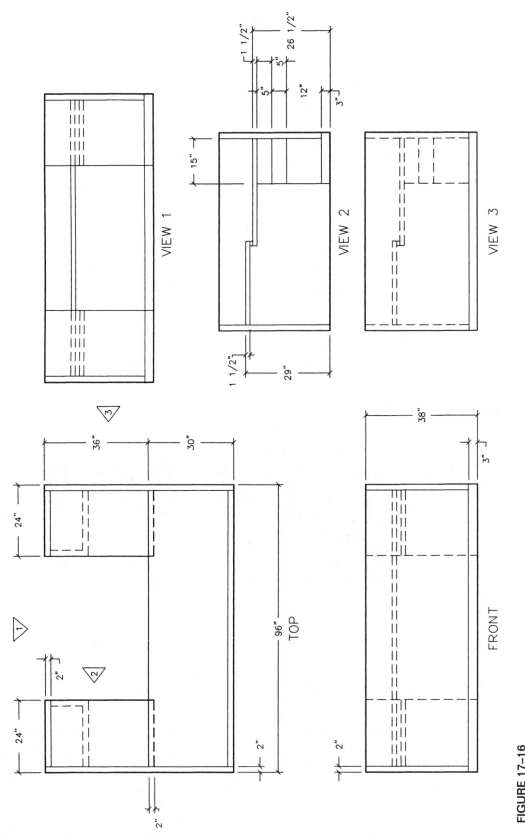

**FIGURE 17-16**
Exercise 17-2: Tenant Space Reception Desk Dimensions

472

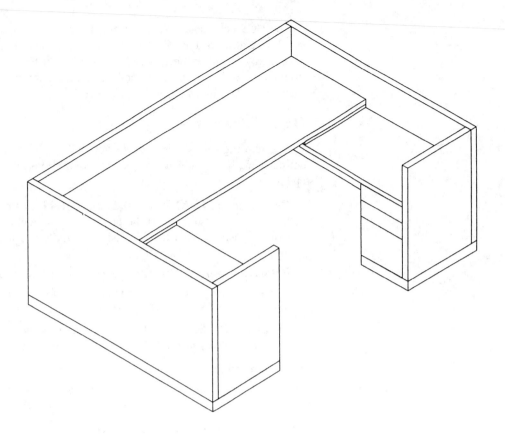

**Note:** When drawing in 3D, use as many different layer colors as needed to help you see the various pieces of the model while you are drawing.

**Note:** When you are drawing in Basic 3D, it does not matter in what order the parts of the model are drawn. In solid modeling order can make a difference.

**Note:** When using a wide polyline to draw an object, remember that the starting and ending points are the middle of the polyline.

**Tip:** If you forget to set elevation and thickness before you draw, you can correct them with Properties from the Modify menu.

corners—which you don't want.) Draw the 66″ polyline to extend to the top of the 24″ polyline and to the bottom of the 96″ polyline. (You will have five of these: two are 66″, two are 22″, and one is 92″.)

□ *Work Surface 1*—Layer 3d-ws1, 2D Solid, 27-1/2″ elevation, 1-1/2″ thickness. (This is the large work surface that measures 28″ × 92″.)

□ *Work Surface 2 (2 each)*—Layer 3d-ws2, 2D Solid, 25″ elevation, 1-1/2″ thickness. (These two measure 22″ × 36″.)

□ *Spacer (2 each)*—Layer 3d-sp, Polyline, 2″ width, 26-1/2″ elevation, 1″ thickness, 22″ long.

□ *Drawer Pedestal (2 each)*—2D Solid (All drawers measure 22″ × 15″.)
Drawer 1: Layer 3d-dr1-3,3″ elevation, 12″ thickness.
Drawer 2: Layer 3d-dr2, 15″ elevation, 5″ thickness.
Drawer 3: Layer 3d-dr1-3, 20″ elevation, 5″ thickness.

Your model should closely resemble Figure 17–17 when you select a viewpoint of 1,1,1 and use the Hide command. In the next part of this exercise, the drawer handles are drawn by relocating the UCS.

## Controlling UCS in Three Dimensions

Thus far, you have been using ELEVATION (ELEV) to locate the base and construction plane of the parts of the 3D models. This exercise shows you how to locate the construction plane by moving the UCS to the desired elevation and orientation.

**Note:** With Release 2002, you can have a different UCS in each viewport. Previous versions of AutoCAD allowed only one UCS, so that all viewports had the same UCS.

Understanding and controlling the UCS is extremely important in creating three-dimensional models. The UCS is the *location and orientation* of the origin of the X, Y, and Z axes. If you are going to draw parts of a 3D model on a slanted surface, you can create a slanted UCS. If you are going to draw a 3D object, such as the handles on the drawer pedestal, you can locate your UCS so that it is flush with the front plane of the pedestal. Thickness is then taken from that construction plane, and the handles can be easily created in the correct location.

The UCS command options Origin, OBject, Previous, Restore, Save, Delete, World, and ? were described in Chapter 10. The options described in this chapter are Move, Origin, ZAxis, 3point, OBject, View, and X/Y/Z. All these options can be selected directly from the menu bar or the UCS toolbar. The Face option will be described in Chapter 18, where 3D solids are used.

## On Your Own

In the following part of this exercise, you will practice with the UCS command options to define new UCS origin locations and orientations. Before continuing with the UCS options:

1. **Return the ELEVATION and THICKNESS settings to 0.** This avoids having the ELEVATION setting affect the position of a model created in a new UCS. The construction plane is controlled by using the UCS command in the following part of this exercise.

2. **Return to the plan view with the world UCS visible in the lower left corner.**

3. **Enter a viewpoint of 1,1,1, and use Hide.** Notice where the World UCS is located on the drawing.

4. **Set UCSICON (not UCS) to Origin; with this setting, the UCS icon is displayed at the origin of any new UCS coordinate system you create.**

### Move and Origin

These UCS command options allow you to define a new UCS by shifting the origin of the current UCS, leaving the direction of its X, Y, and Z axes unchanged.

**Use UCS Move to define a new UCS (Figure 17–18):**

| Prompt | Response |
|---|---|
| Command: | TYPE: **UCS<enter>** (or select from the menu bar or the UCS toolbar) |
| Enter an option [New/Move/orthoGraphic/ Prev/Restore/Save/Del/Apply/?/World]: | TYPE: **M<enter>** |
| Specify new origin point or [Zdepth] <0,0,0>: | **Osnap-Intersection** |
| | CLICK: **the lower left corner of the largest drawer, where it intersects with the kickplate.** |

**Note:** When creating a new UCS, make sure the ELEVATION setting is set to 0.

**FIGURE 17–18**
Use UCS Origin to Define a New UCS

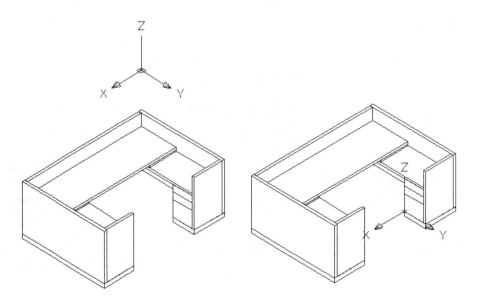

The origin of the World UCS is shifted to the corner of the drawer, but the direction of its X, Y, and Z axes remained unchanged. You can do the same using the Origin option under New. TYPE: **UCS<enter>,** then TYPE: **O<enter>** for origin, and then move the origin in the same manner.

### ZAxis

The ZAxis option allows you to change the direction of the Z axis. On the basis of a new Z axis, AutoCAD determines the direction of the X and Y axes. Before continuing, use the UCS command to return to the World UCS location, as follows.

**Use UCS World to return to the World UCS location:**

| Prompt | Response |
|---|---|
| Command: | TYPE: **UCS<enter>** |
| Enter an option [New/Move/orthoGraphic/<br>Prev/Restore/Save/Del/Apply/?/World]<br><World>: | **<enter>** |

The World UCS returns.

**Use UCS ZAxis to define a new UCS (Figure 17–19):**

**FIGURE 17–19**

Use UCS ZAxis to Define a New UCS

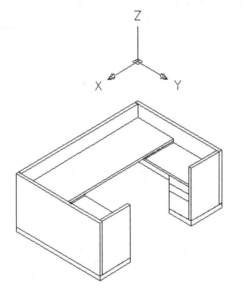
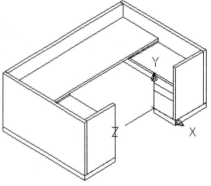

| Prompt | Response |
|---|---|
| Command: | TYPE: **UCS<enter>** |
| Enter an option [New/Move/orthoGraphic/<br>Prev/Restore/Save/Del/Apply/?/World]<br><World>: | TYPE: **ZA<enter>** |
| Specify new origin point <0,0,0>: | **Osnap-Intersection** |
| of | CLICK: **the lower left corner of the largest drawer where it intersects with the kickplate.** |
| Specify point on positive portion of Z-axis<br><default>: | **Use the crosshair of the pointer to reorient the Z axis so it comes "out" from the lower left corner of the pedestal, and click a point** (with ORTHO and SNAP ON). |

The origin of the current UCS is moved to the corner of the drawer, and when the direction of the Z axis is changed, the X and Y axes follow.

**FIGURE 17–20**
Use UCS Y to Define a New
UCS

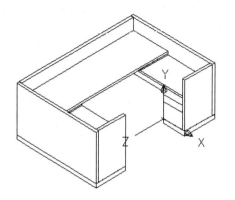
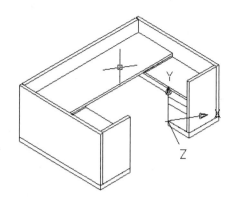

## X/Y/Z

These options allow you to rotate the UCS about any of the three axes. Keep the UCS just created and use the X/Y/Z option in the following exercises to rotate the UCS about the three axes.

**Use UCS Y to define a new UCS by rotating the UCS about the Y axis (Figure 17–20):**

| Prompt | Response |
|---|---|
| Command: | TYPE: **UCS<enter>** (or CLICK: **New UCS-Y)** |
| Enter an option [New/Move/orthoGraphic/ Prev/Restore/Save/Del/Apply/?/World] <World>: | TYPE: **Y<enter>** |
| Specify rotation angle about Y axis <90>: | TYPE: **60<enter>** |
| (The UCS rotates 60° counterclockwise around the Y axis to appear as in Figure 17–20.) | |
| Command: | TYPE: **U<enter>** (to return to the UCS created using the ZAxis option) |

**Use UCS Z to define a new UCS by rotating the UCS about the Z axis (Figure 17–21):**

| Prompt | Response |
|---|---|
| Command: | TYPE: **UCS<enter>** |
| Enter an option [New/Move/orthoGraphic/ Prev/Restore/Save/Del/Apply/?/World] <World>: | TYPE: **Z<enter>** |

**FIGURE 17–21**
Use UCS Z to Define a New
UCS

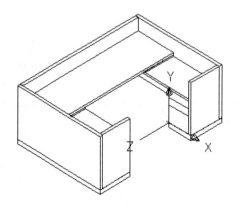
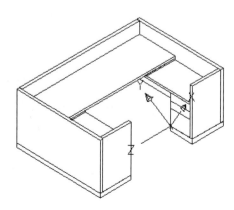

**FIGURE 17–22**
Use UCS X to Define a New
UCS

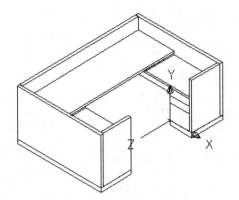 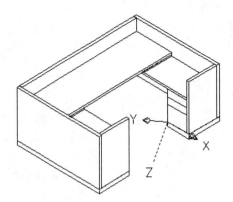

| Prompt | Response |
|---|---|
| Specify rotation angle about Z axis <90>: | TYPE: **60<enter>** |
| (The UCS rotates 60° counterclockwise around the Z axis to appear as in Figure 17–21.) | |
| Command: | TYPE: **U<enter>** (to return to the UCS created by the ZAxis option) |

**Use UCS X to define a new UCS by rotating the UCS about the X axis (Figure 17–22):**

| Prompt | Response |
|---|---|
| Command: | TYPE: **UCS<enter>** |
| Enter an option [New/Move/orthoGraphic/ Prev/Restore/Save/Del/Apply/?/World] <World>: | TYPE: **X<enter>** |
| Specify rotation angle about X axis <90>: | TYPE: **60<enter>** |
| (The UCS rotates 60° counterclockwise around the X axis to appear as in Figure 17–22.) | |
| Command: | **<enter>** |

**Use UCS World to return to the World UCS coordinate system:**

| Prompt | Response |
|---|---|
| Enter an option [New/Move/orthoGraphic/ Prev/Restore/Save/Del/Apply/?/World] <World>: | **<enter>** |

The UCS returns to the World coordinate system.

### View

This option creates a new coordinate system whose X-Y plane is parallel to the display screen. This is the UCS that must be used when a 2D format (border) is to be placed around a 3D drawing. A good way to combine the 3D drawing and the 2D format is to arrange the 3D drawing as you wish it to appear, set the UCS to View, and insert a previously drawn format around it. Also use the View option when you want to add text to your drawing; when "View" is used, you can enter text parallel to the screen while in a 3D viewpoint.

### On Your Own

**1. Create a text style with a Roman Simplex font.**

**Use UCS View to define a UCS parallel to the screen, and annotate the drawing (Figure 17–23):**

**FIGURE 17–23**
Use UCS View to Define a New
UCS Parallel to the Screen

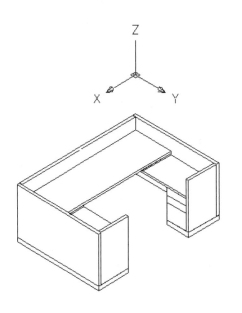
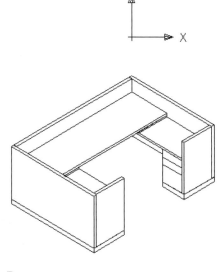

| Prompt | Response |
|---|---|
| Command: | TYPE: **UCS<enter>** |
| Enter an option [New/Move/orthoGraphic/ Prev/Restore/Save/Del/Apply/?/World] <World>: | TYPE: **V<enter>** |
| (The UCS is parallel to your screen.) | |
| Command: | **Single Line Text** (or TYPE: **DT<enter>**) |
| Specify start point of text or [Justify/Style]: | CLICK: **a point below the desk. Allow enough room for 4″ text** (see Figure 17–23). |
| Specify height <default>: | TYPE: **4<enter>** |
| Specify rotation angle of text <0>: | **<enter>** |
| Enter text: | TYPE: **RECEPTION DESK<enter>** |
| Enter text: | **<enter>** |
| (The 3D model of the reception desk is annotated.) | |

## On Your Own

1. **Erase the text "RECEPTION DESK" from the drawing, and return to the World UCS.**

### OBject

The OBject option allows you to define a UCS by pointing to any object except a 3D polyline or polygon mesh. The Y axis of the UCS created with OBject has the same extrusion direction as the object that is selected.

**Use UCS OBject to define a new UCS (Figure 17–24):**

| Prompt | Response |
|---|---|
| Command: | TYPE: **UCS<enter>** |
| Enter an option [New/Move/orthoGraphic/ Prev/Restore/Save/Del/Apply/?/World] <World>: | TYPE: **OB<enter>** |
| Select object to align UCS: | CLICK: **any point on the largest work surface.** |

The work surface was drawn by using the 2D Solid command. The position of the UCS shown in Figure 17–24 may vary from the position of your UCS, because the first point

**FIGURE 17–24**
Use UCS Object to Define a New
UCS

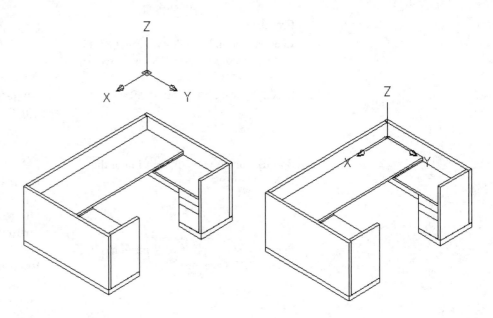

of the solid (when drawn) determines the new UCS origin. The new X axis lies along the line between the first two points of the solid.

See the *AutoCAD Command Reference* for a description of how each entity—arc, circle, dimension, line, point, 2D Polyline, solid, 3D face, text, insert, attribute, and attribute definition—determines the position of the UCS origin when the OBject option is used.

### 3point

This option allows you to change the origin of a new UCS by specifying a new direction for the X and Y axes; the Z axis follows. In the next part of this exercise, you will create a new UCS using the 3point option. This UCS will be used to draw the hardware on the drawers of the left pedestal.

## On Your Own

Return to the World UCS.

**1. Use UCS 3point to define a new UCS (Figure 17–25):**

| Prompt | Response |
|---|---|
| Command: | TYPE: **UCS<enter>** |

**FIGURE 17–25**
Use UCS 3point to Define a New
UCS

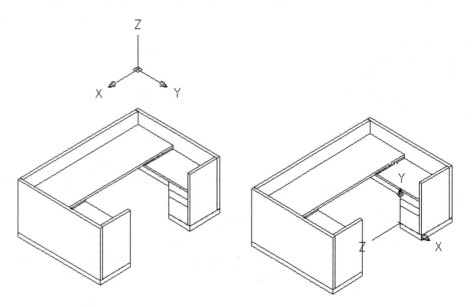

| Prompt | Response |
|---|---|
| Enter an option [New/Move/orthoGraphic/ Prev/Restore/Save/Del/Apply/?/World] <World>: | TYPE: **3<enter>** |
| Specify new origin point <0,0,0>: | **Osnap-Intersection** |
| | CLICK: **the lower left corner of the largest drawer, where it intersects with the kickplate.** |
| Specify point on positive portion of the X-axis < >: | **Osnap-Intersection** |
| | CLICK: **the lower right corner of the largest drawer, where it intersects with the kickplate.** |
| Specify point on positive-Y portion of the UCS XY plane < >: | **Osnap-Intersection** |
| | CLICK: **the upper left corner of the largest drawer, where it intersects with the drawer above it.** |

The newly created UCS appears.

## Thickness (System Variable)

When the UCS coordinate system is used to define the construction plane, the ELEVATION setting must be 0. Otherwise, the ELEVATION defines the construction plane from the current UCS.

You may also set ELEVATION and THICKNESS using the ELEVATION and THICKNESS system variables. The entire word—ELEVATION or TH for THICKNESS—must be typed and entered to set the system variable. Thickness may also be selected from Format on the menu bar.

**Use the THICKNESS (system variable) to set the thickness for the drawer handles:**

| Prompt | Response |
|---|---|
| Command: | **Thickness** (or TYPE: **TH<enter>**) |
| Enter new value for THICKNESS <default>: | TYPE: **1/2<enter>** |

## Drawing in 3D

In the following part of this exercise, the UCS created using the 3point option is used to add the drawer hardware to the drawers of both pedestals. The dimensions for the locations of the drawer hardware are shown in Figure 17–26.

**FIGURE 17–26**
Drawer Hardware Dimensions

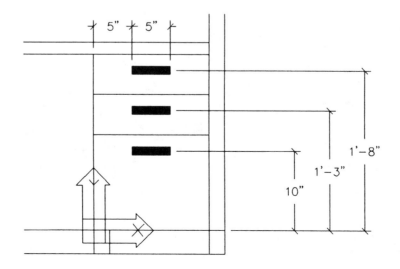

**Note:** If the UCS Icon origin is off screen, or if it is clipped at the viewport edges, it is displayed at the lower left corner of the viewport.

**Warning:** When you are working in 3D, you absolutely must use OSNAP to Move or Insert objects as blocks. An object that appears to be placed on the endpoint of a line, for example, may be in front, behind, below, or above where it appears to be unless OSNAP is used to designate the endpoint of the line.

**Draw the drawer hardware on the left pedestal using the Polyline command:**

| Prompt | Response |
|---|---|
| Command: | TYPE: **PL<enter>** |
| Specify start point: | TYPE: **5,10<enter>** |
| Specify next point or [Arc/Close/Halfwidth/ Length/Undo/Width]: | TYPE: **W<enter>** |
| Specify starting width <0'-2">: | TYPE: **1<enter>** |
| Specify ending width <0'-1">: | **<enter>** |
| Specify next point or [Arc/Close/Halfwidth/ Length/Undo/Width]: | TYPE: **10,10<enter>** |
| Specify next point or [Arc/Close/Halfwidth/ Length/Undo/Width]: | **<enter>** |

The first drawer handle is complete.

## On Your Own

1. **Use the dimensions in Figure 17–26 to complete the drawer handles on the left pedestal.**

2. **Return to the World UCS.**

3. **Select a viewpoint of -1,1,1.**

4. **Use UCS 3point to create a UCS to draw the drawer handles on the right pedestal.**

5. **Using the same dimensions as you used on the left pedestal, draw the handles of the right pedestal drawers.**

If you have done everything correctly, your drawing is complete. Figure 17–27 shows the model with a viewpoint of 1,1,1. Figure 17–28 shows the model with a viewpoint of -1,1,1.

**FIGURE 17–27**
Reception Desk, Viewpoint 1,1,1

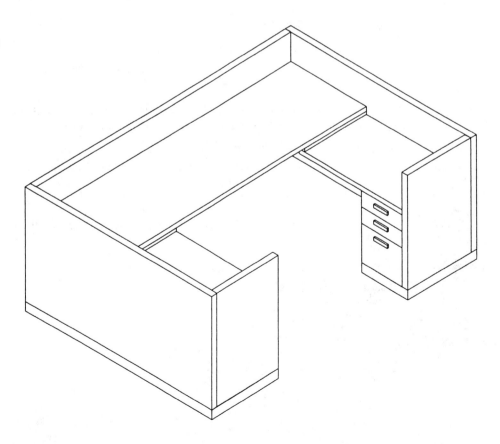

**FIGURE 17–28**
Reception Desk, Viewpoint -1,1,1

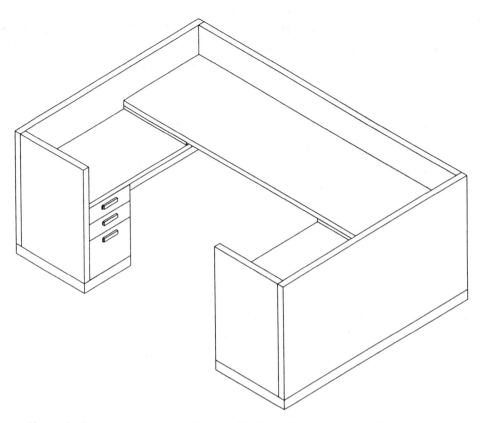

If you find any errors, correct them at this time. You can use the Move command to correct location errors by noting the X, Y, and Z coordinates of the current UCS and moving objects using relative coordinates. For example, the response **@1,0,0** to the "Second point of displacement:" prompt of the Move command moves an object 1″ in the positive X direction. (You may select any point as the base point.)

## PLAN

When you TYPE: **PLAN<enter>**, the prompt is "Enter an option [Current UCS>/Ucs/ World]<current>:". All these options may be selected from the menu bar.

### <Current UCS>

When the Current UCS option is entered, the display is returned to the plan view (VPOINT 0,0,1) with respect to the current UCS.

### UCS (Named UCS)

This option prompts for the "Enter name of UCS or [?]:" and returns the display to the plan view for the named UCS.

### World

This option returns the display to the plan view for the World Coordinate System.

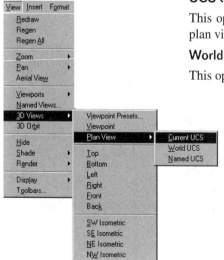

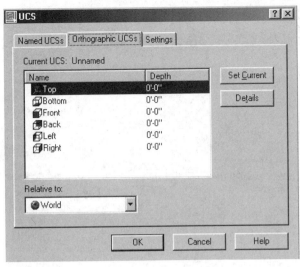
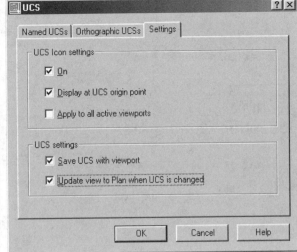

**FIGURE 17–29**
Orthographic UCSs and Settings Tabs of the UCS Dialog Box

### UCSFOLLOW

The UCSFOLLOW system variable may be set so that when a new UCS is created, the display automatically goes to the plan view of the new UCS in the active viewport.

When you TYPE: **UCSFOLLOW<enter>**, the prompt is "Enter new value for UCS-FOLLOW <0>:". When UCSFOLLOW is set to 1, any UCS change automatically causes the screen to return to the plan view of the new UCS. When UCSFOLLOW is set to 0, a UCS change does not affect the display. You can set UCSFOLLOW separately for each viewport. UCS FOLLOW can also be set from the Settings tab of the UCS dialog box (Figure 17–29). CHECK: **Update view to Plan when UCS is changed.**

When part of a 3D model is viewed in plan view, be aware that you are viewing the entire model, *including* any part of it that is in front of the current UCS. For example, when the UCS is on the same plane as the pedestals, the *viewpoint* is from outside the entire reception desk. Therefore, if you perform a Hide operation while the UCS is in this location, the entire pedestal will be hidden by the outside panel of the desk. That is because the pedestals are inside the model. Clipping planes, as described in *Help Auto-CAD 2002,* can be used to remedy this situation if it is a problem.

Otherwise, draw anything that is inside a model while the model is in a 3D view, as you drew the drawer hardware.

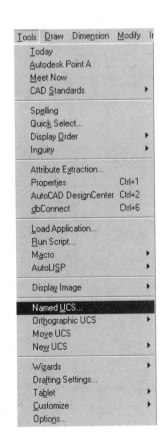

### UCS Dialog Box

You can also click Named UCS... to obtain the UCS dialog box. The desired UCS coordinate system option can be selected from the Orthographic UCSs tab of the UCS dialog box (Figure 17–29), and the Origin point is entered at the prompt. When UCSFOLLOW is set to 1, the plan view of the coordinate system automaticaly appears on the screen; otherwise, TYPE: **PLAN<enter>** to see the plan view. It is easiest to keep your orientation by returning to the plan view of the World UCS before you select a new UCS option from the dialog box.

It is important to understand the difference between the UCS option of Front and the Viewpoint option of Front. You may draw directly on the Front UCS option plan view and know exactly where you are drawing. If you draw on the Viewpoint option of Front and your UCS has not been located correctly on the front of the 3D model, you don't know where you are drawing.

### SAVE

When you have completed Exercise 17–2, save your work in at least two places.

## PLOT

Plot or print Exercise 17–2 at a scale of 1/2″ = 1′-0″, Viewpoint 1,1,1, as shown in Figure 17–27.

## EXERCISE 17–3
## Creating a 3D Model of the Tenant Space Reception Seating Area

Create a 3D model from the views and dimensions given in Figure 17–30. Plot a single view of the model to scale on the Layout1 so that it fits on an 11″ × 8-1/2″ sheet and still fills most of the sheet.

**FIGURE 17–30**

Exercise 17–3: Tenant Space Reception Seating Area Dimensions (Scale: 3/8″ = 1′-0″)

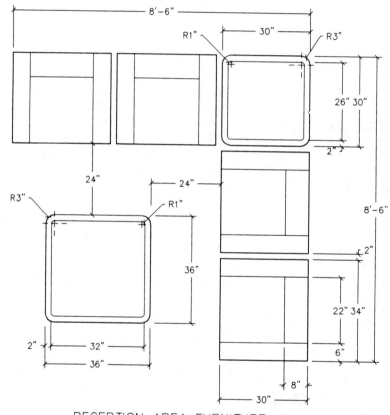

RECEPTION AREA FURNITURE
PLAN VIEW

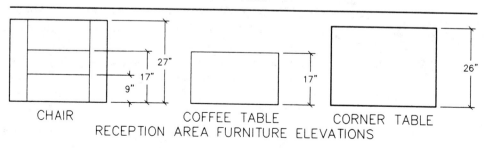

CHAIR          COFFEE TABLE          CORNER TABLE
RECEPTION AREA FURNITURE ELEVATIONS

# EXERCISE 17–4
## Creating a 3D Model of the Tenant Space Conference Room Cabinets

Create a 3D model from the views and dimensions given in Figures 17–31A and 17–31B. Plot a single view of the model to scale on Layout1 so that it fits on an 11″ × 8-1/2″ sheet and still fills most of the sheet.

# EXERCISE 17–5
## Creating a 3D Model of the Tenant Space Conference Room Chair

Create a 3D model from the views and dimensions given in Figure 17–32. Plot a drawing containing four 3D views of the model on Layout1 on an 11″ × 8-1/2″ sheet. The four viewpoints should be:

☐ Above, in front, and to the right
☐ Above, in front, and to the left
☐ Above, behind, and to the right
☐ Above, behind, and to the left

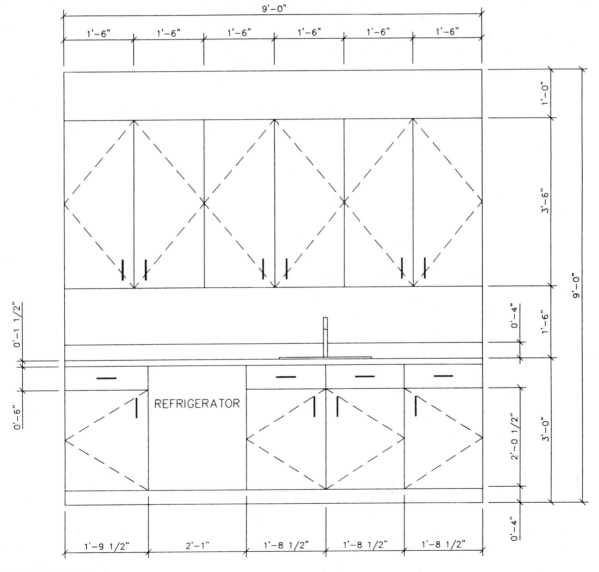

**FIGURE 17–31A**
Exercise 17–4: Tenant Space Conference Room Cabinets Dimensions (Scale: 1/2″ = 1′-0″)

**FIGURE 17–31B**

Exercise 17–4: Tenant Space
Conference Room Cabinets
Dimensions (Scale: 1/2″ = 1′-0″)

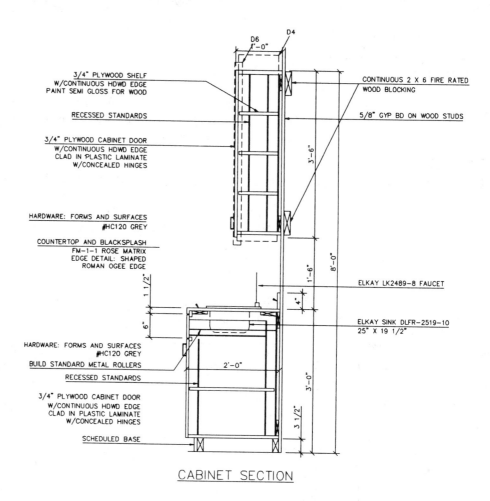

3/4" PLYWOOD SHELF
W/CONTINUOUS HDWD EDGE
PAINT SEMI GLOSS FOR WOOD

RECESSED STANDARDS

3/4" PLYWOOD CABINET DOOR
W/CONTINUOUS HDWD EDGE
CLAD IN PLASTIC LAMINATE
W/CONCEALED HINGES

HARDWARE: FORMS AND SURFACES
#HC120 GREY

COUNTERTOP AND BLACKSPLASH
FM-1-1 ROSE MATRIX
EDGE DETAIL: SHAPED
ROMAN OGEE EDGE

HARDWARE: FORMS AND SURFACES
#HC120 GREY
BUILD STANDARD METAL ROLLERS
RECESSED STANDARDS
3/4" PLYWOOD CABINET DOOR
W/CONTINUOUS HDWD EDGE
CLAD IN PLASTIC LAMINATE
W/CONCEALED HINGES
SCHEDULED BASE

CONTINUOUS 2 X 6 FIRE RATED
WOOD BLOCKING

5/8" GYP BD ON WOOD STUDS

ELKAY LK2489-8 FAUCET

ELKAY SINK DLFR-2519-10
25" X 19 1/2"

CABINET SECTION

**FIGURE 17–32**

Exercise 17–5: Tenant Space
Conference Room Chair
Dimensions (Scale: 1/2″ = 1′-0″)

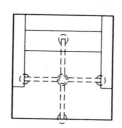

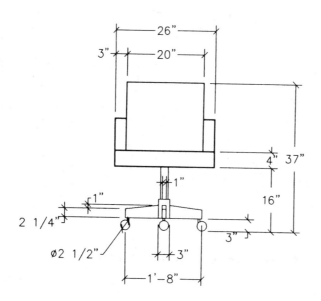

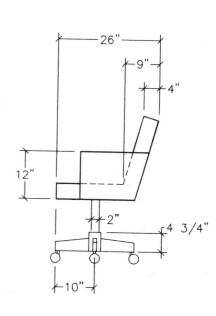

486

# REVIEW QUESTIONS

1. Drawing in three dimensions requires the same concepts of space as drawing in two dimensions.
   a. True
   b. False

2. Thickness values may be set with the use of which of the following commands?
   a. LAYER
   b. TILEMODE
   c. VPORTS
   d. ELEV
   e. VPOINT

3. 3D objects may be selected from which of the following pull-down menus in the menu bar?
   a. View
   b. Tools
   c. Draw
   d. Format
   e. Modify

4. Which of the following viewpoints displays a view to the right in front and above the object?
   a. 1,-1,1
   b. -1,-1,1
   c. -1,1,1
   d. 1,1,-1
   e. 0,0,1

5. Which of the following viewpoints displays a view one unit to the left, one unit in front, and one unit above the object?
   a. 1,-1,1
   b. -1,-1,1
   c. -1,1,1
   d. 1,1,-1
   e. 0,0,1

6. Which is the correct setting to use with the 2D Solid command, to create a 3D object that is 3′ from the floor and 5′ tall?
   a. Elevation 3′, thickness 5′
   b. Elevation 0, thickness 8′
   c. Elevation 5′, thickness 3′
   d. Elevation 8′, thickness -3′
   e. Elevation 0, thickness 5′

7. The Plan command is found on which of the following menus on the View menu of the menu bar?
   a. 3D Views
   b. Viewports
   c. Named Views
   d. 3D Orbit
   e. Display

8. When PLAN<enter> is typed and the default option is selected by pressing <enter> again, Auto-CAD
   a. Displays a plan view of the current UCS
   b. Displays a plan view of the object
   c. Displays a plan view of the World UCS
   d. Displays a plan view of all named UCSs
   e. All the above

9. When the Viewpoint Presets dialog box is used, which of the following angles from the X-Y plane will provide a viewpoint from below the object?
   a. 60
   b. 30
   c. 0
   d. -30
   e. None of these angles can be used.

10. Clicking a point on the AutoCAD compass within the inner and outer circles, above the horizontal line and to the left of the vertical line, produces which of the following views?
   a. Behind, below, and to the left of the object
   b. In front, below, and to the left of the object
   c. Behind, above, and to the left of the object
   d. In front, above, and to the left of the object
   e. Behind, below, and to the right of the object

11. Write the command described in this chapter that allows you to view an object in three dimensions.

   _____

12. Write the command that splits the active viewport into two, three, or four areas.

   _____

13. Write the command that allows you to restore a viewport configuration saved in model space to a display in paper space.

   _____

14. Describe the two different ways to set ELEVATION and THICKNESS.

   _____

   _____

15. Write the command that allows you to change the thickness of an existing entity.

   _____

16. Write the command that allows you to change the elevation of an existing entity.

   _____

17. Describe the uses of model space and paper space in constructing and plotting 3D models.

   Model space _____

   _____

   Paper space _____

   _____

18. List five 3D objects that can be created from the 3D Objects dialog box.

   _____        _____

   _____        _____

   _____

19. Describe how to activate the AutoCAD compass from the VPOINT prompt "Specify a view point or [Rotate] <display compass and tripod>:".

   _____

20. Describe the view obtained with a viewpoint to the right side of a 3D object, at a −45° angle from the X-Y plane.

   _____

# 18 Solid Modeling

## OBJECTIVES

When you have completed this chapter, you will be able to

- ☐ Draw the following primitive solids: box, sphere, wedge, cone, cylinder, torus.
- ☐ Make settings to display solids smoothly.
- ☐ Draw extruded solids.
- ☐ Draw revolved solids.
- ☐ Rotate solids about the X, Y, or Z axis.
- ☐ Form chamfers and fillets on solid edges.
- ☐ Join two or more solids.
- ☐ Subtract one or more solids from another solid.
- ☐ Use the Solidedit command to change existing solids.
- ☐ Form a solid model from the common volume of two intersecting solids.
- ☐ Obtain a perspective view of a complex solid model.
- ☐ Use 3D Orbit and Render to render solids and print the rendered model.

## INTRODUCTION

AutoCAD provides three means of creating 3D models: basic 3D using elevation and thickness, surface modeling, and solid modeling. The previous chapter covered basic 3D. Surface modeling uses commands similar to those used in solid modeling but requires a wire frame on which surfaces are placed to give the illusion of a solid model. Models cannot be subtracted from other models when surface modeling is used, nor can they be joined to form a composite model. Surface modeling is not covered in this book. Solid modeling creates solids that are much more useful and easier to modify than surface models. A solid may be a single object called a *primitive,* or it may be a combination of objects called a *composite*.

### SOLIDS Commands Used to Create Basic Shapes

A primitive solid is a single solid shape that has had nothing added to or subtracted from it. There are six solid primitives (box, sphere, wedge, cone, cylinder, torus) that are the basic shapes often used in solid modeling. They are drawn by using six commands:

| | |
|---|---|
| Box | Sphere |
| Cone | Torus |
| Cylinder | Wedge |

AutoCAD also allows you to form solids by extruding (adding height) and revolving (rotating about an axis) two-dimensional drawing entities such as polylines, circles, ellipses, rectangles, polygons, and donuts. The commands that extrude and revolve drawing entities to form solids are:

Extrude
Revolve

## SOLIDS Commands Used to Create Composite Solids

Composite solids are formed by joining primitive solids, other solids, or a combination of the two. These combinations may also be added to or subtracted from other solids to form the composite model needed. The following commands used to create composite solids are described in this chapter:

**Union**   Allows you to join several solids to form a single solid.

**Intersect**   Allows you to create composite solids from the intersection of two or more solids. Intersect creates a new solid by calculating the common volume of two or more existing solids.

**Subtract**   Allows you to subtract solids from other solids.

**Interfere**   Does the same thing as Intersect except it retains the original objects.

## SOLIDS Commands Used to Edit Solids

**Slice**   Used to create a new solid by cutting the existing solid into two pieces and removing or retaining either or both pieces.

**Section**   Used to create the cross-sectional area of a solid. That area may then be hatched using the Hatch or Bhatch commands with any pattern you choose. Be sure the section is parallel with the current UCS when you hatch the area.

## SOLIDEDIT

The SOLIDEDIT command has several options that allow you to change features of 3D solid objects. These options are shown as separate tools on the Solids Editing toolbar and as separate commands on the Solids Editing menu from the Modify menu on the menu bar.

With SOLIDEDIT, you can change solid objects by extruding, moving, rotating, offsetting, tapering, copying, coloring, separating, shelling, cleaning, checking, or deleting features such as holes, surfaces, and edges.

**When you TYPE: SOLIDEDIT\<enter\>, the following prompt appears:**

Enter a solids editing option [Face/Edge/Body/Undo/eXit] \<eXit\>:

**When you TYPE: F\<enter\> for face, the following options appear for changing surfaces:**

**Extrude**   Allows you to extrude an existing surface or surfaces on a solid along a path.

**Move**   Allows you to move surfaces such as holes or objects in the solid from one point to another.

**Rotate**   Allows you to rotate surfaces in a solid such as slots, or other shapes.

**Offset**   Allows you to create new surfaces by offsetting existing ones.

**Taper**   Allows you to taper surfaces on a solid along a path.

**Delete**   Allows you to delete surfaces (such as holes and other features) from the solid.

**Copy**   Allows you to copy existing surfaces from a solid model.

**coLor**   Allows you to assign a color to any surface of the solid model.

All these options are similar to commands you have already used.

**When you TYPE: E for Edge, the following options appear for changing edges:**

**Copy**   Allows you to copy existing edges from a solid model.

**coLor**   Allows you to assign a color to any edge of the solid model.

**When you TYPE: B\<enter\> for Body, the following options appear for changing the body of the model:**

**Imprint**   Allows you to imprint a shape onto a solid. The object to be imprinted must intersect one or more faces on the selected solid in order for imprinting to be successful. You can imprint the following objects: arcs, circles, lines, 2D and 3D polylines, ellipses, splines, regions, and 3D solids.

**seParate solids**   Allows you to separate some solids that have been joined together to form a composite solid.

**Shell**   Creates a hollow, thin wall with a specified thickness. You can specify a constant wall thickness for all the faces. You can also exclude faces from the shell by selecting them. A 3D solid can have only one shell.

**Clean**   Removes any unused or duplicated geometry from the model.

**Check**   Allows you to verify that the object is a valid solid.

## Other Commands That Can Be Used to Edit Solids

**3D Array**   Used to create three-dimensional arrays of objects.

**Rotate 3D**   Used to rotate solids about X, Y, or Z axis.

**Mirror3D**   Used to create mirror images of solids about a plane specified by three points.

**Trim**   Used to trim lines, polylines and similar entities in 3D space, but this command will not trim a solid shape .

**Extend**   Used to extend lines, polylines and similar entities in 3D space, but this command will not extend a solid shape.

**Fillet**   Used to create fillets and rounds. Specify the radius for the fillet and then click the edge or edges to be filleted.

**Chamfer**   Used to create chamfers. Specify the distances for the chamfer and then click the edge or edges to be chamfered.

**Align**   Used to move a solid so that a selected plane on the first solid is aligned with a selected plane on a second solid.

**Explode**   Used to explode a solid into regions or planes. (Example: An exploded solid box becomes six regions: four sides, a top, and a bottom.) Use care with Explode. When you explode a solid you destroy it as a solid shape.

All the following commands may be used to edit or view solids in the same manner as you have used them previously:

| | |
|---|---|
| Move | Dview |
| Chprop | Vpoint |
| Erase | Mview |
| Scale | Zoom |
| UCS | Pan |

## Settings That Control How the Solid Is Displayed

**FACETRES**   Used to make shaded solids and those with hidden lines removed appear smoother. Values range from 0.01 to 10.0. The default value is 0.5. Higher values take longer to regenerate but look better. If you change this value, you can update the solid to the new value by using the Shade or Hide command again.

**ISOLINES**   Sets the number of lines per surface on solids. Values range from 0 to 2047. The default value is 4. Ten is a good middle ground. If you change this value, you can update the solid to the new value by regenerating the drawing.

# EXERCISE 18–1, PART 1
## Drawing Primitive Solids

Exercise 18–1, Parts 1 through 6, provides step-by-step instructions for using the solid commands just described. These basic commands will also be used to create complex solid models in Exercise 18–2. Upon completion of this chapter, and mastery of the commands included in the chapter, you will have a sound foundation for learning solid modeling.

When you have completed Exercise 18–1, Parts 1 through 6, your drawing will look similar to Figure 18–1.

**FIGURE 18–1**
Exercise 18–1 Complete

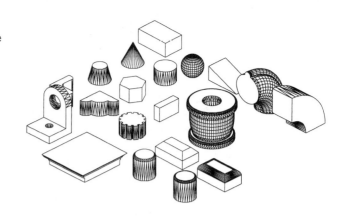

In Part 1 of this exercise you will set FACETRES and ISOLINES and use Box, Sphere, Wedge, Cone, Cylinder, and Torus to draw primitive solids. Turn on the computer and start AutoCAD. The AutoCAD 2002 Today window is displayed.

1. CLICK: **the Create Drawings tab**
2. CLICK: **Wizards**
   CLICK: **Quick Setup**
3. Set drawing Units: **Architectural**
   CLICK: **Next>**
4. Set drawing Width: **11″** × Length: **8-1/2″**
   CLICK: **Finish**
5. **Use SaveAs... to save the drawing on the hard drive with the name CH18-EX1.**
6. Set Grid: **1/2**
7. Set Snap: **1/16**
8. Create the following Layers:

| LAYER NAME | COLOR | LINETYPE | LINEWEIGHT |
|---|---|---|---|
| 3d-w | White | CONTINUOUS | Default |
| 3d-r | Red | CONTINUOUS | Default |
| 3d-g | Green | CONTINUOUS | Default |

9. Set Layer 3d-w current.
10. Use the Vports command to make two vertical viewports. Zoom-All in both viewports to start, then Zoom in closer so your view is similar to the figures shown. Either viewport may be active as you draw. You will need to Zoom-All occasionally in both viewports to see the entire drawing.
11. Use the Vpoint command to set a 1,-1,1 viewpoint for the right viewport.
12. Set elevation and thickness to 0.

## FACETRES and ISOLINES

**Set the FACETRES and ISOLINES variables:**

| Prompt | Response |
|---|---|
| Command: | TYPE: **FACETRES<enter>** |
| Enter new value for FACETRES <0.5000>: | TYPE: **2<enter>** |

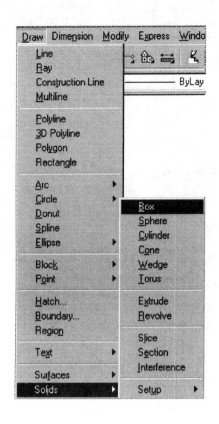

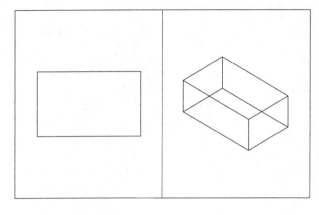

**FIGURE 18–2**
Draw a Solid Box

| Prompt | Response |
|--------|----------|
| Command: | TYPE: **ISOLINES<enter>** |
| Enter new value for ISOLINES <4>: | TYPE: **10<enter>** |

## BOX

**Draw a solid box, 1.2 × .8 × .5 height (Figure 18–2):**

| Prompt | Response |
|--------|----------|
| Command: | **Box** (or TYPE: **BOX <enter>**) |
| Specify corner of box or [CEnter] <0,0,0>: | TYPE: **1/2,7-1/2 <enter>** |
| Specify corner or [Cube/Length]: | TYPE: **1-3/4,8-1/4 <enter>** |
| Specify height: | TYPE: **1/2 <enter>** |

**Center**  Allows you to draw a box by first locating its center.
**Cube**  Allows you to draw a cube by specifying the length of one side.
**Length**  Allows you to draw a box by specifying its length (X), width (Y), and height (Z).

## SPHERE

**Draw a solid sphere, 3/8 radius (Figure 18–3):**

| Prompt | Response |
|--------|----------|
| Command: | **Sphere** (or TYPE: **SPHERE <enter>**) |
| Specify center of sphere> <0,0,0>: | TYPE: **2-3/4,7-3/4<enter>** |
| Specify radius of sphere or [Diameter]: | TYPE: **3/8<enter>** |

**FIGURE 18–3**
Draw a Solid Sphere

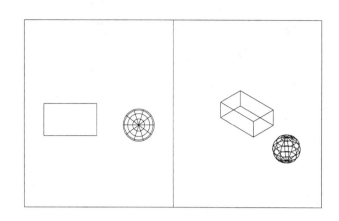

# WEDGE

**Draw a solid wedge, 3/4 × 1-1/4 × 1/2 height (Figure 18–4):**

| Prompt | Response |
|---|---|
| Command: | **Wedge** (or TYPE: **WEDGE <enter>**) |
| Specify first corner of wedge or [CEnter] <0,0,0>: | TYPE: **3-3/4,7-1/2<enter>** |
| Specify corner or [Cube/Length]: | TYPE: **5,8-1/4<enter>** |
| Specify height: | TYPE: **1/2<enter>** |

**FIGURE 18–4**
Draw a Solid Wedge

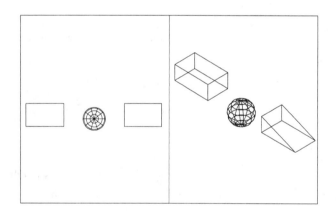

# CONE

**Draw a solid cone, 3/8 radius, 3/4 height (Figure 18–5):**

| Prompt | Response |
|---|---|
| Command: | **Cone** (or TYPE: **CONE <enter>**) |
| Specify center point for base of cone or [Elliptical] <0,0,0>: | TYPE: **1-1/4,6-1/2<enter>** |
| Specify radius for base of cone or [Diameter]: | TYPE: **3/8<enter>** |
| Specify height of cone or [Apex]: | TYPE: **3/4<enter>** |

**FIGURE 18–5**
Draw a Solid Cone

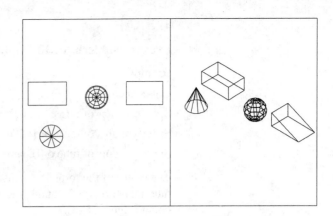

# CYLINDER

**Draw a solid cylinder, 3/8 radius, 1/2 height (Figure 18–6):**

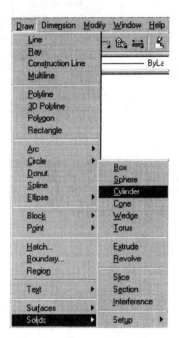

| Prompt | Response |
|---|---|
| Command: | **Cylinder** (or TYPE: **CYLINDER <enter>**) |
| Specify center point for base of cylinder or [Elliptical] <0,0,0>: | TYPE: **2-3/4,6-1/2<enter>** |
| Specify radius for base of cylinder or [Diameter]: | TYPE: **3/8<enter>** |
| Specify height of cylinder or [Center of other end]: | TYPE: **1/2<enter>** |

**FIGURE 18–6**
Draw a Solid Cylinder

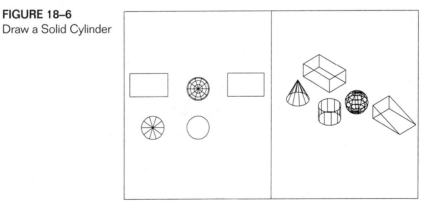

## TORUS

**Draw a solid torus (a 3D donut), 3/8 torus radius, 1/4 tube radius (Figure 18–7):**

| Prompt | Response |
|---|---|
| Command: | **Torus** (or TYPE: **TORUS<enter>**) |
| Specify center of torus> <0,0,0>: | TYPE: **4-3/8,6-1/2<enter>** |
| Specify radius of torus or [Diameter]: | TYPE: **3/8<enter>** |
| Specify radius of tube or [Diameter]: | TYPE: **1/4<enter>** |

The radius of the torus is the distance from the center of the 3D donut to the center of the tube that forms the donut. The radius of the tube is the radius of the tube forming the donut (Figure 18–8).

**FIGURE 18–7**
Draw a Solid Torus

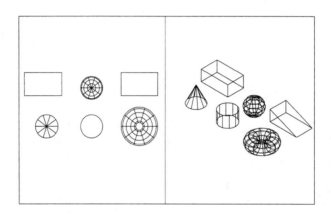

**FIGURE 18–8**
Radius of the Tube and Radius of the Torus

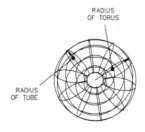

# EXERCISE 18–1, PART 2
## Using Extrude to Draw Extruded Solids

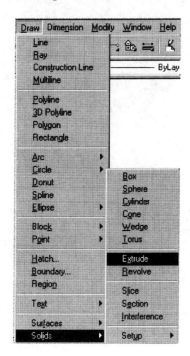

### Draw an Extruded Circle

**Draw a circle (Figure 18–9):**

| Prompt | Response |
|---|---|
| Command: | TYPE: **C<enter>** |
| 3P/2P/TTR/<Center point>: | TYPE: **1-1/4,5<enter>** |
| Diameter/<Radius>: | TYPE: **3/8<enter>** |

**Extrude the circle, 1/2 height, 15° extrusion taper angle (Figure 18–9):**

**FIGURE 18–9**
Extruding and Tapering a Circle

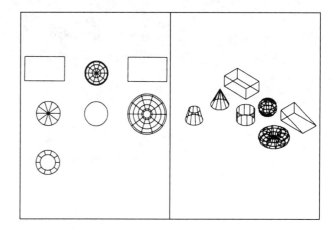

| Prompt | Response |
|---|---|
| Command: | **Extrude** |
|  | (or TYPE: **EXT<enter>**) |
| Select objects: | **Click the circle.** |
| Select objects: | **<enter>** |
| Specify height of extrusion or [Path]: | TYPE: **1/2<enter>** |
| Specify angle of taper for extrusion <0>: | **15<enter>** |

### Draw an Extruded Polygon

**Draw a polygon (Figure 18–10):**

| Prompt | Response |
|---|---|
| Command: | **Polygon** |
|  | (or TYPE: **POL<enter>**) |
| Enter number of sides <4>: | TYPE: **6<enter>** |
| Specify center of polygon or [Edge]: | TYPE: **2-3/4,5<enter>** |
| Enter an option [Inscribed in circle/ Circumscribed about circle] <I>: | TYPE: **C<enter>** |
| Specify radius of circle: | TYPE: **3/8<enter>** |

FIGURE 18–10
Extruding a Polygon

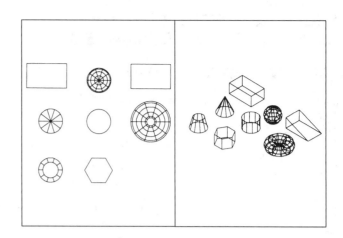

**Extrude the polygon, 1/2 height, 0° extrusion taper angle (Figure 18–10):**

| Prompt | Response |
|---|---|
| Command: | **Extrude** |
| Select objects: | CLICK: **the hexagon.** |
| Select objects: | **<enter>** |
| Specify height of extrusion or [Path]: | TYPE: **1/2<enter>** |
| Specify angle of taper for extrusion <0>: | **<enter>** |

## Draw an Extruded Rectangle

**Draw a rectangle (Figure 18–11):**

| Prompt | Response |
|---|---|
| Command: | **Rectangle** (or TYPE: **REC<enter>**) |
| Specify first corner point or [Chamfer/ Elevation/Fillet/Thickness/Width]: | TYPE: **4-1/4,4-1/2<enter>** |
| Specify other corner point or [Dimensions]: | TYPE: **4-1/2,5-3/8<enter>** |

FIGURE 18–11
Extruding a Rectangle

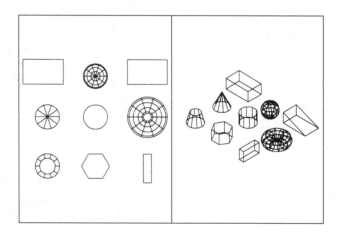

**Extrude the rectangle, 1/2 height, 0° extrusion taper angle (Figure 18–11):**

| Prompt | Response |
|---|---|
| Command: | **Extrude** |
| Select objects: | CLICK: **the rectangle.** |
| Select objects: | **<enter>** |

| Prompt | Response |
|---|---|
| Specify height of extrusion or [Path]: | TYPE: **1/2<enter>** |
| Specify angle of taper for extrusion: | **<enter>** |

## Draw an Extruded Structural Angle

**Draw the outline of the cross section of a structural angle (Figure 18–12):**

| Prompt | Response |
|---|---|
| Command: | TYPE: **L<enter>** |
| Specify first point: | TYPE: **1,3<enter>** |
| Specify next point or [Undo]: | TYPE: **@7/8,0<enter>** |
| Specify next point or [Undo]: | TYPE: **@0,1/4<enter>** |
| Specify next point or [Close/Undo]: | TYPE: **@-5/8,0<enter>** |
| Specify next point or [Close/Undo]: | TYPE: **@0,5/8<enter>** |
| Specify next point or [Close/Undo]: | TYPE: **@-1/4,0<enter>** |
| Specify next point or [Close/Undo]: | TYPE: **C<enter>** |

**Add a 1/8 radius fillet to the outline (Figure 18–12):**

| Prompt | Response |
|---|---|
| Command: | **Fillet** |
| | **(or TYPE: F<enter>)** |
| Current settings: Mode = TRIM, Radius = 0'-0 1/2" | |
| Select first object or [Polyline/Radius/Trim]: | TYPE: **R<enter>** |
| Specify fillet radius <0'-0 1/2">: | TYPE: **1/8<enter>** |
| Select first object or [Polyline/Radius/Trim]: | **D1** (Use the Zoom-Window command if needed to allow you to pick the necessary lines.) |
| Select second object: | **D2** |

## On Your Own (Figure 18–12)

1. **Draw 1/8 radius fillets at the other two intersections shown.**

**Use Edit Polyline (Pedit) to combine all the lines and fillets into a single entity (Figure 18–12):**

**FIGURE 18–12**
Extruding a Structural Steel Angle

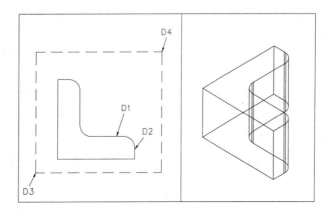

| Prompt | Response |
|---|---|
| Command: | **Edit Polyline** |
| | (or TYPE: **PE<enter>**) |
| Select polyline: | **Click one of the lines forming the structural angle.** |
| Object selected is not a polyline | |
| Do you want to turn it into one? <Y> | **<enter>** |
| Enter an option [Close/Join/Width/Edit vertex/ Fit/Spline/Decurve/Ltype gen/Undo]: | TYPE: **J<enter>** (to select the Join option) |
| Select objects: | **D3** |
| Specify opposite corner: | **D4** |
| Select objects: | **<enter>** |
| 8 segments added to polyline | |
| Enter an option [Open/Join/Width/Edit vertex/ Fit/Spline/Decurve/Ltype gen/Undo]: | **<enter>** (to exit from the Pedit command) |

**Extrude the cross section of the structural angle, 1/2 height, 0° extrusion taper angle (Figure 18–12):**

| Prompt | Response |
|---|---|
| Command: | **Extrude** |
| Select objects: | **Click the polyline.** |
| Select objects: | **<enter>** |
| Specify height of extrusion or [Path]: | TYPE: **1/2<enter>** |
| Specify angle of taper for extrusion: | **<enter>** |

## Draw Two Extruded Shapes

## On Your Own (Figures 18–13 and 18–14)

1. Draw the two shapes shown as Figures 18–13 and 18–14 in the approximate locations shown in Figure 18–1. Draw one section of the knurled knob, Figure 18–14, and then create a polar array using the Array command. When you draw the sec-

**FIGURE 18–13**

Extruding a Molding Shape

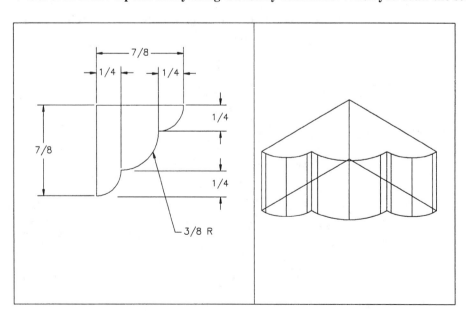

Part IV: Three-Dimensional AutoCAD

FIGURE 18–14
Extruding a Knurled Knob

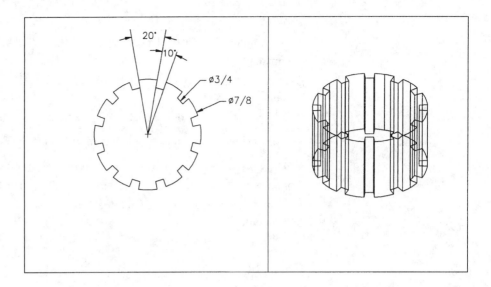

tion, be sure that you draw only what is needed. If you draw extra lines, the Edit Polyline command cannot join the lines into a single polyline.

2. Use the Edit Polyline command to join all entities of each figure into a single polyline.

3. Extrude each figure to a height of 1/2.

# EXERCISE 18–1, PART 3
## Using Revolve to Draw Revolved Solids; Using Rotate 3D to Rotate Solids about the X, Y, and Z Axes

### Draw Revolved Shape 1

**Draw two circles (Figure 18–15A):**

| Prompt | Response |
|---|---|
| Command: | TYPE: **C<enter>** |
| Specify center point for circle or [3P/2P/Ttr (tan tan radius)]: | TYPE: **6-1/4,7-3/4<enter>** |

FIGURE 18–15
Revolving a Shape 90°

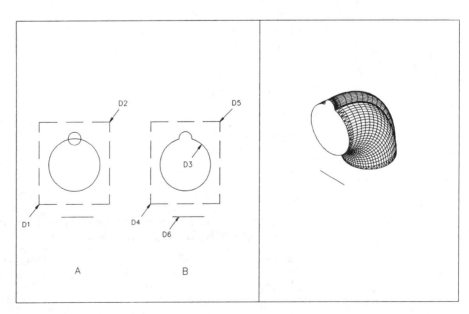

| Prompt | Response |
|---|---|
| Specify radius of circle or [Diameter]: | TYPE: **1/2<enter>** |
| Command: | **<enter>** |
| Specify center point for circle or [3P/2P/Ttr (tan tan radius)]: | TYPE: **6-1/4,8-1/4<enter>** |
| Specify radius of circle or [Diameter] <0'-1/2">: | TYPE: **1/8<enter>** |

**Use the Trim command to trim parts of both circles (Figures 18–15A and 18–15B):**

| Prompt | Response |
|---|---|
| Command: | **Trim** (or TYPE: **TR<enter>**) |
| Current settings: Projection=UCS Edge=None Select cutting edges ... | |
| Select objects: | **D1** (first corner of a window) |
| Specify opposite corner: | **D2** (second corner of a window) |
| Select objects: | **<enter>** |
| Select object to trim or [Project/Edge/Undo]: | **Trim the circles as shown in Figure 18–15B.** (Zoom-Window to get in closer if needed.) |

**Join all segments of the circles into one polyline (Figure 18–15B):**

| Prompt | Response |
|---|---|
| Command: | **Edit Polyline** (or TYPE: **PE<enter>**) |
| Select polyline: | **D3<enter>** |
| Object selected is not a polyline Do you want to turn it into one? <Y> | **<enter>** |
| Enter an option [Close/Join/Width/Edit vertex/ Fit/Spline/Decurve/Ltype gen/Undo]: | TYPE: **J<enter>** |
| Select objects: | **D4** |
| Specify opposite corner: | **D5** |
| Select objects: | **<enter>** |
| 1 segment added to polyline Enter an option [Open/Join/Width/Edit vertex/ Fit/Spline/Decurve/Ltype gen/Undo]: | **<enter>** (to exit from the Edit Polyline command) |

**Draw the axis of revolution (Figure 18–15B):**

| Prompt | Response |
|---|---|
| Command: | **Line** (or Type: **L<enter>**) |
| Specify first point: | TYPE: **6,6-3/4<enter>** |
| Specify next point or [Undo]: | TYPE: **@5/8<0<enter>** |
| Specify next point or [Undo]: | **<enter>** |

**Use Revolve to form a revolved solid created by revolving a single polyline 90° counterclockwise about an axis (Figure 18–15B):**

| Prompt | Response |
|---|---|
| Command: | **Revolve** (or TYPE: **REV<enter>**) |

| Prompt | Response |
|---|---|
| Select objects: | **D3** |
| Select objects: | **<enter>** |
| Specify start point for axis of revolution or define axis by [Object/X (axis)/Y (axis)]: | TYPE: **O<enter>** |
| Select an object: | **D6** (Be sure to click the left end of the line for counterclockwise rotation.) |
| Specify angle of revolution <360>: | TYPE: **90<enter>** |

## Draw a Revolved Rectangle

**Draw a rectangle (Figure 18–16):**

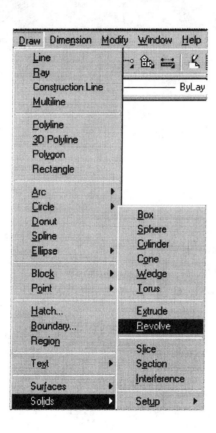

| Prompt | Response |
|---|---|
| Command: | **Rectangle** (or TYPE: **REC<enter>**) |
| Specify first corner point or [Chamfer/ Elevation/Fillet/Thickness/Width]: | TYPE: **7-3/8,7-3/8<enter>** |
| Specify other corner point: | TYPE: **8-1/4,8-1/8<enter>** |

**Draw the axis of revolution (Figure 18–16):**

| Prompt | Response |
|---|---|
| Command: | TYPE: **L<enter>** |
| Specify first point or [Dimensions]: | TYPE: **7-3/8,6-3/4<enter>** |
| Specify next point or [Undo]: | TYPE: **@3/4<0<enter>** |

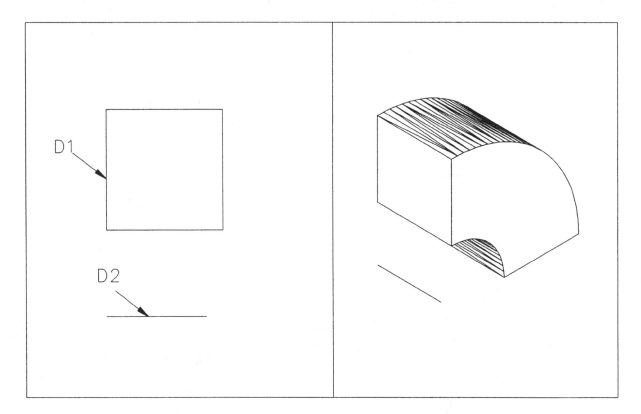

**FIGURE 18–16**
Revolving a Rectangle

| Prompt | Response |
|---|---|
| Specify next point or [Undo]: | <enter> |

**Use the Revolve command to form a revolved solid created by revolving the rectangle 90° counterclockwise about an axis (Figure 18–16):**

| Prompt | Response |
|---|---|
| Command: | **Revolve** |
| Select objects: | **D1<enter>** |
| Select objects: | **<enter>** |
| Specify start point for axis of revolution or define axis by [Object/X (axis)/Y (axis)]: | TYPE: **O<enter>** |
| Select an object: | **D2** |
| | (Click the left end of the line.) |
| Specify angle of revolution <360>: | TYPE: **90<enter>** |

## Draw a Revolved Paper Clip Holder

### On Your Own (Figures 18–17 and 18–18)

1. Draw the cross-sectional shape of the object shown in Figure 18–17 using the Line and Arc commands in the approximate locations shown in Figure 18–1.

2. Use the Edit Polyline command to join all entities of the shape into a single closed polyline.

3. Locate the axis of revolution for the shape in the position shown.

4. Use Revolve to revolve the shape full circle about the axis.

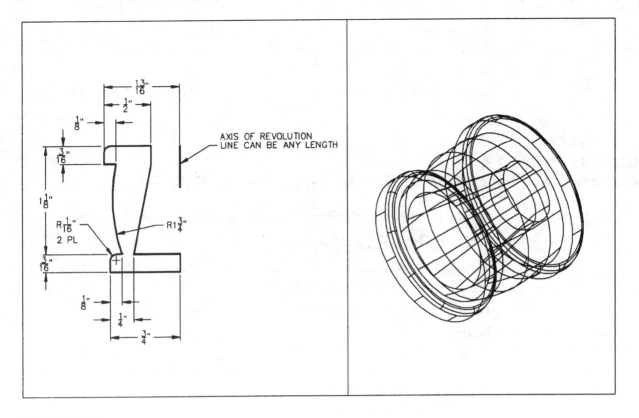

**FIGURE 18–17**
Revolving a Paper Clip Holder

**FIGURE 18–18**
Rotating an Object about
the X Axis

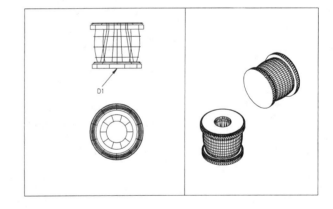

## Rotate 3D

**Use Rotate 3D to rotate the paper clip holder 90° about the X axis so that it assumes the position shown in Figure 18–18:**

| Prompt | Response |
|---|---|
| Command: | **Rotate 3D** |
| | (or TYPE: **ROTATE3D<enter>**) |
| Select objects: | CLICK: **the paper clip holder** |
| Select objects: | **<enter>** |
| Specify first point on axis or define axis by [Object/Last/View/Xaxis/Yaxis/Zaxis/ 2points]: | TYPE: **X<enter>** |

| Prompt | Response |
|---|---|
| Specify a point on the X axis <0,0,0>: | TYPE: **CEN<enter>** |
| of | **D1** |
| Specify rotation angle or [Reference]: | TYPE: **90<enter>** |

# EXERCISE 18–1, PART 4
## Using Chamfer and Fillet to Draw Chamfers and Fillets on Solid Edges

### Chamfer and Fillet the Top Four Edges of Two Separate Boxes

### On Your Own (Figure 18–1)

1. Use Box to draw two boxes measuring 1-1/4 3 3/4 3 1/2 H each, in the approximate locations shown in Figure 18–1.

**Chamfer the top four edges of the first box (Figure 18–19):**

| Prompt | Response |
|---|---|
| Command: | **Chamfer**<br>(or TYPE: **CHA<enter>**) |
| (TRIM mode) Current chamfer<br>Dist1 = 0'-0 1/2", Dist2 = 0'-0 1/2"<br>Select first line or [Polyline/Distance/<br>    Angle/Trim/Method]: | TYPE: **D<enter>** |
| Specify first chamfer distance <0'-0 1/2">: | TYPE: **3/16<enter>** |
| Specify second chamfer distance <0'-0 3/16">: | **<enter>** |
| Select first line or [Polyline/Distance/<br>    Angle/Trim/Method]: | **D1** (Figure 18–19) |
| Base surface selection... | |
| Enter surface selection option [Next/OK<br>    (current)] <OK>: | |

If the top surface of the box turns dotted, showing it as the selected surface, continue. If one of the side surfaces is selected, TYPE: **N<enter>** until the top surface is selected.

**FIGURE 18–19**<br>Chamfering and Filleting Solid<br>Edges

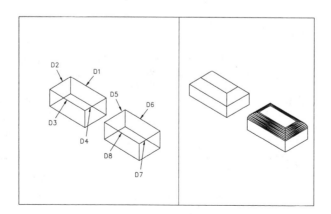

| Prompt | Response |
|---|---|
| Enter surface selection option [Next/OK (current)] <OK>: | <enter> |
| Specify base surface chamfer distance <0'-0 3/16">: | <enter> |
| Specify other surface chamfer distance <0'-0 3/16">: | <enter> |
| Select an edge or [Loop]: | **D1, D2, D3, D4** |
| Select an edge or [Loop]: | <enter> |

**Fillet the top four edges of the second box (Figure 18–19):**

| Prompt | Response |
|---|---|
| Command: | **Fillet** |
| | (or TYPE: **F<enter>**) |
| Current settings: Mode = TRIM, Radius = 0'-0 1/8" | |
| Select first object or [Polyline/Radius/Trim]: | **D5** (Figure 18–19) |
| Enter fillet radius <0'-0 1/8">: | TYPE: **3/16<enter>** |
| Select an edge or [Chain/Radius]: | **D6,D7,D8** |
| Select an edge or [Chain/Radius]: | <enter> |

## Chamfer and Fillet on the Top Edge of Two Separate Cylinders

## On Your Own (Figure 18–20)

1. **Draw two cylinders using Cylinder with a radius of 3/8 and a height of 3/4 in the approximate location shown in Figure 18–1.**
2. **Chamfer the top edge of the first cylinder (Figure 18–20) using chamfer distances of 1/16. CLICK: D1 when you select edges to be chamfered.**
3. **Fillet the top edge of the second cylinder (Figure 18–20) using a fillet radius of 1/16. CLICK: D2 when you select edges to be filleted.**

The edges of the cylinders should appear as shown in Figure 18–20.

**FIGURE 18–20**
Chamfering and Filleting Cylinders

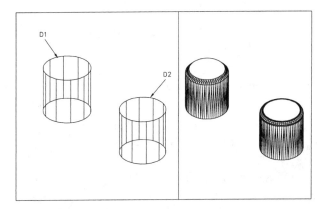

## EXERCISE 18–1, PART 5
## Using Union to Join Two Solids; Using Subtract to Subtract Solids from Other Solids

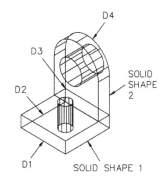

**FIGURE 18–21**
Drawing a Composite Solid

### Draw Solid Shape 1

**Draw solid shape 1 (the base of the shape), and a cylinder that will be the hole in the base (Figure 18–21):**

| Prompt | Response |
|---|---|
| Command: | **Box** |
| Specify corner of box or [CEnter] <0,0,0>: | TYPE: **4-1/2,3/4<enter>** |
| Specify corner or [Cube/Length]: | TYPE: **@1,1<enter>** |
| Specify height: 3 | TYPE: **1/4<enter>** |
| Command: | **Cylinder** |
| | (or TYPE: **CYLINDER<enter>**) |
| Specify center point for base of cylinder or [Elliptical] <0,0,0>: | TYPE: **X<enter>** |
| of | TYPE: **MID<enter>** |
| of | **D1** |
| (need YZ): | TYPE: **MID<enter>** |
| of | **D2** |
| Specify radius for base of cylinder or [Diameter]: | TYPE: **1/8<enter>** |
| Specify height of cylinder or [Center of other end]: | TYPE: **1/2<enter>** (Make the height of the hole tall enough so you can be sure it goes through the model.) |

### Draw Solid Shape 2

### On Your Own

Set the UCS Icon command to ORigin so you will be able to see the USC icon move when the origin is relocated. (TYPE: **UCSICON<enter>**, then **OR<enter>**)

1. Rotate the UCS 90° about the X axis, and move the origin of the UCS to the upper left rear corner of the box (Figure 18–21):

| Prompt | Response |
|---|---|
| Command: | **UCS** |
| Enter an option [New/Move/orthoGraphic/ Prev/Restore/Save/Del/Apply/?/World] <World>: | TYPE: **X<enter>** |
| Specify rotation angle about X axis <90>: | TYPE: **90<enter>** |
| Command: | **<enter>** (to repeat the last command) |
| Enter an option [New/Move/orthoGraphic/ Prev/Restore/Save/Del/Apply/?/World] <World>: | TYPE: **O<enter>** |
| Specify new origin point <0,0,0>: | TYPE: **END<enter>** |
| of | **D3** |

**Draw solid shape 2 (the vertical solid), and a cylinder that will be the hole in the vertical solid (Figure 18–21):**

| Prompt | Response |
|---|---|
| Command: | **Polyline** |
| | (or TYPE: **PL<enter>**) |
| Specify start point: | TYPE: **0,0<enter>** |
| Specify next point or [Arc/Close/Halfwidth/ Length/Undo/Width]: | TYPE: **@1<0<enter>** |
| Specify next point or [Arc/Close/Halfwidth/ Length/Undo/Width]: | TYPE: **@3/4<90<enter>** |
| Specify next point or [Arc/Close/Halfwidth/ Length/Undo/Width]: | TYPE: **A<enter>** |
| Specify endpoint of arc or [Angle/CEnter/ CLose/Direction/Halfwidth/Line/Radius/ Second pt/Undo/Width]: | TYPE: **@1<180<enter>** |
| Specify endpoint of arc or [Angle/CEnter/ CLose/Direction/Halfwidth/Line/Radius/ Second pt/Undo/Width]: | TYPE: **CL <enter>** |
| Command: | **Extrude** (or TYPE: **EXT<enter>**) |
| Select objects: | **Click the polyline just drawn.** |
| Select objects: | **<enter>** |
| Specify height of extrusion or [Path]: | TYPE: **1/4<enter>** |
| Specify angle of taper for extrusion <0>: | **<enter>** |
| Command: | **Cylinder** |
| Specify center point for base of cylinder or [Elliptical] <0,0,0>: | TYPE: **CEN<enter>** |
| of | **D4** |
| Specify radius for base of cylinder or [Diameter]: | TYPE: **1/4<enter>** |
| Specify height of cylinder or [Center of other end]: | TYPE: **1/2<enter>** |

The cylinder is longer than the thickness of the upright piece so you can be sure that the hole goes all the way through it.

Make sure the base of the cylinder is located on the back surface of the upright piece. If the cylinder is located on the front surface of the upright piece, move the cylinder 3/8 in the negative Z direction.

## Union

**Join the base and the vertical shape together to form one model:**

| Prompt | Response |
|---|---|
| Command: | **Union** (from Modify-Solids Editing) |
| | (or TYPE: **UNION<enter>**) |
| Select objects: | **Click the base (shape 1) and the vertical solid (shape 2).** |
| Select objects: | **<enter>** |

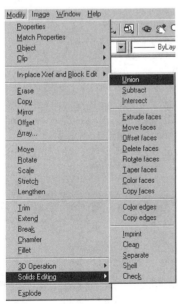

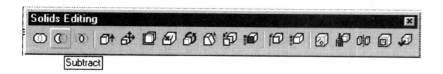

## Subtract

**Subtract the holes from the model:**

| Prompt | Response |
|---|---|
| Command: | **Subtract** (from Modify-Solids Editing) (or TYPE: **SU\<enter>**) |
| Select solids and regions to subtract from... | |
| Select objects: | CLICK: **any point on the model.** |
| Select objects: | **\<enter>** |
| Select solids and regions to subtract... | |
| Select objects: | CLICK: **the two cylinders.** |
| Select objects: | **\<enter>** |

## Hide

**Perform a Hide to be sure the model is correct (Figure 18–22):**

| Prompt | Response |
|---|---|
| Command: | **Hide** (or TYPE: **HI\<enter>**) |

The model should appear as shown in Figure 18–22.

**FIGURE 18–22**
The Completed Model after a Hide

## On Your Own

**1. Return the to the World origin.**

# EXERCISE 18–1, PART 6
# Using Intersection to Form a Solid Model
# from the Common Volume of Two Intersecting Solids

Drawing the solid model in Exercise 18–1, Part 6, demonstrates some powerful tools that can be used to form complex models.

In this exercise two separate solid shapes are drawn (in this case the same shape is copied and rotated so the two shapes are at right angles to each other) and moved so that they intersect. Intersection is used to combine the shapes to form one solid model from the common volume of the two intersecting solids. Figure 18–23 shows the two separate solid shapes, and the solid model that is formed from the common volume of the two solid shapes.

This shape will also be used in Exercise 18–4 to form the cornices at the top of the columns (Figure 18–57).

## Draw Two Extruded Shapes at Right Angles to Each Other

## On Your Own

**1. Zoom out so you can draw the full size shape shown in Figure 18–24 (Zoom .25) in the left viewport. In an open area of the screen draw Figure 18–24 using line and arc or circle commands.**

Part IV: Three-Dimensional AutoCAD

**FIGURE 18–23**
Two Shapes and the Shape
Formed from the Intersected
Volume of the Two Shapes

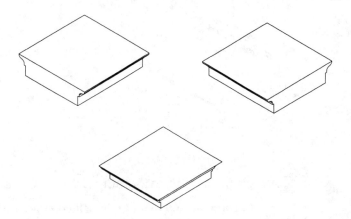

**FIGURE 18–24**
Dimensions for the Extruded
Shapes

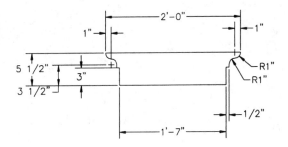

2. **Use Edit Polyline to join all parts of Figure 18–24 to form a single polyline.**

3. **Use the Scale command to scale the polyline to 1/12 its size.** (This is a scale of 1″ = 1′. In Exercise 18–3 you will scale this model to its original size.)

4. **In the right viewport, set UCS to World, copy the shape and and use Rotate 3D to rotate both shapes 90° about the X axis.**

5. **Use Rotate 3D to rotate the shape on the right 90° about the Z axis (Figure 18–25).**

6. **Extrude the shape on the left 2″ with a 0 taper angle (Figure 18–26).**

7. **Extrude the shape on the right 2″ with a 0 taper angle.**

**FIGURE 18–25**
Two Shapes Rotated 90° to Each
Other

**FIGURE 18–26**
Both Shapes Extruded

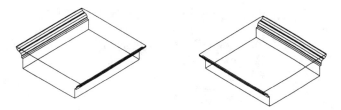

FIGURE 18–27
Moving One Shape to Intersect
with the Other

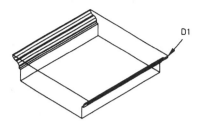
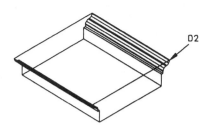

## Move One Solid to Intersect with the Other Solid

**Use the Move command to move the solid on the left to intersect with the other solid (Figure 18–27):**

| Prompt | Response |
|---|---|
| Command: | **Move** |
| Select objects: | CLICK: **the shape on the left.** |
| Select objects: | **<enter>** |
| Specify base point or displacement: | TYPE: **END<enter>** |
| of | **D1** |
| Specify second point of displacement or <use first point as displacement>: | TYPE: **END<enter>** |
| of | **D2** |

## Intersect

**FIGURE 18–28**
The Shape Formed from the Inter-sected Shapes

**Use Intersect to form a solid model from the common volume of the two intersecting solids (Figure 18–28):**

| Prompt | Response |
|---|---|
| Command: | **Intersect** (from Modify-Solids Editing) |
| | (or TYPE: **IN <enter>**) |
| Select objects: | CLICK: **both shapes.** |
| 2 solids intersected | |

The display should appear as shown in Figure 18–28.

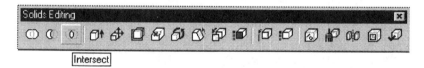

**Perform a Hide to be sure the solid model is correct (Figure 18–29):**

| Prompt | Response |
|---|---|
| Command: | **Hide** (or TYPE: **HI<enter>**) |

The display should appear as shown in Figure 18–29.

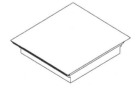

**FIGURE 18–29**
The Intersected Solid after a Hide

## On Your Own

1. **Return the UCS to World so you will not be surprised at the position the model will assume when it is inserted.**

FIGURE 18–30
Wblocking the Intersected Shape

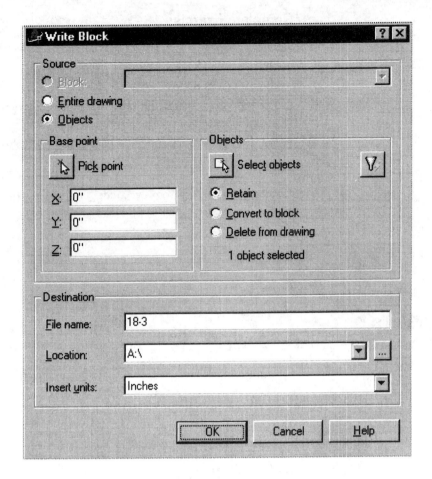

## Wblock the Intersected Model

You should now Wblock the intersected model so you can use it in Exercise 18–4 to form the cornices at the tops of the columns (see Figure 18–48).

**Use Wblock to save the model to a floppy disk (Figure 18–30):**

| Prompt | Response |
| --- | --- |
| Command: | TYPE: **W<enter>** |
| The Write Block dialog box appears: | **Locate the 3-1/2 Floppy [A:]. (CLICK: the three dots to the far right of the location box)** |
| | TYPE: **18-3** in the File name: as shown in Figure 18–30 |
| | CLICK: **Pick Point** |
| Specify insertion base point: | TYPE: **END<enter>** |
| of | CLICK: **the bottom corner of the intersected shape using Osnap-Endpoint. It will be the lowest point on the display.** |
| The Write Block dialog box appears: | CLICK: **Select Objects** |
| Select objects: | CLICK: **the intersected shape** |
| Select objects: | **<enter>** |
| The Write Block dialog box appears: | If Retain is not on, CLICK: **that radio button** |
| | CLICK: **OK** |

The shape now exists on your floppy disk as 18-3.dwg, and it is also on the current drawing.

**Complete Exercise 18–1**

**On Your Own**

1. Use the Move command to move the intersected shape to the approximate location shown in Figure 18–1.

2. Use the Vports command to return to a single viewport of the 3D viewport (Figure 18–1).

3. Set the UCS to View, and add your name to the lower right corner of the drawing.

## PLOT

Plot the 3D viewport from the Model tab on a standard size sheet of paper. Be sure to pick the Hide objects box in the Plot dialog box so the final plot appears as shown in Figure 18–1.

## SAVE

Save the drawing in two places.

# EXERCISE 18–2:
# Creating a Solid Model of Chair 1

In this exercise you will create a solid model of chair 1 (Figure 18–31) using many of the commands you used in Exercise 18–1 and many of the options of the SOLIDEDIT command. Turn on the computer and start AutoCAD. The AutoCAD 2002 Today window is displayed.

1. CLICK: **the Create Drawings tab**

2. CLICK: **Wizards**

   CLICK: **Quick Setup**

3. Set drawing Units: **Architectural**

   CLICK: **Next>**

4. Set drawing Width: **50″** × Length: **50″**

   CLICK: **Finish**

5. Use SaveAs… to save the drawing on the hard drive with the name CH18-EX2.

6. Set Grid: 1

7. Set Snap: 1/2

8. Create the following Layers:

| LAYER NAME | COLOR | LINETYPE | LINEWEIGHT |
|---|---|---|---|
| 3d-r | Red | Continuous | Default |
| 3d-m | Magenta | Continuous | Default |
| 3d-g | Green | Continuous | Default |

9. Set Layer 3d-r current.

10. Use the Viewports command to make two vertical viewports. Zoom-All in both viewports to start, then Zoom in closer as needed. You will need both viewports as aids in creating this model.

11. Use the Vpoint command to set a 1,-1,1 viewpoint for the right viewport.

12. Set FACETRES to 2, ISOLINES to 20.

**FIGURE 18–31**
Exercise 18–2 Complete

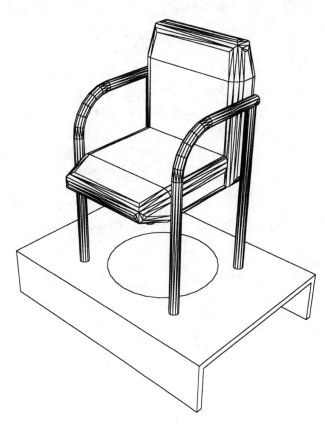

## Draw One Side of the Chair Legs and Arms

**Define a UCS that is parallel to the side of the chair legs and arms:**

| Prompt | Response |
|---|---|
| Command: | TYPE: **UCS<enter>** |
| Enter an option [New/Move/orthoGraphic/ Prev/Restore/Save/Del/Apply/?/World] <World>: | TYPE: **X<enter>** |
| Specify rotation angle about X axis <90>: | **<enter>** |
| Command: | **<enter>** (Repeat UCS) |
| Enter an option [New/Move/orthoGraphic/ Prev/Restore/Save/Del/Apply/?/World] <World>: | TYPE: **Y<enter>** |
| Specify rotation angle about Y axis <90>: | **<enter>** |

**Draw a path for the chair arm and front leg (two lines and a fillet and join them together using Pedit). Draw a circle to form the metal tube, rotate the circle, and extrude it along the path:**

| Prompt | Response |
|---|---|
| Command: | TYPE: **L<enter>** |
| Specify first point: | TYPE: **8,12<enter>** |
| Specify next point or [Undo]: | TYPE: **@0,27<enter>** |
| Specify next point or [Undo]: | TYPE: **@16.5,0<enter>** |
| Specify next point or [Close/Undo]: | **<enter>** |
| Command: | TYPE: **F<enter>** |
| Select first object or [Polyline/Radius/Trim]: | TYPE: **R<enter>** |

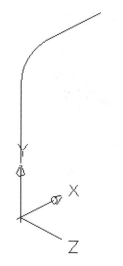

**FIGURE 18–32**
Draw a Path to Extrude a Circle

| Prompt | Response |
|---|---|
| Specify fillet radius <0.5000>: | TYPE: **5<enter>** |
| Select first object or [Polyline/Radius/Trim]: | CLICK: **one of the lines** |
| Select second object: | CLICK: **the other line** |
| Command: | TYPE: **PE<enter>** |
| Select polyline: | CLICK: **one of the lines, Figure 18–32** |
| Object selected is not a polyline<br>Do you want to turn it into one? <Y> | **<enter>** |
| Enter an option [Close/Join/Width/Edit vertex/<br>Fit/Spline/Decurve/Ltype gen/Undo]: | TYPE: **J<enter>** |
| Select objects: | TYPE: **ALL<enter>** |
| Select objects: | **<enter>** |
| 2 segments added to polyline | |
| Enter an option [Close/Join/Width/Edit vertex/<br>Fit/Spline/Decurve/Ltype gen/Undo]: | **<enter>** |
| Command: | TYPE: **C<enter>** |
| CIRCLE Specify center point for circle or<br>[3P/2P/Ttr (tan tan radius)]: | TYPE: **END<enter>** |
| of | CLICK: **the lower end of the vertical line** |
| Specify radius of circle or [Diameter]: | TYPE: **1<enter>** |
| Command: | **Rotate 3D** |
| Select objects: | CLICK: **the circle** |
| Select objects: | **<enter>** |
| Specify first point on axis or define axis by<br>[Object/Last/View/Xaxis/Yaxis/Zaxis/<br>2points]: | TYPE: **X<enter>** |
| Specify a point on the X axis <0,0,0>: | TYPE: **END<enter>** |
| of | CLICK: **the lower end of the vertical line** |
| Specify rotation angle or [Reference]: | TYPE: **90<enter>** |
| Command: | TYPE: **EXT<enter>** |
| Select objects: | CLICK: **the circle** |
| Select objects: | **<enter>** |
| Specify height of extrusion or [Path]: | TYPE: **P<enter>** |
| Select extrusion path: | CLICK: **the polyline** |

The right viewport should appear as shown in Figure 18–33.

## Draw the Cushion of the Chair

**Set a new UCS that is parallel to the World UCS (the cushion of the chair) that has an origin at the bottom of the chair leg:**

| Prompt | Response |
|---|---|
| Command: | TYPE: **UCS<enter>** |
| Enter an option [New/Move/orthoGraphic/<br>Prev/Restore/Save/Del/Apply/?/World]<br><World>: | **<enter>** |

**FIGURE 18–33**
Chair Leg-Arm Extrusion
Complete

**FIGURE 18–34**
Move the UCS

| Prompt | Response |
|---|---|
| Command: | <enter> (Repeat UCS) |
| Enter an option [New/Move/orthoGraphic/ Prev/Restore/Save/Del/Apply/?/World] <World>: | TYPE: **M<enter>** |
| Specify new origin point or [Zdepth] <0,0,0>: | TYPE: **CEN<enter>** |
| of | CLICK: **the bottom of the left chair leg (Figure 18–34)** |

**Set Layer 3d-m current. Draw a box for the chair cushion and extrude and taper the front of it.**

## On Your Own

**1. Set Layer M current.**

| Prompt | Response |
|---|---|
| Command: | **Box** (or TYPE: **BOX<enter>**) |
| Specify corner of box or [CEnter] <0,0,0>: | TYPE: **.75,13,14<enter>** |
| Specify corner or [Cube/Length]: | TYPE: **@18,-13** |
| Specify height: | TYPE: **5<enter>** |
| Command: | TYPE: **SOLIDEDIT<enter>** |
| Enter a solids editing option [Face/Edge/ Body/Undo/eXit] <eXit>: | TYPE: **F<enter>** (for face or surface) |
| Enter a face editing option [Extrude/Move/ Rotate/Offset/Taper/Delete/Copy/coLor/ Undo/eXit] <eXit>: | TYPE: **E<enter>** |
| Select faces or [Undo/Remove]: | CLICK: **D1**, Figure 18–35 |
| Select faces or [Undo/Remove/ALL]: | TYPE: **R<enter>** (to remove any surfaces that you do not want to extrude. You will probably have one that needs to be removed.) |
| Remove faces or [Undo/Add/ALL]: | CLICK: **any extra faces so the model appears as shown in Figure 18–36** |

**FIGURE 18–35**
CLICK: **the Face to Extrude**

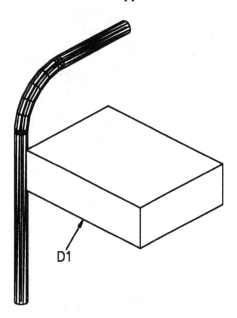

D1

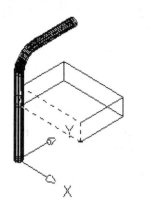

**FIGURE 18–36**
Select the Front Face to Extrude

| Prompt | Response |
|---|---|
| Remove faces or [Undo/Add/ALL]: | <enter> |
| Specify height of extrusion or [Path]: | TYPE: **5<enter>** |
| Specify angle of taper for extrusion <0>: | TYPE: **15<enter>** |
| Enter a face editing option [Extrude/Move/ Rotate/Offset/Taper/Delete/Copy/coLor/ Undo/eXit] <eXit>: | <enter> |
| Enter a solids editing option [Face/Edge/ Body/Undo/eXit] <eXit>: | <enter> |

The model appears as shown in Figure 18–37.

## Draw the Back of the Chair

Draw a box for the back of the chair.

| Prompt | Response |
|---|---|
| Command: | **Box** (or TYPE: **BOX<enter>**) |
| Specify corner of box or [CEnter] <0,0,0>: | TYPE: **END<enter>** (or select Osnap-endpoint) |
| of | CLICK: **D1**, Figure 18–38 |
| Specify corner or [Cube/Length]: | TYPE: **@20,5<enter>** |
| Specify height: | TYPE: **16<enter>** |

**Oops, the back is too long. Correct it by moving the right surface of the box 2″ to the left using solid edit, then Extrude the top face of the back 5″ with a 15° taper as shown in Figure 18–39 and use the Fillet command to round all the box edges.**

## On Your Own

1. **Use the Move Faces option of the Solids Editing (SOLIDEDIT) command to move the right side of the back of the chair 2″ to the left. Be sure that only the right side of the box is selected. Select any point as a base point, then TYPE: @2<180 as the second point of displacement.** You can skip several prompts by using either the Solids Editing toolbar or Solids Editing-Move Faces from the Modify menu on the menu bar. Typing the command shows you the complete structure of the SOLIDEDIT command.

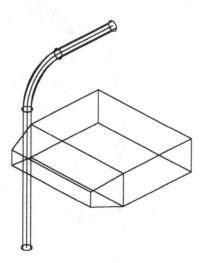

**FIGURE 18–37**
Cushion Extruded

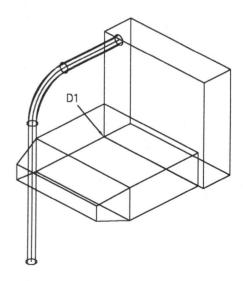

**FIGURE 18–38**
Draw the Box for the Back of the Chair

## FIGURE 18-39
Correct the Back, Extrude Its Top Surface, and Fillet All Sharp Edges 1″

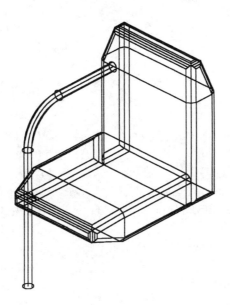

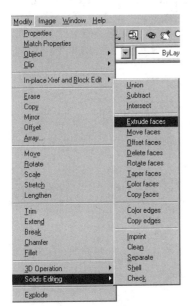

2. **Use the Extrude Faces option of the Solids Editing (SOLIDEDIT) command to extrude the top of the chair back 5″ with a 15° taper.** You can skip several prompts by using either the Solids Editing toolbar or Solids Editing-Extrude Faces from the Modify menu on the menu bar.

3. **Use the Fillet command to round all sharp edges of the chair cushion and back.** TYPE: **F<enter> for fillet,** then TYPE: **R<enter> for radius,** then TYPE: **1<enter>** to set the radius, **then select edges when you get the prompt: "Select an edge or [Chain/Radius]:". Pick the edges of the right side of the cushion, for example, then PRESS <enter>. If you try to select all edges at the same time you will get an error message.**

## Complete the Leg and Arm Assembly

**Set Layer 3d-g current. Draw a circle for one of the back legs, extrude it, and combine front and back legs into a single object using the Union command, Figure 18–40.**

## FIGURE 18-40
Draw a Circle for the Back Leg, Extrude It, and Union It with the Front Leg and Arm

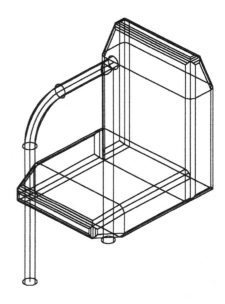

| Prompt | Response |
|---|---|
| Command: | TYPE: **C<enter>** |
| Specify center point for circle or [3P/2P/Ttr (tan tan radius)]: | TYPE: **0,15.5<enter>** (This makes the center point of the circle 15.5″ in the Y direction from the UCS origin.) |
| Specify radius of circle or [Diameter]: | TYPE: **1<enter>** |
| Command: | TYPE: **EXT<enter>** |
| Select objects: | CLICK: **the circle you just drew** |
| Select objects: | **<enter>** |
| Specify height of extrusion or [Path]: | TYPE: **27<enter>** (The back leg is 27″ high.) |
| Specify angle of taper for extrusion <0>: | **<enter>** |
| Command | **Union** (or TYPE: **UNION<enter>**) |
| Select objects: | CLICK: **the chair front leg and the back leg** (This makes the two pieces into a single piece.) |
| Select objects: | **<enter>** |

**Copy the leg assembly to the right side of the chair, Figure 18–41.**

| Prompt | Response |
|---|---|
| Command: | TYPE: **CP<enter>** |
| Select objects: | CLICK: **the chair leg assembly** |
| Select objects: | **<enter>** |
| Specify base point or displacement, or [Multiple]: | CLICK: **any point** |
| Specify second point of displacement or <use first point as displacement>: | TYPE: **@20<0 <enter>** |

**FIGURE 18–41**
Copy the Leg Assembly to the
Right Side of the Chair

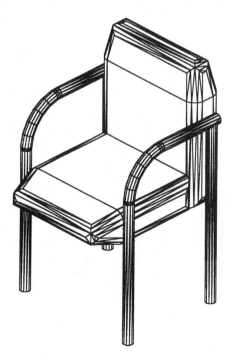

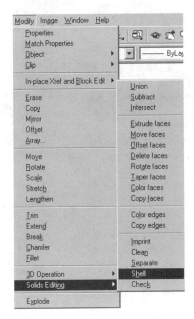

## Draw the Chair Platform

**Draw a box and make a shell out of it:**

| Prompt | Response |
|---|---|
| Command: | TYPE: **BOX<enter>** |
| Specify corner of box or [CEnter] <0,0,0>: | TYPE: **-10,-8,-6<enter>** (Notice that these are absolute coordinates based on the UCS located on the bottom of the front left leg.) |
| Specify corner or [Cube/Length]: | TYPE: **30,23.5,0<enter>** (absolute coordinates again) |
| Command: | **Solids Editing-Shell** |
| Select a 3D solid: | CLICK: **the box you just drew** |
| Remove faces or [Undo/Add/ALL]: | CLICK: **D1 and D2**, Figure 18–42 |
| Remove faces or [Undo/Add/ALL]: | **<enter>** |
| Enter the shell offset distance: | TYPE: **1<enter>** |
| [Imprint/sePparate solids/Shell/cLean/Check/ Undo/eXit] <eXit>: | **<enter>** |

**FIGURE 18–42**
Draw a Box and Make a Shell of It

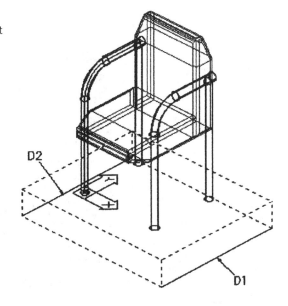

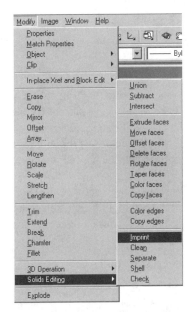

**Draw a circle and imprint it on the shell, Figure 18–43.**

| Prompt | Response |
|---|---|
| Command: | TYPE: **C<enter>** |
| Specify center point for circle or [3P/2P/Ttr (tan tan radius)]: | TYPE: **10,7.75<enter>** |
| Specify radius of circle or [Diameter] <0'-1">: | TYPE: **8<enter>** |
| Command: | **Solids Editing-Imprint** |

**FIGURE 18–43**
Draw a Circle and Imprint It on
the Shell

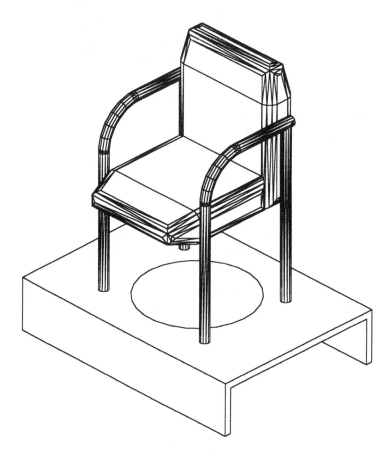

| Prompt | Response |
|---|---|
| Select a 3D solid: | CLICK: **the shell under the chair** |
| Select an object to imprint: | CLICK: **the Circle you just drew** |
| Delete the source object <N>: | TYPE: **Y<enter>** |
| Select an object to imprint: | **<enter>** |
| Enter a body editing option [Imprint/seParate solids/Shell/cLean/Check/Undo/eXit] <eXit>: | **<enter>** |
| Enter a solids editing option [Face/Edge/ Body/Undo/eXit] <eXit>: | **<enter>** |

## 3D Orbit

3D Orbit allows you to obtain a 3D view in the active viewport. The 3D Orbit shows an arcball. An arcball is a large circle with a small circle at each of its four quadrants. When you start 3D Orbit, the target of the view remains stationary while the camera, or your point of view, orbits the target. The center of the arcball (not the center of the model) is the target point. When you move your mouse over different parts of the arcball, the direction in which the view rotates changes.

When 3D Orbit is active, you can right-click in the drawing area to activate the shortcut menu shown in the margin. This menu allows you to render the object and select parallel or perspective views while the object is being orbited. You can also access these options from the 3D Orbit toolbar.

**Use 3D Orbit to render and animate the model you have just completed:**

| Prompt | Response |
|---|---|
| Command: | **3D Orbit** (or TYPE: **3DO<enter>**) |

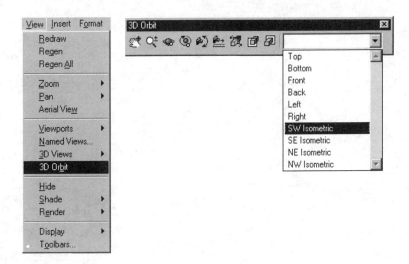

**Prompt**

The acrball with smaller circles at its
quadrants appears:

**Response**

CLICK: **one of the circles, hold down
the click button, and slowly move the
mouse so you get a feel for how the
view changes.** Practice a moment with
each of the quadrant circles.

CLICK: **the down arrow at the right
side of the 3D orbit toolbar and**
CLICK: **SW Isometric**

RIGHT-CLICK: **to obtain the shortcut
menu**

CLICK: **Projection on the shortcut
menu, then** CLICK: **Perspective**

CLICK: **Shading Modes on the
shortcut menu, then** CLICK:
**Gouraud shading**

CLICK: **3D Continuous Orbit on the 3D
Orbit toolbar or the right click menu**

CLICK: **a point at the upper left edge
of the display, hold down the click
button, and describe a very small
circle so the model rotates
continuously.** Experiment with the
continuous orbit display until you feel
comfortable with it.

You may need to return to 3D Orbit and click SW Isometric occasionally to return the
display to a manageable view.

**Prompt**

**Reponse**

CLICK: **3D Orbit and rotate the view
with perspective projection and
Gouraud shading ON to obtain a
view similar to Figure 18–44.**

Click the other commands (3D Swivel, 3D Adjust Distance, and 3D Adjust Clip
Planes) on the 3D Orbit toolbar to see how they operate.

## FIGURE 18–44
Exercise 18–2: Gouraud Shaded, Perspective Projection Using 3D Orbit

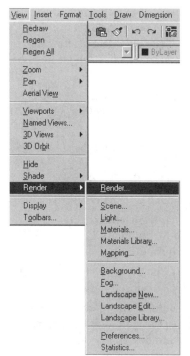

## Printing the Rendered Solid

**Render the drawing again using the Render command:**

| Prompt | Response |
|--------|----------|
| Command: | **Render** (or TYPE: **RENDER<enter>**) |
| The Render dialog box appears: | CLICK: **File in the Destination area** (You are rendering this drawing to a file.) |
| | CLICK: **Render** |
| The Rendering File dialog box appears with the name CH18–EX2 in the File name: text box. | CLICK: **a folder on the hard drive (or a compact or zip drive) and make a note of where you are saving the file** |
| | CLICK: **Save** |

**Insert the rendered file in paper space:**

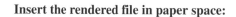

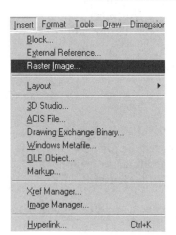

| Prompt | Response |
|--------|----------|
| Command: | CLICK: **Layout1** to enter paper space |
| The Page Setup dialog box appears: | CLICK: **OK** |
| | **Erase the paper space viewport that appears.** (If you get the message that the object is on a locked layer, unlock the layer by CLICKING: on the locked lock in the layer list, then erase it.) |
| Command: | CLICK: **Insert-raster image…** |

Part IV: Three-Dimensional AutoCAD

| Prompt | Response |
|---|---|
| The Select Image File dialog box appears: | Locate your rendered file and CLICK: on it so the name CH18-EX2 appears in the File name: text box. |
| | CLICK: **Open** |
| The Image dialog box appears: | CLICK: **OK** (Checks should appear in Specify onscreen boxes in both the Insertion point and Scale areas.) |
| Specify insertion point (0,0): | CLICK: **a point inside the lower left corner of the dashed lines** |
| Specify scale factor or [Unit] <1>: | Move your mouse very slowly upward to the right to CLICK: **the upper right corner of the image.** (The image will be much larger than the distance you moved the mouse.) |

**Use Dtext (CLICK: Single Line Text or TYPE: DT<enter>) to place your name in the lower right corner of the page using some readable font other than txt.**

**Print or plot the drawing to fit on an 11 × 8 1/2 sheet.**

# EXERCISE 18–3
## Creating a Solid Model of Chair 2

In this exercise you will create a solid model of a chair (Figure 18–45). This chair will be inserted into the structure that you will create in Exercise 18–4. The Prompt/Response format will not be used in this exercise. The steps will be listed with suggested commands for creating this model. Turn on the computer and start AutoCAD. The AutoCAD 2002 Today window is displayed.

1. CLICK: **the Create Drawings tab**
2. CLICK: **Wizards**
3. CLICK: **Quick Setup**
4. Set drawing Units: **Architectural**
   CLICK: **Next>>**
5. Set drawing Width: **5′** × Length: **5′**
   CLICK: **Finish**
6. **Use SaveAs... to save the drawing on the hard drive with the name CH18-EX3.**
7. **Set Grid: 1**
8. **Set Snap: 1/4**
9. **Create the following Layers:**

| LAYER NAME | COLOR | LINETYPE |
|---|---|---|
| 3d-m | Magenta | Continuous |
| 3d-g | Green | Continuous |

10. **Set Layer 3d-m current.**
11. **Use the Vports command to make two vertical viewports. Zoom-All in both viewports to start, then Zoom in closer as needed.** You will find it easier to draw in the left viewport and use the right viewport to determine if the model is proceeding as it should.

**FIGURE 18–45**
Exercise 18–3 Complete

FIGURE 18–46
Dimensions for the Chair

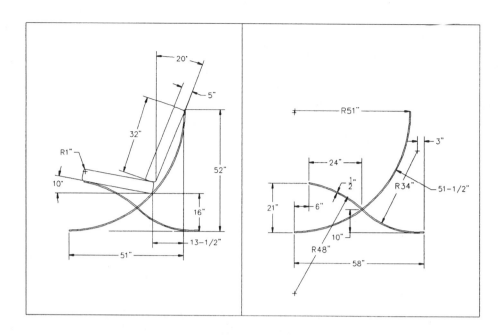

12. Use the Vpoint command to set a 1,-1,1 viewpoint for the right viewport.

13. Set FACETRES to 2; set ISOLINES to 10.

## Draw Two 32″ × 5″ Cushions

1. Draw the cushions in vertical and horizontal positions and rotate them to the positions shown using the dimensions from Figure 18–46. (Both cushions are the same size.)

2. Draw a temporary construction line to locate the bottom of the chair legs.

3. Use Rectangle to draw the bottom cushion in a horizontal position 160 above the temporary construction line. Use the Polyline option of the Fillet command to create the 10 fillet on all four corners at the same time.

4. Use Rotate to rotate the bottom cushion 210° as shown.

5. Use Rectangle to draw the back cushion in a vertical position, and fillet all four corners.

6. Use Rotate to rotate the back cushion 220°.

7. Use Stretch to form the bottom of the back cushion so it fits flush against the bottom cushion.

## Draw Chair Legs and Back Support

1. Set Layer 3d-g current.

2. Draw temporary construction lines as needed to locate the beginning and ending points of the three arcs.

3. Use Arc, Start-End-Radius to draw the three arcs. Be sure to use the Endpoint of the arc with the 48″ radius as the starting point of the arc with the 34″ radius so the two can be joined together to form a single polyline.

4. Use Edit Polyline to join the arcs with the 340 and 480 radii.

5. Use Offset to offset the joined arcs 1/20 down.

6. Use Offset to offset the arc with the 510 radius 1/20 to the right.

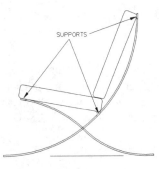

**FIGURE 18–47**
Chair Supports Measuring
2″ × 1/2″

7. Use the Line command to draw lines at the ends of all arcs so that the two metal legs have a thickness.

8. Use Edit Polyline to join all parts of each leg so they can be extruded.

## Draw Chair Supports

1. Draw the three supports in Figure 18–47 in the locations shown.

2. Use the Rectangle command to draw the 2″ × 1/2″ supports in either a vertical or horizontal position as needed.

3. Use the Rotate and Move commands to locate the supports in the positions shown.

## Extrude Cushions, Legs, and Supports

1. Use the Extrude command to extrude the two cushions 36″ in the positive Z direction with a 0 taper angle.

2. Use the Extrude command to extrude the polylines forming the legs 2-1/2″ in the positive Z direction with a 0 taper angle.

3. Use the Extrude command to extrude the supports 31″ in the positive Z direction with a 0 taper angle.

## Move Supports So They Sit on Top of the Legs

1. Use the Move command to move the three supports 2-1/2″ in the positive Z direction (second point of displacement will be @0,0,2-1/2).

## Join Extruded Legs to Form a Single Piece

1. Use the Union command to join the two extruded legs to form a single piece.

## Add the Other Set of Legs

1. Use the Copy command to copy the legs 33-1/2″ in the positive Z direction.

## Rotate Chair to the Upright and Forward Position

1. Use the Rotate 3D command to rotate the chair 90° about the X axis. Click one of the lowest points of the end of one of the chair legs as the Point on the X axis.

2. Use the Rotate 3D command to rotate the chair 90° about the Z axis. Click one of the lowest points of the end of one of the chair legs as the Point on the Z axis.

## Remove Hidden Lines

1. Use the Hide command to remove hidden lines so the chair appears as shown in Figure 18–45.

## Save the Drawing as a Wblock

1. Use the Wblock command to save the drawing on a floppy disk with the name **EX18-3.** Use the bottom of the front of the left leg as the insertion point. CLICK: **Retain** to keep the drawing on the screen.

2. Save the drawing as **CH18-EX3.**

## PLOT

1. Plot or print the drawing at a scale of 1=24 from the Model tab in the center of an 8-1/2″ × 11″ sheet.

2. Do not use Single Line Text to place your name on the drawing. Write your name on this drawing so you can use the drawing in Exercise 18–4.

# EXERCISE 18–4
## Create a Solid Model of a Patio

In this exercise you will create a solid model of an elaborate patio area and insert your chair into it (Figure 18–48). The Prompt–Response format will not be used in this exercise. The steps will be listed with suggested commands for creating this model. Turn on the computer and start AutoCAD. The AutoCAD 2002 Today window is displayed.

1. CLICK: **the Create Drawings tab**
2. CLICK: **Wizards**
3. Set drawing Units: **Architectural**
   CLICK: **Next>**
4. Set drawing Width: **50′** × Length: **40′**
   CLICK: **Finish**
5. **Use SaveAs... to save the drawing on the hard drive with the name CH18-EX4.**
6. **Set Grid: 2′**
7. **Set Snap: 6″**

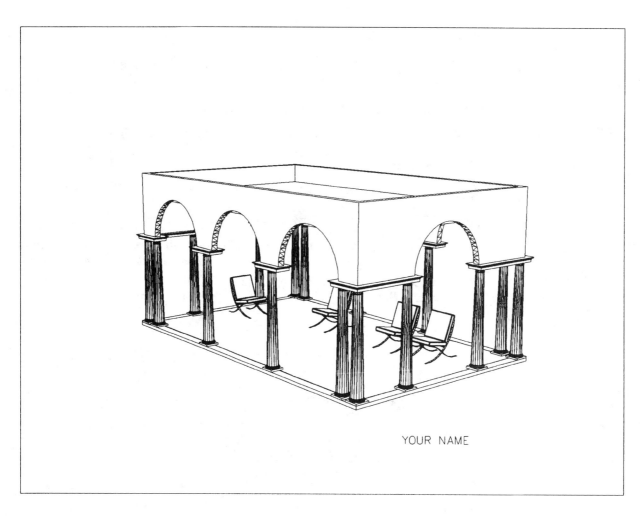

YOUR NAME

**FIGURE 18–48**
Exercise 18–4 Complete

8. **Create the following Layers:**

| LAYER NAME | COLOR | LINETYPE |
|---|---|---|
| 3d-m | Magenta | CONTINUOUS |
| 3d-c | Cyan | CONTINUOUS |

9. **Set Layer 3d-m current.**

10. **Use the Vports command to make two vertical viewports. Zoom-All in both viewports to start, then Zoom in closer as needed.** You will find it easier to draw in the left viewport and use the right viewport to determine if the model is proceeding as it should.

11. **Use the Vpoint command to set a 1,-1,1 viewpoint for the right viewport.**

12. **Set FACETRES to 2; set ISOLINES to 10.**

Let's begin at the bottom and work up.

## Draw the Concrete Pad with a Border Around It

**The concrete pad and the border have to be two separate objects extruded to a height of 4″. Draw the outside edge of the border and extrude it, then draw the inside edge, extrude it, and subtract it from the outside edge. Finally, draw the pad and extrude it (Figure 18–49):**

1. **Use the Rectangle command to draw a rectangle measuring 39′ × 24′. Start the first corner at absolute coordinates 6′,8′.**

2. **Use the Rectangle command to draw a rectangle measuring 37′ × 22′. Start the first corner at absolute coordinates 7′,9′.**

3. **Use the Offset command to offset the 37′ × 22′ rectangle 1/2″ to the inside to form the concrete pad with a 1/2″ space between it and the border.**

4. **Use the Extrude command to extrude all three rectangles 4″ in the positive Z direction, 0 taper angle.**

5. **Use the Subtract command to subtract the inside of the border (the 37′ × 22′ extruded rectangle) from the outside of the border.** You will have to Zoom a window so you can get close enough to pick the correct rectangle to subtract.

**FIGURE 18–49**
The Concrete Pad with a 1′
Border

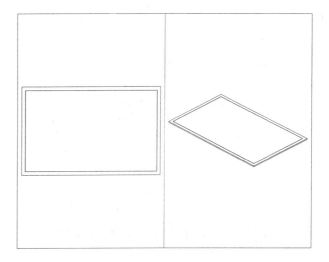

FIGURE 18–50
Draw the Base of the Column

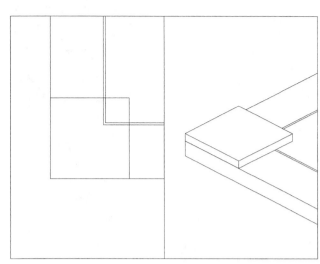

## Draw the Base of the Columns

**Draw the base of the columns on the lower left corner of the drawing. They will be copied after the columns are placed on them (Figure 18–50):**

1. **Zoom in on the lower left corner of the drawing as shown in Figure 18–50 in both viewports.**

2. **Use Box to draw the column base.** The box measures 18″ × 18″ × 2″ height. **Locate the "Corner of box" on the lower left corner of the border as shown. Use Osnap-Endpoint to click the first corner, then @18,18 to specify the other corner.**

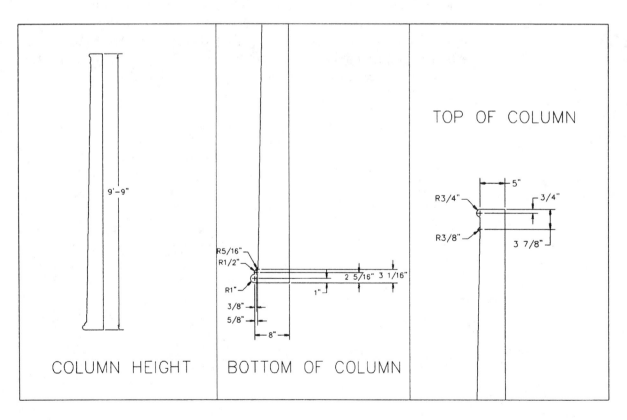

**FIGURE 18–51**
Dimensions for Drawing the Column

**FIGURE 18–52**
The Column Revolved

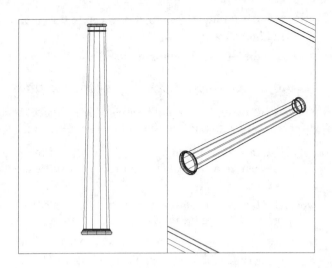

**FIGURE 18–53**
Move the UCS to the Top Lower
Left Corner of the Base

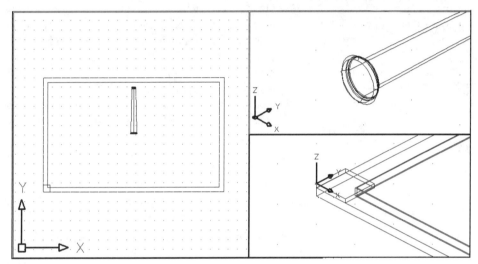

## Draw the Columns

Draw the column and rotate it so it sits on top of the base (Figures 18–51, 18–52, 18–53, 18–54, and 18–55):

1. **Use the dimensions in Figure 18–51 to draw the column in an open area of your drawing. Use the Line and Arc or Circle commands to draw this figure.** It may be easier to use Circle and Trim to draw the arcs on the bottom and top of the column instead of the Arc command.

2. **Use Edit Polyline to join all the parts of Figure 18–51 into a single polyline.**

3. **Use the Revolve command to create the solid column as shown in Figure 18–52.** Select both ends of the vertical line using Osnap-Endpoint as the Axis of revolution.

4. **Use the VPORTS command to split the right viewport into two horizontal viewports (three:left) and Zoom in on the bottom of the column and the box you drew as the column base, as shown in Figure 18–53 in both horizontal viewports.** (You may need to adjust your view in the left viewport.)

5. **Use the UCS command to move your UCS to the lower left corner of the top plane of the base as shown in Figure 18–53.**

6. **Use the Move command to move the column to the center of the base as shown in Figure 18–54. Use Osnap-Center as the Base point, and CLICK: the extreme bottom circular center of the column in the upper right viewport.** TYPE: **9,9** as the second point of displacement to move the column to the center of the base.

**FIGURE 18–54**
Move the Column to the Center
of the Base

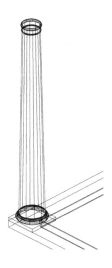

**FIGURE 18–55**
Rotate the Column to Its Upright Position

**Tip:** Be sure the insertion point is positive 9-1/2, negative −9-1/2.

7. **Use the Rotate 3D command to rotate the column 90° about the X axis as shown in Figure 18–55.**

8. **Use the VPORTS command to return the display to two vertical viewports.**

## Add the Cornice at the Top of the Column

**Insert drawing 18–3 (from Exercise 18–1, Figures 18–24 through 18–29) to form the cornice at the top of the column (Figures 18–56 and 18–57):**

1. **Use the Move option of the UCS command to move the UCS to the extreme top of the column as shown in Figure 18–56. Use Osnap-Center to locate the UCS at that point.**

2. **Use the Insert command to insert drawing 18–3 onto the top of the column** (Figure 18–57). Use the following:

   Insertion point: TYPE: **9-1/2** in the X: box and **−9-1/2** in the Y: box. (Be sure to include the minus in the Y: direction.) Leave Z: at 0. (The bottom of the cornice drawing measures 19″, as shown in Figure 18–24. Because you picked the endpoint of the lower corner as the insertion point when you Wblocked the shape, 9-1/2, −9-1/2 will place the center of the shape at the center of the column top. The shape must measure 24″ × 24″ when it is inserted. The arithmetic requires you to subtract 5″ from both measurements and divide by 2.)
   After you have typed the insertion point in the X: and Y: boxes of Insertion point, TYPE: **12** in the X: Scale box and check Uniform Scale.
   (The shape measures 2″ square, so an X scale factor of 12 will make the shape 24″ long.)
   (The shape must be 24″ in the Y and Z directions also so Uniform Scale must be checked.)
   (The height of the original shape was reduced to 1/12 of the 5-1/2″ dimension shown in Figure 18–24, so a scale factor of 12 will make it 5-1/2″ in this drawing.)
   Leave Rotation angle: 0. CLICK: **OK**

3. **Use the Explode command to explode the inserted cornice so it can be joined to form longer cornices.** Explode it only once. If you explode it more than once, you destroy it as a solid.

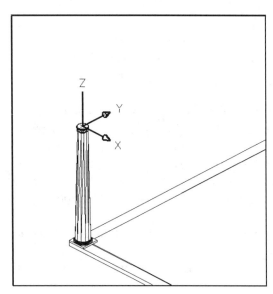

**FIGURE 18–56**
Move the UCS to the Center of the Top of the Column

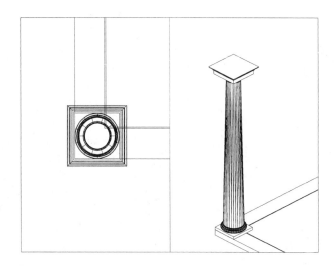

**FIGURE 18–57**
Inserting the Cornice

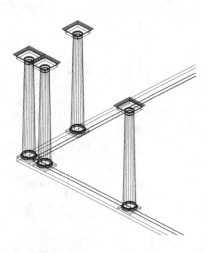

**FIGURE 18–58**
Copy the Base, Column, and Cornice Twice in the X Direction and Once in the Y Direction

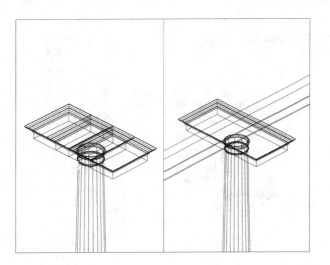

**FIGURE 18–59**
Copy the Cornice in the Positive X Direction and the Negative X Direction and Union of the Three Cornice Shapes

## Draw the Columns and Cornices at the Center and One Corner of the Structure

**Copy the column and cornice to create supports at the center of the structure (Figures 18–58 and 18–59):**

1. **With Ortho ON use the Multiple option of the Copy command and direct distance entry to copy the column, its base, and cornice three times: 2′ and 12′9″ in the positive X direction, and once 6′2″ in the positive Y direction (Figure 18–58).**

2. **With Ortho ON use the Multiple option of the Copy command and direct distance entry to copy the cornice on the column that is to the far right 12″ in the positive X direction and 12″ in the negative X direction so that the cornice on this column will measure 48″ when the three are joined.**

3. **Use Union to join the cornice and the two copies to form a single cornice that is 48″ long (Figure 18–59).**

**Copy the cornice and join all the cornice shapes on the three corner columns to create the L-shaped cornice at the corner of the structure (Figure 18–60):**

1. **With Ortho ON use the Multiple option of the Copy command and direct distance entry to copy the cornice on the corner column six times: 12″ in the positive X direction and 12″, 24″, 36″, 48″, and 60″ in the positive Y direction so that the cornice on the three corner columns will measure 48″ in the X direction and 96″ in the Y direction when all these shapes are joined.**

2. **Use Union to join all the cornice shapes on the three corner columns to form a single L-shaped cornice, Figure 18–60.**

**FIGURE 18–60**
The L-Shaped Cornice after Using the Union and Hide Commands

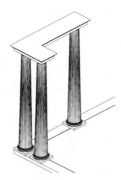

**FIGURE 18–61**
Copying the Columns Using the
Mirror Command

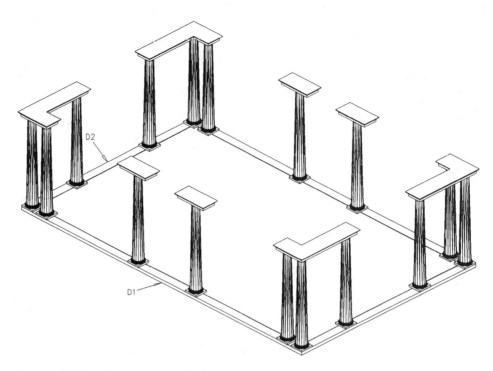

## Draw All the Remaining Columns

**Mirror the existing columns twice to form the remaining columns (Figure 18–61):**

1. **Use the UCS command to return to the World UCS.**
2. **With Ortho ON use the Mirror command to form the columns on the right side of the structure.** Select all existing columns, bases, and cornices. PRESS: **<enter>**, then using Osnap-midpoint, CLICK: **D1** (Figure 18–61) as the first point of the mirror line, then click any point directly above or below D1. Do not delete source objects.
3. **With Ortho ON use the Mirror command to form the columns on the back side of the structure.** Select all existing columns, bases, and cornices. PRESS: **<enter>**, then using Osnap-midpoint, CLICK: **D2** (Figure 18–61) as the first point of the mirror line, then click any point directly to the left or right of D2. Do not delete old objects.

## Draw the Upper Part of the Structure

**Draw the front and rear elevations of the upper structure (Figure 18–62):**

1. **Use the UCS command to rotate the UCS 90° about the X axis.**
2. **Draw the upper part of the structure in an open area.** You will move it to its correct location after it is completed.
3. **Use the dimensions from Figure 18–62 to draw that shape with the Line and Arc or Circle commands.**
4. **Use Edit Polyline to join all the parts of the figure into a single polyline.**
5. **Use the Extrude command to extrude the polyline 8″ in the positive Z direction.**

**FIGURE 18–62**

Dimensions for the Front and
Rear Elevations of the Upper
Structure

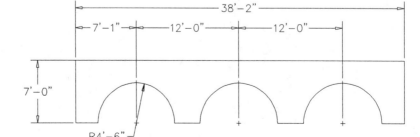

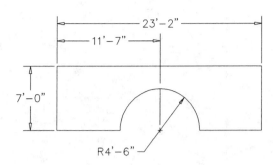

**FIGURE 18–63**
Dimensions for the Left and Right Elevations of
the Upper Structure

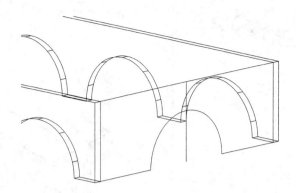

**FIGURE 18–64**
Draw the Right Elevation on the Right Ends of
the Front and Rear Planes

6. Use the Copy command to copy this shape 22'-6" in the negative Z direction (Base point—click any point, Second point of displacement—@0,0,-22'6<enter>).

**Draw the left and right elevations of the upper structure (Figures 18–63 and 18–64):**

1. Use the UCS command to rotate the UCS 90° about the Y axis.

2. Use the dimensions from Figure 18–63 to draw that shape with the Line and Arc or Circle commands across the ends of the front and rear elevations.

3. Draw the right side of the structure on the right ends of the front and rear planes (Figure 18–64).

4. Use Edit Polyline to join all the parts of the figure into a single polyline.

5. Use the Extrude command to extrude the polyline 8" in the negative Z direction.

6. Use the Copy command to copy this shape 37'-6" in the negative Z direction (Base point - CLICK: any point, Second point of displacement - TYPE: @0,0,−37'6<enter>).

**Draw the roof and complete the upper part of the structure (Figures 18–65, 18–66, 18–67, and 18–68):**

1. Make the 3d-c layer current.

2. Use the UCS command to return to the World UCS.

3. Use the Rectangle command to draw a rectangle to form the flat roof inside the upper part of the structure (Figure 18–65):

   First corner—D1
   Other corner—D2

4. Use the Extrude command to extrude the rectangle 8" in the negative Z direction.

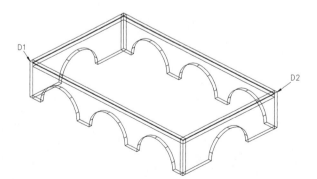

**FIGURE 18–65**
Draw a Rectangle to Form the Roof

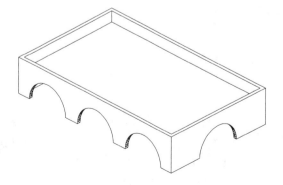

**FIGURE 18–66**
The Completed Upper Structure

**FIGURE 18–67**
Move the UCS to the Top of the
Cornice Corner

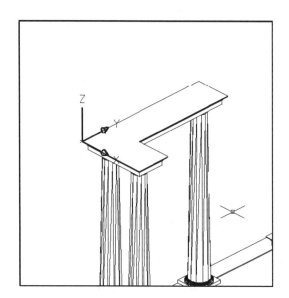

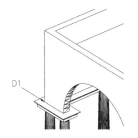

**FIGURE 18–68**
Move the Upper Structure into
Position

5. Use the Move command to move the extruded rectangle 18″ in the negative Z direction (Second point of displacement - TYPE: @0,0,-18<enter>).

6. Use the Union command to join all parts of the upper structure into a single unit.

7. Use the Hide command to make sure your model is OK (Figure 18–66).

8. Use the UCS command to move the origin of the UCS to the endpoint of the lower left cornice (Figure 18–67).

9. Use the Move command to move the endpoint, D1 (Figure 18–68), of the lower right corner of the upper part of the structure to absolute coordinates 8,8,0. Be sure you do not put the @ symbol in front of the coordinates.

## Insert Chairs to Complete the Model

Insert a chair at the correct elevation, copy it, rotate it, and complete Exercise 18–4 (Figures 18–69 and 18–70):

1. Use the UCS command to move the origin of the UCS to the top of the border surrounding the concrete pad, D1 (Figure 18–69).

2. Use the Insert command to insert the chair drawing, A:EX18-3, at absolute coordinates 18′,14′,0.

3. With Ortho ON use the Copy command to copy the chair three times to the approximate locations shown in Figure 18–70.

4. Use the Rotate command to rotate the chair on the far left 90°.

**FIGURE 18–69**
Move the UCS to the Top of the
Border Surrounding the Pad

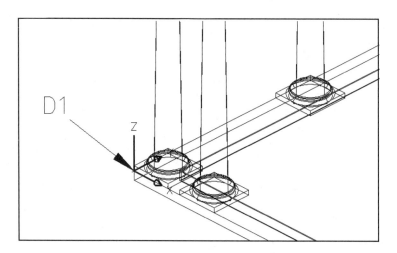

FIGURE 18–70
Locating the Chairs

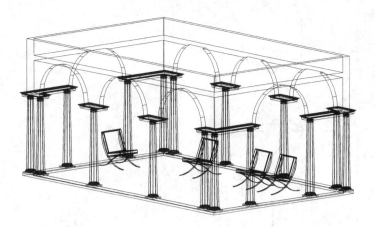

5. Use the 3Dviewpoint-Select... command to select a viewpoint of 315, 10.

6. Use 3D Orbit with Perspective projection to obtain a view similar to Figure 18–48.

7. With the right viewport active, use the SIngle option of the VPORTS command to return the display to a single viewport.

8. CLICK: Layout1.

9. Use the Hideplot option of Mview to remove hidden lines when you plot. Turn Hideplot ON and click the outside edge of the viewport when you are prompted to select objects.

10. Use the Single Line Text command (TYPE: DT<enter>) to place your name in the lower right corner 1/8″ high in the simplex font. Your final drawing should appear as shown in Figure 18–48.

## SAVE

Use the SaveAs command to save your drawing in two places.

## PLOT

Plot or print the drawing at a scale of 1=1.

# EXERCISE 18–5
# Drawing Solid Models of Eight Objects

1. Draw solid models of the eight objects shown in Figure 18–71. Use the dimensions shown in the top and front views of A through H:

   Draw the top view, join it to form a continuous polyline, and extrude it to the height shown in the front view.

   Rotate the UCS 90° about the X axis, draw a rectangle at the angle shown in the front view, extrude it, move it in the Z direction so it covers the area of the extruded top view that must be removed, and subtract it from the extruded top view.

2. Arrange the objects so that they are well spaced on the page and take up most of a 9″ × 7″ area on an 11″ × 8-1/2″ sheet.

3. Your final drawing should show eight solid objects in a viewpoint similar to Exercise 18–1.

4. CLICK: Layout1, place your name in the lower right corner in 1/8″ letters, use Mview-Hideplot to hide lines, and plot or print the drawing on an 11″ × 8-1/2″ sheet at a scale of 1=1.

5. Save your drawing in two places with the name EX18-5.

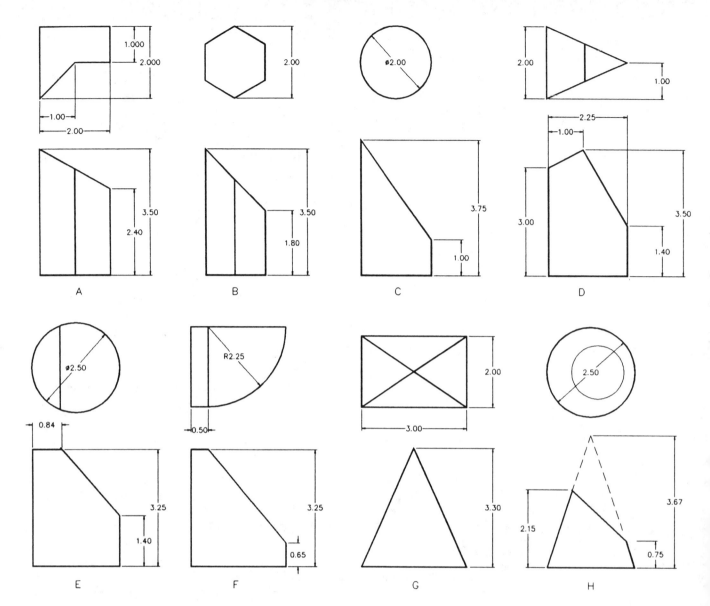

**FIGURE 18-71**
Exercise 18–5: Draw Solid Models of Eight Objects

## EXERCISE 18–6
## Drawing a Solid Model of a Lamp Table

1. Draw a solid model of the lamp table shown in Figure 18–72. Scale the top and front views using a scale of 1″=1′-0″ to obtain the correct measurements for the model.

2. Use Revolve for the table pedestal. Use Polyline and Extrude for one table leg, and duplicate it with Polar Array. The table top can be an extruded circle or a solid cylinder.

3. Use 3D Orbit to obtain a perspective view of your final model and CLICK: **Layout1** before you plot.

4. Place your name in the lower right corner in 1/8″ letters using simplex or an architectural font.

5. Plot the drawing at a scale of 1=1 on an 11″ × 8-1/2″ sheet. Be sure to use the Hideplot option of the Mview command before plotting.

6. Return to the model tab (World UCS current) and Wblock the lamp table to a floppy disk with the name TABLE.

7. Save your drawing with the name EX18-6.

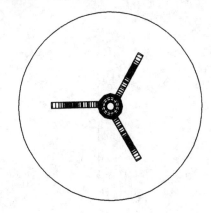

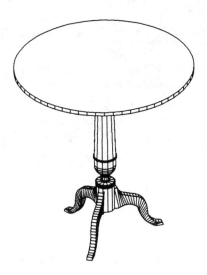

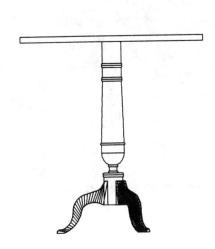

# EXERCISE 18–7
## Drawing a Solid Model of a Sofa

1. Use the dimensions from Figure 18–73 to draw the sofa. Draw two rectangles measuring 27″ × 6″ with 3″ fillets to form the bottom cushion. Extrude them both to a height of 21″, and rotate one 90° about the Y axis.

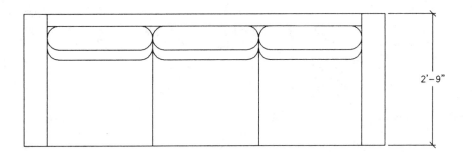

**FIGURE 18–73**
Exercise 18–7: Sofa Dimensions
(Scale: 1/2″ = 1′-0″)

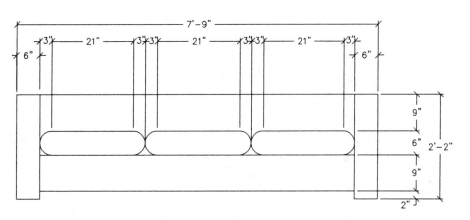

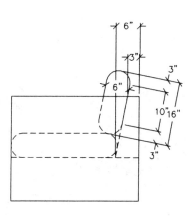

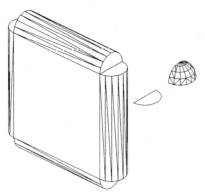

**FIGURE 18–74**
The Parts of the Bottom Cushion

2. Move one of the rectangles to intersect with the other as shown in Figure 18–74. Draw an end cap using a line and an arc with a 3″ radius, join them together, and revolve them 90°as shown. Move the end cap to one corner of the cushion and copy it to the other three corners using the Mirror command. Join all parts of the cushion using the Union command.

3. Draw the back cushions in a similar manner.

4. Draw the arms, back, and base of the sofa using the Rectangle and Polyline commands, and extrude them to the dimensions shown.

5. Copy the cushions and move them to their correct locations using the Move and Rotate 3D commands.

6. Use 3D Orbit to obtain a perspective view of your final model and CLICK: **Layout1** before you plot.

7. Place your name in the lower right corner in 1/8″ letters using simplex or an architectural font.

8. Plot the drawing at a scale of 1=1 on an 11″ × 8-1/2″ sheet. Be sure to use the Hideplot option of the Mview command before plotting.

9. Return to the model tab (World UCS current) and Wblock the sofa to a floppy disk with the name SOFA. CHECK: **Retain** so the drawing stays on the screen.

10. Save your drawing in two places with the name EX18-7.

# EXERCISE 18–8
# Drawing a Solid Model of a Lamp and Inserting It and the Lamp Table into the Sofa Drawing

1. Draw the lamp and the shade from the dimensions shown in Figure 18–75. Use your 1/8″ architect's scale for any dimensions not shown. Make sure the lamp is a closed polyline and the shade is a closed polyline. You will have to give the shade some thickness by offsetting its shape and closing the ends with a line. Then join all parts of the shade to form a closed polyline.

2. Revolve the two polylines to form the lamp.

3. Rotate the lamp 90° about the X axis so it is in an upright position.

4. With the World UCS current Wblock the lamp to a floppy disk with the name LAMP. Use the center of the bottom of the lamp as the insertion point.

5. Open the drawing SOFA that you have Wblocked to the floppy disk.

6. Insert the TABLE and LAMP models from the floppy disk into the SOFA drawing. Place the table to the right of the sofa, and center the base of the lamp on the table top as shown in Figure 18–76.

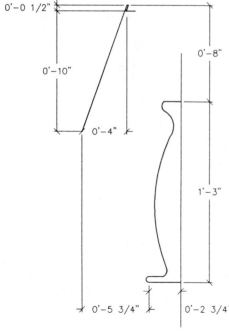

**FIGURE 18–75**
Exercise 18–8: Overall Dimensions of the Lamp (Scale: 1/8″ = 1″)

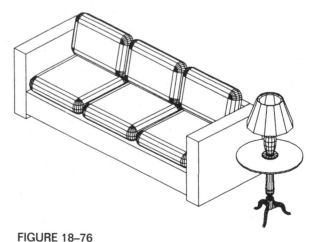

**FIGURE 18–76**
Exercise 18–8: Combine Solid Models

7. Use 3D Orbit to obtain a perspective view of your final model and CLICK: **Layout1** before you plot.

8. Place your name in the lower right corner in 1/8″ letters using simplex or an architectural font.

9. Plot the drawing at a scale of 1=1 on an 11″ × 8-1/2″ sheet. Be sure to use the Hide-plot option of the Mview command before plotting.

10. Save your drawing in two places with the name EX18-8.

# EXERCISE 18–9
# Drawing a Solid Model of the Tenant Space Reception Seating

1. Draw the chair coffee table and corner table with a series of boxes (Figure 18–77).

2. Fillet the vertical edges of the coffee table and corner table.

3. Use the Rectangle command with 1″ fillets to draw the coffee table and corner table inlays. Extrude the rectangles 1″ and place them so they are flush with the top of the tables. Subtract the extruded rectangles from the tables and replace them with other extruded rectangles that are slightly smaller to form the inlays.

**FIGURE 18–77**
Exercise 18–9: Tenant Space
Reception Seating Dimensions
(Scale: 3/8″ = 1′-0″)

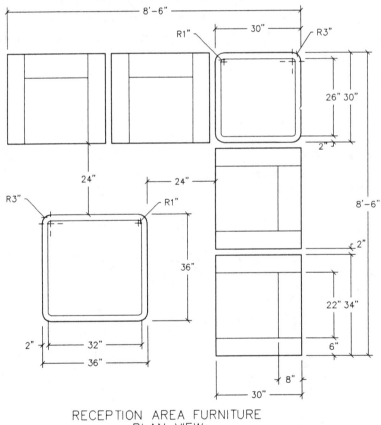

RECEPTION AREA FURNITURE
PLAN VIEW

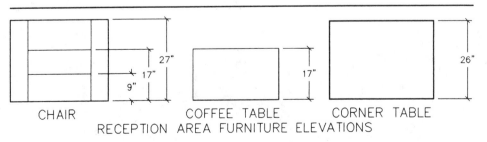

CHAIR                    COFFEE TABLE          CORNER TABLE
RECEPTION AREA FURNITURE ELEVATIONS

4. Use 3D Orbit to obtain a perspective view of your final model and CLICK: the **Layout1** tab before you plot.

5. Place your name in the lower right corner in 1/8″ letters using simplex or an architectural font.

6. Plot the drawing at a scale of 1=1 on an 11″ × 8-1/2″ sheet. Be sure to use the Hideplot option of the Mview command before plotting.

7. Save your drawing in two places with the name EX18-9.

# EXERCISE 18–10
# Drawing a Solid Model of a Conference Chair

1. Use the dimensions from Figure 18–78 to draw the chair. Draw one caster with the solid Sphere command and use the Polar Array command to copy it three times.

2. The chair base can be formed with two cylinders and an extruded polyline copied three times using Polar Array.

3. Draw the bottom and back cushion with a single extruded polyline.

4. Draw the arms with a single extruded polyline.

5. Use 3D Orbit to obtain a perspective view of your final model and CLICK: **Layout1** before you plot.

6. Place your name in the lower right corner in 1/8″ letters using simplex or an architectural font.

7. Plot the drawing at a scale of 1=1 on an 11″ × 8-1/2″ sheet. Be sure to use the Hideplot option of the Mview command before plotting.

**FIGURE 18–78**
Exercise 18–10: Tenant Space
Conference Chair Dimensions

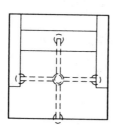

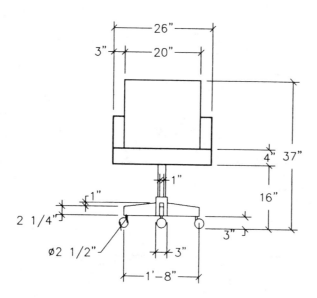

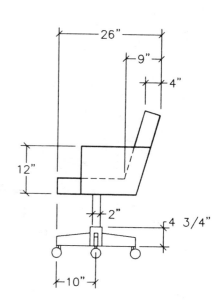

8. Return to model space with Tilemode ON and Wblock the conference chair to a floppy disk with the name C-CHAIR. Use the bottom of one of the casters as the insertion point. Make sure the radio button **Retain** is on before you select objects.

9. Save your drawing with the name EX18-10.

# EXERCISE 18–11
# Drawing a Solid Model of a Conference Table and Inserting Chairs Around It

1. Use the dimensions from Figure 18–79 to draw the conference table. Draw the table bases with the Cylinder command.

2. Draw the table top with the Rectangle command using a 29″ fillet radius. The rectangle will measure 108″ × 58″.

3. Insert the C-CHAIR drawing into the conference table drawing.

4. Copy the chair seven times, and position the chairs as shown in Figure 18–80.

5. Use 3D Orbit to obtain a perspective view of your final model and CLICK: **Layout1** before you plot.

6. Place your name in the lower right corner in 1/8″ letters using simplex or an architectural font.

7. Plot the drawing at a scale of 1=1 on an 11″ × 8-1/2″ sheet. Be sure to use the Hide-plot option of the Mview command before plotting.

8. Save your drawing in two places with the name EX18-11.

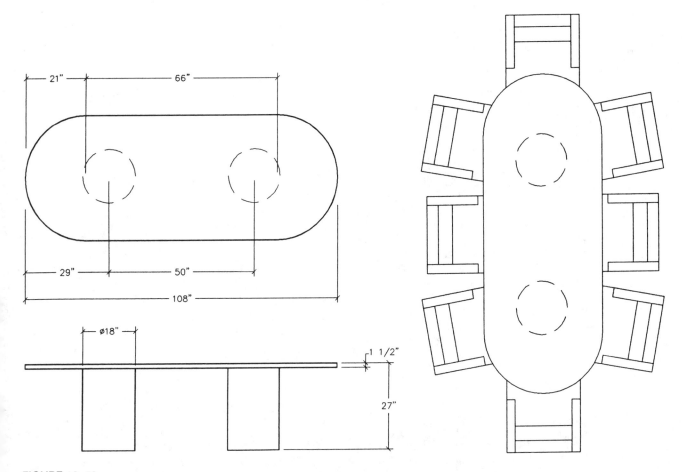

**FIGURE 18–79**
Exercise 18–11: Plan and Elevation Views of the Conference Table (Scale: 3/8″ = 1′-0″)

**FIGURE 18–80**
Exercise 18–11: Conference Table and Chair Locations

# REVIEW QUESTIONS

1. Which of the following is *not* a SOLID command used to draw solid primitives?
   a. Box
   b. Cylinder
   c. Rectangle
   d. Wedge
   e. Sphere
2. Which of the following is used to make rounded corners on a solid box?
   a. Chamfer
   b. Extrude
   c. Intersection
   d. Round
   e. Fillet
3. Which is the last dimension called for when the Box command is activated?
   a. Height
   b. Width
   c. Length
   d. First corner of box
   e. Other corner
4. Which is the first dimension called for when the Sphere command is activated?
   a. Segments in Y direction
   b. Segments in X direction
   c. Radius
   d. Center of sphere
   e. Diameter
5. Which of the following *cannot* be extruded?
   a. Polylines
   b. Circles
   c. Regions
   d. Polygons
   e. Solids
6. Which of the following commands is used to join several polylines into a single entity?
   a. Edit Polyline
   b. Offset
   c. Union
   d. Intersection
   e. Extrude
7. Which of the following is used to make a solid by revolving a polyline about an axis?
   a. Revolve
   b. Extrude
   c. Intersection
   d. Round
   e. Fillet
8. Which of the following adjusts the smoothness of objects rendered with the Hide command?
   a. SURFTAB1
   b. MESH
   c. SEGS
   d. WIRE
   e. FACETRES and ISOLINES
9. Which of the following allows you to rotate an object around an X,Y, or Z axis?
   a. Rotate
   b. Rotate 3D
   c. Extrude
   d. Solrot
   e. Offset
10. Which of the following sets the number of lines on rounded surfaces of solids?
    a. FACETRES
    b. ISOLINES
    c. Union
    d. Fillet
    e. Interfere

11. List six Solid commands used to make solid primitives.

_____    _____    _____

_____    _____    _____

12. List the Solid command used to extrude a polyline into a solid.

_____

13. List the Solid command used to create a new solid by cutting the existing solid into two pieces and removing or retaining either or both pieces.

_____

14. List the Solid command that allows you to join several solids into a single object.

_____

15. List the Solid command used to subtract solids from other solids.

_____

16. List the command and its option that is used to move the UCS icon so that it is displayed at the origin of the current coordinate system.

_____    _____
command                    option

17. List the Solid command used to create a cross-sectional area of a solid.

_____

18. List the command and its option that allows you to view a solid model in perspective mode.

_____    _____
command                    option

19. List the command and the rotation angle that may be used to rotate an object 90° clockwise about the Z axis.

_____    _____
command                    rotation angle

20. List the Solid command used to create an object from the common volume of two intersecting solids.

_____

# Glossary

**Absolute coordinates** The location of a point in terms of distances and/or angles from a fixed origin point.

**Alias** Two names for the same command (Example: L is an alias for LINE).

**Aliasing** The jagged appearance of a curved line or a straight line at an angle.

**Aligned dimension** A dimension that shows the distance between two points at an angle.

**Ambient color** A color produced by ambient light.

**Ambient light** Light that illuminates all surfaces equally.

**Angular dimension** A dimension that measures angles.

**Annotations** Notes, text, tolerances, legends, and symbols.

**ANSI** American National Standards Institute; sets drafting standards.

**Anti-aliasing** A means of shading the main pixels to reduce the appearance of aliasing.

**Array** A rectangular or circular pattern of graphical objects.

**ASCII** American Standard Code for Information Interchange; a standard set of 128 binary numbers representing keyboard information such as letters, numerals, and punctuation.

**Aspect ratio** The ratio of width to height on the display.

**Associative dimensions** Dimensions that automatically update their values when the associated geometry is modified.

**Associative hatching** A hatched area that changes as the shape of the area changes.

**Attribute** Textual information associated with CAD geometry. Attributes can be assigned to drawing objects and extracted from the drawing database. Applications include creating bills of material.

**Attribute extraction file** A text file to which attribute data is written when it is extracted from a drawing.

**Attribute prompt** The text that is displayed as a prompt when a block with an attribute is inserted.

**Attribute tag** The label for which AutoCAD looks when attributes are extracted.

**Attribute template** A file that is used to provide a format for extracted attributes.

**Attribute value** The text that appears on the block when a block with an attribute is inserted.

**AUI** Advanced User Interface; a user–interface enhancement that includes on-screen dialog boxes, a menu bar that can be customized, pull-down menus, and icon menus.

**Autolisp** A programming language contained within the AutoCAD program that is used for writing programs for Auto-CAD commands.

**Baseline dimensioning** A dimension relative to a fixed horizontal or vertical datum or reference.

**Base point** The first point selected when copying, moving, rotating, inserting, and gripping objects.

**Baud rate** See *bps.*

**Bezier curve** A curve defined by a set of control points.

**Binary** The numerical base, base 2, by which computers operate. The electrical circuitry of a computer is designed to recognize only two states, high and low, which easily translate to logical and arithmetic values of 1 and 0. For example, the binary number 11101 represents the decimal number 29.

**Bit (binary digit)** The smallest unit of computer data.

**Board (printed circuit board)** Board onto which components are soldered and connected via etched circuits on the board.

**Boot** To turn the computer on and start a program.

**bps (bits per second)** A unit of transmission; also called baud rate.

**B-spline curve** A curve that passes near a set of control points.

**Buffer** An intermediate storage device (hardware or software) between data handling units.

**Busy lamp** Indicator on the front of a disk drive that lights when the drive is writing to or reading a disk.

**Byte** A string of 8 bits representing 256 different binary values. A kilobyte (Kbyte) is 1024 bytes.

**CAD** Computer-aided design; the use of graphics-oriented computer software for designing and drafting applications.

**Chamfer** A beveled edge or corner between two otherwise intersecting lines or surfaces.

**Chip (integrated circuit)** A miniature circuit made by etching electronic components onto a silicon wafer.

**Clipping** The process of setting the display boundaries of graphical items.

**Clock** Electronic timer used to synchronize computer operations. A clock is an indication of the speed of the computer operations.

**Cold boot** Starting the computer by turning it off and then on again.

**CMYK** Cyan, magenta, yellow, and black (key color); a system of creating colors by specifying the percentage of each of the four colors.

**Command** A word used to initiate a task.

**Com port** A communications port that allows data to flow into and out of the computer. Most communication ports are serial ports. Digitizers and most plotters are connected to communication ports. Most COM ports have pins rather than holes.

**Configuration** A particular grouping of computer hardware as a functional unit. It may also include the allocation of hardware resources and sometimes refers to software parameter settings.

**Continue dimension** A linear dimension that uses the second extension origin of the previous dimension as its first extension origin.

**Coons patch**   A surface between four adjoining edges.

**Coordinate filters**   An AutoCAD feature (also called XYZ point filters) that allows a user to extract individual X, Y, and Z coordinate values from different points in order to create a new, composite point.

**Cpolygon**   A crossing polygon that selects any object crossed by or contained within it.

**CPU**   Central processing unit; it is responsible for arithmetic computations, logic operations, memory addresses, and data and control signal traffic in a computer.

**Crosshair**   A cursor usually made up of two perpendicular lines on the display screen used to select coordinate locations.

**Crossing window**   A window that selects any object crossed by or contained within the window.

**CRT**   Cathode-ray tube; the video display tube used with computers.

**Cursor**   An indicator on the display screen that shows where the next entered data will appear.

**Database**   Related information organized and stored so that it can be easily retrieved and, typically, used in multiple applications. A noncomputer example of a database is the telephone directory.

**Default**   A parameter or variable that remains in effect until changed. It is what a computer program assumes in the absence of specific user instructions.

**Definition points (def points)**   Points that appear when associative dimensions are created.

**DIESEL**   Direct Interpretively Evaluated String Expression Language; a programming language for customizing menu items.

**Diffuse color**   The predominant color of an object.

**Digitizing tablet**   A graphics input device that generates coordinate data. It is used in conjunction with a puck or a stylus.

**Dimensioning variables**   Settings that control the appearance of dimensions.

**Dimension style**   A named group of settings for each dimensioning variable affecting the appearance of a dimension; also called a dimstyle in AutoCAD.

**Dimension text**   The text that appears in the dimension line.

**Direct distance entry**   A method of defining points that allows you to move your cursor to indicate the desired direction, then type the value.

**Directory**   Groups of files identified by a directory name.

**Disk or diskette**   A thin, flexible platter coated with a magnetic material for storing information.

**Disk or diskette drive**   A magnetic device that writes on and retrieves data from a disk.

**Display resolution**   The number of horizontal and vertical rows of pixels that can be displayed by a particular graphics controller or monitor. For example, 640 columns and 350 rows of pixels can be displayed by a standard EGA graphics controller and color monitor.

**Display screen**   A video-display tube or CRT used to transmit graphical information.

**Dithering**   Combining color dots to display more colors than are really available.

**DOS**   Disk operating system; software that controls the operation of disk drives, memory usage, and I/O in a computer.

**Drag**   To dynamically move the virtual image of a graphical entity across the display screen to a new location using a puck, mouse, or stylus.

**Drawing file**   A collection of graphical data stored as a set (file) in a computer.

**Drawing limits**   The page size specified for a drawing. The grid shows the drawing limits.

**Drive**   A device used to read or write information on a disk or diskette.

**DXF**   Drawing interchange file; a file format used to produce an ASCII description of an AutoCAD drawing file.

**Edge**   A command used to change the visibility of a face.

**Edit**   To modify existing data.

**Elevation**   The Z value of an object with reference to the XY plane.

**Embed**   To copy an object from a source document without retaining a link to the program from which the source document was taken.

**Endpoint**   The exact location on a line or curve where it terminates.

**Enter key (<enter>)**   Sometimes called the Return key; it signals the computer to execute a command or terminate a line of text.

**Entity**   An AutoCAD term describing predefined graphical objects that are placed in the drawing using a single command.

**Expansion option**   Add-on hardware that expands power and versatility.

**Expansion slot**   Location inside the system unit for the connection of an optional printed circuit board. Expansion slots for optional boards are available in many computers.

**Explode**   A command that separates blocks and polylines into separate line segments.

**Extents**   The extreme boundary of a drawing without regard to the drawing limits.

**External reference**   A drawing file that is linked (or attached) to another drawing. Also called an Xref in AutoCAD.

**Extrusion**   In AutoCAD, the process of assigning a thickness property to a given entity. The direction of the extrusion is always parallel to the Z axis of the UCS in effect when the entity was created.

**Face**   A bounded section of the surface of a modeled object.

**Feature control frame**   The box surrounding a geometric dimension.

**File**   Information stored by a computer.

**Fill**   Solid coloring covering an area bounded by lines and/or curves.

**Fillet**   A curved surface of constant radius connecting two intersecting surfaces; a 2D representation of the preceding involving two lines or curves and an arc.

**Finite Element Analysis (FEA)**   Numerical technique of approximately determining field variables such as displacements or stresses in a domain. This is done by breaking down the domain into a finite number of "pieces," also called "elements," and solving for the unknowns in those elements.

**Finite Element Modeling (FEM)**   Process of breaking down a geometric model into a mesh, called the finite element mesh model, that is used for finite element analysis.

**Fit tolerance**   The setting that determines how close a B-spline curve passes to the fit points.

**Floppy disk**   A circular plastic disk coated with magnetic material mounted in a plastic holder. It is used by a computer to store information for use later. It can be inserted or removed from a floppy disk drive at will. It is also called a diskette.

**Font**   A distinctive text typeface, usually named and recognized by the aesthetic appearance of its characters.

**Formatting**   Preparing a disk to accept data.

**Freeze** A setting that keeps objects on selected layers from being displayed. A frozen layer is not displayed, regenerated, or plotted. Freezing shortens regeneration time. Objects on a frozen layer are not selected when the ALL selection option is used.

**Function key** A key on the keyboard that can be assigned to perform a task. A function key is typically used as a shortcut to a lengthy string of keystrokes.

**Grid** An area on the graphics display covered with regularly spaced dots used as a drawing aid.

**Grips** Small squares that appear on objects selected before a command is activated. After the grips appear the objects can be edited by selecting one of the squares to make it hot and toggling through the available grip modes.

**Handle** An alphanumeric tag that AutoCAD gives every object.

**Hard copy** A paper printout of information stored in a computer.

**Hard disk** A rigid magnetic storage device that provides fast access to stored data.

**Hardware** The electronic and mechanical parts of a computer.

**Hatching** A regular pattern of line segments, dots, or solids covering an area bounded by lines and/or curves.

**High density** The storage capacity of a disk or disk drive that uses high-capacity disks.

**HLS** Hue, lightness, and saturation; system of defining color by specifying the amount of these three values.

**Hz (hertz)** A unit of frequency equal to one cycle per second.

**Icon** A graphical symbol typically used to convey a message or represent a command on the display screen.

**Interface** A connection that allows two devices to communicate.

**I/O** Input/output; a mechanism by which a computer accepts or distributes information to peripheral devices such as plotters, printers, disk drives, and modems.

**ISO** International Standards Organization, an organization that sets international standards for drawings.

**ISO** An abbreviation for isometric, a view or drawing of an object in which the projections of the X, Y, and Z axes are 30° left, 30° right, and vertical.

**Isometric snap style** A snap style that sets the grid and snap to the isometric angles of 30°, 30°, and 90°.

**K (kilobyte)** 1024 bytes.

**Layer** A logical separation of data to be viewed individually or in combination. Similar in concept to transparent acetate overlays.

**Layout** The tab that allows you to create paper space viewports with scaled insertions of the model space drawing.

**Linetype** A term representing the appearance of a line. For example, a continuous line has a different linetype from that of a dashed line.

**Lineweight** A setting in the Layer Manager that allows you to give lines on any layer a specific width.

**Link** To connect a copy of a source document to the source program so that any changes to the source document are reflected in the copy.

**Load** Enter a program into the computer's memory from a storage device.

**M (megabyte)** One million bytes.

**Macro** A single command made up of a string of commands.

**Memory** An electronic part of a computer that stores information.

**Menu** A display of programs or commands.

**MHz (megahertz)** One million hertz.

**Microprocessor** An integrated circuit "chip" (or set of chips) that acts as the CPU of a computer.

**Mirror** To create the reverse image of selected graphical items.

**Mode** A software setting or operational state.

**Model** A two- or three-dimensional representation of an object.

**Model space** Model space is where model geometry is created and maintained. Typically, entities in model space are drawn to scale of the design feature. Model space is the complement of paper space. See *paper space.*

**Modem (modulator-demodulator)** A device that links computers over a telephone.

**Monochrome** A video display that features different shades of a single color.

**Motherboard** The main printed circuit board in a computer to which all other boards are connected.

**Mouse** A hand-operated, relative-motion device resembling a digitizer puck used to position the cursor on a computer display screen.

**Network** An electronic linking of computers for communication.

**Node** An object snap option that allows the user to snap to points.

**Normal** The same as perpendicular.

**Numerical control (NC)** Programmable automation of machine tools.

**NURBS** Nonuniform rational B-spline curve. A curve or surface defined by control points.

**Object** Also called *entity;* any element such as text, lines, circles, arcs, dimensions, hatching, and polylines used in AutoCAD.

**OLE** Object linking and embedding. Objects from a source document are copied into a destination document. When the object is selected in the destination document, the program used to create the source document is activated.

**Operating system** Also called the disk operating system; software that manages computer resources and allows a user access and control.

**Origin** The intersection point of the axes in a coordinate system. For example, the origin of a Cartesian coordinate system is the point at which the X, Y, and Z axes meet, (0,0,0).

**Orthographic projection** The 2D representation of a 3D object without perspective. In drafting, it is typically the front, top, and right-side views of an object.

**Ortho mode** An AutoCAD setting that permits only horizontal or vertical input from the graphical pointing device (mouse, puck, or stylus).

**Osnap** Object snap, an AutoCAD setting that allows the user to specify point locations based on existing geometry. This allows for the graphic selection of the precise location of midpoints and endpoints of lines, center points and tangent points of circles and arcs, and the like.

**Overwrite** To store information at a location where information is already stored, thus destroying the original information.

**Pan** Redefines the display boundaries without changing magnification. It is similar to panning a camera.

**Paper space** Space in which documentation graphics such as title blocks, some annotation, or borders can reside. Typically, entities are created in paper space to the scale at which they will be plotted. Some 3D features also work in paper space. Working in paper space allows the user to work with nontiled viewports. See *model space.*

**Parallel interface**   Interface that communicates 8, 16, or 32 bits at a time.

**Parallel port**   A connector on the back of the computer that usually has holes rather than pins. This connector always has 25 connections. Most printers are connected to parallel ports.

**Parallel printer**   A printer with a parallel interface.

**PC3 file**   The plotter configuration file. It contains all the specific information needed to operate a particular plotter or printer.

**Peripheral**   An input or output device not under direct computer control.

**Perspective projection**   The simulation of distance by the representation of parallel lines as converging at a vanishing point.

**Pick button**   The button on any pointing device such as a mouse that is used to pick objects on define points—usually the left mouse button.

**Pixels (picture elements)**   Tiny dots that make up a screen image.

**Plan view**   A view perpendicular to a selected face of an object.

**Plot style**   A file containing all the pen assignments, fill style, line endings, and other elements that control how a drawing is plotted.

**Plotter**   A computer-controlled device that produces text and images on paper or acetate by electrostatic, thermal, or mechanical means (with a pen).

**PMP file**   Plot model parameter. This file contains the custom plotter calibration and paper size data to operate a specific printer or plotter.

**Point**   A location or dot in 3D space specified by X,Y, and Z coordinates.

**Point filters**   A means of individually extracting the X,Y, and Z coordinates of points to specify a new point.

**Polar array**   Objects copied about a center point a specific number of times.

**Polar coordinate**   A coordinate specified by a distance and angle from an origin.

**Polygon window**   A selection window in the shape of a polygon. An item must be contained entirely inside the window to be selected.

**Polyline**   An AutoCAD geometric entity composed of one or more connected segments treated as a single entity. Polylines can be converted into curves.

**Port**   A connection on a computer where a peripheral device can be connected.

**Primitive**   A basic geometric model from which more complex models are constructed. Primitives are points and lines in wire frame models, and simple shapes such as blocks, cones, and cylinders in solid models.

**Processor**   A computer on a chip.

**Program**   A detailed list of instructions that will be quickly, precisely, and blindly followed by a computer.

**Prompt**   A message from the computer software requesting a response from the user.

**Puck**   A hand-operated device with one or more buttons (resembling a mouse) that operates in conjunction with a digitizing tablet.

**RAM (random-access memory)**   Temporary read/write memory that stores information only when the computer is on.

**Read**   To extract data from a storage device such as a floppy disk or hard disk.

**Reflection color**   The color of a highlight on shiny material.

**Regenerate**   To recompute the screen coordinates from the drawing database so that the screen is refreshed. Redraw does not recompute, whereas regenerate does.

**Relative coordinates**   Coordinates specified by differences in distances and/or angles measured from a previous set of coordinates rather than from the origin point.

**Return button**   The button on a pointing device used to accept an entry—usually the right mouse button.

**RGB**   Red, green, blue. A system of creating colors using percentages of these three colors.

**Right-hand rule**   Using the fingers of the right hand to remember the relative directions of the positive X, Y, and Z axes of a Cartesian coordinate system. It is particularly useful in Auto-CAD in visualizing UCS orientations.

**ROM (read-only memory)**   Permanent computer memory that cannot be written to.

**RS-232C**   Standard interface cable for serial devices.

**Running object snap**   An object snap mode such as endpoint that is automatically active when a point is selected.

**Save**   To store data on a disk.

**Script file**   A file with the extension .scr created in a text editor that executes a set of AutoCAD commands.

**Selection window**   A window used to select objects. Any object must be contained entirely within the window to be selected.

**Serial interface**   An interface that communicates information one bit at a time.

**Serial port**   A connector on the back of the computer that has pins rather than holes. This connector may have either 9 pins or 25 pins.

**Serial printer**   A printer with a serial interface (receives information one bit at a time).

**Snap**   A means of setting a pointing device to stop at specified intervals on an invisible grid.

**Software**   Computer programs.

**Solid model**   A computer representation of a fully enclosed, three-dimensional shape. Solid models define the space a real object occupies in addition to the surface that bounds the object.

**Stylus**   An input device used like a digitizer puck but that looks like a pen.

**Surface model**   A 3D representation of an object made of a wire frame on which surfaces are attached. A surface model is hollow. A solid model is solid.

**Surface of revolution**   A surface generated by revolving a profile curve around an axis.

**System board**   The main printed circuit board inside the system unit, into which other boards are connected.

**System unit**   The component that contains the computer parts, disk drives, and option boards.

**System variable**   A setting that determines how the AutoCAD program operates.

**Template drawing**   A drawing file with predefined settings.

**Text style**   A collection of settings that determine the appearance of text.

**Thaw**   A setting that displays frozen layers when that layer is also on.

**Thickness**   A setting that gives height (the Z dimension) to certain objects such as solids, circles, and polylines making them 3D objects.

**Tilemode**   An AutoCAD system variable that controls whether viewports are tiled or nontiled when created. When tilemode is

ON, you are in model space—viewports are adjacent and cannot be moved, stretched, or erased.

**Tracking**   A means of locating a point relative to other points on the drawing.

**Unit**   A user-defined distance. It may be inches, meters, miles, and so on.

**User coordinate system**   A movable, user-defined coordinate system used for convenient placement of geometry. It is frequently referred to as the UCS.

**Vector**   A mathematical entity with a precise direction and length.

**View**   A graphical representation of a 2-D drawing or 3-D model from a specific location (viewpoint) in space.

**Viewpoint**   A location in 3-D model space from which a model is viewed.

**Viewport**   A bounded area on a display screen that may contain a view. If a viewport is created when Tilemode is set to 1, then it is tiled. When Tilemode is set to 0, viewports are created with the Mview command. They are nontiled viewports and reside in paper space or model space. See *model space* and *paper space.*

**Virtual screen display**   The area of the display where AutoCAD can zoom in or out without regenerating the drawing.

**Wire frame model**   A 2D or 3D representation of an object consisting of boundary lines or edges of an object.

**World coordinate system**   A fixed coordinate system that defines the location of all graphic items in a drawing or model. It is frequently referred to as the WCS.

**Wpolygon**   See *polygon window.*

**Write**   To record or store information in a storage device.

**Write-enable notch**   Slot on the side of a floppy disk that, when uncovered, permits the disk to be written on.

**Write-protect**   To cover a floppy disk write-enable notch, thus preventing writing on the disk.

**Xref**   See *external reference.*

**X,Y,Z point filters**   A means of individually extracting the X, Y, and Z coordinates of points to specify a new point.

**Zoom**   The process of reducing or increasing the magnification of graphics on the display screen.

# Index

Save, 466
View Slide, 406
VPLAYER command, 393-94
VPOINT command, 459-61
VPORTS command, 384-90, 458
    Restore, 466, 467
    Save, 466
Vslide, 406

## W

Wall section, 267-79
Walls, 166-68
WBLOCK command, 180-82
Web page, 408-10
Wedge command, 489, 494
Wide polylines, 104-6, 109
Width Option, Pedit, 108, 109
Window, 67, 68
Window, crossing, 67, 68
Window menu, 18
Window option of the Plot dialog box, 150
Window Polygon, 67
Windows Clipboard, 23
Windows Desktop, 12, 13
Windows Explorer, 441-44
Windows, Microsoft, starting, 12, 13
Windows, Notepad, 318
Windows, selecting, 67, 68

Wizards, to create a new drawing, 28
Wordpad, Windows, 444, 445
World Coordinate System, 153, 482
Write Block dialog box, 180-82

## X

XBIND command, 321
X,Y coordinates, 54-56
X,Y,Z coordinates, 453
XREF command, 320-21
Xrefs, 320-21
XY plane, 54-56

## Z

Zero radius (fillet or chamfer), 91
Zoom command, 31, 52, 60
    All, 31, 52, 61, 62
    Center, 63
    Dynamic, 62, 63
    Extents, 63
    In, 64
    Out, 64
    Previous, 62
    Realtime, 64
    Scale, 63
    Window, 60, 61

# AutoCAD® for
# Interior Design
# and Space Planning
# Using AutoCAD® 2002